A Reader's Book of Days

A Reader's Book of Days

True Tales from
the Lives and Works of Writers
for Every Day of the Year

Tom Nissley

WITH ILLUSTRATIONS BY

Joanna Neborsky

W. W. NORTON & COMPANY
NEW YORK ∽ LONDON

For information about permission to reproduce selections from
this book, write to Permissions, W. W. Norton & Company, Inc.,
500 Fifth Avenue, New York, NY 10110

For information about special discounts for bulk purchases, please contact
W. W. Norton Special Sales at specialsales@wwnorton.com or 800-233-4830

Manufacturing by Courier Westford
Book design by BTDNYC
Production manager: Anna Oler

ISBN 978-0-393-23962-1 (hardcover)

W. W. Norton & Company, Inc.
500 Fifth Avenue, New York, N.Y. 10110
www.wwnorton.com

W. W. Norton & Company Ltd.
Castle House, 75/76 Wells Street, London W1T 3QT

1 2 3 4 5 6 7 8 9 0

To all my days with
Laura, Peter, and Henry

Contents

Do not remit the practice of writing down occurrences
as they arise, of whatever kind, and be very punctual in
annexing the dates. Chronology, you know, is the eye of
history; and every man's life is of importance to himself.
—DR. JOHNSON TO MRS. YHRALE, September 6, 1777

I hate books and articles which begin with a date of
birth. Altogether I hate books and articles which adopt
a biographical and chronological approach; that strikes
me as the most tasteless and at the same time the most
unintellectual procedure.
—THOMAS BERNHARD, *Concrete*

Introduction

I was the guy in the library with books piled all around him, new ones every day. I'm sure they had a name for me behind the desk. Each morning I'd walk into the stacks with a handful of authors in mind—Colette, Heinlein, Babel, Baldwin, Welty— and come back with as many fat volumes as I could balance on my laptop: biographies, diaries, novels, complete correspondences. I lived between PG and PT in the Library of Congress system, with occasional forays upstairs to BX, D, E, F, and HV and down to QH and Z. I pulled out a half-dozen Brontë books at a time, and I blew the dust off the Franz Werfel biography from the auxiliary stacks that no one had checked out for years.

And every day I foraged for stories: moments in the lives of writers, or the invented lives of their characters, that I could connect to a particular date but also to something larger. Moviemakers have never really known how to dramatize the lives of writers—how many balled-up pages thrown into the trash can you show?—but writers have always left a vivid record of the lives they lived, as well as the ones they imagined. They gossip and despair in their diaries, they grouch and boast in letters, they transform their struggles into fiction. They drive themselves into poverty to write a masterpiece, badger their agents, fall in and out of love, crash cars and planes and motorcycles, stoke feuds, read books they hate and adore, dream of fame and regret it, discover their talent and drink it away.

The book I wanted to create would hold all those things and more, not just the usual almanac staples of births and deaths and publication dates. April 15, after all, isn't just the day that *Robinson Crusoe* was published, Henry James was born, and Edward Gorey died. It's also the day that Walt Whitman mourned the death of Lincoln, Charles Dickens called the Mississippi the "beastliest river in the world," George McGovern's political director told Hunter S. Thompson he was worried about his health, and Thomas Higginson received four poems from a woman named Emily Dickinson with a note that began, "Are you too deeply occupied to say if my Verse is alive?"

In the piles of books around me I looked for historic events (the day Charles Dodgson invented Wonderland for Alice Liddell and her sisters, the night Mary Shelley imagined Frankenstein's monster), but I also had my eye out for moments that were less momentous, the way the days in our lives usually are, and I've filled the corners of this book with reminders (Susan Sontag going to a double feature, Herman Melville playing croquet, David Foster Wallace describing his new tobacco-chewing habit to Jonathan Franzen) of the sheer dailyness of even the most eventful of lives.

Best of all was when I could find these two things—the historic and the humdrum—in the very same event. I knew how important the day Franz Kafka met Felice Bauer was to his literary life, but I didn't know that he stepped on her foot in the revolving door when he dropped her off at her hotel. And June 14, 1950, I learned, is not only the day Charles M. Schulz signed the syndication contract for his new comic strip. It's also the night he came home and celebrated by asking red-haired Donna Mae Johnson to marry him. (She turned him down.)

I spent a whole (and happy) year that way, collecting a year's worth of stories for the 366 daily pages of this book. Caught up as I was in other days—consuming books, at times, as if the dates they contained were their only fruit—I never knew what day it was in my own life. Any book I opened I read with a strange and narrow radar. I skimmed indexes, tracked anecdotes from reference to reference, typed "january," "february," "march," etc., into search boxes, and developed a particular appreciation for epistolary novels and a grudge against writers who didn't date their diary entries (John Cheever, that means you). My first question, when my wife told me about a book she was reading, was always "Does it have any dates?"

Just as many of the best of these tales connect the lives of writers with the books they created, I also wanted to do something in this book that I hadn't seen anywhere else: tell stories from the invented lives of fiction alongside those of the writers themselves. January 8 is the day Jane Austen wrote her sister about dancing with Tom Lefroy on his birthday, but it's also the day Callie, or Cal, Stephanides was born in Jeffrey Eugenides's *Middlesex*. L. Frank Baum finished the book he called then *The Emerald City* on October 9, the same day the mysterious title organization in Arthur Conan Doyle's "The Red-Headed League" closed its doors. Sometimes writers have connected the two themselves, knitting crucial days from their lives into their fiction. Bloomsday, James Joyce's booklong celebration of the day he met Nora Barnacle, is the most familiar example, but Toni Morrison, Truman Capote, and J. K. Rowling are among the many who have made their own birthdays important dates in their novels.

Dates in books, I realized as I combed for them, are a literary tool like any other—dialogue, geography, physical description—to be deployed or withheld according to the effect desired. A novelist might choose, or choose not, to tell you that something happened on October 21, just as she might tell you, or not, that a character has gray eyes or lives in Knoxville. Diaries, biographies, epistolary novels, histories, and explorers' accounts are all built on the bones of dates, as are mysteries, with their reliance on evidence and the tick-tock of police procedure. Memoirs, though, turn out to be concerned more with memory than evidence; it's a rare memoirist, even one as careful as Mary Karr, who gets specific about the days things happened. Science fiction, to my surprise, often uses dates as a way of grounding its speculations, but fantasy rarely does, although Tolkien did pay attention to the calendars of Middle Earth. Poets mostly prefer months to days. (An exception is when they want to mark an occasion in their title: Wordsworth above Tintern Abbey, Yeats after the Easter Rebellion, Frank O'Hara on his lunch hour.) "April" is poetic; "April 18" is not. It's too specific, too pedestrian. It's the stuff of journalism or letters or train schedules, the muckier genres that novels have always dirtied themselves with.

Specific dates carry with them the lure of the real that the novel has always dangled, the stray facticity every good storyteller or con man knows can put a tale over. Some novelists are maestros of the date: Nabokov, Joyce, Philip K. Dick, Zadie Smith. Lovecraft's unnameable horrors are made more dreadful by the precision of the days on which they occur, and much of the pleasure of Conan Doyle's stories of detection comes from the details of their setting: the geography of London, the variety of its carriages, and the exact day—January 4—the five orange pips arrive. In some books a single date becomes a talisman: the August 4ths the sad story in Ford Madox Ford's *The Good Soldier* keeps circling back to, or the memory of an April 27 that becomes a fetish in Orhan Pamuk's *The Museum of Innocence*.

Not every story cares about the calendar, of course. Do you ever know what day—or even month—it is in one of Kafka's novels? Time there is both too urgent and too infinite for the mere particularity of dates. Time has a different character in Virginia Woolf's novels too. *Mrs. Dalloway*, like *Ulysses*, is set on a single day in the middle of June, but she never says which one, leaving us no Dallowayday to celebrate the way we do Joyce's June 16, 1904. In fiction, her sense of time had less to do with what day it was than with, as *Mrs. Dalloway*'s working title put it, *The Hours*, or, as she named one of her essays, "The Moment."

But outside their fiction, Kafka and Woolf were two of the great artists of daily life—Kafka in his diary and especially his letters to his eternal fiancée Felice Bauer, and Woolf in her letters and especially her incomparable diary. They are among those writers whose daily impromptu autobiographies, like the diaries of Pepys, Thoreau, and Victor Klemperer or the letters of Flannery O'Connor or the James family, have become literature too. Then there are those who have the everyday art of their lives recorded by others: Dr. Johnson by his Boswell, of course, but also Herman Melville, who was no diarist but whose days appear again and again in these pages thanks to the blessed obsessiveness of biographers like Jay Leyda and Hershel Parker, and literary characters like Zora Neale Hurston and Jack Kerouac, whose self-creation made their days lastingly vivid.

Now you know how I read to make this book. How should you read it? If you're like me, you'll look up your birthday first. Some readers will simply open it at random, or seek out favorite names in the index, or read a single page on its appointed day before moving on to the next one, or even sit down and read it straight through. Most of all, I hope you will get detoured from this book to start opening some of the other books it's made of. That's what I'm going to do now that I've finished writing it.

Seattle, Washington
March 28, 2013

A Reader's Book of Days

January You'd think more books

would start in January. Does it not feel original

enough to open a story with the new year? Or do

we find more natural beginnings in the spring,

or when we return to work or school after the

summer? What, after all, is born in the dead month

of January besides a new calendar?

There are exceptions. There's Archie Jones, in Zadie Smith's *White Teeth*, roused to life on New Year's Day from his attempt to gas himself in his car in the delivery zone of a halal butcher's shop, and Bridget Jones, sourly recording in her diary the fourteen alcohol units, twenty-two cigarettes, and 5,424 calories she consumed on New Year's Eve the day (and night) before. And there are January beginnings that seem like endings: the death just hours after midnight on January 1, 2021, of the last human born before the species became infertile in P. D. James's *The Children of Men*, and the New Year's deadline haunting Michael Chabon's *The Yiddish Policemen's Union*,

when the crowded but temporary Jewish settlement in Sitka, Alaska, is set to revert to local control.

Calendars do begin in January, although that wasn't always the case. In 1579 March was still, officially at

least, the first month of the year in England, but Edmund Spenser justified beginning his pastoral poem *The Shepheardes Calender* in January because it was the first month after the rebirth of the "decayed world" through the birth of Christ. In colonial America the calendar was a printer's bread and butter: an almanac was often the only book a household would buy during the year, which drew Benjamin Franklin, like many of his fellow printers, to create his own. The first edition of *Poor Richard's Almanack*, which soon became the colonies' favorite, included a tongue-in-cheek prediction that one of his main rivals, the *American Alma-nac*'s compiler Titan Leeds, would die, "by my Calculation made at his Request," at 3:29 P.M. on October 17 of the coming year. (Leeds was not amused, but survived the year.)

In his *Sand County Almanac*, Aldo Leopold was more content to observe than predict, and for him the barely detectable stirrings of January in Wisconsin—the venturing forth of a skunk from hibernation, the skittering of a meadow mouse from the melting shelter of the thawing snow—make observation "almost as simple and peaceful as snow, and almost continuous as cold. There is time not only to see who has done what, but to speculate why."

A Calendar of Wisdom by Leo Tolstoy (1909) ✍ What did Tolstoy, in his last years, believe was the great work of his life? *War and Peace? Anna Karenina?* No, this anthology he spent fifteen years gathering, which mixed his own aphorisms with those of the "best and wisest thinkers of the world," organized by a theme for each day of the year.

At the Mountains of Madness by H. P. Lovecraft (1936) ✍ As the southern summer opens up the South Pole for exploration, a scientific expedition led by professors Dyer and Lake discovers behind a range of unknown Antarctic mountains a vast, dead, and ancient city, one of the most evil and benighted of Lovecraft's inhuman horrors.

"New Year Letter" by W. H. Auden (1940) ✍ With hatreds convulsing the world "like a baffling crime," Auden composed one of his great long poems as a letter to "dear friend Elizabeth," whose hospitality in his adopted home of New York helped him toward this vision of order in art and life during a time of tyranny.

Do Androids Dream of Electric Sheep? by Philip K. Dick (1968) ✍ Many more people know *Blade Runner* than its source novel, set on a single January day in a post-nuclear 1992, which features, rather than Ridley Scott's rainy, neon glamour, Dick's equally thrilling and disturbing brand of stripped-down noir.

Airport by Arthur Hailey (1968) ✍ Arthur Hailey wrote blockbusters like no one else, earnest and fact-filled dramas set in a series of massive industrial monoliths: banks, hotels, power plants, and, in this case, Lincoln International Airport in Illinois during the worst winter storm of the decade, with one jetliner stuck at the end of a runway and another coming in fast with a bomb on board.

"In California: Morning, Evening, Late January" by Denise Levertov (1989) ✍ Levertov's pastoral is unseasonal in the temperate lushness of its California winter, and unsettling in its vision of the industrial forces invading and managing its beauty.

The Children of Men by P. D. James (1992) ✍ Another novel overshadowed by its movie adaptation, *The Children of Men*, in a startling departure from James's Adam Dalgliesh mysteries, uses the premise of a world in which human fertility has disappeared to examine the nature and lure of power.

White Teeth by Zadie Smith (2000) ✍ Smith's debut, which begins with Archie Jones's failed January suicide, has too much life to begin with a death: it overflows with not only the variety of multiethnic London but the exuberance of Smith taking her brilliant talent for its first walk out on the stage.

The Omnivore's Dilemma by Michael Pollan (2006) ✍ One of the omnivore's dilemmas is how to navigate a world whose technology and global trade have accustomed even New Englanders to unseasonal luxuries like sweet corn and asparagus in the middle of January.

January 1

BORN: 1879 E. M. Forster (*Where Angels Fear to Tread, A Room with a View*), London
1919 J. D. Salinger (*The Catcher in the Rye, Franny and Zooey*), New York City
DIED: 2002 Julia Phillips (*You'll Never Eat Lunch in This Town Again*), 57, West Hollywood, Calif.
2007 Tillie Olsen (*Tell Me a Riddle, Silences*), 94, Oakland, Calif.

1803 Perhaps we shouldn't be surprised that the rise of the restaurant in post-revolutionary France coincided with the rise of the restaurant guide. On New Year's Day a man-about-town named Alexandre Balthazar Laurent Grimod de La Reynière published his first *Almanach des Gourmands*, a pocket-sized, almost annual guide to eating aimed, with a slyly decadent style, at the "purely animal pleasures" unleashed by the upheaval of the Revolution (through which Grimod himself had successfully maneuvered, despite his noble birth). The judgments of the *Almanach* were drawn in part from the Jury Dégustateur, a group of gourmands who met weekly at Grimod's mansion for five-hour tasting sessions: the Michelin or Yelp of their day.

1926 Isaac Babel confessed to his diary that he hadn't "done a thing as far as serious literature goes for about ten months, but have simply been hanging around in Moscow in search of big pay-offs."

1947 In a *Guide to Your Child's Development* she has purchased for the purpose, Charlotte Haze notes on the twelfth birthday of her daughter, Dolores, that the girl is fifty-seven inches tall and possesses an IQ of 121. She also completes an inventory of the child's qualities: "aggressive, boisterous, critical, distrustful, impatient, irritable, inquisitive, listless, negativistic (underlined twice) and obstinate." For Charlotte's new husband, Humbert Humbert, this list of epithets is "maddening" in its viciousness toward the girl he calls Lolita and claims to love. But he has his own reasons to revolt at the child's birthdays: after just a few more of them she'll no longer be a "nymphet," and soon after that she'll be—"horror of horrors"—"a 'college girl.'"

1970 Detached from the rhythms of any planet's orbit or rotation, the star-faring trading culture of the Qeng Ho in Vernor Vinge's 1999 Hugo-winning novel, *A Deepness in the Sky*, measures time in seconds rather than days or years: kiloseconds, megaseconds, gigaseconds. When did their clock begin ticking? Not, as many assume, at the moment thousands of earth-years before, when the first human set foot on the moon, but about fifteen megaseconds later, at "the 0-second of one of Humankind's first computer operating systems": the Unix system, which indeed started its counter at midnight on New Year's Day in 1970. It's a telling shift in the history of science fiction, which has mirrored technology by turning its imagination from the exploration of space to the development of machine intelligence.

January 2

BORN: **1951** André Aciman (*Call Me by Your Name*, *Out of Egypt*), Alexandria, Egypt
1956 Lynda Barry (*Ernie Pook's Comeek*, *What It Is*), Richland Center, Wis.
DIED: **2000** Patrick O'Brian (*Master and Commander* and the rest of the Aubrey-Maturin series), 85, Dublin
2008 George MacDonald Fraser (*Flashman* and the rest of the Flashman series), 82, Isle of Man

1960 Donald Malcolm, in *The New Yorker*, on Robert Ruark's *Poor No More*: "With breathtaking ingenuity, he has managed to include between a single set of covers a representative example of nearly every kind of bad novel . . . a sort of Golden Treasury of Commercial Narrative."

1995 "The escape from Glades Correctional Institution seemed the stuff of movies," wrote one local Florida paper, and in time it would be, but only after Elmore Leonard used it to inspire the first big scene in *Out of Sight*, published just a year after the jailbreak. To the real-life story of Cuban inmates tunneling twenty-five yards under the prison chapel, Leonard added the characters of Jack Foley, a recidivist bank robber with even more than the usual Leonard cool who tags along with the Cubans on the way out, and Karen Sisco, a U.S. Marshal who soon discovers her weak spot for charming bank robbers. Two years later George Clooney and Jennifer Lopez, as Jack and Karen, climbed into the trunk of a car and heated up the finest of all Leonard film adaptations, which date back to 1957's *3:10 from Yuma*.

1998 On this day in London, one of the patron saints of entertainingly excessive knowledge, Frank Muir, passed away at the age of seventy-seven. Paired for decades with Dennis Norden, Muir was ubiquitous in postwar Britain as a bow-tied wit both behind the scenes as a writer for BBC Radio and TV and a panelist on the quiz shows *Call My Bluff*, *My Word!*, and *My Music*, the latter two of which introduced him to American audiences via public radio. In their trademark *My Word!* segment, Muir and Norden spun out ingeniously convoluted shaggy-dog tales that ended on a punch-line pun, which were collected in a half-dozen books that, like his anthologies, the *Oxford Book of Humorous Prose* and *The Frank Muir Book: An Irreverent Companion to Social History*—and like his particular brand of learned drollery—are by now well out of print and fashion.

January 3

BORN: 1892 J. R. R. Tolkien (*The Hobbit, The Fellowship of the Ring*), Bloemfontein, Orange Free State

1973 Rory Stewart (*The Places in Between, The Prince of the Marshes*), Hong Kong

DIED: 1923 Jaroslav Hašek (*The Good Soldier Švejk*), 39, Lipnice nad Sázavou, Czechoslovakia

2005 Will Eisner (*The Spirit, A Contract with God*), 87, Lauderdale Lakes, Fla.

1889 In 1888, as he fought off the encroachment of his madness, Friedrich Nietzsche wrote some of his most lasting works: *Twilight of the Idols*, *The Antichrist*, and *Ecce Homo*. By December, though, his self-grandeur was overflowing—he called himself a clown and a god, plotted to destroy the German Reich by provoking a war, and wrote that "quite literally, I hold the future of humanity in my hand." And on this day, just after the turn of the year, he collapsed in Turin, putting his arms—as the stories say, and they seem to be true—around a mistreated workhorse and falling unconscious to the street. It was the letters he wrote to friends the next day, speaking delusions far beyond his earlier grandeur, that brought them to Turin to place him in the psychiatric care under which he spent his last, silent decade.

1951 Precocious in all things, Susan Sontag was just seventeen when, after a short engagement and an even shorter courtship (they became engaged ten days after meeting), she married her twenty-eight-year-old sociology instructor at the University of Chicago, Philip Rieff. "I marry Philip with full consciousness + fear of my will toward self-destructiveness," she recorded in her diary, in a note far more terse than her passionate entries in the same journal on the female lovers she called "H" and "I." Soon after, she would later recall, she read *Middlemarch* for the first time and "realized not only that *I* was Dorothea but that, a few months earlier, I had married Mr. Casaubon." They divorced in 1959.

1992 "Dial and see; just try me." Rick Deckard wants his wife, Iran, to dial their Penfield mood organ to a productive setting this morning—perhaps 481, "awareness of the manifold possibilities open to me in the future," or at least 594, "the desire to watch TV, no matter what's on it"—but she prefers the setting she has planned for the day, "self-accusatory depression." The mood organ is one of the features of the near-future world Philip K. Dick invented for *Do Androids Dream of Electric Sheep?* that Ridley Scott didn't include when he adapted it into *Blade Runner* (the electric sheep of the title, which Deckard keeps as a pet because he can't afford a high-status real animal, didn't make it either), but both book and movie are concerned with the question that drove all of Dick's visionary fiction: in an age of machines, what is real, and what is human?

BORN: **1943** Doris Kearns Goodwin (*Team of Rivals, No Ordinary Time*), Brooklyn
1962 Harlan Coben (*Tell No One, Gone for Good*), Newark, N.J.

DIED: **1986** Christopher Isherwood (*The Berlin Stories*), 81, Santa Monica, Calif.
2005 Guy Davenport (*The Jules Verne Steam Balloon*), 77, Lexington, Ky.

1912 "Two desperate and notorious criminals," reported the *San Francisco Call*, took "French leave" from the Ingleside jail on this day, escaping their steel cells for parts unknown: Harry Davenport, a well-known pickpocket, and "Thomas Callaghan, alias Jack Black, 'dope fiend,' burglar, murderous thug, about to go to Folsom to serve a term of 25 years." Fourteen years later, that same Jack Black was the librarian of that same *San Francisco Call*, having in the meantime reformed himself, more or less, and written *You Can't Win*, a bestselling memoir of his underworld life that was kept alive for decades by the appreciation of William S. Burroughs, who borrowed its style—and a hoodlum character named Jack—for his first novel, *Junky*.

1946 After a four-day bender with his second wife, Margery Bonner, in Cuernavaca, Mexico, the site of the alcohol-soaked dissolution of his first marriage, Malcolm Lowry noticed—and hoped his wife wouldn't—a tree in the Borda Garden carved with the message "Jan and Malcolm December 1936—Remember me."

1958 Lewis Mumford, whose *The Culture of Cities* had made him a leading voice on urban America for two decades, found an ally and a protégée in Jane Jacobs, the Greenwich Village neighborhood activist and writer. "There are half a dozen publishers who'd snap up a ms. of yours on the city," he wrote her on this day. "There's no one else who's had so many fresh and sensible things to say about the city." But when it came out three years later, Jacobs's book, *The Death and Life of Great American Cities*, dismissed *The Culture of Cities* as a city-hating "morbid and biased catalog of ills." Mumford returned fire in *The New Yorker*, praising her fresh and shrewd activism but dismissing her "schoolgirl howlers." Nevertheless, in the same month his review came out, Jacobs and Mumford joined forces to help block Robert Moses's proposed Lower Manhattan Expressway.

1991 It's "like V-E Day and V-J Day all rolled into one" when Frannie Goldsmith has her baby, Peter, in the tiny Free Zone community in Boulder, Colorado. With one immune parent, there's a chance he'll be the first child born in the Free Zone to survive the superflu that wiped out 99.4 percent of humanity since it escaped from a U.S. Army lab, although after a couple of days Peter too starts showing the familiar signs of illness. There are dozens more pregnant women in the Free Zone, so not everything is riding on his survival; nevertheless, the hopes of the small community of survivors—and of all those who have read the thousand or so pages of Stephen King's *The Stand* to that point—rest on his tiny shoulders.

January 5

BORN: 1932 Umberto Eco (*The Name of the Rose, Foucault's Pendulum*), Alessandria, Italy

1938 Ngũgĩ wa Thiong'o (*The River Between, Wizard of the Crow*), Kamiriithu, Kenya

DIED: 1987 Margaret Laurence (*The Stone Angel, The Diviners*), 60, Lakefield, Ont.

1996 Lincoln Kirstein (*What Ballet Is All About*), 88, New York City

1889 Mark Twain's enthusiasm for business ventures was as unquenchable as his judgment was poor. And no investment was more disastrous than the Paige Compositor, a typesetting machine Twain was certain would make such previous innovations as the telephone and the locomotive seem "mere toys, simplicities." Twain took over full ownership of its development in 1886 and on this day thought he had witnessed history: "Saturday, January 5, 1889, 12:20 PM. EUREKA! I have seen a line of movable type, *spaced and justified by machinery*!" The temperamental machine, though, lost the race to market to the more reliable Linotype, and Twain was driven into bankruptcy after $300,000 in losses, believing all the way that James W. Paige, its inventor, was a "Shakespeare of mechanical invention."

1895 Too nervous to attend the opening night of his own play, *Guy Domville*, Henry James, who had spent five years attempting to conquer the London stage, distracted himself by going instead to Oscar Wilde's latest success, *An Ideal Husband*. Returning in time to witness his play's final lines, he missed one hostile exchange—when his hero lamented, "I'm the *last*, my lord, of the Domvilles!" a shout from the audience was said to have replied, "It's a bloody good thing y'are"—but wasn't spared the wrath of the gallery when, in response to the cheers of his friends in the crowd, he took a curtain call and was met with howls and catcalls from the cheap seats. The fiasco—"the most horrible hours of my life"—forever haunted James, but it also cured him for good of the theater bug and returned him to the grand fictional ambitions of his late period.

1920 The successful London stage premiere of A. A. Milne's *Mr. Pim Passes By*, starring Leslie Howard (the future Ashley Wilkes), made the author's fortune before he ever wrote about a silly old bear.

1943 Eleven novels into a career always promising to tip over from critical to popular acclaim, Dawn Powell had an idea for her twelfth. "I could write a novel about the Destroyers," she wrote in her diary, "that cruel, unhappy, ever-dissatisfied group who feed on frustrations (Dorothy Parker, Wolcott Gibbs, Arthur Kober, etc.) . . . If people are in love, they must mar it with laughter; if people are laughing, they must stop it with 'Your slip is showing.'" Five years later, the book became *The Locusts Have No King*, both a satire of ambitious literary New Yorkers that many fans consider her finest and, in her words, a "great true romance" of love held tightly in spite of the Destroyers (and the atom bomb).

January 6

BORN: 1883 Kahlil Gibran (*The Prophet, Broken Wings*), Bsharri, Ottoman Syria
1931 E. L. Doctorow (*Ragtime, The Book of Daniel, The March*), Bronx, N.Y.
DIED: 1944 Ida Tarbell (*The History of the Standard Oil Company*), 86, Bridgeport, Conn.
2000 Don Martin (*Don Martin Steps Out, The Mad Adventures of Captain Klutz*), 68, Miami, Fla.

1892 As homebound women living in the heart of New England's intellectual ferment who turned their brilliance inward in private writings only published and celebrated after their deaths, Emily Dickinson and Alice James have often been compared. James lived just long enough to make the comparison herself, quoting Dickinson's lines with approval in her diary just two months before her death: "How dreary to be somebody / How public, like a frog / To tell your name the livelong day / To an admiring bog!" "Dr. Tucky asked me the other day whether I had ever written for the press" like her brothers Henry and William, she added. "I vehemently disclaimed the imputation. How sad it is that the purely innocuous should always be supposed to have the trail of the family serpent upon them."

1952 Amos Oz ends *A Tale of Love and Darkness*, his memoir of his youth in the early days of Israel, with the event the book has been circling around: his mother's suicide, when she was thirty-eight and Oz was twelve. Worn down by sadness and insomnia while visiting her sister, she spent the day walking the cold and rainy streets of Tel Aviv following her doctor's prescription to "look for handsome young men" and then took all her sleeping pills at some point during the night and never woke up. At their apartment in Jerusalem, meanwhile, her husband and son, who was still a few years away from running off to a kibbutz and changing his name from Klausner to Oz, spent the same evening reading, writing, and playing checkers before going off to bed.

1975 She made her first appearances in the Talk of the Town section of *The New Yorker* as "Sassy Antiguan Jamaica Kincaid," whose observations were quoted extensively by her friend George W. S. Trow; on this day, in a report on lunchtime disco dancers, she confessed her favorite song was "Kung Fu Fighting." But in those days Talk of the Town pieces didn't carry bylines, so it was only when her name *didn't* appear in the magazine that Kincaid really started writing for it. With her first book still almost a decade away, she gathered her forces under the magazine's cloak of anonymity, apprenticing on subjects such as taking the train from Cleveland, a promotional event for cheese, and Boz Scaggs.

1975 John Updike, in *The New Yorker*, on Iris Murdoch's *The Sacred and Profane Love Machine*: "Let it be asked now: What other living novelist in the language is the peer of Iris Murdoch at inventing characters and moving them fascinatingly, at least as long as the book is in our hands?"

January 7

1877 Completed on this day when its author was not yet fifteen, *Fast and Loose: A Novelette* certainly promises illicit fun. As one reviewer noted, "The very title suggests something desperate. Who is fast? What is loose? . . . We prophesy 128 pages of racy trash & are glad to think we shall be wasting our time agreeably." The reviewer, though, was none other than the author, Edith Jones, who not only wrote the book (for the enjoyment of a friend) but attached three wittily scathing reviews—"the whole thing a fiasco," said another—mocking her own efforts. Eight years later, Miss Jones married and became Edith Wharton, but despite this precocious beginning it wasn't until she was thirty-eight that she published her first novel, *The Touchstone*.

1938 Stabbed by an unknown assailant on a Paris street just after midnight, Samuel Beckett woke in the hospital to see his concerned employer, James Joyce, who soon brought him a reading lamp and paid for a private room for his recovery.

1950 "I shall keep a diary." Those words have been known to start a novel—and of course any number of diaries—but in Doris Lessing's *The Golden Notebook*, they don't appear until a third of the way through the story. Finding herself turning a household event into a short story, Anna Wulf asks, "Why do I never write down, simply, what happens? . . . Obviously, my changing everything into fiction is simply a means of concealing something from myself." And so she begins recording her life more directly, in her Blue Notebook. Or so she thinks. In Lessing's nested story of self-discovery, that notebook proves no more satisfactory than the others: "The Blue Notebook, which I had expected to be the most truthful of the notebooks, is worse than any of them."

2000 What was a "McG"? To the cognoscenti, they were portraits of the recently deceased—usually those with only a fleeting or obscure relation to the mainstream of history—crafted on deadline for the *New York Times* obituary page by Robert McG. Thomas Jr. with an unusual and sympathetic enthusiasm for the eccentricities of personality and fate. In the short period of his flourishing in the late 1990s, as celebrated in the collection *52 McGs*, Thomas profiled, among many others, "Lewis J. Gorin Jr, Instigator of a 1930's Craze," "Charles McCartney, Known for Travels with Goats," and "Toots Barger, the Queen of Duckpins' Wobbly World," but on this day his own name came up on the *Times* obit assignment desk. The headline the next day read, "Robert McG. Thomas Jr., 60, Chronicler of Unsung Lives": "The cause was abdominal cancer, said his wife, Joan."

BORN: **1909** Evelyn Wood (speed-reading impresario), Logan, Utah
1942 Stephen Hawking (*A Brief History of Time*), Oxford, England
DIED: **1642** Galileo Galilei (*Dialogue Concerning the Two Chief World Systems*), 77, Arcetri, Italy
1896 Paul Verlaine (*Romances sans paroles*), 51, Paris

1796 The earliest surviving letter by Jane Austen began with birthday greetings to her sister Cassandra, but its strongest sentiments were reserved for one whose birthday was the day before, a young Irishman named Tom Lefroy. At "an exceeding good ball" that night, Jane reported, "I am almost afraid to tell you how my Irish friend and I behaved. Imagine to yourself everything most profligate and shocking in the way of dancing and sitting down together." But in Austen's England, the promising young Lefroy, who in old age confessed a "boyish love" for Austen, couldn't court a woman without property. Marrying an heiress

instead, he returned to Ireland, where, a half century later, long after Austen's death, he became Lord Chief Justice.

1938 At the age of thirty-eight, with his father nearing death, Jorge Luis Borges began his first full-time job, as an assistant at a remote branch of the Buenos Aires Municipal Library. Told by his colleagues to slow his cataloguing of the library's paltry holdings or else they'd all be out of a job, he limited his work to an hour a day and spent the remainder reading and writing while his co-workers talked about sports and women. Though he was despondent at the "menial and dismal existence" he'd made for himself from his aristocratic legacy, during these years he wrote his most distinctive works, the stories of *The Garden of Forking Paths*, including "The Library of Babel," the tale of an archive whose infinite contents drive its librarians to despair.

1960 As she tells us on the first page of Jeffrey Eugenides's *Middlesex*, Callie—or Cal—was born for the first time on this day, as a girl in Detroit. Even before that day, though, two genes, "a pair of miscreants—or revolutionaries, depending on your view," had given her a genetic and genital legacy that would result, fourteen and a half years later, in a discovery that she calls her second birth, as a boy, in a hospital in northern Michigan—Hemingway country, fittingly. But on this day, however complicated her eventual path from Callie to Cal, her father proudly took part in the simple, binary ritual of handing out cigars ribboned in pink.

January 9

BORN: 1901 Chic Young (*Blondie, Dumb Dora*), Chicago
   1908 Simone de Beauvoir (*The Second Sex, The Mandarins*), Paris
DIED: 1324 Marco Polo (*The Travels of Marco Polo*), c. 69, Venice
   1923 Katherine Mansfield (*The Garden Party, The Journals*), 34, Fontainebleau, France

1873 Twenty years after he wrote "Bartleby, the Scrivener" and sixteen since he'd last published a novel, Herman Melville's own position as a self-effacing clerk was given a poignant portrait in a letter from his brother-in-law to George Boutwell, the secretary of the treasury. Was there anything Boutwell could do to assure Melville "the undisturbed enjoyment of his modest, hard-earned salary" of $4 a day as a customs inspector? Making no mention of Melville's forgotten fame as an author, the letter emphasized his principled ability to, like Bartleby, say no: "Surrounded by low venality, he puts it all quietly aside,—quietly declining offers of money for special services,—quietly returning money which has been thrust into his pockets behind his back."

1922 At 74 rue Cardinal Lemoine in the Latin Quarter, Ernest and Hadley Hemingway rented their first Paris apartment.

1927 Writing to his mother that everyone at Oxford was either "rich and vapid or poor and vapid," Henry Yorke, with his first novel already published the previous fall under the name Henry Green, left without his degree to work instead on the shop floor of the Birmingham manufacturer of bathroom plumbing and brewery equipment owned by his father. After two years he rose to management, a career that ran alongside, and even outlasted, his writing life as Henry Green, whose best-known novels—all of them subtle and thrillingly innovative—inhabit both sides of Yorke's life: *Living*, the workers on the factory floor, *Party Going*, the upper class into which he was born, and *Loving*, an upstairs-downstairs tale of both.

1944 Francis T. P. Plimpton, one of the most prominent lawyers in New York City, was a man of great discipline and industry, and expected the same from his children. His eldest, George, was less able to harness his own considerable energies, and when he ran into trouble at Exeter his father sent him on New Year's Day a typed list of eight "Resolutions," twenty-six "Supplementary Resolutions" (among them "I will not day dream" and "I will stand up straight, and walk as if I were carrying a pail of water on my head"), and four justifications for immediate withdrawal from the school, including failure to write his parents "every day." Young George did make an effort—in his letter on this day he reported, "Followed schedule perfectly"—but just weeks before his graduation he was, to his shame, expelled for surprising his housemaster with a Revolutionary War–era musket and yelling, "Bang bang! You're dead."

BORN: 1928 Philip Levine (*What Work Is, Ashes*), Detroit
　1953 Dennis Cooper (*Closer, Frisk, Try, Guide, Period*), Pasadena, Calif.
DIED: 1951 Sinclair Lewis (*Main Street, Babbitt, Elmer Gantry*), 65, Rome
　1961 Dashiell Hammett (*Red Harvest, The Maltese Falcon*), 66, New York City

1776 Published: *Common Sense; Addressed to the Inhabitants of America* by "an Englishman" (R. Bell, Philadelphia). (Its author, Thomas Paine, donated his considerable profits, from 500,000 copies sold in the first year, to the Continental Army.)

1846 Be careful what you ask for. That appears to be the lesson of the "*Corsair* affair," one of the strangest in the odd and passionate philosophical career of Søren Kierkegaard. Stung by attacks on his writing in the *Corsair*, a satirical scandal sheet read by everyone from servants to royalty in Copenhagen, Kierkegaard made a perverse public request for more abuse. He got it, and was especially wounded by caricatures in the paper that depicted him as a hunchbacked eccentric who had the cuffs of his trousers cut at different lengths as a sign of his genius. Once a proud walker of the city who delighted in speaking to anyone he met, Kierkegaard found himself a laughingstock, a wound he nursed for the rest of his life. Even his tailor suggested he take his business elsewhere.

18— The metamorphosis of respectable Dr. Jekyll into murderous Mr. Hyde is a basic scene in our mythology of horror, but in the original tale, Robert Louis Stevenson's *Strange Case of Dr. Jekyll and Mr. Hyde*, it's the reverse transformation that is so terrifying it kills the man who witnesses it. Given the choice, just after midnight on this day, *not* to see the effects of the chemical mixture he has delivered, on Jekyll's request, to Mr. Hyde, Dr. Lanyon replies, "I have gone too far in the way of inexplicable services to pause before I see the end." The end he sees is the terrible Hyde turned before his eyes, "like a man restored from death," into his friend Henry Jekyll. "I must die," Lanyon wrote afterward, "and yet I shall die incredulous."

1953 Writing in her journal at midnight in her parents' house in London, Iris Murdoch recounted one of her first nights with Elias Canetti: "We laughed very much, C. keeping up a stream of pompous-sounding discussion in an audible voice for my parents' benefit in intervals of kissing me violently." For three years they kept up a secret affair and for forty years a friendship, until his death. Dominating both in his arrogance and his intense receptiveness, Canetti seemed to her that night like a "beast" and an "angel," and his presence can be seen in the terrible attraction of characters in many of her novels, from *The Flight from the Enchanter*, published the year after their breakup, to *The Sea, the Sea*, which won the Booker Prize in 1978, three years before Canetti received the Nobel Prize for Literature.

January 11

BORN: 1842 William James (*The Varieties of Religious Experience*), New York City
1952 Diana Gabaldon (*Outlander*, *Dragonfly in Amber*), Arizona
DIED: 1928 Thomas Hardy (*Tess of the d'Urbervilles*, *Jude the Obscure*), 87, Dorchester, England
1980 Barbara Pym (*Excellent Women*, *Quartet in Autumn*), 66, Finstock, England

1842 On New Year's Day, John Thoreau Jr. cut a tiny piece of skin off the tip of his ring finger while stropping his razor. He hardly gave it a thought until seven days later, when he removed the bandage and found the wound had "mortified." The next day, the terrible spasms of lockjaw took hold, and on this day, having calmly said to his friends, "The cup that my father gives me, shall I not drink it?" he died in the arms of his younger brother, Henry, with whom he had founded a grammar school and taken the trip Henry later memorialized in *A Week on the Concord and Merrimack Rivers*. For a time afterward, Henry grieved quietly, but then, on the 22nd, though he had no injury to cause it, he began to suffer from the precise symptoms of lockjaw himself. He convulsed for two days before recovering, and for the rest of his life suffered awful dreams on the anniversary of his brother's death.

1844 Having just struck up a correspondence with the botanist Joseph Dalton Hooker, Charles Darwin broached a delicate subject with an almost shameful hesitancy: "I am almost convinced (quite contrary to opinion I started with) that species are not (it is like confessing a murder) immutable." He added, "I think I have found out (here's presumption!) the simple way by which species become exquisitely adapted to various ends.— You will now groan, & think to yourself 'on what a man have I been wasting my time in writing to.'— I shd, five years ago, have thought so." His hesitancy would remain: it was another fourteen years before he announced his theory in public, and a year after that until the publication of *On the Origin of Species*.

1914 The *Nouvelle revue française* was one of the publishers that rejected the first volume of Marcel Proust's *In Search of Lost Time*—they hardly read it, put off by "its enormous size and because Proust had a reputation as a snob"—but Proust's revenge was quick and sweet. After the book was published André Gide, novelist and editor of *NRF*, wrote with his abject apologies: "For several days I have not put down your book; I am supersaturating myself in it, rapturously, wallowing in it. Alas! why must it be so painful for me to like it so much?" Proust replied that his joy at Gide's change of heart far outweighed the pain of the earlier rejection: "I finally obtained that pleasure, not as I hoped, not when I hoped, but later, and differently, and far more splendidly, in the form of this letter from you. In that form, too, I 'recaptured' Lost Time."

BORN: 1949 Haruki Murakami (*Norwegian Wood*, *1Q84*), Kyoto, Japan
1969 David Mitchell (*Cloud Atlas*, *number9dream*), Southport, England
DIED: 1965 Lorraine Hansberry (*A Raisin in the Sun*, *Les Blancs*), 34, New York City
1976 Agatha Christie (*Murder on the Orient Express*), 85, Wallingford, England

1926 A hurricane brought in the new year, sweeping nearly everything aside on the Samoan island of Ta'u. As the storm rose, Margaret Mead, coming of age herself at twenty-four while she did the fieldwork for what would be her first book, *Coming of Age in Samoa*, was "absorbed in the enormous and satisfying extravagance" of making hard sauce for a holiday fruit cake, but the winds started tearing the village to shreds. Taking refuge with two babies in the bottom of an emptied water tank, Mead rode out the storm and emerged in the morning to a village "weaving furiously" to reconstruct itself. Finally, on this day, in response to frantic telegrams from her teacher and friend Ruth Benedict, who had heard of the hurricane in New York, she wired back a single word, "Well."

1957 Robert Phelps, in the *National Review*, on *The Old Farmer's Almanac*: "The wish for a chronology of significant events is as persistent as it is involuntary . . . Simply to know, to be a squinting, amateur witness to so much precision and progression, is delightful."

1974 A groundbreaking scrapbook of three hundred years of African American history, *The Black Book*, published on this day, is now itself a piece of history, a record of a moment when someone like Toni Morrison, then an editor at Random House and the author of a single novel, had gained the authority to see a project like it into print. Working with collectors who had been gathering the materials for decades, Morrison and Middleton Harris curated a loving hodgepodge of newspaper clippings, minstrel-show placards, slave-auction records, patent diagrams, biographical sketches, voodoo spells, and portraits of the famous and the anonymous. "I was scared," Morrison said at the time, "that the world would fall away before somebody put together a thing that got close to the way we really were."

1997 You don't find out the birthday of one of the most memorable of modern characters until late in the story, when Dave Bowman, stranded on a spacecraft half a billion miles from Earth, realizes he needs to destroy the only other intelligence left on the ship. As he removes its memory blocks, the mind of his companion is reduced to its most basic elements: "I am a HAL Nine Thousand computer Production Number 3. I became operational at the Hal Plant in Urbana, Illinois, on January 12, 1997." If you can't help but hear the disturbingly soothing voice of Douglas Rain speaking those words as you read Arthur C. Clarke's *2001: A Space Odyssey*, don't worry you're doing literature a disservice: *2001* was a rare novel written *alongside* the screenplay, as two versions of the same imagined world.

January 13

BORN: 1940 Edmund White (*A Boy's Own Story*, *The Beautiful Room Is Empty*), Cincinnati
1957 Lorrie Moore (*Self-Help*, *The Gate at the Stairs*), Glens Falls, N.Y.
DIED: 1599 Edmund Spenser (*The Faerie Queen*, *Epithalamion*), c. 46, London
1941 James Joyce (*Ulysses*, *Finnegans Wake*), 58, Zurich

1898 Émile Zola had written on the Dreyfus Affair before, in essays so scathing that *Le Figaro* refused to print any more, but his open letter to French president Félix Faure in the newspaper *L'Aurore*, known immediately by its headline, *"J'accuse"* (given it by the paper's publisher, future prime minister Georges Clemenceau), galvanized the entire country. Putting his life and his position as France's leading novelist on the line amid anti-Semitic riots, Zola defended Major Dreyfus, the Jewish officer who had spent four years on Devil's Island after a trumped-up conviction for treason, and courted arrest for libel by naming those he thought responsible. He was indeed twice convicted, but the force of his essay and the evidence brought out in his libel trials transformed public opinion and led to Dreyfus's exoneration in 1906.

1909 On his first anniversary as a lawyer at the American Bonding Company, Wallace Stevens wrote his future wife, "I certainly do not exist from nine to six, when I am at the office . . . At night I strut my individual state once more—soon in a night-cap."

1934 M. F. K. Fisher, reading Samuel Butler's *The Way of All Flesh*, wished "to have, someday, a style one nth as direct."

1970 It was just a few months after the Stonewall riot, at which he had been a skeptical but interested observer, that Edmund White, on his thirtieth birthday, decided to shake off the shame of not yet having a book to his name by moving to Rome. He didn't make the most of it—his friend and mentor Richard Howard wagged his finger from afar, "Here you are in the central city of Western culture and you've managed to turn it into some kicky version of Scranton"— and when he returned after six months to New York he found that "the 1970s had finally begun," the gay, post-Stonewall '70s, that is: "I couldn't believe how unleashed New York had become."

1987 There may be no better window into the passive-aggressive hothouse of *The New Yorker* during the later William Shawn years than the account in Renata Adler's *Gone* of a mass staff meeting on the day word got out that Shawn, the magazine's editor for thirty-five years, was being replaced. As voices, variously querulous and strident, were raised about whether or not to write a letter of protest to the magazine's owner, Adler, an active courtier in the palace intrigue herself, filtered the inconclusive proceedings through her imperious style, cutting toward her enemies, alternately adoring of and exasperated with Shawn himself, and mournful for a magazine that to her mind, no matter its later incarnations, was now forever gone.

BORN: 1886 Hugh Lofting (*The Story of Doctor Dolittle*), Maidenhead, England
1947 Taylor Branch (*Parting the Waters*), Atlanta
DIED: 1898 Lewis Carroll (*Through the Looking Glass*), 65, Guildford, England
1977 Anaïs Nin (*Delta of Venus, Henry and June*), 73, Los Angeles

1928 Dr. Seuss's first contribution to the common language was not "A person's a person, no matter how small" but "Quick, Henry, the Flit!"—the tagline for his series of ads for Standard Oil's insecticide, which became a '30s catchphrase on radio and in song. (Seuss was hired after the wife of an ad exec saw his cartoon in this day's issue of *Judge*, a satirical weekly, with the punch line "Darn it all, another Dragon. And just after I'd sprayed the whole castle with Flit!") As Seuss often said, his work for the petroleum giant directed the course of his later career: "I would like to say I went into children's book writing because of my great understanding of children. I went in because it wasn't excluded by my Standard Oil contract."

1939 "When I read through this book I'm *appalled* at myself!" Tennessee Williams wrote in his journal just after moving to New Orleans. "It is valuable as a record of one man's incredible idiocy! . . . Am I all animal, all willful, blind, stupid *beast?*"

1973 The date and the year are unnamed, but let's assume that it's on this January Sunday that the New York Giants, starring Billy Clyde Puckett, stud hoss of a running back, and Shake Tiller, semi-intellectual split end and fellow ex-TCU All-American, take on the dog-ass New York Jets in the Super Bowl in front of 92,000, among them Barbara Jane Bookman, a childhood friend to both Giants and "so damned pretty it makes your eyes blur." It's the most amiable of love triangles in the most foul-mouthed of sports classics, Dan Jenkins's *Semi-Tough*, as narrated by Billy Clyde himself with a glass of Scotch and a little tape recorder in his and Shake's "palatial suite here at the Beverly Stars Hotel in Beverly Hills, California."

2010 Tony Judt's essay "Night," in the *New York Review of Books* on this day, began with a statement of fact shocking to readers who had known him only as a prolific historian and essayist: "I suffer from a motor neuron disorder, in my case a variant of amyotrophic lateral sclerosis (ALS): Lou Gehrig's disease." A further shock came on its heels: his disease had progressed enough that he was, more or less, a quadriplegic, living in the cage of his own body, nearly immobile but still able to feel sensation and, with full clarity, think. And so, having recently completed a massive and masterful work of synthetic history, *Postwar*, Judt turned to tiny, hard-won essays of memory, observation, and reflection, composed during his lonely, sleepless nights, dictated during the days, and collected after his death that summer in *The Memory Chalet*.

January 15

BORN: 1622 Molière (*Tartuffe, The Misanthrope*), Paris
1933 Ernest J. Gaines (*A Lesson Before Dying*), Pointe Coupee Parish, La.
DIED: 1893 Fanny Kemble (*Journal of a Residence on a Georgian Plantation*), 83, London
1982 Red Smith (*To Absent Friends, The Red Smith Reader*), 76, Stamford, Conn.

1848 *Douglas Jerrod's Weekly Newspaper* on the new novel by "Ellis Bell": "In *Wuthering Heights* the reader is shocked, disgusted, almost sickened by details of cruelty, inhumanity, and the most diabolical hate and vengeance, and anon come passages of powerful testimony to the supreme power of love."

1895 Poor Hurstwood: his decline in Theodore Dreiser's *Sister Carrie* matches the rise of Carrie, his former protégée, but he's inspired to make one last, ill-fated grab toward his old vitality by a notice in the papers that the Brooklyn streetcar lines, facing a strike by their motormen, are hiring replacements. His day out on the lines, though, is a nightmare: mobs of strikers assault him as a scab in scenes Dreiser based on the massive Brooklyn streetcar strike in January 1895, a strike Dreiser had covered himself for the *New York World*, struggling, much like the striking motormen, against a horde of other bottom-feeding reporters to cobble together a daily living.

1907 Calling the book "a rather strained rhapsody with whaling for a subject," Joseph Conrad declined an offer to write a preface for *Moby-Dick*.

1924 The restless interests of Edmund Wilson—who wrote about everything from Karl Marx to modernist poets to the Zuni to the Dead Sea Scrolls—found perhaps their furthest reach when, having taken work as a press agent for the Royal Swedish Ballet, he interested his employers in *Cronkhite's Clocks*, a work of his own composition that he described in a letter on this day as "a great super-ballet of New York," written for "a Negro comedian and seventeen other characters, full of orchestra, movie machine, typewriters, radio, phonograph, riveter, electromagnet, alarm clocks, telephone bells, and jazz band," as well as, in a starring role, Charlie Chaplin. But Chaplin, making *The Gold Rush* in California at the time, said he only worked on things he created, and that was the end of the ballet.

1959 With his four children, four months' worth of food, five hundred books, and a crew of a dozen or so ready to sail on his hundred-ton schooner, Sterling Hayden, once a wartime OSS agent in the Balkans and once promoted by Paramount Pictures as "the Beautiful Blond Viking God," now bitterly divorced and sour on Hollywood, waited for a judge's permission to set out for the freedom of the South Seas. The judge ruled he couldn't take the children out of the country, but Hayden hoisted anchor anyway and sailed for Tahiti, an adventure he recounted in a memoir named after his ship, *Wanderer*, a brooding, two-fisted tale of the sea and Hollywood ennui published not long before his return to the screen as Gen. Jack T. Ripper in *Dr. Strangelove*.

BORN: **1933** Susan Sontag (*On Photography, Against Interpretation*), New York City
1955 Mary Karr (*The Liars' Club, Cherry, Lit*), Groves, Tex.
DIED: **1794** Edward Gibbon (*The History of the Decline and Fall of the Roman Empire*), 56, London
2009 John Mortimer (*Rumpole of the Bailey*), 85, Turville Heath, England

1605 Published: *El ingenioso hidalgo don Quixote de la Mancha*, the first volume of *Don Quixote,* by Miguel de Cervantes (Francisco de Robles, Madrid)

1632 It is possible that both René Descartes and Thomas Browne were in attendance when Dr. Nicolaes Tulp presented the public dissection Rembrandt immortalized in *The Anatomy Lesson.* The annual "anatomies" were a major social event, and both Descartes and Browne were in Holland then and had great scientific and philosophical interest in the subject (Descartes had made his own animal dissections in search of the sources of memory and emotion). The mere possibility they were there was enough for W. G. Sebald, who in the midst of a meditation on Browne in the early pages of *The Rings of Saturn* claims that Rembrandt, unlike Descartes, was drawn not to the mechanics of the body but to the grotesque, open-mouthed horror of the cadaver, a criminal hanged just an hour before.

NO YEAR Before *The Fountainhead* and *Atlas Shrugged*, Ayn Rand found her first audience on Broadway with a play called *Night of January 16th.* Rand had disowned it by then—on opening night she sat in the back row and yawned "out of genuine boredom"—but with its theatrical gimmick, a trial in which a jury of audience members decided on the guilt or innocence of an accused murderer, the play lasted for six months on Broadway and became a local-theater staple; in a bit of happenstance enjoyed by Robert Coover in his novel *The Public Burning*, the part of District Attorney Flint in the Whittier Community Players production in 1938 was played by local lawyer Richard M. Nixon.

1966 Conrad Knickerbocker, in the *New York Times*, on Truman Capote's *In Cold Blood*: "At a time when the external happening has become largely meaningless and our reaction to it brutalized, when we shout 'Jump' to the man on the ledge, Mr. Capote has restored dignity to the event. His book is also a grieving testament of faith in what used to be called the soul."

1979 "Proceeding with *Bellefleur.* Slowly, as usual." It's the sort of unsatisfied remark you might read in any writer's diary, but in the *Journals* of Joyce Carol Oates, whose productivity—bewildering to everyone but herself—has always threatened to obscure the value of her works, it's incongruous enough that even she took note: "I suppose since I've written 450 pages since Sept. 24 I can't have gone as slowly as it seems." Time feels different to her when she's consumed in her stories, she added: she feels like she's "crawling on her hands and knees" while to everyone else it seems she is sprinting, a "queer unfathomable teasing paradox."

January 17

BORN: 1860 Anton Chekhov ("The Lady with the Dog," *Uncle Vanya*), Taganrog, Russia
1962 Sebastian Junger (*The Perfect Storm, Fire, War*), Belmont, Mass.
DIED: 1964 T. H. White (*The Once and Future King, Mistress Masham's Repose*), 57, Piraeus, Greece
1972 Betty Smith (*A Tree Grows in Brooklyn*), 75, Shelton, Conn.

1904 On Anton Chekhov's forty-fourth birthday (six months before his death), *The Cherry Orchard* had its premiere at the Moscow Art Theatre, directed by Constantin Stanislavsky.

1925 Laura Ingalls Wilder had written for the *Missouri Ruralist*, a farm newspaper, for over a dozen years, but her short article "My Ozark Kitchen," in *Country Gentleman* on this day, was among her first for a national audience. Her move to a wider readership was pushed by her daughter, Rose Wilder Lane, already one of the best-paid freelance writers in the country. "I'm trying to train you as a writer for the big market," Rose wrote. "You must understand that what sold was *your* article, *edited* . . . So that next time you can do the editing yourself." Seven years later Rose edited her mother's childhood stories into a book called *Little House in the Big Woods*, the beginning of a series whose true authorship—by mother or daughter or, most likely, both—has been debated ever since.

1929 For ten years, Olive Oyl, her tiny and ambitious brother, Castor, and her meathead boyfriend, Ham Gravy, had been starring in E. C. Segar's *The Thimble Theatre* in Hearst's *New York Journal*, along with a series of oddball minor characters who cycled in and out of the series. In this day's episode, Castor Oyl went in search of someone to captain a boat he had bought as part of his latest get-rich-quick scheme (involving a good-luck bird named the Whiffle Hen). "Hey there! Are you a sailor?" he shouted at a man on the dock. " 'Ja think I'm a cowboy?" came the reply from a man in a sailor suit with a corncob pipe and massive, tattooed forearms. And so was born Popeye, who soon took over the strip and long outlived his creator, who died of leukemia in 1938.

1971 Joseph Epstein's "liberal" expression of disgust with homosexuality—and its alleged new vogue—in a *Harper's* essay brought post-Stonewall protesters into the *Harper's* offices and pushed Merle Miller, a novelist, reporter, screenwriter, and former *Harper's* editor, to make his own statement in the *New York Times Magazine*. In "What It Means to Be a Homosexual," Miller came out at age fifty-one, recounting a history of being called "sissy," finding love among young outcasts, and living a closeted life in a culture that despised his sexuality, often under the cloak of "toleration." While Epstein declared he could think of nothing worse for his sons than to be gay, Miller closed his piece, which spurred a record 2,000 letters to the *Times*, most of them grateful, by saying, "I would not choose to be anyone or any place else."

BORN: 1882 A. A. Milne (*Winnie-the-Pooh, When We Were Very Young*), London
1925 Gilles Deleuze (*Anti-Oedipus, A Thousand Plateaus*), Paris
DIED: 1936 Rudyard Kipling (*Kim, The Jungle Book*), 70, London
1989 Bruce Chatwin (*In Patagonia, The Songlines*), 48, Nice, France

1902 "As for my not having read Stevenson's letters—my dear child!" Jack London wrote to Anna Strunsky, his fellow Socialist and the woman to whom he would have rather been married. "When the day comes that I have achieved a fairly fit scientific foundation and a bank account of a thousand dollars, then come & be with me when I lie on my back all day long and read, & read, & read, & read."

1939 With E. M. Forster and a young friend of Isherwood's to see them off on the boat train from London, W. H. Auden and Christopher Isherwood left England for America. Well traveled, this time they were leaving for good, each for his own reasons—Auden to escape the cage of his celebrity and Isherwood out of a general restlessness: "I couldn't stop traveling." But their departure, on the eve of war, was seen as a betrayal by some at home. The *Daily Mail* called Auden a "disgrace to poetry," and Evelyn Waugh, in his next novel, *Put Out More Flags*, satirized them as Parsnip and Pimpernell. Arriving to a snowstorm in New York eight days later, the two, friends for a decade and a half and sometimes lovers, soon parted, with Auden settling into the city, and Isherwood heading to California in May.

1947 Raymond Chandler asked his editor at the *Atlantic Monthly* to pass along a message to his zealous copy editor: "When I split an infinitive, God damn it, I split it so it will stay split."

1960 Mikael Blomkvist, crusading editor in Stieg Larsson's Millennium Trilogy, is born.

1969 George Steiner, in *The New Yorker*, on Hermann Hesse: "Why the Hesse vogue? Possibly a fairly rude, simple answer is in order. The young have read little and compared less."

1999 Daphne Merkin, in *The New Yorker*, on A. L. Kennedy's *Original Bliss*: "This is one of those books that makes you curious to meet the author; you wonder how Kennedy came to dream up Helen and Edward and how, at the age of thirty-three, she understands so much about the existential unease that wafts, unremarked on, through ordinary life."

January 19

BORN: 1809 Edgar Allan Poe ("The Raven,"
*The Narrative of Arthur Gordon Pym of
Nantucket*), Boston
   1929 Patricia Highsmith (*The Talented Mr.
   Ripley*), Fort Worth, Tex.
DIED: 1997 James Dickey (*Deliverance,
   Buckdancer's Choice*), 73, Columbia, S.C.
   2011 Wilfrid Sheed (*A Middle Class
   Education*), 80, Great Barrington, Mass.

1813 Among the most unsettling of American tales is "William Wilson," the story of a man haunted from youth by a double who shares his name, his size, his features, and even this date as his birthday. Intimate rivals as schoolboys, the two Wilsons part ways, but the narrator finds, as he leads a life of cruelty and extravagant debauchery across Europe, that his double appears again and again at his side to remind him of his nature in low, insinuating whispers. When, finally, the narrator is driven to murder his twin, he finds, as *Fight Club* fans might not be surprised to hear, that he has murdered himself. In a further blurring of identity, the Wilsons share their birthday (though not its year) with their creator, Edgar Allan Poe.

1921 "So long." "See you tomorrow." For a short time one winter, two boys played together in the unfinished house the father of one of them was building and, when evening came each day, parted with those words, until one day one boy didn't come back. William Maxwell built his short novel *So Long, See You Tomorrow* from two events over a half-century old that still caused him

a vertigo not unlike what you might feel walking along an unfinished beam with the risk of falling below: the death of his mother in 1918 and the sudden absence of his friend Cletus, who didn't return to play after his father killed a man and then himself.

1943 One night at Patsy's Bar and Grill in Harlem, a fellow patron called Langston Hughes over to join him and a friend. As the man explained, with a stubborn fatalism, that he didn't know what kind of cranks he was building in his war-plant job—"I don't crank with those cranks. I just make 'em"— his friend said, "You sound right simple." On this day soon after, Hughes added a new character to his weekly column in the *Chicago Defender*, "My Simple Minded Friend," who commented on the news of the day with the same plain-spoken sensibility and who, over time, developed into Jessie B. Semple, the hero of Hughes's "Simple" stories and the most popular creation in his wide-ranging career.

BORN: **1804** Eugène Sue (*The Mysteries of Paris*), Paris
1959 Tami Hoag (*Night Sins, Kill the Messenger*), Cresco, Iowa

DIED: **1900** John Ruskin (*The Stones of Venice, Modern Painters*), 80, Brantwood, England
2011 Reynolds Price (*A Long and Happy Life, Kate Vaiden*), 77, Durham, N.C.

1006 It's fortunate that any details at all about the life of Murasaki Shikibu have survived the thousand years since she lived, much less that her epic of courtly life, *The Tale of Genji*, has itself endured to be considered by many the first novel. Murasaki was a court nickname for a woman whose real name and birth date aren't certain, but we do know, thanks to a diary entry, that she entered service in the emperor's court on "the twenty-ninth of the twelfth month," the last day of the year in the imperial Japanese calendar and the equivalent in the West, as some scholars measure it, of January 20, 1006. By that point, it's thought, she had already written much of *The Tale of Genji*; its early episodes, meant to entertain the aristocracy, may have been what won their author her place in the empress's entourage.

1775 Samuel Johnson had long been an irascible skeptic of the "Ossian" poems then taking Europe by storm, which the Scottish poet James Macpherson claimed he had translated from the work of a third-century Gaelic bard. Asked in 1763 whether any modern man could have composed such poetry, he growled, "Yes, Sir, many men, many women, and many children." And his final reply in his exchange with the equally fractious Macpherson is legendary: "You want me to retract. What shall I retract? I thought your book an imposture from the beginning . . . Your rage I defy . . . and what I have heard of your morals disposes me to pay regard not to what you shall say, but what you can prove." But though most came to agree with Johnson that the poems were a fraud, their popularity only increased, gaining admirers from Goethe and Wordsworth to Jefferson and Napoleon.

1988 With more pounds of dog food in his backpack than pennies in his pocket and a vague hope of finding a job and a place to stay in California, Lars Eighner, out of work for a year and about to be evicted, set up on the shoulder of Highway 290 west out of Austin, Texas, with his dog Lizbeth and a sign reading, "To L.A. with Dog." Eighner made it to L.A. but soon hitched back to Austin, where he spent the next few years surviving on the streets and writing what became, after his essay "On Dumpster Diving" was an instantly anthologized hit, *Travels with Lizbeth*, a memoir whose wry elegance contrasts with the desperation of his circumstances.

January 21

BORN: 1952 Louis Menand (*The Metaphysical Club*, *American Studies*), Syracuse, N.Y.
1962 Tyler Cowen (*Discover Your Inner Economist*), Kearny, N.J.
DIED: 1932 Lytton Strachey (*Eminent Victorians*, *Queen Victoria*), 51, Ham, England
1950 George Orwell (*1984*, *Animal Farm*, *Homage to Catalonia*), 46, London

1846 "How do you write, o my poet?" Elizabeth Barrett, in a question echoed at thousands of author appearances since, asked Robert Browning, "with steel pens, or Bramah pens, or goosequills or crowquills?" In her case she asked because she had a gift for him, "a penholder which was given to me when I was a child, & which I have used both then & since in the production of various great epics & immortal 'works.'" She had replaced it with a lighter one, and asked, "Will you have it dearest? Yes—because you can't help it."

1849 "Do you know Sarah Helen Whitman?" Horace Greeley wrote his fellow editor Rufus Griswold about a poet of their acquaintance. "Of course, you have heard it rumored that she is to marry Poe. Well, she has seemed to me a good girl, and—you know what Poe is . . . Has Mrs. Whitman no friend within your knowledge that can faithfully explain Poe to her?"

1863 Few of Emily Dickinson's poems were published during her lifetime, but that doesn't mean none of the others had readers. When her uncle Loring Norcross died, a few years after his wife, Emily's beloved aunt Lavinia, Dickinson wrote in sympathy to her cousins Loo and Fanny, and closed the letter, "Good night. Let Emily sing for you because she cannot pray." The twelve lines that followed, which begin "'Tis not that dying hurts us so— / 'Tis living—hurts us more—," were not written for the occasion—death was no stranger to Dickinson, and she had composed them during the previous year—but they were appropriate to a New England January, with their description of the living as birds who, unlike the dead they mourn, don't fly south to a "Better Latitude" when the frost approaches. "We—" she said to her grieving cousins, "are the Birds—that stay."

1870 Philip Henry Gosse was a Victorian naturalist of some repute who, in addition to popularizing the aquarium, spent much of his busy career attempting to reconcile the geologic evidence of the earth's age with the biblical story of creation. For readers, though, he has survived as the other title character in his son Edmund's classic memoir, *Father and Son*. Entrusted after his wife's death with the spiritual development of young Edmund, the elder Gosse and his Protestant sect descended on the child with a spiritual intensity that had the unintended effect of propelling Edmund into fierce secularism, a "horrid, insidious infidelity" that Gosse Sr. lamented in a lengthy letter on this day that his son, more than three decades later, used to close his memoir and to demonstrate their final irreconcilability.

BORN: **1788** Lord Byron (*Don Juan, Childe Harold's Pilgrimage*), London
1937 Joseph Wambaugh (*The New Centurions, The Onion Field*), East Pittsburgh, Pa.

DIED: **1993** Kobo Abe (*The Woman in the Dunes, The Ruined Map*), 68, Tokyo
2003 Bill Mauldin (*Up Front, Back Home*), 81, Newport Beach, Calif.

1824 Even in 1824 the age of thirty-six was not elderly, but for Lord Byron it was. Mired in the rain in Missolonghi, where he had hoped to be the savior of Greek independence but was finding he was mainly its banker, and where a beautiful, black-eyed teenage page named Loukas had similarly shown more interest in his gifts than in his affections, Byron wrote one of his final poems, "On This Day I Complete My Thirty-Sixth Year," in which he declares that since, at his advanced age, he can no longer rouse the hearts of others, he has nothing left but to seek a "Soldier's Grave" in the "Land of honourable Death." And die he did, three months later, though from sepsis, not the sword.

1948 Despite his success in placing his early stories in national magazines, J. D. Salinger still hadn't been embraced by the one he wanted most, *The New Yorker,* which had accepted his first Holden Caulfield story but kept it on the shelf for five years. Finally *New Yorker* editor William Maxwell wrote to Salinger's agent to say, "We like parts of 'The Bananafish' by J. D. Salinger very much, but it seems to lack any discoverable story or point." Salinger eagerly made the extensive changes they requested, and on this day, a year later, their long back-and-forth about the story ended with a final editorial query before "A Perfect Day for Bananafish" could be published: is "bananafish" one word or two?

1956 W. H. Auden, in the *New York Times,* on J. R. R. Tolkien's *The Return of the King*: "Either, like myself, people find it a masterpiece of its genre or they cannot abide it, and among the hostile there are some, I must confess, for whose literary judgment I have great respect."

1967 There may have been more prolific authors in the golden age of the pulp magazines than Harry Stephen Keeler, who died on this day in Chicago, but few possessed an imagination as vast and untethered as his. In dozens of books whose titles—*The Skull of the Waltzing Clown*; *Finger! Finger!*; *Y. Cheung, Business Detective*; *I Killed Lincoln at 10:13!*—only hint at the wonders within, Keeler cast aside traditional notions of plot, character, and consequence in favor of an extravagance of incident and invention, following a theory of fiction he called "webwork" that one of the small army of fans dedicated to resurrecting his work has described as "coincidence porn."

1982 Adam Mars-Jones, in the *TLS*, on Raymond Carver's *What We Talk About When We Talk About Love*: "That's the trick, though: to throw your voice so that it seems to be coming from the furniture, and Carver is an excellent ventriloquist."

January 23

BORN: 1783 Stendhal (*The Red and the Black*, *On Love*), Grenoble, France
1930 Derek Walcott (*Omeros*, *In a Green Night*), Castries, St. Lucia
DIED: 1991 Northrop Frye (*Anatomy of Criticism*, *Fearful Symmetry*), 78, Toronto
2007 Ryszard Kapuściński (*The Emperor*, *The Soccer War*), 74, Warsaw

1759 The French *Encyclopédie* was a compendium of human knowledge but also a radical Enlightenment attack on superstition at a time when revolution was brewing. Finally, after eight years of publication, the royal authorities had enough. "In the shadows of a dictionary which assembles an infinity of useful and curious facts about the arts and sciences," warned the public prosecutor on this day, "one has admitted all sorts of absurdities, of impieties spread by all authors, embellished, augmented, and shockingly obvious," and by summer the project was officially banned. But work continued, for the *Encyclopédie* had important friends as well as enemies. When police searched the house of its editor, Denis Diderot, they found nothing, because the tens of thousands of pages of manuscript had been hidden by the king's chief censor in his own office.

1886 James Ashcroft Noble, in the *Academy*, on Robert Louis Stevenson's *Strange Case of Dr. Jekyll and Mr. Hyde*: "It is, indeed, many years since English fiction has been enriched by any work at once so weirdly imaginative in conception and so faultlessly ingenious in construction as this little tale, which can be read with ease in a couple of hours."

1892 The *Spectator* on Thomas Hardy's *Tess of the d'Urbervilles*: "We confess that this is a story which, in spite of its almost unrivalled power, is very difficult to read, because in almost every page the mind rebels against the steady assumptions of the author, and shrinks from the untrue picture of a universe so blank and godless."

1931 "10:15 p.m. Important discovery . . . found monstrous barrel-shaped fossil of wholly unknown nature . . . Arrangement reminds one of certain monsters of primal myth, especially fabled Elder Things in *Necronomicon* . . . 11:30 p.m. Matter of highest—I might say transcendent—importance . . . Vast field of study opened . . . I've got to dissect one of these things before we take any rest." The wireless dispatches from Dr. Lake's expedition, which has already discovered Antarctic mountains higher than the Himalayas, send the rest of his scientific party into ecstasy with their revelations. But, as readers of H. P. Lovecraft will expect, such hopes soon turn to horror, and the following day, in Lovecraft's *At the Mountains of Madness*, the terror begins as the monstrous Elder Things, awakened, begin their *own* dissections.

1976 Russell Davies, in the *TLS*, on E. L. Doctorow's *Ragtime*: "I am at a loss to say how this most wooden of jigsaws has come to be regarded as a powerful and impressive novel—unless it be by that uncontrollably spawning common consent that takes over when the American public realizes a publicity campaign has got too big to face failure."

BORN: **1776** E. T. A. Hoffmann (*The Nutcracker and the Mouse King*), Königsberg, Prussia

1862 Edith Wharton (*The House of Mirth*, *The Age of Innocence*), New York City

DIED: **1986** L. Ron Hubbard (*Dianetics*, *Battlefield Earth*), 74, Creston, Calif.

2013 Richard G. Stern (*Other Men's Daughters*), 84, Tybee Island, Ga.

1922 A champion of T. S. Eliot since he called "The Love Song of J. Alfred Prufrock" the "best poem I have yet had or seen from an American," Ezra Pound eagerly became the hands-on editor of *The Waste Land* in 1921. Much as Gordon Lish would do with Raymond Carver's stories sixty years later, he pruned half of Eliot's manuscript away, leaving a compact and opaque masterpiece that Eliot largely accepted, saying later that "I should wish the blue penciling . . . to be preserved as evidence of Pound's critical genius." Pound happily accepted credit, writing Eliot on this day to congratulate him on the revisions and attaching a little ditty saying that if readers wanted to know how *The Waste Land* was born, "Ezra performed the Caesarian Operation."

1934 T. H. Mathews, in the *New Republic*, on Dashiell Hammett's *The Thin Man*: a "first-rate murder story," but by writing a more conventional detective tale outside his "gangster-political" milieu, "perhaps Mr. Hammett is coasting."

1949 There are few more evocative accounts of the writing of a book than the notes, terse but full of sentiment, that appear at the end of Marguerite Yourcenar's *Memoirs of Hadrian*. Her "Reflections on the Composition of *Memoirs of Hadrian*" reecounts the story of a love affair—taken up in youth, abandoned, and taken up again in maturity—between a writer and her subject, the Roman emperor Hadrian. Possessed by his character in the 1920s, Yourcenar worked fitfully on the story in the '30s and then put it aside as impossible through most of the '40s until, while sorting through a trunk stored during the war in Switzerland, she came across yellowed

sheets from her lost manuscript, which she immediately took up again in a passion that consumed her for the next three years until *Hadrian* was complete.

1954 In a safari plane crash, Ernest Hemingway ruptured his kidney, spleen, and liver and suffered a concussion, burns, and two crushed vertebrae.

January 25

BORN: 1882 Virginia Woolf (*To the Lighthouse,*
Mrs. Dalloway), London
1950 Gloria Naylor (*The Women of*
Brewster Place), New York City
DIED: 1640 Robert Burton (*The Anatomy of*
Melancholy), 62, Oxford, England
1855 Dorothy Wordsworth (*Grasmere*
Journals), 83, Rydal, England

1533 It's the most storied and significant marriage in European history, but in Hilary Mantel's telling the wedding between Henry VIII and Anne Boleyn, the second wife for whom he rebelled against the pope, takes place "almost in secret, with no celebration, just a huddle of witnesses, the married pair both speechless except for the small admissions of intent forced out of them by the ceremony." Among the witnesses, Thomas Cromwell exchanges threats with his fellow courtier William Brereton, who three years later will be executed, at Cromwell's bidding, along with the new queen. As often as their tale has been told, Mantel gave it new life—with a surprisingly sympathetic Cromwell, one of history's villains, at its center—in the Booker Prize–winning *Wolf Hall* and its Booker-winning sequel, *Bring Up the Bodies*.

1836 Chasing promises of payment for writing he'd already done, Nathaniel Hawthorne moved to Boston at thirty-one to take the editorship of the *American Magazine of Useful and Entertaining Knowledge*, a hodgepodge periodical of mostly regurgitated fact and advice. Writing and editing nearly the entire magazine on his own, he enlisted his older sister, Elizabeth, to help. "Concoct, concoct, concoct," he wrote her on this day. "I make nothing of writing a history or biography before dinner. Do you the same." Promised $500 for a year's work, he lasted half the year and only received $20. Giving up in exhaustion and dismay, he realized, as he wrote his younger sister, "this world is as full of rogues as Beelzebub"—his cat—"is of fleas."

1851 The *Spectator* on the poems of Elizabeth Barrett Browning: "Like all bad artists, she never knows when she has said enough, and does not spend sufficient time upon her poems to make them short. She labours under the mistake that two-hundred-and-forty pence make a pound in the coinage of Parnassus."

1973 Mary McCarthy, in the *New York Review of Books*, on David Halberstam's *The Best and the Brightest*: "Despite the tone of concern and commitment, the book has less to contribute to the public interest . . . than to consumer appetites for unauthorized prowls down the corridors of power."

January 26

BORN: 1929 Jules Feiffer (*Feiffer, Little Murders*), Bronx, N.Y.
1945 Thom Jones (*The Pugilist at Rest, Cold Snap*), Aurora, Ill.
DIED: 1996 Harold Brodkey (*First Love and Other Sorrows*), 65, New York City
2000 Jean-Claude Izzo (*Total Chaos, Chourmo, Solea*), 54, Marseille, France

1901 Unable at first to interest a publisher in her tale of a mischievous rabbit, Beatrix Potter undertook to print privately an edition of 250 of *The Tale of Peter Rabbit* herself, in one copy of which she wrote a eulogy for the real-life model for her hero: "In affectionate remembrance of poor old Peter Rabbit, who died on the 26th. of January 1901 at the end of his 9th. year. He was bought, at a very tender age, in the Uxbridge Road, Shepherds Bush, for the exorbitant sum of 4/6 . . . [W]hatever the limitations of his intellection or outward shortcomings of his fur, and his ears and toes, his disposition was uniformly amiable and his temper unfailingly sweet. An affectionate companion and a quiet friend."

1931 On a winter's evening, Charles Fort, who would much rather have been sitting in the New York Public Library or at his kitchen table in the Bronx adding to the tens of thousands of tiny slips of paper he had filled with notes about phenomena unexplained by science, was induced to make his way down to the Savoy Plaza Hotel, where he was surprised by the first meeting of the Fortean Society, an organization founded to promote Fort's odd brand of mystical skepticism of science and religion, which he outlined in compendiums such as *Lo!* and *The Book of the Damned*. Among the society's founders: Ben Hecht, Booth Tarkington, and Theodore Dreiser, who called Fort "the most fascinating literary figure since Poe." Among the unconvinced: H. G. Wells, who thought him "one of the most damnable bores who ever cut scraps from out of the way newspapers."

1963 At the end of a stay in New York at the height of her American success, Muriel Spark threw herself a farewell party and set about matchmaking between two fellow *New Yorker* contributors. Her shy new friend Shirley Hazzard was just thirty-two and hardly known as a writer, while Francis Steegmuller was a fifty-seven-year-old widower of rather magnificent reputation as a translator and writer, but Spark thought they should marry and, after a two-hour conversation at the party and a year's courtship, they did, beginning a literary alliance of rare charm and endurance. When they returned from their honeymoon, Spark sent a photo of her apartment building with the inscription "The Scene of the First Encounter between Shirley Hazzard and Francis Steegmuller by Muriel Spark. (Her best book ever.)"

January 27

BORN: 1832 Lewis Carroll (*Alice's Adventures in Wonderland*), Daresbury, England
1957 Frank Miller (*Batman: The Dark Knight Returns, Sin City*), Olney, Md.
DIED: 2009 John Updike (*Rabbit at Rest, The Witches of Eastwick*), 76, Danvers, Mass.
2010 J. D. Salinger (*The Catcher in the Rye, Nine Stories*), 91, Cornish, N.H.

1837 In an echo of the climactic duel in his poem *Eugene Onegin*, in which the dandy Onegin kills the poet Lansky, Alexander Pushkin was mortally wounded in the abdomen from a dozen paces away by Georges-Charles d'Anthès, an exiled French gallant who had publicly courted Pushkin's wife, Natalya, for years (before surprising St. Petersburg society by marrying her plainer sister). With his return shot, Pushkin, who spurred the duel by insulting d'Anthès after he flirted with Natalya at a ball, managed only to break two of his rival's ribs. Two days later, ending a short career that later saw him acclaimed as Russia's greatest poet, he succumbed in his library at home; it is said that when a doctor suggested he see his friends before he died, he looked at the books surrounding him and replied, "Farewell, my friends."

1939 Samuel Beckett asked Stanley Hayter to engrave a stone from the Liffey River for the upcoming fifty-seventh birthday of James Joyce.

1945 "So for us even the hour of liberty rang out grave and muffled, and filled our souls with joy and yet with a painful sense of pudency, so that we should have liked to wash our consciences and memories clean from the foulness that lay upon them." On this day, nine days after the German abandonment of the Auschwitz concentration camp, Russian troops arrived to find only a few thousand prisoners remaining, among them Primo Levi, left behind from the murderous Nazi evacuation because of his scarlet fever. That "hour of liberty," such as it was, stands as the hinge between Levi's two memoirs, *Survival in Auschwitz* and *The Re-awakening* (or *If This Is a Man* and *The Truce*, in their better British titles), published sixteen years apart but linked by the day that ends one book and begins the next.

1979 Though he was only thirty-one, still at the peak of a Hall of Fame goaltending career, Ken Dryden went into the 1978–79 season knowing it would be his last in pro hockey. *The Game*, his memoir of that final season, acclaimed ever since as the great hockey book (if you like your sports books heavier on analysis than action), doesn't reach its emotional peak at the season's end, when Dryden's Montreal Canadiens won their fourth straight Stanley Cup, but midway through, when the Canadiens traveled to Boston for another hard-fought game against the Bruins, their great rivals, and Dryden—whose cerebral stardom made him the Bill Bradley of hockey—was reminded that every Ali needs a Frazier to push him to greatness.

January 28

BORN: **1873** Colette (*Chéri, Claudine at School, Gigi*), Yonne, France
1936 Ismail Kadare (*The General of the Dead Army*), Gjirokastër, Albania
DIED: **1939** W. B. Yeats (*The Tower*, "The Second Coming"), 73, Menton, France
1996 Jerry Siegel (*Superman*), 81, Los Angeles

1728 On this evening Jonathan Swift received a message he had been dreading, announcing the death of Esther Johnson and, with it, the end of the great friendship of his life. They met when he was twenty-one and she just eight: he tutored her as a child, nicknaming her Stella, and when she reached maturity she followed him to Dublin. Biographers doubt the rumors they were married in secret and generally trust Swift's assertions of their celibacy, but the passion between them was unmistakable: as Swift wrote to a friend, "Believe me that violent friendship is much more lasting, and as much engaging, as violent love." After her death, Swift confessed in "On the Death of Mrs. Johnson" that he was too heartsick to attend her funeral, and indeed had to move away from a window through which he could see the light from the church where it was being held.

1856 In *Beloved*, Toni Morrison made a ghost story out of one of the most haunting public episodes in the history of American slavery. On a snowy January night, a family of eight slaves in Boone County, Kentucky, took horses and a sled from their masters and broke for freedom across the frozen Ohio River to Cincinnati. Just hours later, though, a posse tracked them down to the house where they were hiding and entered to find Margaret Garner, having cut the throat of her two-year-old daughter, threatening to kill her other children to keep them from being returned to slavery. Garner's dramatic trial became a cause célèbre, and her story was retold by Harriet Beecher Stowe in *Dred*. Morrison discovered the story in a newspaper clipping when editing two documentary books in the early '70s, but chose to learn no more about Garner as she imagined her characters Sethe and Beloved. "The rest," she said, "was novel writing."

1913 A long morning trip by train and elephant, after an exhausting night in which he made his last declaration of love to his friend Syed Ross Masood, left E. M. Forster susceptible to the echoes of the Barabar Caves, an experience he'd turn during the next decade into the pivotal Marabar Caves scene in *A Passage to India*.

January 29

BORN: 1927 Edward Abbey (*Desert Solitaire,
The Monkey Wrench Gang*), Indiana, Pa.
1939 Germaine Greer (*The Female
Eunuch*), Melbourne, Australia
DIED: 1963 Robert Frost (*North of Boston,
New Hampshire*), 88, Boston
2004 Janet Frame (*Owls Do Cry, An Angel
at My Table*), 79, Dunedin, New Zealand

1888 The last years of Edward Lear were melancholy, as was the entire life of the man known for his nonsense, afflicted as he was by epilepsy and depression. He had after years of travels settled in San Remo on the Italian Mediterranean, and as his heart wore down in his last years he buried his friend and servant Giorgio Cocali and his cat Foss but did have the pleasure of finishing his series of two hundred illustrations of his great friend Tennyson's poems. And though the funeral after his death on this day was a lonely affair, too sudden and distant for any of his English friends to make it, he also left a wall covered with the photographs of his loved ones, as he described in his last letter to the Tennysons: "There! it ain't everybody as has such friends! Goodbye, E. L."

1898 The *Spectator* on H. G. Wells's *The War of the Worlds*: "Any man can be original if he may be also vague and inexpressive. Mr. Wells when he is most giving wings to his imagination is careful to be concrete and specific."

1934 "Wealthy Tarleton Powers, fearing death by a gang headed by 'the Top,' sends for Secret Agent X-9—despite X-9's presence Powers is mysteriously shot! On with the story!" Newspaper readers of the new comic strip *Secret Agent X-9* might indeed have required this recap after its busy first week, which launched with a flurry of publicity and inexplicable action. Trying to compete with the success of *Dick Tracy* and *Dan Dunn, Secret Operative 48*, King Features had paired Dashiell Hammett, then at the top of his game as a detective novelist, with young illustrator Alex Raymond. The results, featuring a two-fisted government agent moonlighting as a private eye, were disappointing, though: Hammett left the strip after a year (and never wrote another novel), and Raymond soon followed, to focus on *Flash Gordon*.

1944 Emporia, Kansas, is a town of modest size, and it was even smaller when William Allen White, a native of the town, came home, after working as a reporter in Kansas City, to buy the *Emporia Gazette* in 1895 at the age of twenty-seven. The following year, his editorial attack on populist politics, "What's the Matter with Kansas?" (a title echoed a century later by Kansas native Thomas Frank), made him nationally known. But though he kept his national profile through editorials, bestselling books, and his role as a Progressive force in Republican politics, he refused offers to leave Emporia for a bigger pond, and by the time of his death on this day, he was already a figure of nostalgia, "the small-town boy," in the words of *Life*, "who made good at home."

BORN: 1912 Barbara W. Tuchman (*The Guns of August, A Distant Mirror*), New York City

1931 Shirley Hazzard (*The Transit of Venus, The Great Fire*), Sydney, Australia

DIED: 2006 Wendy Wasserstein (*The Heidi Chronicles*), 55, New York City

2007 Sidney Sheldon (*The Other Side of Midnight*), 89, Rancho Mirage, Calif.

1890 Not every battle on the American frontier was bloody. The historian Angie Debo, who was born on this day near Beattie, Kansas, before moving with her family at age ten to Oklahoma, where she spent the balance of her ninety-eight years, made a specialty of what she called "the second stage of dispossession of the Indians," when the rifle "was replaced by the legislative enactment and court decrees of the legal exploiter, and the lease, mortgage and deed of the land shark." With few academic jobs open to a woman, Debo worked mainly as a freelance historian, digging through bureaucratic archives to write a series of books including *And Still the Waters Run: The Betrayal of the Five Civilized Tribes*, which pointed enough fingers at prominent, living Oklahomans that the University of Oklahoma Press dropped its contract for the book, which had to be published out of state.

1913 Leaving poultry farming and teaching behind at thirty-eight, Robert Frost, a self-described "Yank from Yankville," moved his family to England and set about a poetic career with new ambition. On this day, the same day the page proofs for his first book, *A Boy's Will*, arrived, a new British friend sent the calling card of a fellow American he ought to see, Ezra Pound. By March Pound was writing with pride to the editors of *Poetry*, "Have just discovered another Amur'kn. VURRY Amur'k'n, with, I think, the seeds of grace." Frost began by calling Pound his "dazzling friend" but soon chafed against his "bullying" patronage, resisting, unlike T. S. Eliot, Pound's strong editorial hand and resenting Pound's portrait of him as a fellow poor and bitter exile.

1935 The day Richard Brautigan died is shrouded in mystery, since his body wasn't found until more than a month after he shot himself at the age of forty-nine, but the day of his birth is not exactly brightly illuminated either, by himself least of all. Brautigan was born on this day to a waitress in Tacoma, who never told the man she had left months before that he had a son. Known as Dick Porterfield, after his stepfather, for much of his childhood, Brautigan left the Northwest for California at age twenty-one and never looked back, writing great quantities of poetry and fiction before striking the generational mother lode with the idiosyncratic bestseller *Trout Fishing in America*, after which he spent two decades alternately chasing after and rejecting the success he had improbably found.

January 31

BORN: 1915 Thomas Merton (*The Seven Storey Mountain*), Prades, France
1923 Norman Mailer (*The Naked and the Dead, Advertisements for Myself*), Long Branch, N.J.
DIED: 1956 A. A. Milne (*The House at Pooh Corner, Now We Are Six*), 74, Hartfield, England
2007 Molly Ivins (*Molly Ivins Can't Say That, Can She?*), 62, Austin, Tex.

1852 John Payne Collier was among the most productive of Shakespeare scholars and the most destructive. Indefatigable in both his authentic research and his forgeries, he left later generations a tangled record of true discoveries and misleading falsehoods, as well as the enduring mystery of why so prominent and able a writer would have been so easily tempted by corruption. On this day his career reached its highest and lowest points when he announced in the *Athenaeum* the discovery of the "Perkins Folio," a tattered Second Folio of Shakespeare's works that included thousands of handwritten notations presumed to be by an "Old Corrector" with direct knowledge of the playwright's intentions, but shown within the decade to be a modern fraud, most likely by Collier's own hand.

1903 John Masefield, in the *Speaker*, on Joseph Conrad's *Youth and Two Other Stories* (including "Heart of Darkness"): "His narrative is not vigorous, direct, effective, like that of Mr. Kipling. It is not clear and fresh like that of Stevenson, nor simple, delicate, and beautiful like that of Mr. Yeats. It reminds one rather of a cobweb abounding in gold threads."

1928 On assignment to collect African American folk material, Zora Neale Hurston took up temporary residence at the Everglades Cypress Lumber Company in Florida.

1938 Hans Fallada had endured his share of persecution in the early years of the Nazi regime—his bestselling novel *Little Man, What Now?* was removed from libraries, and the authorities declared him an "undesirable author"—but perhaps the most terrifying episode began when the Nazi propaganda chief, Joseph Goebbels, wrote in his diary on this day that Fallada's new novel, *A Wolf Among Wolves*, was "a super book." Taken up by Goebbels, Fallada spent the rest of the regime in a delicate and miserable negotiation with the Reich, reluctantly altering his next novel toward a pro-Nazi storyline and then spending the war years in an insane asylum, acquiring scarce supplies in the guise of writing an anti-Semitic novel but composing instead a condemnation of life under the Nazis, published after the war as *The Drinker*.

February

By the time it gets to February, in the northern parts of North America at least, there's a weariness to the winter. The days are longer but often no warmer, hibernation's novelty has long worn out, and the fruits of the harvest are running low. Thoreau, writing on the coldest day of 1855, noted the old saying that "by the 1st of February the meal and grain for a horse are half out." (He spent the rest of that frozen month skating on the local rivers.) "It is February," writes Anne Carson from even farther north. "Ice is general."

But the calendar calls to break the ice with romance in the middle of the month. Why February 14? There are a handful of historical St. Valentines whose martyrdom became associated with that day, but scholars have found little evidence that they or the date was linked to a celebration of romantic love until the late fourteenth century, when Geoffrey Chaucer, first artificer of so much in our language, joined St. Valentine's Day to match-making in a number of poems, most prominently in the mating of birds in his *Parliament of Fowls*, "on Seynt Valentynes day, / Whan every foul cometh there to chese his make."

But even he might not have been thinking of love in February: one of those scholars has argued at length that Chaucer had in mind a festival for a St. Valentine in Italy in May, a date whose suitability for romance might, if you do the gestational math, explain why February is also known as a month for birthdays. James Joyce was born on the 2nd, and on his forti-eth birthday Shakespeare & Company published the first edition of *Ulysses* in Paris. Toni Morrison was born on the 18th in 1931, the very same day that insurance agent Robert Smith, in the opening paragraph of *Song of Solomon*, promises to jump from the top of Mercy Hospital and fly across Lake Superior on his own wings. The February birthdays of Freder-ick Douglass and Abraham Lincoln are the reason Carter G. Woodson chose its second week for Negro His-tory Week, later institutionalized as Black History Month. And lovers of calendars and coincidence have long marveled that perhaps the two great-est figures in the English-speaking nineteenth century, Lincoln and Charles Darwin—neither known foremost for his writing but each a communicator of great power—were born an ocean apart on the same day, February 12, 1809.

Persuasion by Jane Austen (1818) ✎ Austen readers looking for a love story in the month of valentines have many choices, but her last novel, the story of an overlooked but independent woman finding love despite obstacles of her own creation, offers perhaps the most moving moment in all her work, the unexpected delivery of a love letter upon which all depends.

Far from the Madding Crowd by Thomas Hardy (1874) ✎ There are plenty of obstacles between Bathsheba Everdene and true love in Hardy's breakthrough novel, beginning with an idle and frolicsome Valentine's Day joke that turns deadly serious and is followed by—this being Hardy, after all—yet more dead bodies in her path.

Life and Times of Frederick Douglass by Frederick Douglass (1881; 1892) ✎ The third autobiography of Douglass, who chose to celebrate his unrecorded birthday on Valentine's Day, doesn't carry the compact power of his original 1845 slave narrative, but it's a fascinating and ambivalent self-portrait of a half-century in the public life that the bestselling *Narrative* launched.

Charlie and the Chocolate Factory by Roald Dahl (1964) ✎ Every day is more or less the same at the Buckets' tiny ramshackle house—watery cabbage soup for dinner and the winter wind whistling through the cracks—until young Charlie Bucket finds a dollar in the snow and then a Golden Ticket in his Wonka bar.

The Left Hand of Darkness by Ursula K. LeGuin (1969) ✎ One of the most challenging and imaginative of love stories takes place entirely in winter, as an envoy from Earth has to learn to negotiate an ice-bound planet populated by an androgynous people who can take the role of either sex during their monthly heat.

Moortown Diary by Ted Hughes (1979) ✎ These poems from the decade Hughes and his third wife took to farming in North Devon, the country of her birth, are journal entries hewn rough into verse, wet and wintry like the country and full of the blood and being of animals.

The Breaks of the Game by David Halberstam (1981) ✎ February is doldrums season in the National Basketball Association, well into the slog of the schedule but still far from the urgency of the playoffs, and few have captured the everyday human business of the itinerant professional athlete better than Halberstam in his portrait of the '79-'80 Trailblazers' otherwise forgettable season.

Ravens in Winter by Bernd Heinrich (1989) ✎ Over four Maine winters, showing as much ingenuity and persistence as his intelligent subjects and an infectious excitement for the drama of the natural world—the "greatest show on earth"—Heinrich tried to solve the mystery of cooperation among these solitary birds, better known as literary symbols than as objects of study.

February 1

BORN: 1902 Langston Hughes (*The Weary Blues, Montage of a Dream Deferred*), Joplin, Mo.
1957 Gilbert Hernandez (*Love and Rockets, Palomar*), Oxnard, Calif.
DIED: 1851 Mary Shelley (*Frankenstein, The Last Man*), 53, London
2012 Wisława Szymborska (*View with a Grain of Sand*), 88, Krakow, Poland

1853 Fitz-James O'Brien, in *Putnam's Monthly*, on Herman Melville's *Pierre*: "He totters on the edge of a precipice, over which all his hard-earned fame may tumble with such another weight as *Pierre* attached to it."

1929 Published: *Red Harvest* by Dashiell Hammett (Knopf, New York)

NO YEAR At ten o'clock sharp outside the factory gates five children appear with their grown-up chaperones: Augustus Gloop, Veruca Salt, Violet Beauregard, Mike Teavee, and Charlie Bucket, one day after he found a dollar in the snow (fifty pence in the original British edition) and the final Golden Ticket inside his second Wonka's Whipple-Scrumptious Fudgemallow Delight. By the end of the day, of course, only Charlie and his Grandpa Joe remain, and from up in the great glass elevator they can see Augustus (slimmer after being squeezed through a pipe), Violet (her face still purple—nothing to be done about that!), Veruca (covered in garbage), and Mike (stretched out so tall on the gum-stretching machine every basketball team will want him), each driving away with a lifetime's supply of candy from the chocolate factory Charlie soon will own.

1963 Among the many unintended consequences of the 114-day New York newspaper strike—new magazine careers for Gay Talese and Tom Wolfe, slow sales at florists without obituaries to announce the dead—was the realization of five editors and writers, Robert Silvers, Barbara and Jason Epstein, Elizabeth Hardwick, and Robert Lowell, that with publishers starved to promote their books it was the perfect time to launch a book review. The first issue of the *New York Review of Books*, published on this day, carried a star-studded table of contents, including poems by Lowell, John Berryman, and Adrienne Rich, Mary McCarthy on *Naked Lunch*, Susan Sontag on Simone Weil, Philip Rahv on Solzhenitsyn, Berryman on Auden, Auden on David Jones, Steven Marcus on Salinger, and Lowell on Robert Frost, who had died just three days before.

2002 Bored with his "office job" as *The New Yorker*'s fiction editor and in search of another immersive adventure after his hooligan-like-me memoir, *Among the Thugs*, Bill Buford talked himself into a lowly kitchen job at Babbo, the three-star Manhattan restaurant run by his friend Mario Batali. His education began, as he recalled it in *Heat*, when he was directed by the dismissive prep chef to his first task: boning ducks, something he vaguely remembered having done as a home cook once a decade ago. Two dozen mangled ducks later, he had sliced his forefinger so deeply that the plastic glove he put on over a Band-Aid so he could keep working had filled with blood like a water balloon.

February 2

BORN: **1882** James Joyce (*Dubliners*, *A Portrait of the Artist as a Young Man*), Rathgar, Ireland
    1940 Thomas M. Disch (*Camp Concentration*, *334*), Des Moines, Iowa

DIED: **1826** Jean Anthelme Brillat-Savarin (*The Physiology of Taste*), 70, Paris
    2002 Claude Brown (*Manchild in the Promised Land*), 64, New York City

1902 E. M. Forster broke his right arm falling down the steps of St. Peter's in Rome.

1922 To say that James Joyce's *Ulysses* was published on this day is a little like saying that it's the story of a man out for a walk one day in Dublin. It was a little more complicated than that. Many sections of the book had already appeared in the *Little Review* and the *Egoist* (and caused a stir, both aesthetically and legally, leading the book to be banned as obscene in the U.K. and U.S. until the '30s). But dates, like many details, were obsessively important to Joyce, and so it was crucial to him that the book be published on this day, his fortieth birthday. So it was, barely: two copies were delivered by train to Paris in the morning to Sylvia Beach, his publisher, who displayed one in her shop, Shakespeare & Company, while Joyce took the other out to celebrate their shared birthday, wearing a new ring he'd promised himself for the occasion. Endless printers' errors kept the rest of the first edition of 1,000 coming slowly to its subscribers, and to this day bickering scholars continue to publish "correct" editions, each claiming to be the first to match the author's original intentions.

1941 For a time, chickadee 65287 was destined for immortality. At their farm in the "sand countries" of central Wisconsin, the family of Aldo Leopold was banding birds, as they did every winter, and on this day they caught the chickadee with band number 65287 for the fourth straight year, the most of any bird they tracked. That fall, drafting one of his first nature essays, Leopold paid tribute to 65287 and its lively longevity: "Everyone laughs at so small a bundle of large enthusiasms." But in December he had to revise the essay, after a different chickadee, number 65290, returned to the family trap for the fifth straight year, and when Leopold's essays were collected after his death in *A Sand County Almanac*, it was chickadee 65290 that Leopold's millions of readers would get to know.

February 3

BORN: 1874 Gertrude Stein (*Three Lives, The Making of Americans*), Allegheny, Pa.
1947 Paul Auster (*The Invention of Solitude, City of Glass*), Newark, N.J.
DIED: 1468 Johannes Gutenberg (Gutenberg Bible), c. 70, Mainz, Germany
1988 Robert Duncan (*The Opening of the Field*), 69, San Francisco

1898 Timofey Pnin lives a life in between: between the Russia of his birth and the American college campus where he plies his marginal, untenured trade as a professor, and between the Russian language that still rules his tongue and the English he can't get his mouth around. He's even lost between birthdays: his original birthday, on this date in the old-style Justinian calendar, was made obsolete by the Russian Revolution, and now it "sidled by in a Gregorian disguise (thirteen—no, twelve days late)." Pnin shared this birthday slippage with his creator, Valdimir Nabokov, who, born on April 10, 1898, in the old calendar, celebrated his modernized birthday on both April 22 and 23, since the gap between the Justinian and Gregorian calendars had increased from twelve to thirteen days in 1900.

1936 Walking through northern England on a "frightfully cold" day to research *The Road to Wigan Pier*, George Orwell made a detour to Rudyard Lake as a tribute to Rudyard Kipling, who had died two weeks before and whose parents had named him after this favorite picnic spot.

1971 Was it just bad luck when Frank Serpico caught a .22 bullet in the cheek while trying to make an undercover drug buy in a Williamsburg tenement just before midnight, or was he set up, as payback for testifying against endemic corruption in the New York Police Department? Not all his luck was bad: the bullet veered away from his spinal cord and stopped just short of his carotid artery, and Officer Serpico survived to receive the NYPD's Medal of Honor for, in his words, being "stupid enough to have been shot in the face." Before Al Pacino played him onscreen and indelibly embodied his hip-cop-in-Greenwich-Village style, his story was told by Peter Maas in *Serpico*, a million-seller that left unanswered the question of whether his fellow cops had anything to do with what happened that night in Brooklyn.

1975 "This was a safe and friendly area," William S. Burroughs observed about the thirteenth row of seating at Madison Square Garden, where he was enjoying his first Led Zeppelin concert on assignment from *Crawdaddy!* magazine, "but at the same time highly charged." He was attending the show as preparation for an interview with Jimmy Page, and to his pleasure he "found the audience well-behaved and joyous, creating the atmosphere of a high school Christmas play." The next day at his apartment, he offered Page a session in his Reichian orgone accumulator, which the guitarist declined, and a cup of tea, which he accepted, and they discussed soccer riots, Moroccan trance music, death rays, Brian Jones, and the possibility of constructing an actual stairway to heaven.

February 4

BORN: 1921 Betty Friedan (*The Feminine Mystique*), Peoria, Ill.

1925 Russell Hoban (*Turtle Diary, Bread and Jam for Frances*), Lansdale, Pa.

DIED: 1975 John R. Tunis (*The Kid from Tomkinsville, Iron Duke*), 85, Essex, Conn.

2006 Betty Friedan (*The Second Stage*), 85, Washington, D.C.

1818 Sir Walter Scott, whose wildly popular historical romances created a vogue for Scottish culture in modern Britain, took on a real-life quest with some of the romance, though little of the danger, of his heroic tales of *Waverley* and *Ivanhoe*. The Scottish crown jewels, known as the Honours of Scotland, had been unseen for a century and were feared lost or transported out of the kingdom until, on this day, Scott and a dozen officials unlocked doors of iron and wood to reach the depths of Edinburgh Castle, where, in a chamber covered six inches thick in dust, they raised the lid of a chest to find intact the crown, sword, scepter, and mace of Scotland.

1882 Oscar Wilde's cheeky tour of America set the good people of Boston against each other. Colonel T. W. Higginson, reformer, soldier, and Emily Dickinson's patient patron, criticized on this day the local ladies who had welcomed into their homes this author of "mediocre" poems whose "nudities do not suggest the sacred whiteness of an antique statue, but rather the forcible unveiling of some insulting innocence." In reply, Julia Ward Howe, already famous for her "Battle Hymn of the Republic," defended Mr. Wilde—"a young man in whom many excellent people have found much to like"—as well as her own hospitality: "If, as alleged, the poison found in the ancient classics is seen to linger too deeply in his veins," the cure was not scolding "but a cordial and kindly intercourse with that which is soundest, sweetest and purest in our own society."

1882 The death, in Leo Tolstoy's *The Death of Ivan Ilyich*, of Ivan Ilyich.

1906 Following the death of Charles Tyson Yerkes, the scandal-courting streetcar magnate whose unapologetic malignity shocked even that robber-baron age (his reply to payoff allegations: "Why not give us the fifty-year franchise we ask for and thus stop the bribery?"), the *New York World* declared on this day that only the late Balzac could have captured his life in fiction: "The tale is too intricate and various and melodramatic for any living novelist who writes the English language." Theodore Dreiser, though, had been keeping a file on Yerkes for years and soon used the arc of his career as the basis for his Trilogy of Desire—*The Financier, The Titan*, and *The Stoic*—which traced the horrifying and fascinating rise and fall of streetcar king Frank Cowperwood.

1938 Sixteen years before *The Lord of the Rings* was published, J. R. R. Tolkien sent "A Long-expected Party," the first chapter "of a possible sequel to *The Hobbit*," for his publisher and, more importantly, his publisher's teenage son, an early fan of *The Hobbit*, to read.

February 5

BORN: 1914 William S. Burroughs (*Junky*, *Naked Lunch*), St. Louis
1948 David Wallechinsky (*The Book of Lists*, *The People's Almanac*), Los Angeles
DIED: 1937 Lou Andreas-Salomé (*Looking Back*, *The Freud Journal*), 75, Göttingen, Germany
1972 Marianne Moore (*Collected Poems*), 84, New York City

1909 Futurism may have been primarily a movement in art, but it was nothing without its writing—its poems but most of all its manifestoes—and on this day the first such bomb was thrown when the *Gazzetta dell'Emilia* of Bologna became the first of more than a dozen newspapers across Europe to print the "Manifesto of Futurism," an eleven-point declaration that began, "We intend to sing the love of danger, the habit of energy and fearlessness." Signed by Filippo Tommaso Marinetti, the tireless and impudent impresario of the movement, the manifesto further celebrated the "beauty of speed," the destruction of museums, the excitement of crowds, factories, and revolution, and the glory of war—"the world's only hygiene." The latter enthusiasm in particular didn't wear well over the following European decades.

1917 Dr. Franz Kafka, after seven years as a law clerk at the Workmen's Accident Insurance Institute in Prague, requested a promotion and a raise to the "fourth bracket of the third salary classification."

1960 Sent a novel called *Confessions of a Moviegoer* by an agent, perhaps because he had just become the movie critic for the *New Republic*, Stanley Kauffmann, an editor at Knopf, sent an encouraging rejection letter to its author, first-time novelist Walker Percy, and then worked with him on revisions through the next six months. On this day, though, he wrote Percy again, saying he had been unable to convince his fellow editors to accept the novel without a thorough rewriting. Knopf did finally take the novel, but let Kauffmann go soon after, leaving *The Moviegoer*, its revised title, as an unwanted orphan on its list until, to everyone's surprise, it won the National Book Award in 1962, despite not having been nominated by its own publisher.

2003 Jonathan Coe spent what would have been B. S. Johnson's seventieth birthday composing one of the most difficult scenes of his biography of the writer, his death. A rather traditional novelist himself, Coe met the challenge of telling the story of Johnson's life—and his suicide at age forty in 1973—with an inventively structured and brilliantly sympathetic biography, *Like a Fiery Elephant*, that shares some of the impatience with formal conventions of its subject, who held in contempt any writer who stuck to the form of the nineteenth-century novel—how could they, after *Ulysses*? Johnson created his own, lonely avant-garde in books like *The Unfortunates*, which he presented as twenty-seven separately bound sections shuffled in a box, and *Albert Angelo*, in which he cut a hole through two pages so readers could see through to an event later in the story and broke in on page 161 with an authorial howl, "OH, FUCK ALL THIS LYING."

BORN: **1898** Melvin Tolson (*Harlem Gallery, Dark Symphony*), Moberly, Mo.
1955 Michael Pollan (*The Omnivore's Dilemma*), Long Island, N.Y.

DIED: **1989** Barbara W. Tuchman (*The Guns of August, The First Salute*), 77, Greenwich, Conn.
1994 Jack Kirby (*Fantastic Four, X-Men*), 76, Thousand Oaks, Calif.

1853 According to his first biographer, February 1853 was a momentous time for Horatio Alger Jr. Living in Paris, the timid Harvard grad was introduced to the sinful pleasures of the body by a plump café chanteuse named Elise. "I was a fool to have waited so long," he told his diary on the 4th, and on this day he added, "She says she knows I wanted to." But in truth there was no diary, no Elise, and no trip to Paris: his French initiation, like nearly everything else in *Alger: A Biography Without a Hero*, was concocted by its author, Herbert R. Mayes, in 1927. Mayes planned the book as a spoof, but he kept quiet as it was taken seriously by reviewers and became the authoritative source on the life of the once-popular master of juvenile uplift stories. Only fifty years later did he confess, as Gary Scharnhorst and Jack Bales detailed in their own Alger biography, that he had invented almost everything in what he called a "miserable, maudlin piece of claptrap."

1910 Writing was rarely easy for Joseph Conrad, and his health was often poor, but his struggles with both peaked with the novel he called *Razumov* (after its main character) until settling on *Under Western Eyes*. In December 1908 he told his agent the novel was complete, but a year later, with the book still not done, the agent threatened to stop the weekly £6 checks he sent the heavily indebted author. Furious, Conrad submitted the full manuscript in late January and immediately broke down, overcome by a nervous breakdown and his chronic gout. By this day, his wife, Jessie, wrote to friends, "he lives mixed up in the scenes and holds converse with the characters." The novel's sales did little to relieve his debt; not until his next book, *Chance*, did he find the success and relative security he had struggled toward for years.

1964 Ralph Ellison, in the *New York Review of Books*, on LeRoi Jones's *Blues People*: "The tremendous burden of sociology which Jones would place upon this body of music is enough to give even the blues the blues."

February 7

BORN: 1812 Charles Dickens (*David Copperfield*, *Dombey and Son*), Landport, England
1932 Gay Talese (*Honor Thy Father*, *Thy Neighbor's Wife*), Ocean City, N.J.
DIED: 1958 Betty MacDonald (*The Egg and I*, *Mrs. Piggle-Wiggle*), 49, Seattle
1995 James Merrill (*The Changing Light at Sandover*), 68, Tucson, Ariz.

1584 Someone must have denounced Domenico Scandella to the authorities, because he was arrested by the Holy Office and on this day was interrogated by the Inquisition for his blasphemy. Scandella was just a poor miller of fifty-two, but he had long been known in his town for the scandalous, self-taught ideas he'd argue to anyone who'd listen, among them that the Virgin Mary could not have been a virgin and that the earth had formed out of a mass of chaos like cheese out of milk, after which "worms appeared in it, and these were the angels." The records of his interrogations and of the trial fifteen years later that resulted in his execution provided Carlo Ginzburg a rare chance, in his influential and entertaining microhistory *The Cheese and the Worms*, to piece together one of the lower-class lives that were often unrecorded and largely untouched by the Renaissance.

1968 At the center of Michael Herr's *Dispatches*, his immersed, anguished, and stylish book about the Vietnam War, is a long chapter called "Khe Sanh." Khe Sanh was a combat base in the mountains near the border with Laos, an outpost, surrounded by North Vietnamese, that grew in strategic importance as the war continued until, in Herr's words, it "became like the planted jar in Wallace Stevens' poem. It took dominion everywhere." For some time the feeling of an uneasy, bunkered truce held there, while reporters like Herr read *The Battle of Dienbienphu* and *Hell in a Very Small Place* to prepare for the siege they expected, but on this day the mood got darker. A nearby Special Forces camp called Langvei had been overrun, with "weapons and tactics which no one imagined" the North Vietnamese had. And now all Khe Sanh was consumed by the terrible thought: "Jesus, they had tanks. Tanks!"

1980 A basketball fan with a hazy sense of NBA history, when told that one of the great basketball books was written about a season with the late-'70s Portland Trailblazers, might assume that David Halberstam's *The Breaks of the Game* is about the Blazers' 1977 championship team. But it isn't, or rather it's about that team three years later, as they succumbed to the entropic forces of injury, age, success, and the business of professional basketball, which all came to a head on one late-season road trip to San Diego, when two of the title team's stalwarts, Maurice Lucas and Lionel Hollins, were traded away as the Blazers prepared to play against their former star, Bill Walton, hobbled himself by a broken foot. "We were pretty good once, weren't we, Bill?" Hollins asked Walton after the trades. "Yeah," Walton replied. "We were pretty good."

BORN: **1850** Kate Chopin (*The Awakening, Bayou Folk*), St. Louis

1955 John Grisham (*The Firm, The Client, A Time to Kill*), Jonesboro, Ark.

DIED: **1998** Halldór Laxness (*Independent People*), 95, Reykjavik, Iceland

1999 Iris Murdoch (*Under the Net, The Black Prince*), 79, Oxfordshire, England

1918 Taking its name from a handful of short-lived Civil War newspapers, *The Stars and Stripes* was founded by the American Expeditionary Force in World War I France as a paper written by soldiers for soldiers. Among the shoestring editorial staff were Captain Franklin P. Adams, already a famous humor columnist stateside, and the young Private Harold Ross, who would found *The New Yorker* seven years later. Joining them soon after was the unlikely figure of Sergeant Alexander Woollcott, a plump drama critic who for years afterward would dine out at New York's Algonquin Round Table on tales of his reporting exploits in "the theater of war."

1926 Fiction doesn't get more speculative than "How Much Shall We Bet?," a tale in *Cosmicomics*, Italo Calvino's collection of scientific fables, in which two proto-beings, Qfwfq and his old friend (k)yK, gamble idly on the universe as it develops. From the most basic of wagers—will matter condense into atoms?—Qfwfq progresses, out of boredom and curiosity, toward recklessly arcane predictions set billions of years in the future:

the winner of an Arsenal vs. Real Madrid match, a treaty between Turkey and Japan, and, most poignantly, the sort of question that novelists have to decide every day: "On February 8, 1926, at Santhià, in the Province of Vercelli . . . Signorina Giuseppina Pensotti, aged twenty-two, leaves her home at quarter to six in the afternoon: does she turn right or left?"

1946 Married and ambitious, Kenneth and Margaret Millar worked closely together on their writing, trading ideas and edits, but by early 1946 Margaret had six mystery novels to her name while Kenneth, detoured by grad school and the navy, had just one. When Margaret's sixth, *The Iron Gates*, became a bestseller and sold to the movies, he wrote anxiously from his ship to the new family breadwinner, chafing at being a "complacent gigolo": "Don't you see that a man whose wife makes more money than he . . . is in a difficult dilemma?" She signed her testy reply "Margaret Mil*lar*," emphasizing the pronunciation she would use from then on to differentiate her name from that of her husband, who soon found his own success under a completely different pen name, Ross Macdonald.

1958 Introducing herself as "the author of a three act dramatic play on Negro family life," twenty-seven-year-old Lorraine Hansberry wrote Langston Hughes for permission to use a phrase of his for her title, *A Raisin in the Sun*.

February 9

BORN: 1940 J. M. Coetzee (*Waiting for the Barbarians*, *Disgrace*), Cape Town, South Africa

1944 Alice Walker (*The Color Purple*, *Meridian*), Eatonton, Ga.

DIED: 1906 Paul Laurence Dunbar (*Lyrics of Lowly Life*), 33, Dayton, Ohio

1979 Allen Tate (*Collected Poems*, *Stonewall Jackson*), 79, Nashville, Tenn.

1878 After showing a deficit in his accounts for more than a decade, Harper's sent notice to Herman Melville that thanks to sales of 190 copies of his novels in the past year they now owed him $64.38 in royalties.

1879 Rather than send his older brother Orion a letter his wife thought was too cruel, Samuel Clemens sent it to William Dean Howells instead, with the command, "You *must* put him in a book or a play right away." Exasperated and fascinated by his brother's improvident restlessness—Orion had passed through five religions as well as atheism, worked at newspapering, chicken farming, lawyering, and cross-country lecturing as "Mark Twain's Brother," and now asked for a raise in the $500 annual pension Clemens was giving him—Clemens professed to Orion his "ineradicable faith in your unsteadfastness."

1927 "Having no longer, I think, any claims to beauty," Virginia Woolf had her hair "shingled," that is, cut. "In front there is no change; behind I'm like the rump of a partridge."

1976 When John Edgar Wideman learned his younger brother Robby was wanted for murder and armed robbery, "the distance I'd put between my brother's world and mine," he wrote, "suddenly collapsed." After three months Robby's fugitive whereabouts were still unknown, but Wideman, whose career as a Rhodes scholar, novelist, and professor had brought him from the Homewood neighborhood of Pittsburgh to the University of Wyoming, felt sure his brother was approaching, and on this day he wrote Robby a long unmailed letter, sensing his presence "just over my shoulder." Two days later, his brother called from a Laramie bowling alley and Wideman drove down in his Volvo to pick him up for his last night of freedom. Afterward, as Robby began a life sentence for murder, Wideman expanded his letter into *Brothers and Keepers*, a memoir in dialogue of their parallel lives.

1977 "Eva, my love, it's over," Stieg Larsson wrote his girlfriend, Eva Gabrielsson. "As I leave for Africa, I'm aware of what's waiting for me . . . I think this trip might lead to my death." At twenty-two Larsson, a science fiction fanzine editor and Trotskyite, was setting out for Africa, where he would put his Swedish national service training to use by teaching a group of female guerrilla fighters in the Eritrean People's Liberation Front to fire mortars in their independence struggle against Ethiopia. Certain he'd die there, he made out the only will of his life before leaving, a will that, at his death twenty-seven years later with his Millennium Trilogy yet to be published, left Gabrielsson, still his girlfriend, without control of his estate, his works, or even their shared apartment.

BORN: **1898** Bertolt Brecht (*The Threepenny Opera*, *Life of Galileo*), Augsburg, Germany
1930 E. L. Konigsburg (*From the Mixed-Up Files of Mrs. Basil E. Frankweiler*), New York City

DIED: **1957** Laura Ingalls Wilder (*Little House in the Big Woods*), 90, Mansfield, Mo.
1992 Alex Haley (*Roots*, *The Autobiography of Malcolm X*), 70, Seattle

1828 Mrs. Frances Trollope's disappointment with her adopted home of Cincinnati, where she and three of her children arrived on this day (her youngest son, the future novelist Anthony, stayed in England), became one of the scandals of the century. The raw frontier town had been advertised to her as a "wonder of the West," but for two heavily indebted years she struggled to build a glamorous department store there. Only after she returned to England did she make her fortune with *Domestic Manners of the Americans*, a sharp-tongued and coolly observant bestseller both in England and in the United States, where "the more it was abused the more rapidly did the printers issue new editions."

1879 Horse thief, bank robber, murderer, and national hero, Ned Kelly was hanged in Melbourne in his mid-twenties but lived on in Australia as a legend of bush rebellion against the colonial authorities, helped in part by a notorious letter he handed in to a small-town newspaper on this day after robbing the local bank. Ferociously bitter toward his enemies—the "big ugly fat-necked wombat headed big bellied magpie legged narrow hipped splaw-footed sons of Irish Bailiffs or english landlords which is better known as Officers of Justice or Victorian Police"—and righteous in the cause of the poor, the Jerilderie Letter has a raw and vivid charisma that gave Peter Carey a voice for *The True History of the Kelly Gang*, his Booker Prize–winning 2000 re-creation of Kelly's short and infamous career.

1971 "You can play guitar, right?" "Yeah, I like to play guitar." "Well, could you play a car crash with an electric guitar?" That was the extent of Lenny Kaye's job interview to accompany Patti Smith in her first poetry reading at St. Mark's Church in New York City, as recalled in *Just Kids*, her National Book Award–winning memoir of her bohemian youth. That first reading, with Kaye's electric feedback behind her, sent her on a long and fruitful detour from writing into rock 'n' roll: the first lines of "Oath," a poem she read that night, would soon be transformed into the first lines of "Gloria," the opening song on her debut album, *Horses*: "Christ died for somebody's sins / But not mine."

February 11

BORN: 1944 Joy Williams (*Taking Care, The Quick and the Dead*), Chelmsford, Mass.
1968 Mo Willems (*Don't Let the Pigeon Drive the Bus!*), New Orleans
DIED: 1650 René Descartes (*Discourse on the Method*), 53, Stockholm
1963 Sylvia Plath (*Ariel, Crossing the Water*), 30, London

1860 In Europe, after serving as American consul in Liverpool, Nathaniel Hawthorne made a literary discovery he was eager to share with his American publisher, James T. Fields: "Have you ever read the novels of Anthony Trollope? They precisely suit my taste; solid and substantial, written on the strength of beef and through the inspiration of ale, and just as real as if some giant had hewn a great lump out of the earth and put it under a glass case, with all its inhabitants going about their daily business and not suspecting that they were made a show of." When Fields dined with Trollope in London a few months later and passed along Hawthorne's praise, Trollope was so pleased he copied it down so he might carry it around with him.

1917 When Virginia Woolf, the patrician novelist still early in her public career, and Katherine Mansfield, a vulgar young New Zealander with an unsavory reputation, finally met, their early encounters, at least on Woolf's side, were not auspicious: she wrote her sister on this day that Mansfield was "a forcible and utterly unscrupulous character" and later recalled her first impression that she "stinks like a—well, civet cat that had taken to street walking." But their short friendship was intense and immeasurably influential, each finding in the other a woman she could speak with about her work as with no one else, and when Woolf learned of Mansfield's death from tuberculosis in 1923, she wrote, "It seemed to me there was no point in writing. Katherine won't read it. Katherine's my rival no longer."

1992 "By the second week in February," begins one of the single-page comic-strip tales in Ben Katchor's *Julius Knipl, Real Estate Photographer*, "the city's wholesale calendar salesmen pack up their samples and enter a state of self-induced hibernation." Now they can sleep late, "luxuriate in the passage of unmarked time," encounter their products hanging, ignored, on the walls of restaurants and small businesses, and leave the seasonal work to the Christmas-decoration salesmen. Katchor's Knipl strips, populated by liquid-soap technicians, freelance clarinetists, former elastic-waistband entrepreneurs, and the underemployed but always curious Mr. Knipl himself, imbue the minor industries and fading establishments of their unnamed city with a profound, though paunchy, elegance.

BORN: 1809 Charles Darwin (*On the Origin of Species*), Shrewsbury, England
1938 Judy Blume (*Are You There God? It's Me, Margaret*; *Forever*), Elizabeth, N.J.
DIED: 1984 Julio Cortázar (*Hopscotch*, *Blow-Up*), 69, Paris
2000 Charles M. Schulz (*Peanuts*), 77, Santa Rosa, Calif.

NO YEAR Joining the African American migration from the South to the South Side of Chicago, Richard Wright found work at the city's massive post office and wrote his first novel, *Cesspool*, a violent and raunchy satire of the lives of postal worker Jake Jackson and his friends that places the mechanical tedium of their mail sorting and their talk of sex, food, and Joe Louis in ironic counterpoint to the solemn uplift of radio celebrations of Lincoln's birthday. The book found no takers; one agent replied, "I have a suspicion that you may have been under the influence of Joyce's *Ulysses* in attempting to relate the events in one day in the life of a negro, and while I can see excellent possibilities in such treatment, you have unfortunately not realized any of them." Only in 1963, after Wright's death, was the novel published, under the new title *Lawd Today*.

1976 The best of friends when they both lived in Barcelona during the "Boom" in Latin American fiction, Mario Vargas Llosa and Gabriel García Márquez had already begun to drift apart, thanks to both politics and personality, when they met in Mexico City at the premiere of *Survivors of the Andes*, a film of a Uruguayan plane crash (the same one recounted in *Alive*) for which Vargas Llosa had written the screenplay. "Brother!" cried García Márquez and raised his arms for an embrace, but Vargas Llosa punched his old friend in the face and knocked him to the ground, shouting, "That's for what you said"—or "did," according to other witnesses—"to Patricia," Mario's wife. They were the last words either writer—both Nobel laureates now—has spoken to the other.

1989 The death of Thomas Bernhard by assisted suicide on this day, after years of illness, was, by his request, not revealed to the public until four days later, following a small private funeral. Also revealed was Bernhard's final joke on the native country he had spent his career despising: a will that stipulated that none of his writings "shall be produced, printed, or even just recited within the borders of the Austrian state, however that state defines itself, for the duration of the legal copyright." But like the artistic efforts of so many of his novels' characters, this last gesture was a failure: ten years after his death, Bernhard's heirs let the ban on production of his plays in Austria lapse, allowing his compatriots to enjoy, once again, his mockery of them.

1996 Walter Kirn, in *New York*, on David Foster Wallace's *Infinite Jest*: "It's as though Paul Bunyan had joined the NFL or Wittgenstein had gone on 'Jeopardy!' The novel is that colossally disruptive. And that spectacularly good."

February 13

BORN: 1903 Georges Simenon (*Tropic Moon*, *The Hotel Majestic*), Liège, Belgium
1945 Simon Schama (*Citizens*, *Rembrandt's Eyes*), London

DIED: 1571 Benvenuto Cellini (*Autobiography*), 70, Florence, Italy
1952 Josephine Tey (*The Daughter of Time*, *The Franchise Affair*), 55, London

1605 The great exception to the contempt in which "literature by committee" is usually held is the King James Bible, a thoroughly bureaucratic undertaking fulfilled by a largely forgotten staff of dozens. Given their marching orders by the king in 1604, the translators were divided into six "companies," among them the Second Oxford Company, which had perhaps the most crucial assignment of all: the Gospels, as well as the Acts of the Apostles and Revelation. A group of men versed in both the holy word and the worldly power struggles of the English Church, they met for the first time on this day in the Merton College rooms of the most worldly of them all, Sir Henry Savile, the only translator not to have taken holy orders and a true man of the Renaissance, as curious about mathematics and the unsettling ideas of Copernicus as he was about holy writ.

1945 Held in Dresden as a German prisoner during the final convulsions of World War II, Kurt Vonnegut witnessed the Allied firestorm that consumed the city beginning on this night. For twenty years he tried to turn the experience into fiction—"I came home in 1945, started writing about it, and wrote about it, and *wrote about it*, and WROTE ABOUT IT"—before arriving at the jumbled and fragmented form of *Slaughterhouse-Five*, a novel that, amid its time travel and green spacemen, returns relentlessly to the inexplicable carnage of those days, echoed in the life of a time-traveling American prisoner who knows that "I, Billy Pilgrim, will die, have died, and always will die on February thirteenth, 1976," the anniversary of the bombing.

1953 We have no autobiographical evidence of Archimedes shouting "Eureka!" in the streets and only secondhand reports of Newton's falling apple, but thanks to *The Double Helix*, James Watson's account of the discovery of the structure of DNA, we do have, firsthand, the story of the day when Watson and his colleague Francis Crick solved the puzzle of the genetic molecule. Watson's memoir, written fifteen years after the discovery, remains fresh with the brashness of its author's youth, but even the unapologetically ambitious Watson confessed he was left "slightly queasy" when Crick, no less brash than he, burst into the Eagle, their regular Cambridge pub, and announced to "everyone within hearing distance that we had found the secret of life."

1974 Six weeks after *The Gulag Archipelago* was first published in the West, Aleksandr Solzhenitsyn was forcibly exiled from the USSR and flown by the KGB to Frankfurt, where he was given five hundred German marks and driven to the country home of his friend Heinrich Böll.

BORN: **1856** Frank Harris (*My Life and Loves*), Galway, Ireland
1944 Carl Bernstein (*All the President's Men*), Washington, D.C.

DIED: **1975** P. G. Wodehouse (*The Code of the Woosters*), 93, Southampton, N.Y.
2010 Dick Francis (*Dead Cert, Nerve, Forfeit*), 89, Grand Cayman Island

1886 "I have assigned my surname and family crest to medicine," Anton Chekhov wrote to a friend, "and I shall cleave to that until my dying day. As for authorship, sooner or later I'll have to give it up. Besides, medicine takes itself seriously, and requires a different label from toying with literature."

1932 Vladimir Nabokov, in goal as always, played his first match with a new Russian émigré soccer team in Berlin. A few weeks later, after he was knocked unconscious by a team of factory workers, his wife, Vera, put an end to his soccer career.

1935 Samuel Beckett wrote to Tom McGreevy on Jane Austen, "Now I am reading the divine Jane. I think she has much to teach me."

1971 In Oaxaca, Mexico, Clifford Irving got the call he had flown there to receive, from a "friend of Octavio's," the code name for Howard Hughes, the pathologically reclusive billionaire who soon agreed—without shaking hands, of course—to collaborate with Irving on an authorized biography. Or at least that's the story Irving told his editors at McGraw-Hill a few days later, leading them to eagerly advance $500,000 for "the most fantastic project of the decade." In reality, as would be scandalously revealed a year later, his Oaxaca trip was just one element in an elaborate hoax: rather than meeting with Hughes, he spent Valentine's Day there trysting with his mistress, the Danish pop star Nina van Pallandt.

1989 At a memorial service in London for the writer Bruce Chatwin, Paul Theroux leaned forward and said to his friend Salman Rushdie, sitting in the pew in front of him, "I suppose we'll be here for you next week, Salman." It was Valentine's Day, and that morning a BBC reporter had called Rushdie and asked, "How does it feel to know that you have just been sentenced to death by Ayatollah Khomeini?" Khomeini's fatwa against Rushdie and "all those involved in" the publication of his novel *The Satanic Verses* drove the author into hiding for much of the next decade, which he later wrote about in *Joseph Anton*, a memoir named after the police alias he created from the first names of Conrad and Chekhov.

February 15

BORN: 1948 Art Spiegelman (*Maus*, *Raw*, *Breakdowns*), Stockholm
1954 Matt Groening (*Life in Hell*), Portland, Ore.
DIED: 1988 Richard Feynman (*Surely You're Joking, Mr. Feynman!*), 69, Los Angeles
1998 Martha Gellhorn (*The Face of War*), 89, London

1912 In her first sentence in *The Freewoman*, a spirited new feminist journal, nineteen-year-old Cecily Fairfield came out with a bang: "There are two kinds of imperialists—imperialists and bloody imperialists." But by her second review, an attack on the anti-suffragist novelist Mrs. Humphry Ward, Fairfield decided, for the sake of her mother, to take a pseudonym. "Rebecca West born February 15, 1912," she wrote in her scrapbook, borrowing a name from an outspoken character in Ibsen's play *Rosmersholm*, and she quickly made a name for West with similarly stylish lines like these: "Mr Harold Owen is a natural slave, having no conception of liberty nor any use for it. So, as a Freewoman, I review his antifeminist thesis, *Woman Adrift*, with chivalrous reluctance, feeling that a steam engine ought not to crush a butterfly."

1941 J. D. Salinger embarked as a member of the entertainment staff of the SS *Kungsholm*, a Swedish American Line cruise ship.

2001 The wheels were already starting to loosen on the Enron juggernaut when new CEO Jeff Skilling spent an agitated twenty minutes on the phone with *Fortune* reporter Bethany McLean, insisting that his company's finances were "*not* a black box" before hanging up on her. On this morning, the next day, Enron CFO Andy Fastow flew to New York to unconvincingly address her concerns, finally ending their meeting with a confidential aside, "I don't care what you say about the company. Just don't make me look bad." Soon after, McLean's headline in *Fortune*, the magazine that had named Enron "America's Most Innovative Company" for each of the last six years, read, "Is Enron Overpriced?" In 2003, after Enron had collapsed in scandal and bankruptcy, her conversations with Skilling and Fastow became one of the more astonishing episodes in her history, co-written with Peter Elkind, of Enron's rise and fall, *The Smartest Guys in the Room*.

2301 It's a bitter winter morning when Ben Reich, the richest (and angriest) man in New York City, wakes up screaming once again. With a quick glance at his multi-clock he can take in, simultaneously, the time in the eight nearby inhabited worlds from Venus to Triton, but all that's on his mind is one man, his great rival Craye D'Courtney. Telepathic surveillance may have kept the city murder-free for seventy-five years, but Reich has just allowed himself a forbidden thought: he must kill D'Courtney. Winning the first Hugo Award in 1953, Alfred Bester's *The Demolished Man* helped usher in modern science fiction with a high-wire story of predatory corporations and mind-reading that paved the way for the coming innovations of Philip K. Dick and William Gibson.

BORN: **1838** Henry Adams (*The Education of Henry Adams, Democracy*), Boston
1944 Richard Ford (*The Sportswriter, Rock Springs*), Jackson, Miss.

DIED: **1992** Angela Carter (*The Bloody Chamber, Wise Children*), 51, London
2012 Anthony Shadid (*Night Draws Near, House of Stone*), 43, Syria

1845 and 1904 As Ian Frazier notes in *Travels in Siberia*, the two Americans who have written most influentially about Russia shared the same name and the same birthday, fifty-nine years apart. The younger of the two, George F. Kennan, the diplomat and architect of the Cold War "containment" strategy, was born in 1904 and named after his first cousin twice removed, George Kennan, born in 1845, who wrote *Tent Life in Siberia*, an affectionate and dramatic account of his adventures as a twenty-year-old from Ohio helping to survey a telegraph line across Russia. Two decades later, the elder Kennan returned to write *Siberia and the Exile System*, a scathing indictment of the tsar admired by both Twain and Tolstoy.

1946 V. S. Pritchett, in the *New Statesman and Nation*, on George Orwell's *Critical Essays*: "To say, for example, that Mr. Orwell's mind appears to be fixed in the boyish satisfactions and rebellions of 1910, tells us nothing about his quality. We all have to be fixed somewhere."

1985 There was no single day when John M. Hull went blind. From childhood, the dark shadows in his vision waxed and waned, but they finally grew until he could no longer tell day from night. His memoir, *Touching the Rock*, begins after that point, a record of complete blindness written by someone who once knew full sight but found himself forgetting what it was like. It's a modestly extraordinary book, a diary of acute and often surprising philosophical and physical observations, among them the basic lesson of this February day that snow is dangerous for the blind not, as many assume, because it's slippery, but because it makes the whole world disappear, muffling sounds and blanketing the landmarks that make the world navigable by ear and touch.

February 17

BORN: **1930** Ruth Rendell (*A Demon in My View*, *A Fatal Inversion*), London
1955 Mo Yan (*Life and Death Are Wearing Me Out*), Gaomi, China

DIED: **1994** Randy Shilts (*And the Band Played On*), 42, Guerneville, Calif.
2006 Sybille Bedford (*A Legacy*, *Jigsaw*, *Quicksand*), 94, London

1847 After Thomas Dunn English called him "thoroughly unprincipled, base and depraved . . . not alone an assassin in morals, but a quack in literature," Edgar Allan Poe was awarded $225 in damages for libel, as well as six cents for costs.

1903 "No one can advise or help you—no one." That paradoxical disclaimer is at the heart of perhaps the most beloved book of writing advice, Rainer Maria Rilke's *Letters to a Young Poet*, which Franz Kappus, the young poet of the title, published after Rilke's death. Kappus was a nineteen-year-old student at a military academy in Vienna when he discovered that Rilke had preceded him, miserably, there. He sent Rilke some poems to critique, but in reply the poet—who was only twenty-seven himself—had less to say about how to write than how to live. Young poets have been looking within themselves and asking, "*Must* I write?" ever since.

1903 Early in a marvelously varied career that included writing *The Autobiography of an Ex-Colored Man* and running the NAACP, James Weldon Johnson left his position as a grade-school principal in Jacksonville to take a chance on Broadway songwriting with his brother, Rosamond, and the performer Bob Cole. They were an immediate success (on this day, the *New York Sun* called them the "ebony Offenbachs"), and their biggest hit, "Under the Bamboo Tree," has had as long a life—quoted by T. S. Eliot in *The Waste Land* and sung by Judy Garland in *Meet Me in St. Louis* and Steve Martin in *The Man with Two Brains*—as another of the Johnson brothers' compositions, "Lift Ev'ry Voice and Sing," which came to be known as the Black National Anthem.

1922 Rilke took an interest in another younger writer, asking their mutual publisher, Kurt Wolff, to tell him of anything new from Franz Kafka, known for just a few stories at that point: "I am among his most devoted readers."

1974 In the early '70s Ted Hughes and his third wife, Carol, both raised on farms, bought a farm of their own in her wet and rough home country of North Devon. The notes he took there, he found, were liveliest when set down immediately; if he tried recollecting and refashioning them in tranquility, in the usual poetic process, they lost what freshness they'd captured. And so the lyrics collected in *Moortown Diary* are as rough as the country, among them "February 17," the story of a lamb he hacked stillborn from its mother at sunrise, and "Feeding out-wintering cattle at twilight," in which the poet, delivering hay to cows at the other end of the same day, stumbles through wind and "night-thickness" so strong he seems lucky to have escaped with his life.

BORN: **1929** Len Deighton (*The Ipcress File, Berlin Game*), London

1957 George Pelecanos (*King Suckerman, Hard Revolution*), Washington, D.C.

DIED: **1546** Martin Luther (*Ninety-five Theses, Luther Bible*), 62, Eisleben, Germany

2009 Tayeb Salih (*Season of Migration to the North*), 80, London

1931 Toni Morrison is one of the least auto-biographical of novelists—after admitting to an audience in her home state of Ohio that she had canceled a contract for a memoir because she wasn't interested enough in her own childhood, she said, "People say to write what you know. I'm here to tell you, no one wants to read that, 'cause you don't know anything. So write about something you don't know"—but on the opening page of *Song of Solomon* she tucked a small link to herself into an otherwise fantastic event: the day that Robert Smith, the North Carolina Mutual Life Insurance agent, announces he will take off from the cupola of Mercy Hospital at three in the afternoon and "fly away on my own wings" is February 18, 1931, the date of Morrison's own birth in Lorain, Ohio.

1949 Flannery O'Connor was just twenty-three, with a few short stories accepted by magazines, but she knew what she wanted, and it wasn't being treated like "a slightly dim-witted Camp Fire Girl." That's how she thought John Selby, an editor at Rinehart, had addressed her when he told her that her resistance to criticism was "most unbecoming in a writer so young." In a reply on this day, she resisted further: "I am amenable to criticism but only within the sphere of what I am trying to do; I will not be persuaded to do otherwise. The finished book, though I hope less angular, will be just as odd if not odder than the nine chapters you have now." The odd book, when finished, she called *Wise Blood*; it was published instead by Harcourt, Brace.

1975 The understanding of one of the classics of European literature, studied intensely for three-quarters of a century, was upended when Chinua Achebe, the most acclaimed West African novelist, presented as the Chancellor's Lecture at the University of Massachusetts "An Image of Africa: Racism in Conrad's *Heart of Darkness*." Cutting through the novel's layers of irony with the blunt statement "Conrad was a bloody racist," Achebe argued that even while portraying the horrors of European colonialism, Conrad couldn't imagine a full humanity for Africans. "Africa," he said, "is to Europe as the picture is to Dorian Gray—a carrier unto whom the master unloads his physical and moral deformities so that he may go forward, erect and immaculate."

February 19

BORN: 1958 Helen Fielding (*Bridget Jones's Diary, Cause Celeb*), Morley, England
1964 Jonathan Lethem (*The Fortress of Solitude, Motherless Brooklyn*), Brooklyn
DIED: 1951 André Gide (*The Counterfeiters, The Immoralist*), 81, Paris
1952 Knut Hamsun (*Hunger, The Growth of the Soil*), 92, Grimstad, Norway

1834 Fantastic stories of whales were general in New England, even among those who didn't go to sea. On this day Ralph Waldo Emerson noted in his journal the tale he had heard while sharing a stagecoach with a sailor, of "an old sperm whale which he called a white whale which was known for many years by the whalemen as Old Tom & who rushed upon the boats which attacked him & crushed the boats to small chips in his jaws." Seventeen years later, of course, Herman Melville built a novel around such a white whale, but he didn't need to depend on Emerson's tale for it. Melville had sailed for whales himself, and knew, as he writes in *Moby-Dick*, of the legendary giants—Timor Tom, New England Jack, Don Miguel—whose death-dealing had made them celebrities with an "ocean-wide renown."

1895 The idea of university creative writing programs was still decades away when Frank Norris left the University of California to spend a year at Harvard, but in English 22, a two-semester course taught there by Lewis E. Gates, he found what the annual herds of MFA students are looking for. Writing open-ended weekly themes, Norris drafted the first pages of both *Vandover and the Brute* and, most memorably, *McTeague*, the novel he dedicated to Gates, "its Godfather and Sponsor." One of the teaching assistants in the course, though, didn't approve of Norris's vivid style. "Morbid and repulsive," he wrote about one passage, and in response to Trina McTeague's death scene—she expired "with a rapid series of hiccoughs, that stirred the great pool of blood in which she lay"—he commented, "Not a toothsome subject."

1924 "To me you are the last Englishman," D. H. Lawrence wrote to E. M. Forster. "And I am the one after that."

1958 In the lonely, exhausted quiet of Ash Wednesday in New Orleans after the end of Mardi Gras, John Rechy realized he had to get out of town. A young woman at the Delta Airlines counter lent him the money to fly back home to El Paso, and the next day, "grasping for God knows what," he wrote a letter to a friend looking back on the weeks of carnival that had brought to a head his restless years of traveling and hustling around the country. The letter, which he discarded, retrieved, and revised, became a story, "Mardi Gras," published in the *Evergreen Review*, and in 1963 the story became *City of Night*, a raw and yearning novel that was a walk-on-the-wild-side bestseller and a barrier-breaking touchstone for gay writing in America.

1963 Published: *The Feminine Mystique* by Betty Friedan (Norton, New York)

February 20

BORN: **1926** Richard Matheson (*I Am Legend,*
The Shrinking Man), Allendale, N.J.
1941 Alan Furst (*Night Soldiers, Dark Star*),
New York City

DIED: **1895** Frederick Douglass (*Narrative of*
the Life), c. 77, Washington, D.C.
2005 Hunter S. Thompson (*Fear and*
Loathing on the Campaign Trail '72), 67,
Woody Creek, Colo.

1824 With his family living beyond the
means of his father's salary as a navy clerk,
his older sister studying piano at the Royal
Academy of Music, and his mother's plan
to open a school a complete failure, it was
left to Charles Dickens, just turned twelve,
to be put out to work pasting labels onto
shoe-polish pots at six shillings for a sixty-
hour week. His family's humiliating descent
from middle-class gentility continued when
his father was imprisoned on this day for an
unpaid debt to a baker of £40. A few months
later, John Dickens was out of prison, but
Charles remained at work, perhaps for a
year, a traumatic episode that shaded the
rest of his life and inspired, most directly,
David Copperfield.

1843 Published: *Enten—Eller* [*Either/Or*] by
Søren Kierkegaard (Reitzel, Copenhagen)

1943 Beautiful, rich, and vivacious, the
celebrity debutantes Oona O'Neill (daughter of the playwright) and Carol Marcus
(the original for Holly Golightly in *Break-*
fast at Tiffany's) attracted publicity and
men, including, in Oona's case, the young
Jerry Salinger, not yet published in *The*
New Yorker, and in Carol's, William Saroyan. Stationed in Georgia during the war,
Salinger wrote long love letters to O'Neill,
who showed them to Marcus, who, fearing she wasn't witty enough for her own
writer beau, copied passages from them into
her letters to Saroyan. O'Neill and Salinger's romance fizzled (she soon wed Charlie
Chaplin), but on this day Marcus married
Saroyan for the first of two times, despite his
disappointment at the "lousy glib letters" she
had cribbed from Salinger.

1965 Malcolm X checked in with Alex
Haley about the manuscript for his *Auto-*
biography, which Haley reported would be
sent to Doubleday in a week. Doubleday,
though, canceled the book's contract after
Malcolm X was assassinated the next day.

1974 Philip K. Dick had certainly had
visions before, but when a young woman
rang his doorbell on this day to deliver prescription Darvon after his oral surgery he
tipped over into what he later described
as "total psychosis." Her "fascinating gold
necklace," with a fish symbol he connected
to the early Christians, spurred in him a
month-long experience of wakefulness and
urgent immortality he referred to thereafter
as "2-3-74" (for February and March 1974).
The vision inspired his late novels *Valis, The*
Divine Invasions, and *The Transmigration of*
Timothy Archer as well as an 8,000-page collection of writings he called his *Exegesis*, in
which he obsessively recorded his immersion in an exploded reality straight out of
his own fiction.

February 21

BORN: 1962 David Foster Wallace (*Infinite Jest,*
Girl with Curious Hair), Ithaca, N.Y.
1962 Chuck Palahniuk (*Fight Club, Choke,*
Lullaby), Pasco, Wash.
DIED: 1677 Baruch Spinoza (*Ethics,*
Theological-Political Treatise), 44, The
Hague, Netherlands
1998 Angie Debo (*And Still the Waters*
Run, Geronimo), 98, Enid, Okla.

1599 The day after performing before
Queen Elizabeth at Richmond Palace (perhaps in a revival of *A Midsummer Night's*
Dream or an early performance of *As You*
Like It), seven members of the Lord Chamberlain's Men signed a thirty-one-year lease
on a marshy lot in Southwark along the
Thames. Among the seven was William
Shakespeare, playwright and actor, who
made the risky investment of about £70 for
a one-tenth share as part of the first agreement that gave London actors ownership
of their own stage. Using timber claimed
in December from their previous theater
on the other side of the Thames, their new
home, known as the Globe, was built over
the next few months, opening during the
summer with a performance of either *Henry*
V or *Julius Caesar.*

1864 William James, having given up
painting for medical school, wrote a friend,
"I embraced the medical profession a couple
of months ago. My first impressions are that
there is much humbug therein."

1911 Marcel Proust, a new subscriber to
the "theatrophone" service that broadcast
performances over telephone wires, listened
to the Opéra-Comique's performance of
Debussy's *Pelléas et Mélisande* from his
bedroom.

1980 "Bizarre letter from Mom today,"
Alison Bechdel, off at college, noted in her
diary. With two undemonstrative English
teachers as parents, Bechdel's family life
often seemed conducted—even within the
same house—through reading and writing:
shared books, private diaries. So it was fitting that when Bechdel came out as a lesbian to her parents, she did so in a letter,
and that her mom answered in the same
way. "I have had to deal with this problem,"
her mother cryptically replied, "in another
form that almost resulted in catastrophe." A
few days later she revealed the truth about
Bechdel's father, whose closeted gay life, in
parallel with his daughter's, would become
the subject of Bechdel's graphic memoir,
Fun Home, itself an intricate construction
of documents and literary references.

February 22

BORN: 1892 Edna St. Vincent Millay (*A Few Figs from Thistles*), Rockland, Maine
1938 Ishmael Reed (*Mumbo Jumbo*, *Flight to Canada*), Chattanooga, Tenn.
DIED: 1810 Charles Brockden Brown (*Wieland*, *Arthur Mervyn*), 39, Philadelphia
1973 Elizabeth Bowen (*The Death of the Heart*, *The Heat of the Day*), 73, London

1632 The book that Galileo Galilei presented to his patron, the Grand Duke of Tuscany, on this day has come to be known as the *Dialogue Concerning the Two Chief World Systems*, but it originally carried a lengthier and more delicately phrased subtitle: "Where, in the meetings of four days, there is discussion concerning the two Chief Systems of the World, Ptolemaic and Copernican, propounding inconclusively the philosophical and physical reasons as much for one side as the other." The pope's censor in Rome had approved the book, but when Pope Urban VIII himself found his belief in an Earth-centered universe defended unconvincingly in the book by a character named Simplicio, he wasn't fooled by the spurious evenhandedness of the title and had the book banned and Galileo tried for heresy.

1882 On this day was born Eric Gill, a singular artist the clarity of whose works, in sculpture, ink, and type, was brought forth from a life of contradiction and idiosyncratic conviction. Deeply religious and heretically hedonistic, Gill created for himself and his small community a life of work and worship and love and sex—including, as was revealed long after his death, incest with both his sisters and his daughters—that produced some of the most memorable public sculpture in twentieth-century Britain, a series of books of autobiography and philosophy (including *Trousers and the Most Precious Ornament*, which argued that pants restricted the male organ—he preferred tunics and smocks), and two of the most elegant and lasting of modern typefaces, Perpetua and Gill Sans, the latter of which, with its deliberate echoes of Edward Johnston's London Underground face, was a natural choice for the titles of Penguin's classic midcentury paperbacks.

1938 On his thirteenth birthday, Edward Gorey joined the crowd at a Sonja Henie ice show in a snowball-throwing riot.

1947 Nine years in the writing—through poverty, alcohol, and a fire that burned his squatter's beach shack—and rejected by a dozen publishers, Malcolm Lowry's *Under the Volcano* was finally released to a reception that met even Lowry's hopes for his great work. "It has not let me alone," John Woodburn wrote most rapturously in the *Saturday Review* on this day. "In the street, in my room, where it has set its sorrowful music to the metronome of my clock, in the company of many or only one, it has been with me insistently." The praise left Lowry, who had traveled from Vancouver Island to New York for the release, nearly paralyzed, drinking immensely even by his standards and returning greetings at a party that night with grinding teeth and silence. His long-awaited success was, he wrote a friend, "just like a great disaster."

February 23

BORN: 1633 Samuel Pepys (*Diary*), London
   1868 W. E. B. Du Bois (*The Souls of Black Folk*), Great Barrington, Mass.
DIED: 1821 John Keats ("Ode to a Nightingale," "Ode on Melancholy"), 25, Rome
   1968 Fannie Hurst (*Imitation of Life*, *Back Street*), 78, New York City

1798 Written in a ten-week frenzy and published when its author was just twenty, Matthew Lewis's Gothic romance, *The Monk*, caused a sensation with the unprecedented detail—or, in Coleridge's disturbed phrase, the "libidinous minuteness"—with which it described its horrors. As his book gained popularity, Lewis, who had become a Member of Parliament—"Yes! the author of the Monk signs himself a LEGISLATOR! We stare and tremble," cried Coleridge—began to regret his own excess, removing the most offensive passages and changing, for instance, "ravisher" to "intruder" in later editions, and, on this day, writing to his father in apology for his youthful indiscretion, "TWENTY is not the age at which prudence is most to be expected."

1942 Unlike some of his fellow Jewish writers, Stefan Zweig had stayed well ahead of the Nazis. In 1934, the most translated author in Europe at the time, he left Austria for London, and in 1940, with Germany moving across Europe, Zweig, calling his occupation "formerly writer, now expert in visas," moved again with his wife, to New York and then Brazil. But even at a distance his horror at the collapse of Europe and his sense that the world he knew had ended was overwhelming. Though he found Brazil peaceful and wrote an optimistic travelogue about his new home, *Brazil: A Land of the Future*, Zweig took a lethal dose of veronal with his wife a few days after visiting Rio for a night of Carnival. On this day, the following afternoon, their bodies were discovered in their bedroom.

1981 It was the most startling and memorable moment in recent Spanish history: two hundred Civil Guards, armed with submachine guns, entered Spain's Congress of Deputies, led by Lieutenant Colonel Antonio Tejero, who took to the rostrum in his tricornered hat, gun in hand, and declared a coup. Thirty years later, the novelist Javier Cercas felt that the moment was already fading into fiction, even though the coup had been caught on film. Its being televised, Cercas argued, was "at once its guarantee of reality and its guarantee of unreality." At first Cercas tried to defeat that unreality by writing a novel about February 23, but, like the coup itself, it failed, and out of his failure he wrote *The Anatomy of a Moment* instead, a compelling history told with the skills of a novelist but also with a thorough skepticism about the forces that want to turn history into myth.

BORN: 1903 Irène Némirovsky (*Suite Française, David Golder*), Kiev
1943 Kent Haruf (*Plainsong, The Tie That Binds*), Pueblo, Colo.
DIED: 1999 Andre Dubus (*Voices from the Moon*), 62, Haverhill, Mass.
2006 Octavia Butler (*Kindred, Parable of the Sower*), 58, Lake Forest Park, Wash.

1938 Jorge Guillermo Borges died, soon after making a final request that his son, Jorge Luis, rewrite his only novel, *El Caudillo*: "I put many metaphors in to please you, but they are very poor and you must get rid of them."

1950 After updating Stanley Unwin, the publisher of *The Hobbit*, for more than a dozen years on the piecemeal progress of its sequel, which had grown into an epic far beyond the scope of the earlier book, J. R. R. Tolkien reported, with some horror, that it was finally done: "Now I look at it, the magnitude of the disaster is apparent to me. My work has escaped from my control, and I have produced a monster: an immensely long, complex, rather bitter, and very terrifying romance, quite unfit for children (if fit for anybody)." In part, he was sandbagging, since he'd decided he wanted to move to a different publisher, but when his other suitor said that *The Lord of the Rings* "urgently demanded cutting," Tolkien returned to Unwin's firm, though neither expected more than modest sales for the massive, three-volume novel.

1954 With the hardcover edition of Kurt Vonnegut's first novel, *Player Piano*, going out of print, his editor sent a last, tiny royalty check to Vonnegut's agent with the note "I hope it helps this guy out, and I'm only sorry that it's not for a larger amount."

1963 Asked to contribute to a special issue of the *Sunday Times* in London on "As Others See Us," Jean Genet submitted "What I Like About the English Is That They Are Such Liars."

1972 "NOVELIST, neo-surrealist, 24, male, genius," read an ad in the *New York Review of Books* personals. "Desires female patron. Expenses absolutely minimal. Platonic relationship. Will move to NY if no offers in Frisco."

1998 "You really are such a repulsive pervert, David." David Boring is not even twenty, but he has the posture and the resigned acceptance of his compulsions of an old man when his story begins on this day in Daniel Clowes's graphic novel, which bears his pedestrian name. He lives with his lesbian friend Dot, who makes drily appreciative comments like the one above, and he narrates his adventures in a self-consciously hard-boiled style that seems inappropriate to his humdrum life until things begin to happen: the murder of a friend, a brush with death, an encounter with a woman who fulfills his every fetish, and the impending end of the world on a remote island, none of which alters David's drab affect, but which create an oddly engrossing tale of chance and compulsion.

February 25

BORN: 1949 Jack Handey (*Deep Thoughts,
What I'd Say to the Martians*), San Antonio
1962 John Lanchester (*The Debt to
Pleasure, Capital*), Hamburg, Germany
DIED: 1983 Tennessee Williams (*A Streetcar
Named Desire*), 71, New York City
2001 A. R. Ammons (*Sphere, Garbage*), 75,
Ithaca, N.Y.

1830 The savviest stage management for the premiere of Victor Hugo's drama *Hernani* at Paris's venerable Comédie Française took place off the stage as the young Hugo, angling to become the icon of the Romantic movement, organized his youthful supporters in the audience. Some hired and some recruited, they came to the performance dressed in their outlandishly outdated fashions, banqueted for hours in the theater before the curtain rose, and then wildly cheered Hugo's subversions of the rules of classical French theater while the so-called knee-heads, the balding old guard, hissed. (Watching a later performance, Hugo happily noted all the crowd's reactions, from "laughter" to "sniggering," in the margins of his script.) So began the "Battle of *Hernani*," a theatrical revolution that lasted for the run of the show, just a few short months before the July Revolution that overthrew Charles X, France's last Bourbon king.

1917 It was "the last day of old Russia": with the February Revolution under way, the Berberovs held one final evening party, with dancing, singing, and ice cream until 5 a.m., but already their daughter, Nina Berberova, had moved on to the new Russia. With the zestful impatience that characterized her entire life, both in Russia and then in exile in Paris and America, she wrote about the day of the party a half-century later in her memoir, *The Italics Are Mine*: "I am seventeen, I am nobody—I accept it as that ground on which I will sprout . . . The past? I don't need it. The breaking up of the old? I don't want even to remember those bits and broken pieces . . . Someone near me says that all is lost, but I don't believe this, I never will."

1956 "A small note after a large orgy," began a rather long entry in Sylvia Plath's journal on February 26. The night before, at a party for a poetry review in Cambridge, England, she met "the one man in the room who was as big as his poems, huge, with hulk and dynamic chunks of words." The man, Ted Hughes, poured her a drink and kissed her, and she "bit him long and hard on the cheek" so that when they came back out into the party "blood was running down his face." He'd never come looking for her again, Plath thought then—her date, as they stumbled home from the party, called Hughes "the biggest seducer in Cambridge" but "oh, to give myself crashing, fighting, to you," she wrote. They were married in June.

BORN: 1907 Milton Caniff (*Terry and the Pirates*, *Steve Canyon*), Hillsboro, Ohio
1956 Michel Houellebecq (*The Elementary Particles*, *Platform*), Réunion
DIED: 1969 Karl Jaspers (*Philosophy of Existence*), 86, Basel, Switzerland

1870 Shortly after being named a justice of the peace, Wyatt Outlaw, one of the leading African American politicians in North Carolina's Alamance County, was lynched on this day by a mob of Ku Klux Klansmen outside the county courthouse where Judge Albion W. Tourgée, the most prominent white Republican in the state, presided. A decade later, writing out of anger and despair at the end of Reconstruction and the violent suppression of black civil rights, Tourgée recast Outlaw's murder as one of the central events in *A Fool's Errand*, a caustic autobiographical novel that caused an immediate publishing sensation, drawing comparisons—which still hold true—to Twain for its sharp satire and Stowe for the moral fervor that made it the *Uncle Tom's Cabin* of the postwar era.

1922 Colette, the music-hall-performer-turned-novelist, appeared onstage for the first time in ten years as Lea in the hundredth performance of the adaptation of her novel *Chéri*.

1981 For thirty years, *The New Yorker* rejected every story Richard Yates (or his agent) sent them. Sometimes they encouraged him to try again, but on this day the magazine's fiction editor, Roger Angell, shut the door. Having declined his "mean-spirited" story "A Natural Girl" three days before, Angell wrote Yates's agent that "Liars in Love" "didn't even come close." "It seems clearer and clearer to me," he added, in a letter Yates would sourly read aloud to visitors in the last years of his life, "that his kind of fiction is not what we're looking for." Not everyone agreed: Richard Ford later included "Liars in Love" in *The Granta Book of the American Short Story*, and in 2001, eight years after his death, Yates finally made *The New Yorker* when they published "The Canal," an early story they had rejected with a form letter in 1952.

1984 Miami in the '80s had the lurid glamour of bright pastels and easy violence: the Miami of *Scarface* and Crockett and Tubbs, and of Edna Buchanan, the hard-boiled *Miami Herald* police reporter who became as big as the stories she covered. Murder was cheap in south Florida, and Buchanan tried to cover it all with the motto "Every murder is major to the victim," including Rosario Gonzalez, a young model who went missing on this day during the Miami Grand Prix. Buchanan tracked down the most likely suspect, a rich sports-car enthusiast named Christopher Wilder, but the cops didn't, and he embarked on a cross-country murder spree that ended with his death in Vermont, one of the dozens of stories she collected in *The Corpse Had a Familiar Face*, a year after she won the Pulitzer Prize for General News Reporting in 1986.

February 27

BORN: 1902 John Steinbeck (*The Grapes of Wrath, East of Eden*), Salinas, Calif.
1934 N. Scott Momaday (*House Made of Dawn, The Way to Rainy Mountain*), Lawton, Okla.
DIED: 1977 Edward Dahlberg (*Bottom Dogs, Because I Was Flesh*), 76, Santa Barbara, Calif.
2008 William F. Buckley (*God and Man at Yale, Saving the Queen*), 82, Stamford, Conn.

1872 After word got out that railroad freight rates for oil had just been jacked up for every producer in Pennsylvania's oil region except the members of a shadowy outfit named the South Improvement Company, 3,000 angry oilmen filled the Titusville Opera House, including Franklin Tarbell, whose livelihood, like everyone else's there, was about to be destroyed. Thirty years later, Tarbell's daughter, Ida, who had watched her father storm off to the meeting, told the story of the Oil War of 1872 as part of her *History of the Standard Oil Company*, a tireless feat of reporting that launched the age of muckraking journalism by tying Titusville and countless other schemes to the ruthless machinations of the country's richest man, John D. Rockefeller.

1952 When Allen Ginsberg struck up a correspondence with his fellow New Jerseyan William Carlos Williams—"from me, an unknown young poet, to you, an unknown old poet, who live in the same rusty county of the world"—he first sent him samples of traditional, rhymed poems. Williams didn't much like them, so two years later Ginsberg pulled out some "short crappy scraps" from his journals and tried those instead. Those the old poet liked (he also liked Ginsberg's letters, which he later quoted at length in the fourth book of *Paterson*), and his enthusiastic response on this day—"You *must* have a book. I shall see that you get it. Don't throw anything away. These are *it*."—led Ginsberg to write his pals Jack Kerouac and Neal Cassady that this was their big break: "We'll have a huge collected anthology of American Kicks and Mental Muse-eries."

2008 At 11:43 at night in his apartment in Malmö, Sweden, with his second wife and their three children sleeping in the rooms around him as if they had been placed there by alien spirits, Karl Ove Knausgaard looks at the deep furrows in his forehead and cheeks and asks, "What has engraved itself on my face?" with the sort of perplexed intensity toward his past and present that characterizes *My Struggle*, a six-volume autobiographical novel that became an immediate phenomenon in his native Norway. Written rapidly with close attention to the banal minutiae of everyday life, *My Struggle* nevertheless gathers a great personal and philosophical power from Knausgaard's commitment to an honest and exhaustive account of his life, an "act of literary suicide," in his own words, that made him a literary celebrity at age forty-three but unsure if he'd ever write again.

BORN: **1533** Michel de Montaigne (*Essays*), Château de Montaigne, France
1970 Lemony Snicket/Daniel Handler (*A Series of Unfortunate Events*, *The Basic Eight*), San Francisco

DIED: **1916** Henry James (*The Ambassadors*, *The Wings of the Dove*), 72, London
1930 C. K. Scott Moncrieff (translator of *Remembrance of Things Past*), 40, Rome

1571 In one of the best-known—and most productive—midlife crises in literary history, Michel de Montaigne retreated from the Bordeaux Parlement after thirteen years as a magistrate to a tower library where he could read every day a message painted on the wall in Latin: "In the year of Christ 1571, at the age of thirty-eight, on the last day of February, anniversary of his birth, Michel de Montaigne, long weary of the servitude of the court and of public employments, while still entire, retired to the bosom of the learned Virgins, where in calm and freedom from all cares he will spend what little remains of his life now more than half run out. If the fates permit he will complete this abode, this sweet ancestral retreat; and he has consecrated it to his freedom, tranquility, and leisure."

1815 Alexandre Dumas set the pivotal moment in his action-packed tale *The Count of Monte Cristo* on the day before Napoleon returned from exile to France to reclaim his command. On that day, young Edmond Dantès, an upstanding and talented sailor who has just celebrated his wedding, is framed for conspiring to overthrow the king in favor of the returning emperor and condemned for life to an island fortress known as the Château d'If. Fourteen years later to the very day, Edmond escapes from the château in a burial sack, takes on a new identity as the wealthy Count of Monte Cristo, and begins to seek his revenge against those who unjustly imprisoned him.

1939 The short and unheralded life of "dord" came to an end on this day when an editor of *Webster's New International Dictionary* noticed that a tiny entry on page 771 was missing its etymology. It turned out on further investigation that "dord" had no etymology because it wasn't a word. In 1931 a slip reading "D or d, cont. density," which meant to add "density" to the list of terms abbreviated as "D," was misread as "Dord" and filed as a separate word. Soon, through sheer inertia, "dord" acquired a part of speech, "n.," and a pronunciation, "(dôrd)," and found its way into early editions of the dictionary before it was discovered. "Probably too bad," wrote *Webster's* editor in chief Philip B. Gove in 1953, hinting at the open-mindedness that would make the next edition of *Webster's* the most controversial dictionary in American history, "for why shouldn't *dord* mean 'density'?"

2005 In the finals of the first annual Tournament of Books, created by the *Morning News* as a complement (or alternative) to the NCAA basketball tournament, David Mitchell's *Cloud Atlas* defeated Philip Roth's *The Plot Against America* by a vote of ten to five.

February 29

BORN: **1908** Dee Brown (*Bury My Heart at Wounded Knee*), Alberta, La.
1952 Tim Powers (*The Anubis Gates, On Stranger Tides*), Buffalo, N.Y.

DIED: **1940** E. F. Benson (*Mapp and Lucia, Dodo, David Blaize*), 72, London
2012 James Trager (*The People's Chronology*), 86, New York City

1876 "Dear Sir," George Bernard Shaw, age nineteen, began his letter to his employer, "I beg to give you notice that at the end of next month, I shall leave your office." Young Shaw had proved so conscientious a clerk at his real estate firm that his salary had quadrupled in four years, but he was done with the job, and with Dublin. "My reason," he continued, "is that I object to receive a salary for which I give no adequate value. Not having enough to do, it follows that the little I have is not well done." When he arrived in London for good in April, he declared that "on no account will I enter an office again."

NO YEAR On a wintry day during the last snowfall of the year, a "singular person fell out of infinity" into the village of Iping. Bundled thoroughly against the cold, he arrived at the inn, threw down a couple of sovereigns, and demanded a room, a fire, and, above all, privacy. But curiosity will have its way, sovereigns or no, especially when the stranger reveals that his head is thoroughly bandaged under his hat and scarf and undertakes mysterious "experiments" behind the locked door of his room. Soon the villagers learn the truth of the title of H. G. Wells's novel *The Invisible Man*, a tale that methodically demonstrates how easily one of humanity's most desired discoveries can become a curse.

NO YEAR It's easy to lose track of time on Thomas Mann's Magic Mountain, although Hans Castorp, the earnest engineer, tries to keep to the calendar. But even the calendar's orderly structure offers him a day without rules: Mardi Gras, a holiday when Hans can cast his propriety aside and confess his love to Clavdia Chauchat, even—gulp—going so far as to address her by the informal pronoun! It was, as he explains later, "an evening outside of any schedule, almost outside the calendar, an hors d'oeuvre, so to speak, an extra evening, a leap-year evening, the twenty-ninth of February." Whether it was actually the twenty-ninth of February, that magical day on which Fat Tuesday occasionally does fall, Mann doesn't say, but then why, when speaking of such a day, would you want to concern yourself with mere facts?

March

Emily Dickinson liked March: it brings a light like no other time of the year, a color "that science cannot overtake / But human nature feels." "Come in!" she wrote. "Oh, March, come right upstairs with me / I have so much to tell." But she also knew the dangers of the life that March's thaw awakens: when the "snows come hurrying in from the hills" they can flood the banks of that "Brook in your little heart" that "nobody knows." "Why, look out for that little brook in March," she warned: it might wash out all your bridges.

We don't know quite what to do with March. We're excited and frightened by its power and variability. Do we really think that the lion it comes in as can lie down with the lamb it becomes? It seems appropriate that halfway between the month's two ends, where the lion and lamb meet, are the ides of March, full of Shakespeare's storms and portents. Casca, one of those plotting the death of Julius Caesar, witnesses not only the "tempests" and "threatening clouds"

of a "world too saucy with the gods" but also a real March lion strolling unnaturally through Rome, "who gazed upon me and went surly by." Even the only lamb mentioned in *Julius Caesar* hides violence in its mildness: Brutus, arguing with Cassius after Caesar is dead, calls himself "a lamb / That carries anger as the flint bears fire."

March's name came from Mars, the god of war, marking the time of year when Rome would take up arms again after the winter. But armies take a while to muster: with few exceptions, history's great battles have taken place later in the spring or in summer or fall, not March. *The Red Badge of Courage* does open in early spring, with the Union Army awakening "as the landscape changed from brown to green," but their first promises of action prove false. Stephen Crane is thought to have based his account—famously grounded in no war experience of his own—on the Battle of Chancellorsville, which didn't commence until the last day of April.

In some years, like the one described in Walker Percy's *The Moviegoer*, Mardi Gras comes late enough to fall in March, and in others an early Easter arrives before the end of the month, but in almost every year March includes most of the Lenten days between Fat Tuesday and Easter Sunday, and so, amid all this first growth and awakening, March is for many a season of, in George Herbert's words, "sweet abstinence." *The Moviegoer* takes place mostly during Mardi Gras, but it ends on Ash Wednesday and carries some of its spirit of repentance.

Oddly, the best-known novels with "March" in their titles have nothing to do with the month: *Middlemarch*, though it sounds like a synonym for the day of Caesar's death, refers to a town, not a time. (It's a fall book more than anything.) And in 2006, the Pulitzer Prize for Fiction went to Geraldine Brooks's *March*, about the March girls' absent father in *Little Women*, while one of the finalists it beat out, E. L. Doctorow's *The March*, already the winner of the National Book Critics Circle and PEN/Faulkner prizes, is the story of Sherman's march through the South, which took place in the fall, not the spring, of 1864.

Julius Caesar by William Shakespeare (1599) ∽ There may be no literary character more famously forewarned than this would-be emperor, who, in his own play, is spoken of far more than he speaks himself and dies halfway through the action.

David Copperfield by Charles Dickens (1850) ∽ On a Friday in March at the stroke of midnight, a baby boy is born to the widow Copperfield, into "a world not at all excited about his arrival," thereby beginning—with "all that David Copperfield kind of crap"—Dickens's favorite of his novels, and his most personal.

Anne of Green Gables by L. M. Montgomery (1908) ∽ It's still winter on Prince Edward Island when Anne Shirley's birthday arrives every March, allowing her to eagerly mark the next milestone in what remains one of the most beloved coming-of-age stories.

The Long Ships by Frans Bengtsson (1941–45) ∽ With the first stirrings of spring, set sail from Scandia in search of plunder with Red Orm and his restless Vikings on their yearly raids in Bengtsson's epic, based on the Icelandic sagas but fully modern in its detached good humor.

Rabbit, Run by John Updike (1960) ∽ Updike's Rabbit Angstrom novels grew, a book at a time, into an unplanned epic with each book tied to a season. The first one begins, appropriately, in spring, with Rabbit still young enough to feel the aches of age for the first time.

The Moviegoer by Walker Percy (1961) ∽ Binx Bolling's story is set in New Orleans during Mardi Gras, but Binx does his best to avoid the hoo-ha, distracting himself instead with drives along the Gulf Coast with his secretaries and with the movies, whose "peculiar reality" contrasts with the potent sense of unreality he's burdened with.

Caesar by Adrian Goldsworthy (2006) ∽ To sweep away the mist of legend and prophecy, turn to this portrait of the ruthless but many-sided general and dictator whose name remains a synonym for leadership.

Animal, Vegetable, Miracle by Barbara Kingsolver (2007) ∽ The Kingsolver family chose to begin their "food sabbatical"—a year of living only on what they grew, or close to it—in late March, with the arrival of the first Virginia asparagus. By the following March they were looking forward to reclaiming a few imported luxuries in their diet but were otherwise well fed and gratifyingly educated by the acre that had sustained them.

March 1

BORN: 1913 Ralph Ellison (*Invisible Man,
Going to the Territory*), Oklahoma City
1917 Robert Lowell (*Life Studies, For the
Union Dead*), Boston
DIED: 1978 Paul Scott (*The Raj Quartet,
Staying On*), 57, London
1983 Arthur Koestler (*Darkness at Noon,
The Ghost in the Machine*), 77, London

1921 At the Mi-carême Ball, the last big charity event of the Atlanta social season, Margaret "Peggy" Mitchell, a young debutante, scandalized society by performing an "Apache dance" inspired by the Valentino movies of the day, in which an undergraduate beau from Georgia Tech flung her shrieking about the ballroom of the Georgian Terrace and gave her a suggestive kiss. The newspapers were still talking of the sensation months later, and the following year society columnist "Polly Peachtree" marveled at Mitchell's "pretty wit" and "fearlessness," which had given her "more honest-to-goodness suitors than almost any other girl in Atlanta." But Mitchell once again confounded social expectations by going from debutante to working reporter at the *Atlanta Journal*, and soon she began a secret project: an epic novel of the Civil War.

1937 "He's my enemy," Jane Auer told a friend after first meeting Paul Bowles in the lobby of New York's Plaza Hotel. Despite (or because of) this strong reaction, the next time they met she invited herself along on Bowles's impromptu trip to Mexico and immediately called her mother, who said to Bowles, "If my daughter's going to Mexico with you, I think I should meet you first, don't you think?" They did meet, Mrs. Auer immediately approved—perhaps because it had been so hard to get her daughter to look for a suitor—and on this day Jane and Paul got on a bus for Mexico. Nearly a year later they were married, beginning a thirty-five-year personal and artistic alliance, through lovers of both sexes, that proved remarkably durable.

1938 Anaïs Nin was an unknown author when her lover Henry Miller declared in the *Criterion* that the diary she'd been keeping since age eleven was "a monumental confession which when given to the world will take its place beside the revelations of St. Augustine, Petronius, Rousseau, Proust, and others." Nin was ambivalent about giving that confession to the world—"I have tried both to uncover the secret and hide myself. Henry's essay in the *Criterion* gave me away," she wrote (in her diary, of course)— but with her consent Miller announced that "by March 1st 1938, failing a world war or a collapse of the monetary systems of the world," he would publish the diary's first volume. But he couldn't raise the funds, and the diaries remained unpublished until 1966 (unexpurgated editions didn't appear until after her death, in 1986).

1969 Anatole Broyard, in the *New York Times,* on Philip Roth's *Portnoy's Complaint*: "The book is a kind of *Catch-22* of sexuality, and much funnier," but Jewish comics like Lenny Bruce and Nichols and May "were working Portnoy's territory more than ten years ago."

BORN: **1904** Dr. Seuss (*The Cat in the Hat, Horton Hears a Who!*), Springfield, Mass.
1931 Tom Wolfe (*The Electric Kool-Aid Acid Test*), Richmond, Va.
1942 John Irving (*A Prayer for Owen Meany*), Exeter, N.H.
DIED: **1930** D. H. Lawrence (*Women in Love, Lady Chatterley's Lover*), 44, Vence, France
1982 Philip K. Dick (*Do Androids Dream of Electric Sheep?*), 53, Santa Ana, Calif.

1909 Living in London, across the world from her family in New Zealand, and carrying the child of a young man who declined to marry her, Katherine Mansfield abruptly accepted the proposal of her older, thoroughly respectable singing teacher, George Bowden, and wed him at the Paddington registry office on this day. That night, though, she had a change of heart, and after breakfast the next morning, their marriage unconsummated, she left him, and later that year she lost the baby. The encumbrances of English law and decorum delayed their divorce, and her subsequent marriage to John Middleton Murry, for nearly a decade.

1936 Samuel Beckett, unsure of his career path, applied to study with Sergei Eisenstein at the Moscow State School of Cinematography. (He never heard back.)

1976 Did Ishmael Reed really finish writing *Flight to Canada* a minute after midnight on Fat Tuesday in room 127 of the Tamanaca Hotel in New Orleans, as the last page of his novel implies? If so, it was a fitting way to spend Mardi Gras: *Flight to Canada* is a novel made for Carnival, upending history while never forgetting

it, putting Abe Lincoln ("Gary Cooper-awkward") and Harriet Beecher Stowe in a gleefully anachronistic plot alongside Raven Quickskill, a fugitive slave and poet who takes a "non-stop jumbo jet" to the North, and Princess Quaw Quaw Tralaralara, an Ivy League grad who earns a living doing "ethnic dances" for grant money and who, come to think of it, would be right at home sitting poolside at the actual teepee-themed Tamanaca in downtown New Orleans.

1976 John Cheever and his son wrote a parody of Gabriel García Márquez together (they both "think he's terrible").

2004 Declaring, "I've waited two years for this. You spat on my book!" Richard Ford spat on Colson Whitehead at a literary party, two years after Whitehead panned *A Multitude of Sins* in the *New York Times*. Whitehead later remarked, "This wasn't the first time some old coot had drooled on me."

2011 It was unprecedented for Prime Minister Ahmed Shafik to answer unscripted questions on a discussion panel on Egyptian TV, but the moment became even more historic when a fellow panelist, Alaa Al Aswany, longtime pro-democracy activist, practicing dentist, and the country's leading novelist since the publication of his bestseller *The Yacoubian Building* in 2002, challenged him about the government's murders of protesters in Tahrir Square. After their exchange escalated into a shouting match— "This is unacceptable!" "You are the one who is unacceptable!"—Aswany demanded that Shafik resign. And the next morning, to the country's surprise, he did.

March 3

BORN: 1756 William Godwin (*Caleb Williams, Political Justice*), Wisbech, England
1926 James Merrill (*The Changing Light at Sandover*), New York City
DIED: 1982 Georges Perec (*Life, a User's Manual*; *A Void*), 45, Ivry-sur-Seine, France
1994 John Williams (*Stoner, Butcher's Crossing*), 71, Fayetteville, Ark.

1896 "How are your stomachs, gentlemen?" It's not the unsettling height of the watchtowers of the unfinished Williamsburg Bridge, far above the black waters of the East River, that Police Commissioner Theodore Roosevelt warns his visitors about, but the mutilated body of a boy. Caleb Carr's *The Alienist* places Roosevelt, a reforming top cop just a few years away from the White House, in the middle of a murder mystery notable for both the imaginative brutality of its crimes and its lovingly detailed evocation of a particular moment in the history of New York City: the tenements packed with immigrants, the muscular reforms of the Progressives, the advent of modern psychology and forensics, and, of course, the green turtle soup *au clair* at Delmonico's.

1900 W. L. Alden, in the *New York Times*: "The other day I read Conrad's 'Heart of Darkness,' which was published in Blackwood's Magazine. Good Heavens! How that man can write! The scene of the story is laid on the Congo, and in truth there is very little story to it, but how it grips and holds one!"

1923 T. S. Eliot's new poem, *The Waste Land*, was so impenetrable, speculated the Books column in the debut issue of *Time* magazine, that it might be a hoax.

1924 After spending the morning scrambling to finish his final draft of "Imprisoned with the Pharaohs," a *Weird Tales* horror story ghostwritten for Harry Houdini, H. P. Lovecraft rushed off to join Sonia Haft Greene in ill-fated matrimony.

1958 Dan Pinck, in the *New Republic,* on Jack Kerouac's *The Subterraneans*: "Were there any sign in any of his three books that Kerouac possessed an intellect, it might be possible to consider *The Subterraneans* as a joke of his on the public and on the critics. It is not a joke. Kerouac is simply ignorant, but a name-dropper supreme."

1983 When the physician on duty on this day at the Merced Community Medical Center in California diagnosed Lia Lee, an eight-month-old girl in the throes of a seizure, with epilepsy, her Hmong family had already made the same diagnosis. But their understanding of the disease and its treatment was far different than Lia's doctors', and that difference becomes tragic in Anne Fadiman's *The Spirit Catches You and You Fall Down*, which takes its name from the translation of *qaug dab peg*, the Hmong name for Lia's condition. Fadiman's own sensitivity to the power of cultural differences has made her subtle portrait of good intentions clashing across a chasm of misunderstanding required reading for medical students across the country and one of the most indelible works of American journalism.

2005 Published: *Never Let Me Go* by Kazuo Ishiguro (Faber & Faber, London)

March 4

BORN: 1948 James Ellroy (*American Tabloid*, *L.A. Confidential*), Los Angeles
1965 Khaled Hosseini (*The Kite Runner*), Kabul, Afghanistan
DIED: 1963 William Carlos Williams (*Paterson*), 79, Paterson, N.J.
1986 Elizabeth Smart (*By Grand Central Station I Sat Down and Wept*), 72, London

1845 With countless novels published under his name filling the newspapers and bookshops of France, the prolific Alexandre Dumas drew the envy and ire of rivals, including the young writer Eugène de Mirecourt, who published a pamphlet, *Fabrique des Romans*, accusing Dumas of running a "novel factory" and lashing his workers like slaves. Dumas successfully sued Mirecourt for libel, and he also asked his most prominent collaborator, Auguste Maquet, to write a testimonial letter on this day that proudly listed the many works they wrote together (including *The Three Musketeers* and *The Count of Monte Cristo*) and disavowed any further compensation for his work. Nevertheless, after their relationship soured, Maquet himself sued Dumas a dozen years later for a share of their work; once again, Dumas won in court.

1857 Young Samuel Clemens thought a lot about the romance of piloting a Mississippi steamboat, but not much about its difficulty: "I supposed that all a pilot had to do was to keep his boat in the river, and I did not consider that that could be much of a trick, since it was so wide." But when on this afternoon, in the crowded waters along the levee at New Orleans, the pilot of the *Colonel Crossman* said, "Here, take her; shave those steamships as close as you'd peel an apple," and handed over the wheel, Clemens, who had begged himself into an apprenticeship as a cub pilot, didn't last long, panicking and steering the boat out into the rougher open water, avoiding the traffic but drawing an earful from his master, the beginning of his river education in Mark Twain's *Life on the Mississippi*.

1866 Collapsed in a cave in the mountains of Arizona, Captain John Carter, a Confederate-vet-turned-prospector who has just struck a valuable vein of gold, finds himself transformed. Rising naked from his lifeless body, he is "drawn with the suddenness of thought through the trackless immensity of space" to a landscape he immediately recognizes as Mars but which, as he soon learns, its inhabitants call "Barsoom." And so Edgar Rice Burroughs, in "Under the Moons of Mars," his first published story (his second was "Tarzan of the Apes"), introduced the character of John Carter of Mars, whose relative strength on the smaller planet leads him, after many journeys through the portal of death between Earth and its red neighbor, to be proclaimed "Warlord of Barsoom."

1974 On the cover of the debut issue of *People* magazine: Mia Farrow as *The Great Gatsby*'s Daisy Buchanan.

March 5

BORN: **1870** Frank Norris (*McTeague, The Octopus, The Pit*), Chicago
1948 Leslie Marmon Silko (*Ceremony, Storyteller*), Albuquerque, N.M.
DIED: **1966** Anna Akhmatova (*Requiem, Poem Without a Hero*), 76, Leningrad
2003 John Sanford (*The People from Heaven*), 98, Montecito, Calif.

1046 When the Persian bureaucrat Nasir Khusraw set out for Mecca on this day (by his calendar the 23rd day of Sha'ban in the year 437) from his home in Merv, at that time one of the great trading cities of the world, it was not his first journey. Earlier in the year, on a business trip to a nearby city, he'd spent a month "constantly drunk on wine." But in a dream at the end of his binge he was transformed: waking from what he called a sleep of forty years, he took leave from his job and began a seven-year pilgrimage that took him to Mecca four times, a circuitous journey through the Middle East he later recorded in the *Safarnama*, or the *Book of Travels*, a memoir consulted ever since for its meticulous descriptions of eleventh-century Cairo and Jerusalem and for its rare insight into the mind of a traveler during the Islamic golden age.

1807 Arrested as a Prussian spy by the French while traveling through Berlin, Heinrich von Kleist was imprisoned in the granite dungeon in the Fort de Joux, the same prison where the Haitian revolutionary Toussaint L'Ouverture died four years before.

1982 The plum role of Ignatius J. Reilly in the long-rumored movie adaptation of John Kennedy Toole's *A Confederacy of Dunces* has been slated for nearly every weight-challenged funnyman in Hollywood: John Candy, Chris Farley, Divine, John Goodman, Will Ferrell, Zach Galifianakis. But first on the list was John Belushi, until he overdosed at the Chateau Marmont on this day, not long before a scheduled studio meeting on the picture (also set to star Richard Pryor as Burma Jones). That's not the only intriguing role from recent fiction Belushi's death derailed: he was also lined up to play Ellerbee, the Job figure in Stanley Elkin's *The Living End*, with Ken Russell directing and Peter O'Toole, naturally, cast as God.

2004 A. S. Byatt, in the *Guardian*, on David Mitchell's *Cloud Atlas*: "David Mitchell entices his readers on to a rollercoaster, and at first they wonder if they want to get off. Then—at least in my case—they can't bear the journey to end."

March 6

BORN: 1885 Ring Lardner (*You Know Me Al, Haircut*), Niles, Mich.
1927 Gabriel García Márquez (*One Hundred Years of Solitude*), Aracataca, Colombia
DIED: 1888 Louisa May Alcott (*Little Women, Jo's Boys, Little Men*), 55, Boston
1982 Ayn Rand (*Atlas Shrugged, The Fountainhead*), 77, New York City

1718 In one of the clearer bits of timekeeping in a story whose digressions continually confound chronology, Tristram Shandy introduces his *Life and Opinions* by tracing his troubles to the moment of his conception, "in the night, betwixt the first Sunday and the first Monday in the month of March." He can place the date precisely because of the regularity of his father's habits, which included the winding of the large house-clock on the first Sunday of every month, a task he combined, for the sake of efficiency, with other husbandly duties. Such a habit, Tristram has reason to believe, caused his mother to interrupt his begetting with the question, "Have you not forgotten to wind up the clock?"—a disruption he is certain caused the unfortunate scattering of his animal spirits just at the moment of their transmission from father to son.

1831 Cadet Edgar Allan Poe was expelled from West Point for "gross neglect of duty" and "disobedience of orders."

1928 After pulling a skylight down on his head in Paris, Ernest Hemingway required stitches.

1943 Especially after the death of his mother when he was fourteen, William Styron was close and affectionate with his father, an engineer with an appreciation for the arts, but on this day during his freshman year at Davidson, "taken aback" by a letter full of criticism, he replied to his father on fraternity stationery. "Pop, I realize that I have done very little to further my 'scholastic record,' if you can call it that," his "worthless son" wrote. "The only consolation I have is that I have made no academic failing large enough to actually 'flunk me out' of school."

1948 Ross Lockridge Jr. piled success on success before his suicide, earning the highest grade average in the history of Indiana University and winning a $150,000 prize from MGM and a Book-of-the-Month Club main selection for his thousand-page debut novel, *Raintree County*. But on the day before his book reached the top spot on one national bestseller list (where it was soon joined by his Bloomington neighbor Alfred Kinsey's *Sexual Behavior in the Human Male*), Lockridge, exhausted into depression by seven years of work on the book, battles with his publisher, a backlash of bad reviews, and perhaps by the anticlimax he found at the end of his frantic ambition, shut the doors of his garage and turned on his car.

1975 Donald Davie, in the *New York Review of Books*, on A. R. Ammons's *Sphere*: "How could I be anything but exasperated by it, profoundly distrustful, sure I was being bamboozled, sure I was being threatened? And how is it, then, that I was on the contrary *enraptured*?"

March 7

BORN: 1952 William Boyd (*A Good Man in Africa*, *Any Human Heart*), Accra, Gold Coast

1964 Bret Easton Ellis (*Less than Zero*, *American Psycho*), Los Angeles

DIED: 1274 Thomas Aquinas (*Summa theologiae*, *Summa contra gentiles*), c. 49, Fossanova, Papal States

1897 Harriet Jacobs (*Incidents in the Life of a Slave Girl*), 84, Washington, D.C.

1835 The merchant brig *Pilgrim* had been on the California coast for two months, gathering cow hides at the tiny Mexican ports of Santa Barbara, Monterey, and San Pedro, and all was not well on board. Nothing was done well or fast enough for the captain, who directed a special ire at a slow-moving sailor named Sam. "I'll flog you, by God!" he declared. "I'm no negro slave," replied Sam. "Then I'll make you one!" shouted the captain. Looking on, Richard Henry Dana, who had left Harvard and signed on to the *Pilgrim* as a common sailor, vowed then that he would "do something to redress the grievances and relieve the sufferings of that poor class of beings, of whom I then was one." His seafaring memoir, *Two Years Before the Mast*, published in 1840, was a stirring bestseller, and he followed it with years of work as a lawyer for sailors and fugitive slaves.

1919 Back home in Illinois from the European war, glad to show off his leg full of shrapnel and expecting that the pretty nurse he'd fallen in love with in a Milan hospital would be joining him stateside, Ernest Hemingway received a letter written on this day telling him otherwise. Turning "Kid," her pet name for her young soldier—she called herself "Mrs. Kid"—into a patronizing pat on the head, Agnes von Kurowsky, twenty-seven to his nineteen, wrote, "I can't get away from the fact that you're just a boy—a kid," and revealed she planned to marry an Italian lieutenant (who soon threw her over in turn). They never met again, but Hemingway turned again and again to this first romance in his fiction, most memorably in the love affair between Lieutenant Frederic Henry and the doomed nurse Catherine Barkley in *A Farewell to Arms*.

NO YEAR March 7 is a noteworthy date in the otherwise lamentable life of the narrator of Flann O'Brien's novel *The Third Policeman*, for that is the day he discovered the great but erratic thinker de Selby. De Selby's theories, explained in preposterously long footnotes that threaten at times to take over the novel, propose that, among other notions, night is caused by "accumulations of 'black air'" and the earth is "sausage-shaped," providing a comic undertone to a twisted murder mystery whose hilarity otherwise turns decidedly toward the menacing. Considered too strange to find a publisher during O'Brien's abbreviated lifetime, it has found a rabid core of readers ever since.

BORN: 1931 John McPhee (*Coming into the Country, Oranges*), Princeton, N.J.
1960 Jeffrey Eugenides (*Middlesex, The Virgin Suicides*), Detroit

DIED: 1941 Sherwood Anderson (*Winesburg, Ohio; Poor White*), 64, Colón, Panama
1999 Adolfo Bioy Casares (*The Invention of Morel*), 84, Buenos Aires

1870 Though her cousins William and Henry James found it hard to imagine the "extinction of that immense little spirit," Minny Temple died of tuberculosis in Pelham, New York, at the age of twenty-four. William responded with silence, leaving a page of his diary blank except for a drawing of a tombstone. Henry, though, was immediately moved in the opposite direction, writing his brother in a lengthy letter, "The more I think of her the more perfectly satisfied I am to have her translated from this changing realm of fact to the steady realm of thought." Her reckless vitality inspired his later heroines Isabel Archer (in *The Portrait of a Lady*) and Milly Theale (in *The Wings of the Dove*), and he ended his memoir *Notes of a Son and Brother*, in some of his last published words, by remembering that her death marked "the end of our youth."

1914 From childhood, Fernando Pessoa wrote in a chorus of different voices, each with a separate name and identity, but one day in Lisbon—he later called it "the triumphal day of my life"—those voices seemed to take over "in a sort of ecstasy whose nature I could not define." Standing at the chest of drawers where he liked to write, he poured out thirty or more poems under the names Alberto Caeiro, Ricardo Reis, and Álvaro de Campos (and his own name as well), identities that, he felt, took form within him as he wrote. For two more decades, while working as a translator of business correspondence in the city, Pessoa wrote under the influence of more than seventy such identities, constructing a vast assemblage of poems and prose that was largely unknown during his lifetime but after his death caused him to be recognized as the great Portuguese writer of the century.

NO YEAR Margaret Ann Simon's twelfth birthday starts out perfect but ends up rotten. She gets a savings bond and a plane ticket to Florida from her grandma and the new Mice Men record from her fellow Pre-Teen Sensations, Nancy, Janie, and Gretchen, and, maybe best of all, uses her mom's deodorant for the first time. But then Mr. Benedict assigns her to a project group with Laura Danker (with the big *you know whats*), Norman Fishbein (a drip!), and Philip Leroy (#1 in her Boy Book), who pinches her on the arm and says, "That's a pinch to grow an inch. And you know where you need that inch!" After Judy Blume's *Are You There God? It's Me, Margaret*, sixth grade (or at least books about sixth grade) would never be the same.

March 9

BORN: 1892 Vita Sackville-West (*The Edwardians*, *All Passion Spent*), Kent, England
1918 Mickey Spillane (*I, the Jury*; *Vengeance Is Mine!*), Brooklyn
DIED: 1918 Frank Wedekind (*Spring Awakening*, *Pandora's Box*), 53, Munich
1994 Charles Bukowski (*Ham on Rye*, *Post Office*), 73, San Pedro, Calif.

1776 Published: *An Inquiry into the Nature and Causes of the Wealth of Nations* by Adam Smith (Strahan & Cadell, London)

1864 Like pretty much everyone in Thomas Pynchon's *The Crying of Lot 49*, Mike Fallopian is both a connoisseur of underground paranoia and an underground paranoiac himself. Mike's particular bag is March 9, 1864, a "day now held sacred" by his fellow members of the ultra-right-wing Peter Pinguid Society in honor of a proto–Cold War confrontation in the waters off San Francisco between Confederate and Russian ships that, truth be told, feels more like a foggy Gulf of Tonkin moment than a real Fort Sumter exchange. And what was the extent of the martyrdom of Peter Pinguid, the Confederate commander? No, he wasn't lost at sea. He endured a more Pynchonian fate: he left the service and made a fortune speculating in L.A. real estate.

1874 Willam Ewart Gladstone, after handing over the British government to his rival Benjamin Disraeli, turned in his leisure to reading Disraeli's first novel, published nearly fifty years before: "Finished *Vivian Grey*. The first quarter extremely clever, the rest trash."

1929 E.E.K., in the *New Statesman*, on Marcel Proust's *Cities of the Plain*: "As a rule there is but little to reconcile one to the repulsiveness of the theme; and the young man who inspects these earth-worms so curiously is such a worm himself that one finds oneself preferring the scrutinised to the scrutiniser."

1963 Two pairs of men, each partners for a little more than a week, converged curbside on Carlos Avenue in Hollywood: Ian Campbell and Karl Hettinger, cops working felony car theft from an unmarked vehicle, and Greg Powell and Jimmy Smith, planning a felony themselves that night, though not the capital crime they ended up committing. Joseph Wambaugh was an LAPD cop too, with two police novels, including the bestselling *The New Centurions*, under his belt, when he turned to nonfiction in 1973 with *The Onion Field*, the story of a traffic stop a decade earlier that turned, on one criminal's impulse, into a double kidnapping and then the murder of a police officer in the farm country between Los Angeles and Bakersfield.

BORN: **1903** Clare Booth Luce (*The Women*),
New York City
1920 Boris Vian (*Foam of the Daze*), Ville-
d'Avray, France
DIED: **1940** Mikhail Bulgakov (*The Master and
Margarita*), 48, Moscow
1948 Zelda Fitzgerald (*Save Me the Waltz*),
47, Asheville, N.C.

1302 Convicted in absentia in January by a
rival political faction on trumped-up charges
of financial corruption, Dante Alighieri
found his temporary exile from Florence
made permanent on this day when it was
decreed that he would be burned to death if
he ever returned to his home city. He never
did, and he spent the last two decades of his
life in a wandering exile he never failed to
speak of as bitter and despairing but that, in
releasing him from the duties and intrigues
of politics, allowed him to become what
he calls in his *Divine Comedy* "a party by
yourself." While traveling through Verona,
Arezzo, Padua, Venice, Lucca, and elsewhere, he conceived of and composed the
Inferno, *Purgatorio*, and *Paradiso*, finally
completing his masterwork in the tranquility of Ravenna.

1812 On what exact morning was it that
Lord Byron "awoke and found himself
famous"? We can't say—the only source
for the quotation, which has acquired its
own considerable fame, is Thomas Moore's
1830 biography—but his celebrity did suddenly blossom with the publication on this
day of the first two cantos of *Childe Harold's Pilgrimage*, the poetic memoir of his
journey across Europe the previous two
years. In three days the complete printing
of 500 expensive quarto editions sold out,
and within six years 20,000 more afford-
able copies had been sold, a bestseller by any
standard at the time. Moore was as shocked
as his friend Byron: "His fame had not to
wait for any of the ordinary gradations, but
seemed to spring up, like the palace of a
fairy tale, in a night."

1964 To the Credit Department at Marshall Field & Co., Moses Herzog writes, "I
am no longer responsible for the debts of
Madeleine P. Herzog. As of March 10, we
ceased to be husband and wife." The ceasing
wasn't Herzog's idea: his wife, dressed for
the moment and glowing with her decision,
had informed him that she had never loved
him, never could, and wanted a divorce.
(What she didn't tell him at the time was
that she had taken up with his best friend,
Valentine Gersbach, he of the wooden
leg and the full head of red hair.) And so
Herzog, perhaps Saul Bellow's greatest creation, is left alone with his fine but restless
mind, writing unsent letters in his head full
of explanation, injustice, and confusion and
trying to think of whether there's an escape
from thinking.

March 11

BORN: 1916 Ezra Jack Keats (*The Snowy Day*, *Whistle for Willie*), Brooklyn
1952 Douglas Adams (*The Hitchhiker's Guide to the Galaxy*), Cambridge, England
DIED: 1969 John Wyndham (*The Day of the Triffids*), 65, Petersfield, England
1970 Erle Stanley Gardner (*The Case of the Velvet Claws, The Case of the Sulky Girl*), 80, Temecula, Calif.

1661 Samuel Pepys returned home to find that his wife had a new set of teeth, which with he was quite pleased.

1818 Published: *Frankenstein* by Mary Shelley (Lackington, Hughes, London)

1933 Thomas Lanier Williams, age twenty-one and the creator much later, under the name "Tennessee," of Blanche DuBois, inquired of Harriet Monroe, the editor of *Poetry*, "Will you do a total stranger the kindness of reading his verse?"

1935 "A short story can be written on a bottle," F. Scott Fitzgerald wrote to his editor Maxwell Perkins, but "it has become increasingly plain to me that the very excellent organization of a long book or the finest perceptions and judgment in time of revision do not go well with liquor." In a hopeful and almost surely false postscript, he added, "I haven't had a drink for almost six weeks and haven't had the faintest temptation yet." Later in the year, still scrambling to pay his debts by writing magazine stories—including a series of medieval tales he thought could make a book called *The Count of Darkness*—Fitzgerald "cracked like a plate," suffering a harrowing alcoholic breakdown that gave him one of his last great subjects.

1936 T.S.M., in the *New Republic*, on Dorothy L. Sayers's *Gaudy Night*: "Isn't it possible to write a murder story and have it taken seriously as literature? Well, there's always 'Tess of the d'Urbervilles' and 'The Brothers Karamazov.' But when it comes to Miss Sayers' kind, I'd rather take mine straight. Give me an Edgar Wallace."

1965 Published: *I Lost It at the Movies* by Pauline Kael (Atlantic–Little, Brown, Boston)

1966 In an author's note at the opening of Joyce Carol Oates's fourth novel, *them*, she claims, with an apparent sincerity that many readers took as the truth, that her story was based on the confessions of a former night student of hers named Maureen Wendall. Nevertheless, it's a surprising moment when, in the middle of her otherwise straightforward narrative, Maureen, the main character of the book, speaks directly to the author. "Dear Miss Oates. The books you taught us are mainly lies I can tell you," Maureen writes. and it feels like a cry not just against the poverty and violence of her life, but against the story her author is trying make that life fit into.

2001 Jim Squires, in the *New York Times,* on Laura Hillenbrand's *Seabiscuit*: "If plans to make a film of the story work out, and if the film is as good as the book, the horse's name may once again be known to almost everyone."

BORN: **1922** Jack Kerouac (*On the Road, Visions of Cody*), Lowell, Mass.

1970 Dave Eggers (*A Heartbreaking Work of Staggering Genius, Zeitoun*), Boston

DIED: **2001** Robert Ludlum (*The Bourne Identity, The Osterman Weekend*), 73, Naples, Fla.

2003 Howard Fast (*Citizen Tom Paine, Spartacus*), 88, Greenwich, Conn.

1714 *The Rape of the Lock*, Alexander Pope reported, had sold 3,000 copies in four days, a sensational amount at the time.

1851 Arriving at the home of Nathaniel Hawthorne and family at dusk, Herman Melville was "entertained with Champagne foam—manufactured of beaten eggs, loaf sugar, & champagne."

1906 George Bernard Shaw's feminism was loud, imperious, and idiosyncratic, and on at least one occasion, an interview he gave to the novelist and suffragette Maud Churton Braby, published in the *Tribune* on this day, it was militant. "If I were a woman," he puckishly declared, "I'd simply refuse to speak to any man or do anything for men until I'd got the vote. I'd make my husband's life a burden, and everybody miserable generally. Women should have a resolution—they should shoot, kill, maim, destroy—until they are given a vote." In later years, when the numbers of women voting had hardly budged their numbers in Parliament, he made a further suggestion: "The representative unit must not be a man *or* a woman. Every vote, to be valid, must be for a human pair, with the result that the elected body must consist of men and women in equal numbers."

1991 Lisbeth Salander refers to it as "All the Evil," although there's plenty more evil to go around in Stieg Larsson's Millennium Trilogy. But the effects of the events on this day—which are described in a suppressed report that's only revealed partway through the trilogy's middle book, *The Girl Who Played with Fire*—are endless: Lisbeth's father was maimed for life, her mother could no longer take care of her children, her twin sister was put in foster care. And twelve-year-old Lisbeth herself, confined to the St. Stefan's Psychiatric Clinic for Children, acquired an official diagnosis that put her in the power of the very sort of men she was already learning to arm herself against.

1999 Denis Donoghue, in the *TLS,* on Harold Bloom's *Shakespeare*: "Bloom's theory, an opportunistic mixture of Blake, Emerson, Nietzsche, and Freud, for which I hold none of those sages to blame, is one of the most nefarious instruments of American individualism, and an ideology that provokes and gratifies one's most selfish impulses."

2009 Geoffrey Wolff, in the *New York Times,* on Blake Bailey's *Cheever*: "The business of this biography is to explore the varieties and costs of unreliability not only in the expression of art, but also in the society of family and the prison of an obsessed self. This mission makes Bailey's biography of Cheever both arresting and disturbing, a disturbance of the peace, if you will."

March 13

BORN: **1892** Janet Flanner (*Paris Was Yesterday*, *Paris Journal*), Indianapolis
1958 Caryl Phillips (*The Final Passage*, *Crossing the River*), St. Kitts
DIED: **1971** Rockwell Kent (*Wilderness*, *N by E*, *Salamina*), 88, Plattsburgh, N.Y.
2009 James Purdy (*Eustace Chisholm and the Works*, *Malcolm*), 94, Englewood, N.J.

1601 The traces left in the archives by the daily life of William Shakespeare are famously scant and, for the most part, dry and businesslike, hardly hinting at the full-bodied humanity of his plays and poems. But among the property and tax records there is one mention that, in its identity-shifting japery, seems taken directly from one of his comedies. In his gossipy diaries, London lawyer John Manningham told the story of an Elizabethan groupie who, taken by Richard Burbage's performance as Richard III, invited him home after the show. "Shakespeare, overhearing their conclusion, went before, was intertained, and at his game ere Burbidge came. Then message being brought that Richard the 3d. was at the door, Shakespeare"—answering "from the capon's blankets," as Stephen Dedalus retells the story in *Ulysses*—"caused returne to be made that William the Conquerour was before Rich the 3."

1929 Published: *The Innocent Voyage* (later *A High Wind in Jamaica*) by Richard Hughes (Harper & Row, New York)

1929 W.T., in the *New Republic*, on Elizabeth Bowen's *The Last September*: "Blind parasites of every land will discover their lineaments in her mirror."

2001 Chapter four of Michael Pollan's *The Omnivore's Dilemma* is a Western of sorts. Pollan, in the process of tracking where his—and our—food comes from, follows the classic romance of a cattle drive: in this case the journey of steer 534, a calf he purchased at the Blair Ranch in South Dakota. Born on this day in late winter, 534 fed for six months on the grass of the Great Plains before being trucked to a massive feedlot in Kansas, a city of 37,000 temporary residents—known as a Confined Animal Feeding Operation—where he beefed up to a thousand pounds on a year-long, unnatural diet of corn, antibiotics, and fat and protein supplements while standing in the grayish mud of his and his neighbors' manure, a "short, unhappy life" that "represents the ultimate triumph of industrial thinking over the logic of evolution."

2012 *Encyclopædia Britannica* announced the end of its print edition.

BORN: 1920 Hank Ketcham (*Dennis the Menace*), Seattle
1923 Diane Arbus (*Family Albums, Revelations*), New York City
DIED: 1883 Karl Marx (*Capital, The Eighteenth Brumaire of Louis Napoleon*), 64, London
2003 Amanda Davis (*Wonder When You'll Miss Me*), 32, McDowell County, N.C.

44 B.C. It's a stormy night, full of portents, on the day that Caesar returns in triumph, declines the crown of Rome three times, and hears the soothsayer's warning, "Beware the ides of March!" Cassius, fearing Caesar's growing power, gathers a conspiracy against him and even uses the weather for his purposes. The "dreadful night," he says to one ally, is heaven's warning of a monster in the Capitol who "thunders, lightens, opens graves, and roars." Brutus, the most necessary and ambivalent conspirator, spends the night awake, tormented by the morrow's action. "Is not to-morrow, boy, the ides of March?" he asks a servant before the morning. "Look in the calendar, and bring me word." The boy returns with news the day has already turned: "Sir, March is wasted fifteen days."

1858 "My dear Beth died at three this morning," Louisa May Alcott recorded. Elizabeth, the third Alcott sister and the quietest, had contracted scarlet fever two years before, much like the last illness of Beth, the third March sister—and the only one whose name matches her model in the Alcott family—in *Little Women*. Alcott also noted a "curious thing": that just after Beth breathed her last, "I saw a light mist rise from the body, and float up and vanish in the air." Her mother saw the same, and the family doctor explained, "It was the life departing visibly." The following day, her sister's pallbearers included "Mr. Emerson" and "Henry Thoreau."

1889 At Clongowes school in Dublin, soon after he turned seven, James Joyce was given four "pandies on his open palm," punished, not for the last time, for the infraction of "vulgar language."

2004 Will Blythe, in the *New York Times*, on Tom Perrotta's *Little Children*: "'Little Children' raises the question of how a writer can be so entertainingly vicious and yet so full of fellow feeling."

80 F.E. As the eightieth anniversary of the new era approaches in Isaac Asimov's *Foundation*, the future has been calculated, but by a science no one left can understand. All the residents of the Foundation, an outpost on the periphery of the crumbling Galactic Empire, have to go on is the archived knowledge they've inherited and the veiled prophecies left by the great seer Hari Seldon, who estimated, with 98.4 percent probability, that the Foundation would develop according to the Plan over its first eighty years. His predictions have proved correct, but even when his second prophecy is revealed on this anniversary day, it explains little more, for too much advance knowledge would upset the balance of his calculations. "Gentlemen, nine hundred and twenty years of the Plan stretch ahead of you. The problem is yours!"

March 15

BORN: 1852 Lady Gregory (*Cuchulain of Muirthemne*), Roxborough, Ireland
1918 Richard Ellmann (*James Joyce, Oscar Wilde, Yeats*), Highland Park, Mich.
DIED: 1937 H. P. Lovecraft (*The Shadow Over Innsmouth*), 46, Providence, R.I.
1983 Rebecca West (*Black Lamb and Grey Falcon*), 90, London

1945 At the tail end of a war nearly won, fighting over a small piece of ground in Alsace, Second Lieutenant Paul Fussell, twenty years old, was wounded in the back and leg by shrapnel that killed the two soldiers lying next to him atop a German bunker. Fussell's combat career ended that day, but the war, and his fury at the way it ground men up, stayed with him for the rest of his life. Returning to the world of words he'd been drawn to before he was drafted, he wrote a series of books driven by the fierce skepticism his time in the army had given him, including the one that made his name, *The Great War and Modern Memory*, a gripping and deeply personal account of the experience of the world war before his that nonetheless, as he says, "was an act of implicit autobiography."

NO YEAR Maqroll doubts that the remote lumber mill that's his destination will actually make his fortune, but like a modern Quixote he sets out nevertheless, a passenger on a tiny barge that battles the current of the fictional Xurandó River with "asthmatic obstinacy" and a captain never less than half-drunk. "It's always the same at the start of a journey," Maqroll writes in his diary. "Then comes a soothing indifference that makes everything all right. I can't wait for it to arrive." When Álvaro Mutis, a poet—and a South American executive for American oil and film companies—for four decades, wrote the story of Maqroll's journey, his first long fiction, he sent it to his agent with the message "I don't know what the devil this is." What it became was *The Adventures and Misadventures of Maqroll*, an open-ended series of tales that made Mutis, late in life, one of the most celebrated South American novelists.

1958 Best known in later years as an uncompromising historian of the horrors of Soviet Communism, Robert Conquest in the '50s was a poet and, with his friends Kingsley Amis and Philip Larkin, a tireless prankster. Conquest took the fun furthest of all, most memorably with Larkin, to whom, knowing the shy poet's extracurricular reading interests, he mailed a warning, claiming to be from the Scotland Yard Vice Squad, that Larkin might be prosecuted under the Obscene Publications Act. After a nervous day at his solicitor's, Larkin angrily sent the £10 legal bill to Conquest on this day, with the suggestion "Why can't you play your japes on David Wright or Christopher Logue or some bastard who wd benefit from a cold sweat or two? Instead of plaguing your old pals." Even the louche Amis recalled the episode with a slight horror.

March 16

BORN: 1952 Alice Hoffman (*Practical Magic, Here on Earth*), New York City
1961 Todd McFarlane (*Spawn, Amazing Spider-Man*), Calgary, Alb.
DIED: 1898 Aubrey Beardsley (*The Yellow Book, Lysistrata*), 25, Menton, France
1940 Selma Lagerlöf (*The Wonderful Adventures of Nils*), 81, Värmland, Sweden

1924 With Gertrude Stein and Alice B. Toklas as godmothers, John Hadley Nicanor Hemingway, the first child of Ernest Hemingway, born in October, was baptized in Paris.

1937 The children call themselves by the private names he's given them: Looloo, Ernest-Paynim-Pigsney-Princeps, Sawbones, and Samulam. And they call him Father, Dad, and one he's chosen for himself, Sam-the-Bold. The packet of family letters that arrives for Samuel Clemens Pollitt is full of what he calls the "un-news" of family life—"We are well. Mother is not well."—and of the language their father has given them in his charismatic, autocratic way, as their creator and destroyer. Christina Stead gave Samuel Pollitt a name of her own in the title of her great (and autobiographical) novel, *The Man Who Loved Children*. To call that description ironic—at least with the thin, tinny definition of irony we have these days—doesn't quite do justice to the vast distance between what Sam Pollitt imagines for himself and what he does.

NO YEAR Nicholas Ray's *In a Lonely Place*, with Humphrey Bogart as a short-tempered screenwriter who may be a killer, doesn't share much with Dorothy B. Hughes's 1947 noir novel it was based on, beyond character names, the L.A. garden apartment setting, and the oppressive presence of male violence, always on the edge of breaking through. Bogie's Dixon Steele is accused of only one murder, but in Hughes's original at least six women, one a month beginning on the night before St. Patrick's Day, have been taken by the "Strangler." It's not long before we know who the culprit is, but we're left to wonder if Laurel Gray, the redheaded femme fatale, will have the brains to get out of what she gets herself into.

1997 Laura Miller, in the *New York Times*, on David Foster Wallace's *A Supposedly Fun Thing I'll Never Do Again*: "This collection . . . reveals Mr. Wallace in ways that his fiction has of yet managed to dodge: as a writer struggling mightily to understand and capture his times, as a critic who cares deeply about 'serious' art, and as a mensch."

March 17

BORN: 1904 Patrick Hamilton (*The Slaves of Solitude, Hangover Square*), Hassocks, England
1948 William Gibson (*Neuromancer, Pattern Recognition*), Conway, S.C.
DIED: 180 Marcus Aurelius (*Meditations*), 58, Vindobona, Roman Empire
2005 Andre Norton (*Witch World, The Stars Are Ours!*), 93, Murfreesboro, Tenn.

1846 Published: *Typee: A Peep at Polynesian Life* by Herman Melville (Wiley and Putnam, New York)

1871 "That book," Robert Chambers would say near the end of his life, "was my death-blow." Those few who remember Chambers might imagine the book he meant was *Vestiges of the Natural History of Creation*, a bestselling sensation of Victorian speculative science that drew the ire of clergymen and the ridicule of scientists, although Darwin credited the book's half-baked concept of the "transmutation of species" with preparing the public for his own theory of evolution. Chambers, a prominent Scottish publisher, kept his authorship of the controversial *Vestiges* secret until after his death on this day, but the book he said killed him was another, a labor of love called *The Book of Days*, an exhaustively researched multivolume miscellany of anecdotes and biographies from history, literature, religion, and science, which he organized, perversely, by the days of the calendar.

1974 In the latest and last of the reclamations of Jean Rhys during her unhappy lifetime, A. Alvarez in the *New York Times* wrote that "she is, quite simply, the best living English novelist": "There is no one else now writing who combines such emotional penetration and formal artistry or approaches her unemphatic, unblinking truthfulness."

2002 Michael Pye, in the *New York Times*, on Jamie O'Neill's *At Swim, Two Boys*: "Love between men is for once not a limit but a starting point. It does not require excuses or boasts or provocation. It can be tragic and comic, but all in the context of the wider world of rebellion, courage, idiocy and history. "

2011 Two days after they were captured by soldiers loyal to Muammar el-Qaddafi, four *New York Times* journalists, including Pulitzer winner Anthony Shadid, were able to get word out that they were alive. The four had entered the country without a visa to cover the uprising against Qaddafi; caught at a checkpoint, they were spared execution when one soldier said, in Arabic, "No, they're American." (Their Libyan driver, they later learned, was killed.) They were released four days later, but the following February, Shadid, an Oklahoma City native who had covered the Middle East for nearly two decades, snuck across yet another border to report on the rebellion in Syria, where he died from an asthma attack brought on by his allergy to horses. His *Times* photographer, Tyler Hicks, one of those captured with him in Libya, carried his body back across the border to Turkey after his death.

March 18

BORN: **1927** George Plimpton (*Paper Lion, Edie, The Paris Review*), New York City
1932 John Updike (*Rabbit, Run; The Centaur; Couples*), Reading, Pa.
DIED: **1768** Laurence Sterne (*The Life and Opinions of Tristram Shandy, Gentleman*), 54, London
1986 Bernard Malamud (*The Fixer, The Magic Barrel*), 71, New York City

1819 Picking up a cricket bat for the first time, John Keats took a ball in the face. The leech a friend applied to his eyelid did not prevent a black eye.

1897 An enthusiastic and talented amateur naturalist, Beatrix Potter cultivated a particular interest in mycology, the perennially unglamorous study of fungi. Working in the field and in her kitchen—and making drawings whose lovely detail her later readers would not be surprised to see—she developed a rare ability to germinate spores and surmised that lichens were the product of symbiosis between fungi and algae, an idea, now confirmed, that few believed at the time. The established botanists of her day did little to encourage a self-educated woman; after one encounter she huffed in her journal, "It is odious to a shy person to be snubbed as conceited, especially when the shy person happened to be right, and under the temptation of sauciness." On this day, though, she was allowed to submit a paper, "On the Germination of the Spores of *Agaricineae*," to be presented at the general meeting of the prestigious Linnean Society, though Potter, as a woman, was not allowed to attend. Decades later, the society officially acknowledged that Miss Potter had been "treated scurvily" by some of its members.

1939 R. D. Charques, in the *TLS*, on Flann O'Brien's *At Swim-Two-Birds*: "Mr. Flann O'Brien will hardly be surprised if a reviewer is at a loss how to describe this book of his."

1960 Raymond Carver, the co-editor of the new literary magazine at Chico State College in Northern California, was, according to a profile in the school paper on this day, one of the "most harried-looking people on campus." Twenty-one but married for three years already, with a baby girl and boy and a wife who, as she did for years, was working to support them, Carver had signed up in his second year of school for English 20A, Creative Writing. His professor, John Gardner, new to the school, was just twenty-six himself and, like Carver, still more than a decade away from the books that would make him famous, but he had a PhD and plenty of theories about writing fiction, and his ambition and his standards for what fiction should be made his student "wild with discovery."

March 19

BORN: 1809 Nikolai Gogol (*Dead Souls*, *The Nose*), Sorochyntsi, Russian Empire
1933 Philip Roth (*The Ghost Writer*, *The Counterlife*), Newark, N.J.

DIED: 1950 Edgar Rice Burroughs (*Tarzan of the Apes*, *A Princess of Mars*), 74, Encino, Calif.
2008 Arthur C. Clarke (*2001*, *2010*, *Rendezvous with Rama*), 90, Colombo, Sri Lanka

1914 *Chance*, late in Joseph Conrad's hard-working and chronically indebted career, was his first great popular success, but not with his friend Henry James, who in a two-part article beginning on this day criticized the book as the work of "a beautiful and generous mind in conditions comparatively thankless." Conrad later said it was "the *only* time a criticism affected me painfully."

1924 Edmund Wilson, in the *New Republic*, on Wallace Stevens's *Harmonium*: "When you read a few poems of Mr. Stevens, you get the impression from the richness of his verbal imagination that he is a poet of rich personality, but when you come to read the whole volume through you are struck by a sort of aridity."

1944 Pablo Picasso broke the tedium and anxiety of the first winter of the German occupation of Paris in 1941 by composing in three days his first and only play, *Desire Caught by the Tail*. A nonsense farce in the tradition of the Surrealists and *Ubu Roi*, the play didn't receive a performance until a reading on this day at the apartment of the anthropologist Michel Leiris, with Picasso, Georges Braque, and Georges Bataille in the audience and an all-star cast that included Albert Camus as the narrator, Leiris as "Big Foot," Jean-Paul Sartre as "Round Morsel," and Simone de Beauvoir and Raymond Queneau as "the Cousin" and "the Onion," who at one point enter singing, "Oboy . . . We're bringing you shrimps! Oboy, oboy, we're bringing you shrimps!" It is unlikely, under the wartime conditions, that the stage directions calling for a giant bathtub full of soapsuds and a bed covered in fried potatoes were followed.

1962 The publication date of her first book, *Sex and the Single Girl*, was still two months away, but Helen Gurley Brown (future editor of *Cosmopolitan*) and her publicist Letty Cottin (a future founding editor of *Ms.*) had high hopes for one way to make her sure-to-be-controversial guide a hit: provoking someone to ban the book. "I don't know how to get a public denunciation—a nice, strong, snarly, vocal one—from some religious leader," Brown wrote on this day, "but it is a possibility." They sent advance copies to the Little Rock public library, Catholic groups, and the Daughters of the American Revolution, but no one took the bait, which perhaps was a sign that America in the early '60s was ready for Brown after all. Without any help from the censors, the book was an immediate bestseller.

1963 The *New York Times* on Anthony Burgess's *A Clockwork Orange*: "a tour-de-force in nastiness, an inventive primer in total violence, a savage satire on the distortions of the single and collective minds."

March 20

BORN: 43 B.C. Ovid (*Metamorphoses, Ars amatoria*), Sulmo, Roman Republic
1937 Lois Lowry (*The Giver, Number the Stars*), Honolulu
DIED: 1727 Isaac Newton (*Principia Mathematica*), 84, Kensington, England
1962 C. Wright Mills (*The Power Elite, White Collar*), 45, West Nyack, N.Y.

1784 Just after midnight, a "puny, seven months' child" named Catherine is born. Two hours later, her sickly mother, also named Catherine, dies without ever having wakened to meet her daughter. In the morning the mother's fair and mild husband, Edgar, lies prostrate beside her corpse, while Heathcliff, her true love, rages outside in the garden, dashing his savage brow against a tree. Sixteen years later, young Cathy celebrates her birthday—always neglected by mourning over her mother's death—with a ramble on the moors, where she meets her estranged uncle, that same Heathcliff, and in the tightly confined drama of Emily Brontë's *Wuthering Heights*, the sins of one generation—and perhaps their hopes—can once again be passed on to the next.

1827 Unable to pay his gambling debts at the University of Virginia and, by his own account, "roaming the streets" of Richmond, Edgar Allan Poe pleaded for money from his adoptive father, who refused.

1846 Elizabeth Barrett, having received *The Raven and Other Poems* from Poe, who dedicated the book to her though they had never met, wrote to a friend for advice: "What is to be said, I wonder, when a man calls you the 'noblest of your sex'? 'Sir, you are the most discerning of yours.'"

1963 Having published six novels with Jonathan Cape, Barbara Pym received word by post that they were not interested in her seventh, *An Unsuitable Attachment*. ("While we have not exactly lost any money," a second letter explained, "we have not made any as a result of publishing these six novels.") Unable, in the era of James Bond and the Beatles, to find another publisher for her stories of spinsters and jumble sales, Pym didn't publish another novel until 1977, when her nomination as the most underrated novelist of the century in the *TLS* sparked a revival of interest in her work. When *An Unsuitable Attachment* was finally released after her death a few years later, one reviewer wrote, "The publisher must have been mad to reject this jewel."

1987 Ludo Newman has been counting down to his sixth birthday all year, but he's concerned less with his birth than with his conception. As a birthday gift, along with the *Oxford-Duden Japanese Pictorial Dictionary*, his mother allows him to ask as many questions as he wants. He has just one: "Who is my father?" Of the many recent novels told through the eyes of precocious youngsters, Helen DeWitt's *The Last Samurai*, about a boy in search of his father and the mother trying to educate him, is the most brilliant, an intellectual and emotional adventure worthy of comparison with Ludo and his mom's favorite Kurosawa film, *The Seven Samurai*.

March 21

BORN: 1905 Phyllis McGinley (*Times Three, Husbands Are Difficult*), Ontario, Ore.
1949 Slavoj Žižek (*The Sublime Object of Ideology*), Ljubljana, Slovenia
DIED: 1997 Rev. W. Awdry (*Thomas the Tank Engine*), 85, Rodborough, England
2013 Chinua Achebe (*Arrow of God, Anthills of the Savannah*), 82, Boston

NO YEAR Why has Mrs. Badger in Dickens's *Bleak House* wed all three of her husbands "upon the twenty-first of March at eleven in the forenoon," in the proud words of husband number three? "I had become attached to the day," she explains.

1868 Standing on an Antarctic peak at noon on the Southern Hemisphere's autumnal equinox, Captain Nemo unfurls a black flag bearing a golden *N* and claims the polar continent in his name as the sun begins its half-yearly journey to the other side of the earth. "Disappear, O radiant orb! Retire beneath this open sea, and let six months of night spread their shadows over my new domains!" he declares before returning with his fascinated captive, Professor Aronnax, to his magnificent submarine, the *Nautilus*, and resuming the undersea peregrinations that are his restless fate in Jules Verne's *20,000 Leagues Under the Sea*.

1888 "Good-night, Mister Sherlock Holmes," says a "slim youth in an ulster" to the detective outside his Baker Street lodgings, in the final, cheeky sally of a day that ranks among the most memorable in Holmes's career. The "youth" is none other than the incomparable Irene Adler, the diminutive opera singer and would-be blackmailer of "A Scandal in Bohemia." Or, rather, she's now Mrs. Irene Norton, for by that time of the day Holmes has already, in bedraggled disguise, served as a witness at her impromptu wedding, before later, disguised this time as a clergyman, gaining entrance to her home and causing her to reveal where she had secreted her incriminating photograph. It's only on the following day that Holmes, realizing that she had seen through his disguises and outwitted him in turn, begins to refer to her, with uncharacteristic sentiment, as "*the* woman."

1915 Oak Park High School sophomore Ernest Hemingway pledged in his school notebook to "do pioneering or exploring work in the 3 last great frontiers Africa, central south America or the country around and north of Hudson Bay."

1972 Elizabeth Bishop had been trying to compose the letter for weeks. "It's hell to write this," she told her great friend Robert Lowell, "so please first do believe I think *Dolphin* is magnificent poetry." But out of love and admiration, she warned him he'd gone too far in using—and changing—his wife Elizabeth Hardwick's letters in his poems. "One can use one's life as material—one does, anyway—but these letters—aren't you violating a trust?" she asked. "*Art just isn't worth that much.*" Even Lowell, after first thinking her concerns "extreme paranoia," later admitted to her, after the poems (and Hardwick herself) were savaged in the press, that perhaps, in this case, the art wasn't worth it.

March 22

BORN: 1908 Louis L'Amour (*Hondo, The Rustlers of West Fork*), Jamestown, N.D.
1947 James Patterson (*Kiss the Girls, 1st to Die*), Newburgh, N.Y.
DIED: 1758 Jonathan Edwards ("Sinners in the Hands of an Angry God"), 54, Princeton, N.J.
1832 Johann Wolfgang von Goethe (*Wilhelm Meister's Apprenticeship*), 82, Weimar, Germany

1540 Following a furious and vengeful six-year campaign of robbery, arson, and pillage across Saxony after he failed to gain redress in the courts for the theft of two horses by a nobleman, the merchant Hans Kohlhase and his associate Georg Nagelschmidt were broken on the wheel in Berlin. Two and a half centuries later, Heinrich von Kleist transformed Kohlhase's chronicle into one of the most relentless and efficient narrative machines ever constructed: *Michael Kohlhaas*, a tale of justice pursued at any cost whose influence continued to flourish in the twentieth century, as one of Franz Kafka's favorite stories and as a model for E. L. Doctorow's *Ragtime*, the name of whose hero, Coalhouse Walker, is a nod to "Kohlhaas."

1861 One of many office seekers descending on the new president, Herman Melville met Lincoln at a White House party soon after his inauguration: "Old Abe is much better looking [than] I expected & younger looking. He shook hands like a good fellow—working hard at it like a man sawing wood at so much per cord."

1897 "Errand," Raymond Carver's story of the final illness of Anton Chekhov, begins on this evening when, as Chekhov dines with a friend at the finest restaurant in Moscow, "suddenly, without warning, blood began gushing from his mouth." It was the first hemorrhage of Chekhov's tuberculosis, and the story soon moves to the night of his death seven years later when an unnamed young Russian runs two errands, one for a bottle of champagne and the other for a mortician. A tale far in both space and time from Carver's usual settings, "Errand" was the last published in his lifetime: within a year of writing it Carver coughed up blood himself, the first sign of the cancer that killed him in 1988, after which he was eulogized as "America's Chekhov."

NO YEAR The diary entries of Lorelei Lee, a character inspired by a "golden-haired birdbrain" Anita Loos saw entrancing every man on the cross-country train to Hollywood, became the smash novel of 1926, *Gentlemen Prefer Blondes*. Among the first of those smitten with Lorelei is an English novelist who, as Lorelei records on this day, takes an interest in her education by sending her some of his own novels, which "all seem to be about middle age English gentlemen who live in the country over in London and seem to ride bicycles." He also sends a complete set of Joseph Conrad, about which she's more hopeful: "I have always liked novels about ocean travel," she notes, "because I always say that a girl never really looks as well as she does on board a steamship, or even a yacht."

March 23

BORN: 1956 Julia Glass (*Three Junes, The Whole World Over*), Boston
1964 Jonathan Ames (*The Extra Man, Wake Up Sir!*), New York City
DIED: 1842 Stendhal (*The Charterhouse of Parma*), 59, Paris
1992 Friedrich von Hayek (*The Road to Serfdom*), 92, Freiburg, Germany

1917 In the year since his arrest for refusing to continue teaching at the University of Ghent during the German occupation of Belgium, the historian Henri Pirenne had lectured to hundreds in the prison barracks. But when he was transferred to house arrest in a small village (for having abused the "hospitality of Germany"), he embarked on another project, a long-dreamed-of *History of Europe*, which he began on this day and which, in his isolation, he composed entirely from memory. He was able to cover the thousand years from the end of the Roman Empire to the early Renaissance before the armistice ended his exile, and his *History*, which wasn't published until after his death, remains wonderfully lively and bewilderingly authoritative, even without the knowledge of the heroic conditions under which it was written.

1925 "Scattered cases of uneasy but formless nocturnal impressions appear here and there" in H. P. Lovecraft's "The Call of Chthulu."

1944 Published: *Dangling Man* by Saul Bellow (Vanguard, New York)

1986 As bad reviews go, it could have been worse. Alice Hoffman, writing in the *New York Times*, called Richard Ford a "daring and intelligent novelist" with "an extraordinary ear for dialogue," but she thought his third novel, *The Sportswriter*, was "a risk that ultimately does not pay off." Ford, though, had a lot riding on the book—and he was right to, since it became his breakthrough—and that wasn't what he, or his wife, wanted to read. So they took Hoffman's own latest novel out in their Mississippi backyard, shot it, and mailed her the results. "People make such a big deal out of it—shooting a book," he shrugged years later. "It's not like I shot her." Hoffman, meanwhile, had her own ways of dealing with hostile reviewers, tweeting the home phone number of the "moron" in the *Boston Globe* who called her 2009 novel *The Story Sisters* "tired" and "contrived."

BORN: **1916** Donald Hamilton (*The Silencers*, *The Ravagers*), Uppsala, Sweden
1919 Lawrence Ferlinghetti (*A Coney Island of the Mind*), Yonkers, N.Y.
DIED: **1976** Ernest Howard Shepard (illustrator of *Winnie-the-Pooh*), 96, Midhurst, England
1993 John Hersey (*Hiroshima*, *The Wall*), 78, Key West, Fla.

1857 Idling in Paris, Tolstoy wrote to a friend in Russia on this day, "I can't foresee the time when the city will have lost its interest for me, or the life its charm." But by the time he finished the letter the next day, it had. What happened? On that morning, he was "stupid and callous enough" to attend an execution by guillotine: "If a man had been torn to pieces before my eyes it wouldn't have been so revolting as this ingenious and elegant machine by means of which a strong, hale and hearty man was killed in an instant." Disgusted with Paris, he couldn't sleep for days and soon left the city, and his disgust transformed his outlook in a way that never left him. "The law of man—what nonsense!" he wrote that day. "The truth is that the state is a conspiracy designed not only to exploit, but above all to corrupt its citizens."

1956 In the home stretch of the Grand National, with the thirty jumps of the steeplechase cleared, his nearest rival sixteen lengths back, and a record time for the race just seconds away, Devon Loch looked, to borrow the title of his jockey Dick Francis's first novel, a "dead cert." But suddenly the horse, owned by the Queen Mother and a favorite of the crowd, collapsed, uninjured, as the field, and the championship, passed him by. While Devon Loch's inexplicable slip may not be, as one Liverpool paper claimed, "the greatest tragedy in the history of sport," it has remained one of its most enduring enigmas. His jockey, Francis, once England's champion rider, retired soon after, and in 1962 *Dead Cert* became the first of his over forty bestselling racetrack mysteries.

2005 Nine chapters into the unfinished manuscript published as David Foster Wallace's final novel, *The Pale King*, arrives what might be a disconcerting element: an "Author's Foreword," claiming to be a message from the "real author, the living human holding the pencil," self-identified as "David Wallace, age forty, SS no. 975-04-2012," writing on the "fifth day of spring, 2005." Disconcerting because no one expects a foreword on page 68 and because this David Wallace's bona fides don't quite match those we can look up about the author, who, among other things, was forty-three in 2005. But at the same time it's the most comfortable part of the book, a familiar triple-back-flip postmodern move that brings into the story the characteristic DFW voice, full of qualifying subclauses and massive footnotes. In that sense perhaps it's an authentic message from the author after all.

March 25

BORN: 1347 St. Catherine of Siena (*Letters,*
The Dialogue of Divine Providence), Siena,
Italy
1925 Flannery O'Connor (*Everything That*
Rises Must Converge), Savannah, Ga.
DIED: 1951 Oscar Micheaux (*The Conquest,*
The Homesteader), 67, Charlotte, N.C.
2009 John Hope Franklin (*From Slavery to*
Freedom), 94, Durham, N.C.

1769 Thomas Chatterton, only sixteen but already an experienced artificer of "ancient" manuscripts, thought that Horace Walpole, the wealthy politician who had passed off a novel, *The Castle of Otranto*, as an old Italian manuscript before revealing it as his own, might have some interest in writings by a medieval monk he claimed to have discovered. Walpole replied politely, but when Chatterton sent more and revealed his age, Walpole sniffed a forgery and recommended the boy stick to his apprenticeship. Furious, Chatterton shot back, "I am obliged to you sir, for your advice and will go a little beyond it, by destroying all my useless lumber of literature and by never using my pen but in the law." His revenge was posthumous: after Chatterton's suicide the next year, Walpole's rejection was blamed for driving the young poet to his death.

1811 For publishing a pamphlet titled *The Necessity of Atheism*, Percy Bysshe Shelley and his friend Thomas Jefferson Hogg were expelled from Oxford.

1914 Heading straight from Greenwich Village to Juarez on a magazine assignment to cover a possible revolution in Mexico in 1913, poet and bohemian journalist John Reed, twenty-six years old, soon managed to ingratiate himself with the bandit-turned-general Pancho Villa and his tattered troops. His reports back, as Villa's increasingly disciplined army advanced toward Mexico City, were full of the romance of his own adventurous exploits as well as Villa's, and they made him immediately famous as an "American Kipling," with his college friend Walter Lippmann writing him in awe on this day, "I want to hug you, Jack. If all history had been reported as you are doing this, Lord—I say that with Jack Reed reporting begins."

1968 Spoiler alert! Jason Bourne—the amnesiac with the skills (and Swiss bank account) of a trained assassin who reconstructs his life while fending off a series of killers across Europe in *The Bourne Identity*, the first installment in Robert Ludlum's Bourne Trilogy and the high point of modern espionage action—is not actually Jason Bourne. The real Jason Charles Bourne was a double agent for the North Vietnamese, shot on this day in the jungles of Tam Quan by an operative for the top-secret elite American unit known as Medusa. Which means the man we know as "Jason Bourne" is actually . . .

2004 Michael Chabon, in the *New York Review of Books*, on Philip Pullman's *His Dark Materials*: "The question of whether or not *His Dark Materials* is meant or even suitable for young readers not only remains open but grows ever more difficult to answer as the series progresses."

BORN: 1941 Richard Dawkins (*The Selfish Gene, The God Delusion*), Nairobi, Kenya
1943 Bob Woodward (*All the President's Men, The Brethren*), Geneva, Ill.
DIED: 1892 Walt Whitman (*Leaves of Grass, Specimen Days*), 72, Camden, N.J.
1959 Raymond Chandler (*The Lady in the Lake, The Long Goodbye*), 70, La Jolla, Calif.

1830 Six and a half years after Joseph Smith said he was directed by the angel Moroni to a book of golden plates buried in a hill in Manchester, New York, and roughly fifteen centuries after the prophet Mormon was said to have engraved the plates with a hieroglyphic account of his people's history in the Americas, the Book of Mormon first went on sale at the shop of its printer, E. B. Grandin, in Palmyra, New York. Translated from its ancient language by Smith by means of a "seer stone" he placed at the bottom of his hat, this new scripture, he claimed, was just a fragment—like the Bible—of the divine records left of God's work through human history. Eleven days later, on the authority of the book and the continuing revelations granted him by God, Smith founded the Church of Christ, soon renamed the Church of Jesus Christ of Latter-day Saints.

1969 Who was B. Traven, the secretive author of a series of novels set among the exploited in the 1920s and '30s? Was he Otto Feige, the son of a potter born in Germany? Or Ret Marut, a German (or maybe American) anarchist and actor last seen when he was released from prison in England? Or Traven Torsvan, a reclusive innkeeper in Mexico known as El Gringo? Or Hal Croves, who showed up on the set when John Huston was filming Traven's best-known book, *The Treasure of the Sierra Madre*, and introduced himself as Traven's "agent"? Or perhaps all of the above. The theories are many, but most now believe that when Hal Croves died in Mexico City on this day, B. Traven died with him, and perhaps all his other identities as well.

1980 Headline writers could hardly resist the obvious when Roland Barthes, the French theorist best known for his essay "The Death of the Author," died on this day at sixty-five. A month and a day before, walking back from a luncheon hosted by France's next president, François Mitterand, he stepped into the rue des Ecoles and was struck down by a laundry van. He spent the next month in the hospital before succumbing, leaving behind an unfinished essay on Stendhal in his typewriter, the book *Camera Lucida*, which had just been published to hostile reviews but would become a classic, and his *Mourning Diary*, which, published much later, revealed the grieving for his beloved mother that some friends thought had already taken his will to live.

2000 Robert Kelly, in the *New York Times*, on Mark Z. Danielewski's *House of Leaves*: "I fell for it—the scholastic, footnoted, typographical fun house aspect of the book. I love the difficult, since it makes the easy seem finally possible."

March 27

BORN: 1901 Carl Barks (*Walt Disney's Comics and Stories*), Merrill, Ore.
   1950 Julia Alvarez (*How the Garcia Girls Lost Their Accents*), New York City
DIED: 1989 Malcolm Cowley (*Exile's Return, Blue Juniata*), 90, New Milford, Conn.
   2006 Stanislaw Lem (*Solaris, Memoirs Found in a Bathtub*), 84, Krakow, Poland

1915 The *New Republic* on James Joyce's *Dubliners*: "He is a sanely reflective observer of a pettily bourgeois city, and he proves his sympathy chiefly by his attentiveness to disregarded men and women, his fidelity to life in its working clothes."

1922 On a visit to his parents in Berlin for the Easter holidays during his last year of university at Cambridge, Vladimir Nabokov boxed playfully with his beloved father and, in pajamas before bed, talked with him about his brother and the opera *Boris Godunov*. The next evening, while his mother plays solitaire and Vladimir reads poetry after a "heavenly day," the phone in the hall will ring: "Something terrible has happened to your father." A car will rush them to a meeting of Russian émigrés where the elder Nabokov has been shot while disarming a Russian monarchist attempting to assassinate the speaker. Vladimir's last memory of his father will be the sight of his hand passing him newspapers through an open door on his way to bed the night before.

1964 Wilfrid Sheed, in *Commonweal*, on Betty Friedan's *The Feminine Mystique* and Simone de Beauvoir's *The Second Sex*: "Thus it comes about that the louder Simone de Beauvoir and Mrs. Friedan shout the funnier they seem . . . It is quite possible that serious injustice has been done to women: yet there remains a strange aura of frivolity about the whole question."

2004 In which Sherlock Holmes adventure is a renowned scholar, after warning of an unnamed "American" trying to destroy him, found garroted in his bedroom? "The Purloined Archives"? "The Deceased Irregular"? "The Thwarted Biography"? None of the above: it happens in "Mysterious Circumstances," the opening chapter in *The Devil and Sherlock Holmes*, David Grann's collection of his *New Yorker* reporting. The circumstances surrounding the death of Richard Lancelyn Green, the foremost expert on the life and works of Sir Arthur Conan Doyle, were indeed mysterious—cryptic messages, lost manuscripts, an ancient curse, and the murderous use of a shoelace on a victim who wore only slip-on shoes—and Grann makes of them a Holmes-worthy case that points to a surprising cause for these well-arranged clues.

BORN: 1936 Mario Vargas Llosa (*Aunt Julia and the Scriptwriter*), Arequipa, Peru
    1940 Russell Banks (*Continental Drift, The Sweet Hereafter*), Newton, Mass.
DIED: 1941 Virginia Woolf (*The Waves, A Room of One's Own*), 59, Lewes, England
    2000 Anthony Powell (*A Dance to the Music of Time*), 94, Frome, England

1860 The *New York Times* on Charles Darwin's *On the Origin of Species*: "Shall we frankly declare that, after the most deliberate consideration of Mr. Darwin's arguments, we remain unconvinced? The book is full of a most interesting and impressive series of minor verifications; but he fails to show the points of junction between these, and no where rises to complete logical statement."

1886 After "five years of knocking about in newspapers," supplementing his small income as a doctor by churning out short sketches under the pen name Antoshe Chekhonte, Anton Chekhov received a letter that came "like a flash of lightning": a note from D. V. Grigorovich, an established literary man from the generation of Turgenev and Dostoyevsky, that declared he had "real talent" and would commit "a grievous moral sin" if he neglected it. In a grateful reply, Chekhov confessed he had taken his talent lightly—"I don't remember a single story at which I worked for more than a day, and 'The Sportsman,' which you liked, I wrote in a bathing-shed!"—and promised to reform. To a literary friend, though, he was more blasé about the praise, saying that "the old boy . . . has rather laid it on with a trowel."

1888 "At Walt's this evening," Horace Traubel began. They had known each other for a decade, but on this day Traubel began to record his visits with Walt Whitman. The poet was sixty-eight, slowed by a stroke but still dynamic. His young Boswell was twenty-nine, a printer and poet in the spirit of his hero, whose last four years he chronicled, unprettified as Whitman requested, in the nine volumes of *With Walt Whitman in Camden*.

1939 At age twenty-three, after just a year of grad school at Columbia, Alfred Kazin outlined in a Guggenheim grant application his ambitious plan for a history of American writing over the previous forty years. He got his Guggenheim, and spent four years—while the world outside convulsed into war—researching in the great reading room of the New York Public Library. The result was *On Native Grounds*, which brought its "boy wonder" author, the son of Yiddish-speaking immigrants, an almost unheard-of reception—"Now and then the publication of a book is not only a literary but a moral event," gushed the *New York Herald Tribune*—and remains one of the best accounts of its era.

1963 Following the failure of his historical novel *Mignon* after twelve years of labor, James M. Cain sold off his thousand-book research collection on the Civil War.

2012 To mark his seventy-sixth birthday, Mario Vargas Llosa announced he would donate his 30,000-book personal library to his hometown of Arequipa, Peru.

March 29

BORN: 1957 Elizabeth Hand (*Waking the Moon, Generation Loss*), Yonkers, N.Y.
1961 Amy Sedaris (*Wigfield, I Like You, Simple Times*), Endicott, N.Y.
DIED: 1772 Emanuel Swedenborg (*Heaven and Hell, True Christian Religion*), 84, London
1957 Joyce Cary (*The Horse's Mouth, Mister Johnson*), 68, Oxford, England

1944 On this day, Anne Frank's diary became an autobiography. Gathered around their radio, the eight residents of the hidden apartment in Amsterdam heard a minister from the Dutch government in exile suggest that the letters and diaries of the people of Holland could provide a record for the future of what the war had been like. "Of course," she wrote that night, "they all made a rush at my diary immediately," but no one more quickly than Anne herself. "Just imagine," she continued, "how interesting it would be if I were to publish a romance of the 'Secret Annex.' The title alone would be enough to make people think it was a detective story." From that day, she continued to write her daily letters to "Kitty," but she also went back through the past two years, revising and shaping her account, no longer writing to herself but to history.

1948 The U.S. Supreme Court struck down on this day a New York law that banned "pictures and stories of deeds of bloodshed, lust or crime," but only in the hope that more specific and effective laws could be passed against the "evil" of gore-splattered and wildly popular comic books. On the same day, in a *Time* article headlined "Puddles of Blood," a new standard-bearer for those laws appeared: psychiatrist Fredric Wertham, who cited the pathogen of comic books as a direct cause of juvenile delinquency. Wertham first made his name by setting up a free psychiatric clinic in Harlem, supported by his friends Richard Wright and Ralph Ellison, but, as David Hajdu describes in *The Ten-Cent Plague*, through his Senate testimony, his book *Seduction of the Innocent*, and his influence on a new Comics Code he became best known as the scourge of the comics industry.

1975 If you lived in Baltimore then, you'd still remember their story, even after thirty years: "The Bethany girls. Easter weekend, 1975." Two sisters, one fifteen and one a few days short of twelve, took the bus to the Security Square Mall and never came back. But now one of them has returned, or so she says: Heather Bethany, who has been living under an identity she won't reveal—just one of a series of names she's taken in her life—and who tells a story about what happened to her and her older sister that no one who hears it is quite willing to believe. Like many a cold case, the twisty and character-rich mystery in Laura Lippman's *What the Dead Know* is full of long-held secrets, and it holds a solution few of its survivors thought they'd live to see.

BORN: 1820 Anna Sewell (*Black Beauty*), Great Yarmouth, England
1928 Tom Sharpe (*Wilt, Riotous Assembly, Porterhouse Blue*), London
DIED: 1964 Nella Larsen (*Quicksand, Passing*), 72, Brooklyn
1967 Jean Toomer (*Cane, The Blue Meridian*), 72, Doylestown, Pa.

1925 "Of all the poisonous, foul, ghastly places," P. G. Wodehouse wrote from the French Riviera, "Cannes takes the biscuit with absurd ease."

1926 H. L. Mencken, editor of the *American Mercury*, traveled to Boston to get himself arrested for selling the April 1926 issue of his magazine to the Reverend J. Frank Chase, described in that very issue as "a Methodist vice-hunter of long practice and great native talent." Whatever Chase thought of that, he had the issue banned in Boston because of the "filthy and degrading descriptions" in another article, Herbert Asbury's reminiscence of a prostitute in his Missouri hometown who serviced her clients in the local cemeteries. For the amusement of the reporters he'd invited, Mencken bit the half-dollar Chase gave him, and when a judge overturned the arrest two days later he celebrated with Harvard students. Asbury, meanwhile, took advantage of the publicity to start a career as his generation's most celebrated chronicler of American vice in *The Gangs of New York, The Barbary Coast*, and elsewhere.

1935 Clifton Fadiman, in *The New Yorker*, on William Faulkner's *Pylon*: "I've read it twice, once slowly and again in a burst of desperate speed, on the assumption that the first time I might not have seen the forest for the trees. It has licked me a dozen ways. Reaction analysis: one part repulsion, one part terror, one part admiration, three parts puzzlement, four parts boredom."

1972 The air was so electric at a George Wallace rally at Serb Hall in Milwaukee that Hunter S. Thompson, in *Fear and Loathing on the Campaign Trail '72*, had a sense that "the bastard had somehow levitated himself and was hovering above us. It reminded me of a Janis Joplin concert."

1997 Larry Wolff, in the *New York Times*, on W. G. Sebald's *The Emigrants*: "Sebald has created an end-of-century meditation that explores the most delicate, most painful, most nervously repressed and carefully concealed lesions of the last hundred years."

March 31

BORN: 1823 Mary Chesnut (*Mary Chesnut's Civil War*), Statesburg, S.C.
1914 Octavio Paz (*The Labyrinth of Solitude, Collected Poems*), Mexico City
DIED: 1797 Olaudah Equiano (*The Interesting Narrative of the Life of Olaudah Equiano*), c. 51, London
1855 Charlotte Brontë (*Jane Eyre, Shirley*), 38, Haworth, England

1903 "A TOURNAMENT FOR READERS!" blared a full-page advertisement in the *Times* of London. The contestant who best answered sixty general-interest questions would win the grand prize: a scholarship to Oxford or Cambridge (or, in the case of a lady winner, Girton College). In the following weeks, the advertising campaign revealed its sponsor: the tenth edition of the *Encyclopædia Britannica*, the only book in the world that "contains all human knowledge from the time when the Temple of El-lil was built at Niffer," part of a promotional push by which two Americans, the encyclopedia's new publisher, Horace Everett Hooper, and its breathless ad writer, Henry Haxton, brought hundreds of thousands of *Britannica* sets into middle-class British homes.

1934 From his father, "the one man I hate as utterly as I love you" (he wrote his wife), Wallace Stegner received a present of shirts and ties.

1934 "I should like to meet the pilgrim halfway," Marianne Moore wrote to her friend Ann Borden, a librarian at Vassar who had a young poetical "protégée" who wanted to meet the famous poet. And so Miss Moore came in from Brooklyn and met Elizabeth Bishop, the Vassar senior, at the New York Public Library, where Bishop overcame her nerves enough to invite Moore to the circus. Moore replied that she "*always* went to the circus," sealing a friendship that lasted another thirty-eight years, until the older poet's death. On a Saturday soon after (perhaps this one), Bishop fed brown bread to the elephants at Madison Square Garden while Moore, whose elephant-hair bracelet needed repair, leaned over the rope to snip a few replacement hairs with her nail scissors.

NO YEAR For a man knocked out by the side of a road the night before in Raymond Chandler's *Farewell, My Lovely*, Philip Marlowe can get a lot done in a day: a morning visit from a pretty amateur sleuth who gives him three marijuana cigarettes she palmed off a dead body; a couple of sour conversations with cops; and house calls on a slack-faced widow with a tiny revolver, a lapis-eyed blonde who gives him a smile he "could feel in my hip pocket," and an ageless, soulless psychic. The evening brings another battering, a visit from a cop he calls "Hemingway" because he "keeps saying the same thing over and over until you begin to believe it must be good," and finally a slug that knocks him back out. And he still doesn't have a client in the case—only his dangerous curiosity.

1942 Sketching the structure of her wartime novel *Suite Française*, Irène Némirovsky noted that while Tolstoy wrote from the distance of history, "I work on burning lava."

April is, by proclamation and curriculum now, the poet's month. "April" (or "Aprill") is the third word of one of the first great poems in the English language, *The Canterbury Tales*, and the first word in what does its best to feel like the last great English poem, *The Waste Land*. April— "spungy," "proud-pied," and "well-apparel'd" April—is also, along with its springtime neighbor May, the most-mentioned month in Shakespeare, and has given a poetic subject to Dickinson, Larkin, Plath, Glück, and countless others. Why? Do we like its promise of rebirth, its green and messy fecundity? Its hopefulness is easy to celebrate or, if you're T. S. Eliot, cruelly undercut, rooting his lilacs in the wasteland of death.

Eliot wasn't the only one a little tired of the ease of April's imagery. In 1936 Tennessee Williams received a note from a poetic acquaintance, a high school student named Mary Louise Lange who had recently won "third honorable mention" in the junior division of a local contest. "Yes, I think April is a fine month to write poetry," she mused. "All the little spear-points of green pricking up, all the little beginnings of new poetic thoughts, all the shafts of thoughts that will grow to future loveliness." A few days later, Williams, oppressed by the springtime St. Louis heat, despairing of his own youthful literary prospects, and perhaps distracted by all those "spear-points" and "shafts," confessed to his diary that he was bored and lonely enough to consider calling on her: "Maybe I'll visit that little girl poet but her latest letter sounded a little trite and affectatious—'little spear points of green'—It might be impossible."

In our man-made calendars, the yearly rebirth of Easter arrives most often in April, and novelists from Faulkner in *A Fable* to Richard Ford in *The Sportswriter* have been drawn to the structure and portent of Holy Week. Publishers annually bring us new spring books on religion and on the green pastimes of baseball and golf. But the April date most prominent in our lives now is associated more with death than birth: April 15, the American tax day since 1955. Lincoln, who died that day, had Whitman to mourn him, but Tax Day found few literary chroniclers until David Foster Wallace's last, unfinished novel, *The Pale King*, which turns the traditional celebrations of the eternal seasons into the flat, mechanical repetition of modern bureaucratic boredom. In the IRS's Peoria Regional Examination Center where Wallace's characters toil, the year has no natural center, just a deadline imposed by federal fiat and a daily in-box of Sisyphean tasks, a calendar that in its very featureless tedium provides at least the opportunity to test the human capacity for endurance and even quiet heroism.

The Canterbury Tales by Geoffrey Chaucer (late 14th century) ✎ When you feel the tender shoots and buds of April quickening again, set out in the company of Chaucer's nine and twenty very worldly devouts, in what has always been the most bawdily approachable of English literature's founding classics.

The Confidence-Man by Herman Melville (1857) ✎ It's no coincidence that the steamboat in Melville's great, late novel begins its journey down the Mississippi on April Fool's Day: *The Confidence-Man* is the darkest vision of foolishness and imposture—and one of the funniest extended jokes—in American literature.

"When Lilacs Last in the Door-yard Bloom'd" by Walt Whitman (1865) and *The Waste Land* by T. S. Eliot (1922) ✎ Whitman's elegy, composed soon after Lincoln's murder, heaps bouquets onto his coffin, and a livelier and more joyful vision of death you're not likely to find. You certainly won't in *The Waste Land*, written after a war equally bloody and seemingly barren of everything but allusions (to Whitman's funeral lilacs among many others).

The Sportswriter by Richard Ford (1986) ✎ Beginning with a Good Friday reunion with his ex-wife on the anniversary of their son's death, Ford's indelible ex-sportswriter Frank Bascombe reckons with balancing the small, heart-lifting pleasures of everydayness with the possibilities of disappointment and tragedy that gape underneath them.

The Age of Grief by Jane Smiley (1987) ✎ Smiley's early novella is still her masterpiece, a story of a family swept through by flu and a young marriage struggling to survive the end of its springtime that's as close to an American version of "The Dead" as anyone has written.

My Garden (Book): by Jamaica Kincaid (1999) ✎ "How vexed I often am when I am in the garden, and how happy I am to be so vexed": Midway through life, Kincaid started planting in her yard in most "ungardenlike" ways, and her garden book is willful and lovely, made of notes in which she cultivates her hatreds as passionately as her affections.

The Likeness by Tana French (2008) ✎ Ireland's French crafted an intrigue with equal elements of the Troubles and *The Secret History* in her second novel, in which Detective Cassie Maddox is seduced by the mid-April murder of a student who had been playing with an identity disturbingly close to her own.

The Pale King by David Foster Wallace (2011) ✎ Don't expect a novel when you open up *The Pale King*, culled from manuscripts Wallace left behind at his suicide. Read it as a series of experiments in growing human stories out of the dry soil of bureaucratic tedium, and marvel when real life, out of this wasteland, suddenly breaks through.

April 1

BORN: 1929 Milan Kundera (*The Unbearable Lightness of Being*), Brno, Czechoslovakia
1942 Samuel R. Delany (*Dhalgren, Nova*), New York City
DIED: 1950 F. O. Matthiessen (*American Renaissance*), 48, Boston
1966 Flann O'Brien (*The Third Policeman, At Swim-Two-Birds*), 54, Dublin

NO YEAR The most sustained April Fool's joke in the history of American literature begins with the appearance in St. Louis of a mute stranger in a cream-colored suit stepping on board the steamboat *Fidèle* bound for New Orleans. Meet the title character of Herman Melville's *The Confidence-Man: His Masquerade*, set on April Fool's Day and published—by coincidence, apparently—on that day too in 1857. Its unrelenting skepticism was met with confusion and indifference, and the once-popular Melville didn't publish another novel in the remaining thirty-four years of his life. It took another century before *The Confidence-Man* was rediscovered as one of his most radical and brilliant inventions.

1936 After serving seven and a half years for robbery, Chester Himes, his stories already published in *Esquire*, was released from the London Prison Farm in Ohio.

1956 On the morning of April Fool's Day, Edward Abbey began his first workday as a national park ranger by stepping out of his government trailer and watching the sun rise over the canyonlands of Arches National Monument in Moab, Utah. Outfitted with trailer, truck, ranger shirt, tin badge, and five hundred gallons of water, Abbey was left more or less alone for six months, which he recorded in journals he typed up a decade later into the manuscript of *Desert Solitaire*, a cantankerous appreciation of the wild inhumanity of nature and a warning against the encroaching "Industrial Tourists" the park was already being prepared for.

1960 There was "something intensely surprising" about witnessing the birth of his daughter Frieda, Ted Hughes later wrote a friend, and "also something infinitely disastrous and shocking about it."

1978 Haruki Murakami had worked day and night for four years at his small jazz club in Tokyo called the Peter Cat when, with an inexplicable and impulsive simplicity that seems right out of his fiction, he decided to try something new. He was drinking a beer in the grassy embankment beyond the outfield fence at a Yakult Swallows baseball game when Dave Hilton, a new American player on the Swallows, hit a double down the left-field line, right on the sweet spot of his bat, and Murakami thought, "You know what? I could try writing a novel." He had no idea what the book would be about, but by the fall he finished *Hear the Wind Sing*. The next spring the novel won a magazine contest he forgot he'd entered, and his writing career began.

2010 Sebastian Junger, in the *New York Times*, on Karl Marlantes's *Matterhorn*: "It's not a book so much as a deployment, and you will not return unaltered."

BORN: 1725 Giacomo Casanova (*Story of My Life*), Venice, Italy

1805 Hans Christian Andersen ("The Little Mermaid," "The Red Shoes"), Odense, Denmark

DIED: 1966 C. S. Forester (Horatio Hornblower series, *The African Queen*), 66, Fullerton, Calif.

1796 Of the "authentic" documents from the life of William Shakespeare—original manuscripts of *Lear* and *Hamlet*, a love letter and poem to Anne Hathaway, an awkwardly scrawled note from Queen Elizabeth—that poured forth from a mysterious old chest William Henry Ireland claimed to have found, the most audacious forgery was *Vortigern*, an unknown play said to be in the Bard's hand whose sole performance at Drury Lane on this evening quickly turned into farce. Even the play's performers smelled a fraud by then, and when the star, John Kemble, repeated the line "And when this solemn mockery is ended," with a leer at the audience, a bedlam of derision ensured the humiliation of Ireland, the play's discoverer and its true author.

1894 In reply to a letter from his father, the Marquess of Queensberry, about his "loathsome and disgusting relationship" with Oscar Wilde, Lord Alfred Douglas wired back, "What a funny little man you are."

1913 Kurt Wolff, Franz Kafka's new publisher, wrote to the author, "Please be good enough to send me a copy or the manuscript of the bedbug story."

1957 "I was overwhelmed to get the little book, filched from the library, and I hope I deserve it," E. B. White wrote in thanks to his Cornell classmate H. A. Stevenson. "What a book, what a man!" The man was William Strunk Jr., and the book was *The Elements of Style*, a privately printed (and stapled) writing manual from 1918 known to Strunk's Cornell students as "the little book." In July White wrote an appreciation of the book and its bold strictures in *The New Yorker* and sent it to an editor at Macmillan to see if they might bring it back into print. Before long, "the little book," with White's edits and additions, was known instead, to a much wider audience, as "Strunk and White."

1990 The remains of Jack Arthur Dodds, which fit tidily into a screw-top plastic jar the size of a pint glass, may not be as unwieldy as the coffin that carried the body of Addie Bundren in *As I Lay Dying*, and Graham Swift's narrative pyrotechnics may be more modest than William Faulkner's, but *Last Orders*, his quiet and generous story of four men fulfilling Jack's final request by carrying his ashes to the sea, gathers a weight of its own while following a funereal path similar to the one Faulkner laid down. On their pilgrimage, which begins with pints and a shot in Bermondsey and ends in wind and rain on a pier in Margate, some secrets are revealed between these old friends, but far more stay buried where they have been for years, to be confessed only to us.

April 3

BORN: 1593 George Herbert (*The Temple*), Montgomery, Wales

1916 Herb Caen (*San Francisco Chronicle* columnist), Sacramento, Calif.

DIED: 1971 Manfred Lee (half of the Ellery Queen pseudonym), 66, Waterbury, Conn.

1991 Graham Greene (*The End of the Affair*), 86, Vevey, Switzerland

1878 Dining at Zola's new house with Flaubert and Edmond de Goncourt, the novelist Alphonse Daudet compared the grouse to "an old courtesan's flesh marinated in a bidet."

1882 It was still the evening of the same day as the killing when Bob Ford, with eager and self-regarding confidence, took the stand at the inquest and testified that from six feet away that morning he had shot the outlaw Jesse James while he was unarmed and dusting a picture frame. He hadn't confessed so freely, though, when he made his escape after the gunshot, according to Ron Hansen's meticulously researched and imagined novel, *The Assassination of Jesse James by the Coward Robert Ford*. "Bob, have you done this?" James's freshly widowed wife wailed. "I swear to God that I didn't," he replied, and then ran to the telegraph office with his brother to wire the governor of Missouri, who had authorized a $10,000 reward for his death or capture, "I have killed Jesse James. Bob Ford."

1920 Zelda Sayre, the daughter of Anthony Dickinson Sayre, justice of the Supreme Court of Alabama, and Minerva Machen Sayre, of Montgomery, Alabama, wed Francis Scott Key Fitzgerald, the son of Edward Fitzgerald, formerly of Procter & Gamble, and Mollie McQuillan Fitzgerald, of St. Paul, Minnesota, at St. Patrick's Cathedral in Manhattan. The bride was a graduate of Sidney Lanier High School; the groom was graduated from Princeton University and recently published his first novel, *This Side of Paradise*.

1952 Julia Child, the wife of an American diplomat in Paris, reading what she called an "able diatribe" by Bernard DeVoto in *Harper's* on the poor quality of American kitchen knives, sent DeVoto a French paring knife in appreciation. In thanks, DeVoto's wife, Avis, replied to Child on this day with a long, friendly letter on cutlery and cuisine, and so began a correspondence and collaboration that resulted in the publication nearly a decade later of the first volume of Child's groundbreaking *Mastering the Art of French Cooking*. Meanwhile, *As Always, Julia*, the collection of letters between Child and DeVoto published in 2010, is itself a minor classic of food writing and friendship.

BORN: **1914** Marguerite Duras (*The Lover, The Ravishing of Lol Stein*), Saigon
1928 Maya Angelou (*I Know Why the Caged Bird Sings*), St. Louis
DIED: **1991** Max Frisch (*I'm Not Stiller, Homo Faber*), 79, Zurich, Switzerland
2013 Roger Ebert (*The Great Movies, Life Itself*), 70, Chicago

1846 Gustave Flaubert sat with the body of his deceased friend Alfred Le Poittevin for two days and two nights and then wrapped him in shrouds and placed him in his coffin for burial.

1886 A close friendship begun over thirty years before, when Émile Zola, age fourteen, met a "large, ungainly boy" named Paul Cézanne in boarding school in Aix-en-Provence, ended with a chilly note on this day from the painter to the novelist that began, "I have just received *L'Oeuvre*, which you arranged to send me." *L'Oeuvre*, Zola's fictional portrait of a novelist's relationship with a painter resembling Cézanne and his fellow Impressionists who descends into madness and failure, drew the ire of Monet, Renoir, and Pissarro, while Cézanne, who had long chafed under Zola's more rapid success, said nothing more to his old friend about the book. In fact, the two of them never spoke to nor saw each other again.

1924 No one was entirely happy when Mabel Dodge Luhan, whose bohemian magnetism drew D. H. and Frieda Lawrence—among many other writers and artists—to Taos, New Mexico, took a run-down ranch she had given her son and bestowed it on Frieda instead. The Lawrences did enjoy being homeowners for the first time in their restless lives but felt beholden to Luhan, so in exchange they gave her the manuscript of *Sons and Lovers*, which Luhan took as an offense to her generosity and which the Lawrences later discovered, to their dismay, was worth far more than the ranch. D. H. Lawrence's tuberculosis prevented him from staying there long, but after his death in 1930 Frieda made the ranch her permanent home.

1925 Carl Sandburg telegraphed news of his Lincoln biography to his wife, Paula, "Harcourt wires book serial rights sold to *Pictorial Review* for $20,000. Fix the flivver and buy a wild Easter hat."

1968 Many stories move with a weary fate toward the assassination of Martin Luther King. Charles Johnson's *Dreamer*, the imagined story of a man hired to double for King, nears its close on the balcony of Memphis's Lorraine Motel, as does Taylor Branch's three-volume history, *America in the King Years*, which devotes seven of its nearly 3,000 pages to the hours between King's last public words, "Mine eyes have seen the glory of the coming of the Lord," and his final ones in private, "Ben, make sure you play 'Precious Lord, Take My Hand,' in the meeting tonight. Play it real pretty." Meanwhile, George Pelecanos's *Hard Revolution*, the most ambitious of his encyclopedic series of DC crime novels, builds toward the aftermath of the assassination, when violence swept through the nation's capital along with the news.

April 5

BORN: 1588 Thomas Hobbes (*Leviathan*),
Westport, England
1920 Arthur Hailey (*Airport, Hotel,
Wheels*), Luton, England
DIED: 1997 Allen Ginsberg (*Howl, Kaddish*),
70, New York City
2005 Saul Bellow (*Herzog, Humboldt's
Gift, Ravelstein*), 89, Brookline, Mass.

1832 Despite his vow to quit gambling, William Makepeace Thackeray played cards until four in the morning, losing eight pounds, seven shillings.

1919 Katherine Mansfield wrote to Virginia Woolf that her cat, Charlie Chaplin, had given birth to kittens named Athenaeum and April.

1919 After a performance of his play *Judith,* Arnold Bennett lamented, "Terrible silly mishaps occurred with the sack containing Holofernes's head in the third act, despite the most precise instructions to the crowd."

1936 By the time of the elaborate Founder's Day festivities at the Tuskegee Institute, three years after he arrived from Oklahoma City as an eager and optimistic music major, Ralph Ellison had soured on the college and turned his interests to literature, so he listened to the language of the featured speaker with a skeptical but attentive ear. The speaker was Dr. Emmett J. Scott, the longtime right-hand man of Tuskegee's charismatic founder, Booker T. Washington, and his tribute to Washington that day planted the seeds of the oration of Rev. Homer A. Barbee—"Thus, my young friends, does the light of the Founder still burn"—in *Invisible Man*, the novel that made Ellison one of Tuskegee's best-known alumni.

1952 "In lots of the books I read," deputy sheriff Lou Ford opines, "the writer seems to go haywire every time he reaches a high point." That won't happen with his story, Ford promises us: "I'll tell you everything." And tell everything he does in *The Killer Inside Me*, the blackest of Jim Thompson's string of sly and brutal noir novels from the '50s and '60s. Most obsessively of all, Ford confesses that on the 5th of April in 1952 he killed Amy Stanton, the woman who thought she was about to marry him. It's neither the first nor the last death Ford orchestrates; the final one, in an explosion of shots and shouts, is his own.

1969 Lester Bangs was selling shoes in El Cajon, California, and taking classes at San Diego State when a cover profile of the MC5 in *Rolling Stone* led him to buy their debut, *Kick Out the Jams*. He thought the record was a derivative fraud, though, and wrote *Rolling Stone* to tell them so, adding that he could write as well as anyone they had. They agreed, at least enough to print his review in their April 5 issue, launching Bangs on a critical career that matched the live-fast, die-young arc of his rock heroes. Bangs's reviews and manifestos, collected in *Psychotic Reactions and Carburetor Dung*, read like uninhibited mash notes from a love affair with rock 'n' roll: passionate, besotted, and angry; vigilant for signs of betrayal but animated at all times by the hope of transcendence.

April 6

BORN: 1866 Lincoln Steffens (*The Shame of the City*), San Francisco
1926 Gil Kane (*Green Lantern*, *The Atom*), Riga, Latvia
DIED: 1992 Isaac Asimov (*I, Robot*; *Foundation*), 72, New York City
2005 Frank Conroy (*Stop-Time*, *Body and Soul*), 69, Iowa City, Iowa

1862 The Battle of Shiloh at the end of the Civil War's first year was the bloodiest by far in American history and marked a new stage in the war's carnage that stunned the nation. Despite the Union's ultimate victory after two days of fighting, blame was spread widely, and most of it settled on Lew Wallace, a major general at age thirty-four, whose "lost division" spent the battle's first day marching back and forth behind the front lines following an ambiguous message from General Grant. Wallace was relieved of his command and for the next two decades protested his scapegoating, with satisfaction coming only when Grant acknowledged Wallace's innocence in a reluctant footnote in his *Memoirs* and when Wallace's fame for his bestselling 1880 novel, *Ben-Hur*, finally eclipsed his infamy at Shiloh.

1924 After finishing chapter eighteen of *An American Tragedy,* Theodore Dreiser had two hot dogs and a cup of coffee at a restaurant at Fourteenth Street and Seventh Avenue and then walked in the rain to Fifty-ninth Street, full of "many odd thoughts about the city."

1934 M. F. K. Fisher, having "settled at a steady pace of about fifteen pages at a time," read *Ulysses* on the beach at Laguna, occasionally turning herself "neatly to brown on both sides in the sun." Later, she made a chocolate cake.

1987 For a few years in the mid-'80s, Jonathan Franzen found an ideal job for a frugal young writer: working weekends reading data at a Harvard seismic lab, which supported him and his wife while he wrote his first novel, *The Twenty-Seventh City*, the rest of the week. It also gave him a subject for his rich and undercelebrated second novel, *Strong Motion*, whose story hinges on clusters of small earthquakes in the Boston area that may or may not be caused by the pumping of industrial waste into deep underground wells. The first of the tremors, despite its mild 4.7 magnitude, claims on this day its only victim, the step-grandmother of his protagonist, Louis Holland, when it knocks her off a barstool.

April 7

BORN: 1770 William Wordsworth (*The Prelude*, "Tintern Abbey"), Cockermouth, England

1931 Donald Barthelme (*Snow White*; *Come Back, Dr. Caligari*), Philadelphia

DIED: 1836 William Godwin (*Caleb Williams*), 80, London

1977 Jim Thompson (*The Killer Inside Me*, *Pop. 1280*), 70, Los Angeles.

1874 "Look here—what day is Easter this year?" "Why, of course, the first week in April. Why?" "I'm going to be married in a month." A half hour before, Newland Archer had been convincing the beautiful and worldly Countess Olenska to abandon their promises to others and be together when a telegram from his fiancée arrived: "Parents consent wedding Tuesday after Easter at twelve Grace Church eight bridesmaids please see Rector so happy love May." In *The Age of Innocence*, Edith Wharton's great novel of renunciation, Newland keeps his promise to May to marry, though he doesn't forget the countess, who, after all, has just told him, "I can't love you unless I give you up."

1919 Though he started with high hopes on this day, working on commission as the advertising manager of the *Little Review*, Hart Crane managed to sell only two ads, for Mary Garden Chocolates and "Stanislaw Portapovitch—Maître de Danse" over the next several months before giving up.

1935 While John Dos Passos filmed the proceedings, Ernest Hemingway shot himself through both legs when a bullet ricocheted that was meant to kill a shark they had hooked onboard.

1962 The ideas suggested by Robert A. Heinlein's *Stranger in a Strange Land* took hold with surprising speed after it was published in 1961: "grok" soon entered the language, and some readers began to take its vision of religion, sex, and justice as gospel. On this day two college friends, Tim Zell and Lance Christie, having been "seized with an ecstatic sense of recognition" by the novel, performed a water-sharing ceremony modeled after the book and later formed the Church of All Worlds, which called science fiction the "new mythology of our age." Heinlein kept a polite distance from such acolytes, and in 1972 responded to a letter from Zell by saying, "Anyone who takes that book as *answers* is cheating himself. It is an invitation to think—not to believe."

1967 "I do not plan to be a 79-year-old lollipop, Mr. Rich," fifty-eight-year-old M. F. K. Fisher wrote her sixty-three-year-old boyfriend, Arnold Gingrich, publisher of *Esquire*. "Even for you. If I should live that long, I'll be a bag of bones, probably rather bent and even more probably racked with arthritic pains, irascible in a barely controlled manner, very impatient of human frailties and quirks, concentrated on my own determination to stay vertical and free. Not an exactly lovable picture!"

1967 The new film critic of the *Chicago Sun-Times*, Roger Ebert, debuted with a review of an "obscure French movie," *Galia*: it opens with shots of the ocean, he noted, but "it's pretty clear that what is washing ashore is the French New Wave."

BORN: **1909** John Fante (*Ask the Dust*), Denver, Colo.

1955 Barbara Kingsolver (*Animal Dreams*, *The Lacuna*), Annapolis, Md.

DIED: **1958** George Jean Nathan (*The Smart Set*, *The American Mercury*), 76, New York City

1979 Breece D'J Pancake (*The Stories of Breece D'J Pancake*), 26, Charlottesville, Va.

1809 With remarkable but characteristic patience, it wasn't until six years after her novel *Susan* was purchased by the publisher Richard Crosby that Jane Austen inquired about her manuscript. "I can only account for such an extraordinary circumstance," she wrote, in a tone of passive indignation adopted by countless thwarted authors before and since, "by supposing the MS by some carelessness to have been lost." Replying on this day, Crosby asserted that "there was not any time stipulated for its publication, neither are we bound to publish it," and offered to sell it back to her for the £10 he had paid. Not for another seven years did Austen take him up on the offer, and not until after her death was the novel published, her brother having changed its title to the more distinctive *Northanger Abbey*.

1877 Henry James deplored the social desert of London during Easter week to his sister Alice: "'Every one' goes out of town . . . and a gloomy hush broods over the place."

1928 "Never you mind," Dilsey tells her daughter, who is ashamed of her mother's open weeping as they walk from church on Easter Sunday. "I seed de beginnin, en now I sees de endin." For "April 8, 1928," the final section of *The Sound and the Fury*, William Faulkner stepped back from the voices of the three Compson brothers who had told the tale of their family's decline to that point. He gave the story over to the voice of an outside narrator, and gave the center of it not to Caddy, the fourth Compson child, but to Dilsey, the black cook who has witnessed the Compsons' rise and fall and who, as head of her own family, represents, perhaps, the rebirth promised by Easter.

1999 Lionel Shriver's agent, after reading the manuscript of *We Need to Talk About Kevin* and deciding there was no way she could sell "a book about a kid doing such maxed-out, over-the-top, evil things, especially when it's written from such an unsympathetic point of view," suggested that Shriver only "allude to" the events of this day rather than describe them in the detail that she does near the book's end. But Shriver didn't cut the full description of Kevin Khatchadourian's school massacre—ripped from the headlines at the time and reflected in them more than once since—and, though her book was rejected by dozens more agents and editors, it eventually found a sizable readership for its story of an incorrigibly sociopathic child and a mother haunted by the question of whether her son made her a bad mother, or her mothering made a bad son.

April 9

BORN: 1821 Charles Baudelaire (*Les Fleurs du mal, Paris Spleen*), Paris
1929 Paule Marshall (*Brown Girl, Brownstones; Praisesong for the Widow*), Brooklyn
DIED: 1553 François Rabelais (*Gargantua and Pantagruel*), c. 58, Paris
1997 Helene Hanff (*84, Charing Cross Road*), 80, New York City

1909 The day Robert Peary and Mathew Henson reach what they think is the North Pole in E. L. Doctorow's *Ragtime* doesn't match the historical record, which says it happened on April 6 (and which also says Henson's name was "Matthew"), but then again, in Doctorow's account Peary and Henson aren't sure from their instrument readings whether they are even at the exact pole (and historians since have largely decided that they weren't). Nevertheless, "Give three cheers, my boy," Doctorow's Peary tells Henson. "And let's fly the flag." Composed in a naive, declarative style and populated with a cast that mixes the historically iconic (Peary, Houdini, Emma Goldman) with the anonymously generic (Mother, Father, Mameh, Tateh), each so abstracted as to be both merely and vividly representative of their times, *Ragtime* embraces the mythmaking at the heart of the historical novel.

1932 Bruno Schulz, at a conference for teachers of handicrafts in Stryj, Poland, presented a lecture titled "Artistic Formation in Cardboard and Its Application in School."

1971 It's a one-sided love affair. On one side, Miss Helen Sweetstory, author of *The Six Bunny-Wunnies and Their Pony Cart*, *The Six Bunny-Wunnies Go to Long Beach*, and so on, and on the other, Snoopy, aspiring author of "It Was a Dark and Stormy Night" and Miss Sweetstory's biggest fan, who decides on this day to write his beloved a fan letter. He sends mash notes and she replies with form letters, but he still believes that a) she loves him and b) she's going to introduce him to her agent. After all, "famous authors like to receive manuscripts from unknown writers." Only the discovery that Miss Sweetstory owns twenty-four cats is enough to break his fever. Enough, he tells Linus: "Back to Hermann Hesse."

1986 May Sarton returned to her journal for the first time after a stroke at age seventy-three: "There in my bed alone the past rises like a tide, over and over, to swamp me with memories I cannot handle. I am as fragile and naked as a newborn babe."

BORN: **1934** David Halberstam (*The Best and the Brightest*), New York City
1941 Paul Theroux (*The Great Railway Bazaar*), Medford, Mass.

DIED: **1955** Pierre Teilhard de Chardin (*The Phenomenon of Man*), 73, New York City
1966 Evelyn Waugh (*Scoop, Brideshead Revisited*), 62, Combe Florey, England

1881 Having chosen months of bed rest for a bladder infection instead of an operation so he could keep delivering his monthly installments of his new novel, *A Laodicean*, to *Harper's* magazine, Thomas Hardy set foot outside his house for the first time since October.

1903 Less than three months into a penniless Paris adventure at age twenty-one, during which his mother in Dublin pawned household goods to keep him from starving, James Joyce received a telegram reading, "Mother dying come home father." (He did; she was.) Much later, that same message, included in *Ulysses* as a telegram received by Stephen Dedalus, would end up at the center of scholarly controversy, with some Joyceans arguing that the original typesetters had mistakenly corrected Joyce's typically punning revision of his own life, and that the text should read, as it does now in some editions, "Nother dying come home father."

1925 Despite his last-minute requests to change its "rather bad than good" title to "Trimalchio in West Egg," "Gold-Hatted Gatsby," or "Under the Red White and Blue," F. Scott Fitzgerald's third novel was published on this day by Scribner's as *The Great Gatsby*. Ten days later his editor, Max-well Perkins, cabled Fitzgerald in Paris, "Sales situation doubtful excellent reviews"; even some admiring reviewers, though, thought *Gatsby*, with its shiny surfaces, "trivial" story, and too-timely slang, would prove "a book of the season only." The sales did allow Fitzgerald to pay off a substantial debt to his publisher, but they failed to reach the levels of his previous novels, and even at his death fifteen years later copies from the small second printing of *Gatsby* remained unsold.

1926 Perhaps only half in jest, H. L. Mencken suggested that losing presidential candidates should be executed and tossed into the Potomac.

1961 Susan Sontag attended a double feature of *I Am a Fugitive from a Chain Gang* and *The Maltese Falcon* at Manhattan's New Yorker theater.

1967 In the "cold late spring of 1967," Joan Didion took her notebook and her eye for entropy to meet some of the young people who were gathering in San Francisco, where she found, along with restless anarchists, trip-seeking teenagers, and a five-year-old sampling acid, a plaintive public notice beginning, "Last Easter Day / My Christopher Robin wandered away. / He called April 10th / But he hasn't called since." In her resulting dispatches, published in the *Saturday Evening Post* under the cover line "The Hippie Cult: Who They Are, What They Want, Why They Act That Way," and later as the title essay in *Slouching Toward Bethlehem*, Didion diagnosed the end of the Summer of Love before it had even begun.

April 11

BORN: 1901 Glenway Wescott (*The Pilgrim Hawk*), Kewaskum, Wis.
1949 Dorothy Allison (*Bastard Out of Carolina, Cavedweller*), Greenville, S.C.
DIED: 1970 John O'Hara (*Appointment in Samarra, BUtterfield 8*), 65, Princeton, N.J.
1987 Primo Levi (*The Periodic Table, The Drowned and the Saved*), 67, Turin, Italy

1681 A friend offered to cure Samuel Pepys's fever if he sent nail clippings and locks of hair.

1773 Boswell and Johnson dined on "a very good soup, a boiled leg of lamb and spinach, a veal pye, and a rice pudding."

1819 Keats and Coleridge met just once, by chance, while both were walking on this day on Hampstead Heath. The young Keats was impressed and amused by the great, white-maned man, then under a doctor's care for opium addiction: "In these two miles he broached a thousand things," among them nightingales, dreams, mermaids, and sea monsters. "I heard his voice as he came towards me—I heard it as he moved away—I heard it all the interval." Coleridge, meanwhile, was so busy talking he hardly noticed this "loose, slack, not well-dressed youth," but later he would claim to have felt "death in the hand" of the young poet, who was felled by tuberculosis less than two years later.

1953 William Peden, in the *Saturday Review*, on two collections by young *New Yorker* short-story writers: J. D. Salinger is "occasionally too aware of the fact that he is a monstrous clever fellow," while John Cheever's "less spectacular" stories often "improve with rereading, which is not usually true of a Salinger piece."

1954 In Paris, Julia Child tried to make a beurre blanc for sea bass that, to her "quite hurt surprise," just wouldn't blanc.

1961 In Jerusalem, Hannah Arendt, on assignment from *The New Yorker*, attended the first day of the trial of former Nazi Adolf Eichmann for his role in organizing the Holocaust. Writing her husband in New York (who, like her, had fled the Nazis) she expressed an immediate disgust for Eichmann, a "ghost in a glass cage," as well as for the entire theater of the trial. Her coldly ironic account of the proceedings, *Eichmann in Jerusalem*, published two years later, ignited a controversy (one that still simmers) about her portrait of the "banality of evil" and of the role of Jewish Councils during the war.

1965 Undaunted by a plea from William Shawn that it would "thrust" the *New York Herald Tribune* "into the gutter," *New York* magazine, then the *Trib*'s Sunday supplement, gleefully published "Tiny Mummies!," the first of a two-part series by the young Tom Wolfe that mocked *The New Yorker* as a musty monastery led by the rumpled, whispering Shawn, reverently preserving the traditions—and the endless luxury advertising pages—of a magazine that, Wolfe argued, had never been that good to begin with.

BORN: 1916 Beverly Cleary (*Henry Huggins, Beezus and Ramona*), McMinnville, Ore. 1947 Tom Clancy (*The Hunt for Red October, Patriot Games*), Baltimore, Md.

DIED: 1988 Alan Paton (*Cry, the Beloved Country*), 85, Botha's Hill, South Africa 1991 James Schuyler (*The Morning of the Poem, A Nest of Ninnies*), 67, New York City

1802 The letter has been lost to history, but Dorothy Wordsworth's biographers have guessed, based on her response in her journals—"Every question was like the snapping of a little thread about my heart—I was so full of thought of my half-read letter and other things"—that on this day she learned of her beloved brother William's engagement to her dear friend Mary Hutchinson. The perennial fascination with discerning the boundaries of affection among poet, sister, and wife—they continued to share a household for nearly fifty years—has extended to the poem he wrote this same day, "Among all lovely things my Love had been": was the Love he spoke of meant for his fiancée, his sister, or both?

1850 When Charlotte Brontë's publishers sent her a box of books including three by Jane Austen, they might not have known she already had an opinion on the author. "I should hardly like to live with her ladies and gentlemen in their elegant but confined houses," she had written George Henry Lewes two years before when he recommended her next book after *Jane Eyre* be less "melodramatic" and more like Austen. And reading *Emma* in 1850 didn't change her mind: "Her business is not half

so much with the human heart as with the human eyes, mouth, hands and feet," she explained on this day, "but what throbs fast and full, though hidden, what the blood rushes through, what is the unseen seat of Life and the sentient target of Death—*this* Miss Austen ignores." She added, "If this is heresy—I cannot help it."

1871 From his window, Edmund de Goncourt rooted for the French army against the "odious tyranny" of the revolutionary Paris Commune.

1903 On Easter Sunday, Jack London accidentally cut off the tip of his thumb.

2010 Operating out of a tiny office in New York's Bellevue Hospital with the mandate to bridge the gap between medicine and literature, the Bellevue Literary Press had published just a couple of dozen books when one of its first fiction releases, Paul Harding's *Tinkers*, was plucked from obscurity for the 2010 Pulitzer Prize for Fiction, the first small-press book to win in almost twenty years. Even before its prize *Tinkers* had stirred word-of-mouth enthusiasm for the intensity of its attention to memory and the senses, with Transcendentalist echoes that make it a spiritual cousin to the Pulitzer winner of five years before, *Gilead*, by Harding's former teacher Marilynne Robinson.

2010 Eight years after Yann Martel's *Life of Pi* won the Booker Prize, the *New York Times*'s Michiko Kakutani called his follow-up novel, *Beatrice and Virgil*, "every bit as misconceived and offensive as his earlier book was fetching."

April 13

BORN: 1906 Samuel Beckett (*Waiting for Godot, Molloy*), Dublin
1909 Eudora Welty (*The Collected Stories, Delta Wedding*), Jackson, Miss.
DIED: 1993 Wallace Stegner (*Angle of Repose, Crossing to Safety*), 84, Santa Fe, N.M.
2006 Muriel Spark (*The Prime of Miss Jean Brodie, Memento Mori*), 88, Florence, Italy

1877 Never shy of concocting literary publicity, the young Guy de Maupassant placed an unsigned squib into the *République des lettres* advertising a dinner at which "six young and enthusiastic naturalists destined for celebrity" would honor their masters, Flaubert, Zola, and Edmond de Goncourt, with a menu inspired by their works, including "Potage purée *Bovary*" and "Liqueur de *l'Assommoir*." The dinner place, at Paris's Restaurant Trapp; the menu, though, was likely fictional, and of the young writers only two, J.-K. Huysmans and, naturally, Maupassant himself, would achieve any lasting literary celebrity.

1924 Among the few facts known about one of the most widely read, or at least distributed, authors in American history is his birth date. Born on this day in Los Angeles, Jack T. Chick, by his own account, was a troublemaking youth with a hobby in drawing until he found the Lord and published *Why No Revival?*, the first "Chick tract" in a series that now numbers in the hundreds, with over half a billion "soul winning" copies in print. Tiny, vivid comic books preaching hellfire for sinners and nonbelievers, especially for the Vatican's minions of Satan, Chick tracts can traditionally be found piled up at bus stations and in the collections of hipsters transfixed by the vigor of the hate they contain.

1924 In response to Franz Kafka's question about his tubercular larynx, "I wonder what it looks like inside?" his nurse responded, "Like the witch's kitchen."

1929 Reader "H.W." wrote to the *New Statesman*, regarding Proust's *Cities of the Plain*, that sexual "inversion" "does not belong to fiction, in spite of the prevailing craze for decadent literature."

1933 Robert M. Coates, in *The New Yorker*, on Nathanael West's *Miss Lonelyhearts*: "the crispest and the cleverest, the most impishly ironical and sharply epigrammatic book I've read in months and months."

1940 In the third of his fifty-eight years as a staff writer at *The New Yorker*, Joseph Mitchell profiled McSorley's, the oldest saloon in New York City, an establishment that trafficked largely in ale, onions, gloomy fellowship, and vigilantly sustained traditions, including a refusal to admit women that would stand until the Supreme Court intervened. A few years later, the business gave its name to Mitchell's first book, *McSorley's Wonderful Saloon*, a collection of portraits of the city's eccentrics and battered bohemians who, like McSorley's and Mitchell himself, pursued their idiosyncrasies with unassuming persistence.

1963 Flannery O'Connor confessed to a friend, "The other day I postponed my work an hour to look at W. C. Fields in *Never Give a Sucker an Even Break*."

BORN: 1897 Horace McCoy (*They Shoot Horses, Don't They?*), Pegram, Tenn.
1961 Daniel Clowes (*Ghost World, Eightball*), Chicago

DIED: 1964 Rachel Carson (*The Sea Around Us, Silent Spring*), 56, Silver Spring, Md.
1986 Simone de Beauvoir (*The Second Sex, The Mandarins*), 78, Paris

1824 When he returned to Philadelphia after years on the American frontier, John James Audubon hoped he might find a publisher for his paintings of the country's birds. He found admirers, but Alexander Lawson, likely the only American engraver who could have handled the job as Audubon imagined it, was not among them. Roused from his bed to meet the artist, Lawson told him his pictures "were ill drawn, not true to nature, and anatomically incorrect." When Audubon protested later, "Sir, I have been instructed seven years by the greatest masters in France," Lawson replied, "Then you have made damned bad use of your time." Rebuffed in Philadelphia, Audubon had to travel to Great Britain to find the engravers and patrons to produce his lavish *Birds of America*.

1865 In *Henry and Clara*, the first of his novels set in the political history of Washington, D.C., Thomas Mallon dramatized the night on which a forgotten couple was taken up and then tossed aside by the caprices of history. Already a bit of a scandal as a stepbrother and -sister engaged to be married, Henry Rathbone and Clara Harris, the Lincolns' guests in their box at Ford's Theatre, were bloodied bystanders at the assassination and were never the same afterward, Henry in particular. Stabbed nearly to death by the fleeing Booth, he slowly went mad and eighteen years later staged a bizarre reenactment of the tragedy with his wife as victim.

1923 James Joyce attended a rugby match between France and Ireland at Stade Colombes in Paris.

1939 For the first time, George Orwell's goat Muriel gave a full quart of milk.

1952 Published: *Invisible Man* by Ralph Ellison (Random House, New York)

1965 Certain he had written an unprecedented masterpiece, Truman Capote had to postpone completing the final section of his "nonfiction novel," *In Cold Blood*, for nearly two "excruciating" years while the machinery of justice moved to its conclusion. Finally, though, Perry Smith, one of Capote's main characters, wrote him that "April 14 you know is the date to drop thru the trap door," and just after midnight on that day Smith and Dick Hickock were indeed hanged by the state of Kansas, giving Capote, in attendance at the request of the condemned, an ending for the book that begins with their murders of the Clutter family four and a half years before.

1975 Kenneth Tynan took tea in London with Mel Brooks, who had "stubby self-confidence radiating from every pore."

April 15

BORN: 1843 Henry James (*Portrait of a Lady,*
The Ambassadors), New York City
1878 Robert Walser (*Jakob von Gunten,*
The Robbers), Biel, Switzerland
DIED: 1942 Robert Musil (*The Man Without*
Qualities), 61, Geneva, Switzerland
2000 Edward Gorey (*The Gashlycrumb*
Tinies), 75, Hyannis, Mass.

1719 Published: *The Life and Strange Sur-*
prizing Adventures of Robinson Crusoe of
York, Mariner by Daniel Defoe (W. Taylor,
London)

1842 Charles Dickens, traveling in the
American Midwest, called the Mississippi
the "beastliest river in the world."

1862 Col. Thomas Wentworth Higginson,
the abolitionist, poet, and essayist, must have
expected some response from the aspiring
authors he addressed in his April "Letter
to a Young Contributor" in the *Atlantic*
Monthly, but nothing like the short note he
received, written in a peculiar bird-scrawl
that began, "Are you too deeply occupied to
say if my Verse is alive?" It appeared to be
unsigned until he discovered a small sub-
envelope within that contained a card with
the shyly penciled name "Emily Dickinson."
Enclosed also were four poems, and his
curious and encouraging response, as well
as the ambivalence about publishing them
he shared with their author, led to a three-
decade correspondence with Dickinson, she
playing a coy "Scholar" and he bewildered
and moved by the flights of her mind.

1865 Working in Washington during the
war, Walt Whitman developed an affectionate and personal admiration for President
Lincoln, whom he often saw riding into
town, but when news came of his assassination, Whitman was back in New York,
where Broadway was "black with mourning" and the sky dripped with "heavy, moist
black weather." Turning his thoughts to
poetry, he composed a number of memorials
in the following months, including "O Captain, My Captain," which gained an immediate popularity Whitman came to regret,
and the great, exuberant elegy "When Lilacs
Last in the Door-yard Bloom'd."

1924 Rand McNally published the first edition of their bestselling road atlas, titled,
for the time being, the *Rand McNally Auto*
Chum.

1972 Hunter S. Thompson was intent on
staying outside the clubby pack of politi-
cos and journalists while covering the 1972
Democratic primaries for *Rolling Stone*,
but when his favored underdog, Senator
George McGovern, suddenly became the
front-runner, the lines got a little blurred,
as in a friendly phone exchange included
in *Fear and Loathing on the Campaign Trail*
'72, which began with McGovern's young
political director, Frank Mankiewicz, fresh
from a surprise win in Wisconsin, declaring, to Thompson's surprise, "We have it
locked up!" and ended with Mankiewicz,
after hearing Thompson's difficulties finding a Wisconsin doc to inject him with his
preferred cocktail of remedies, saying with
concern, "Hunter, I get the feeling that
you're not very careful about your health."

April 16

BORN: 1871 J. M. Synge (*The Playboy of the Western World*), Rathfarnham, Ireland
1922 Kingsley Amis (*Lucky Jim*, *The Old Devils*), London
DIED: 1689 Aphra Behn (*The Rover*, *Oronooko*), 48, England
1994 Ralph Ellison (*Invisible Man*, *Shadow and Act*), 80, New York City

1911 Apsley Cherry-Garrard and the Scott Antarctica party spent Easter in a "howling blizzard," dining on tinned haddock and "cheese hoosh" and reading *Bleak House*.

1912 On a foggy night in London, only a day after news of the sinking of the *Titanic*, an odd and "quaint" figure surprised the editor of *Nash's Magazine* in his darkened office: Joseph Conrad, the novelist and former seaman, who was agitated at the blame quickly falling on the crew of the ship. Would they publish an article by him? Four hours later, a cable from the magazine's New York office replied, "Who is Conrad? Do not want his story." (Undaunted, Conrad vented his anger at the arrogance of building a "45,000 ton hotel of thin steel plates to secure the patronage of, say, a couple of thousand rich people" in the *English Review* instead.)

1933 Precariously and unrewardingly employed as an art teacher in his hometown of Drohobycz, Poland, Bruno Schulz found an outlet for the vivid world inside his head in stories he embroidered with a richly mythologized history of the town. His friends pressed to get them published until finally the timid Schulz traveled to Warsaw to present them to a well-known writer, Zofia Nałkowska, and waited, trembling, for her response. It came by telephone just before he had to leave for his return train: "This is the most sensational discovery in our literature!" By the end of the year, the collection was published as *Cinnamon Shops*; not until 1963, two decades after Schulz's murder by an SS soldier in Drohobycz, was it translated into English and acclaimed in the United States as *The Street of Crocodiles*.

1963 "My dear fellow clergymen": so began the message Martin Luther King scribbled in the margins of newspapers in the Birmingham jail, where he was held for defying an injunction against protest in the city. While demonstrators in the streets of Birmingham faced the police dogs and fire hoses of the arch-segregationist "Bull" Connor, King expressed a growing frustration with those who had at times been his allies, the "white moderates" who had counseled patience rather than protest in their own open letter four days before. Little noted at the time, King's passionately reasoned "Letter from Birmingham Jail" became his best-known piece of writing after the Birmingham campaign, with its dramatic images of assaulted protesters, grew into one of the most influential of the civil rights movement.

1972 Charlie Brown told Peppermint Patty that the "secret to living is owning a convertible and a lake."

2002 Published: *Everything Is Illuminated* by Jonathan Safran Foer (Houghton Mifflin, Boston)

April 17

BORN: **1885** Isak Dinesen (*Seven Gothic Tales, Out of Africa*), Rungsted, Denmark
1928 Cynthia Ozick (*The Shawl, The Puttermesser Papers*), New York City

DIED: **1790** Benjamin Franklin (*Autobiography, Poor Richard's Almanack*), 84, Philadelphia
1986 Bessie Head (*A Question of Power*), 48, Serowe, Botswana

1907 Edgar Rice Burroughs, still five years away from creating Tarzan and John Carter of Mars, was promoted to manager of the Stenographic Department at Sears, Roebuck, and Co. in Chicago.

1926 Experiencing "silent convulsions of joy" as his train from New York approached his ancestral home in Rhode Island, H. P. Lovecraft could hardly contain his "surges of ecstasy" at his arrival at "HOME—UNION STATION—PROVIDENCE!!!!" "There *is* no other place for me," he wrote. "My world is Providence." For two years he'd been doomed to the heterogeneous metropolis of Brooklyn, whose "hateful chaos" of "non-Nordic" races spurred in him what one biographer has called a "genocidal frenzy." Released to the relative purity of Rhode Island (and from the marriage that had taken him to New York), Lovecraft never moved away again and in the next decade before his death channeled his genius for disgust into the most memorably unsettling of his tales of horror.

1926 Carrying an amateur camera but hoping to become a writer, Walker Evans, like so many other Americans of his generation, arrived in Paris in search of an artistic education and a bohemian life. Somehow, though, despite becoming a regular at Sylvia Beach's Shakespeare & Company bookshop, he missed out on the "moveable feast." Lonely and shy, he connected with none of the famed expatriates, and when offered an introduction to James Joyce refused it in fear of meeting the great man. But while he wrote little, he read a lot, and at the Paris cafés he learned how to observe: "I got my license at the Deux Magots," he later wrote. "Stare. It is the way to educate your eye and more. Stare, pry, listen, eavesdrop. Die knowing something."

1982 Dying of cancer, John Cheever steered his son Fred away from a career he was considering: "On librarians I do speak with prejudice. The profession in general has always seemed to me like the legitimization and financing of an impulse to collect old socks."

2002 At the Elliott Bay Book Company in Seattle, Ben Marcus, author of the excellent *Age of Wire and String*, graciously corrected the author of this book, who had confused him with Ben Metcalf, author of the superb essay "American Heartworm."

BORN: 1918 André Bazin (*What Is Cinema?*),
Angers, France

1959 Susan Faludi (*Backlash*, *Stiffed*),
Queens, N.Y.

DIED: 1945 Ernie Pyle (*Here Is Your War*,
Brave Men), 44, Iejima, Japan

1964 Ben Hecht (*The Front Page*, *A Child
of the Century*), 70, New York City

NO YEAR They may not be the details you recall most vividly from your school reading, but *The Canterbury Tales* contain as much useful information about medieval astronomy, a fascination of Chaucer's, as they do about the methods for cuckolding a carpenter. In his introduction to the Man of Law's Tale, for instance, the Host mentions the only specific date in the poem— "the eightetethe of Aprill"—and estimates from the latitude and the length of shadows that it is ten in the morning. Scholars ever since have speculated about the actual dates of this fictional pilgrimage, placing it anywhere from 1385 to 1394 and giving it any length from four days and three nights to a single day's journey taken at a canter, a word derived, after all, from the "Canterbury gallop" used by monks on their way to the cathedral.

1800 "If you really must beat the measure, sir, let me entreat you to do so in time, and not half a beat ahead." Such is the cold, whispered greeting that Stephen Maturin gives to Lieutenant Jack Aubrey—soon to become Captain Aubrey—in their first meeting, at a concert in Port Mahon, Minorca, in the opening pages of Patrick O'Brian's *Master and Commander*. They part equally coldly that night but are reconciled the following morning by their common musical enthusiasm and a shared pot of chocolate. Soon Aubrey asks Maturin to be the ship's surgeon on his new command, the HMS *Sophie*, and their durable alliance of opposites—Aubrey large, bluff, and cheerful; Maturin small and introspective—provides the emotional backbone of the twenty further volumes in O'Brian's beloved Aubrey-Maturin series.

1927 Fitzgerald wrote Hemingway that the first line of "In Another Country," "In the fall the war was always there but we did not go to it any more," was "one of the most beautiful prose sentences I have ever read."

1981 "She ate the egg. Then another egg." And that's when June Kashpaw began to decide that her bus ticket out of town would be just as good any other day and she could stick around with the man who had bought her a beer and peeled her an egg, and then another, and then another. The eggs felt lucky, and this man could be different. "You got to be," she breathed to him. "You got to be different." Got to be or not, he turns out to be beside the point: it's June who feels different, pure and naked like an egg under her crackling skin, and able to walk across the fields in the deep April snow, even as it buries her, in the sudden blizzard that opens Louise Erdrich's *Love Medicine*.

April 19

BORN: 1900 Richard Hughes (*A High Wind in Jamaica*, *In Hazard*), Weybridge, England
1943 Rikki Ducornet (*The Jade Cabinet*), Canton, N.Y.
DIED: 1824 Lord Byron (*Childe Harold's Pilgrimage*), 36, Missolonghi, Ottoman Empire
1882 Charles Darwin (*On the Origin of Species*), 73, Downe, England

1854 Henry David Thoreau declined a neighbor's offer of a two-headed calf: "I am not interested in mere phenomena."

1862 Lionel Tennyson, age eight, explained to a visitor to the household, Lewis Carroll, the conditions under which he would show Carroll some poems he had written: Carroll must play chess with him, and must allow Lionel to give him "one blow on the head with a mallet."

1891 Following the line "I am sleepy, and the oozy weeds about me twist," Herman Melville, seventy-one years old and five months from his death, added the words "End of Book." He may have intended that line, the final one in a ballad called "Billy in the Darbies," as the end of his book, but the book itself, *Billy Budd*, was unfinished and would remain so. The first novel he'd written in three decades, it was only discovered as a manuscript among his papers after nearly three more decades, when it was acclaimed as his last masterpiece.

1913 The *Athenaeum* on Sigmund Freud's *Interpretation of Dreams*: "The results he reaches are hardly commensurate with the labour expended, and reveal a seamy side of life in Vienna which might well have been left alone."

1951 Noel Coward had "nearly finished *Little Dorrit*—what a beastly girl, but what a wonderful novel."

1956 The long friendship between Albert Murray and Ralph Ellison began in New York during the war when they realized they both, as southern transplants and African American writers, "had accepted the challenge of William Faulkner's complex literary image of the South," as Murray later put it. But by 1956 they were losing patience with Faulkner. "Nuts!" Ellison wrote from Rome about Faulkner's "Go slow now" essay about civil rights in *Life*. "He thinks that Negroes exist simply to give ironic overtone to the viciousness of white folks." Murray, replying on this day from Casablanca, where he was stationed with the air force, was more blunt: "Son of a bitch prefers a handful of anachronistic crackers to everything that really gives him a reason not only for being but for writing. I'm watching his ass but close forevermore."

BORN: 1950 Steve Erickson (*Days Between Stations, Zeroville*), Los Angeles
1953 Robert Crais (*L.A. Requiem, The Two-Minute Rule*), Independence, La.
DIED: 1912 Bram Stoker (*Dracula, The Lair of the White Worm*), 64, London
1996 Christopher Robin Milne (*The Enchanted Place*), 75, Totnes, England

1746 Giacomo Casanova was a seducer not just of women but of patrons. Born poor, he had by the age of twenty-one already been a lawyer, a clergyman, a soldier, and finally a mediocre violinist when, after fiddling at a wedding in Venice, he retrieved a letter a nobleman dropped while stepping into his gondola. The nobleman offered him a ride home but suffered a stroke along the way, and Casanova, taking charge of his recovery and convincing him meanwhile that he was a master of the occult, made himself so useful that the nobleman—a Venetian senator, it turned out—adopted him as a son and, "at one bound," as he recalled in his *Story of My Life*, raised him into the idle pleasures of the nobility.

1827 Charles and Alfred Tennyson, ages eighteen and seventeen, celebrated the publication of *Poems by Two Brothers* by riding to the coast and shouting their verses into the wind and waves.

1926 When *The Autobiography of an Ex-Colored Man* appeared in 1912, its author, James Weldon Johnson, thought it would make more of a splash published anonymously so it could be taken as the true confession of a black narrator who had passed into the white world. As it turned out, the novel hardly made a splash at all, receiving few sales or reviews (although the *Nashville Tennessean* did go to the trouble of declaring its title an impossibility: "once a negro, always a negro"). It was only in the following decade, during the flourishing of the Harlem Renaissance, that Blanche Knopf wrote Johnson on this day, "There is no question that we want *The Autobiography of an Ex-Colored Man*," bringing back into print one of the subtlest and most challenging examinations of identity in American fiction.

1936 William Faulkner piloted a Waco F biplane in his first solo flight.

1984 At five in the morning on Good Friday in the opening pages of Richard Ford's *The Sportswriter*, Frank Bascombe climbs over the cemetery fence behind his house to meet his ex-wife in remembrance of the birthday of their son, Ralph. Four years before, Ralph died at the age of nine, and two years after that Frank and "X," as she's known in the book, were divorced. Frank has brought a poem to read this year at Ralph's grave: Theodore Roethke's "Meditation," a poem he likes and she dislikes for its assurance of the happiness that can be found in the everyday, an assurance that will be tested throughout *The Sportswriter* and the Bascombe novels that follow, *Independence Day* and *The Lay of the Land*.

April 21

BORN: 1816 Charlotte Brontë (*Jane Eyre,
Villette*), Thornton, England
1838 John Muir (*The Mountains of
California*), Dunbar, Scotland
DIED: 1910 Mark Twain (*Life on the
Mississippi, Pudd'nhead Wilson*), 74,
Redding, Conn.
1946 John Maynard Keynes (*The General
Theory of Employment, Interest, and
Money*), 62, Firie, England

129 Many have noticed that on April 21, the traditional anniversary of the founding of Rome, the open oculus at the top of the rotunda in the city's Pantheon causes a circle of sunlight to shine on the temple's doorway. Did the emperor Hadrian, who oversaw the building's completion, arrange to have his ceremonial entrance on this date so illuminated? In Marguerite Yourcenar's novel *Memoirs of Hadrian*, the emperor speaks with pride of the temple's dedication and of the "disk of daylight . . . suspended there like a shield of gold." As she mentions in her fascinating afternotes to the novel, Yourcenar visited the Pantheon herself on that same day of the year to check where the sunlight would fall.

1883 In remarks he'd later disown, Oscar Wilde described Algernon Swinburne as "a braggart of vice, who has done everything he could to convince his fellow citizens of his homosexuality and bestiality, without being in the slightest degree a homosexual or a bestializer."

1992 "It was," Mr. McAlister, the faculty adviser to the Student Government Association, has to admit, "the most interesting election I'd seen in my nine years at Winwood." There's Tracy Flick, smoldering with "110 pounds of the rawest, nakedest ambition" (and fresh off a scandalous fling with her English teacher); Paul Warren, the genial varsity fullback and Mr. M's secret protégé; and the wild card, Paul's sister, Tammy, whose campaign slogan is "Who cares about this stupid election?" And there's Mr. M himself, who drops two crucial votes in a trash can on election day and ruins his life. Before Reese Witherspoon and Matthew Broderick made Tracy and Mr. M their own, there was Tom Perrotta's *Election*, a breezily challenging novel about messy American democracy in the Bush-Clinton era.

1995 A mentor to his favorite cartoonists but competitive with them all, Charles M. Schulz developed a particularly affectionate friendship with Lynn Johnston, whose *For Better or For Worse* approached his *Peanuts* in popularity for a time. Her realistic strip, like few others, followed its characters through real time, and eventually Johnston had to deal with death, beginning with the sheepdog Farley, who died in this day's strip after rescuing little April Patterson from a swollen river. "You cannot kill off the family dog," Schulz told Johnston when she first previewed the storyline for him. "If you do this story, I am going to have Snoopy get hit by a truck and go to the hospital, and everybody will worry about Snoopy, and nobody's going to read your stupid story."

BORN: 1899 Vladimir Nabokov (*Laughter in the Dark, Lolita*), St. Petersburg, Russia
1923 Paula Fox (*Desperate Characters, Borrowed Finery*), New York City
DIED: 1984 Ansel Adams (*Parmelian Prints of the High Sierra*), 82, Monterey, Calif.
1996 Erma Bombeck (*The Grass Is Always Greener over the Septic Tank*), 69, San Francisco

1848 Having forgotten her birthday the day before, Charlotte Brontë lamented, "I am now 32. Youth is gone—gone—and will never come back."

1910 One of Sigmund Freud's most famous—and favorite—patients was one he only knew from a book. Daniel Paul Schreber, a judge in Leipzig who had suffered a mental breakdown, wrote *Memoirs of My Nervous Illness* to argue (successfully) for release from his asylum in 1902; Freud was so intrigued by his account he jokingly wrote Carl Jung on this day that Schreber "should have been made a professor of psychiatry and director of a mental hospital." It's no surprise he was drawn to the book: Schreber's fantastic and detailed visions—of turning into a woman, of being penetrated by rays and by crowds of people, of his "soul murder" at the hands of his former doctor—provide a rich text for Freud's analysis in *The Schreber Case* of the source of the patient's paranoia. (Surprise: it's his father.)

1949 After his ex-con friend Little Jack Melody crashed his car in a police chase—with Ginsberg and a load of stolen jewelry and furs in the back seat—twenty-one-year-old Allen Ginsberg was arrested for grand larceny and attempting to run over a policeman.

1951 The legend of Jack Kerouac's frenzied composition of *On the Road* both is and isn't true. He spent years drafting and revising the novel, but it is true that for three weeks, ending on this day, he typed a complete, 125,000-word draft on a 120-foot roll of paper he had taped together. Soon after, he proudly unrolled the scroll in the office of Robert Giroux, to that point his champion in New York publishing, who replied, "How the hell can the printer work from this?" His revised version finally saw print in 1957, but fifty years later the draft was published as *On the Road: The Original Scroll*, with the characters Dean Moriarty and Carlo Marx restored to their original names, Neal Cassady and Allen Ginsberg.

1973 *Concrete Island* is not the only novel of J. G. Ballard's that begins with an automobile crash. But unlike the erotic violence of *Crash*, this accident, in which a blown tire sends Robert Maitland's Jaguar onto the embankment of a highway interchange in central London, leaves its victim unscathed. And what follows is less a story of violence than of isolation, of a man marooned in the midst of a metropolis. Unable at first to attract a rescuer from the flow of traffic, as he's left to his own resources and those of his few tramp neighbors, he becomes unwilling to leave his concrete island on any terms but his own.

April 23

BORN: 1895 Ngaio Marsh (*Enter a Murderer*), Christchurch, New Zealand
1942 Barry Hannah (*Airships, Geronimo Rex*), Meridian, Miss.
DIED: 1915 Rupert Brooke (*1914 and Other Poems*), 27, Skyros, Greece
1996 P. L. Travers (*Mary Poppins*), 96, London

1374 Has a poet been more glamorously compensated than when Edward III, during the feast of St. George at Windsor Castle, granted Geoffrey Chaucer a pitcher of wine a day for life, to be picked up daily from the king's butler? It is not certain that the reward—extravagant even for its time—was for poetry; some have connected it instead to his recent mission to Florence or his new position as controller of the Wool Custom. Whatever its cause, the impracticality of the gift was such that four years later Edward's successor, Richard II, turned it into a regular cash payment.

1616 Did Shakespeare and Cervantes, the two great founders of modern literature, really die on the same day, as is often said? Not quite: Shakespeare died on this day in the old Julian calendar, while Cervantes died eleven days earlier, on April 22 in the Gregorian calendar, and was buried on the 23rd.

1857 Nearing forty, Henry David Thoreau might have felt he had encountered his own youthful self in the person of a twenty-year-old woman when he met Kate Brady. An admirer of *Walden* and a lover of nature, she told Thoreau that like him she wanted to "live free." "Her own sex, so tamely bred, only jeer at her for entertaining such an idea," Thoreau wrote a week later, "but she has a strong head and a love for good reading, which may carry her through." Then, as if to banish any thought that she might be a companion for him, he added, "How rarely a man's love for nature becomes a ruling principle with him, like a youth's affection for a maiden, but more enduring! All nature is my bride."

1916 His new job as head of the Surety Claims Department of the Hartford Accident and Indemnity Company often took Wallace Stevens, who had just begun publishing poems in literary journals, on the road, and on Easter Sunday he wrote his wife from Miami. "Florida," he reported, "is not really amazing in itself but in what it becomes under cultivation . . . There are brilliant birds and strange things but they must be observed," the stirrings of a thought he'd expand and complicate twenty years later in his portrait, in "The Idea of Order at Key West," of a singer who "Knew that there never was a world for her / Except the one she sang and, singing, made."

1975 Longtime correspondents Barbara Pym and Philip Larkin met in person for the first time for lunch, Pym having informed Larkin beforehand, "I shall probably be wearing a beige tweed suit or a Welsh tweed cape if colder. I shall be looking rather anxious, I expect."

BORN: 1815 Anthony Trollope (*Barchester Towers, The Way We Live Now*), London
1940 Sue Grafton (*"A" Is for Alibi, "B" Is for Burglar*), Chicago

DIED: 1731 Daniel Defoe (*Robinson Crusoe, Moll Flanders*), c. 70, London
1942 L. M. Montgomery (*Anne of Green Gables, Emily of New Moon*), 67, Toronto

1814 Edward Barrett sent his eight-year-old daughter, Elizabeth, ten shillings in exchange for a poem "on virtue," calling her the "Poet Laureate of Hope End."

1895 "I had resolved on a voyage around the world, and as the wind on the morning of April 24, 1895, was fair, at noon I weighed anchor, set sail, and filled away from Boston." Not far past the docks, Joshua Slocum, piloting the thirty-seven-foot sloop *Spray* alone, passed a steamship that had broken on the rocks and noted, "I was already farther on my voyage than she." Slocum sailed 46,000 more miles before returning to New England over three years later as the first to circumnavigate the globe solo. By then the newspapers that had been his early sponsors had lost interest in his dispatches, but his full account, published as *Sailing Alone Around the World*, was an immediate international success and remains one of the finest of adventure yarns.

1916 The factions of Irish nationalism were many, and when word reached him in England of the Rising in Dublin against the British that began on this Easter Monday, W. B. Yeats didn't think much of some of the conspirators—a dreamer, a drunk, and a madwoman among them, he thought. But by May, when British firing squads began executing the rebels, he had already composed the famous refrain—"a terrible beauty has been born"—of the poem "Easter, 1916," which he would complete in September. It wasn't until 1920, though, with World War I over and the Irish War of Independence begun, that he found the times right to publish his ambivalent song of martyrdom.

1944 With *Under the Volcano*, his own novel of alcoholic descent, still unpublished, Malcolm Lowry wrote a friend, "Have you read a novel *The Lost Weekend* by one Charles Jackson, a radioman from New York? It is perhaps not a very fine novel but admirably about a drunkard and hangovers and alcoholic wards as they have never been done (save by me of course)."

1963 Eight years after he first mocked up a tiny book called *Where the Wild Horses Are*, Maurice Sendak drafted the opening lines of what would be his first solo picture book. The story began, "Once a boy asked where the wild horses are. Nobody could tell him," and it involved a magic garden and a mother who turned into a wolf. Within a month, though, the horses had become "things"— "I couldn't really draw horses," Sendak said—inspired by the frightening relatives who invaded his childhood home on Sundays, saying, "You're so cute I could eat you up," and in the fall *Where the Wild Things Are* was published, to great consternation and delight.

April 25

BORN: 1949 James Fenton (*The Memory of War*), Lincoln, England
1952 Padgett Powell (*Edisto, The Interrogative Mood*), Gainesville, Fla.
DIED: 1944 George Herriman (*Krazy Kat*), 63, Los Angeles
2006 Jane Jacobs (*The Death and Life of Great American Cities*), 89, Toronto

387 St. Augustine may have invented the modern autobiography with his *Confessions*, but his own autobiography, or at least the modern part of it, ends midway through that book with the words describing this day: "And we were baptized, and anxiety for our past life vanished from us." To that point Augustine's path has taken him through sin and spiritual yearning to the moment when he saw the light in a garden in Milan; a year later that serene vision of his sins absolved was granted by his baptism in the same city. The *Confessions* still has four books remaining at that point, but the confessing is over: the rest is less about Augustine the man than about his God.

1811 Jane Austen, asked by her sister about *Sense and Sensibility*, soon to be published, replied, "I am never too busy to think of S&S. I can no more forget it, than a mother can forget her sucking child."

1929 With his second novel on its way, Henry Green was able to make his engagement with Mary Biddulph official when their fathers, after months of negotiation, settled on an £1,800 annual income for the young couple.

1931 "Constant Reader," in *The New Yorker*, on Dashiell Hammett's *The Glass Key*: "All I can say is that anybody who doesn't read him misses much of modern America . . . Dashiell Hammett is as American as a sawed-off shotgun."

1983 It took only three days for one of the greatest scoops in modern journalism to unravel. On April 22, the German newsweekly *Stern* announced the discovery of a treasure trove for historians: the diaries kept by Adolf Hitler between 1932 and 1945, which had been authenticated in a Swiss bank vault by experts swayed by the sight of over sixty handwritten notebooks, a number no forger, surely, would have had the audacity or stamina to fabricate. The next day the distinguished historian Hugh Trevor-Roper wrote that history as we knew it would "have to be revised," but by the 25th, when *Stern* and *Newsweek* first published excerpts, the fraud was coming undone. (Among the clues: the *A* in the Gothic initials "AH" glued onto each volume was, in fact, an *F*.) The diaries, it was soon revealed, were a collaboration between journalist Gerd Heidemann and career forger Konrad Kujau.

2008 Michel Faber, in the *Guardian,* on James Kelman's *Kieron Smith, Boy*: "I suspect Kelman knew exactly what he was doing. And what he has done here is both revolutionary and very, very dull."

April 26

BORN: 1889 Ludwig Wittgenstein (*Tractatus Logico-Philosophicus*), Vienna
1914 Bernard Malamud (*The Natural*, *The Fixer*), Brooklyn
DIED: 1991 A. B. Guthrie Jr. (*The Big Sky*, *The Way West*), 90, Choteau, Mont.
2004 Hubert Selby Jr. (*Last Exit to Brooklyn*, *Requiem for a Dream*), 75, Los Angeles

1336 Did the poet Petrarch invent mountaineering when he ascended Mont Ventoux? Some historians have claimed it, but some have questioned whether he climbed the mountain—best known now as one of the great cyclist's challenges in the Tour de France—at all. The fame of his adventure rests on an account he claimed to have written the night of his descent: full of earthly pleasure at the view from the 1,912-meter summit, he opened his pocket copy of St. Augustine's *Confessions* and was chastened and exalted by the passage he turned to by chance: "And men go to admire the high mountains, the vast floods of the sea, the huge streams of the rivers, the circumference of the ocean and the revolutions of the stars—and desert themselves."

1853 Reading Montaigne in bed, Flaubert wrote to Louise Colet: "I know of no more soothing book, none more conducive to peace of mind. It is so healthy, so down to earth!"

1884 Leo Tolstoy, one of Russia's best-known men, set out to visit a bookshop in Moscow but turned back when no one on the streetcar would change a ten-ruble note. "They all thought I was a swindler."

1942 After his daring entrance into the war, in which he crashed his plane in the Sahara and then joined his RAF squadron in the dogfights of the Battle of Athens, Roald Dahl's posting to Washington, D.C., seemed dull. But when C. S. Forester, whose Horatio Hornblower maritime adventures Dahl had loved as a child, asked him to sit down and describe his exploits so Forester could write them up for the *Saturday Evening Post*, Dahl was transformed. "For the first time in my life," he said, "I became totally absorbed in what I was doing." Forester saw it too: he passed Dahl's draft, unedited, on to the magazine, which published it in August and began Roald Dahl's new career as a writer.

2007 Colm Tóibín must surely have been alluding to the opening scene in Ian McEwan's *Enduring Love* when he wrote admiringly in the *London Review of Books* of McEwan's control of tone in *On Chesil Beach*, "It is like putting just enough air in a hot-air balloon to allow it to fly, making sure, however, that it can land as well."

April 27

BORN: 1759 Mary Wollstonecraft (*Vindication of the Rights of Women*), London
1898 Ludwig Bemelmans (*Madeline, Hotel Splendide*), Meran, Austria-Hungary
DIED: 1882 Ralph Waldo Emerson (*Nature, Self-Reliance*), 78, Concord, Mass.
1932 Hart Crane (*The Bridge, White Buildings*), 32, Gulf of Mexico

1934 Unable to interest New York publishers in his proposal for a new bird guide, twenty-four-year-old naturalist and painter Roger Tory Peterson discovered that the head of the Massachusetts Audubon Society, Francis Allen, was also a senior editor at the Boston house of Houghton Mifflin. Allen was immediately interested but, as Peterson told it, tested Peterson's illustrations by asking a Harvard ornithologist to identify the pictured birds from the other end of a long conference table. The paintings passed the test, and Peterson's *Field Guide to the Birds* was published on this day in the following year. The first printing of 2,000 copies sold out in a week; by Peterson's death in 1996, he had sold over seven million bird guides.

1948 Gore Vidal reminded Christopher Isherwood, whom he had just met in Paris, "of a teddy bear, sometimes of a duck"; he also seemed "a pretty shrewd operator."

1959 "Poor thing," Robert Lowell wrote Elizabeth Bishop about a visit from Theodore Roethke, "mammoth yet elfinlike, hairless, red-faced, beginning the day with a shot of bourbon, speechless except for shrewd grunted asides—behind him nervous breakdowns, before him—what?"

1975 On April 27, 2012, four years after his novel *The Museum of Innocence* was published, Orhan Pamuk opened an actual Museum of Innocence in Istanbul, in a house he purchased and filled (at a cost he estimated as equal to his Nobel Prize) with thousands of objects—school reports, hairclips, cigarette stubs—from the imagined affair between the novel's two lovers, Kemal and Füsun. For years, as he wrote their story, he stocked the museum as well, and the opening celebrated the thirty-seventh anniversary of the moment that launched their affair (and its long, melancholy aftermath), when Kemal's future wife admired a handbag in the window of a posh boutique, causing him to return the next day to buy the bag and see Füsun, a young cousin working there who had grown beautiful since he'd seen her last.

1979 Rebecca Stead's *When You Reach Me* swept a handful of prizes for young readers, including the 2010 Newbery Medal, thanks to its intensely evoked atmosphere of late-'70s Upper West Side Manhattan and its ingenious (and affecting) time-travel plot. At the center of the story's chronological swirl one date holds firm: April 27, 1979, the day Miranda's mom is scheduled to be a contestant on Dick Clark's *$20,000 Pyramid*, just as a mysterious correspondent from the future had predicted in his final note to Miranda. And on that day, as her mom's round in the Winner's Circle begins, all the clues Miranda has been unraveling through the story begin to fall into place.

April 28

BORN: 1926 Harper Lee (*To Kill a Mockingbird*), Monroeville, Ala.
1953 Roberto Bolaño (*The Savage Detectives*, *Distant Star*), Santiago, Chile
DIED: 1992 Iceberg Slim (*Trick Baby*, *Pimp*), 73, Los Angeles
1997 Ann Petry (*The Street*, *The Narrows*), 88, Old Saybrook, Conn.

1873 After a night out with Flaubert, George Sand had had enough of her "young friend": "I'm very fond of him, but he gives me a splitting headache. He doesn't like noise, but he doesn't mind the din he makes himself."

1937 Sherwood Anderson watched from the stands at the Polo Grounds as the Dodgers, behind Van Lingle Mungo, topped the Giants, 3–2.

1952 How do you make a spider beguiling? A pig, or a little girl: no problem. But Garth Williams's greatest challenge in illustrating E. B. White's *Charlotte's Web* was drawing Charlotte herself in a way that would be both natural and appealing. Williams sketched Charlotte with a variety of anthropomorphic eyes, eyebrows, and mouths—at one point going so far as to borrow the face of the Mona Lisa—but White and his editor, Ursula Nordstrom, pushed him to make her more "spider-y," and on this day Nordstrom sent White, who felt that "the book must at all odds have a beguiling Charlotte," the latest batch of Williams's sketches, agreeing that their heroine should look "less like a person": "After all, Charlotte *is* a spider."

1962 On this morning, two detectives arrested Kenneth Halliwell and Joe Orton for stealing seventy-two library books and cutting pages from 1,653 art books to decorate the walls of their flat. The two

had also doctored dozens of library book covers—replacing Henry VIII's head with a monkey's, for instance, and adding mildly obscene jacket blurbs to Dorothy Sayers novels. For these crimes the "frustrated authors," in the words of the prosecutor, were sentenced to six months in prison, which changed their lives. Halliwell attempted suicide shortly after their release, while Orton, finally unlocking the detachment and anger his writing needed, wrote a series of hit plays over the next five years, beginning with *Entertaining Mr. Sloane*, before being murdered by Halliwell in the same flat.

1966 Muriel Spark watched her horse Lifeboat, which she bought from the queen, race at Fontwell Park.

April 29

BORN: 1931 Robert Gottlieb (editor of *Catch-22* and *The New Yorker*), New York City
DIED: 1997 Mike Royko (*Boss*; *I May Be Wrong, but I Doubt It*), 64, Chicago
2011 Joanna Russ (*The Female Man*, *Picnic on Paradise*), 74, Tucson

1863 and 1933 The seventy years of Constantine Cavafy's life, between his birth on this day in 1863 and his death on the same day in 1933, were spent largely outside the public eye. Though he wrote in Greek, he lived nearly all his life in Alexandria, Egypt, where his father, an export merchant, had compiled a fortune that was mostly lost by Cavafy's youth. For over thirty years he worked as a clerk in the Irrigation Office of the Ministry of Public Works, while living, like Borges, with his mother, pursuing an active, though secret, homosexual life, and writing poems that, over time, found a voice of distilled irony to express his passions for the vanished byways of classical Greece and the beauty of men.

1939 In his mid-thirties, James Beard left Portland, Oregon, for New York City to make one last attempt at a theater career. Like many actors, he found more work in catering, and he joined with his friends Bill and Irma Rhode to launch Hors d'Oeuvre, Inc., which on this day attracted the notice of the *Herald Tribune*'s urbane columnist Lucius Beebe. Bill got the public credit from Beebe—"He has turtle livers flown in from Florida, the finest of Danish hams and caviars, anchovies, lobsters and game pastes in every known combination"—but the next year Beard, to Rhode's fury, adapted the company's name into his first cookbook, *Hors d'Oeuvre and Canapés*. Their partnership soon dissolved, but Beard's book remained in print for decades as he became the dean of American food writers.

1940 Tennessee Williams "saw a silly picture called *1,000,000 Years B.C.*"

1946 Published: *The Portable Faulkner* by William Faulkner, edited by Malcolm Cowley (Viking, New York)

1974 When President Richard Nixon announced on this day that, in response to a House subpoena, he would release 1,200 pages of edited transcripts of the taped White House discussions of the Watergate break-in, "blemishes and all," he made an offering not only to history but to readers as well. The transcripts and the tapes, which continued to trickle out over the following decades and are best collected in Stanley I. Kutler's *Abuse of Power*, are a rich trove of conversation made under stress, full of conspiracy, self-dealing, and indirection. "In many places on the tapes," the president said in his address, "there were ambiguities," and there are, if not always where he claimed. What could be more compelling for a reader than a book full of both smoking guns and ambiguous gaps, with an eighteen-and-a-half-minute absence at its heart that rivals the great unnameables of Beckett, Lovecraft, or Dickinson in its power and mystery?

BORN: 1877 Alice B. Toklas (*The Alice B. Toklas Cookbook*), San Francisco
1945 Annie Dillard (*Pilgrim at Tinker Creek, The Maytrees*), Pittsburgh
DIED: 1982 Lester Bangs (*Psychotic Reactions and Carburetor Dung*), 33, New York City
1994 Richard Scarry (*What Do People Do All Day?*), 74, Gstaad, Switzerland

1574 Rich and bored, the young Mathilde de La Mole, daughter of the employer of Julian Sorel, Stendhal's antiheroic upstart in *The Red and the Black*, has cultivated a passion for what she supposes to have been a more heroic age, mourning the day, April 30, 1574, when her ancestor Boniface de La Mole was beheaded for a daring threat to the Crown. Julian finds her black mourning gown flattering, and soon, encouraged by his own romantic imitation of Napoleon, they fall for each other. Later in their story, the legend that La Mole's severed head was buried by his lover (herself the subject of Alexandre Dumas's *La Reine Margot*) will have its ironic echo.

1746 Samuel Johnson, until then a literary journeyman of moderate reputation, submitted to a group of booksellers "A Short Scheme for Compiling a New Dictionary of the English Language," leading to a contract in June for the substantial sum of £1,575. "The great Labour is yet to come," he wrote, "the labour of interpreting these words and phrases, with brevity, fulness, and perspicuity," and indeed, it was only after nine years of "harmless drudgery" that *A Dictionary of the English Language,* a nearly one-man production that remained the standard English dictionary for almost two hundred years, was published and made his fame.

1861 Jilted by Ashley Wilkes, Scarlett O'Hara marries Charles Hamilton the day before Ashley's wedding to Charles's sister Melanie, as both grooms prepare to go off to war.

1926 Working with an unprecedented fluency, Virginia Woolf wrote most of the first section of *To the Lighthouse* in a few months in early 1926, and on this day recorded in her diary that she had finished the first part and begun the lyrical middle interlude, "Time Passes," in which she gave herself the "most difficult abstract" challenge of writing of time and a place without characters. After dashing out the first two pages, she wondered, "Is it nonsense, is it brilliance?"

1966 After a party celebrating both the twenty-first birthday of his wife, Mimi Baez, with whom he'd recorded two folk-rock albums, and the release of his first novel, *Been Down So Long It Looks Like Up to Me*, Richard Fariña said, "Let's go for a ride!" and climbed behind a casual acquaintance onto the back of his red Harley-Davidson Sportster. You can guess what happened next. Up in the Carmel hills over the Pacific, the bike failed to navigate a curve at a speed later estimated at ninety and threw Fariña off, killing him instantly. Less than two months later, his friend Bob Dylan nearly met the same fate when he crashed his Triumph 500 near Woodstock, New York.

May is blooming and fertile, spring in
its full flower. Unlike the storms of March and
the "uncertain glory" of April, Shakespeare's
May, with its "darling buds," is always sweet, and
ever the month for love. Traditionally—before
the international labor movement claimed May
1st in honor of the Haymarket riot—May Days
were holidays of love too, white-gowned fertility
celebrations. It's on a May Day that Thomas
Hardy, always attuned to ancient rites, introduces
Tess Durbeyfield, whose "bouncing handsome
womanliness" among the country girls
"under whose bodices
the life throbbed
quick and warm"
still reveals flashes
of the child she
recently was.

May has long been the month for mothers as well as maidens, even before Anna Jarvis chose the second Sunday in May in 1908 for Mother's Day to honor the death of her own mother. The mother of them all, the Virgin Mary, was celebrated for centuries as the Queen of May, and in "The May Magnificat" Gerard Manley Hopkins reminds us that "May is Mary's month," and asks why. "All things rising," he answers, "all things sizing / Mary sees, sympathizing / with that world of good, / Nature's motherhood."

May's meanings can get to be too much, though. When the mother in *The Furies*, Janet Hobhouse's fictional memoir of a life caught up in isolated family dependence, chooses Memorial Day to end her own life, her daughter mournfully riffs on May in an overdetermined frenzy of meaning: "month of mothers, month of Mary, month of heroes, the beginning of heat and abandonment, of the rich leaving the poor to the cities, May as in Maybe Maybe not, as in yes, finally you may, as in Mayday, the call for help and the sound of the bailout, and also, now that I think of it, as in her middle name, Maida."

The "may" in "May" had another meaning for Elizabeth Barrett, who wrote to Robert Browning from her invalid's bed during the "implacable weather" of March that "April is coming. There will be both a May & a June if we live to see such things, & perhaps, after all, we may." She wasn't only speaking of better weather coming: since they began to write each other in January they had spoken of meeting in person for the first time—he especially—but she, without refusing, had put him off, excusing herself as "a recluse, with nerves that have been all broken on the rack, & now hang loosely." When May arrived, she wrote him, "Shall I have courage to see you soon, I wonder! . . . But oh, this make-believe May—it can't be May after all!" And then on May 20 she met him, beginning a secret courtship, against her father's wishes, that ended in their elopement in September of the following year.

RECOMMENDED READING FOR MAY

Alice's Adventures in Wonderland by Lewis Carroll (1865) ∽ She may have met a March Hare that was mad as a hatter, but it was in the month of May—the birthday month of Alice Liddell, Charles Dodgson's model for his heroine—that Alice followed a rabbit with a watch in his waistcoat pocket down a hole and began her adventures underground.

Tess of the d'Urbervilles by Thomas Hardy (1891) ∽ Angel is first drawn, fleetingly, to young Tess at a May Day dance at Whitsun time. By late spring two years later, her womanly blossoming is almost overwhelming—she's working alongside him as a *milkmaid*, for goodness sake— but by then Hardy has arranged their fates to make her bloom a cruel joke on both of them.

Death in Venice by Thomas Mann (1912) ∽ A false taste of summer in May in his northern home drives the middle-aged writer Gustav Aschenbach south for freshness and inspiration to Venice, where he will be drawn into an impotent attraction to a young Polish boy amid the humid miasma of cholera.

Lucky Jim by Kingsley Amis (1954) ∽ There's no better cure for end-of-term apathy than the campus novel that, for better or worse, launched the genre (along with Randall Jarrell's *Pictures from an Institution*, published the same year). But it may make you never want to go back to class at all, especially if you're lecturing, miserably, on medieval history at a provincial English university.

"The Whitsun Weddings" by Philip Larkin (1964) ∽ Amis based *Lucky Jim* on, and dedicated it to, his good friend Larkin, who made his own mark on postwar British culture with this ambivalent ode to the hopeful mass pairing-up of springtime, three years before the Kinks captured the same lonely-in-the-city melancholy in "Waterloo Sunset."

Frog and Toad Are Friends by Arnold Lobel (1970) ∽ The lesson of "Spring," the opening tale in Lobel's thrillingly calm series for early readers, is, apparently, that there is honor in deception, as Frog fools hibernating Toad into joining him on a fine April day by tearing an extra page off the calendar to prove it is, in fact, May.

Awakenings by Oliver Sacks (1973) ∽ Awed equally by chemistry and human adaptability, Sacks recorded in the second book of his remarkable career the moment in May 1969 when he began to administer a new "miracle drug" to a few dozen patients subdued for decades by a rare illness contracted in the '20s.

Reborn: Journals & Notebooks, 1947–1963 by Susan Sontag (2008) ∽ "I AM REBORN IN THE TIME RETOLD IN THIS NOTEBOOK," sixteen-year-old Sontag scribbled on the inside cover of her journal for May 1949, marking a moment when she was colossally precocious— *re*reading Mann, Hopkins, and Dante— and falling in love for the first time, with a young woman in San Francisco.

May 1

BORN: 1923 Joseph Heller (*Catch-22*, *Something Happened*), Brooklyn
1924 Terry Southern (*Candy*, *The Magic Christian*), Alvarado, Tex.
DIED: 1700 John Dryden (*MacFlecknoe*, *Marriage à la Mode*), 68, London
1978 Sylvia Townsend Warner (*Lolly Willowes*), 84, Maiden Newton, England

1841 Reviewing Dickens's *Barnaby Rudge* in the middle of its serialization, Edgar Allan Poe correctly predicted the identity of the murderer.

1908 About to give his "The Poet of Democracy" lecture to a local literary society in Appleton, Wisconsin, Carl Sandburg confessed, "A sort of deviltry possesses me at times among these—to talk their slangiest slang, speak their homely, beautiful home-speech about all the common things—suddenly run a knife into their snobbery—then swing out into a crag-land of granite and azure where they can't follow but sit motionless following my flight with their eyes."

1934 The early comic-book adventures of Tintin are unthinkingly accepting of European stereotypes of foreign lands (in the regrettable *Tintin in the Congo*, to be precise), but when Hergé, Tintin's young Belgian creator, turned to China as a subject for his fifth tale, his Catholic advisers wisely recommended he be less culturally careless, and introduced him to a visiting Chinese sculptor named Chang Chong Chen on this day. The two young artists hit it off immediately, and Hergé paid tribute to their friendship with a character named after his friend in *The Blue Lotus*. Nearly a half-century later, fact and fiction reversed: after Hergé had Tintin search for his old friend Chang in *Tintin in Tibet*, the real-life Chang, having survived the Cultural Revolution, reappeared in Belgium for a well-publicized reunion with Hergé.

1935 Israel Joshua Singer was always ahead of his younger brother, Isaac Bashevis: born a decade earlier, he was the first to find success in writing and the first to immigrate to America (where his novel *Yoshe Kalb* had already become a popular play). When his brother followed him to New York on this day, Israel Joshua met him at the dock, and a photograph of the two together appeared in the *Forward*, the city's Yiddish newspaper where the elder brother worked, with the caption, "Two Brothers and Both Writers." For years Isaac worked at the *Forward* under his brother's shadow, but after Israel's sudden death of a heart attack in 1944, it was the younger Singer who continued at the paper for more than half a century, and who won the Nobel Prize for Literature in 1978.

1941 If *The Escapist* had ended its run before this day, it would doubtless have disappeared like its countless, disposable comic-book peers. But all that changed, because on the 1st of May, in Michael Chabon's *The Adventures of Kavalier & Clay*, Joe Kavalier and Sammy Clay saw *Citizen Kane*. Afterward, their ambition aflame with the possibilities of narration matched with image, Joe looked over at Sammy and said, "I want to do something like *that*."

BORN: 1838 Albion W. Tourgée (*A Fool's Errand, Bricks Without Straw*), Williamsfield, Ohio
1900 W. J. Cash (*The Mind of the South*), Gaffney, S.C.

DIED: 1519 Leonardo da Vinci (*Treatise on Painting, Notebooks*), 67, Amboise, France
1963 Van Wyck Brooks (*The Flowering of New England*), 77, Bridgewater, Conn.

1970 Though a son of Louisville himself, Hunter S. Thompson tried to put family ties aside when he returned for the ninety-sixth running of the local horse race. His self-appointed job was to pin down the "whole doomed atavistic culture that makes the Kentucky Derby what it is," which meant embarking on a "vicious, drunken nightmare" inside the press box and out. He and his bearded British illustrator, Ralph Steadman, along for the ride for the first time, managed to miss, more or less, both the race itself and whatever crowd violence there was (the violence seemed mainly to be in Thompson's head), but his scabrous report, "The Kentucky Derby Is Decadent and Depraved," published in the short-lived *Scanlan's Monthly*, became the first Thompson piece to earn the adjective he'd proudly wear the rest of his life: "gonzo."

1981 Jim Williams did not deny that he shot Danny Hansford in the office of his carefully restored and furnished Savannah mansion shortly after midnight. He just said Danny shot first (and second and third). It wasn't this murder that drew John Berendt

to Savannah to write *Midnight in the Garden of Good and Evil*: he had already fallen for the city and its mix of gossipy gentility and down-market style, and he already knew both the deceased, a volatile young hustler, and the wealthy man who would be convicted twice and acquitted once of shooting him. He was there to hear the tongues wagging before and after the crime, which is what makes his book so delicious—and kept it on the bestseller list for over four years.

1984 No one would think of George Orwell as a poet of the pastoral (he was drawn more to disgust), but listen to him: "Under the trees to the left of them the ground was misty with bluebells. The air seemed to kiss one's skin. It was the second of May." Readers of *1984* will likely recall this thrillingly unlikely rural interlude, when Winston meets Julia alone for the first time and she flings her scarlet chastity sash from the Junior Anti-Sex League aside in a sun-dappled forest grove. Of course their joys won't last—Winston knows they won't—but the liquid song of a thrush they hear in that grove stands in the novel as an uncorrupted life force that somehow exists outside the power of Big Brother.

1989 David Foster Wallace's new habit of chewing tobacco, he explained to Jonathan Franzen, "is stupid and dangerous, and involves goobing big dun honkers every thirty seconds."

May 3

BORN: 1469 Niccolò Machiavelli (*The Prince, Discourses on Livy*), Florence, Italy
1896 Dodie Smith (*I Capture the Castle, The 101 Dalmatians*), Whitefield, England
DIED: 1991 Jerzy Kozinski (*Being There, The Painted Bird*), 57, New York City

1810 Lord Byron did like to swim, and he liked to write about what he had swum. In 1809 he crossed the wide mouth of the Tagus River, near Lisbon, a feat his traveling companion John Hobhouse considered more daring than the one, undertaken a year later, that brought him greater fame, not least by his own efforts. Following the Greek myth of the youth Leander who swam every night to his lover, Hero, across the Hellespont, the strait dividing Europe from Asia, Byron and a ship's lieutenant attempted the crossing themselves. Driven back once by cold and current, they tried again a week later and made the four-mile crossing in a little more than an hour, an achievement he celebrated in a short poem and mentioned again nearly a decade later in *Don Juan*. The hazardous current, he wrote to one friend, made him "doubt whether Leander's conjugal powers must not have been exhausted in his passage to paradise."

1939 Malcolm Cowley, in the *New Republic*, on John Steinbeck's *The Grapes of Wrath*: "What one remembers most of all is Steinbeck's sympathy for the migrants—not pity, for that would mean he was putting himself above them; not love, for that would blind him to their faults, but rather a deep fellow feeling."

1978 After a visit to the Eastman archives in Rochester spent watching the silent films of Louise Brooks, "this shameless urchin tomboy, this unbroken, unbreakable porcelain filly" whose image had "run through my life like an unbroken thread," Kenneth Tynan returned for a second day of conversations at a nearby apartment building with a tiny, elderly woman, barefoot in a nightgown and bed jacket: Louise Brooks. "You're doing a terrible thing to me," she said. "I've been killing myself for twenty years, and you're going to bring me back to life." For three days she recalled her years of notoriety and obscurity, flirted with her younger fan, and shared her own love of the movies, with Tynan taking notes for his classic *New Yorker* profile "The Girl in the Black Helmet," which became the introduction to Brooks's own sharp-witted book of memoir and film criticism, *Lulu in Hollywood*.

BORN: **1939** Amos Oz (*Black Box, A Tale of Love and Darkness*), Jerusalem
1949 Graham Swift (*Waterland, Shuttlecock, Last Orders*), London
DIED: **1973** Jane Bowles (*Two Serious Ladies, In the Summer House*), 56, Malaga, Spain

1852 "What day of the month is it?" asked the Hatter, looking at his watch. "Alice considered a little, and then said, 'The fourth.' 'Two days wrong!' sighed the Hatter. 'I told you butter wouldn't suit the works!'" It's only natural that sensible Alice would know this date—it was the birthday of the girl who inspired the tale, Alice Liddell. She was ten when Charles Dodgson first told the story to the Liddell sisters on a rowboat, thirteen when he published *Alice's Adventures in Wonderland* under the name Lewis Carroll, and nineteen when its sequel, *Through the Looking-Glass,* appeared, which included an acrostic poem that spells out "Alice Pleasance Liddell."

1896 Why did Edith Wharton and her husband purchase a brownstone in an unfashionable Upper East Side neighborhood? "On account of the bicycling," she explained.

1928 Virginia Woolf found her fame "becoming vulgar and a nuisance. It means nothing; and yet takes one's time. Americans perpetually."

1929 "You must be married at once very obtrusively," Evelyn Waugh advised Henry Green on learning of his engagement. "A fashionable wedding is worth a four column review in the *Times Literary Supplement* to a novelist."

1953 Under the supervision of Dr. Humphry Osmond, a Saskatchewan psychiatrist who later coined the term "psychedelic," Aldous Huxley took mescaline for the first time at his home in Los Angeles. Overcome at first by lassitude, he walked with his wife and Osmond to the World's Biggest Drug Store at Beverly and La Cienega boulevards, where, in an aisle of art books, the brushstrokes of Botticelli overwhelmed him with a splendor that made a drive later that evening to see the hilly vistas over Hollywood an anticlimax by comparison, a vision that became the centerpiece of his account of the experience, *The Doors of Perception.*

1976 Mike Royko had been battling the Daley Machine in his *Chicago Daily News* column for years, so making fun of Frank Sinatra and his "army of flunkies" for the free, around-the-clock police protection the Chicago police provided the singer at his hotel was no big deal. But Ol' Blue Eyes didn't think it was funny, writing Royko on this day to call him a "pimp" and ask "why people don't spit in your eye three or four times a day." Royko obligingly printed the letter in his next column and then auctioned off the original to the highest bidder, Vie Carlson of Rockford, Illinois. Three decades later, Vie, whose son Brad, as it happens, was in the music business too, drumming for Cheap Trick under the stage name Bun E. Carlos, brought her letter onto the PBS show *Antiques Roadshow*, where it was appraised at $15,000.

May 5

BORN: 1813 Søren Kierkegaard (*Either/Or,*
Fear and Trembling), Copenhagen
1818 Karl Marx (*The German Ideology,*
The Communist Manifesto), Trier, Prussia
DIED: 1988 Michael Shaara (*The Killer Angels,*
For Love of the Game), 59, Tallahassee,
Fla.
1997 Murray Kempton (*Part of Our Time,*
The Briar Patch), 79, New York City

1593 With London scourged by plague and war, some looked for scapegoats among the city's immigrants, and on this night a vicious poem was posted on the wall of a Dutch church, warning "you strangers that inhabit this land" that "we'll cut your throats, in your temples praying." The poem's authors are unknown, but they were surely playgoers: the poem was signed "Tamberlaine," the murderous hero of one Christopher Marlowe play, and it alluded to two of his other violent dramas: *The Jew of Malta* and *The Massacre of Paris*. The quarters of playwright Thomas Kyd were searched, but they turned up evidence of a different crime: atheist papers that Kyd, under torture, said were Marlowe's. Ordered arrested for heresy on the 18th, Marlowe was dead on the 30th, killed in a mysterious brawl that has ever since been suspected to be an assassination.

1857 At a dinner at Boston's Parker House, assembled by the publisher Moses Phillips, eight leading literary men, including Emerson, Longfellow, Lowell, and Oliver Wendell Holmes, met to found the *Atlantic*. "Imagine your uncle at the head of such guests," blushed Phillips to his niece two weeks later. "It was the proudest moment of my life."

1862 Arthur Blomfield, in search of a "young Gothic draughtsman who could restore and design churches and rectory-homes," hired as an architectural assistant at £110 a year twenty-one-year-old Thomas Hardy, who had arrived in London three weeks before.

1943 Five days after his discharge from the army after recovering from a nervous breakdown, Mervyn Peake wrote to a friend he had made just before the war, Graham Greene, "I'll be able to concentrate on Gormenghast. It's a grand feeling." Already known by this time as a painter and as "the greatest illustrator of his day," Peake had spoken before to Greene of the novel he'd been working on. But when he sent him the final draft a few months later, Greene's response was devastating: "I was very disappointed in a lot of it and frequently wanted to wring your neck because it seems to me you were spoiling a first class book by laziness." Greene hadn't given up on the book, though—he suggested they "duel" about it over whiskey—and after Peake's thorough revisions it was published as *Titus Groan*, the first volume in his long-loved cult classic, the Gormenghast Trilogy.

1946 Caroline Gordon, in the *New York Times*, on *The Portable Faulkner*: "He writes like a man who so loves his land that he is fearful for the well-being of every creature that springs from it."

BORN: **1856** Sigmund Freud (*The Interpretation of Dreams*), Freiberg in Mähren, Austrian Empire
1914 Randall Jarrell (*The Woman at the Washington Zoo*), Nashville, Tenn.
DIED: **1862** Henry David Thoreau (*The Maine Woods*), 44, Concord, Mass.
1919 L. Frank Baum (*The Wonderful Wizard of Oz, Ozma of Oz*), 62, Hollywood, Calif.

1850 Emily Dickinson—at least at the age of nineteen—wasn't always a homebody by choice. With her mother laid up by acute neuralgia, Dickinson sat attentively by her side and remained there even when temptation called. "I heard a well-known rap," she wrote a teenage confidant, "and a friend I love *so* dearly came and asked me to ride in the woods, the sweet still woods, and I wanted to exceedingly—I told him I could not go, and he said he was disappointed, he wanted me very much." She conquered her tears, calling it "a kind of helpless victory," and returned to her work, "humming a little air" until her mother was asleep, but then she "cried with all my might." The young man who invited her out has never been identified.

1871 When the great man arrived in the Yosemite Valley, the word went out: "Emerson is here!" John Muir joined the crowd around him but was too awed to approach. Later, though, he sent a note inviting Emerson to stay for "a month's worship" in the woods, and the next morning Emerson rode up to the hill to meet the young man. No longer shy, Muir made an eager guide and insisted that on his last night in the valley the author of "Nature," though sixty-seven, more than twice his age, camp out with him under the giant trees of the Mariposa Grove. Emerson agreed, but when evening came those less adventurous in his party urged him instead into the staler comforts of an inn, disappointing Muir that his hero "was now a child in the hands of his affectionate but sadly civilized friends."

1908 The imaginative materials that Marcel Proust would weave into the volumes of *In Search of Lost Time* started to come together in 1908. "Sickened" by his efforts to pastiche the styles of Balzac, Flaubert, and others, he turned instead to writing a series of fragmentary pieces. The subjects might have seemed disconnected, but his later readers would certainly recognize in them the connective tissue of his vast novel. "I have in hand," he described the elements to a friend either on this day or the previous one, "a study on the nobility, a Parisian novel, an essay on Sainte-Beuve and Flaubert, an essay on women, an essay on pederasty (not easy to publish), a study on stained-glass windows, a study on tombstones, a study on the novel."

1948 Italo Calvino, in *L'Unità*, on Primo Levi's *Se questo è un uomo* (*Survival in Auschwitz*): a book of "authentic narrative power, which will remain . . . amongst the most beautiful of the literature of the Second World War."

May 7

BORN: 1931 Gene Wolfe (*The Book of the New Sun*), New York City
1943 Peter Carey (*Oscar and Lucinda*), Bacchus Marsh, Australia
DIED: 1941 Sir James George Frazer (*The Golden Bough*), 87, Cambridge, England
1994 Clement Greenberg ("Avant-Garde and Kitsch"), 85, New York City

1911 The life of Albert Mathé, French journalist, began in 1943 at the age of thirty-two, when false papers and an identity card under that name were created by the French Resistance for Albert Camus, including a forged birth certificate that said Mathé was born on this day in Choisy-le-Roi, France, far from Camus's own birthplace in Algeria. Camus had begun the war as a declared pacifist and spent its first years working on his novels *The Stranger* and *The Plague* while considering returning to Algeria, but late in 1943 he committed himself to staying in German-occupied Paris and joined the newspaper of the Resistance, *Combat*, as a writer and editor.

1932 At the height of his most prodigiously creative period, with *The Sound and the Fury* and *As I Lay Dying* recently published and *Light in August* on its way, William Faulkner reported for work as a screenwriter at the Culver City offices of Metro-Goldwyn-Mayer. Bleeding from a small head wound—he said he had been struck by a cab—he announced: "I've got an idea for Mickey Mouse" (not, as it happened, an MGM property). Or, he suggested, he could write for newsreels; "newsreels and Mickey Mouse, these are the only pictures I like." And then he went missing. The studio assumed he'd gone home to Mississippi, but two days later he reappeared, claiming to have been wandering in Death Valley, and commenced with the work that would occupy him—and take time away from his fiction—for much of the next dozen years.

1933 It's almost the same name, "a mere translation of the German compound," but for Marjorie Morgenstern, a sophomore at Hunter College sure she's destined to become a famous actress, it's a "white streak of revelation," "a name that could blaze and thunder on Broadway." "MARJORIE MORNINGSTAR," she prints in pencil in her Hunter College biology notebook. "Marjorie Morningstar, May 7, 1933," she tries signing in a sophisticated hand. A bestseller when it was published in 1955, Herman Wouk's *Marjorie Morningstar* has had a longer life than most blockbusters, winning readers for generations even though—or perhaps because—it's the story of Marjorie's transformation not into Marjorie Morningstar, star of stage and screen, but into Mrs. Milton Schwartz.

1948 Orville Prescott, in the *New York Times*, on Norman Mailer's *The Naked and the Dead*: "Mr. Mailer is as certain to become famous as any fledgling novelist can be. Unfortunately, he is just as likely to become notorious."

1968 After Allen Ginsberg, accompanying himself on harmonium, performed the Hare Krishna chant on *Firing Line*, host William F. Buckley drawled, "That's the most *unhurried* Krishna I've ever heard."

BORN: **1937** Thomas Pynchon (*The Crying of Lot 49, Gravity's Rainbow*), Glen Cove, N.Y.

1943 Pat Barker (*Regeneration, Union Street*), Thornaby-on-Tees, England

DIED: **1880** Gustave Flaubert (*Sentimental Education*), 58, Rouen, France

2012 Maurice Sendak (*Where the Wild Things Are, In the Night Kitchen*), 83, Danbury, Conn.

1897 "Silly these philanderings," Beatrice Webb wrote about her friend George Bernard Shaw. "He imagines that he gets to know women by making them in love with him. Just the contrary . . . His sensuality has all drifted into sexual vanity, delight in being the candle to the moths, with a dash of intellectual curiosity to give flavour."

1948 As he turned up the hill from Cannery Row, a few blocks from the Pacific Biological Laboratories he had founded, Ed Ricketts was blindsided in his 1936 Buick by the evening train from San Francisco. An indefatigable marine researcher and a larger-than-life presence in Monterey, Ricketts was at the center of an intellectual and social circle that included Joseph Campbell, Henry Miller, and, most prominently, John Steinbeck, who collaborated with Ricketts on *Sea of Cortez*, a travelogue and research record of their expedition in the Gulf of California, and made him famous as the model for "Doc" in *Cannery Row*. "The greatest man in the world is dying," Steinbeck drunkenly told a friend in New York as he waited for a flight west, "and there is nothing I can do."

1998 "Um." Stephen Glass hesitated. "I'm increasingly beginning to think I was duped." On this morning, Glass and his *New Republic* editor, Charles Lane, were on a call with two outside reporters who thought Glass's latest piece—on a fifteen-year-old hacker who blackmailed software companies after breaking into their databases, shouting, implausibly, "I want a Miata! I want a lifetime subscription to *Playboy*! Show me the money!"—was fabricated. Lane thought so too, and later that day he had Glass drive him to the building in suburban Bethesda where he claimed a "National Association of Hackers" conference had been held and where, clearly, no such thing had taken place. By the end of the day, Glass was suspended, and by the end of its investigation, the *New Republic* determined that at least two-thirds of the articles Glass had written for them were faked in some way.

NO YEAR Katniss Everdeen starts making dangerous bargains early in Suzanne Collins's *Hunger Games*. Near-starving on her family's scavenged diet, she can hardly wait until she reaches her twelfth birthday on this day, when she can sign up at the District 12 Justice Building for yearly credits for grain and oil for herself, her sister, and her mother. All she has to do in return: add three more slips of paper with her name on them to the big glass ball on reaping day, raising the chance she'll be selected for the dubious privilege of representing her district in the annual Hunger Games, from which only one of twenty-four children emerges alive.

May 9

BORN: 1920 Richard Adams (*Watership Down*, *Shardik*), Newbury, England
1938 Charles Simic (*The World Doesn't End*), Belgrade, Yugoslavia
DIED: 1981 Nelson Algren (*The Man with the Golden Arm*), 72, Sag Harbor, N.Y.
2008 Nuala O'Faolain (*Are You Somebody?*, *My Dream of You*), 68, Dublin

1931 "I was aware of the risk I was taking in opening Tanne's letter to you," Ingeborg Dinesen wrote to her son, Thomas, on this day. "Tanne" was her daughter, Karen, the Baroness Blixen, who was returning, reluctantly, to Denmark after the failure of her coffee farm in Kenya. The letter her mother opened was blunt—Karen would rather die than rejoin the bourgeois life she led, she declared, and she needed money from her family to begin her new life as a writer—but lovely too, with a clear-eyed sense of the beauty of the world she was leaving behind. It's a tone she captured again in the opening of *Out of Africa*, written in Denmark after she took the pen name Isak Dinesen: "I had a farm in Africa, at the foot of the Ngong Hills."

1939 Christopher Isherwood made his first visit to Washington, D.C.: "There is something charming, and even touching, about this city. For the size of the country it represents, it is absurdly small. The capital of a nation of shrewd, conservative farmers."

1950 A year and a half before, L. Ron Hubbard had written his fellow science fiction novelist Robert Heinlein that "I will soon, I hope give you a book . . . which details in full the mathematics of the human mind, solves all the problems of the ages, and gives six recipes for aphrodisiacs and plays the mouth organ with the left foot." And on this day Hubbard published a book that, mouth organ aside, more or less made those same claims: *Dianetics: The Modern Science of Mental Health*. John W. Campbell, the editor of *Astounding Science Fiction*, who published an advance excerpt of the book, thought the problems of the ages had indeed been solved. "I know dianetics is one of, if not the greatest, discovery in all Man's written and unwritten history," he wrote one author, and predicted to another it would win Hubbard the Nobel Peace Prize.

NO YEAR Pierre Broussard may be seventy, and he may have only been a "paper shuffler" when he committed his crimes of wartime collaboration all those years ago, but his vigilance is not to be taken lightly, especially when an assassin is on his trail. T. is the second man they've sent to do the job: the first ended up dead at the bottom of a ravine. Brian Moore was himself past seventy when *The Statement*, the second-to-last novel in his varied and always interesting career, came out, and in concocting this taut philosophical thriller he proved as wily and observant as his villain, Broussard, a former Nazi collaborator who has been protected by the Church ever since the war and now finds the walls closing in around him.

BORN: **1933** Barbara Taylor Bradford (*A Woman of Substance*), Leeds, England
1939 Robert Darnton (*The Forbidden Best-Sellers of Prerevolutionary France*), New York City

DIED: **1990** Walker Percy (*The Moviegoer, The Last Gentleman*), 73, Covington, La.
2003 Leonard Michaels (*I Would Have Saved Them if I Could*), 70, Berkeley, Calif.

1849 On one side: Washington Irving and Herman Melville, who, along with forty-seven other local dignitaries, implored William Charles Macready, the noted English actor, to attempt *Macbeth* again and assured his safety from the nativist hooligans who drove him off the stage at the Astor Place Opera House the night before with a barrage of eggs and vegetables and cries of "Down with the English hog!" On the other side: Ned Buntline, dime novelist, street bully, and future heavy-drinking temperance activist, who roused a mob of 10,000 supporters of Macready's rival American thespian Edwin Forrest into the theater and the surrounding streets. Macready survived the performance, but two dozen or so ruffians and bystanders were killed by soldiers shooting into what became known as the Astor Place Riot.

1907 Kenneth Grahame, banker and writer, had been telling bedtime stories about moles and water-rats to his difficult son, Alastair (known to all as "Mouse"), for a few years, but he first began to write them down in a birthday letter to Mouse, who had been dispatched with his governess on a separate holiday from his parents. Along with gifts and apologies for not being there with him, Grahame added news of the character who would soon become the center of *The Wind in the Willows* (and whose impulsive behavior may have been inspired by young Alastair himself): "Have you heard about the Toad? He was never taken prisoner at all." He had stolen a motor-car and vanished "without even saying Poop-poop! . . . I fear he is a bad low animal."

1957 Explaining she was "too well educated for the job," Zora Neale Hurston's supervisor fired her from her last full-time employment, as a library clerk in the space program at Patrick Air Force Base in Cocoa Beach, Florida.

2001 James Wood, in the *New Republic*, on J. M. Coetzee's *Disgrace*: "It sometimes reads as if it were the winner of an exam whose challenge was to create the perfect specimen of a very good contemporary novel."

2012 David Rakoff's essays were hard to separate from his voice; many of them began, in fact, as monologues on *This American Life*, the radio show he contributed to from its beginnings in the mid-'90s. Along the way, he told stories of the cancer that had first struck him at age twenty-two and then returned two decades later, and in his last appearance on the show, at a live performance recorded on this day, three months before he died, Rakoff, once a dancer, with his left arm rendered useless by his tumor and surgery, danced again, alone onstage, to Nat King Cole's "What'll I Do?"

May 11

1831 On May 12 New York's *Mercantile Advertiser* announced a notable arrival in the city the previous day: "We understand that two magistrates, Messrs. de Beaumont and de Tonqueville, have arrived in the ship *Havre*, sent here by order of the Minister of the Interior, to examine the various prisons in our country, and make a report on their return to France." The two men did indeed produce a report on American prisons after their journey through the young republic, but two years later, one of them, whose name was properly spelled Alexis de Tocqueville, published the first volume of the book that was his true purpose for the visit, *Democracy in America*. (In 2010, Peter Carey used the travelers' descriptions of their arrival in New York in his novel inspired by de Tocqueville, *Parrot and Olivier in America*.)

1924 Drawn to a new apartment in Brooklyn Heights by his first love, a Danish sailor whose father lived in the building, Hart Crane was also attracted by another local feature: the view of the Brooklyn Bridge, "the most superb piece of construction in the modern world," he wrote his mother on this day. "For the first time in many weeks I am beginning to further elaborate my plans for my Bridge poem." The connection of his new home to what would become his masterwork, *The Bridge*, only increased when he learned that his own windows were the very ones from which Washington Roebling, invalided by an accident during the building of the support towers, had overseen by telescope the construction of the bridge he and his father had designed.

1996 The climb should have been over. At around seven the night before, Jon Krakauer had stumbled back to his tent after summiting Everest and descending through a gathering storm. But when he woke this morning he learned that one of his guides, Andy Harris, had disappeared; another, Rob Hall, was still on the summit ridge; and three or more of the climbers they had led were dead. By the end of this sunny, windy, and miserable day of searching and waiting, eight climbers were lost on the mountain—and two miraculously saved—and Krakauer was left, in despair and guilt, to sort out what went wrong in *Into Thin Air*.

BORN: 1812 Edward Lear (*The Owl and the Pussycat, A Book of Nonsense*), Holloway, England
1916 Albert Murray (*The Omni-Americans, Stomping the Blues*), Nokomis, Ala.
DIED: 1907 J.-K. Huysmans (*Against Nature, The Damned*), 59, Paris
2008 Oakley Hall (*Warlock, The Downhill Racers*), 87, Nevada City, Calif.

1897 Before he met Lou Andreas-Salomé, the thirty-six-year-old married intellectual who had been called by Friedrich Nietzsche—once her spurned suitor—"the *smartest* woman I ever knew," at a friend's Munich apartment on this day, René Maria Rilke, only twenty-one, had courted her with anonymous notes and poems, and after their meeting he continued his seduction with a flurry of letters. Within weeks they were lovers—she admiring his "human qualities" more than his poems—and by the fall she had convinced him to change his name from the affected-sounding René to the "beautiful, simple, and German" Rainer.

1904 Following disappointing sales for his previous two books, *The House Behind the Cedars* and *The Marrow of Tradition*, Houghton Mifflin turned down Charles W. Chesnutt's new novel, *The Colonel's Dream*, regretting that "the public has failed to respond adequately to your other admirable work in this line." Agreeing with Houghton that "the public does not care for books in which the principal characters are colored people," Chesnutt concentrated instead on his thriving legal stenography business, setting aside a literary career that had made him the most prominent African American novelist yet and that later generations would recognize produced some of the most incisive fiction of its era.

1948 Adventurer Apsley Cherry-Garrard, author of *The Worst Journey in the World*, purchased the "Aylesford copy" of a Shakespeare First Folio for £7,100.

1957 Margaret S. Libby, in the *New York Herald Tribune*, on Dr. Seuss's *The Cat in the Hat*: "Restricting his vocabulary to a mere 223 words (all in the reading range of a six- or seven-year-old) and shortening his verse has given a certain riotous and extravagant unity, a wild restraint that is pleasing."

1961 A fire in the Hollywood Hills destroyed the home of Aldous and Laura Huxley, sparing only a few clothes and books, a violin, the manuscript of Aldous's *Island*, and, oddly, their firewood.

2009 It had been over three years since George R. R. Martin promised in a postscript to *A Feast of Crows*, the long-awaited and frustratingly unresolved fourth volume of his Song of Fire and Ice series, that the fifth book in the series would be done within a year, and his readers were getting restless, commenting impatiently online and creating entire websites with names like *Finish the Book, George*. Finally on this day his fellow author Neil Gaiman weighed in, responding to a reader who asked if Martin and fellow series authors had a responsibility to the readers waiting for their next book with the memorable phrase "George R. R. Martin is not your bitch." In 2011, book five in the series, *A Dance with Dragons*, was published.

May 13

BORN: 1907 Daphne du Maurier (*Rebecca,*
Jamaica Inn), London
1944 Armistead Maupin (*Tales of the City,*
The Night Listener), Washington, D.C.
DIED: 1916 Sholem Aleichem (*Tevye and His*
Daughters), 57, New York City
2001 R. K. Narayan (*Malgudi Days, The*
English Teacher), 94, Chennai, India

1860 With Garibaldi and his Redshirts just days away from conquering Sicily for united Italy, Don Fabrizio, an aging Sicilian prince, can foresee the inevitable but is unwilling to abandon his familiar pleasures, unlike his favorite nephew, Tancredi, who joins with the Redshirts in hopes of saving the aristocracy: "If we want things to stay as they are," he tells his uncle, "things will have to change." Giuseppe di Lampedusa, himself a Sicilian prince, wrote *The Leopard*, based on the life of his grandfather, at the end of a solitary, bookish life. Rejected by publishers before his death in 1958, it became the most popular and admired Italian novel of the century, a subtle and graceful portrait of character in the middle of historical upheaval.

1871 "You will not understand at all," Arthur Rimbaud, age sixteen, wrote his teacher and mentor George Izambard, but for a poet "the idea is to reach the unknown by the derangement of all the senses."

1937 J. R. R. Tolkien agreed that illustrations could be added to the U.S. edition of *The Hobbit*, so long as they were not "from or influenced by the Disney studios (for all whose works I have a heartfelt loathing)."

1958 Unlike Hamlet's birth, on the same day his father defeated old Fortinbras, the birth of Edgar Sawtelle on this date marked no special occasion, except the arrival of a first child to a mother and father who'd begun to think they might never have one. But the Sawtelles' family drama soon mirrors Hamlet's, with the suspicious death of Edgar's father and the quick insinuation of his uncle Claude into the bed of his mother, Trudy. David Wroblewski built *The Story of Edgar Sawtelle* from the bones of Shakespeare's tragedy, but he added another lineage: "the Sawtelles" refers both to Edgar's family and to the breed of dogs they have raised, bred for a near-telepathic level of companionship that mute Edgar understands better than anyone else. And like young Fortinbras entering the scene of slaughter at *Hamlet*'s end, those canine Sawtelles will remain to survive the collapse of the Sawtelle line.

1961 William Maxwell, in *The New Yorker*, on a reissue of Francis Kilvert's *Diary*: "The day-by-day record he kept is not all of equal interest; it is not above silliness; it contains sentiments that are not now acceptable (some are even shocking) and a good many 'literary' descriptions that don't come off. But these are minor flaws, no journal is without them, and so long as English diaries are read, Kilvert's humble and uneventful life will not pass altogether away."

BORN: 1930 María Irene Fornés (*And What of the Night?*), Havana

1965 Eoin Colfer (*Artemis Fowl*), Wexford, Ireland

DIED: 1912 August Strindberg (*Miss Julie, The Red Room*), 63, Stockholm

1979 Jean Rhys (*Wide Sargasso Sea*), 88, Exeter, England

1920 Katherine Mansfield, in the *Athenaeum*, on Compton Mackenzie's *The Vanity Girl*: "We should not waste space upon so pretentious and stupid a book were it not that we have believed in his gifts and desire to protest that he should so betray them."

1944 For half a dozen years, Ayn Rand tried to meet with Frank Lloyd Wright to discuss the novel she was writing about an architect. "My hero is not you," she assured him. "But his spirit is yours." Wright proved elusive, and said he didn't like the name "Roark" or Roark's red hair in the sample she sent, but she forged on with the book, and in April 1944 she received a letter from Wright. "My Dear Miss Rand: I've read every word of *The Fountainhead*. Your thesis is *the* great one," he wrote. "So I suppose you will be set up in the marketplace and burned as a witch." "Thank you," she replied on this day, but she wasn't worried: "I think I am made of asbestos." And then she came to the point: "Now, would you be willing to build a house for me?" (He designed one, but it was never built.)

1962 "I was cured all right": Alex's cheekily ironic final line in Stanley Kubrick's *A Clockwork Orange* matches the ending that first greeted American readers of Anthony Burgess's novel. But the original U.K. edition (published on this day) includes an additional, more hopeful chapter in which Alex contemplates giving up the droogs and becoming a husband and father someday. That chapter was restored to all editions in the 1980s after Burgess complained that his American editor had cut it against his will, but the editor remembered otherwise; Burgess, he said, didn't like the "Pollyanna ending" then any more than he did. The controversy was unresolved, but Burgess's ambivalence about the ending is clear in a note written just before the final chapter on his 1961 typescript of the novel: "Should we end here? An optional 'epilogue' follows."

202- Packed with characters, locations, and narrative styles, *A Visit from the Goon Squad*, Jennifer Egan's prize-sweeping novel (or collection of linked stories, if you prefer), is also a book of empty spaces, the long, unnarrated stretches of time between her stories that connect them as strongly as the events she describes. In the penultimate chapter—told in PowerPoint slides—time stretches out into the 2020s, when the teenage son of Sasha Blake, the character with whom the novel began, has become obsessed with the pauses in pop songs, the one- or two-second gaps—when the song seems to be over but isn't—that hold within their empty spaces the emotions of anticipation, release, and relief.

May 15

BORN: 1890 Katherine Anne Porter (*Pale Horse, Pale Rider*), Indian Creek, Tex.
1967 Laura Hillenbrand (*Seabiscuit, Unbroken*), Fairfax, Va.
DIED: 1886 Emily Dickinson (*Poems*), 55, Amherst, Mass.
1996 John Hawkes (*The Beetle Leg, The Lime Twig*), 72, Providence, R.I.

1853 The Reverend Arthur Nicholls, his proposal of marriage rejected by Charlotte Brontë, broke down while officiating at a public communion service. (She accepted his renewed suit the following year.)

1939 The fame of Isaac Babel in the Soviet Union and abroad could not protect him when Stalin's secret police finally came to the door of his dacha on this morning and took him to the Lubyanka prison, where he endured six months of interrogation and was forced to write a bloodstained confession before being summoned in January to a twenty-minute nighttime trial in the private offices of Lavrenti Beria, the chief of Stalin's secret police. He was executed in the early hours of the following morning, though his family was not told of his death until fourteen years later. "I was not given time to finish," he was heard to say at his arrest, a plea he repeated to Beria when he made his final request, "Let me finish my work."

1950 Mountain climbing was a different affair in those days. When Maurice Herzog and his team of French climbers set out for the Himalayas, they had no reliable map and weren't even sure which mountain they would attempt. After weeks of exploring, they ruled out the apparently inaccessible peak of Dhaulagiri and settled on the still-mysterious Annapurna, for which Herzog set out on this morning. He returned more than a month later, having lost his toes and most of his fingers to frostbite and having become with Louis Lachenal the first to scale an 8,000-meter peak. Higher peaks have since been conquered, but Herzog's *Annapurna* remains at the pinnacle of mountaineering lore.

1956 Circumstance—the discovery of a letter not meant to be sent, a mishap with a hot air balloon—can be almost as dangerous as desire in the world of Ian McEwan. In *The Innocent*, Leonard Marnham, a young Englishman in divided Berlin at the height of the Cold War, didn't plan to be running around the city with two equipment cases filled with the dismembered body of the ex-husband of his German fiancée, Maria, but circumstance and desire brought him to that desperate point. And on this day they bring him to another, when, as Maria waves to him from across the airport as he leaves for London, he sees an American friend of theirs arrive unexpectedly at her side, and he makes a sudden decision that irreparably alters the rest of their lives.

1981 Valentine Cunningham, in the *TLS*, on Salman Rushdie's *Midnight's Children*: "What makes it so vertiginously exciting a reading experience is the way it takes in not just the whole apple cart of India but also, and this with the unflagging zest of a *Tristram Shandy*, the business of being a novel at all."

May 16

BORN: 1912 Studs Terkel (*Division Street, Hard Times*), New York City
1929 Adrienne Rich (*Diving into the Wreck*), Baltimore, Md.
DIED: 1928 Edmund Gosse (*Father and Son, Gossip in a Library*), 78, London
1984 Irwin Shaw (*The Young Lions; Rich Man, Poor Man*), 71, Davos, Switzerland

1683 Having lived alone for four and twenty years (by the reckoning of his wooden calendar) after his shipwreck off an unknown island in the Americas, Robinson Crusoe is startled by the sound of a gunshot offshore. He imagines another ship is in distress and sets a fire to signal to its survivors, but when he comes in sight of the wreck he can see there are none. Consumed by longing that one, just one, could have survived to give him a Christian companion, he salvages what he can from the ship in the following days. Shirts and fire tongs are of great use, but the bags full of gold pieces? In his isolation, they are of no more value than the dirt under his feet.

1836 On the marriage bond for his wedding to his cousin Virginia Clemm, Edgar Allan Poe and his witness, Thomas W. Cleland, attested that the bride "is of the full age of twenty-one years." She had not yet turned fourteen.

1863 At the time, *Romola*, George Eliot's fourth novel, seemed likely to mark the height of her success. She turned down £10,000 to serialize the book, "the most magnificent offer ever yet made for a novel," but accepted a similar amount later, setting herself a double challenge: write a novel under the deadline pressure of a magazine, and set it not in present-day England, like her others, but in fifteenth-century Florence. The book was a struggle—"I began *Romola* as a young woman," she said, "I finished it an old woman"—and on this day, nearing the end, she wrote in her journal about the death of her villain with understandable high spirits, "Finished Part XIII. Killed Tito in great excitement!"

1934 John Dos Passos, in the *New Republic*, on Robert Cantwell's *The Land of Plenty*: "To tell truly, and not romantically or sentimentally, about the relation between men and machines, and to describe the machine worker, are among the most important tasks before novelists today. The job has only begun. I think Robert Cantwell is as likely to discover a method of coping with machinery, which is now the core of human life, as any man writing today."

May 17

BORN: 1873 Dorothy Richardson (*Pointed Roofs*, *Pilgrimage*), Abington, England
1939 Gary Paulsen (*Hatchet*, *Harris and Me*), Minneapolis

DIED: 1987 Gunnar Myrdal (*The American Dilemma*), 88, Danderyd, Sweden
2007 Lloyd Alexander (*The Black Cauldron*), 83, Drexel Hill, Pa.

1824 In the drawing room of the publisher John Murray, six men committed one of literature's most notorious acts of destruction. The body of Lord Byron, their "mad, bad, and dangerous to know" friend, was on its way back from Greece, where he had died of fever, and they were in possession of a document that could determine his legacy: his *Memoirs*, entrusted to his friend Tom Moore. Moore wanted them published, but after days of argument John Cam Hobhouse, Byron's oldest friend, who hadn't read the memoirs but feared the effect of their scandalous content on "Lord Byron's honor & fame" (and perhaps on his own political career), won out. To Moore's dismay that Hobhouse could destroy the book "without even opening it, as if it were a pest bag," the pages were torn from their bindings and fed to the fire.

1890 In the *Aberdeen Saturday Pioneer*, a short-lived newspaper in South Dakota he largely wrote himself (and the latest in a series of failed business ventures), L. Frank Baum on this day published "Beautiful Displays of Novelties which Rival in Attractiveness the Famed Museums of the World," an appreciation of a budding art form: the store display window. His interest in the subject didn't end there. In 1907 he founded both *The Show Window: A Journal of Practical Window Trimming for the Merchant and Professional* and the National Association of Window Trimmers of America, launching a promising career he only gave up when his children's books, beginning with *Father Goose* and continuing on to Oz, allowed him to devote himself to writing at the age of forty-four.

1922 Robert Littell, in the *New Republic*, on F. Scott Fitzgerald's *The Beautiful and Damned*: "Mr. Fitzgerald has a very small allowance of tenderness, and even less of pity, but for every pint of them his mixture contains gallons of blistering hatred. He hates, to be sure, just the things that I do, but it is a perilous mood to maintain."

1928 Evelyn Waugh wrote to the *TLS* with a complaint: "Your reviewer refers to me throughout as 'Miss Waugh.' My Christian name, I know, is occasionally regarded by people of limited social experience as belonging exclusively to one or other sex; but it is unnecessary to go further into my book than the paragraph charitably placed inside the wrapper for the guidance of unleisured critics, to find my name with its correct prefix of 'Mr.'"

BORN: **1048** Omar Khayyam (*Rubaiyat*),
Nishapur, Iran
1944 W. G. Sebald (*The Emigrants, The Rings of Saturn*), Wertach, Germany
DIED: **1909** George Meredith (*The Egoist, Modern Love*), 81, Box Hill, England
2006 Gilbert Sorrentino (*Mulligan Stew, Aberration of Starlight*), 77, Brooklyn

1916 Though often placed on May 16, 1915—perhaps so it would fall exactly forty years to the day before James Agee's own early death—it was on this morning that Hugh James Agee, known as Jay, driving at high speed, turned his Ford over on the Clinton Pike on his way back to Knoxville and died in the crash. His adoring son James, just six and known then as Rufus, spent much of his life putting the events of that day into words, culminating in *A Death in the Family*, his autobiographical novel that won the Pulitzer Prize for Fiction when it was released unfinished after his own death, in which he remembered seeing his father's body at the funeral two days later: "His face looked more remote than before and much more ordinary and it was as if he were tired or bored."

1943 At the Lincoln University commencement ceremonies, Langston Hughes, on the stage to receive an honorary doctorate from his alma mater, "got both hungry and sleepy" as Carl Sandburg spoke on Abraham Lincoln for three and a half hours.

1945 On this afternoon, Laura Chase, age twenty-five, sharply turned the wheel of her sister's car with her white-gloved hands and drove off the side of a Toronto bridge into the ravine below. Laura's death, reported first by her sister, Iris, and then in the flat tones of the *Toronto Star*, is just the first piece in the ingeniously constructed puzzle of Margaret Atwood's Booker Prize–winning novel, *The Blind Assassin*, a nest of boxes made of family and national history, science fiction, and newspaper reports that finally reveals at its center the traditional fictional engines of passion and betrayal.

2000 Was it as a gambler or a journalist that James McManus felt himself luckier when, having gone to Las Vegas to cover the World Series of Poker for *Harper's*, he found himself at the final table of the WSOP's no-limit hold-'em main event? Parlaying $4,000 the magazine hadn't intended as a bankroll into play-in fees, McManus, a forty-year veteran of home poker games, played his way into the main event and then outlasted dozens of the game's legends to join, among others, T. J. Cloutier, author of McManus's instructional bible, *Championship No-Limit and Pot-Limit Hold'em*, at the final table. McManus's eventual fifth-place finish (and $247,760 prize) made for the ultimate insider account, which, in *Positively Fifth Street*, he expanded to include the story that brought him out to Nevada in the first place, the murder of Vegas scion Ted Binion.

May 19

BORN: 1932 Elena Poniatowska (*Massacre in Mexico; Here's to You, Jesusa*), Paris
1941 Nora Ephron (*Heartburn, Wallflower at the Orgy*), New York City
DIED: 1864 Nathaniel Hawthorne (*The Blithedale Romance*), 59, Plymouth, N.H.
1935 T. E. Lawrence (*Seven Pillars of Wisdom, The Mint*), 46, Dorset, England

1821 The *Literary Gazette* on Percy Bysshe Shelley's *Queen Mab*: "We have spoken of Shelley's genius, and it is doubtless of a high order; but when we look at the purposes to which it is directed, and contemplate the infernal character of all its efforts, our souls revolt with tenfold horror at the energy it exhibits, and we feel as if one of the darkest of the fiends had been clothed with a human body, to enable him to gratify his enmity against the human race, and as if the supernatural atrocity of his hate were only heightened by his power to do injury."

1857 In a scene, recorded on this day in the *Goncourt Journals*, that encapsulates much of nineteenth-century French literary life, the poet Charles Baudelaire, "coming out of a tart's rooms," met the critic Charles-Augustin Sainte-Beuve. "Ah! I know where you're going!" said Baudelaire. "And I know where you've been," replied Sainte-Beuve. "But look," he added, "I'd rather go and have a chat with you," and so they retired to a café, where Sainte-Beuve declared his disgust with philosophers and their interest in the immortality of the soul, which they know "doesn't exist any more than God does," in an atheistic tirade so fierce, in the words of the Goncourts, "as to bring every game of dominoes in the café to a stop."

1906 The *Spectator* on Upton Sinclair's *The Jungle*: "This is not a book to be read for pleasure or recreation. It deals with the elementary problems of life so frankly that it can only be recommended with a grave caution, since there are scenes in it so horrible as to leave an indelible impression on the mind of the reader."

1927 T. E. Lawrence spent the last half of his life attempting to escape his fame as "Lawrence of Arabia," or at least manage it from a distance. Having had his cover blown when he first attempted to disappear into the ranks by enlisting in the Royal Air Force as "John Hume Ross," he signed up again as "T. E. Shaw" and by 1927, as *Revolt in the Desert*, the abridged version of his memoir *Seven Pillars of Wisdom*, was selling tens of thousands of copies a week, he was stationed as an aircraftman second class in Karachi, overhauling engines while corresponding with Churchill, E. M. Forster, and Bernard Shaw (who may have inspired his assumed name). In one letter he explained his time abroad as "exile, endured for a specific purpose, to let the book-fuss pass over"; in another, on this day, he wrote, "I languish for my sins in publishing a little bit of the *Seven Pillars* called *Revolt in the Desert*."

BORN: 1806 John Stuart Mill (*Autobiography, On Liberty*), London

1952 Walter Isaacson (*Steve Jobs, Einstein, Benjamin Franklin*), New Orleans

DIED: 1956 Max Beerbohm (*Zuleika Dobson*), 83, Rapallo, Italy

2002 Stephen Jay Gould (*The Mismeasure of Man*), 60, New York City

1845 "Thursday, May 20, 1845, 3-4½ p.m." With this notation, which became his standard habit to mark their visits, Robert Browning recorded on the envelope of her most recent letter his first meeting with Elizabeth Barrett at her home—indeed, in her bedroom, for she was an invalid—on Wimpole Street. He had first written her in January in a letter that began, "I love your verses with all my heart, Miss Barrett," but there were many barriers in the way of their meeting: her famously tyrannical father, violently skeptical of the prospect of marriage for his sickly daughter, as well as her own fear that she'd merely "make a company-show of an infirmity" for Browning and "hold a beggar's hat for sympathy." Meet they did, though, on this afternoon, the first of ninety visits—always with her father safely out of the house—before their elopement to Italy.

1915 E. M. Forster had chicken pox.

1953 Andrew Sean Greer's *The Story of a Marriage* is not the story of the marriage that takes place on this day between Annabel DeLawn and William Platt, just before William, finally drafted, is shipped out to train for the war in Korea. The book is, instead, the story of Pearlie and Holland Cook, married a few years earlier, after Holland's own war in the Pacific. But as Pearlie learns, no marriage—not her marriage, at least—is between just two people. In Greer's intricate and often indirect tale, she discovers that her beautiful husband has drawn desire to him from more sources than her, and returned it too, and so she forces another couple together—Annabel and William—in the hope that her husband will then focus his desire on just one.

1990 Harry Bosch's Sunday morning begins with a call about a body in a pipe, the body of a man he knew twenty years before. When Michael Connelly, a young crime reporter on the *Los Angeles Times*, introduced LAPD Detective Harry Bosch in his first novel, *The Black Echo*, he gave Bosch a history of high-profile cases that had made him a pariah in his own department. The body in the pipe takes him even further back, to the nightmare of his time as a "tunnel rat" in Vietnam, in a case where the strongest clues were planted years before, the last of which Bosch, fittingly, tracks down at the funeral of a fellow soldier at a veterans cemetery on Memorial Day.

NO YEAR In *Fifty Shades of Grey,* Christian Grey sends Ana Steele, after her final exam on Thomas Hardy, a three-volume first edition of *Tess of the d'Urbervilles* that must be worth a fortune.

May 21

BORN: 1688 Alexander Pope (*The Rape of the Lock, The Dunciad*), London
1926 Robert Creeley (*For Love, Hello, Later*), Arlington, Mass.
DIED: 1926 Ronald Firbank (*Valmouth, The Flower Beneath the Foot*), 40, Rome
2000 Barbara Cartland (*The Elusive Earl, Not Love Alone*), 98, Hatfield, England

1749 Writing on this day to her young lover, the marquise du Châtelet described the daily regimen she had to follow to finish her life's work, her translation of Newton's *Principia Mathematica*, by her deadline, the birth of her fourth child less than four months away: wake at eight or nine and work till three; stop for coffee and then work again from four to ten, when she dined alone and took time to talk with Voltaire, the former lover with whom she was sharing a Paris house; and then back to work from midnight to five in the morning. She did finish the book, just before she died, as she had feared, of complications from the birth of her daughter. Her book nearly perished too, but was finally published ten years later, and it remains the standard translation of Newton in France.

1813 By the time Henri Beyle rejoined Napoleon's army at the Battle of Bautzen, the witty urban dandy was sick of war. He had survived the disastrous retreat from Russia the previous winter, and the prospect of observing more carnage, even from a comfortable distance, made him ill. "It's like a man who has drunk too much punch and has been forced to throw it up; he is disgusted with it for life." Of the battle, in which over 200,000 soldiers clashed and 20,000 were lost, he wrote, "We see quite well, from noon to three o'clock, everything that can be seen of a battle, which is to say, nothing," a vision he doubtless recalled when, writing under his pen name of Stendhal two decades later, he described the chaos of Waterloo in the early pages of *The Charterhouse of Parma*.

1924 One of the details in "Tiny Mummies," Tom Wolfe's mockery of *The New Yorker*, that most irritated those it mocked was its gleeful furtherance of the long-standing rumor that William Shawn, *The New Yorker*'s editor, had as a child in Chicago been considered as a possible victim by the murderers Leopold and Loeb before they killed his classmate Bobby Franks on this day. Was it so? Wolfe claimed he saw in court records the name "William" on a list prepared by the killers, but Renata Adler, in *Gone*, was adamant there was no such thing, and the magazine's most recent historian, Ben Yagoda, called the story "nonsense." But Lillian Ross, in her memoir of her long, secret relationship with Shawn, said Shawn told her Leopold and Loeb had indeed come to his house and looked him over "as a candidate for what they were going to do." The deeply private Shawn, of course, never said a word about it on the record.

BORN: **1859** Arthur Conan Doyle (*A Study in Scarlet*, *The Sign of the Four*), Edinburgh
1907 Hergé (*Red Rackham's Treasure*, *Tintin in Tibet*), Etterbeek, Belgium
DIED: **1885** Victor Hugo (*Les Misérables*, *The Hunchback of Notre Dame*), 83, Paris
2010 Martin Gardner (*The Ambidextrous Universe*), 95, Norman, Okla.

1867 Fleeing the grasping of creditors and family, Fyodor Dostoyevsky and his new wife, Anna, embarked on a European trip funded by pawning the jewelry and silver of her dowry. Dostoyevsky held out a mad hope that he might cure their debts at the roulette table, and early in the trip he set out alone for the resort town of Bad Homburg, planning to return in just a few days. After nearly a week of losing, he wrote his wife, "If one plays coolly, calmly and with calculation, *it is quite impossible to lose!* I swear—it is an absolute impossibility!" (The problem, he added, was that he couldn't keep calm.) He assured her he was leaving Homburg, though if he could just stay four more days he'd be certain to win everything back! He did stay, continued to lose, and over their next few years of travel pawned their wedding rings countless times.

1942 When Naomi Nakane sits down in 1972 to read the unsent letters her aunt Emily wrote to Naomi's mother thirty years before, it's like finding her "childhood house filled with rooms and corners I've never seen." Written from Vancouver to Japan, where Naomi's mother had returned to take care of their own mother before the attack on Pearl Harbor divided the countries by war, the letters begin with Emily's wariness at the early signs that some Canadians think the Japanese families among them are enemies and end abruptly when the family packs to leave their home on this day for a tiny abandoned town in the interior, the first step in an odyssey of exclusion that lasts well beyond the war in Joy Kogawa's novel *Obasan*, based in part on her own family's history.

1944 J. R. R. Tolkien, still a decade from publishing *The Lord of the Rings*, mentioned to a friend that he had brought Frodo "to the very brink of Mordor," while Gollum, he added, "continues to develop into a most intriguing character."

1980 Children's book editor Ursula Nordstrom confessed to her author Mary Stolz her wish she "could look EXACTLY like Dick Cavett": "I dote on his neat, tidy spare face."

May 23

1948 In an "outrageously decrepit bi-motor" airplane with fifteen cases of Moose Brand Beer stowed in the canoe lashed to the plane's belly, Farley Mowat was flown three hundred miles northwest from Churchill, Manitoba, into Canada's northern Barrenlands with a government mission to "spend a year or two living with a bunch of wolves." Or that's how he tells the story of his arrival in *Never Cry Wolf*, one of two controversial, bestselling books, along with *People of the Deer*, he wrote about his first time in the barrens. The books, fierce and funny, drew attention to the mistreatment of, respectively, wolves and the local Inuit, and drew plenty of fire to Mowat, especially from the government officials with whom he engaged in spirited combat in both tales.

1980 At a garden party in Connecticut, two men met for the first time: Ian Hugo, who was married to Anaïs Nin from 1923 to her death in 1977, and Rupert Pole, who for much of that time was also married to Nin. Hugo hadn't known about Pole, while Pole had known about Hugo but had thought their marriage was over, and for almost thirty years Nin had shuttled secretly between the two, Hugo in New York and Pole in Los Angeles. (When she died, the *New York Times* listed Hugo as her husband in her obituary, while the *Los Angeles Times* listed Pole.) Both men, of course, had accommodated other lovers of hers at times—Henry Miller not the least of them—and when Hugo died a few years after their belated meeting, it was Pole who, at Hugo's request, scattered his ashes in Santa Monica Bay.

2003 Erich von Däniken, who was a hotel manager when he wrote *Chariots of the Gods?*, the improbable 1968 bestseller that argued that the wonders of ancient civilization had been left behind by extraterrestrial visitors (and that, in later editions, confidently abandoned the question mark in its original title), returned to his roots in tourism when he opened Mystery Park, a theme park in Interlaken, Switzerland, in which seven pavilions explained the evidence of ancient aliens, from Stonehenge to the Mayan calendar. Three years later, citing poor attendance, the park closed.

BORN: 1928 William Trevor (*The Old Boys, Felicia's Journey*), Mitchelstown, Ireland
1963 Michael Chabon (*The Amazing Adventures of Kavalier & Clay*), Washington, D.C.

DIED: 1543 Nicolaus Copernicus (*On the Revolutions of the Celestial Spheres*), 70, Frombork, Poland
1996 Joseph Mitchell (*McSorley's Wonderful Saloon*), 87, New York City

1939 Alex Haley began a twenty-year career in uniform by enlisting in the Coast Guard.

1944 In a London car accident, Ernest Hemingway acquired a concussion and a gash in his scalp.

1945 Indicted for treason in 1943 for his support of Fascist Italy, Ezra Pound turned himself in to American authorities after the Italian surrender and on this day was driven to a makeshift prison camp in Pisa, where, for three weeks, he was held in an open cage of steel mesh before being moved to a nearby tent. Having called Hitler "a Jeanne d'Arc, a saint" after his arrest, Pound was hardly repentant, but in his captivity he wrote—first on a sheet of toilet paper in his cage and then on a typewriter he was granted as a privilege—what became known as the *Pisan Cantos*, ten new sections in his ongoing poetic project that reflect on his imprisonment and the lost poetic friends of his past and that contain some of his most lyrical passages, particularly the promise that "What thou lovest well remains, / the rest is dross."

1954 "Why can't Johnny read?" was one of the most anxious pleas of the '50s, and in *Life* magazine on this day, John Hersey laid the blame on the "insipid" *Dick and Jane*–style primers that bored beginning readers out of their little minds. Among his solutions: bring in "wonderfully imaginative" illustrators like Dr. Seuss or Walt Disney. In response, a publisher asked Seuss to "write me a story that first-graders can't put down," challenging him to limit his vocabulary to 225 different words from a basic list of 348. Seuss stretched it to 236 words and came up with *The Cat in the Hat*, whose sales soon rivaled those of *Peyton Place*, although purchases by schools lagged as some considered it too unruly for classroom use.

1963 The meeting seemed to go terribly. On the invitation of Attorney General Robert Kennedy, James Baldwin brought a group including playwright Lorraine Hansberry, Lena Horne, Rip Torn, and Jerome Smith, a young activist beaten badly during the Freedom Rides, to Kennedy's Manhattan apartment to discuss civil rights. The tension peaked when Smith said he couldn't fight for a country that didn't protect him from racial violence and Kennedy said if an Irish Catholic like his brother could become president blacks could too in forty years (he was off by five). Hansberry replied that if Kennedy couldn't understand Smith's position then "there's no alternative to our going in the streets." Kennedy thought he'd been ambushed, and Baldwin's group left in despair, but later Kennedy acknowledged the meeting as a watershed in his understanding of the moral urgency of civil rights.

May 25

BORN: 1938 Raymond Carver (*Will You Please Be Quiet, Please?*), Clatskanie, Ore.
1949 Jamaica Kincaid (*Annie John*, *A Small Place*), St. John's, Antigua
DIED: 1693 Madame de La Fayette (*The Princess of Cleves*), 59, Paris
2008 George Garrett (*Death of the Fox*, *The Finished Man*), 78, Charlottesville, Va.

1793 Twice in a week the works of William Godwin were greatly underestimated. First came Prime Minister William Pitt, who decided on this day not to prosecute Godwin for *Political Justice*, his lengthy and pricey radical treatise, because "a three guinea book could never do much harm among those who had not three shillings to spare." (The book, in fact, sold well and widely in many forms and had an enormous effect on Romantic poets and radicals alike.) And then on the 31st Godwin's friend James Marshal returned the manuscript of Godwin's novel *Caleb Williams*, saying, "I should have thrust it in the fire. If you persist, the book will infallibly prove the grave of your literary fame." The novel, in fact, was an immediate triumph, recognized then as one of the great novels of its age and now as the ingeniously constructed first "thriller."

1900 After the Spanish-American War, William James reflected on his former student Theodore Roosevelt, "a combination of slime and grit, sand and soap" that could "scour anything away, even the moral sense of the country."

1910 The best-known note James sent to another of his notable students, Gertrude Stein—the one that said, "Dear Miss Stein—I understand perfectly how you feel," excusing her from the philosophy final she had abandoned in favor of a nice spring day and giving her the top grade in the class—may have been apocryphal, but the great pragmatist did write to her on this day, just months before he died. He had enjoyed the early pages of *Three Lives*—"This is a fine new kind of realism—Gertrude Stein is great!" he thought—but then could go no further. "You know how hard it is for me to read novels . . . As a rule reading fiction is as hard to me as trying to hit a target by hurling feathers at it. I need *resistance*, to cerebrate!"

1944 "I could not stand *Gaudy Night*," J. R. R. Tolkien admitted to his son Christopher. "I followed P. Wimsey from his attractive beginnings so far, by which time I conceived a loathing for him (and his creatrix) not surpassed by any other character in literature known to me."

1994 Of the many revelations in Andre Agassi's appropriately titled memoir, *Open*, one of the most enjoyable (for the reader) takes us netside after a hard-fought loss to the Austrian Thomas Muster at the French Open, when Muster reached over and tousled Agassi's hair. Or, rather, his hairpiece, which Agassi had been wearing secretly for years. "I stare at him with pure hatred," he recalled. "Big mistake, Muster. Don't touch the hair." He vowed he'd never lose to "Muster the hair-musser" again, and he never did.

May 26

BORN: **1954** Alan Hollinghurst (*The Folding Star*, *The Line of Beauty*), Stroud, England
1974 Ben Schott (*Schott's Original Miscellany*), London
DIED: **1976** Martin Heidegger (*Being and Time*), 86, Freiburg, Germany
2003 Kathleen Winsor (*Forever Amber*, *Star Money*), 83, Manhattan

1827 Edgar Allan Poe enlisted in the army under the name Edgar A. Perry.

1897 Published: *Dracula* by Bram Stoker (Constable, London)

1911 "Polish was being spoken nearby." So intrudes, quietly, the presence that will soon consume the life of Gustav Aschenbach in Thomas Mann's novella *Death in Venice*. Aschenbach has just arrived, lonely and aimless, at his hotel in Venice when he notices a group of young people speaking Polish, among them Tadzio, a "perfectly beautiful" boy "of perhaps fourteen," with long curls, an opulent sailor suit, and the appearance of being pampered. Mann too

once arrived in Venice (on this day) and saw a beautiful boy, who has since been traced to Władysław Moes, ten at the time (Mann was only thirty-five then, not the fifty-plus of Aschenbach) and who can be seen in a photograph on the beach in Gilbert Adair's *The Real Tadzio*, his delicate features almost obscured by the gigantic bow of his beach costume.

1953 On assignment as a summertime guest college editor at *Mademoiselle*, Sylvia Plath interviewed Elizabeth Bowen at May Sarton's house in Cambridge.

1985 In the *New York Times Book Review* on this day, critic Ken Tucker reviewed a book that wasn't a book yet and helped to make it one. Since 1980 Art Spiegelman had been telling the story of his father's survival of the Holocaust in "Maus," a series in his avant-garde comics magazine, *Raw*, and, after countless rejections—including a particularly obtuse one by Knopf's Robert Gottlieb, who said they were publishing enough "comic strip-cartoon type books" already—had even found a publisher for the whole series at Pantheon, but when Tucker's piece came out, calling "Maus" an "unfolding literary event" that few were aware of, Pantheon was convinced to release the first half of the book ahead of schedule, to surprising acclaim that made it one of the most important books of the decade.

BORN: 1894 Dashiell Hammett (*Red Harvest*, *The Maltese Falcon*), St. Mary's County, Md.

1894 Louis-Ferdinand Céline (*Journey to the End of the Night*), Courbevoie, France

1912 John Cheever (*The Wapshot Scandal, Stories, Journals*), Quincy, Mass.

DIED: 1564 John Calvin (*The Institutes of the Christian Religion*), 54, Geneva, Switzerland

1949 Robert Ripley (*Believe It or Not!*), 58, New York City

1891 Arthur Rimbaud's right leg was amputated.

1943 Rising before dawn, Second Lieutenant Louis Zamperini, with a jeep to pace him on the runway in Oahu where he was stationed, ran a 4:12 mile, just seconds off the NCAA record he'd set while training for the 1940 Olympics that were canceled by the war. By the end of the same day, after their B-24 crashed in the Pacific while searching for another downed plane, Zamperini and his fellow airmen "Phil" Phillips and Francis McNamara were drifting in the ocean on two rafts lashed together, circled by sharks. Zamperini and Phillips survived a record forty-seven days afloat before coming ashore in the Marshall Islands, where they became prisoners of the Japanese. And only then, as Laura Hillenbrand masterfully recounts in *Unbroken*, did their true ordeal begin.

1963 After a series of profiles of Malcolm X, including a prominent interview in *Play-boy*, Alex Haley, despite his mainstream career and integrationist politics, had gained enough of the trust of the Nation of Islam's fiery spokesman that Malcolm agreed to collaborate with him on a book. On this day they agreed to split the proceeds of what became *The Autobiography of Malcolm X* equally, with Malcolm requesting that his share go directly to the Nation's Mosque No. 2 in Chicago, the flagship congregation led by his mentor Elijah Muhammad. He also drafted a dedication to Muhammad, who "made me the man that I am today." Neither the dedication, nor the share of the proceeds, survived Malcolm's break with the Nation and his subsequent assassination by three of its members.

1979 "Remember, it's YOUR prom; make it one to remember always!" With over 400 dead in the town and the school gymnasium a charred and blood-soaked ruin, it's not likely that anyone—assuming they survived it—will forget the 1979 Ewen High School senior prom anytime soon. Stephen King was scraping by as a high school English teacher in Maine, selling stories to men's magazines to help support his young family, when he wrote a few pages about a telekinetic girl bullied in the school showers. He threw them in the trash, but his wife, Tabitha, pulled them out, and they became the opening of *Carrie*, King's first published novel and, after a lucrative sale of the paperback rights, his own ticket out of high school.

BORN: 1908 Ian Fleming (*Casino Royale, Live and Let Die*), London

1912 Patrick White (*Voss, The Vivisector, Riders in the Chariot*), London

DIED: 1843 Noah Webster (*An American Dictionary of the English Language*), 84, New Haven, Conn.

1849 Anne Brontë (*Agnes Grey, The Tenant of Wildfell Hall*), 29, Scarborough, England

1899 Though reclaimed as a classic by later generations, Kate Chopin's *The Awakening* was scorned by reviewers of its day as "morbid," "vulgar," and "nauseating" for its apparent refusal to judge the unruly passions of Edna Pontellier. One young reviewer, the twenty-three-year-old Willa Cather, did admire Chopin's style but thought her "trite and sordid" theme made Emma's story merely "a Creole *Bovary*." Chopin, meanwhile, responded to her critics with a shrug of her shoulders—"I never dreamed of Mrs. Pontellier making such a mess of things and working out her own damnation as she did," she drily commented—but her short professional writing career never recovered from the attacks before she died five years later.

1948 England! It's the word that rushed Hortense Roberts and Gilbert Joseph into what is more of a business partnership than a marriage. Five days after they met, the banns were published; three weeks later they were wed, each "astonished to see the other looking so elegant," and the next day Gilbert sailed on the *Empire Windrush* for England, funded by the prudent savings Hortense had offered along with her hand. Six months later, in Andrea Levy's *Small Island,* Hortense too left their island of Jamaica to join him on the larger one of Great Britain, in an immigrants' alliance in which their disappointment at what they find in their idealized England is leavened by their ability to adapt.

1955 On a slow train to London from his home in Hull, Philip Larkin, traveling alone, noticed that the train filled at each stop with couples just wed on Whit Saturday who were heading into the city for their honeymoons. "Every time you stopped fresh emotion climbed aboard," he'd later say. For three years after—taking the same trip each year to refresh the experience—he worked on transforming his journey into the ten stanzas of one of his longest poems, "The Whitsun Weddings," which, with its lonely vision of new marriages aimed into an unknown future like arrows shot into the sky, became the poem that more than any other evoked a sense of community for postwar Britain, though it was written by a man legendary for his misanthropy.

May 29

BORN: 1880 Oswald Spengler (*The Decline of the West*), Blankenburg, Germany
1935 André Brink (*A Dry White Season, An Act of Terror*), Vrede, South Africa
DIED: 1911 W. S. Gilbert (*The Mikado, H.M.S. Pinafore*), 74, London
1970 John Gunther (*Inside U.S.A., Death Be Not Proud*), 68, New York City

1847 Apologizing for his delay in writing to a colleague, the young historian Francis Parkman blamed "the extremely bad state of my eyes," which had forced him to design a wooden frame fixed with wires to guide his pencil so he could write without looking at the page. Energetic and ambitious, Parkman had traveled through the West in 1846 but returned to a debilitating nervous condition that left him blind, distracted, and prostrate most of his days. Nevertheless, he persisted in writing his first two books, *The Oregon Trail* and *The Conspiracy of Pontiac*, under remarkable conditions, having friends read to him for periods "never, without injury, much exceeding half an hour" and making notes with his wire-guided method at a rate that "averaged about six lines a day."

1895 With his parents still hoping that Marcel Proust might find a respectable profession, and with Proust himself perhaps imagining it might not interfere with his literary activities, he took an examination on this day to become an unpaid assistant at the Bibliothèque Mazarine. When he didn't like his assignment, he pleaded ill health and requested a better one; the chief librarian replied, "If he was so weak that he was unable to endure five hours of work every other day, he was wrong to apply." Proust made just a few appearances in the library before being granted a series of sick leaves that lasted until 1900, after which no more pretense was made that he would have any career other than a literary one.

1925 As the valedictorian of his ninth-grade class at Smith Robertson Elementary School in Jackson, Mississippi, Richard Wright wrote a graduation speech, but his black principal, W. H. Lanier, had no intention of letting him use his own words. "Listen, boy, you're going to speak to both *white* and colored people that night," he said with a laugh in Wright's memoir *Black Boy*. "What can you alone think of saying to them?" Lanier threatened to cut off his promising path to Jackson's black educated class, but Wright, already set on leaving for Chicago, said, "I want to learn, professor. But there are some things I don't want to know." Nervous and halting, he gave his own speech and then walked home alone, readier than ever to leave his old life behind.

1966 Madeleine Chapsal, in *L'Express*, on Michel Foucault's *Les mots et les choses* (a review that made the book a French bestseller): "A young man has come on the intellectual scene in order to announce the excellent news: the death of Man and, at the same time, the renewal of the one who invented him, then destroyed him, the *Philosopher*. This demands notice."

BORN: **1951** Garrett Hongo (*The River of Heaven, Volcano*), Volcano, Hawaii
1955 Colm Tóibín (*The Master, Brooklyn*), Enniscorthy, Ireland
DIED: **1593** Christopher Marlowe (*Tamburlaine, Doctor Faustus*), 29, Deptford, England
1960 Boris Pasternak (*Doctor Zhivago*; *My Sister, Life*), 70, Peredelkino, Russia

1887 After an evening of exasperation at the prospect of strikes and socialism, the wealthy and idle Julian West falls into a deep sleep from which he arises to the news that he has slumbered in a trance for more than a century. West wakes in the year 2000 to a society prosperous beyond his grandest dreams, in which the labor question has been solved and women have been released from both housework and the absurd encumbrances of Victorian dress. A homegrown American *Utopia*, Edward Bellamy's *Looking Backward: 2000–1887* joined *Uncle Tom's Cabin* and *Ben-Hur* as the runaway bestsellers of the nineteenth century, inspiring "Bellamy Clubs" across the United States with its vision of a society where, with private property abolished, work and goods would be shared equally by its citizens.

1961 The *fukú* didn't begin with Rafael Trujillo, and it certainly didn't end with his assassination—with or without the help of the CIA—on this day. A curse brought to the New World, and to the island of Hispaniola in particular, by Columbus or by the enslaved shipped in from Africa, the fukú thrived through the generations as a contagion of calamity and injustice, and when JFK okayed the assassination of the murderously ferocious Trujillo, the Curse of the New World became the Curse of the Kennedys, or so Junot Díaz suggests in the dread-soaked overture to *The Brief Wondrous Life of Oscar Wao*, a novel he offers as a sort of counterspell to his island's legacy of doom.

1971 Dee Brown was neither a Native American nor a native of the American West. He grew up in Arkansas on tales of the frontier and, alongside a career as a librarian, published fifteen books before *Bury My Heart at Wounded Knee*. Subtitled "An Indian History of the American West," *Bury My Heart* was really a history of the three bloody decades, from 1860 to 1890, when white settlers and soldiers eroded the so-called permanent Indian frontier for good. The time was right for the book: in his *New York Times* review, N. Scott Momaday compared the Wounded Knee massacre to My Lai, and it hit #1 on the *Times* bestseller list on this day alongside counterculture classics like *The Greening of America* and *The Female Eunuch* and spent nearly the rest of the year at the top. Two years later, Lakota activists reclaimed its title's embattled territory with their seventy-three-day occupation of the town of Wounded Knee.

1999 Gary Krist, in the *New York Times*, on A. M. Homes's *Music for Torching*: "To say that I loved A. M. Homes's 'Music for Torching' would be a ridiculously inadequate description of my feelings about this nasty and willfully grotesque novel."

May 31

BORN: 1819 Walt Whitman (*Leaves of Grass, Democratic Vistas*), West Hills, N.Y.
1974 Adrian Tomine (*Optic Nerve, Shortcomings*), Sacramento, Calif.
DIED: 1991 Angus Wilson (*Anglo-Saxon Attitudes*), 77, Bury St. Edmunds, England
1995 Stanley Elkin (*George Mills, The Franchiser*), 65, St. Louis

NO YEAR "I should like to see you when you're tired and satiated. I shall prefer you in that state." What a quiet and diabolical seduction Henry James places at the center of his *Portrait of a Lady*! Everybody desires Isabel Archer—who wouldn't?—but only Gilbert Osmond, the villainous aesthete, has the languorous confidence to tell her just before they part in Rome that he loves her but can let her go. Isabel, meanwhile, thinks of her latent passion like her new-found wealth: "It was there like a large sum stored in a bank—which there was a terror in having to begin to spend. If she touched it, it would all come out." She may hold back both her money and her desire for now, but in time Gilbert will have them all.

1889 When David McCullough decided, after a dozen years as an editor, to tell a story of his own, he turned to the great Johnstown Flood, close to his childhood home of Pittsburgh. Writing and researching on nights, weekends, and lunch hours for three years, he published *The Johnstown Flood* in 1968, and the success of his absorbing account of the disaster—the deadliest in American history to that point—and the scandalous negligence of the wealthy Pittsburgh resort owners that caused it gave him the courage to set out as a full-time writer of history. Not wanting to become "Bad News McCullough," though, he declined immediate offers to write about the Chicago fire and the San Francisco earthquake.

1906 A bystander at the attempted assassination of Spain's King Alfonso by anarchists, Ezra Pound left the country in fear he would be connected to it.

1939 Christopher Isherwood, in the *New Republic*, on Robert Penn Warren's *Night Rider*: "So important is the theme of this novel and so considerable its achievement, that I almost wish he would rewrite it—as George Moore used to—ten years from now, when the powers already apparent in his first attempt have come to full maturity."

2001 Murray Thwaite, the title patriarch in Claire Messud's novel *The Emperor's Children*, has only one child, his daughter, Marina, but he also looms as an idol to be worshipped or toppled by what feels like a whole generation of young people, including Marina's best friend, Danielle, who on this evening accepts Murray's suggestion that he come up to her apartment. It's a measure of the warmth of Messud's satire that while she certainly shows her emperor, a legendary and self-satisfied liberal journalist, to be wearing no clothes (and literally so on this evening), he's a human and complex character who nearly earns the affection he initially inspires in his young admirer.

June is sickly sweet; it's insipid. Is that because it's so warm, or because it rhymes so easily? June, moon, spoon, balloon . . . But while Robert Burns happily rhymed his "red, red rose / That's newly sprung in June" with a "melody / that's sweetly played in tune," Gwendolyn Brooks burned off any sugar in the terse rhythms of "We Real Cool": her "Jazz June" is followed by "Die soon." Thoughts of death in summer haunt—or enliven— Wallace Stevens's "Sunday Morning" too. His heroine's "desire for June" gains its vitality from the inevitable darkening of evening. "Death," he writes, "is the mother of beauty."

June is called "midsummer," even though it's the beginning, not the middle, of the season. The days are longest, and the summer stretches hopefully ahead. Shakespeare's *Midsummer Night's Dream* is a comic fantasy of lovers diverted and united that ends, more or less, with a group wedding, the traditional end for a comedy and a ceremony traditionally celebrated in June. Marriage plots are supposed to reconcile all differences, but of course not every wedding ties things up so neatly. In Dorothy Baker's *Cassandra at the Wedding*, the approaching June marriage of her twin sister seems to Cassandra like an abandonment, a crisis that flays open her own vivid but uncertain identity. And Mary McCarthy's *The Group* begins rather than ends with a June wedding, the first among its set of Vassar grads and hardly an auspicious one (the book will come full circle to end with the funeral of its long-divorced bride).

The wedding in *The Group* takes place just a week after that other modern June ritual, graduation day—or, as it's more evocatively known, commencement, an ending that's a beginning. It's an occasion that brings out both hope and world-weariness in elders and advice givers. It brought David Foster Wallace, in his 2005 Kenyon College commencement address reprinted as *This Is Water*, perhaps as close as he ever came to the unironic statement his busy mind was long striving for. But the grammar-school graduation speech is an especially potent scene in African American literature. There's the narrator's friend "Shiny" in James Weldon Johnson's *Autobiography of an Ex-Colored Man*, speaking to a white audience like "a gladiator tossed into the arena and bade to fight for his life," and Richard Wright, in his memoir *Black Boy,* giving a rough speech he'd composed himself instead of the one written for him. Ralph Ellison's Invisible Man is invited to give his class speech before his town's leading white citizens, only to find himself instead pitted in a "battle royal" with his classmates, while in Maya Angelou's *I Know Why the Caged Bird Sings*, a young student follows a white dignitary's patronizing words to the graduates with an unprompted and subversive leading of the "Negro national anthem," "Lift Ev'ry Voice and Sing" (whose lyrics were written by none other than James Weldon Johnson).

Suite Française by Irène Némirovsky (1942/2004) ✎ After reading Colette's account of the forced migration from the German occupation of Paris, Némirovsky remarked, "If that's all she could get out of June, I'm not worried," and continued work on her own version, "Storm in June," the first of the two sections of her fictional suite she was able to complete.

Ubik by Philip K. Dick (1969) ✎ It's June 1992, a few days before Resurrection Day, when Glen Runciter comes into the Beloved Brethren Moratorium to commune with his late wife, Ella, suspended in a half-life of extended cognition. But Ella's connection is deteriorating, and soon time itself is falling apart as well in one of Dick's most unsettling explosions of reality.

Jaws by Peter Benchley (1974) ✎ Is the greatest beach read ever the one that could keep you from ever wanting to go into the water again?

The Public Burning by Robert Coover (1977) ✎ We've never quite known what to do with *The Public Burning*, Coover's wild American pageant starring Nixon, the Rosenbergs, and a foul and folksy Uncle Sam: it's too long, too angry, too crazy, and, for the publishers' lawyers who said it couldn't be released while its main character, the recently deposed president, was still alive, it was too soon.

Sleepless Nights by Elizabeth Hardwick (1979) ✎ Like *Ubik*, *Sleepless Nights* begins anchored in a hot, blinding June but soon fragments across time, in this case into memories from the narrator's life—which closely resembles Hardwick's—and stories from the lives of others, a method that has the paradoxical effect of heightening time's power.

Clockers by Richard Price (1992) ✎ It's often said that no modern novel can match the storytelling power of *The Wire*, but its creators drew inspiration from Price's novel of an unsolved summertime murder in the low-level New Jersey crack trade, and for their third season they added Price to their scriptwriting team.

When the World Was Steady by Claire Messud (1995) ✎ Bali is hot in June, but dry; the Isle of Skye is gray and wet, at least until the weather makes yet another change. Messud's first novel follows two English sisters just on the far side of middle age who find themselves on those distant and different islands, reckoning with the choices they've made and suddenly open to the life around them.

Three Junes by Julia Glass (2002) ✎ *Three Junes* might well be called "Three Funerals"—each of its three sections, set in summers that stretch across a decade, takes place in the wake of a death. But the warm month in her title hints at the story inside, and the way her characters hold on to life wherever they find it.

June 1

BORN: 1932 Christopher Lasch (*The Culture of Narcissism*), Omaha, Neb.
1937 Colleen McCullough (*The Thorn Birds*), Wellington, Australia

DIED: 1952 John Dewey (*Democracy and Education*), 92, New York City
1968 Helen Keller (*The Story of My Life*), 87, Easton, Conn.

NO YEAR Oyster soup, sea bass and barracuda, a calf's head in oil and a gigantic roast goose, rice pudding, stewed prunes, and strawberry ice cream, lemonade and a case of champagne that the groom calls "the best beer I ever drank": Frank Norris's 1899 novel *McTeague* is unmatched as a tale of excess, greed, and desire, and the feast celebrating the wedding of McTeague, the brutish dentist, and Trina, his tiny bride, is just one of its orgies of consumption. At its end, with the partygoers gone and their new apartment dark, empty, and quiet, the couple is left alone in their new life together, with nothing more to consume but each other. "Oh, you must be good to me—very, very good to me, dear," Trina whispers to McTeague, "for you're all that I have in the world now."

1932 Colette opened a beauty institute in Paris, featuring her own cosmetics and creams. (It closed a year later.)

1974 The speakers at the gala reopening of Sandstone, an open-sexuality resort in Topanga Canyon, California, included Dr. Alex Comfort, author of the bestselling *Joy of Sex*, Al Goldstein, publisher of *Screw* magazine, and Gay Talese, who was under contract to write a book on sex in America and who, for months at a stretch, had lived at Sandstone. The scandal of Talese's enthusiastic research on the sexual revolution has always overshadowed that book, *Thy Neighbor's Wife*, but the book itself delves into its subject with a calm curiosity that's best evoked in the final chapter, where "Gay Talese" enters the narrative in the third person, enjoying massage parlors and orgies as both observer and participant, and never entirely separating the two.

1976 "The telephone rings at four. 'This is C.B.C. John Updike has been in a fatal automobile accident. Do you care to comment?'" Bewildered and weeping, John Cheever couldn't get back to sleep after the news, and in his journal sketched a eulogy. "He was a prince," he wrote, though they had often been anxious and envious rivals. "One misses his brightness—one misses it painfully." But in the daylight, the prank was revealed: an unnamed novelist was the caller, Updike was still alive, and he lived long enough to eulogize Cheever at his funeral six years later.

BORN: 1840 Thomas Hardy (*The Return of the Native*), Stinsford, England
1929 Norton Juster (*The Phantom Tollbooth, The Dot and the Line*), Brooklyn
DIED: 1961 George S. Kaufman (*The Man Who Came to Dinner*), 71, New York City
1989 Frederic Prokosch (*The Asiatics*), 89, Le-Plan-de-Grasse, France

1816 William Hazlitt, in *The Examiner*, on Samuel Taylor Coleridge's *Christabel*: "He is a man of that universality of genius, that his mind hangs suspended between poetry and prose, truth and falsehood, and an infinity of other things, and from an excess of capacity, he does little or nothing."

1910 The ghosts of Albany remember Francis Phelan when he returns, in William Kennedy's *Ironweed*, and so do some of the living, including the family he left behind twenty-two years ago, after his baby son died from his negligence. "You don't just pop up one day with a turkey and all is forgiven," says his daughter, Peg, and Francis would be the first to agree. But there's something like forgiveness in an old letter from her he finds upstairs, the only one he had kept in his former life as a traveling ballplayer. "Dear Poppy," she wrote on this day, "I suppose you never think that you have a daughter that is waiting for a letter since you went away."

1963 Former car thief Jacky Maglia, a protégé of Jean Genet, won a race in Belgium in a Lotus that Genet had paid for with a sizable loan from his publisher.

1977 Not yet forty, Raymond Carver had hit bottom and sobered up before, but never for long. After his first book of stories, *Will You Please Be Quiet, Please?*, was nominated for a National Book Award in March, he stayed sober for a few weeks, but at the booksellers convention in San Francisco he went on a final bender. Drunk and hungover at the same time, he drove his publisher to Sausalito for lunch and Bloody Marys, and after the publisher offered him $5,000 to write a novel, his first book advance, Carver went to the bathroom to cry and then to the liquor store to celebrate. But on this day four days later, at a bar in Arcata, California, he took the last drink of his life.

1978 After not seeing his difficult father, Vladek, for a couple of years, Art Spiegelman went out to Queens to remind him he still wanted to draw a comic book about his life in Poland during the war. Spiegelman had begun to record his father's memories six years before, but now he sat down with him in earnest and began sketching out the pages that he would fashion, over the next thirteen years, into the two volumes of *Maus*, the history of his father's survival of the war and Auschwitz. "I want to start with Mom. Tell me how you met," Art asks in *Maus*. "I lived then in Czestochowa," Vladek begins, "a small city not far from the border of Germany . . ."

June 3

BORN: 1930 Marion Zimmer Bradley (*The Mists of Avalon*), Albany, N.Y.
1936 Larry McMurtry (*Lonesome Dove, The Last Picture Show*), Archer City, Tex.
DIED: 1924 Franz Kafka (*The Trial, The Castle*), 40, Kierling, Austria
1992 Bill Gaines (publisher of *Mad*, EC Comics), 70, New York City

1906 Neither D. H. Lawrence, the son of a miner, nor Jessie Chambers, the daughter of a tenant farmer, had reason to expect a literary life, but they read hungrily together anyway in a teenage idyll. Then, just after his family told him to either propose to Jessie or drop her—he did neither—Lawrence began to write, and on this Whitsun holiday he showed her the first pages of a novel. For the next half-dozen years she was his reader, editor, and agent, submitting his poems for publication and, after their relationship unhappily turned romantic, commenting on his manuscript of *Sons and Lovers*. "Astonishing misconception," she wrote in the margin about one description of Miriam, whose portrayal, modeled after her, she later said "gave the death-blow to our friendship."

1933 Clifton Fadiman, in *The New Yorker*, on Jules Romains's *Men of Good Will*: "He is one of the few living writers who point unhesitatingly straight toward the future. At some later date, when the little ones ask you 'Grandfather, what did you do before the revolution?,' perhaps the only answer many of us will be able to make will be 'I was a contemporary of Jules Romains.'"

NO YEAR "There's nothing so dark as a railroad track in the middle of the night," and that's where Walter Huff finds himself after dropping off the back of a slow-moving train dressed as H. S. Nirdlinger, the man whose wife he sold an accident insurance policy to in February, and the man whose neck he just broke. James M. Cain didn't think much of *Double Indemnity*—he wrote it fast for money, to satisfy his editors' hunger for another *Postman Always Rings Twice*—but thanks in part to their portrayal by Fred McMurray and Barbara Stanwyck in Billy Wilder's 1944 film version, Huff and Phyllis Nirdlinger (renamed Dietrichson in the movie) remain one of the most memorably doomed couples in American literature.

1969 Kingsley Amis, never shy of a commercial publishing idea that matched his enthusiasms (for example, his pseudonymous *Book of Bond, or Every Man His Own 007*), pitched an especially attractive idea to his agent Pat Kavanagh on this day: a series "On Drink and Drinking" that combined personal interest with sales potential. Best of all, he "could get something like six months' drink off tax, which would be a tremendous achievement." The result was the slim classic *On Drink*, with its complaints on the troublesomeness of wine, advice for dealing with hangovers (read Kafka and have sex on waking—not in that order), and a recipe for "The Lucky Jim" (one part vermouth, two parts cucumber juice, and a dozen parts of the cheapest British vodka you can find).

BORN: 1955 Val McDermid (*A Place of Execution*), Kirkcaldy, Scotland
1972 Joe Hill (*20th Century Ghosts, Heart-Shaped Box*), Hermon, Maine
DIED: 1967 J. R. Ackerley (*My Dog Tulip, My Father and Myself*), 70, London
2010 David Markson (*Wittgenstein's Mistress, Reader's Block*), 82, New York

1908 At the ceremony in the Pantheon to inter the remains of his most famous defender, Émile Zola, Alfred Dreyfus, in an attempted assassination, was shot in the arm.

1940 Published: *The Heart Is a Lonely Hunter* by Carson McCullers (Houghton Mifflin, Boston)

1949 "The fur can easily be removed," C. S. Lewis responded to a reader concerned both about the mention of fur coats in *The Lion, the Witch, and the Wardrobe* and about the danger of children getting stuck in wardrobes. "Much more serious is the undesirability of shutting oneself into a cupboard. I might add a caution—or wd. this only make things worse?" In later editions of the book, Lewis indeed added a caution, five of them throughout the story, in fact, to always leave the door open when hiding in a wardrobe.

1972 Timothy Crouse was the *other* correspondent *Rolling Stone* assigned to cover the 1972 presidential campaign. Hunter S. Thompson's *Fear and Loathing on the Campaign Trail '72* stands as an inimitable landmark of political journalism, if that's what you call it, but *The Boys on the Bus*, Crouse's look in the mirror at the pack of reporters following the campaign, may have been more influential, in both its free-wheeling gossip and its foreshadowing of the way the media has increasingly made itself the story. Foremost among its larger-than-life characters is R. W. "Johnny" Apple Jr., the talented and tireless man from the *New York Times* who launched into a self-congratulatory monologue to Crouse over poached eggs and caviar at the Beverly Wilshire on the Sunday before the California primary: "Believe it or not, they gave me an unlimited travel budget at the *Times* . . ."

2002 Unlike the NFL and NBA drafts, the Major League Baseball amateur draft takes place in a near-vacuum, a selection of players nobody's heard of and, for the most part, nobody ever will. But the 2002 baseball draft is the first big scene in the biggest baseball book of the last four decades, Michael Lewis's *Moneyball*, with maverick Oakland A's exec Billy Beane and his staff giddily drafting diamonds in the rough no one else wanted. It's a heady moment—"This is maybe the funnest day I have ever had in baseball," Beane says—but its victories were less evident a decade later: most of the picks, like most others in baseball's talent crap-shoot, never panned out, including Jeremy Brown, the hard-hitting, overweight catcher who played five games for the A's in 2006 and then retired, weary of all the publicity that followed him as a *Moneyball* poster boy.

June 5

BORN: **1939** Margaret Drabble (*The Waterfall, The Millstone*), Sheffield, England
1958 Geoff Dyer (*Out of Sheer Rage, But Beautiful*), Cheltenham, England
DIED: **1900** Stephen Crane (*The Red Badge of Courage*), 28, Badenweiler, Germany
2012 Ray Bradbury (*Dandelion Wine, The Illustrated Man*), 91, Los Angeles

1826 An epochal moment in the hothouse creative atmosphere of the Brontë parsonage occurred with the arrival of a dozen toy soldiers, brought home for young Branwell Brontë by their father and shared by him with his sisters, ages ten, seven, and six. They quickly named their favorites—Bonaparte or Sneaky (Branwell), Wellington (Charlotte), Parry (Emily), and Ross (Anne—Ross was "a queer little thing very much like herself," remembered Charlotte)—and around them constructed a fantasy world, named variously Glasstown, Angria, and Gondal, inspired by the personalities and geography they read about in their beloved *Blackwood's Magazine*. Few troves of juvenilia have received the fascinated attention the Brontë children's "plays" and tiny handmade books have brought ever since.

1909 While he built a career in law and insurance in his twenties and early thirties, Wallace Stevens wrote almost nothing for the public. His writing was done in letters to Elsie Moll, the woman he courted, and in two birthday collections of poems he prepared for her, a "Book of Verses" in 1908 and a "Little June Book" in 1909, soon after which they married. (Stevens's parents, who disapproved of their son marrying a woman who had been too poor to finish high school, did not attend.) When her husband's work began to appear in literary journals in 1914, Elsie was shocked and disappointed that he published the poems he had written for her, a skepticism toward his vocation that continued throughout their marriage.

1940 Ever since J. B. Priestley threatened Graham Greene with a libel suit for a nasty portrait of a bestselling novelist in *Stamboul Train* he thought was based on him, Greene had had it in for Priestley and his "graceless sentences." Until this day, that is, when Priestley, drafted by the BBC to speak on the radio after the disastrous but heroic evacuation of over 300,000 Allied soldiers from Dunkirk, spoke in his Yorkshire baritone of the rescue—"typically English" in both "its folly and its grandeur"—paying memorable tribute to the "fussy little" pleasure steamers that had been diverted from Brighton holiday-making to the hell of war. Priestley's weekly addresses made him, with Churchill, the voice of British resistance in the war's first year, and "for those dangerous months," Greene later wrote, "he was unmistakably a great man."

1977 Three days sober, Raymond Carver wrote his publisher to propose the subject of his first novel, which he would never write: a World War I adventure involving the German navy in East Africa, "*The African Queen* seen from the other side."

1980 Draco Malfoy, bully in the Harry Potter series, is born.

BORN: 1875 Thomas Mann (*Buddenbrooks,
Death in Venice*), Lübeck, Germany
1923 V. C. Andrews (*Flowers in the Attic,
Petals on the Wind*), Portsmouth, Va.

DIED: 1961 Carl Jung (*Man and His Symbols,
The Red Book*), 85, Zurich
1982 Kenneth Rexroth (*One Hundred
Poems from the Japanese*), 76, Santa
Barbara, Calif.

1761 Famed though they might be for
the line of stones with which their survey-
ing divided Maryland from Pennsylvania, Charles Mason and Jeremiah Dixon
first met on another expedition of similar
public fascination: their observation on this
day, from the Cape of Good Hope, of the
first transit of Venus across the sun in over
a hundred years, an event that allowed a
more accurate measure of the distance from
the earth to the sun and that, in *Mason &
Dixon*, Thomas Pynchon's serious goof on
the Age of Enlightenment, sets off an entire
craze: Transit-of-Venus Wigs ("a dark little
round Knot against a great white powder'd
sphere"), Transit-of-Venus Pudding ("a singular black Currant upon a Circular Field
of White"), and a popular sailors' song,
"'Tis ho, for the Transit of Venus!"

1780 William Blake was a visionary thinker
in a revolutionary age, but even as a young
man was not one for mass movements.
He was twenty-two and newly admitted
to the Royal Academy of Arts when Lord
George Gordon, with the cry "No Popery!,"
inflamed Protestant mobs in London against
the lessening of restrictions against Catho-
lics by Parliament. For days rioters pillaged

the city, and on this day they marched on
Newgate Prison. Blake was walking near
the house of his old engraving master when
he was caught up in the front ranks of the
advancing mob and carried along with it,
likely against his will, to Newgate, where
the crowd burned the prison and freed its
inmates, and where Blake himself was fortunate to escape without injury or arrest.

1951 In the summer of 1939, and William
Saroyan celebrated his first Broadway hit,
The Time of Your Life, by buying a new
Buick and driving to California with his
young cousin Ross Bagdasarian, who had
played a bit part in the show. Along the way
they composed a song, based on an Armenian tune with words mainly by Saroyan,
"Come On My House (I'm Gonna Give
You Candy)." A dozen years later, "Come
On-a My House," released on this day and
sung with an Italian accent (so she'd sound
a little Armenian) by Rosemary Clooney,
became the hit of the summer of 1951. The
royalties gave a much-needed boost to Saroyan's income, but Bagdasarian had another
hit coming: in 1958, under the name Dave
Seville, he created and voiced Alvin, Simon,
and Theodore and recorded "The Chip-
munk Song."

1997 Paul Quinn, in the *TLS*, on Philip
Roth's *American Pastoral*: "Roth is com-
pelled to forgo the usual randy, rebellious,
wiseacre persona for the much more difficult task of inhabiting a decent, compliant,
doomed consciousness; his achievement is
to show a happily shallow man's enforced
depths."

June 7

BORN: 1952 Orhan Pamuk (*The Black Book*, *My Name Is Red*, *Snow*), Istanbul
1954 Louise Erdrich (*Love Medicine*, *The Round House*), Little Falls, Minn.
DIED: 1967 Dorothy Parker (*Enough Rope*, *Here Lies*), 73, New York City
1970 E. M. Forster (*Howards End*, *A Passage to India*), 91, Coventry, England

NO YEAR The death, in *Little Women*, of Pip the canary.

1909 "I'm no bum," Richard Marquard told the firemen who found him, asleep and penniless after five days riding the rails, in their Chicago firehouse. "I'm a ballplayer." They believed him enough to chip in $5 to help him get home from a failed tryout in Iowa, and Marquard, just sixteen, vowed he'd pay them back when he made it big. Two years later, when his Giants came to town to play the Cubs on this day, Marquard, known by then as Rube, the nickname he'd carry to the Hall of Fame, did as promised, part of the story of his fast rise to the big leagues he told Lawrence Ritter, the baseball-loving economics professor who tracked down the sport's aging early stars to record their stories in 1966's *The Glory of Their Times*, a landmark book whose first appearance now stands as far in the past as Ritter's subjects were from the ancient games they recalled.

1943 Malcolm Cowley, in the *New Republic*, on T. S. Eliot's *Four Quartets*: "*Four Quartets* is one of those rare books that can be enjoyed without being understood."

1967 Hubertus Bigend, the Belgian proprietor of Blue Ant, a mysterious ad agency that traffics in cool, may not be the main character of any of William Gibson's novels *Pattern Recognition, Spook Country*, and *Zero History*, but he presides over them all as a ubiquitous and vaguely malign presence, looking like "Tom Cruise on a diet of virgins' blood and truffled chocolates." The Bigend Trilogy, as Gibson has called the books, marked the first time that the science fiction visionary wrote about the present, so it's fitting that Bigend may be the first character in literary history whose fictional Wikipedia entry (which appears in *Spook Country*, from which his birth on this date was gleaned) was later quoted in his actual Wikipedia entry.

NO YEAR A few hours before, she was a person. Now she's evidence. Once a Harvard grad and once a doctor, Lori Petersen is now just a body for another doctor, Dr. Kay Scarpetta, to work on with forceps and thermometer, already considering how this murder scene resembles the other three "Mr. Nobody," her serial strangler, has left behind. Patricia Cornwell was working in the state medical examiner's office in Richmond (as a writer, not a doctor) when she created Scarpetta, the chief medical examiner of Virginia, in *Postmortem*, an award-winning mystery debut that opened the door both to crime series led by strong-willed professional women and to the ongoing fascination with forensics in fiction, film, and television.

June 8

BORN: **1903** Marguerite Yourcenar (*Memoirs of Hadrian*, *The Abyss*), Brussels
1947 Sara Paretsky (*Blood Shot*, *Blacklist*), Ames, Iowa
DIED: **1876** George Sand (*Indiana*, *Mauprat*, *Consuelo*), 71, Nohant, France
1889 Gerard Manley Hopkins ("The Wreck of the Deutschland"), 44, Dublin

1290 We know little more about Beatrice Portinari than that she was the daughter of one wealthy Florentine banker and the wife of another, and that she died on this day at the age of twenty-four. After her death, though, she gained a kind of immortality as the "Beatrice" of the poems of Dante Alighieri, who claimed to have loved her since he met her as a child (though he had met her only once since, when she greeted him on the street while walking with a friend). In his *Vita nuova*, he courted sacrilege by worshipping this earthly woman, concluding, "After she had departed this life, the whole city was left as though widowed, shorn of all dignity." And in his *Divine Comedy* she rises again, to take over from the pagan Virgil as Dante's immortal guide through the heavens of Paradise.

1949 Published: *1984* by George Orwell (Secker & Warburg, London)

1977 Marilynne Robinson has often mentioned the PhD dissertation she wrote at the University of Washington on Shakespeare, but only to say it was the task she stole time away from to experiment with "extended metaphors," written for no purpose but the freedom of their thought. Those metaphors turned into her first novel, the singular, visionary *Housekeeping*, but she didn't entirely neglect her schoolwork, turning in a 257-page thesis on this day called "A New Look at Shakespeare's *Henry VI, Part II*: Sources, Structure, Meaning," which can still be found in the stacks of the UW library, and which makes the rather unambitious argument, with little sign of the elegant ferocity of her later essays, that this neglected work was actually a "good, sound play."

1978 Invited to give the commencement address at Harvard after two years of living in exile in the United States, Aleksandr Solzhenitsyn proclaimed that the West, with all its material abundance, was weakened by cowardice, decadence, mediocrity, and spiritual exhaustion.

June 9

BORN: 1954 Gregory Maguire (*Wicked*, *Confessions of an Ugly Stepsister*), Albany, N.Y.

1956 Patricia Cornwell (*Postmortem*, *Body of Evidence*), Miami, Fla.

DIED: 1870 Charles Dickens (*Great Expectations*, *A Tale of Two Cities*), 58, Higham, England

1974 Miguel Angel Asturias (*Men of Maize*, *The President*), 74, Madrid

1865 The inattention of a work crew on this day caused six of the seven first-class coaches in the express train from the English Channel to plunge into a gap in the rails in Staplehurst, England. Left dangling over the abyss in the seventh were the young actress Ellen Ternan, her mother, and her secret paramour, Charles Dickens, who crawled out through a window and spent the next few hours ministering to the victims below with water he carried from the river with his top hat and brandy he retrieved from the carriage. He also retrieved the manuscript of the latest installment of *Our Mutual Friend*, and when the novel was published later that year, Dickens rather light-heartedly mentioned the rescue of his book in a final note, but the carnage of the crash, in which ten died and two score were seriously injured, haunted him the rest of his life, as did the near-discovery of his relationship with Miss Ternan.

1941 At the time, neither Vladimir nor Vera Nabokov knew how to drive, so when Stanford University offered Vladimir a summer teaching position, they accepted the suggestion of one of his Russian-language students, Dorothy Leuthold, that she drive them from New York to California in her new car. At a stop at the Grand Canyon, Vladimir, never without a butterfly net, had the thrill of his lepidopteral career when on a trail just under the canyon's rim Dorothy disturbed into flight an unknown brown butterfly. Bringing two specimens back to the car, he found Vera had caught two of the same, and in a paper the following year he named the new species, the first he had identified, after their traveling companion, *Neonympha dorothea*.

1976 The mud came from somewhere. When Dana Franklin disappears from her California apartment and then reappears a few seconds later, wet, muddy, and frightened, having spent the time in between on a riverbank she doesn't recognize, where she saves a drowning boy and is nearly shot by his father, she and her husband try to hold to the facts of what, unbelievably, has happened: the mud had to come from somewhere. And when it happens again and again, she adds to her facts: she travels when the boy is in danger, she returns when *she's* in danger, and the place she goes to is on Maryland's Eastern Shore in 1815, where, as a black woman, she must live as a slave. Most of Octavia Butler's fiction was set in the future, but with *Kindred* she brought her readers bodily into the past in a story that grounds the fantastic, uneasily, in the matter-of-fact.

BORN: 1915 Saul Bellow (*The Adventures of Augie March*), Lachine, Quebec
1925 James Salter (*A Sport and a Pastime, Light Years*), New York City

DIED: 1949 Sigrid Undset (*Kristin Lavransdatter*), 67, Lillehammer, Norway
2011 Patrick Leigh Fermor (*A Time of Gifts*), 96, Dumbleton, England

1928 Among the hidden private references in the dream cityscape of *In the Night Kitchen*—allusions to Maurice Sendak's friends, his childhood addresses, his dog, and the hospital where he recovered from a heart attack—is a carton labeled "COCOANUT," "Patented June 10th, 1928," the date of the author's birth.

1964 In 1955, Flannery O'Connor quickly replied to a letter from a woman she didn't know who asked about the presence of God in her work. "I would like to know who this is who understands my stories," she wrote, beginning an exchange of hundreds of letters with an Atlanta clerk named Betty Hester, who chose to be identified only as "A" when O'Connor's letters were first published in *The Habit of Being*. They wrote about God, as Hester joined the Catholic Church but then lost her faith, and they wrote about their lives and their reading, trading books and opinions in a correspondence that lasted until her last letter to Hester, in which she wrote on this day from the hospital, "I sure don't look like I'll ever get out of this joint."

1992 When Joe Sacco first arrived in Gorazde in 1995, the Bosnian war wasn't over, but the worst days of the siege seemed to be. In a few years Gorazde, once a small Yugoslav city, had become an "enclave" of mostly Muslim Bosnians, besieged by the surrounding ethnic Serbs as the Yugoslav federation was torn apart. While peace talks continued in Ohio, Sacco drank, smoked, and listened to the Bosnians—who, unlike him, couldn't take the UN's protected Blue Route out of their city—as they recounted the horrors of the siege and waited for their lives to resume. With each of the dates, mostly in 1992, they mentioned—May 4, May 22, June 10, April 17—came a terrible story that Sacco, the pioneering comics journalist, turned into the grim testimony and dark laughter of *Safe Area Gorazde*.

1997 Though he later had one of his characters, Aidan Donahue in *The Song Is You*, commit the mortifying game-show sin of blurting out an inadvertent anti-Semitic slur after winning three games on *Jeopardy!*, Arthur Phillips, then a "speechwriter from Boston" and not yet a published novelist, made it unscathed through his own run on America's Favorite Quiz Show™, winning five games before retiring (as the show then required in the pre–Ken Jennings era) as an undefeated champion. Perhaps his finest moment came in his third game, when he swept the "Shakespearean Characters" category, revealing an expertise he'd later use in his fifth novel, *The Tragedy of Arthur*, which includes a complete, and completely made up, lost Shakespeare play by the same name.

June 11

BORN: **1925** William Styron (*Sophie's Choice*, *Darkness Visible*), Newport News, Va.
1947 Allan Gurganus (*Oldest Living Confederate Widow Tells All*), Rocky Mount, N.C.
DIED: **1936** Robert E. Howard (Conan the Barbarian), 30, Cross Plains, Tex.
1998 Catherine Cookson (*The Fifteen Streets*), 91, Newcastle, England

1687 Robinson Crusoe returns to England after thirty-six years.

1850 Death is general throughout Cormac McCarthy's *Blood Meridian*, meted out and suffered and sparing no one save Judge Holden—the judge who, he says himself, will never die. But for everyone and everything else in the story the end is ever-present. The marauders in Glanton's gang, whose murderous swarming across the Southwest makes up much of the novel, band together and disband without sentiment or permanence, and on this day the fighter known as the "kid," long gone from the gang himself, witnesses a moment emblematic of many others. Standing in a crowd at a public hanging, he watches as "abruptly two bound figures rose vertically from among their fellows to the top of the gatehouse and there they hung and there they died." That the two figures are Toadvine and Brown, men he'd traveled and killed with, holds hardly any more value for the kid than that they are all fellows in the same fate.

1865 Friedrich Nietzsche was hardly the only twenty-year-old to lose his faith in God, but few have done it with such eloquent finality, or such lasting influence. Having announced his apostasy to the distress of his family, he replied (in a joking and affectionate letter otherwise full of news of a music festival) to his sister's defense of the Christian faith she thought they had shared, "Is it the most important thing to arrive at that particular view of God, world and reconciliation that makes us feel most comfortable? . . . Here the ways of men divide: if you wish to strive for peace of soul and happiness, then believe; if you wish to be a disciple of truth, then inquire."

1906 "Here you are," W. C. Fields greeted Winsor McCay in their shared dressing room before the *Little Nemo* cartoonist made his vaudeville debut as a "lightning-sketch" artist. "A little scotch for my little Scotch friend."

1927 "Alceste," in *The New Yorker*, on Mary Agnes Best's *Thomas Paine*: "When Roosevelt . . . called Paine 'a filthy little atheist,' he was following in the footsteps of all Paine's traducers. There is nothing wrong with the statement except three facts: Paine was not an atheist; he was not a little man, either physically or mentally; and he was neither careless or dirty in his habits and appearance."

2000 W. S. Di Piero, in the *New York Times*, on W. G. Sebald's *Vertigo*: "Sebald is a thrilling, original writer. He makes narration a state of investigative bliss."

BORN: 1892 Djuna Barnes (*Nightwood, Ladies Almanack*), Cornwall-on-Hudson, N.Y.
1929 Anne Frank (*The Diary of a Young Girl*), Frankfurt, Germany
DIED: 1936 Karl Kraus (*Die Fackel, The Third Walpurgis Night*), 62, Vienna
1972 Edmund Wilson (*Axel's Castle, To the Finland Station*), 77, Talcottville, N.Y.

1857 When no one came to shave him on his first morning as a guest at the country home of Charles Dickens, Hans Christian Andersen sent for his host's eldest son to perform the service. This may have put him on the wrong side of the Dickens children, who found his stay interminable. As Kate Dickens remembered, "He was a bony bore, and stayed on and on." Having suggested he would visit for a week or two, Andersen stayed for five, and though he entertained the children with his ingenious paper cutouts, he could tell they despised him. Their busy father was friendlier, but after Andersen finally went home to Denmark, Dickens posted a card in his guest room that read, "Hans Andersen slept in this room for five weeks—which seemed to the family AGES!"

1915 Theodore Dreiser, in the *New Republic*, on *The Good Soldier* by Ford Madox Ford: "The interlacings, the cross-references, the re-re-references to all sorts of things which subsequently are told somewhere in full, irritate one to the point of one's laying down the book."

1963 On the day that Medgar Evers, the Mississippi field representative of the NAACP, was shot in the back outside his home in Jackson, James Baldwin was writing *Blues for Mister Charlie*, a play about another notorious murder of a black man in Mississippi. When he learned of Evers's death he "resolved that nothing under heaven would prevent me from getting this play done." Meanwhile, when Evers's fellow Jackson resident Eudora Welty heard of the murder, she wrote "Where Is the Voice Coming From?," a story told from the mind of the killer that was published in *The New Yorker* within weeks. When later that year Byron De La Beckwith, from a higher class than the poor white Welty had imagined as the murderer, was arrested for the crime (he wasn't convicted until 1994), a Faulkner-reading friend told her, "You thought he was a Snopes, but he was a Compson."

1971 Charles Joseph Samuels, in the *New Republic*, on Kurt Vonnegut: "He can tell us nothing worth knowing except what his rise itself indicates: ours is an age in which adolescent ridicule can become a mode of upward mobility."

June 13

BORN: 1752 Fanny Burney (*Evelina, Cecilia, Camilla*), King's Lynn, England
1888 Fernando Pessoa (*The Book of Disquiet*), Lisbon
DIED: 1965 Martin Buber (*I and Thou, The Way of Man*), 87, Jerusalem
1998 Reg Smythe (*Andy Capp*), 80, Hartlepool, England

1863 Darwin's *Origin of Species* took a year or so to make its way to New Zealand, but once it did, Samuel Butler, who had taken up sheep farming there to escape the English upbringing he'd later savage in the posthumous novel *The Way of All Flesh*, pounced on its ideas. On this day, in the essay "Darwin Among the Machines," he declared our machines would be the next to evolve, leaving humans where horses and dogs were today: "There is nothing which our infatuated race would desire more than to see a fertile union between two steam engines." He extended the idea in his utopian satire, *Erewhon*, and it took hold again a century and a half later, as the intelligence of machines grew, in books like George Dyson's *Darwin Among the Machines*.

1954 Saul Bellow, in the *New York Times*, on Ben Hecht's *A Child of the Century*: "His manners are not always nice, but then nice manners do not always make interesting autobiographies, and this autobiography has the merit of being intensely interesting."

1963 Kenzaburō Ōe was already known as the precocious, rebellious voice of his postwar generation in Japan when he and his wife were presented with a grim dilemma: their son was born with a growth from his skull that their doctors said would kill him if left untouched but turn him into a vegetable if removed. The Ōes' decision to operate and, against cultural traditions, integrate Hikari, their handicapped child, into their lives transformed Ōe's writing life immediately, beginning with his novel *A Personal Matter*, in which a young father has to decide what to do with his "monster" child. Ōe's great subject remained his son, who against all expectations found a vocation in musical composition that made him nearly as well known around the world as his Nobel Prize–winning father.

1965 Long delayed by a Polish bureaucracy annoyed that a national sex symbol wanted to marry a *New York Times* correspondent who had already been threatened with expulsion for his reporting, the wedding between Elżbieta Czyżewska and David Halberstam took place in Warsaw before Czyżewska rushed off to receive the Golden Mask award as Poland's most popular TV actress for 1965. Halberstam, who had left his Pulitzer-winning work in Vietnam to report from behind the Iron Curtain, finally wore out his welcome and was thrown out of the country at the end of the year; Czyżewska followed him but struggled to find acting work in her adopted country, where her vividly Eastern European use of English was said to inspire the speech patterns of the title character in her friend William Styron's *Sophie's Choice*.

June 14

BORN: 1899 Yasunari Kawabata (*Snow Country, A Thousand Cranes*), Osaka, Japan
1941 John Edgar Wideman (*Brothers and Keepers*), Washington, D.C.
DIED: 1936 G. K. Chesterton (*The Man Who Was Thursday*), 62, Beaconsfield, England
1986 Jorge Luis Borges (*The Garden of Forking Paths*), 86, Geneva, Switzerland

1728 It's a measure of the outrage stirred up by a small satirical pamphlet called *The Dunciad*, which mocked the horde of London scribblers as followers of the goddess of Dulness, that its author, Alexander Pope, had to take out a newspaper advertisement on this day asserting that, despite the claims of a rival pamphlet titled *A Popp upon Pope*, he had *not* been whipped on his "naked Posteriors" by two assailants in a park along the Thames, nor was he carried away bleeding in a lady friend's apron. Though his biographer calls publishing *The Dunciad* the "greatest folly" of Pope's career, the poet likely would have been gratified to know that being named in his satire would end up as most of his targets' only claim to literary immortality.

1949 Phillies first baseman Eddie Waitkus survived World War II amphibious landings in New Guinea and the Philippines, but he barely came out alive from a night at the Edgewater Beach Hotel in Chicago, when Ruth Ann Steinhagen, a nineteen-year-old obsessed with Waitkus since his days with the Cubs, asked him up to her room and shot him in the chest with a rifle. Waitkus returned to the Phillies lineup within a year, though, and was still playing in 1952

when Bernard Malamud transformed the incident into mythology in *The Natural*, in which Roy Hobbs, an unknown pitching prospect who has just struck out the legendary Walter "the Whammer" Whambold in a carnival dare, is shot by the mysterious Harriet Bird in her hotel room.

1950 Fresh from signing a national syndication contract for his new comic strip, *Li'l Folk*, Charles Schulz celebrated with a steak dinner on the train from New York and, upon arriving in the Twin Cities, went directly to the home of Donna Mae Johnson, the petite, red-haired fellow employee at Art Instruction, Inc., he'd been courting for months, and proposed. She replied, "I don't want to marry anybody, I just wish everybody would leave me alone," but in October, the same month Schulz's strip made its newspaper debut—with a new name, *Peanuts*, that he'd always despise— she married Schulz's rival, her childhood sweetheart Al Wold. Forty years later, a grandmother and still Mrs. Al Wold, she would be discovered as the original for Charlie Brown's eternal unrequited crush, the Little Red-Haired Girl.

1951 Rachel Carson, author of the year's surprise bestseller, *The Sea Around Us*, agreed to write the liner notes to Leopold Stokowski and the NBC Symphony Orchestra's recording of Debussy's *La mer*.

1998 In one of the forty meals he took at Jack's Outback in Yarmouthport, Massachusetts, this month, Edward Gorey ordered two poached eggs, ham, white toast, and fruit cup.

June 15

BORN: 1914 Saul Steinberg (*The Discovery of America*), Râmnicu Sărat, Romania
1939 Brian Jacques (*Redwall, Castaways of the Flying Dutchman*), Liverpool
DIED: 1941 Evelyn Underhill (*Mysticism, The Spiritual Life*), 65, London
1984 Meredith Willson (*The Music Man*), 82, Santa Monica, Calif.

1904 Five days after he met Nora Barnacle in the street and one day after she stood him up for their first date, James Joyce sent her a note: "I may be blind. I looked for a long time at a head of reddish brown hair and decided it was not yours. I went home quite dejected." They met the next day.

1935 "Wouldn't Old Jules snort if he knew that his story won the $5,000 Atlantic Monthly press prize?" Two days after a telegram arrived announcing the prize for *Old Jules*, Mari Sandoz's biography of her pioneer father, Sandoz wrote her mother with the news. On his deathbed Jules Sandoz had made a request to his daughter, "Why don't you write my life some time?"—a surprising suggestion because just a few days before he had scribbled a note to her: "You know I consider artists and writers the maggots of society." Despite his domineering distaste for her work, she kept to her vocation, indefatigably chronicling the settlers of the sandhills of Nebraska and—in books like *Crazy Horse* and *Cheyenne Autumn*—those they displaced.

1952 Though he had been commissioned only to write a three-hundred-word review, Meyer Levin's enthusiasm for Anne Frank's *Diary of a Young Girl* convinced the editors of the *New York Times Book Review* to give him their entire front page on this day. His praise—"It is so wondrously alive, so near, that one feels overwhelmingly the universalities of human nature"—led the book's first edition to be sold out in a week. It also spurred a rush to adapt the diary for the stage, which Levin was already enmeshed in, since he had agreed with Frank's father, Otto, to turn it into a play himself. When his version of the play was rejected, though, he refused to let go, and spent the final thirty years of his life consumed in a single-minded combat with Frank and others that even he called, in a 1973 memoir, *The Obsession*.

2001 Misha Vainberg, the grossly overweight and U.S.-educated son of the 1,238th-richest man in the new Russia, prefers improvising hip-hop rhymes to declaiming Pushkin while relaxing at an upscale nightspot in downscale St. Petersburg, until news arrives that his Beloved Papa has been murdered. The crimes of that same papa were what stranded Misha in his homeland in the first place—knocking off a businessman from Oklahoma is no way to get your son an American visa—but his death sends Misha on a renewed quest to return to the complacent pleasures of the States and to his South Bronx sweetheart, across the barely-stranger-than-truth landscape of Gary Shteyngart's surprisingly poignant satire, *Absurdistan*.

BORN: 1937 Erich Segal (*Love Story, The Death of Comedy*), Brooklyn
1938 Joyce Carol Oates (*them, We Were the Mulvaneys*), Lockport, N.Y.
DIED: 1944 Marc Bloch (*French Rural History*), 57, Saint-Didier-de-Formans, France
2006 Barbara Epstein (editor, *The New York Review of Books*), 77, New York City

1816 When was *Frankenstein* made? (The story, that is, not the monster.) The moment of Mary Shelley's creation has been nearly as enshrouded in legend as the "dreary night of November" when Victor Frankenstein gave the reanimating jolt to his monster. It was, as the story goes, a wet and dreary June in Switzerland when Lord Byron suggested to his guests—Dr. Polidori, who had just sprained his ankle, and the scandalously not-yet-married couple, Percy Shelley and Mary Godwin—that they each write a ghost story. As Mary Shelley recalled it later, after the men told their stories she had a vision in her bedroom of a scientist terrified by his creation as it begins to stir with the spark of life. Terrified too by her vision, she rose to the sight of moonlight over the Alps, a detail that a Texas astronomer has, with methodical literal-mindedness, traced to a single possible hour for her inspiration, between two and three in the early morning of June 16.

1904 James Joyce went on his first outing with his future wife, Nora Barnacle, a rooming-house chambermaid he'd met in the street six days before. They went walking at Ringsend, where, at least as he reminded her in a letter five years later, "it was you who slid your hand down down inside my trousers" while "gazing at me out of your quiet saintlike eyes."

1904 Buck Mulligan shaves himself; Mr. Deasy tells anti-Semitic jokes; Stephen Dedalus says God is "a shout in the street," picks his nose, analyzes *Hamlet*, owes George William Russell money, and drinks absinthe; Leopold Bloom grills a kidney, steps over a hopscotch game, samples *Sweets of Sin* from a bookcart, buys it for his wife, and tidies up after fireworks on the beach; Patrick Dignam is laid to rest; J. J. O'Molloy asks Myles Crawford for a loan; Blazes Boylan places a losing bet on Sceptre, peeks down the front of a shopgirl's blouse, and cuckolds Bloom; Bantam Lyons picks the winning longshot Throwaway; John Eglinton doubts that Shakespeare was a Jew; Martin Cunningham takes up a collection for the widowed Mrs. Dignam; Cissy Caffrey asks Bloom the time; Gerty MacDowell raises her skirt; Mortimer Edward Purefoy is born to Mina; John Howard Parnell plays chess against himself; Ben Dollard sings "The Croppy Boy"; and Bob Doran passes out on the bar in James Joyce's *Ulysses*.

1965 "When you write that you have never lied to her about what she might expect, I think you exaggerate," John Cheever advised Frederick Exley, whose wife had just returned to him. "Neither you nor I nor anyone else can describe the volcanic landscapes a poor girl strays into when she marries a literary man."

June 17

BORN: 1871 James Weldon Johnson (*The Autobiography of an Ex-Colored Man*), Jacksonville, Fla.
1880 Carl Van Vechten (*Nigger Heaven, Firecrackers*), Cedar Rapids, Iowa
DIED: 1947 Maxwell Perkins (editor of Fitzgerald, Hemingway, Wolfe), 62, Stamford, Conn.
1992 Frederick Exley (*A Fan's Notes, Pages from a Cold Island*), 63, Alexandria Bay, N.Y.

1904 After midnight in James Joyce's *Ulysses*, Stephen Dedalus flourishes his ashplant, smashes a chandelier, and gives Corley a loan; Leopold Bloom buys a luke-warm pig's crubeen and a cold sheep's trotter at a late-night butcher and feeds a stray dog, gives Zoe Higgins his potato and retrieves it, and makes cocoa for Stephen; Stephen and Bloom pee in Bloom's garden and look at the stars; Bloom kisses Molly's rear and falls asleep; and Molly wakes and thinks of Blazes Boylan, lieutenants Mulvey and Garvey, and the time Bloom asked to marry her and she said yes.

1943 The elderly Norwegian novelist Knut Hamsun, passionate in his hatred of Eng-land and fervent in his belief in the German spirit, sent the medal for his Nobel Prize for Literature to Joseph Goebbels as a gift to the Nazi cause, saying to the propaganda chief, "I know of no one, Minister, who has so idealistically and tirelessly written and preached the case for Europe, and for man-kind, year in and year out, as yourself." Less than a week later, in a speech in Vienna (in English, oddly enough), he declared, "Eng-land must be brought to her knees!" and on the 26th he was granted an audience with Hitler himself. The meeting, however, was a debacle. Hamsun, nearly deaf and weep-ing, berated Hitler for the brutality and "Prussian ways" of the German occupation of Norway. The Führer shouted in reply, "Quiet, you understand nothing of this!" and the meeting was over.

1959 Frank O'Hara had seen Billie Holiday sing a few times in her last years of decline, and in early 1959, he stood by the bathroom door at the Five Spot when her pianist, Mal Waldron, accompanied a poetry reading by Kenneth Koch and Holiday, despite being banned from performing in bars after her heroin conviction, stepped up to sing. On this day just a few months later, with police waiting outside her hotel room to arrest her again, Holiday was dead, and O'Hara, writ-ing poems during the lunch hour of his job at the Museum of Modern Art, gathered the moments of his afternoon into "The Day Lady Died": the train schedule to Long Island, a shoeshine, the "quandariness" of choosing a book, the sweat of summer, and the memory of how Lady Day once took his breath away.

1960 Anthony Cronin, in the *TLS*, on Samuel Beckett's *Molloy, Malone Dies*, and *The Unnameable*: "Critics have applied the words 'despairing' and 'unbearable' to Mr. Beckett's work, yet the true despair is to cease from contemplation of the mystery, and the true gaiety that which is born of the courage to contemplate the worst. Mr. Beckett has seen the gorgon's head; but he has not been turned to stone."

BORN: 1953 Amy Bloom (*Come to Me, Away*), New York City

1957 Richard Powers (*Galatea 2.2, The Echo Maker*), Evanston, Ill.

DIED: 1902 Samuel Butler (*The Way of All Flesh, Erewhon*), 66, London

2010 José Saramago (*Blindness, The Stone Raft*), 87, Tías, Canary Islands

1815 "Depend upon it, there is no such place as Waterloo!" Jonathan Strange, the personal magician to the Duke of Wellington, possesses many powers in Susanna Clarke's prodigiously inventive historical fantasy, *Jonathan Strange & Mr. Norrell*—glimpsing faraway armies in his silver basin, bringing rain to slow Napoleon's progress, moving the city of Bruxelles to North America for the day—but they don't include a thorough knowledge of Belgian geography. There *is* such a place as Waterloo, and on its muddy, bloody fields (the mud his own doing) Strange pits his magic against the nearly supernatural powers of the French emperor. By nightfall the French are in ragged retreat, but Wellington's victory table, surrounded by acres of dead no spells could save, is somber and nearly empty.

1918 Joe Zmuda, one of the hundred-plus souls who tell their stories in *Working*, the best known of Studs Terkel's unparalleled oral-history collections, isn't working anymore. Retired for ten years, he was a felt cutter for fifteen years and before that a shipping clerk for twenty-five more. And before that? "I was a roving Romeo." He can recall one day in particular—"I have a very, very good, darn good memory": June 18, 1918, when he and a friend went dancing and met two sisters. He kissed one, and she told him and anyone else who could hear, "If I don't marry you, Joe, I'll never marry another person in this world." Did they marry? No. Did she marry anyone else? He doesn't say, but for her seventieth birthday—just the other day—he "called her up, wished her a happy birthday, and that's all. I could have married her, but—."

1936 James Agee was halfway through a letter to his mentor, Father James Harold Flye, when he broke in and added, "Later: I must cut this short and do a week's worth in next 20 hours or so: have been assigned to do a story on: a sharecropper family (daily & yearly life)." He was ecstatic at the assignment, and thrilled about the photographer he'd be working with, Walker Evans. "Best break I ever had on *Fortune*," he added, though he had doubts about his own ability to pull it off and, prophetically, "*Fortune*'s ultimate willingness to use it." The magazine ultimately rejected what he and Evans submitted about the three tenant farmers they visited, and for the next five years Agee doggedly reworked the material into what became the one-of-a-kind book *Let Us Now Praise Famous Men*.

1982 At age seventy in Ossining, New York; age eighty in Franklin Park, New Jersey; and age ninety in New York City, respectively, John Cheever, Granville Hicks, and Djuna Barnes died.

June 19

BORN: 1945 Tobias Wolff (*This Boy's Life, The Barracks Thief*), Birmingham, Ala.
1947 Salman Rushdie (*Midnight's Children, The Satanic Verses*), Bombay
DIED: 1937 J. M. Barrie (*Peter Pan, The Admirable Crichton*), 77, London
1993 William Golding (*Lord of the Flies*), 81, Perranarworthal, England

1948 Robert Lowell, in the *Nation*, on William Carlos Williams's *Paterson, Book Two*: "It is a book in which the best readers, as well as the simple reader, are likely to find *everything*."

1953 It was "a queer sultry summer, the summer they executed the Rosenbergs," and Sylvia Plath, like her character Esther Greenwood in *The Bell Jar*, was "supposed to be having the time of my life," spending a month in Manhattan as one of a team of collegians chosen to guest-edit the August issue of *Mademoiselle*. But she was miserable, and the impending electrocution of the atomic spies became the focus of her anxieties, as it does for Esther. One fellow editor remembered Plath at breakfast the morning of the execution asking "how I could eat when the Rosenbergs were about to be fried just like the eggs on my plate." In her journal, Plath recorded another editor yawning nastily about the prospect, much as in the novel her colleague Hilda's "pale orange mouth opened on a large darkness" to say, "I'm so glad they're going to die."

1972 It was the day after the Watergate break-in went public, and White House counsel John Dean was busy putting out fires. He knew one conversation was too toxic to have indoors, so he took G. Gordon Liddy, who had organized the break-in, out to Seventeenth Street to talk about what had gone wrong. And there, next to the Ellipse and across from the Corcoran Gallery of Art, in an exchange that appears in both *Blind Ambition*, Dean's riveting memoir, and *Will*, Liddy's own bestseller, Dean suggested to Liddy that they not speak about the matter any more and Liddy replied, "I want you to know one thing, John. This is my fault. I'm prepared to accept responsibility for it. And if somebody wants to shoot me on a street corner, I'm prepared to have that done. You just let me know when and where, and I'll *be* there."

2008 Novelist and Seattle SuperSonics season-ticket holder Sherman Alexie testified in the city's lawsuit to stop the team's move to Oklahoma City that "I want two more years of the Greek gods."

BORN: 1905 Lillian Hellman (*The Children's Hour, Pentimento*), New Orleans
1952 Vikram Seth (*A Suitable Boy, The Golden Gate*), Kolkata, India
DIED: 1995 E. M. Cioran (*The Temptation to Exist, The Trouble with Being Born*), 84, Paris
1999 Clifton Fadiman (*The Lifetime Reading Plan, Party of One*), 95, Sanibel, Fla.

1901 Edward Cullen was born, a fact he revealed to Bella Swan a century later as "the light of the setting orb glittered off his skin in ruby-tinged sparkles."

1925 The *New Statesman* on Ivy Compton-Burnett's *Pastors and Masters*: "It is astonishing, amazing. It is like nothing else in the world. It is a work of genius. How to describe it—since there is nothing of which to take hold?"

1945 In a car crash on the way to the airport in New York, Ernest Hemingway bruised his head and broke four ribs.

1958 It would have disappointed Herbert Bayard Swope greatly to learn that his wonderful name is by now largely forgotten. The greatest reporter of his time, the preposterously dynamic editor of the *New York World* in its heyday, and the intimate and peer of the powerful throughout the first half of the twentieth century, Swope, who died on this day, might best be remembered now as a model for F. Scott Fitzgerald's Gatsby, or at least for Gatsby's parties. At the endless all-night affairs Swope threw at his Great Neck mansion, gamblers and prizefighters mingled with debutantes, Supreme Court justices, and the Fitzgeralds themselves in what Swope's wife called "an absolutely seething bordello of interesting people." Ring Lardner, who lived across the way, complained that he had to go into New York to get any writing done, thanks to all the guests roaming the woods.

NO YEAR It's Sunday on the first weekend of the summer season, and husbands are lying asleep on the beach at Amity, Long Island, while their wives read Helen MacInnes and John Cheever and their kids play in the surf. A boy of six on a raft kicks idly a few times to bring himself back toward shore, while below the great fish rises, drawn to the surface by the vibrations. By the end of the afternoon, a great white shark "as large as a station wagon" will have taken its second and third victims in a week and an entire summer of tourism will be in danger. Meanwhile, it's safe to say that any actual husbands and wives on the shores of Long Island in 1974 left their MacInnes and Cheever back at the cottage in favor of the book everyone was reading that summer: Peter Benchley's *Jaws*.

1999 Adam Goodheart, in the *New York Times*, on David Foster Wallace's *Brief Interviews with Hideous Men*: "Calling Wallace's talent unruly doesn't go nearly far enough. It is fiendish, infantile; it takes as much pleasure in acts of destruction as it does in creation."

June 21

BORN: 1905 Jean-Paul Sartre (*Nausea, No Exit, Being and Nothingness*), Paris
   1948 Ian McEwan (*Atonement, The Cement Garden*), Aldershot, England
DIED: 2002 Timothy Findley (*The Wars, Not Wanted on the Voyage*), 71, Brignoles, France
   2003 Leon Uris (*Exodus, Trinity, Mila 18*), 78, Shelter Island, N.Y.

528 Finding himself, inexplicably, in ancient England and, more specifically, near-naked in a dungeon sentenced to be burned at the stake at noon the following day, Hank Morgan, Mark Twain's *Connecticut Yankee in King Arthur's Court*, has an inspiration. "Tell the king," he thunders, "that at that hour I will smother the whole world in the dead blackness of midnight; I will blot out the sun." As it happens, Hank knows the only solar eclipse in the sixth century will begin at three minutes after noon on the very day of his execution, and when his prophecy is fulfilled he is untied from the stake and named the king's right-hand man. Meanwhile, the eclipse also confirms, to his own Yankee skepticism, that he has indeed been transported thirteen centuries into the past.

1858 A. S. Byatt launches *Possession*, her Booker Prize–winning literary romance, with the discovery by a young scholar of two letters to an unknown woman, written on this day in the unmistakable hand of the great (and fictional) Victorian poet Randolph Henry Ash, whose comic circumlocutions and crossed-out words betray a hidden passion: "I cannot but feel . . . ~~that~~ ~~you must in some way share my eagerness that further conversation could be mutually profitable that we must meet~~." Those submerged desires, revealed after a century and a half, set off an academic and romantic quest both endearingly musty and cuttingly modern, in which Byatt's scholars manage, despite their intellectual self-consciousness, to unearth their own buried passions.

1941 Irène Némirovsky planned five sections for her *Suite Française*, the set of novels she imagined as a *War and Peace* for the German occupation of France, to be written as the events unfolded. The second of these, "Dolce," she saw as a short, sweet interlude in the drama, with the relations between occupying German soldiers and their unwilling hosts in a French village culminating on this day in a celebration the Germans arrange on the anniversary of their regiment's arrival in Paris. The villagers look on, happy almost in spite of themselves, and the sweetness is not false, but neither will it last: the Nazi invasion of the Soviet Union will soon draw these soldiers to the Eastern Front. And "Dolce" would be the last section of the novel Némirovsky completed before she was arrested and sent to Auschwitz in 1942.

1964 "I sometimes think that you do not really understand what will be the effect of this book. There has never been, at least not in our time, any other book like it," Alex Haley wrote to Malcolm X about his *Autobiography*. "Do you realize that to do these things you will have to be alive?"

BORN: 1856 H. Rider Haggard (*King Solomon's Mines, She*), Bradenham, England

1964 Dan Brown (*The Da Vinci Code, Angels & Demons*), Exeter, N.H.

DIED: 1947 Jim Tully (*Beggars of Life, Circus Parade*), 61, Los Angeles

1992 M. F. K. Fisher (*The Art of Eating, How to Cook a Wolf*), 83, Glen Ellen, Calif.

YEAR 1342 (by Shire-reckoning) Bilbo Baggins, in *The Hobbit*, returns to Bag-End.

1945 Former high school athletes don't fare too well in American literature, so it's with a vague sense of doom that we read, in the opening pages of Philip Roth's *American Pastoral*, of Seymour "Swede" Levov, whose exploits in football, basketball, and baseball—along with his blond hair and blue eyes—made him the "household Apollo of the Weequahic Jews." Does his downfall come when he joins the marines the day after his graduation on this day from Weequahic High? No, the atom bomb saves him. Does it come when he turns down a contract with the Giants to join his father's glove business, or when he marries Miss New Jersey 1949? Well, not right away, but give it time. His apparent American pastoral will yet meet what Roth calls the "indigenous American berserk."

1958 "Son, your mother's been killed," they told ten-year-old James Ellroy when he got out of a cab his divorced dad had put him in and found police cars around his mother's house in suburban L.A. Photographers posed him in a toolshed for the news stories and called him "brave." In his memoir, *My Dark Places*, forty years later, Ellroy, blunt and luridly obsessive as always, turned noir inside-out with his true-crime investigation into his mother's unsolved murder, not just acknowledging that the violent men and redheaded women in his own fiction were born that day, but wallowing in it, telling the story of Jean Ellroy's cheap death—and his own rage and budding perversity—with the same hepcat brutality of his novels.

1975 Though Frank Conroy was best known for a book about himself, his memoir *Stop-Time*, when he profiled the Rolling Stones for the *New York Times Magazine* on this day he left out a personal moment other writers would have made their lead: finding no Stones home at the Long Island estate they were renting from Andy Warhol, Conroy, who had often supported himself as a jazz pianist, sat down and started playing some Thelonious Monk. He was so caught up in the music that when a drummer joined in he didn't look up until fifty bars later, and when he did, he didn't recognize him—he had never had much interest in rock music. The drummer, Charlie Watts, recognized him, though: he reminded Conroy they had played together two decades before at a jazz club in London.

June 23

BORN: 1894 Alfred Kinsey (*Sexual Behavior in the Human Male, Sexual Behavior in the Human Female*), Hoboken, N.J.
  1961 David Leavitt (*Family Dancing, The Indian Clerk*), Pittsburgh
DIED: 1836 James Mill (*The History of British India*), 63, London
  1956 Michael Arlen (*The Green Hat*), 60, New York City

1959 Was Boris Vian killed by a movie? It makes for a good story: ten minutes into a screening of the film adaptation of his novel *I Spit on Your Graves*, Vian stood up, protested, "These guys are supposed to be American? My ass!" collapsed of a heart attack, and died. The story may be apocryphal—although, as Louis Malle wrote about his old friend, "like anything else, the cinema can kill"—but Vian did die at the movie in Paris on this day at age thirty-nine, after a lifetime of heart trouble in which he packed decades of ambition into the time on earth he knew would be short. He had written *I Spit on Your Graves*, for example, in two weeks on a dare; passed off at first as the translated work of an African American writer named Vernon Sullivan, it made him wealthy and famous after it was banned by the French government.

1975 It's eight o'clock in the evening, and Percival Bartlebooth, a reclusive English millionaire, has died in his third-floor flat holding the last piece to a nearly finished jigsaw puzzle, a W-shaped piece for an X-shaped hole. Isabelle Gratiolet is building a house of cards, Cinoc is eating a tin of pilchards, and Geneviève Foulerot is taking a bath. Two kittens and a dog named Poker Dice are sleeping. The elevator is broken. And Serge Valene, just a few weeks before his death, shares his tiny room with a nearly blank canvas on which he has long planned to paint the lives of his fellow residents in their Paris apartment building. In his novel *Life, a User's Manual*, Georges Perec set himself the same task, using a battery of playful mathematical methods to populate the rooms of 11 rue Simon-Crubellier with a host of very human lives but leaving an unfinished puzzle of its own.

1979 It's the summer of gas shortages, of knowing "the great American ride is ending," but Rabbit Angstrom, for a change, is sitting pretty. Ten years after getting laid off from his Linotype machine and twenty after he was demoing kitchen gadgets in five-and-dimes, Rabbit is selling Toyotas, the little cars everybody wants, at the dealership he and his wife, Janice, inherited from her father-in-law. "I did not know, when I abandoned to motel sleep the couple with a burnt-out house and a traumatized child," John Updike has written about the space between *Rabbit Redux* and *Rabbit Is Rich*, his third Rabbit novel, which begins on this day, "that they would wake to such prosperity."

1996 On the island of Hokkaido, Haruki Murakami ran the sixty-two miles of his first and only ultramarathon in eleven hours and forty-two minutes.

June 24

BORN: 1842 Ambrose Bierce (*The Devil's Dictionary*), Meigs County, Ohio
1937 Anita Desai (*Clear Light of Day*, *In Custody*), Mussoorie, India
DIED: 1909 Sarah Orne Jewett (*The Country of the Pointed Firs*), 59, South Berwick, Maine
1969 Frank King (*Gasoline Alley*), 86, Winter Park, Fla.

1937 After his sister, Rose, later the model for Laura in *The Glass Menagerie*, was diagnosed the day before with what would later be called schizophrenia, Tennessee Williams worried in his journal about her sanity and his own. In the evening, he "lay cowering on my bed for a while and then got up with the reflection that nobody ever died from being strong."

1967 "Alma," Ennis del Mar says to his wife by way of explanation, "Jack and me ain't seen each other in four years." Four years ago, they had parted at the end of their summer on Brokeback Mountain and Ennis found his insides so wrenched by Jack's sudden absence he had to stop at the side of the road and dry heave in the snow. And now, on the landing outside Ennis and Alma's little apartment over a laundry, they're drawn together with such a jolt that Jack's teeth draw blood from Ennis's mouth. It's the first of many—but not enough—reunions in Annie Proulx's "Brokeback Mountain," a love story that made its first, iconic appearance in *The New Yorker* in 1997.

1969 Literature and trash met atop the *New York Times* fiction bestseller list during this week, but which was the bigger scandal? *Portnoy's Complaint*, the story of a boy's love for his mother (and a slab of liver) by Philip Roth, later the most honored writer of his generation, or *The Love Machine*, the *Valley of the Dolls* sequel by Jacqueline Susann, whose former editor had just called her "a poor imitation of about 25 other authors" in the *New York Times*? Susann, who knocked *Portnoy* off the top of the list this week, was happy to rustle up a rivalry, telling Johnny Carson that Roth was "a fine writer, but I wouldn't want to shake hands with him." Roth, meanwhile, was said to shrug to friends later, "After all, it wasn't as if André Malraux said it to François Mauriac."

NO YEAR The *Urus* is scheduled to sail from New York on this day with a cargo of fertilizer for Costa Rica, or at least that's what five men—a waiter, a cook, and three ordinary seamen—have been told before they fly from Managua to New York, happy to have found work on the ship. What they find on a Brooklyn pier, though, is a rusted-out hulk that is anything but seaworthy and that becomes for them a sort of offshore purgatory, stranding them in a stateless, unpaid limbo from which one sailor begins making intrepid forays into the borough beyond in Francisco Goldman's marvelously humane second novel, *The Ordinary Seaman*.

June 25

BORN: 1903 George Orwell (*Homage to Catalonia*, *The Road to Wigan Pier*), Motihari, India
1929 Eric Carle (*The Very Hungry Caterpillar*), Syracuse, N.Y.
DIED: 1984 Michel Foucault (*Discipline and Punish*, *Madness and Civilization*), 57, Paris
1997 Jacques Cousteau (*The Silent World*, *The Living Sea*), 87, Paris

1947 Published: *Het Achterhuis* (*The Secret Annex*) by Anne Frank (Contact, Amsterdam)

1948 It's a small house, but it's his as long as he can keep paying the bank what he owes, and what Easy Rawlins owes is sixty-four dollars by the end of the month. That's why, when the big white man with the white Panama hat and white suit and bone-white shoes and eyes so pale they look like robins' eggs comes into Joppy's looking for someone to track down a young woman named Daphne Monet—"Not bad to look at but she's hell to find"—Easy takes the job, not quite knowing what he's getting mixed up in. "Easy," the man says, in Walter Mosley's debut, *Devil in a Blue Dress*, "walk out your door in the morning and you're mixed up in something. The only thing you can really worry about is if you get mixed up to the top or not."

1949 Diana Trilling, in the *Nation*, on George Orwell's *1984*: "Whereas 'Animal Farm' was too primitive a parable to capture the emotions it wished to persuade, the new book exacerbates the emotions almost beyond endurance."

1966 The issue of *Time* magazine asking "Is God Dead?" is still on the table in her obstetrician's waiting room when Rosemary Woodhouse starts to put the pieces together in Ira Levin's *Rosemary's Baby*. The helpful—too helpful!—couple down the hall in 7A, always so insistent she doesn't skip her vitamin drink; her doctor, who wears the same pungent good-luck charm the neighbors gave her; and even her husband, whose acting career took off after his rival went blind: they are witches, all of them, and they want her baby. When she gives birth just after midnight on this day—"exactly half the year 'round from you-know"—they tell her the baby died, but she knows better, and when she enters apartment 7A she learns the truth about her child: "He has His Father's eyes."

2195 How near is the theocratic, woman-controlling near future of the Republic of Gilead in Margaret Atwood's *The Handmaid's Tale*? Near enough to our time that the women can still smell the sweat in the converted gym where they sleep, but far enough that the messages carved in a desk—*J.H. loves B.P. 1952*, *M. loves G. 1972*—seem "incredibly ancient." And for the twenty-second-century scholars at the Twelfth Symposium on Gileadean Studies who meet on this day in the novel's sardonically hopeful epilogue, it's far enough in the past that they speak of the Republic as almost incomprehensibly distant, a "great darkness" of the past that shouldn't be judged or censured, just understood.

June 26

BORN: 1892 Pearl S. Buck (*The Good Earth, Pavilion of Women*), Hillsboro, W.Va.

1969 Lev Grossman (*The Magicians, The Magician King*), Lexington, Mass.

DIED: 1793 Gilbert White (*The Natural History and Antiquities of Selborne*), 72, Selborne, England

1961 Kenneth Fearing (*The Big Clock, Dead Reckoning*), 58, New York City

NO YEAR The plan required five men: Kelp fakes a seizure to distract one guard at the New York Coliseum, and Murch crashes a car into the main entrance to draw the rest, which gives Dortmunder, Greenwood, and Chefwick time to nab the Balabomo Emerald and get out of the building. And it all might have worked if Greenwood hadn't gotten lost on the way out and, desperate, swallowed the giant gem. So now Dortmunder needs a new plan: spring Greenwood, and the emerald, out of jail. It won't be the last plan he needs. Donald E. Westlake began *The Hot Rock* as one of the hard-boiled Parker novels he wrote as Richard Stark, but it "kept turning funny," so instead he launched a new series under his own name featuring bumbling crook John Dortmunder.

1980 Which moment in Steven Bach's *Final Cut* marked the end of a filmmaking era: when Michael Cimino, two weeks into shooting *Heaven's Gate*, was already ten days behind schedule and a couple of million dollars over budget, or when the first reviews came in, which compared the film to "a forced, four-hour walking tour of one's own living room"? Or was it this day, when Cimino delivered his first cut of the film, a year and a half late and five and a half hours long: "I felt bludgeoned," Bach, the studio production chief in charge of the movie, wrote about the screening, "by vainglory and excess." Although some have since reclaimed it as a neglected masterpiece, *Heaven's Gate* is still inseparable from Bach's classic insider account of the insanity of Hollywood.

1996 Friendly, foul-mouthed, and fearless, Veronica Guerin found in her short journalism career that she could get almost anyone to talk to her. When she was shot in the leg in her Dublin home after she identified the mastermind of a $4 million airport robbery, she found out from her sources who had ordered the hit and then went on crutches to tell him she wasn't afraid. But a year and a half later, as she continued to report on Ireland's drug trade—and two days before she was to give a speech called "Dying to Tell a Story: Journalists at Risk"—two men on a motorcycle pulled up behind her car and finished the job. Of those suspected, only one has yet been convicted of her murder.

1997 Published: *Harry Potter and the Philosopher's Stone* by J. K. Rowling (Bloomsbury, London)

2005 Terrence Rafferty, in the *New York Times*, on Michael Cunningham's *Specimen Days*: "a book that is, in the sheer obstinacy of its wrongheadedness, itself an almost suicidal act of courage."

June 27

BORN: 1936 Lucille Clifton (*Good Woman, Blessing the Boats*), Depew, N.Y.
  1953 Alice McDermott (*That Night, Charming Billy*), Brooklyn
DIED: 1980 Carey McWilliams (*Factories in the Field*), 74, New York City
  2001 Tove Jansson (*Finn Family Moomintroll, The Summer Book*), 86, Helsinki

1787 Few stories of a writer finishing a book are as romantic or as well known—to earlier generations of readers, at least—as the final hour of Edward Gibbon's twenty years of labor on *The History of the Decline and Fall of the Roman Empire*. "Between the hours of eleven and twelve" in the evening he put his pen down at last and took a stroll under the acacias in Lausanne, Switzerland, feeling joy at the prospect of freedom and fame but then melancholy at leaving the *History*, his "old and agreeable companion." The acacias themselves became a monument to his work: Byron helped himself to a leaf on a visit, and Thomas Hardy marked the 110th anniversary of the moment with a poem, "Lausanne: In Old Gibbon's Garden: 11–12 pm."

1880 Dr. John H. Watson is struck in the shoulder by a bullet at the Battle of Maiwand, forcing his return from service in Afghanistan to London, where he soon takes shared lodgings at 221B Baker Street.

NO YEAR There may be no American writer better known for just a few pages of her work than Shirley Jackson, who despite writing one of the great ghost stories, *The Haunting of Hill House*, and a bestselling collection of proto-Bombeck household tales, *Life Among the Savages*, is known primarily for the events of the "clear and sunny" morning of June 27, when the men, women, and children of an unnamed village assemble to conduct a lottery. With its matter-of-fact narration, "The Lottery" remains among the most terrifying of tales, whose effect on its original *New Yorker* readers, who wrote to the magazine by the hundreds after it appeared, must have only been heightened by the date of the issue it appeared in: June 26, 1948.

1951 "I haven't the slightest doubt but that if this novel had any other name on it than that of Howard Fast," began Angus Cameron's report to his fellow editors at Little, Brown on Fast's latest book, *Spartacus*, "it would become a best seller." But Fast had just spent three months in prison for contempt of Congress for refusing to name names before the Un-American Affairs Committee, and so, given the tenor of the times—the Rosenbergs were executed eight days before—Little, Brown turned down the book. So did every other publisher Fast approached, so instead he published *Spartacus* himself, sending out Cameron's report—to Cameron's dismay—in an appeal for orders. *Spartacus* sold nearly 50,000 copies in three months, and nine years later the film version, with Dalton Trumbo of the Hollywood Ten as screenwriter, helped end the Hollywood blacklist soon after Crown ended Fast's exile from major publishing by reprinting the novel.

June 28

BORN: 1712 Jean-Jacques Rousseau
(*Confessions*, *Émile*), Geneva
1947 Mark Helprin (*Winter's Tale*, *A Soldier of the Great War*), New York City
DIED: **1985** Lynd Ward (*God's Man*, *The Biggest Bear*), 80, Reston, Va.
2001 Mortimer Adler (*How to Read a Book*), 98, Palo Alto, Calif.

1889 Alice James, a great admirer of the novels and the courageously nonconformist life of George Eliot (and never one to mince opinions in her diaries), was disappointed in the *Life* of the novelist, edited by Eliot's widower, John Cross, that came out soon after her death: "But what a monument of ponderous dreariness is the book! What a lifeless, diseased, self-conscious being she must have been! . . . She makes upon me the impression, morally and physically, of mildew, or some morbid growth—a fungus of a pendulous shape, or as of something damp to the touch." James was not alone in her disappointment, although Prime Minister William Gladstone was rather less vivid when he merely, but famously, remarked, "It is not a Life at all. It is a Reticence, in three volumes."

1898 "It is especially disagreeable for me," Leo Tolstoy, who had largely left fiction behind for philosophy in his last decades, wrote in his diary, "when people who have lived little and thought little, do not believe me, and not understanding me, argue with me about moral problems. It would be the same for which a veterinary surgeon would be hurt, if people who were not familiar with his art were to argue with him."

1991 Charles Tomlinson, in the *TLS*, on Pablo Neruda's *Canto General*: "Neruda does not really trust us as readers. There are times when it even seems that he would like to transform us into the simple people he often talks about, so that he could play the village explainer, thus reducing us all to a role of purely passive and loving acceptance."

1997 Lindsay Fraser, in the *Scotsman*, on J. K. Rowley's [*sic*] *Harry Potter and the Philosopher's Stone*: "What distinguishes this novel from so many other fantasies is its grip on reality. Harry is a hugely likeable child, kind but not wet, competitive but always compassionate."

2006 It had to happen sometime. When Henry DeTamble was first given a tour of his new workplace, Chicago's Newberry Library, he shied at the sight of one element no one else gave a thought to: the Cage, a fenced-off, four-storey shaft in the center of a stairwell. "You can't get into it," he's told, but all he can think is, "I won't be able to get out." And now it's happened: he's found himself, naked and cold, at the bottom of the Cage, but at least his explanation to his co-workers becomes more convincing when his present, clothed self shows up too, outside the Cage. As he patiently explains, Henry has the rare but increasingly common condition of chrono-impairment; he is, as you might have guessed, the husband of Audrey Niffenegger's *Time Traveler's Wife*.

June 29

BORN: 1798 Giacomo Leopardi (*Canti, Zibaldone*), Recanati, Italy

1900 Antoine de Saint-Exupéry (*The Little Prince, Night Flight*), Lyon, France

DIED: 1861 Elizabeth Barrett Browning (*Sonnets from the Portuguese*), 55, Florence, Italy

1990 Irving Wallace (*The Chapman Report, The Book of Lists*), 74, Los Angeles

NO YEAR Witty, wearily grandiose, and distinctly unreliable, Frederick Charles St. John Vanderveld Montgomery—"Freddie" to everyone except himself—takes advantage of the forced leisure of his incarceration for the murder of a servant girl to confess his sins, with a chilling emptiness, in John Banville's *The Book of Evidence*. The emptiness is not limited to himself, though: he operates in a world of decadent and diluted wealth in which, in his own mind at least, everyone stands at the same icy and bewildered remove from any sense of morality or even identity. For ten days after the crime he hid in plain sight at the home of an art dealer he knows, a perverse interlude that ended with a sad, drunken party on this night and then the next morning the knock of the police on the door, which gave him his last hope of finding meaning.

NO YEAR Patrick Kenzie greets the dawn in a chair. He's been sitting up and brooding all night in the apartment of a stranger because he has a job to do and because he doesn't have anything better to go home to. His job: finding a woman named Jenna Angeline and the documents he's been told she ran off with when she skipped out on her job as a cleaning woman in the Massachusetts State House. He's found Jenna and extracted a grudging promise to see the documents, but by the end of the day, his assignment will have blown up into something else entirely, putting him in danger and on the front page of the Boston papers in *A Drink Before the War*, Dennis Lehane's first novel and the debut of his flirty and flawed investigators, Kenzie and his partner Angie Gennaro.

NO YEAR In his stories, Edward P. Jones maps Washington, D.C., with a precision that often reaches the detail of individual street addresses. Even in "Lost in the City," the title story in his first collection, when Lydia Walsh hands two twenties to the cabbie she called to take her to the hospital where her mother has died and tells him to get her lost instead, he keeps driving past places she knows too well: 1122 5th Street, where her father died when she was four; 457 Ridge Street, where she and her mother took a downstairs apartment; the spot on Rhode Island Avenue, a Safeway now, where they lived on the same floor as a woman driven crazy by the certainty her husband would leave her. The addresses have a concrete persistence, much like the people Jones writes about, the District's lifelong residents who are often ignored in favor of their city's high-profile transients.

BORN: 1685 John Gay (*The Beggar's Opera*), Barnstaple, England

1911 Czesław Miłosz (*The Captive Mind, Collected Poems*), Szetejnie, Russian Empire

DIED: 1973 Nancy Mitford (*The Pursuit of Love*), 68, Versailles, France

2003 Robert McCloskey (*Blueberries for Sal*), 88, Deer Isle, Maine

1835 "$100 REWARD will be given for the apprehension and delivery of my Servant Girl, HARRIET," read a notice placed in the Norfolk, Virginia, *American Beacon* by Dr. James Norcom. "As this girl absconded from the plantation of my son without any known cause or provocation, it is probable she designs to transport herself to the North." She had indeed absconded, in fear of Norcom's designs on her, but hadn't gone far: for the next seven years, Harriet Jacobs hid in a crawlspace in the attic of her grandmother's house less than a block from Norcom's office, before she was able to escape north and, in 1861, publish *Incidents in the Life of a Slave Girl*, an account little noticed at the time but rediscovered and acclaimed in the 1980s, when the improbable details of Jacobs's escape were also confirmed.

1950 On this day, "right in the middle of the twentieth century," Fleur Talbot, in Muriel Spark's *Loitering with Intent*, sensed her life change. Sitting in a park, she felt "more than ever how good it was to be a woman and an artist there and then." The following day her feelings were confirmed when a publisher accepted her first novel, placing a satisfying seal on the previous ten months, whose often terrible events came to resemble, with a precision that neither surprised nor dismayed her, the ones she had already described in the book. Fleur's story (which bears some resemblance to Spark's own early history as a writer) is a delicious and sharp-witted tale of the novelist's amoral hunger for experience—preferably that of others. As Fleur herself admits, "I do dearly love a turn of events."

1962 It may have been young, disillusioned reporters like David Halberstam, Neil Sheehan, and Peter Arnett who grabbed the biggest headlines with their skeptical early dispatches from the American ensnarement in Vietnam, but it was the veteran Homer Bigart, already twice a battlefront Pulitzer winner and holder of no illusions to begin with, who showed them the way. As William Prochnau relates in *Once Upon a Distant War*, just before leaving the country in disgust on this day Bigart turned a quiet—too quiet—South Vietnamese mission in search of Vietcong guerrillas into a lesson for the young Sheehan. "For God's sake, let's go home," Sheehan complained. "Nothing happened. There's no story." "No story, kid? That's the story, k-k-kid," Bigart stuttered back in contempt. "It doesn't *work*."

1967 A New Jersey justice of the peace, grumbling because he missed a day of golf to perform the ceremony, interrupted his marriage of writers Kenneth Tynan and Kathleen Halton to tell one of the witnesses, Marlene Dietrich, "I wouldn't stand with your ass to an open door in this office, lady."

July Perhaps this chapter should be titled "Messidor" or "Thermidor" instead: July is the month of revolutions, and why shouldn't a revolution sweep away the calendar as well? Along with the new metric system for weights and measures (which proved longer-lived), the French Republic introduced a new calendar that not only founded a new Year I in 1792, the first year of the Republic, but created twelve new months of three ten-day weeks each. (The five or six days left over became national holidays, *les jours complémentaires*, at the end of the year.)

New names were given to each month by the poet Fabre d'Églantine, among them Messidor (from "harvest") and Thermidor (from

"heat"), which overlapped the traditional days of July (British wags were said to have suggested "Wheaty" and "Heaty" as local equivalents).

Each day of the year had an individual name too, inspired by plants, animals, and tools: for instance, Alexandre Dumas (b. July 24, 1802), was born on Bélier (Ram), the 5th of Thermidor in Year X. Luckless Fabre d'Églantine, meanwhile, was executed for corruption by his own revolution on Laitue (Lettuce), the 16th of Germinal in Year II. (He handed out his poems on the way to the guillotine.)

America's calendar was unaffected by its own revolution, except for the new Fourth of July celebration (which didn't become an official federal holiday until 1870). For reading on the Fourth, along with the documents of the founders and the endless stream of biographies and histories, you can turn to Ross Lockridge Jr.'s nearly forgotten epic, *Raintree County,* which uses the single day of July 4, 1892, to look back on a century of American history, while George Pelecanos's *King Suckerman* crackles to a final showdown at the Bicentennial celebration in Washington, D.C., and Frank Bascombe, in Richard Ford's *Independence Day* (a Pulitzer winner like *Raintree County*), attempts a father-son reconciliation with a July Fourth weekend visit to those shrines to American male bonding, the baseball and basketball Halls of Fame. And soldier-turned-antiwar-activist Ron Kovic really was, as he titled his memoir, *Born on the Fourth of July*.

For a classic small-town Independence Day story of the kind that may only exist in memory and fiction, there is the tug-of-war in John D. Fitzgerald's *The Great Brain Reforms*. Based on his own childhood in Utah at the turn of the last century, the eight Great Brain books embed the Tom Sawyer–like schemes of Fitzgerald's older brother (also named Tom) in a vividly imagined community, in which the Fitzgeralds are minority "Gentiles" among Mormon settlers, and in *The Great Brain Reforms*, the town's annual Fourth of July celebration, with its parade, picnic, and tug-of-war across the irrigation canal between Gentile and Mormon kids, offers yet another chance for Tom to swindle the locals, not long before he encounters a rare and temporary comeuppance that makes this fifth book the finest and most dramatic in the series.

The Federalist Papers by Alexander Hamilton, James Madison, and John Jay (1788) ❧ Anybody can have a revolution: the real achievement of the American experiment was building a system of government that could last, as argued for in these crucial essays on democracy and the balance of powers.

Crime and Punishment by Fyodor Dostoyevsky (1866) ❧ It's an exceptionally hot July, and the student Raskolnikov is subject to fevers, but what is most chilling about his crimes—to him as much as anyone—is their cold-bloodedness, that they erupted from the deliberations and inexplicable resolutions of his own mind.

The Worst Journey in the World by Apsley Cherry-Garrard (1922) ❧ No Antarctic tourist would choose the height of the southern winter for a visit, but that's when emperor penguins nest, and so Cherry-Garrard and two companions set out on a foolhardy scientific expedition across the Ross Ice Shelf in the darkness of the Antarctic July, the "Winter Journey" that became the centerpiece of Cherry-Garrard's classic account of the otherwise doomed Scott Expedition.

The Killer Angels by Michael Shaara (1974) ❧ "It rained all that night. The next day was Saturday, the Fourth of July." Those are the final words of *The Killer Angels*, but there's no danger of spoiling the story of Shaara's Pulitzer-winning novel of Gettysburg, the battle that more than any other reclaimed the Union that had been founded four score and seven years before.

Saturday Night by Susan Orlean (1990) ❧ Orlean's first book, a traveling celebration of the ways Americans spend their traditional night of leisure—dancing, cruising, dining out, staying in—follows no particular season, but it's an ideal match for July, the Saturday night of months, when you are just far enough into summer to enjoy it without a care for the inevitable approach of fall.

Paris Stories by Mavis Gallant (2002) ❧ What better way to celebrate Canada Day and Bastille Day (and Independence Day too, for that matter) than with the stories of Montreal's great expatriate writer, who left for Paris empty-handed except for the plan to make herself a writer of fiction before she was thirty, and has been publishing her stories in *The New Yorker* for six decades since.

Call Me by Your Name by André Aciman (2007) ❧ "This summer's houseguest. Another bore." Hardly: the young American academic who intruded on Elio's family's Italian villa set off a summer's passion whose intensity upended his life and still sears his memory in Aciman's elegant story of remembered, inelegant desire.

Gone Girl by Gillian Flynn (2012) ❧ Five years are all it's taken for the marriage of Amy and Nick, a once-high-flying media couple, to curdle, and Amy's disappearance on their wedding anniversary, July 5, sets off this twisted autopsy of a marriage gone violently wrong.

BORN: 1869 William Strunk Jr. (*The Elements of Style*), Cincinnati
1915 Jean Stafford (*The Mountain Lion*, *The Collected Stories*), Covina, Calif.
DIED: 1896 Harriet Beecher Stowe (*Uncle Tom's Cabin, Dred*), 85, Hartford, Conn.
1983 Buckminster Fuller (*Nine Chains to the Moon, Synergetics*), 87, Los Angeles

1660 Samuel Pepys brought home a "fine Camlett cloak, with gold buttons, and a silk suit": "I pray God to make me able to pay for it."

1858 Neither author was present—Alfred Russel Wallace was specimen-hunting in Malaysia, and Charles Darwin was mourning the death of his tenth and last child—when their papers on natural selection were presented at a meeting of the Linnean Society in London on this day. Squeezed onto the program by Darwin's friends after Wallace had surprised Darwin with an essay whose ideas matched the ones Darwin had been long developing, the papers caused little remark at the time, and the revolution they represented only began to be recognized when they were published in August, two months before Wallace, still in the jungles of Asia, learned they had been made public at all.

1916 "CECIL TEUCER VALANCE MC," the tomb reads, with the dead man chiseled in marble in "magnificently proper" style, "FELL AT MARICOURT JULY 1 1916." The death of Cecil Valance, the young poet taken before his time like so many in the First World War, is the event at the center of Alan Hollinghurst's novel *The Stranger's Child*, but it hardly seems to have happened at all, or at least Cecil, in all his unformed, demanding magnificence, seems hardly to have existed. His few poems will last, enough to make an industry at least, but the endless attempts to retrieve Cecil's presence to accompany them are doomed. As one of those who loved him says gloomily ten years later, "One sees the anniversaries stretching out for ever."

1923 Young reporter Margaret Mitchell, while interviewing Rudolf Valentino, was carried through a window by the screen star amid "gasps of admiration from a crowd of ladies." "But," he told her, "there are as many men that come to see me as the ladies."

1931 There may be no other American novel that mentions money so often as James M. Cain's *Mildred Pierce*. Nearly every page has a sum or a calculation, from the pennies Mildred pinches when she's trying to get by as a single mother in the early days of the Depression to the extravagances she can't deny herself and her monstrous daughter when their careers both take off. The book's early chapters are haunted by the first day of July, the due date of the mortgage Mildred's shiftless husband put on their house, which drives her to start her own pie-making business and to turn, not for the last time, to Wally, her husband's old partner and her indifferent lover, for a loan.

1950 After banging his head docking his fishing boat in Cuba, Ernest Hemingway needed three stitches.

July 2

BORN: 1877 Hermann Hesse (*Siddhartha,
Steppenwolf*), Calw, Germany
1919 Jean Craighead George (*My Side of
the Mountain*), Washington, D.C.
DIED: 1904 Anton Chekhov (*The Three
Sisters*), 44, Badenweiler, Germany
1961 Ernest Hemingway (*For Whom the
Bell Tolls*), 61, Ketchum, Idaho
1977 Vladimir Nabokov (*Pnin, Pale Fire*),
78, Montreux, Switzerland

1861 Searching for the Great Comet of 1861 in the "murky" London sky, George Eliot reported she could only see the red light of a "distant gin-shop."

1863 Told from the documents of history and from the gallant perspective of the officers whose names—Longstreet, Chamberlain, Lee, Armistead, Buford—have been tied to the Battle of Gettysburg ever since, Michael Shaara's novel *The Killer Angels* has been embraced as one of the most vivid accounts of the Civil War's turning point. The battle's own turning point comes on this middle day, as the armies engage in their full force. "We *must* attack," Lee tells Longstreet, and so they do, even though Longstreet soon finds that the Union forces he thought were on Cemetery Ridge had moved forward into the orchard below. Meanwhile, the Union's Colonel Vincent, who won't survive his wounds from the day, tells Chamberlain up on Little Round Top, "Looks like you're the flank, Colonel," which means one thing: "You must defend this place to the last."

1925 On a summer day at a hotel in Santa Fe, Willa Cather happened on a privately published biography, *The Life of the Right Reverend Joseph P. Machebeuf*, by a fellow priest named Father Howlett. After reading through the night in a frenzy of inspiration, by the following day Cather had already mapped out the story of *Death Comes for the Archbishop*, which took the lives of Machebeuf and Jean-Baptiste Lamy as the models for its portrait of the missionary fathers Vaillant and Latour. We don't have an exact date for Cather's inspiration, but by early July she was already writing her friend Mabel Dodge Luhan that she was on the hunt for old priests from the area for further research, and by November *Death Comes for the Archbishop* was completed.

1977 On June 21, 1977, the Japanese ship *Tsimtsum* leaves Madras, India, for North America with a cargo of sedated zoo animals and a family of former zookeepers on board, including sixteen-year-old Pi Patel. None of them will reach their destination, though. After an explosion sinks the ship on this day, only Pi, a hyena, an orangutan, a zebra, and a Bengal tiger named Richard Parker—and soon only Pi and Richard Parker—are left to share a lifeboat, on which, if his story is to be believed, Pi and the tiger survive another 226 days before landing in Mexico. It is, admittedly, an unlikely story, but then everything about Yann Martel's novel *Life of Pi* is unlikely: that the novel could actually succeed with such a preposterous premise, and that such a novel, by an unknown Canadian writer, could win the U.K.'s most prestigious literary award, the Booker Prize.

July 3

BORN: **1883** Franz Kafka (*The Metamorphosis, Amerika*), Prague
1937 Tom Stoppard (*Arcadia, Rosencrantz and Guildenstern Are Dead*), Zlin, Czechoslovkia
DIED: **1904** Theodor Herzl (*The Jewish State, The Old New Land*), 44, Edlach, Austria
2001 Mordecai Richler (*The Apprenticeship of Duddy Kravitz*), 70, Montreal

1778 After Voltaire's death in May, Wolfgang Amadeus Mozart wrote to his father: "That godless archvillain Voltaire has died like a dog, like an animal—that's his reward!"

1910 Considering himself at age sixteen already educated beyond the capabilities of the University of Wisconsin, on his third day there Ben Hecht ran off to Chicago, where his audition as a reporter for the *Chicago Daily Journal*, at least as he remembered it in his lively memoir, *A Child of the Century*, consisted of the impromptu composition of a humorous poem about a bull that swallowed a bumblebee. Hired, he received his first introduction to the line of work he'd fondly immortalize in the play (and then film) *The Front Page* when his new editor, after telling him to report for work the next morning at six, answered his objection that the following day was the Fourth of July, "Allow me to contradict you, Mr. Hecht. There are no holidays in this dreadful profession you have chosen."

1929 Edmund Wilson, in the *New Republic*, on D. H. Lawrence's *Lady Chatterley's Lover*, nineteen years before Wilson's own novel, *Memoirs of Hecate County*, was upheld as obscene by the U.S. Supreme Court: "His courageous experiment . . . should make it easier for the English writers of the future to deal more searchingly and plainly, as they are certainly destined to do, with the phenomena of sexual experience."

1941 July 1941 was the darkest month in P. G. Wodehouse's sunny life. Released in June from nearly a year in a German internment camp, which he described as "really great fun," he recorded a series of radio broadcasts in Berlin with the encouragement of the Nazi authorities. They were a disaster. Bafflingly naive about his hosts and the war, which he seemed to think was one big Edwardian comedy, his comments were taken at home as signs of irresponsibility or even collaboration. Among the most furious was his fellow clubman and humorist A. A. Milne, who, long envious of Wodehouse's more durable success, attacked him on this day for thinking politics was what "the grown-ups talk about at dinner when one is hiding under the table." Wodehouse later got his mild revenge on Milne with his portrait of Rodney Spelvin, a hapless poet who hovered about his son's nursery gathering material for "horribly whimsical" verses about a boy named "Timothy Bobbin."

2006 James Wood, in the *New Republic*, on John Updike's *Terrorist*: "Updike should have run a thousand miles away from this subject—at least as soon as he saw the results on the page."

July 4

BORN: 1804 Nathaniel Hawthorne (*The Scarlet Letter, Twice-Told Tales*), Salem, Mass.
1918 Eppie Lederer (Ann Landers) and Pauline Phillips (Dear Abby), Sioux City, Iowa
DIED: 1761 Samuel Richardson (*Pamela, Clarissa*), 71, London
1826 Thomas Jefferson (*Notes on the State of Virginia*), 83, Charlottesville, Va.

1846 Charlotte Brontë submitted the Brontë sisters' first three manuscripts (*The Professor, Wuthering Heights*, and *Agnes Grey*) to H. Colborn, beginning a year of rejection by London publishers.

1855 Published: *Leaves of Grass* by Walt Whitman (self-published, Brooklyn)

1862 Charles Dodgson frequently took the Liddell sisters, Lorina, Edith, and Alice, on rowboat outings on the Thames, but one "golden afternoon" in July was especially remembered for the story he told the girls, in which he sent his "heroine straight down a rabbit-hole, to begin with, without the least idea what was to happen next." Alice, the youngest, asked him to write out the adventures of her namesake, but it was another two years, during which the Liddells made a mysterious break with him that may or may not have been caused by his interest in their daughter, before he presented her with a hand-written and -illustrated pamphlet he called *Alice's Adventures Under Ground*. When the story appeared in print as *Alice's Adventures in Wonderland* a year later, Dodgson asked his publisher to send a copy to Alice Liddell on July 4, the anniversary of their outing.

1922 "Few people love the writings of Sir Thomas Browne," Virginia Woolf wrote in 1923, "but those who do are the salt of the Earth." Over the centuries the fans of Browne's *Religio Medici* and *Urn Burial*, his 1658 meditation on fate and death provoked by the recent unearthing of ancient Roman graves, have included Dr. Johnson, Coleridge, Poe, Emerson, Melville, Joyce, Borges, and W. G. Sebald, who in *The Rings of Saturn* noted the odd but appropriate fact that Browne's own bones suffered a fate entirely in keeping with his essay's melancholy meditations about mortality: disinterred by mistake in 1840, his skull was kept on display in a Norwich hospital until on this day it was buried once again in his tomb.

1935 No American writer was more closely identified with his editor than Thomas Wolfe with Maxwell Perkins, known for wrestling Wolfe's giant manuscripts into bestselling novels, and Wolfe grew to resent it, finally making a public break with Perkins and his publisher, Scribner's. But when Wolfe was dying in a Seattle hospital at age thirty-seven, he reached out to his old editor, and in his final written words he fondly reminded Perkins of the Fourth of July three years before when Wolfe arrived home from Europe to find himself famous. Perkins was waiting for him at the dock, and they spent the night celebrating, capped by the dignified editor leading a climb up a fire escape to the garret in which Wolfe had written *Look Homeward, Angel*, and where Wolfe that night scrawled on the wall, "Thomas Wolfe lived here."

BORN: **1958** Bill Watterson (*Calvin and Hobbes*), Washington, D.C.
1972 Gary Shteyngart (*The Russian Debutante's Handbook*), Leningrad, USSR

DIED: **1948** Georges Bernanos (*Diary of a Country Priest*), 60, Neuilly-sur-Seine, France
1991 Howard Nemerov (*The Winter Lightning*), 71, University City, Mo.

1814 "While wading thro' the whimsies, the puerilities, and unintelligible jargon of this work," Thomas Jefferson wrote to John Adams after finishing Plato's *Republic* for the first time, "I laid it down often to ask myself how it could have been that the world should have so long consented to give reputation to such nonsense as this?"

1911 When Lucy Maud Montgomery, whose first Anne of Green Gables books had given her financial independence at age thirty-six, finally married the minister Ewen Macdonald on this day after rejecting a number of suitors, she had a pang of ambivalence: "I felt a sudden horrible inrush of *rebellion* and *despair*," she wrote in her journal. "I *wanted* to *be free*!" That ambivalence hasn't prevented her uncle's home on Prince Edward Island from becoming a shrine where hundreds of couples, mostly from Japan, where interest in "Anne of Red Hair" was strong enough to support a Canadian World theme park in the '90s, enact their own wedding ceremonies in the same parlor where Montgomery had hers.

1922 Edmund Wilson, in the *New Republic*, on James Joyce's *Ulysses*: "Since I have read it, the texture of other novelists seems intolerably loose and careless; when I come suddenly unawares upon a page that I have written myself I quake like a guilty thing surprised."

1925 In Paris, Edith Wharton, though she had admired *The Great Gatsby*, had a disastrous tea with F. Scott Fitzgerald. Wharton was stiffly formal; Fitzgerald, thirty-four years her junior, most likely was drunk.

NO YEAR When Uncle Rondo threw a package of firecrackers into her bedroom at 6:30 in the morning, that was the last straw. They had all ganged up on her: Mama slapped her face and Papa-Daddy called her a hussy, all because Stella-Rondo came home on the Fourth of July—separated from Mr. Whitaker and with a baby named Shirley-T. she claimed was adopted—and turned them all against her. So Sister packed up the radio, the Hawaiian ukelele, and all the preserves she had put up, and headed down to the China Grove post office for good the next day, in Eudora Welty's "Why I Live at the P.O.," first published in the *Atlantic* in 1941.

1949 At a writer's conference in Utah, Vladimir Nabokov met, and liked, Ted Geisel, Dr. Seuss, "a charming man, one of the most gifted people" there.

1974 After dreaming for three months of a "vast and important" book in his own library, Philip K. Dick tracked down the only book in his collection that matched the dream: *The Shadow of Blooming Grove: Warren G. Harding in His Times*, seven hundred pages long and "the dullest book in the world."

July 6

BORN: 1946 Peter Singer (*Animal Liberation, Practical Ethics*), Melbourne, Australia
1952 Hilary Mantel (*Wolf Hall, Bring Up the Bodies*), Glossop, England
DIED: 1962 William Faulkner (*Light in August; Absalom, Absalom!*), 64, Byhalia, Miss.
2005 Ed McBain/Evan Hunter (*The Blackboard Jungle, The Mugger*), 78, Weston, Conn.

1483 "Ha! Am I king? 'Tis so. But Edward lives." Shakespeare packed considerable drama into the nine words Richard III, perhaps his most vivid villain, speaks on taking the throne. His play, like most historians, accuses Richard of the murder of the princes Edward and Richard of Shrewsbury, his young rivals for the crown. But the boys' disappearance remains unsolved, and Richard has had his defenders, including Josephine Tey, in whose ingenious historical mystery, *The Daughter of Time*, Scotland Yard inspector Alan Grant, restlessly confined to a hospital room by a broken leg, builds a case that the real Richard III, crowned on this day, was honorable, innocent, and, for that matter, not even a hunchback.

1882 Vincent van Gogh was a passionate reader, self-taught and voracious, and his letters—which are literature themselves—mention hundreds of writers and books he'd read: Hugo, Dickens, Maupassant, *Uncle Tom's Cabin*, *Bouvard and Pecuchet*. No writer is mentioned more often than Émile Zola, the French novelist (and champion of Impressionist painters), beginning with a letter to his brother, Theo, in which, in a discussion of capturing the "curious grays" of Paris at night, Van Gogh speaks of the novelist as a fellow painter: "In *Une page d'amour* by Émile Zola I found several townscapes painted or drawn in a masterly, masterly fashion . . . I'm very definitely going to read *everything* by Zola, of whom I had only known a few fragments up to now."

1943 Philip Larkin wrote to a friend about Diana Gollancz: "I like publishers' daughters. Oh I do like publishers' daughters! The more we mix together, etc. I'd like to brush some of the dust off her myself."

1945 Among those lost in a plane crash off Newfoundland on this day was Colonel Denis Capel-Dunn, returning with the British delegation from the signing of the United Nations Charter in San Francisco. Capel-Dunn rose to a high rank in wartime intelligence and might have been headed for even higher office, but instead he found another sort of notoriety nearly a half-century later when Anthony Powell, the novelist whom Capel-Dunn had hired and then quickly fired as a military secretary during the war, acknowledged that he used his former boss as a model for Kenneth Widmerpool, the "fabulous monster"—ludicrously fat, extravagantly ambitious, and ridiculously boring—who is the most memorable invention in the vast cast of characters in Powell's twelve-volume series, *A Dance to the Music of Time*.

1953 Michael Straight, in the *New Republic*, on a new translation of Colette's *Chéri*: "Colette's preoccupation is of course with women, and she despises all of them but one."

BORN: 1907 Robert A. Heinlein (*Stranger in a Strange Land*, *Starship Troopers*), Butler, Mo.

1933 David McCullough (*Truman*, *John Adams*), Pittsburgh

DIED: 1930 Arthur Conan Doyle (*The Hound of the Baskervilles*), 71, Crowborough, England

1999 Julie Campbell (*Trixie Belden and the Secret of the Mansion*), 91, Alexandria, N.Y.

1806 A month and a half after his first son was born, James Mill threw down a challenge to a fellow new father: "I intend to run a fair race with you in the education of a son. Let us have a well-disputed trial which of us twenty years hence can exhibit the most accomplished & virtuous young man." (His competitiveness might be explained by the fact that the other father was William Forbes, who had married Wilhelmina Stuart, the love of Mill's youth he was barred from marrying by his lower-class status.) If a race it was, it's impossible to imagine that Mill didn't win: the prodigious education of his son, John Stuart Mill—reading Greek at three and thoroughly versed in the classics

by twelve, when he began assisting his father with his *History of India*—remains a legend in British education.

1938 In a letter full of reading advice, F. Scott Fitzgerald wrote his sixteen-year-old daughter, Scottie, "*Sister Carrie*, almost the first piece of American realism, is damn good and is as easy reading as a True Confession."

NO YEAR Granner Weeks has had eighty-two birthdays before this one, but she's still as excited as a child waiting for Santa about the party she always arranges, with flags and fireworks and cake. There used to be two parties in the same week, until she convinced her husband, Buck, to combine them. "All right by me," he said, agreeable as always. "You won't mind gettin your presents three days early?" "I ain't thinking of changing my day," she replied. "I was thinking it would be easier to change the country's day." Granner's birthday party is only one of the things that bring the people of Marshboro, North Carolina—and one notable outsider—together in Jill McCorkle's second novel, *July 7th*, which is set on, and named after, McCorkle's own birthday.

2005 David Kipen, in the *San Francisco Chronicle*, on Jonathan Coe's *Like a Fiery Elephant: The Story of B. S. Johnson*: "It's as if Paul McCartney wrote a song about John Cage, and it made you want to listen to them both all over again."

July 8

BORN: 1929 Shirley Ann Grau (*The Keepers of the House*), New Orleans
   1952 Anna Quindlen (*Black and Blue, One True Thing*), Philadelphia
DIED: 1822 Percy Bysshe Shelley (*Prometheus Unbound*), 29, Gulf of Spezia, Italy
   1939 Havelock Ellis (*Sexual Inversion, My Life*), 80, Hintlesham, England

1848 Alarmed that their novels *Jane Eyre, Wuthering Heights,* and *Agnes Grey*, written under the pseudonyms of Currer, Ellis, and Acton Bell, were being taken as the work of a single author, Charlotte and Anne Brontë—after failing to convince their shy sister, Emily, to join them—set out on the train for London to establish their identities to their publishers. They resisted requests, though, to announce publicly that the Bell brothers, whose violent and passionate books had caused a popular scandal, were in fact three tiny country spinsters. Meanwhile, reviews of Anne's second novel, *The Tenant of Wildfell Hall*, published the same day, warned of the Bells' "morbid love of the coarse," a warning that may have contributed to the book's immediate success, and to Charlotte's suppression of the book after Anne's death.

1940 W. H. Auden, in the *New Republic*, on *The Wartime Letters of Rainer Maria Rilke: 1914–1921*: "Now in this second and even more dreadful war, there are few writers to whom we can more profitably turn, not for comfort—he offers none—but for strength to resist the treacherous temptations that approach us disguised as righteous duties."

1980 At eight in the morning after a sleepless and tormented night, Raymond Carver wrote a 2,000-word letter to his editor, Gordon Lish, that carries the compressed and complex emotional weight of his best stories. Surprised by the massive cuts Lish had made to the stories in his upcoming collection, *What We Talk About When We Talk About Love*, Carver pleaded for Lish to either reinstate the lost material or cancel the book. He was grateful to Lish for helping him become one of the most admired story writers in the country, but if the book was published as edited, he said, "I'm liable to croak." Just two days later he wrote a conciliatory follow-up letter, and the stories were published largely as Lish had edited them, but later, in his final collection, Carver returned three of the stories to their original form.

1983 Harriett Gilbert, in the *New Statesman*, on *Granta 8: Dirty Realism*, the influential issue collecting stories by Carver, Richard Ford, Bobbie Ann Mason, Tobias Wolff, and other Americans: "This realism's 'dirtiness' has little to do with decadence or ripe, organic decay. It is closer to the sadness of yesterday's rubbish being blown down an empty street. But it also contains an element that synopsis cannot convey—a terrible edge of violence, a violence that slowly runs its thumb down the blade of each hard, tight sentence."

BORN: **1933** Oliver Sacks (*Awakenings, Uncle Tungsten*), London
1951 Larry Brown (*Dirty Work, Joe, Father and Son*), Oxford, Miss.

DIED: **1797** Edmund Burke (*Reflections on the Revolution in France*), 68, Beaconsfield, England
1977 Loren Eiseley (*The Immense Journey, The Firmament of Time*), 69, Philadelphia

1846 "Ah Flush!, Flush!—he did not hurt you really?" Elizabeth Barrett inquired. "The truth is he hates all unpetticoated people, and though he does not hate *you*, he has a certain distrust of you." The unpetticoated person in question, of course, was Miss Barrett's suitor, Robert Browning, and Flush was her dog, the spaniel who found a further literary fame when Virginia Woolf, exhausted after finishing *The Waves*, amused herself by writing a "Life" of the Brownings' dog, including a dog's-eye retelling of this day: "At last his teeth met in the immaculate cloth of Mr. Browning's trousers!" *Flush* was a popular success, but it soon lost its humor for Woolf, who called it a "silly book" about an "abominable dog."

1875 The police surveillance of Fyodor Dostoyevsky, in place since his return from Siberian exile sixteen years before, ended.

1937 Though they were two of the prize horses in the stable of the great editor Maxwell Perkins at Scribner's, Thomas Wolfe and F. Scott Fitzgerald had never had much to say to each other, so Wolfe was surprised to receive a letter out of the blue from Fitzgerald, although he wasn't surprised at Fitzgerald's advice, which he'd heard many times before: he should discipline his "unmatchable" talent by leaving more stuff out of his vast novels. Wolfe's response, naturally, was eight times as long, but it is a marvel of disciplined and cordial dissent, claiming his place among Shakespeare, Cervantes, and Dostoyevsky, the "great putter-inners" (rather than "taker-outers") of literature, and declaring that he was heading into the woods to do the best work of his life. (He'd be dead within the year, though, and Fitzgerald wasn't far behind him.)

1937 "It is indeed getting more and more difficult, even pointless, for me to write in formal English," Samuel Beckett wrote in German to Axel Kaun, a friend in Berlin, declaring he wanted to tear the language apart "in order to get to those things (or the nothingness) lying behind it." At least in this letter he had the "consolation," he added, "of being allowed to violate a foreign language as involuntarily as, with knowledge and intention, I would like to do against my own language, and—Deo juvante—shall do." A decade later, Beckett abandoned his native English to write in French, beginning with *Molloy*, *Malone Dies*, and *Waiting for Godot*.

1961 James Dickey, in the *New York Times*, on Allen Ginsberg's *Kaddish*: "Confession is not enough, and neither is the assumption that the truth of one's experience will emerge if only one can keep talking long enough in a whipped-up state of excitement. It takes more than this to make poetry. It just does."

July 10

BORN: **1871** Marcel Proust (*In Search of Lost Time*), Auteuil, France
1931 Alice Munro (*Open Secrets, The Love of a Good Woman*), Wingham, Ont.

DIED: **1993** Ruth Krauss (*A Hole Is to Dig, The Carrot Seed*), 91, Westport, Conn.
2007 Doug Marlette (*Kudzu, The Bridge*), 57, Holly Springs, Miss.

1666 Less than two months before the Great Fire of London, a smaller blaze swept through Anne Bradstreet's home in North Andover, Massachusetts, destroying her family's library—massive for the time—of eight hundred volumes and leading her to write the "Verses upon the Burning of Our House, July 10, 1666" that bless that grace of God that "gave and took": "It was his own it was not mine / Far be it that I should repine."

1792 Daughter of one minister to Louis XVI and lover of another, the novelist, political theorist, and brilliant conversationalist Madame de Staël was sympathetic to the French Revolution and was no admirer of Louis XVI and Marie Antoinette, who despised her in return. But around this time, after her disgust at the rabble that forced their way into the Tuileries Palace in late June, she concocted a plan for the escape of the royal couple to England. She would buy an estate in Normandy, across the Channel from England, and travel there a number of times with servants who resembled the king and queen, and then make the same journey a few weeks later with the royal family disguised as the servants. Word was returned from the palace, though, that the queen, whether out of naiveté, fatalism, or distrust of her would-be rescuer, declined the offer.

1873 In the final argument of their two-year relationship, Paul Verlaine, in a drunken rage, shot Arthur Rimbaud in the arm.

1958 Jack Kerouac was the jock of the Beats, and though a broken leg derailed his football career at Columbia he kept up another sporting interest through his entire life, playing hundreds of games a year in a homemade baseball simulation of his own devising that used cards and a chart on the wall he'd throw things at to determine the plays. Even after *On the Road* made him one of the best-known writers of his generation, he continued to type up news reports (later archived in *Kerouac at Bat*) about his invented teams and players, including an issue on this day of his *Baseball News* that announced that young "Sugar Ray" Sims, hitting .368 in the Cuban League, had been brought up by the fourth-place St. Louis Blues to replace first baseman Joe Boston, who had broken his arm in the shower at home.

1960 Frank H. Lyell, in the *New York Times*, on Harper Lee's *To Kill a Mockingbird*: "Movie-going readers will be able to cast most of the roles very quickly, but it is no disparagement of Miss Lee's winning book to say that it could be the basis of an excellent film."

BORN: 1899 E. B. White (*Charlotte's Web*, *Here Is New York*), Mount Vernon, N.Y.
1967 Jhumpa Lahiri (*Interpreter of Maladies*, *The Namesake*), London
DIED: 1966 Delmore Schwartz (*In Dreams Begin Responsibilities*), 52, New York City
2012 Donald J. Sobol (*Encyclopedia Brown, Boy Detective*), 87, Miami, Fla.

1790 From his deathbed, Adam Smith oversaw the burning of over a dozen uncompleted volumes, including manuscripts for planned "great works" on literature and government.

1890 To the consternation of friends and family, Anton Chekhov, dissatisfied with his literary life in Moscow and looking for some kind of heroic action as he turned thirty, resolved to travel to the far eastern island of Sakhalin to inspect the penal colony there. After an arduous three-month journey—the last 3,000 miles by horse-drawn coach—he arrived in July carrying no more authority than his journalist's credentials but soon received permission to tour the entire island, which he did, filling out over 10,000 self-designed census cards (still archived at the Russian State Library) about the prisoners, and describing their miserable conditions in an influential report, about which he wrote, "I'm glad that this rough convict's smock will hang in my fictional wardrobe."

1942 On this morning, three days after all books by Jewish authors were banned from sale in occupied France, Irène Némirovsky took a walk in the woods in the village of Issy-l'Évêque, where she had fled from Paris in 1940. She brought with her the second volume of *Anna Karenina*, the *Journal* of Katherine Mansfield, and an orange, and sat "in the middle of an ocean of leaves, wet and rotting from last night's storm, as if on a raft." That same day, she wrote her editor, "I've written a great deal lately. I suppose they will be posthumous books but it still makes the time go by." Two days later she was seized by the French police and four days after that shipped in a cattle car to Auschwitz, where she died a month later, sixty years before *Suite Française*, the book she left unfinished, was discovered and published.

NO YEAR Everyone is in place: the glum pianist is playing Rachmaninoff, the liver lady has put her slabs of liver to sizzle in the pan, the boring couple is moving the Hoover around, the motorcycle enthusiast is clanging in the courtyard, and the staff is all ready behind the scenes for the first reenactment. After months of preparation and rehearsal, the narrator of Tom McCarthy's *Remainder* can finally step out of his flat into a world "zinging with significance." A provocative (and diabolically approachable) experiment in fiction, in which a man injured in an accident uses his legal settlement to construct a complex simulation to recreate the fleetingly intense moments of reality his unreliable memory can recall, *Remainder* exposes the limits and seductions of memory and the tyranny of unlimited power.

July 12

BORN: 1817 Henry David Thoreau (*Walden, Civil Disobedience*), Concord, Mass.
1904 Pablo Neruda (*Twenty Love Poems and a Song of Despair*), Parral, Chile
DIED: 1536 Erasmus (*In Praise of Folly, On Civility in Children*), 69, Basel, Switzerland
2010 Harvey Pekar (*American Splendor*), 70, Cleveland Heights, Ohio

1794 On the 24th day of Messidor in Year II of the French Republic (according to the new calendar proclaimed by the Revolution), Jean Anthelme Brillat-Savarin, having been forced from his post as small-town mayor by the Jacobins, sailed for the United States, where among his most memorable adventures, recounted thirty years later in his food-lover's classic, *The Physiology of Taste*, was the shooting of a wild turkey in Connecticut. While his host proclaimed the advantages of American liberty in terms that would perhaps have drawn more interest from his countryman Tocqueville, Brillat-Savarin, a man of less abstract appetites, concerned himself instead with his host's four "buxom" daughters and with the pressing dilemma: "how best I should cook my turkey."

1951 The army patrol had been missing in Korea for less than four days when they encountered a marine outfit near Haeju and were returned to their own unit, where they happily testified that their sergeant, Raymond Shaw, had engaged and destroyed the enemy and saved the lives of his men—minus poor Ed Malvole and Bobby Lembeck—and that, though none of them could stand Sergeant Shaw a week before, they now believed, to a man, that he was the finest, bravest, most admirable person they'd ever known. Those missing four days, of course, in Richard Condon's delirious Cold War fantasia, *The Manchurian Candidate*, were spent under the expert care of Yen Lo, the brilliant Pavlovian psychologist, who left the soldiers' brains washed almost clean—except for those nightmares Major Marco keeps having—and transformed sour, arrogant Raymond Shaw into a war hero and a programmed assassin.

1980 "Dear Madame Bonamitan, In reply to your letter of July twelfth 1980, it gives us great pleasure to inform you . . ." In reply to which letter? Sonore had written so many, on so many days, or rather Ti-Cirique, the local man of letters, had written them for her, sprinkling her appeals for work with literary quotations of woe from Hugo, Racine, and Lautréamont. Finally this letter came in return, and with it an offer of temporary employment with the city office of urban services. But what interest had the city in her shanty neighborhood, called Texaco, a name borrowed or wrested or stolen from the oil refinery in whose shadow it arose: was it just a "pocket of insalubrity" to be cleared and cleansed? From that question grows the story of Patrick Chamoiseau's *Texaco*, a full-throated and many-voiced defense of the motley Creole vigor and misery-built history of Chamoiseau's island of Martinique.

1980 A bolt of lightning exploded Farley Mowat's chimney on Cape Breton and showered his Volvo with shards of brick.

BORN: **1894** Isaac Babel (*Red Cavalry, Odessa Tales*), Odessa, Russian Empire

1934 Wole Soyinka (*Ake, Death and the King's Horseman*), Abeokuta, Nigeria

DIED: **1946** Alfred Stieglitz (*Camera Work*), 82, New York City

1983 Gabrielle Roy (*The Tin Flute, Street of Riches*), 74, Quebec City

1798 The poem's full title is "Lines written a few miles above Tintern Abbey, on revisiting the banks of the Wye during a tour, July 13, 1798," and William Wordsworth would later say with pride that he had composed it fully in his head on a walk of four or five days with his sister, Dorothy, before writing it down. Presented as a reflection on the time since his last visit to the Wye five years before, when he was "in the hour of thoughtless youth," it reveals, more particularly, the power and anxiety felt by someone who has just finished his first book. *Lyrical Ballads*, his collaboration with Samuel Taylor Coleridge, was already complete, they thought, but Wordsworth quickly inserted "Tintern Abbey" at its end, making a sort of afterword that showed he'd already outgrown the rest of his works in the collection.

1890 Vastly prolific and sourly misanthropic, Ambrose Bierce established himself as one of the best-known newspapermen on the West Coast when William Randolph Hearst hired him to write for his newly acquired *San Francisco Examiner* in 1887, where he contributed columns, essays, and stories, including one story, published on this day, that has likely been read more times than all his other writing combined. Anthologized and adapted almost to the point of oblivion in the years since, "An Occurrence at Owl Creek Bridge" still packs a clean wallop, held together as it is by, in a phrase Bierce cut from the final paragraph after this first appearance of the story, "as stout a rope as ever rewarded the zeal of a civilian patriot in war-time."

1928 Was there a real Charlie Chan? Earl Derr Biggers, who introduced the detective as a secondary character in 1925's *The House Without a Key*, habitually deflected reports that Chan was modeled on an intrepid Honolulu detective named Chang Apana, but he came to embrace the idea after the two met in Hawaii. The Charlie Chan of the six books and forty-seven movies was urbane and fat, known for his fortune-cookie aphorisms, while Apana, as described in *Charlie Chan*, Yunte Huang's dual biography of the man and the character, was a wiry ex-ranchhand who once wielded a five-foot bullwhip to round up a den of illegal gamblers (according to a Honolulu newspaper report on this day) and thought his English was too poor for him to accept a cameo role in the Charlie Chan movies he was offered.

July 14

BORN: 1916 Natalia Ginzburg (*The City and the House*), Palermo, Italy
1966 Brian Selznick (*The Invention of Hugo Cabret*), East Brunswick, N.J.
DIED: 1817 Germaine de Staël (*Delphine*; *Corinne, or Italy*), 51, Paris
1984 Ernest Tidyman (*Shaft*, *Shaft's Big Score*), 56, London

1831 The governor of New York, hosting the French visitors Alexis de Tocqueville and Gustave de Beaumont, ran into his house for a gun after sighting a squirrel, but "the big man," in Beaumont's words, "had the clumsiness to miss him four times in succession."

1914 F.H., in the *New Republic*, on Edith Wharton's *Summer*: "A good shipwreck, moral or physical, is by no means the least satisfactory of fictional themes, but no author has a right to run up and down the shore line waving a harmless heroine to destruction."

1920 In Isaac Babel's *1920 Diary*, the tersely observant record of his travels with brutal Cossack troops in the Bolshevik war against Poland that became the basis for his stories in *Red Cavalry*, a downed American pilot makes a single, memorable appearance, "barefoot but elegant, neck like a pillar, dazzlingly white teeth," chatting with Babel about Bolshevism and Conan Doyle. Babel was right to suspect his name, Frank Mosher, was fake: the pilot, Captain Merian C. Cooper, had found the name written in his second-hand underwear. Meanwhile, in a fact Elif Batuman has great fun with in

The Possessed, her romp through Russian literature, Captain Cooper went on to his own fame as the director of *King Kong*, and in the movie's climactic scene he can be seen in the air again as the pilot of one of the planes attacking the giant ape.

1931 The "curious dismembered volume" that Henry Frobisher mentions he has discovered in a letter on this day also, winkingly, describes the novel his story is part of, David Mitchell's *Cloud Atlas*. "To my great annoyance," Frobisher complains, "the pages cease, midsentence." He's referring to a journal written during the California gold rush by a traveler named Adam Ewing that he's come across in the library of a Belgian château, but pages ceasing abruptly is the common affliction of five of *Cloud Atlas*'s six stories, which are folded inside each other like the leaves of a book, with Frobisher's letters making up chapters two and ten and Ewing's journal chapters one and eleven, each story linked with the next by bonds both arbitrary and meaningful.

1956 In high school in Chicago, he was the prodigy, leading his friend Saul Bellow "by the nose," one classmate said. Among the New York intellectuals, he was, Irving Howe remembered, "our golden boy, more so than Bellow." But Isaac Rosenfeld soon became a bohemian cautionary tale, the young man whose brilliance had taken him into a thicket of filthy basement apartments and homemade Reichian orgone boxes by the time he died at his desk of a heart attack on this day at thirty-eight.

BORN: 1892 Walter Benjamin (*Illuminations, The Arcades Project*), Berlin
1949 Richard Russo (*Empire Falls, Straight Man*), Johnstown, N.Y.
DIED: 1999 Gina Berriault (*Women in Their Beds, The Son*), 73, Greenbrae, Calif.
2003 Roberto Bolaño (*2666, By Night in Chile, Amulet*), 50, Barcelona

1677 or 1684 The illustrated adventures of Tintin take place in an abstracted geography bearing only an incomplete resemblance to our own. The intrepid boy reporter's travels take him to countries you could once easily find on a map—Egypt, Tibet, the Soviet Union—but also to more fanciful nations like Syldavia and San Theodoros. And then there is Marlinspike Hall, the ancestral home of Sir Francis Haddock so gloriously regained by his descendant Captain Haddock at the end of *Red Rackham's Treasure*. Where can it be found? For English readers, an envelope address in *The Secret of the Unicorn* places the mansion in England, granted to Sir Francis on this day in 1677 by Charles II. But in the original French editions, *le château de Moulinsart* is in Belgium, a gift on the same day in 1684 from Louis XIV. Blistering barnacles, which is to be believed?

1955 With the delivery of the mail on this day J. P. Donleavy thought his literary career was over. Included was a parcel from Paris containing two copies of his first novel, *The Ginger Man*, which only then did he learn his publisher, the Olympia Press, had included in their smutty "Traveller's Companion Series" alongside such offerings as *Tender Was My Flesh, School for Sin*, and *White Thighs*. Vowing revenge, Donleavy spent the next twenty years battling with Maurice Girodias, Olympia's publisher, over the international rights to his novel, which became more valuable every year as the notorious book became a bestseller. Finally, vengefully, Donleavy bought control of Olympia, his enemy, at a bankruptcy auction, but even then the litigation between them continued.

1988 "I can imagine you at forty," Emma says to Dexter. "I can picture it right now." She has the future Dexter figured out: a tiny sports car, a little paunch, a tan like a basted turkey. And he's sure he has Emma's number as well, as an artsy campus radical: Chagalls and manifestos on the wall, *The Unbearable Lightness of Being* at the side of the bed. We think we know what's coming in the story too, after these opposites spend a night together in an Edinburgh flat, but David Nicholls has some surprises in store. In his novel *One Day* Nicholls revisits Emma and Dexter on July 15 every year for two decades and within that structure tells the story of their mostly parallel, sometimes passionately intersecting lives in a convincing way, by creating two people who you can imagine spend all the other days of the year thinking about each other.

1995 Amazon.com sold its first book, a copy of Douglas Hofstadter's *Fluid Concepts and Creative Analogies: Computer Models of the Fundamental Mechanisms of Thought*.

July 16

BORN: 1920 Anatole Broyard (*Intoxicated by My Illness, Kafka Was the Rage*), New Orleans
1928 Anita Brookner (*Hotel du Lac, Look at Me*), London

DIED: 1995 May Sarton (*Mrs. Stevens Hears the Mermaids Singing*), 83, York, Maine
1995 Stephen Spender (*World Within World, The Temple*), 86, London

1948 With Jean Genet's many arrests for thievery and other crimes threatening to send him to prison for life just as his novels—often veiled portraits of his life outside the law—were becoming celebrated, Jean Cocteau and Jean-Paul Sartre published an open letter on this day to French president Vincent Auriol requesting a pardon for Genet, so he could devote himself to his work. The pardon was granted, and Genet never returned to prison, but he also never wrote another novel and for a half-dozen years he wrote almost nothing at all, a fallow period perhaps caused, as his biographer Edmund White has suggested, by the unfamiliarity of his acceptance by society, which only increased with the publication in 1952 of Sartre's massive analysis of his life and work, *Saint Genet*.

1951 Published: *The Catcher in the Rye* by J. D. Salinger (Little, Brown, Boston)

1969 John Updike had rarely encountered the present tense in fiction when he tried it out in *Rabbit, Run*. It felt "exhilaratingly speedy and free," and it remained a perfect match for the Rabbit series, in which, at the end of every decade, Updike checked in on his flawed hero as he was transformed by time and by the times. In the second book, *Rabbit Redux*, the headlines from that turbulent era begin to invade the lives of his small-town Pennsylvania characters with a bewildering insistence, although as the novel

opens, the private news that Rabbit's father has for him—that Rabbit's wife is having an affair—still dwarfs the event in the background on the TV, the endless replays of Apollo 11 blasting off for the moon.

BORN: **1902** Christina Stead (*The Man Who Loved Children*), Rockdale, Australia
1951 Mark Bowden (*Black Hawk Down, Guests of the Ayatollah*), St. Louis
DIED: **1790** Adam Smith (*The Wealth of Nations*), 67, Edinburgh
2001 Katherine Graham (*Personal History*), 84, Boise, Idaho

NO YEAR When Agatha Christie was challenged by a friend to try writing one of the detective stories she enjoyed so much, she began with the crime. And an ingenious one it was: in the early hours of July 17, Emily Inglethorpe, a wealthy matriarch who had just married a much younger man whom her family considered a fortune-hunting bounder, went into violent convulsions that finally killed her, an intricately planned murder whose details are revealed only when the Belgian detective Hercule Poirot, stranded nearby as a wartime refugee, is brought into the case. Written when Christie was twenty-five, *The Mysterious Affair at Styles* sat unread at her future publisher, the Bodley Head, for two years; finally published to superb reviews in 1921, it introduced Poirot to the world and earned its author £25.

1948 P. H. Newby, in the *New Statesman and Nation*, on Raymond Queneau: "To the inexperienced eye a thoroughbred racehorse looks much too thin to be healthy. One can make the same mistake over good writing. Raymond Queneau's *A Hard Winter* is only half the length of an average novel, but it is twice as effective. The speed, grace and intelligence of the writing give shock after shock of pleasure."

1960 "There's a difference between knowing and yapping." That's the law of the house when the narrator of Alice Munro's "Before the Change" returns from Toronto to stay with her father for a time. Some things—many things, nearly everything—are better off not spoken about, especially the women who come to see her father, the local doctor, in the evenings. But sometimes, to her "dismay and satisfaction," she finds herself speaking to him of the unspoken subjects: saying the word "abortion," for instance, or, in the last thing she tells him before his death, that she herself on July 17 had a baby and gave it away, and isn't that ironic, given what she has finally realized about why those women come under the cover of night to see him.

1996 Everybody knew that Jack and Susan Stanton in the novel *Primary Colors* stood for Bill and Hillary Clinton. The question was: who was Anonymous, the secret author of one of the few political novels in memory to which the adjective "acclaimed" could legitimately be attached? Finally, six months after the book hit the bestseller lists and five months after *Newsweek* columnist Joe Klein heatedly denied early reports that pointed the finger at him, Klein fessed up at a press conference hastily arranged after a handwriting analysis of a manuscript of the book revealed him as the author after all, thereby bringing upon himself just the sort of temporary journalistic fury he had decried in his novel.

July 18

BORN: 1937 Hunter S. Thompson (*Fear and Loathing in Las Vegas*), Louisville, Ky.
1969 Elizabeth Gilbert (*Eat, Pray, Love*; *The Last American Man*), Waterbury, Conn.

DIED: 1817 Jane Austen (*Emma, Northanger Abbey, Persuasion*), 41, Winchester, England
1899 Horatio Alger Jr. (*Ragged Dick, Luck and Pluck*), 67, Natick, Mass.

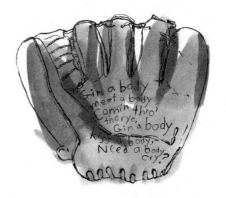

1818 Writing to a friend of his disappointment that women, whom he had thought were ethereal, superior creatures, turned out to be roughly equal to men, Keats declined to say any more: "After all I do think better of Womankind than to suppose they care whether Mister John Keats five feet high likes them or not."

1946 You'd have gotten into a fistfight with Stradlater too, if he'd come back to your room after a date and given you a hard time for writing a composition for him about how your brother Allie used to write poems on his baseball glove in green ink to give him something to read in the outfield, when you were supposed to write it about a room or a house—it was a goddam *favor*—and on top of that he'd just come back from a date with Jane Gallagher, who used to keep all her kings in the back row when she played you in checkers and who was the only one you'd ever shown Allie's glove, which you kept ever since Allie died of leukemia on this day and you broke all the windows in the garage with your fist, in J. D. Salinger's *The Catcher in the Rye*.

2008 At first, Abdul bolted. Not far: just to the storeroom attached to his family's shack, where he listened to the police officers arrive next door as he perched as silently as he could on the tower of garbage that, sorted for resale, represented their liquid capital. But the next morning he ran instead to the police station, to turn himself in for a crime he hadn't committed—that no one had committed—of driving their neighbor to light herself on fire. Will Abdul get justice? It might be a central question in a different book, or a different place, but in Katherine Boo's *Behind the Beautiful Forevers*, the product of three and a half years of reporting in a tiny slum neighborhood in the shadow of Mumbai's luxury hotels and international airport, justice is an afterthought, overwhelmed by the contingencies of poverty, corruption, disease, and personality, and the rough judgments of good and bad fortune.

BORN: **1893** Vladimir Mayakovsky (*The Bedbug*), Baghdati, Russian Empire
1952 Jayne Anne Phillips (*Machine Dreams, Lark and Termite*), Buckhannon, W.Va.

DIED: **2005** Edward Bunker (*Education of a Felon, Dog Eat Dog*), 71, Burbank, Calif.
2009 Frank McCourt (*Angela's Ashes, Teacher Man*), 78, New York City

1374 Petrarch died, bequeathing Boccaccio fifty florins to buy a dressing gown to warm him during "winter study and lucubrations by night."

1850 After four years in Europe as a foreign correspondent for the *New York Tribune*, the last three of which she'd also spent aiding the democratic revolution in Rome, Margaret Fuller returned to the United States with Giovanni Angelo Ossoli, the Italian revolutionary she may have married, and their son, Nino. But in the early hours of this morning, a freak hurricane drove their ship into a sandbar off Fire Island and, while locals gathered to watch from the shore without organizing a rescue, the Ossolis drowned. Five days later, Henry David Thoreau arrived at the beach, sent by Fuller's friend Emerson to search for any sign of their bodies or possessions, in particular the manuscript of Fuller's book on the Roman revolution, which her admirers had hoped would have been the great work they always expected her intellect would produce.

1896 The sight of a thistle on this day, broken and dusty but still flowering on the edge of a plowed field at midsummer, evoked in Leo Tolstoy a memory of forty years before and sparked his great final story, "Hadji Murat," at a time when he had largely abandoned fiction for philosophy. In 1852 Tolstoy had fought in the tsar's army against Muslim Chechen guerrillas, among the most famous of whom was Hadji Murat, an admirable warrior who allied himself for a time with the Russians against a Chechen rival but then escaped, only to be killed by the Russians, his head brought back as a trophy for the decadent empire. "It stood firm," Tolstoy wrote of the hardy thistle that reminded him of Murat, "and did not surrender to man who had destroyed all its brothers around it."

NO YEAR "Do you mind if I marry Wilf? she asks." She is Lydia, an actress and filmmaker, and even though she's only marrying Wilf in a movie, Gabriel, the narrator of Michael Winter's *This All Happened* and the man who has been talking about marrying her for the two years they've been together, does mind, enough that his jealousy evokes the strongest pang of love he's felt all year. Gabriel began the year with two resolutions: "to decide on Lydia and to finish a novel." The novel, we quickly realize, is the diary we're reading, and deciding on Lydia (or waiting for Lydia to decide for him) is just one of its subjects. Set in the tiny bohemia of St. John's, Newfoundland, *This All Happened* is a year's record that conceals in its day-by-day meandering a subtle and sharp portrait of jealousy, friendship, and creative ambition.

July 20

BORN: 1924 Thomas Berger (*Little Big Man*, *Neighbors*, *The Feud*), Cincinnati
1933 Cormac McCarthy (*Blood Meridian*, *The Road*), Providence, R.I.
DIED: 1912 Andrew Lang (*The Blue Fairy Book*), 68, Banchory, Scotland
1945 Paul Valéry (*La Jeune Parque*, *Monsieur Teste*), 73, Paris

1754 Robert Louis Stevenson always said that *Treasure Island* began with a map he sketched to entertain his stepson. At first he called the story it inspired *The Sea Cook*; only when it neared publication did the book take the name of the map itself, and not until the book's second edition did it include a woodcut of the map, which featured a detail written in its margins but not mentioned in the text of the story, "Given by above J.F. to Mr W. Bones Maste of ye Walrus Savannah this twenty July 1754 W B." Perhaps it's fitting that, like the treasure in the story, this lucrative creation was long fought over: for years, though Stevenson denied it, his stepson claimed that he had drawn the original map himself.

1928 With roughly 95 percent voting in favor, a local civic league in California's San Fernando Valley officially named its town Tarzana, after the local estate of Tarzan of the Apes creator Edgar Rice Burroughs.

1945 Patrick O'Brian was both an intensely private man and a fabulist about his own history, so not until after his Aubrey-Maturin series of naval adventures had become internationally beloved was it widely revealed that he had lived the first thirty-one years of his life under a different name, Patrick Russ, legally changing his last name to O'Brian on this day, just weeks after his second marriage. Why the change? He never explained, but along with his original name he left behind a first marriage and a child, animal tales he published as a teenager, and various financial crises. Over time, with the new name, he created a new identity—Irish, Catholic, and experienced at sea—that more closely matched the stories he was writing.

1969 "The day man landed on the moon," Philip Larkin noted, "I landed in the Nuffield," a hospital in Hull, for the removal of a nasal polyp.

2019 Nothing dates as quickly as a vision of the future. Few writers have been as eager to look far ahead as the novelist Arthur C. Clarke, and in 1986 he assembled a book called *July 20, 2019* that imagined daily human (and robot) life on the fiftieth anniversary of the moon landing. Read in retrospect as the day of its prophecy approaches, the book offers plenty of errant predictions—moon colonies, computer-controlled waterbeds, West Germany at war with the Soviet Union—although many of its other, sensibly incremental ideas are not as far from the world we know. What's most noticeable, though, is how much Clarke's 2019 *looks* like 1986: even with all the airbrushing in the world, it's still hard to imagine oneself out of one's own time.

BORN: **1899** Ernest Hemingway (*The Sun Also Rises, A Farewell to Arms*), Oak Park, Ill.

1899 Hart Crane (*The Bridge, White Buildings*), Garrettsville, Ohio

1966 Sarah Waters (*Tipping the Velvet, Fingersmith*), Neyland, Wales

DIED: **1796** Robert Burns ("A Red Red Rose," "To a Louse"), 37, Dumfries, Scotland

1938 Owen Wister (*The Virginian, Roosevelt*), 78, Saunderstown, R.I.

1940 In May, H. A. Rey put aside his book illustrations so he and his wife, Margret, German Jews who had met in Brazil and returned to Paris, could begin preparing to leave France ahead of the Nazi invasion. In June, the Reys left Paris on bicycles H. A. had built from spare parts, carrying manuscripts and drawings in their baskets, including one, about a mischievous monkey, called *The Adventures of Fifi*. On this day they sailed from Lisbon for Rio, in October they arrived in New York, and in November they signed a contract for four books based on the work they had brought with them from France, including *Fifi*, which was soon renamed *Curious George*.

1974 On the forty-fourth and final day of Brian Clough's disastrous reign as manager of Leeds United, the soccer club that had once been his bitterest rival, he discussed his firing on a TV panel show nearly as dramatic and unlikely as his decision, seven weeks before, to manage the club. Joining him on the panel was none other than the man he hated and had replaced: former Leeds manager Don Revie, happy to dance on Cloughie's grave in the most polite of sporting language. It's a scene that David Peace, in his fictional version of Cloughie's ordeal, *The Damned Utd*, could hardly resist, and their tense exchange, preening and vulnerable and nearly verbatim, makes a fitting end to a novel whose propulsive and obsessive treatment of its subject has led many to call it the greatest novel on English football.

1980 "Kaufman meeting—disaster." By the beginning of the eighties, William Goldman, Oscar-winning screenwriter of *Butch Cassidy and the Sundance Kid* and *All the President's Men*, knew his way around Hollywood enough to sense that his first meeting with Philip Kaufman, the director of his next movie, *The Right Stuff*, had gone terribly. And he was right: of the 148 pages of Goldman's script, Kaufman, more interested in the story of test pilot Chuck Yeager than in the Mercury astronauts, wanted to keep six. Who won? As Goldman wrote in *Adventures in the Screen Trade*, his beloved—and not unloving—memoir of Hollywood, "Whenever someone asks, 'How much power does a screenwriter have?' my mind goes only to those terrible days in Los Angeles. The answer, now and forever: in the crunch, none."

2002 Craig Seligman, in the *New York Times*, on Adam Haslett's *You Are Not a Stranger Here*: "Haslett may have talent to burn and the grades to get him into Yale, but his prose exudes a desolation so choking that it can come only from somewhere deep inside."

July 22

BORN: 1936 Tom Robbins (*Even Cowgirls Get the Blues*), Blowing Rock, N.C.
1948 S. E. Hinton (*The Outsiders; That Was Then, This Is Now*), Tulsa, Okla.
DIED: 1990 Manuel Puig (*Kiss of the Spider Woman*), 57, Cuernavaca, Mexico
1996 Jessica Mitford (*Hons and Rebels*), 78, Oakland, Calif.

1848 John Forster, *Examiner*, on W. M. Thackeray's *Vanity Fair*: "We are seldom permitted to enjoy the appreciation of all gentle and kind things which we continually meet within the book, without some neighbouring quip or sneer that would seem to show the author ashamed of what he yet cannot help giving way to."

1951 This month the Oxford University Press published a natural history of the ocean by a little-known researcher at the U.S. Fish and Wildlife Service, whose only previous book, a decade before, had earned her just $689.17 in royalties. Thanks, though, to a three-part serialization in *The New Yorker* and the enthusiasm of readers for her poetic approach to explaining the science of the oceans, Rachel Carson's *The Sea Around Us* quickly hit the *New York Times* nonfiction bestseller list. This week was her second on the list, and helped by a National Book Award in January (and despite her academic publisher's struggles to keep up with demand), she remained there for a then-record eighty-six weeks, thirty-two of them at #1.

1975 The economy's going haywire—the prime rate yo-yoing, the cost of sugar and gas accelerating—and Ben Flesh's body is too, ravaged by multiple sclerosis. And so the great franchiser is selling everything—his Baskin-Robbinses, his HoJos, his Western Autos—and putting all his chips in a single Travel Inn in Ringgold, Georgia, ideally situated halfway between Chicago and Disney World: two storeys, 150 rooms, opening for business on this day. Stanley Elkin's *The Franchiser* is an American road novel in which all the roads, or at least the roadside attractions, look the same: trademarked golden arches, trademarked orange roofs, and trademarked turquoise towers, multiplying like the empire of Ben Flesh, who has, until now, embodied their insatiable logic of growth.

1990 *Army Man*, "America's Only Magazine," was priced at $15 for six photocopied issues mailed from the editor's condominium in Boulder, Colorado, but it only lasted for three. On this day, George Meyer, who moved to Boulder when he soured on TV writing after stints with David Letterman and *Saturday Night Live*, wrote the subscribers to his homemade comedy newsletter, "I have some news for you, and I'm not going to sugar-coat it. I might varnish it . . . no, I'm not even going to varnish it. *Army Man* is suspending publication." *Army Man* was already becoming a word-of-mouth legend, but Meyer was too busy to continue: he had been hired to write for *The Simpsons* along with *Army Man* contributors Jon Vitti and John Schwartzwelder. It was Schwartzwelder who wrote what Meyer has called "the quintessential *Army Man* joke: 'They can kill the Kennedys. Why can't they make a cup of coffee that tastes good?'"

BORN: 1888 Raymond Chandler (*The Big Sleep*; *Farewell, My Lovely*), Chicago
1907 Elspeth Huxley (*The Flame Trees of Thika*, *Red Strangers*), London
DIED: 2002 Chaim Potok (*The Chosen*, *My Name Is Asher Lev*), 73, Merion, Pa.
2009 E. Lynn Harris (*Invisible Life*, *Just as I Am*), 54, Los Angeles

1943 The romance of a poet dying young is difficult to resist, and Max Harris, the editor of the Australian poetry journal *Angry Penguins*, didn't resist it at all when he received a packet of poems by an unknown writer named Ern Malley from someone claiming to be Malley's sister, who said her brother had left the poems behind when he died on this day at age twenty-five. In truth, though, Malley was a product of the imaginations of James McAuley and Harold Stewart, who, fed up with the experiments of modern poetry, composed the seventeen Malley poems, which they considered nonsense, in their army barracks in a single day. Harris took the bait and devoted a special issue to announcing his discovery, and the hoax soon exploded into Australia's greatest literary scandal, but the biggest joke of all may be that the "fake" poems of Ern Malley have outlasted those of anyone involved.

1969 Through a haze of sleeping pills, Jacqueline Susann watched Truman Capote tell Johnny Carson on *The Tonight Show* that she "looks like a truck driver in drag."

Mrs. Susann
7/23/69
1 Tablet Nightly to Aid Sleep

1986 When he came to, on the center median of I-93 out of Boston, Andre Dubus first carefully explained to the police officer that he had three guns and was licensed to carry them. Then the pain hit. Dubus had pulled his car over to assist a woman and her brother who had just hit an abandoned motorcycle in the highway and had helped them to the median when another driver, avoiding the wreck, swerved off the highway and killed the brother and crushed Dubus's legs. Dubus, recognized already as one of his generation's finest short-story writers, lost one leg and the use of the other and lived in pain and depression for much of the last thirteen years of his life, but he continued to write, often about the accident and its consequences, saying more than once that having learned he had saved the woman by pushing her out of the way of the car, "Now I can never be angry at myself for stopping that night."

July 24

BORN: 1802 Alexandre Dumas *père* (*The Three Musketeers*), Villers-Cotterêts, France
1916 John D. MacDonald (*The Deep Blue Good-by*), Sharon, Pa.
DIED: 1969 Witold Gombrowicz (*Ferdydurke, Trans-Atlantyk*), 64, Vence, France
1991 Isaac Bashevis Singer (*Enemies, a Love Story; The Slave*), 91, Surfside, Fla.

1895 Sigmund Freud's *Interpretation of Dreams* had sold only a handful of copies when the doctor wrote to his colleague Wilhelm Fleiss, "Do you suppose that someday one will read on a marble tablet on this house: 'Here, on July 24, 1895, the secret of the dream revealed itself to Dr. Sigm. Freud.' So far there is little prospect of it." Freud's dream that fateful night, about a patient named Irma, was central to his book, where he interpreted it as an expression of his desire not to be blamed for her continuing symptoms. (Later analysts have argued Freud's anxiety in the dream was in fact about his friend Fleiss, who had nearly killed Irma by leaving a foot and a half of gauze in her nose during an operation.) Freud's self-fulfilling prophecy was indeed fulfilled when a marble tablet was erected at the site in 1963.

1901 William Sydney Porter, already writing stories under the name O. Henry, was released from prison after serving thirty-nine months for embezzling from his former employer, the First National Bank in Austin, Texas.

NO YEAR At a crime scene just after midnight, detectives banter until they find that the man down is one of their own, 87th Precinct detective Mike Reardon. When Evan Hunter began his 87th Precinct series with *Cop Hater* in 1956, making your detective a cop instead of a private eye or an elderly spinster was a new idea, as was basing a mystery series around a group of investigators (some of whom, like Detective Reardon, might die) rather than a single character. Also new was the name Hunter chose as his pseudonym for the series so there wouldn't be any confusion with his "serious" novels like *The Blackboard Jungle*: Ed McBain. Hunter chose the name casually, but over time, as his 87th Precinct series grew to more than fifty police procedurals, its fame eclipsed his own.

1959 Russell Hoban was an illustrator and ad copywriter as well as a fledgling children's book author when he submitted a picture-book manuscript called *Who's Afraid?* to his editor, Ursula Nordstrom. "I'm afraid it's going to need a lot more work, Russ," she told him, advising him to rethink the pacing as well as the species of his young heroine, Frances: "I sort of wish any other creature but a vole which looks like a mouse. I think it is terribly difficult to draw ATTRACTIVE mice." Over the following months both problems were solved, as Hoban reconstructed the story (and renamed it *Bedtime for Frances*) and illustrator Garth Williams did away with the voles: as Nordstrom informed Hoban in a later letter, "He has decided to make these people badgers."

BORN: 1902 Eric Hoffer (*The True Believer, The Passionate State of Mind*), New York City

1905 Elias Canetti (*Auto-da-Fé, Crowds and Power*), Ruse, Bulgaria

DIED: 1834 Samuel Taylor Coleridge (*Kubla Khan*), 61, Highgate, England

1966 Frank O'Hara (*Meditations in an Emergency*), 40, Fire Island, N.Y.

1914 At age eleven, while sailing from Barcelona to New York, Anaïs Nin began her diary.

1938 When his German publishers asked about his ancestry, J. R. R. Tolkien drafted a response saying that "if I am to understand that you are enquiring whether I am of Jewish origin, I can only reply that I regret that I appear to have no ancestors of that gifted people." He has been glad of his German name, he added, but "if impertinent and irrelevant inquiries of this sort are to become the rule in matters of literature, then the time is not far distant when a German name will no longer be a source of pride."

1967 Invited by the Kerner Commission to contribute to its official report on the riots in Detroit that left forty-three dead and thousands of buildings destroyed, John Hersey chose instead to report from the city on his own. Soon he focused on one event: the death during the riots of three black men at the hands of white policemen. In *The Algiers Motel Incident*, as he had with *Hiroshima* two decades before, Hersey immersed himself in the lives of those present at the scene on this night, but in this book he stepped forward for the first time as a character in his own reporting. "This account is too urgent, too complex, too dangerous to too many people," he wrote, for him to hide behind "the luxury of invisibility."

1969 A neurologist's medical notes took on the flavor of the fables of Sleeping Beauty or Rip Van Winkle when a group of patients in a New York hospital who had been reduced for decades to catatonic dormancy after contracting "sleeping sickness" in the '20s were treated with a new drug, L-DOPA, that caused them, in powerfully individual ways, to awaken. With the sensitive curiosity that has since become his trademark, their young neurologist Oliver Sacks told their stories in *Awakenings*, including that of Rose R., who, unlike others whose awakenings held for the rest of their lives, woke fully for just a few vivid weeks that peaked on this day when, "joyous and elated, and very salacious," she regained her lively personality, with, in Sacks's words, an "extraordinary sense of 1926-ness," fully immersed in the events and personalities of the year she went to sleep.

1976 On a plane in the Philippines while her husband made *Apocalypse Now*, Eleanor Coppola started reading volume five of the *Diary of Anaïs Nin*. "I almost never read. I have stopped being embarrassed about it only recently. I hardly ever watch television. I am not sure exactly how I get my information."

July 26

BORN: 1856 George Bernard Shaw (*Man and Superman, Major Barbara*), Dublin
1894 Aldous Huxley (*Brave New World, Crome Yellow*), Godalming, England
DIED: 1934 Winsor McCay (*Little Nemo in Slumberland*), c. 64, Brooklyn
1957 Giuseppe di Lampedusa (*The Leopard*), 60, Rome

1849 The industrious Anthony Trollope, employed by the post office in Ireland, set out to solve the mystery of currency vanishing in the local mails by scratching a sovereign with a knife, enclosing it in a letter, and tracking its course. When it disappeared after passing through the town of Tralee, a search was made and the coin found in the possession of a young postmistress. At her trial in July, Trollope was the principal witness for the prosecution, and the transcript of his witty exchanges on the stand with the defense counsel would have been quite at home in any of his Barchester Chronicles, punctuated as it is by notations of "(laughter)," "(loud laughter)," and "(tremendous laughter)," and ending with the paired salutations "Good morning, triumphant Post Office Inspector" and "Good morning, triumphant cross-examiner."

1860 "Hooray!!!!!" Wilkie Collins wrote his mother, four weeks before the final episode of *The Woman in White* was to appear in his friend Dickens's magazine, *All the Year Round*. "I have this instant written at the bottom of the four hundred and ninetieth page of my manuscript the two noblest words in the English language—The End."

1910 In his first decade in the business, George Herriman had experimented with more than a dozen comic-strip series, from *Rosy Posy—Mama's Girl* to *Major Ozone's Fresh Air,* when, looking to fill up some white space at the bottom of his latest strip, *The Dingbat Family*, he drew a tiny mouse throwing something—a brick?—at a little black cat that was minding its own business. And so began the simplest and most enduring drama in comics: Ignatz Mouse, in fury or contempt, hurling a brick at Krazy Kat, who takes it as a token of affection from his beloved. After three years dwelling in a slot under the Dingbats, Krazy and Ignatz got their own strip, and for over thirty years of *Krazy Kat* Herriman composed endless variations on this barest of dramatic structures: mouse, cat, and brick.

2002 A. S. Byatt, in the *Guardian*, on Gustave Flaubert's *Madame Bovary*: "Our sympathy for her is like our sympathy for a bird the cat has brought in and maimed. It flutters, and it will die."

BORN: 1916 Elizabeth Hardwick (*Sleepless Nights*), Lexington, Ky.

1939 William Eggleston (*William Eggleston's Guide*), Memphis, Tenn.

DIED: 1946 Gertrude Stein (*The Autobiography of Alice B. Toklas*), 72, Neuilly-sur-Seine, France

1948 Susan Glaspell (*Fidelity*, *A Jury of Her Peers*), 72, Provincetown, Mass.

1656 "Cursed be he by day and cursed be he by night; cursed be he when he lies down, and cursed be he when he rises up; cursed be he when he goes out, and cursed be he when he comes in," read the decree of expulsion of Baruch Spinoza for heresy from the Jewish community in Amsterdam on this day. "We order that no one should communicate with him orally or in writing, or show him any favor, or stay with him under the same roof, or within four ells of him, or read anything composed or written by him."

1921 Telling him to stop his "lazy loafing" and "trading on your handsome face" and become a real man, "with brawn and muscle, moral as well as physical," Grace Hemingway evicted her son Ernest, newly turned twenty-one, from her Michigan cottage.

1966 The regular mail flights made Wednesdays the high point of the week for Edward Hoagland, who recorded in *Notes from the Century Before* the "exuberant, staccato summer" he spent in the former gold-rush outposts of northwest British Columbia, where he could still glimpse the old ways, especially with a man named Dan McPhee, who had spent thirty-five years in the bush as road-maintainer, trapper, deputy, gravedigger, and the only socialist in Telegraph Creek, and whose hospitality Hoagland flew back to enjoy on this day. A man in town, seeing him back, asked, "What do you have, some sort of a gold mine here?" Hoagland laughed and said "no, thinking yes."

2007 Roz Kaveney, in the *TLS*: "If *Harry Potter and the Deathly Hallows* is, for all its weaknesses, a far more satisfying work than some of its predecessors, it is because J. K. Rowling is an intelligent writer for whom writing the most popular children's books in history has been an education in responsibility and power not unlike that of her boy wizard hero."

2010 Schonberg's *Lives of the Great Composers* ($7.50), Djuna Barnes's *Nightwood* ($7.50), Stephen Joyce's copy of *Dead Souls* (price unknown): a month after the novelist David Markson died, browsers started noticing books from his personal library—with his underlines and comments in the margins—on the eighteen miles of bookshelves at the Strand in New York. Alex Abramovich was first tipped off when a friend passed on Markson's marginal comments on *White Noise* ("I've finally solved this book, it's sci-fi!"), and he posted about his finds on the *LRB* blog, where the comments section soon included his further purchases on this day (Montaigne's *Essays* [$7.50]) and a lengthy debate about whether Markson's library should be reconsolidated or, as the author seemed to intend, dispersed among his fellow patrons of the Strand.

July 28

BORN: 1866 Beatrix Potter (*The Tale of Peter Rabbit*), London
1959 William T. Vollmann (*Europe Central, Imperial*), Los Angeles
DIED: 1995 Don Carpenter (*Hard Rain Falling, Turnaround*), 64, Mill Valley, Calif.
1996 Roger Tory Peterson (*Field Guide to the Birds of North America*), 87, Old Lyme, Conn.

1841 The discovery in the Hudson River of the body of a young woman, soon identified as that of Mary Rogers, a beautiful cigar-shop clerk who had disappeared three days before, became the story of the summer in the New York newspapers. A year later, when no murderer had been found, Edgar Allan Poe proposed to solve the crime himself, through the person of C. Auguste Dupin, the fictional detective he had introduced in "The Murders in the Rue Morgue" (considered by many the first detective story). Transposing the details of the murder to Paris, Poe claimed in "The Mystery of Marie Roget" to have pointed to the culprit merely by following the evidence in newspaper accounts. Despite his efforts, the crime remains unsolved to this day.

1945 There's a balance in summer in this remote New Mexico canyon, "a seasonal equation of well-being and alertness," from the urgent speed of roadrunners in the canyon's depths to the golden eagles nesting on its highest peaks. They have "tenure in the land" in N. Scott Momaday's *House Made of Dawn*, unlike the domesticated latecomers, the farm animals and house cats, whose place in the canyon can be blown away like dust. Poised uneasily somewhere between them is Abel, a young Indian back from the war who on this day finds himself unable to speak to his grandfather in "the old rhythm of the tongue." Later in the day, though, alone in the canyon and looking down on the valley below, he finds himself approaching a peace he is still years from achieving.

1969 From the index to Stephen Davis's rock-excess classic, *Hammer of the Gods: The Led Zeppelin Saga*, "Seattle, Washington, Shark Episode, 78–80."

1974 It's just a two-hour drive from Islington to Stratford-upon-Avon, but when Richard Adams piled his daughters (with their Shakespearean names, Juliet and Rosamond) into the car to go see *Twelfth Night*, eight-year-old Juliet demanded, "Now Daddy, we're going on a long car journey, so we want you to while away the time by telling us a completely new story, one that we have never heard before and without any delay. Please start now!" When, at Juliet's further insistence, he wrote the story down—and greatly expanded it—in spare evenings and holidays from his civil service job, he named it *Hazel and Fiver*, after two of its rabbit characters, but the publisher who took the novel after many others had rejected it thought a better title might be *Watership Down*. On this day, two years after it was first published, *Watership Down* spent the last of its thirteen weeks at #1 on the *New York Times* fiction bestseller list.

July 29

BORN: **1805** Alexis de Tocqueville (*Democracy in America*), Paris

1965 Chang-Rae Lee (*A Gesture Life, Native Speaker*), Seoul, South Korea

DIED: **1833** William Wilberforce (*A Letter on the Abolition of the Slave Trade*), 73, London

1979 Herbert Marcuse (*One-Dimensional Man*), 81, Starnberg, Germany

1835 Charlotte Brontë began work as a teacher at Miss Wooler's School.

1890 In the evening, after writing two and a half pages of a novel he later tore up, George Gissing "broke down with wretchedness."

1935 Fresh out of college, with literary aspirations but ten siblings to support, Brian O'Nolan was one of just a few of the hundreds who had applied with him to be sworn on this day into the bureaucratic safety of the Irish Civil Service. O'Nolan's position offered enviable economic security but also required him to divert his spare-time literary activities into an endless pro-liferation of pseudonyms, including Myles na gCopaleen, whose satirical "Cruiskeen Lawn" columns in the *Irish Times* made him a household name in Dublin during his life-time, and Flann O'Brien, whose inventively subversive novels *At Swim-Two-Birds* and *The Third Policeman* belatedly placed him in the company of Joyce and Beckett as Ire-land's great modern novelists.

1943 "On the 29th of July, of 1943," James Baldwin begins "Notes of a Native Son," his stepfather, whom Baldwin called his father, died, three days before the riots in Harlem that left an apocalyptic landscape of broken glass along the route to his burial. Baldwin had struggled to understand his father, the "most bitter man I have ever met," until the year before, when Baldwin, at nineteen, worked in defense plants in New Jersey. "I acted in New Jersey as I had always acted, that is as though I thought a great deal of myself—I had to *act* that way," but the results "were, simply, unbelievable": a "unanimous, active, and unbearably vocal hostility" against him (and his race) that gave him a "rage in his blood," a rage that, finally, made him his father's son.

July 30

BORN: 1818 Emily Brontë (*Wuthering Heights*), Thornton, England
1924 William Gass (*Omensetter's Luck, The Tunnel*), Fargo, N.D.
DIED: 1992 Joe Shuster (*Superman*), 78, Los Angeles
2012 Maeve Binchy (*Circle of Friends, Tara Road*), 72, Dublin

1915 Confronted by game wardens with a dead blue heron in his boat on Walloon Lake in Michigan, fifteen-year-old Ernest Hemingway denied that he had shot the bird. He later admitted his crime to a judge and paid a $15 fine.

1918 Captain Hubert Young, tasked with revising the supply plan for the capture of Damascus according to the scheme of T. E. Lawrence, chafed against "the sight of the little man reading the *Morte d'Arthur* in a corner of the mess-tent with an impish smile on his face."

1935 Support for the innovation was hardly unanimous—George Orwell called it a "disaster" for publishers, authors, and booksellers—but the reaction of the market was immediate when Allen Lane introduced the first ten books in his new Penguin line of six-penny paperbacks (a fifteenth of the price of the standard hardcover). Reordered by booksellers within days, the Penguins, whose trademark mascot was chosen for its "dignified flippancy," went on to sell three million copies in their first year from a list that began with André Maurois's *Ariel* and included in its first batch Hemingway's *A Farewell to Arms* and Agatha Christie's *The Mysterious Affair at Styles,* as well as less widely remembered releases such as Beverley Nichols's *Twenty-Five,* Eric Linklater's *Poet's Pub,* and Susan Ertz's *Madame Claire.*

2007 There is no wilderness anymore, not even within the Aldo Leopold Wilderness in New Mexico's Black Range, where Philip Connors has taken to spending his summers as a solo fire lookout in a tower perched over the tree line. His diary of one summer there, *Fire Season*, is a thoughtful portrait of the beauty of solitude but also a vivid on-the-ground (or, rather, fifty-five feet off the ground) report on the ethics and strategy of managing nature, in which the mistakes have been both large and small, from the often misguided history of fire prevention across the West to Connors's own failed attempt on this day to rescue a fawn that may not have needed rescuing, which ends, to his misery and shame, in the death of the fawn and, fittingly, a fire.

BORN: **1919** Primo Levi (*If This Is a Man, The Truce*), Turin, Italy

1965 J. K. Rowling (*Harry Potter and the Philosopher's Stone*), Yate, England

DIED: **1784** Denis Diderot (*Jacques the Fatalist, Rameau's Nephew*), 70, Paris

2000 William Maxwell (*So Long, See You Tomorrow*), 91, New York City

1771 Benjamin Franklin was sixty-five, an old man by his own estimation but still caught up in the ferment of his time, when he took advantage of two weeks' leisure at the home of the bishop of St. Asaph in Hampshire, England, to begin his *Autobiography*, most likely on this day. Tradition has it that each evening he read the day's draft for the entertainment of the bishop's family, but those first pages were formally addressed to another audience: his son William, at that time the governor of New Jersey. But by the time Franklin took the project up again a dozen years later—"The Affairs of the Revolution occasion'd the Interruption," he explained, understandably—he made no more mention of William, whose loyalty to the British crown had caused an irreparable break with his father in the meantime, as he worked aggressively for the suppression of the rebellion of which his father was a leader.

1943 Wounded by machine-gun fire on the Solomon Islands on this day in World War II, Private Rodger W. Young, in the words of his Medal of Honor history, "continued his heroic advance, attracting enemy fire and answering with rifle fire," providing cover for his platoon to escape an attack he didn't survive. Two years later, Broadway composer and fellow private Frank Loesser, wanting to write a song to celebrate the infantry, composed "The Ballad of Rodger Young," which became a hit for Burl Ives and Nelson Eddy, and which stayed in the ears of Robert A. Heinlein as he wrote *Starship Troopers* in the late '50s: the song's refrain echoes through the compartments of the starship itself, christened the *TFCT Rodger Young*.

1980 According to the prophecy of Sybill Trelawney, as recalled in *Harry Potter and the Order of the Phoenix*, "the one with the power to vanquish the Dark Lord" was "born to those who have thrice defied him, born as the seventh month dies." There are two wizard children who match the profile—Neville Longbottom, born on July 30, and Harry Potter, born a day later (and exactly fifteen years after his creator J. K. Rowling's own date of birth)—but of course only Harry has been marked by the Dark Lord himself as his equal and his nemesis.

2005 Joe Queenan, in the *New York Times*, on Edward Klein's *The Truth About Hillary: What She Knew, When She Knew It, and How Far She'll Go to Become President*: "If Klein purposely set out to write the sleaziest, most derivative, most despicable political biography ever, he has failed both himself and his readers miserably. 'The Truth About Hillary' is only about the 16th sleaziest book I have ever read."

August is the only month whose name is also an adjective. But is August august? There's nothing majestic or venerable about it. It's sultry and lazy. It's the height of the dog days, named after the dog star, Sirius, which was thought to reign over the hottest time of the year with a malignity that brings on lassitude, disease, and madness. "These are strange and breathless days, the dog days," promises the opening of *Tuck Everlasting*, "when people are led to do things they are sure to be sorry for after."

It's not only the heat that can drive one mad; it's the idleness. Without something to keep you occupied, there's a danger your thoughts and actions will fall out of order. It was during the dog days of August when W. G. Sebald set out on a walking tour in the east of England in *The Rings of Saturn*, "in the hopes of dispelling the emptiness that takes hold of me whenever I have completed a long stint of work." But he couldn't just enjoy his freedom; he became preoccupied by it, and by the "paralyzing horror" of the "traces of destruction" his leisured observation

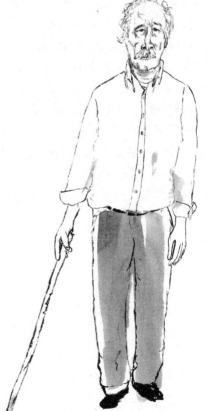

opened his eyes to. It strikes him as no coincidence at all that exactly a year later he checked into a local hospital "in a state of almost total immobility."

What evil can restlessness gin up in August? "Wars begin in August," Benny Profane declares in Pynchon's *V.* "In the temperate zone and twentieth century we have this tradition." The First World War, one of the more thorough examples of modernity's instinct for destruction, was kicked off with two shots in Sarajevo in late June, but it was only after a month of failed diplomacy that, as the title of Barbara W. Tuchman's definitive history of the war's beginning described them, the guns of August began to fire. "In the month of August, 1914," she wrote, "there was something looming, inescapable, universal that involved us all. Something in that awful gulf between perfect plans and fallible men." In some editions, *The Guns of August* was called *August 1914*, the same title Aleksandr Solzhenitsyn

used for his own book on the beginning of the war, a novel about the calamitous Battle of Tannenberg that exposed the rot under the tsar and helped bring on the years of Russian revolution.

Not everyone is idle or evil in August. Many stay behind as the cities empty out in the heat, as Barbara Pym reminds us in *Excellent Women*, the best known of her witty and modestly willful novels of spinsters and others left out of the plots novelists usually concern themselves with. "'Thank goodness *some* of one's friends are unfashionable enough to be in town in August,'" William Caldicote says to Mildred Lathbury when he sees her on the street toward the end of the month. "'No, I think there are a good many people who have to stay in London in August,'" she replies, "remembering the bus queues and the patient line of people moving with their trays in the great cafeteria."

Arthur Mervyn by Charles Brockden Brown (1799) ⁖ The deadly yellow fever epidemic of 1793 in Philadelphia inspired Brockden Brown's Gothic fever dream of a novel, in which disease is but one of the anxious urban dangers threatening the young hero.

Light in August by William Faulkner (1932) ⁖ Faulkner thought he would call his tale of uncertain parentage "Dark House" until he was inspired instead by those "few days somewhere about the middle of the month when suddenly there's a foretaste of fall" and "a luminous quality to the light" to name it instead after the month in which most of its tragedy is set.

All the King's Men by Robert Penn Warren (1946) ⁖ Embedded in Warren's tale of compromises and betrayals is a summer interlude between Jack Burden and Anne Stanton, the kind of young romance during which, as Jack recalls, "even though the calendar said it was August I had not been able to believe that the summer, and the world, would ever end."

The Member of the Wedding by Carson McCullers (1946) ⁖ It's the last Friday of August in that "green and crazy summer when Frankie was twelve years old," and on Sunday her brother is going to be married. In the two days between, Frankie does her best to do a lot of growing up and, by misdirection, she does.

Excellent Women by Barbara Pym (1952) ⁖ It's hard to state how thrilling it is to see the expectations and supposed rules of the novel broken so quietly and confidently: not through style or structure but through one character's intelligent self-sufficiency, and through her creator's willingness to pay attention to her.

The Guns of August by Barbara W. Tuchman (1962) ⁖ It only added to the aura surrounding Tuchman's breakthrough history of the first, error-filled month of the First World War that soon after it was published John F. Kennedy gave copies of the book to his aides and told his brother Bobby, "I am not going to follow a course which will allow anyone to write a comparable book about this time [called] *The Missiles of October.*"

The Rings of Saturn by W. G. Sebald (1995) ⁖ A book—call it a memoir or a travelogue or a novel—grounded in an August walk through Suffolk, although Sebald could hardly go a sentence without being diverted by his restless curiosity into the echoes of personal and national history he heard wherever he went.

Kitchen Confidential by Anthony Bourdain (2000) ⁖ In August, in a seaside village in southwest France, Bourdain tasted his first oyster, pulled straight from the ocean, and everything changed: "I'd not only survived—I'd *enjoyed.*"

August 1

BORN: 1815 Richard Henry Dana (*Two Years Before the Mast*), Cambridge, Mass.
1819 Herman Melville (*Typee, Moby-Dick*), New York City

DIED: 1743 Richard Savage (*The Bastard, The Wanderer*), c. 46, Bristol, England
1963 Theodore Roethke (*The Lost Son, The Waking*), 55, Bainbridge Island, Wash.

1866 On his forty-seventh birthday, Herman Melville played croquet. His sister, observing from a hammock, noted, "Herman was quite a hand at it."

1928 Harold Coxe, in the *New Republic*, on the *Mémoires de Joséphine Baker*: "They are stimulating in a certain freshness and absurdity which is not often to be found, and they make you feel that, waiving prejudice, you would like Miss Baker."

1950 "To go abroad could fracture one's life," V. S. Naipaul later wrote about the moment when, headed to Oxford at age seventeen, he left Trinidad and flew for the first time to New York to meet his ship to London. His attention having already turned toward the future, away from the family he wouldn't see for another six years, he wrote his observations in a diary bought for that purpose—asking the stewardess to sharpen his pencil "to taste the luxuriousness of air travel"—but made no note then of the family farewell at the Trinidad airport nor of his first meal in New York: a roasted chicken brought from home, whose humble consumption—eaten without fork or plate over the trash basket in his hotel room, ashamed of the smell and the oil—he would nevertheless still intensely recall when he returned to his past in the autobiographical novel *The Enigma of Arrival*.

1956 In the hours after midnight sometime in April, Jean Shepherd, the radio host whose improvised, late-night monologues had drawn a cult audience, suggested a stunt, a prank of his fellow "Night People" against the "Day People" and their regimented lives. He sent his listeners out to ask in bookstores for a fictitious title, *I, Libertine* by Frederick R. Ewing, and they did in numbers enough to create a buzz in the publishing world for a book that didn't exist. The stunt didn't end there: as the *Wall Street Journal* and *Village Voice* reported on this day, publisher Ian Ballantine, embracing the hoax, arranged with Shepherd and novelist Theodore Sturgeon to write a book to match the title, a pastiche of eighteenth-century bawdiness that Ballantine released in the fall with a press run of 130,000 copies.

1963 Richard Chopping, commissioned to paint a toad for the original cover of Ian Fleming's *You Only Live Twice*, reported back to Fleming's editor that, "proud, do-it-yourself masochist" that he was, he had spent the previous day trudging through the swamps of Suffolk to find a suitable specimen, which now lived on mealworms under a glass dome in his studio.

August 2

BORN: **1924** James Baldwin (*Notes of a Native Son*, *Giovanni's Room*), New York City
1942 Isabel Allende (*The House of the Spirits*), Lima, Peru

DIED: **1988** Raymond Carver (*Cathedral*, *Fires*), 50, Port Angeles, Wash.
1997 William S. Burroughs (*The Soft Machine*), 83, Lawrence, Kans.

1779 Fanny Burney's play *The Witlings* seemed to amuse its audience of family and friends at its first reading, but afterward her beloved father and their close family friend Samuel Crisp, fearing scandal from its satire, wrote her what she called a "hissing, groaning, catcalling epistle," demanding she suppress it. Burney, already celebrated as the author of the novel *Evelina*, was stunned— "I expected many objections to be raised—a thousand errors to be pointed out—and a million of alterations to be proposed," she wrote her father, "but the suppression of the piece were words I did not expect"—but accepted their judgment. "I shall wipe it from my memory," she promised bitterly, though in fact she recycled much of its plot for her next novel, *Cecilia*, from whose text Jane Austen soon borrowed a title phrase, *Pride and Prejudice*.

1805 In the first of over two hundred annual Eton-Harrow cricket matches, the longest-running rivalry in the sport, Lord Byron made 7 and 2 for the Harrow eleven. "Byron played very badly," his captain noted; afterward, according to Byron, players from both teams made a drunken spectacle in a box at the Haymarket Theatre.

1845 Replying to his mother, who had been unhappy with a previous letter critical of the Old Testament, William Makepeace Thackeray asked: "What right have you to say I am without God because I can't believe that God ordered Abraham to kill Isaac or that he ordered the bears to eat the little children who laughed at Elisha for being bald. You don't believe it yourself."

1891 Ill from tuberculosis after a lengthy trip to Africa, the African American historian George Washington Williams died in London on this day at the age of forty-one. A year before, reporting from the Congo, he had published a blistering open letter to the colony's overseer, Leopold II of Belgium, about the "deceit, fraud, robberies, arson, murder, slave-raiding, and general policy of cruelty" of his administration, the final public act in Williams's short but remarkable career. Though W. E. B. DuBois later remembered him as "the greatest historian of the race" and John Hope Franklin called him "one of the small heroes of the world," Williams, whose unprecedented, thousand-page *History of the Negro Race from 1619 to 1880* is one of the landmarks of African American scholarship, has largely been left out of the history that he was the first in so many cases to record.

1947 Gabriel Marcel, in the *TLS*, on Albert Camus's *La peste*: "No doubt translations will soon appear; and then it may be that the book will be recognized as the most important which has appeared in France since the impressive novels of M. Malraux."

August 3

BORN: 1920 P. D. James (*Death in Holy Orders, The Children of Men*), Oxford, England
1943 Steven Millhauser (*Martin Dressler, Edwin Mullhouse*), New York City
DIED: 1924 Joseph Conrad (*Nostromo, Victory*), 66, Bishopsbourne, England
2008 Aleksandr Solzhenitsyn (*The Gulag Archipelago*), 89, Moscow

1890 When John Addington Symonds encountered the "Calamus" poems, with their celebration of love between men, in Walt Whitman's *Leaves of Grass* in the 1860s, he said they "made another man of me." For the next two decades he wrote to Whitman—and sometimes exasperated him—with his admiration, but finally on this day, with both their lives nearly over, he made his questions as explicit as he could: did Whitman agree that "those semisexual emotions and actions which no doubt do occur between men" were *not* entirely "prejudicial to social interests"? Whitman denied such "morbid inferences" should be made from his poetry and replied that the "one great difference between you and me, temperament & theory, is *restraint*." He also asserted, by the way, that "tho' always unmarried I have had six children," a fact otherwise undocumented in his biography.

1915 Jack Burden is just a historical researcher in search of the truth, or so he tells himself while in the sullied employ of Governor Willie Stark, the charismatic despot of Robert Penn Warren's *All the King's Men*. The governor expects, correctly, that even the upstanding Judge Irwin, the hero of Jack's youth, has a secret worthy of blackmail, and at the end of a trail across the South of old stock transactions, real estate records, and the recollections of elderly women, Jack finds it, in a letter written on this day whose plainspoken revelations cause Jack's last illusions about the nature of men, or of one man in particular, to collapse.

1916 Harold Hannyngton Child, in the *TLS*, on O. Henry: "Reading him is like catching prawns with the hands. With infinite patience you close your hands over the prey, and at the very last second, when the hole for escape is all but closed, flick! the quarry has gone."

2003 "This is America," one immigrant chides another in Joseph O'Neill's *Netherland*. "Hit the ball in the air, man." The first immigrant is Chuck Ramkissoon, a Trinidadian whose restless, self-made schemes include the building of a quality cricket ground in the far reaches of Brooklyn; the second is Hans van den Broek, a Dutch Wall Street analyst (and middling batsman) who has been drawn into Chuck's outerborough world. "It's not how I bat," Hans protests, but on this day, in the last game of the season, he finds his free-swinging form. "I'd done it," he thinks. "I'd hit the ball in the air like an American cricketer; and I'd done so without injury to my sense of myself." For a moment—though it turns out to be fleeting—Hans can imagine that yes, "I am at last naturalized."

BORN: 1961 Barack Obama (*Dreams from My Father*), Honolulu

1965 Dennis Lehane (*A Drink Before the War*, *Mystic River*), Boston

DIED: 1875 Hans Christian Andersen ("Thumbelina," "The Ugly Duckling"), 70, Copenhagen

2003 James Welch (*Fool's Crow*, *Winter in the Blood*), 62, Missoula, Mont.

1866 John Morley, in the *Saturday Review*, on Algernon Swinburne's *Poems and Ballads*: "No language is too strong to condemn the mixed vileness and childishness of depicting the spurious passion of a putrescent imagination, the unnamed lusts of sated wantons, as if they were the crown of character and their enjoyment the great glory of human life."

1892 Angela Carter is best known for her merrily subversive transformations of traditional European fables in books like *The Bloody Chamber*, but she turned the folk tales of America inside-out as well. Those legends are, of course, of a more recent vintage: the drunken lurchings of Edgar Allan Poe, the frontier dramas of Indian captivity narratives and John Ford Westerns, and, most vividly, the murders of Lizzie Borden's father and stepmother on this day for which Borden was acquitted by a jury but convicted by popular opinion. Carter's retelling of Lizzie's story, "The Fall River Axe Murders," is a fever dream of New England humidity and repression that will cause you to feel the squeeze of a corset, the jaw-clench of parsimony, and the hovering presence of the angel of death.

1913 The date of August 4 runs through the life of Florence Dowell like a line of fate, or of determination. She was born on that day, and on that day in 1901 she married John Dowell, the narrator of Ford Madox Ford's *The Good Soldier*. On August 4ths in between she set off on a trip around the world and made herself the mistress of a cabin boy. And on this August 4, Florence takes a lethal dose of prussic acid and lies down, for the last time, on their hotel bed, after which her husband comes to learn the truth of the Dowells' friendship with Edward and Leonora Ashburnham and understands that what had seemed to him "nine years of uninterrupted tranquility" were, he now assures us, "the saddest story I have ever heard."

1947 After approaching land for the first time in ninety-seven days and nearly 4,000 nautical miles across the Pacific, Thor Heyerdahl and his Scandinavian crew spent this day maneuvering their raft *Kon-Tiki* to avoid a reef while offering cigarettes to the Polynesian islanders who came by canoe to investigate. Four days later they landed on another island, planting a South American coconut to symbolize Heyerdahl's theory that South Americans on such rafts could have populated the islands, and completing an adventure tale that became a bestseller named after their raft.

1961 Orville Prescott, in the *New York Times*, on Robert A. Heinlein's *Stranger in a Strange Land*: a "disastrous mishmash of science fiction, laborious humor, dreary social satire, and cheap eroticism."

August 5

BORN: 1850 Guy de Maupassant (*Bel-Ami*, "Boule de Suif"), Dieppe, France
1934 Wendell Berry (*Jayber Crow*, *The Unsettling of America*), Henry County, Ky.

DIED: 1895 Friedrich Engels (*The Condition of the Working Class in England*), 74, London
2009 Budd Schulberg (*What Makes Sammy Run?*), 95, Quogue, N.Y.

1920 Writing *Jacob's Room* every morning, Virginia Woolf felt "each day's work like a fence which I have to ride at, my heart in my mouth till it's over, and I've cleared, or knocked the bar out."

1925 The legend of B. Traven began with the publication in a German socialist newspaper of *The Cotton-Pickers*, a series of stories of proletarian life that the author claimed were drawn from his own experiences. On this day, writing to his publisher from Mexico, Traven expanded on the legend, describing the tropical torments under which he worked—"one's bleeding hands and legs and cheeks, stung through and through by mosquitoes and other hellish insects"—while adamantly deflecting any

attempts to identify himself to the public. An explosion of novels under his name in the next decade, including *The Death Ship* and *The Treasure of the Sierra Madre*, made Traven internationally known, only increasing interest in the author's identity despite, or because of, his insistence that the work, not the man, should matter.

1944 When the motorcycle he was riding with photographer Robert Capa came under fire in France, Ernest Hemingway threw himself into a ditch and suffered a concussion on a boulder.

2006 *What It Is*, the title of Lynda Barry's 2008 book, either begs or answers the question, "What is it?" What is the book itself? It's a scrapbook and/or a memoir and/or a guidebook to creativity, and far better than any of that sounds. But, more importantly, what is "it"? Depending on the page in the book, "it" is images, or experiences, or reflection, or thoughts, or writing, or any other word we have for things that can open up a feeling of "aliveness," that by distraction or discipline or some combination of the two allow us to pay attention to what's around us, and to ourselves. Part personal collage, part storytelling along the lines of her old *Ernie Pook's Comeek*, part activity book, *What It Is* is a book-long pep talk that leads by example. For instance, as she records on page 193, Lynda Barry spent this entire day drawing people dancing.

BORN: 1934 Diane di Prima (*Loba, Memoirs of a Beatnik*), Brooklyn
1934 Piers Anthony (*A Spell for Chameleon, Split Infinity*), Oxford, England
DIED: 2010 Tony Judt (*Postwar, The Memory Chalet*), 62, New York City
2012 Robert Hughes (*The Fatal Shore, The Shock of the New*), 74, Bronx, N.Y.

1666 Recently widowed but still well connected at the court of Charles II, Aphra Behn entered the king's service as a spy. Sent to Antwerp to report on English exiles plotting against Charles after the Restoration (and to turn one of them, William Scott, an old friend, back to loyalty), she made her first report on this day, on the initial meeting between "Celladon" and "Astrea," her code names for Scott and herself. Less than a year later she returned to London so deeply in debt she was sent to prison, after which she turned to a profession as unlikely for a woman then as espionage. As a poet, playwright, and novelist—sometimes under the same name, "Astrea"—she became, in Vita Sackville-West's definitive phrase, "the first woman in England to earn her living by her pen."

1945 When the great, silent flash came over the city, Miss Toshiko Sasaki was at her office desk, Dr. Masakazu Fujii and Dr. Terufumi Sasaki were in their hospitals, Mrs. Hatsuyo Nakamura was at the window in her kitchen, Father Wilhelm Kleinsorge was reading a magazine in his underwear, and the Reverend Mr. Kiyoski Tanimoto was at the doorway of a house in the suburbs. Soon after the Japanese surrender, John Hersey gathered the stories of these six survivors of the atomic blast into *Hiroshima*, a spare, declarative account that was given an entire issue of *The New Yorker*, read aloud for four straight nights on ABC radio, and sent for free to all Book-of-the-Month Club members, although the Allied occupying authorities kept it from circulating in Japan.

1989 At 9:46 in the morning on this day John Updike was still alive, and suddenly to Nicholson Baker that meant he had to write about him *now*. Baker had made vague plans before to examine his "obsession with Updike," but he had thought it would be better done when his subject was dead. But now, having seen the way his thoughts about Donald Barthelme, after Barthelme's death a few weeks before, had congealed into "sad-clown sorrowfulness" or "valedictory grand-old-man reverence," Baker felt he had to capture his admiration for Updike while it was still anxious and dangerous, while the man and his writing were still alive. Most anxious of all, as Baker wrote in his strange and delightful book *U and I, "if he dies, he won't know how I feel about him."*

1997 The San Antonio Historic Design and Review Commission ruled that the shade of purple Sandra Cisneros had painted her house (Sherwin Williams Corsican Purple) was not historically appropriate to the King William Historic District, though, as she argued, it evoked a local history a thousand years older than the district.

August 7

BORN: 1942 Garrison Keillor (*Lake Wobegon Days, WLT*), Anoka, Minn.
1953 Anne Fadiman (*The Spirit Catches You and You Fall Down*), New York City
DIED: 1941 Rabindranath Tagore (*Gitanjali, The Home and the World*), 80, Calcutta
1995 Brigid Brophy (*Hackenfeller's Ape, Black Ship to Hell*), 66, Louth, England

1836 The "opening salvo" of New England Transcendentalism came in the form of a book of conversations with children. In 1835, Elizabeth Peabody, a teacher at the Temple School of Bronson Alcott (whose students did not yet include his daughter Louisa May), published *Record of a School,* composed from the open-ended dialogues of Alcott and his students. But by the time her book, and thereby his school, became acclaimed for their brilliance, their partnership had soured. The final straw for Peabody, who resigned from the school on this day, was Alcott's next book, *Conversations with Children on the Gospels*, whose frank discussions of the physical basis of creation—six-year-old Josiah Quincy commented that the body was formed out of "the naughtiness of other people"—were condemned in the Boston press as "one third absurd, one third blasphemous, and one third obscene," leading three-quarters of the school's pupils to withdraw.

1958 There are two Chaneysville incidents in *The Chaneysville Incident*: one, more a part of legend than history, in which thirteen slaves, about to be captured as they made their way through southern Pennsylvania on the Underground Railroad, chose to take their own lives rather than give them up again to slavery, and a second, on this day more than a century later, when Moses Washington, a black moonshiner and a man of mysterious wealth and local power, "went hunting and came home dead." In David Bradley's novel, it becomes the obsessive burden of Moses's son John, a professor of history, to return to his hometown and unearth the truth behind both incidents and the connection between them, a task that will require his scholarly skills as well as the full measure of his humanity to fulfill.

1974 It was a moment that felt lighter than air, but as substantial as the towers themselves. Two days before Nixon resigned, a man appeared in the space between the tops of Manhattan's Twin Towers, balanced on a cable that was nearly invisible from the street below, where "the whole August morning was blown wide open, and the watchers stood rooted," as Colum McCann describes it in *Let the Great World Spin*, his novel of New York stories drawn together by the man on a wire above them. From above, the man on the wire himself, Philippe Petit, had this view: "The city has changed face. Its maddening daily rush has transformed into a magnificent motionlessness. It listens. It watches. It ponders." That's how he remembered the moment in *To Reach the Clouds*, the memoir of his daring coup, which he published the year after the towers came down.

August 8

BORN: 1922 Gertrude Himmelfarb (*The Roads to Modernity*), Brooklyn
1931 Roger Penrose (*The Road to Reality*), Colchester, England
DIED: 1984 Ellen Raskin (*The Westing Game*), 56, New York City
2008 Ted Solotaroff (*Truth Comes in Blows*), 79, East Quogue, N.Y.

1920 Katherine Mansfield, in the *Athenaeum*, on E. M. Forster's "Story of a Siren": "So aware is he of his sensitiveness, of his sense of humour, that they are become two spectators who follow him wherever he goes, and are for ever on the look-out for a display of feeling."

NO YEAR "Oh yes, I've no doubt in my mind that we have been invited here by a madman—probably a dangerous homicidal maniac," Mr. Justice Wargrave remarks. Ten of them, including the judge—all strangers to each other except a married couple—have arrived for either a summer holiday or summer employment at remote

Indian Island, where, by a voice on gramophone, they are charged with each having caused the death of someone in their past. And then, one by one, they begin to die. *And Then There Were None* (which has had nearly as many nursery-rhyme titles as it has victims) is perhaps the most intricate in Agatha Christie's career of homicidal puzzles, a locked-room mystery that takes place on an entire island, and one, she later admitted, she was tremendously pleased to have constructed.

1969 When her friend Rex Reed decided he was too tired to go out that night, Jacqueline Susann called Sharon Tate, who had starred in the movie of her book *Valley of the Dolls*, and told her she wouldn't be able to make her dinner party.

1969 The murders of seven people, including actress Sharon Tate, over two nights in the Los Angeles hills went unsolved for nearly four months, but in early 1971 Vincent Bugliosi, an L.A. prosecutor, obtained guilty verdicts against Charles Manson and three of his followers. That same year Ed Sanders, Beat poet and former member of the Fugs, writing from within the counterculture that had curdled into evil in Manson's hands, told the story of the crimes in *The Family*, and in 1974 *Helter Skelter*, Bugliosi's own massive, fact-heavy account of the murders and the prosecution—part *Warren Report* and part *In Cold Blood*—became a massive bestseller and one of the pop-culture tombstones marking the end of the '60s.

August 9

BORN: 1922 Philip Larkin ("The Whitsun Weddings," *High Windows*), Coventry, England

1949 Jonathan Kellerman (*When the Bough Breaks*), New York City

DIED: 1967 Joe Orton (*Entertaining Mr. Sloane, Loot*), 34, London

2008 Mahmoud Darwish (*Unfortunately, It Was Paradise*), 67, Houston, Tex.

1853 From the seaside, George Eliot wrote that the "sacraments" of swimming and beer-drinking have been "very efficacious."

1912 "Will you stand by me in a crisis?" P. G. Wodehouse wrote apologetically to Arthur Conan Doyle. "A New York lady journalist, a friend of mine, is over here gunning for you. She said 'You know Conan Doyle, don't you?' I said, 'I do. It is my only claim to fame'. She then insisted on my taking her to see you . . . Can you stand this invasion? If so, we will arrive in the afternoon."

1925 "You are right about Gatsby being blurred and patchy," F. Scott Fitzgerald wrote to John Peale Bishop. "I never at any one time saw him clear myself—for he started as one man I knew and then changed into myself—the amalgam was never complete in my mind."

1945 "Did I tell you what Jean-Paul Sartre said about your work? He's a little man with bad teeth, absolutely the best talker I ever met," Malcolm Cowley wrote to William Faulkner. *"Pour les jeunes en France, Faulkner c'est un dieu."* Faulkner, mired in Hollywood with his books out of print, could hardly have minded being called a god, nor did he resist Cowley's pitch in the same letter to construct a *Portable Faulkner*, a one-volume anthology that would introduce his writing as an interconnected Mississippi saga and also give a "bayonet prick in the ass of Random House to reprint" his books. Faulkner agreed—"By all means let us make a Golden Book of my apocryphal county"—and *The Portable Faulkner*, published to great success in 1946, followed by Faulkner's Nobel Prize in 1949, cemented his reputation as, indeed, a god among American novelists.

1984 Walter Tevis, who described himself as a "good American writer of the second rank," died on this day at the age of fifty-six, with his novels obscured by the glare of the movies a few of them had become, by his cussed indifference to keeping to a single genre of storytelling, and perhaps by his own blunt self-effacement. His promising first novel, *The Hustler*, became a hit movie with Paul Newman and Jackie Gleason. His second, *The Man Who Fell to Earth*, confounded expectations with its switch to science fiction but became the source for David Bowie's most vivid screen role. Tevis then spent seventeen years mostly teaching and drinking, but in his last years he turned again to writing and published a flurry of books, including the *Hustler* sequel, *The Color of Money*, and two novels, *The Queen's Gambit* and *Mockingbird*, that have developed devoted followings without the benefit, or curse, of a movie adaptation.

BORN: 1962 Suzanne Collins (*The Hunger Games, Catching Fire*), Hartford, Conn.
1963 Andrew Sullivan (*Virtually Normal*), South Godstone, England
DIED: 1948 Montague Summers (*The History of Witchcraft and Demonology*), 68, Richmond, England

1914 In early August, as the European powers gathered themselves for battle, two speedy German ships of war, the *Goeben* and the *Breslau*, were pursued east across the Mediterranean by a fleet of British cruisers that exchanged fire with the Germans but couldn't prevent their escape to the waters of their new Turkish ally. As Barbara W. Tuchman mentioned in *The Guns of August*, "the daughter, son-in-law, and three grandchildren of the American ambassador Mr. Henry Morgenthau" observed the gunfire from a "small Italian passenger steamer," and Morgenthau's daughter gave an account of the confrontation to the German and Austrian ambassadors in Constantinople on this day. What Tuchman didn't mention is that the eyewitness was her own mother, and that the "three grandchildren" on the steamer were her sisters, Josephine and Anne, and herself, age two.

1945 Graham Greene, in the *Evening Standard*, on George Orwell's *Animal Farm*: "If Mr Walt Disney is looking for a real subject, here it is: it has all the necessary humour, and it has, too, the subdued lyrical quality he can sometimes express so well. But it is perhaps a little too real for him?"

1958 Glenn Gould was not averse to placing his idiosyncratically brilliant piano career in a literary context, as in a self-interview he conducted in which he suggested to himself that the Salzburg Festspielhaus, where he played a concert on this day, would, with its "Kafka-like setting at the base of a cliff," be a perfect site for "the martyr's end you so desire." And others have been equally willing to use him as a character, most memorably in Thomas Bernhard's novel, *The Loser*, the story of two gifted piano students driven to give up the instrument (and in one case to suicide) by the greater talent of their fellow student Gould. Bernhard plays loose with the details of Gould's life, but he too mentions a Salzburg concert and imagines, as Gould did, a sort of martyrdom to music: in his story Gould dies of a stroke, not while sleeping as in real life, but while playing the Goldberg Variations.

1967 Among Kurt Vonnegut's advice to a friend coming to teach at the Iowa Writers' Workshop: "Go to all the football games," "Cancel classes whenever you damn please," and "Don't ball undergraduates. Their parents are still watching."

2012 Contemplating retirement after fifty-five years as a book dealer and hoping to "seed the clouds" of the used-book market, Larry McMurtry opened Booked Up, his four-building store in his hometown of Archer City, Texas, to what he called, in a nod to one of his early novels, the Last Book Sale, selling off two-thirds of his 400,000-book stock by auction.

August 11

BORN: 1897 Louise Bogan (*The Blue Estuaries*), Livermore Falls, Maine
1922 Mavis Gallant (*From the Fifteenth District*), Montreal
DIED: 1890 John Henry Newman (*Apologia pro vita sua*), 89, Edgbaston, England
1979 J. G. Farrell (*Troubles, The Siege of Krishnapur*), 44, Bantry Bay, Ireland

NO YEAR Ever since the strange wreck of a ship nearby, with no apparent survivors save an immense dog that bounded out of sight, the beautiful Lucy Westenra has had restless nights, and in the early, dark hours of August 11 her dear friend Mena wakes to discover Lucy's bed empty and Lucy nowhere to be found. Searching for her out on the cliffs, Mena sees in the ruined abbey across the harbor something dark bending over a white figure, but when she reaches the abbey Lucy is alone and sleeping. All seems well the next morning, in the best-known novel by Irish theatrical manager Bram Stoker, *Dracula,* except for those two pinpricks on Lucy's neck, which Mena must have caused when she clumsily used a safety pin to wrap a shawl around her in the night.

1937 When Max Eastman wrote in "Bull in the Afternoon," his lengthy takedown of his old friend Ernest Hemingway's *Death in the Afternoon* in the *New Republic* in 1933, "that Hemingway lacks the serene confidence that he *is* a full-sized man," and compared his literary style to "wearing false hair on the chest," it was, well, like waving a red flag in front of his subject. Hemingway fumed and wrote public letters asserting his "potency," and four years later, when he found Eastman in his editor Maxwell Perkins's office, he pulled open his shirt to reveal his full, authentic pelt. Before long the two men were grappling on the floor. They continued their battle for days in the New York papers, with Eastman claiming he had stood the younger man on his head while Hemingway offered a rematch: for $1,000, they would be left alone in a room and "the best man unlocks the door."

1994 There may never have been a more inspired pairing of book reviewer and subject than when the *New York Review of Books* commissioned Nicholson Baker to review volume one (*A–G*) of the *Historical Dictionary of American Slang*, edited by J. H. Lighter. Baker, the author of both the micro-epics *The Mezzanine* and *Room Temperature* and the highbrow smut of *Vox* and, later, *House of Holes*, was like a pig in, uh, slop, celebrating the way the reference book made worn lingo like "broke-dick" and "dingleberry" freshly funny again—thanks in part to the recurring, deadpan punch line "(usu. considered vulgar)"—and constructing a homemade grid charting the various combinations of prefixes (cheese-, dirt-, scum-) and suffixes (-ball!, -bag!, -wad!) that the ingenuity of human insult had, so far, concocted.

August 12

BORN: 1937 Walter Dean Myers (*Fallen Angels, Monster*), Martinsburg, W.Va.
1964 Katherine Boo (*Behind the Beautiful Forevers*), Washington, D.C.
DIED: 1955 Thomas Mann (*The Magic Mountain, Doctor Faustus*), 80, Zurich
1964 Ian Fleming (*Dr. No, Chitty-Chitty-Bang-Bang*), 56, Canterbury, England

1803 With Napoleon's armies massing on the other side of the English Channel, Britain hastily deployed troops in the towns along the coast, including Felpham, the tiny Sussex village where William Blake had moved a few years before, and where he had an altercation with a Private Scho-field that nearly cost him his freedom. The soldier claimed Blake had shouted words of sedition, "Damn the King. The soldiers are all slaves," and that Blake's wife added that she would fight for Napoleon "as long as I am able." Blake was no admirer of the king, but he was quickly acquitted at trial when no witnesses would support the soldier. In his later poetry, he would celebrate "sweet Felpham," and forever curse "Skofield" as a "minister of evil."

1967 It is nearly impossible to think of Scott Spencer's third novel without being reminded of the young Brooke Shields or without hearing Diana Ross and Lionel Richie breathe its title, *Endless Love*, in your mind's ear, but behind that gauzy scrim there's a novel that engages directly with the kind of overwhelming teen passion usually left to pop songwriters. The story begins with a fire, a small flame that David Axel-rod lights on the porch of the girl—and the entire family—he loves, for no better reason than that they would come out and see him. The flame becomes a blaze, and years later, he tells us, "the night of August 12, 1967, still divides my life." Much of the power of Spencer's story, though, is that even years later David doesn't seem that far from the seventeen-year-old who acted that night "in full obedience to my heart's most urgent commands."

1984 Published: *Bright Lights, Big City* by Jay McInerney (Vintage Contemporaries, New York)

2006 He wrote the book, David Grossman said later, with the hope it would somehow protect his sons. As Jonathan, the elder son, and then Uri, the younger, enlisted for their military service, Grossman wrote *To the End of the Land*, the story of an Israeli mother of a soldier, who sets out on a hike through the Galilee with the similar hope that her absence from home will keep away from her door the messengers who deliver the army's bad news. But the book couldn't keep them from Grossman's own door: early on this morning the news arrived that Uri and three soldiers he commanded had been killed by a Hezbollah rocket, just a day before a cease-fire Grossman himself had argued for in a public speech. After sitting shiva, Grossman saw the novel to its finish: "What changed, above all," he wrote, "was the echo of the reality in which the final draft was written."

August 13

BORN: 1940 Michael Herr (*Dispatches*, *Walter Winchell*), Syracuse, N.Y.
   1961 Tom Perrotta (*Election*, *Little Children*), Garwood, N.J.
DIED: 2004 Julia Child (*Mastering the Art of French Cooking*), 91, Montecito, Calif.
   2012 Helen Gurley Brown (*Sex and the Single Girl*), 90, New York City

1841 Skeptical and solitary, Nathaniel Hawthorne was always an unlikely candidate for utopia, and within months of joining the Transcendentalist experiment in communal living at Brook Farm he was lamenting that the work left him even less energy for writing than before. "Even my Custom-House experience was not such a thraldom and weariness," he wrote his fiancée on this day. "Dost thou think it a praiseworthy matter that I have spent five golden months in providing food for cows and horses? Dearest, it is not so." Leaving in the fall, he lightly satirized the commune a decade later in *The Blithedale Romance*, which those who had stayed loyal to the farm resented though it gave their short-lived experiment an immortality.

1912 When he arrived at his friend Max Brod's house this evening to discuss how to arrange the pieces for his first book to send to the publisher the next day, Franz Kafka was surprised and disconcerted to find a visitor, a cousin of the family, "sitting at the table" though she "looked to me like a maid-servant." Her name was Felice Bauer, and he was, apparently, repelled and attracted at once: coldly assessing her "bony, empty face" and her "blond, somewhat stiff, unattractive hair" in his diary while admitting that "by the time I was seated, I had already formed an immutable opinion." Saying goodbye at her hotel he stumbled into a revolving door with her and nearly stepped on her foot, and the next day he apologized to Brod for any stupidity with his manuscript that night: "I was completely under the influence of the girl." A month later he wrote his first of over five hundred letters to her, promising—falsely, as it would turn out—that he was an "erratic letter writer" and "never expect[ed] a letter to be answered by return," and closing with words that would be innocuous, were he not Franz Kafka: "You might well give me a trial."

1974 It was the opening day of the Bread Loaf Writers' Conference in Vermont, but one of the star faculty members, John Gardner, scheduled to teach at Bread Loaf for the first time, was nowhere in sight and unreachable until, some days later, he arrived in a new Mercedes he had purchased with the proceeds from one of his recent bestsellers. Shortly after, drunk, he wrecked the Mercedes in a ditch, but despite—or because of—this entrance, he became the dominant presence at Bread Loaf for most of the next decade: combative and charismatic, holding court and hungrily engaging with students' manuscripts, until, in the fall of 1982, he died when he crashed his Harley-Davidson near Binghamton, New York.

August 14

BORN: **1947** Danielle Steel (*The Promise, Fine Things*), New York City

1950 Gary Larson (*The Far Side*), Tacoma, Wash.

DIED: **1951** William Randolph Hearst (publisher, *New York Journal*), 88, Beverly Hills, Calif.

1963 Clifford Odets (*Waiting for Lefty, Awake and Sing!*), 57, Los Angeles

1881 According to the memoir of his wife, the naturalist Ernest Thompson Seton hated two men: the late General George Armstrong Custer, for the usual reasons, and his own father, who, following Ernest's twenty-first birthday, brought out his massive cash book and computed the amount, beginning with the doctor's fee for his birth, he had spent on his son through his life: $537.50. "Hitherto I have charged no interest," he continued. "But from now on I must add the reasonable amount of six percent per annum. I shall be glad to have you reduce the amount at the earliest opportunity." And repay him Seton did, though not before using the next money he earned to leave his Toronto home as quickly as he could, for Manitoba.

1919 Richard Aldington, in the *TLS*, on Marcel Proust's *À la récherche du temps perdu*, vols. 1 and 2: "That which is novel in M. Proust is the deliberate avoidance of the search for novelty. He is the antithesis of a man like Gauguin, always wandering about to find '*quelques éléments nouveaux*.'"

1947 "So how *did* your grandmother die?" "Natural causes." "What?" "Flood." In his memoir *Running in the Family,* Michael Ondaatje recounted his family's history in Sri Lanka in stories that retain the polished, elliptical style of legend, including the life and death of his grandmother Lalla. An eccentric, alcoholic widow who lived according to means she no longer possessed, Lalla imagined a great death for herself and found it: as storm waters rose around her, she spent this day playing cards and drinking indoors, stayed up through the night—the same night on which, though Ondaatje doesn't mention it, neighboring India took her independence—and then in the morning walked out her door and was swept away by the floods.

2008 Zadie Smith, in the *New York Review of Books*, on *The BBC Talks of E. M. Forster*: "To love Forster is to reconcile oneself to the admixture of banality and brilliance that was his, as he had done himself. In this book that blend is perhaps more perfectly represented than ever before. Whether that's a good thing or not is difficult to say."

August 15

BORN: 1771 Walter Scott (*Ivanhoe*, *Rob Roy*, *Waverley*), Edinburgh
1885 Edna Ferber (*So Big*, *Show Boat*, *Giant*), Kalamazoo, Mich.
DIED: 2009 Richard Poirier (*A World Elsewhere*), 83, New York City
2012 Harry Harrison (*Make Room! Make Room!*), 87, Brighton, England

1788 In the *Almanach des honnêts gens*, a radical new calendar in which the French poet and revolutionary Sylvain Maréchal replaced the saints' names honored in the Christian calendar with the names of philosophers, poets, scientists, and even a courtesan, he left one day blank for future generations to fill: August 15, the date of his own birth.

1947 No literary character is more beholden to the "occult tyrannies" of the calendar than Saleem Sinai, a.k.a. "Snotnose, Stainface, Baldy, Sniffer, Buddha, and even Piece-of-the-Moon," who was born in the city of Bombay not only on the day of India's independence from the British Empire (and its partition from Pakistan), but at its very moment, at the midnight hour between August 14 and 15. In *Midnight's Children*, his second novel, Salman Rushdie, who himself was born in Bombay two months before Saleem, embraced the narrative possibilities offered by a child born along with his country, going beyond mere symbolism by imagining his hero as one of a handful of children whose midnight births brought them each a superpower, as if they were the X-Men of independent, divided India.

1973 Passing herself off as Zora Neale Hurston's niece to discourage "foot-dragging" among those who could tell her something about the late writer, who had died in poverty and obscurity thirteen years before, Alice Walker arrived in Eatonville, Florida, the tiny, all-black town Hurston had grown up in. Soon she and a fellow Hurston scholar, Charlotte Hunt, were directed to the graveyard in nearby Fort Pierce where Hurston had been buried without a stone to mark her and, wading into knee-high, snake-friendly weeds, chose a spot for the small monument Walker commissioned reading, "Zora Neale Hurston, 'A Genius of the South.'" Walker's moving, bittersweet account of their adventure, "In Search of Zora Neale Hurston," appeared in *Ms.* in March 1975 and sparked the revival of interest in Hurston that continues to this day.

1982 As someone whose best-known book, and lifelong project, is called *Ten Thousand Lives*, Ko Un has lived a fair amount of lives himself. A Buddhist monk in his twenties and a poet and teacher (and suicidal alcoholic) in his thirties, he became a leader of the resistance against the South Korean military dictatorship and spent much of his forties in prison, where, in solitary confinement under a life sentence, he began in the darkness of his cell to imagine the faces of all the people he'd known and compose his ongoing poem about their lives as well as those of figures from legend and history. Released from prison under a general amnesty on this day, he has become, in his fifties, sixties, and seventies, the most acclaimed Korean poet.

BORN: **1902** Georgette Heyer (*The Black Moth, The Grand Sophy*), London
1902 Wallace Thurman (*The Blacker the Berry*), Salt Lake City
DIED: **1949** Margaret Mitchell (*Gone with the Wind*), 48, Atlanta
1998 Dorothy West (*The Wedding, The Living Is Easy*), 91, Boston

1884 Hugo Gernsback, who was born in Luxembourg on this day, cultivated early interests in electronics, Mars, and the United States, and immigrated to the latter in 1903, where, a fan of Mark Twain, he called himself "Huck" and quickly became a radio entrepreneur. Building a fleet of electronics magazines, he published fiction along with the science, including his own novel *Ralph 124C41+*, one of the founding books of modern science fiction, though it has been described since as "pitiable," "simply dreadful," and "appallingly bad." In 1926 he launched *Amazing Stories*, the first magazine devoted to what he called "scientifiction," starting a ten-year run in which he published many of the early innovators of science fiction while frustrating them with his pathological unwillingness to pay for their work.

1898 When the unnamed narrator of Tayeb Salih's *Season of Migration to the North* returns to his village along the Nile after seven years studying in Europe, he wants it to be as it was when he left: the people, his familiar bed, the sound of the wind through the palm trees. But there is a stranger in the village, a man called Mustafa

Sa'eed, to whom he's drawn by an unspoken mutual interest until Mustafa stuns him first by reciting a Ford Madox Ford poem at the end of a drunken evening and then by thrusting a bundle of documents into his hands, including a birth certificate and passport showing years of European travel and a birth date on this day. Mustafa soon disappears from the village, but not before burdening the narrator with the tragic story of his own travels north. For years after, like a figure out of Poe, Mustafa haunts him as a phantom, a double whose legacy he feels doomed to follow.

1922 You'd think Virginia Woolf would have been an ideal reader for *Ulysses*. Almost exactly Joyce's age, she was similarly weary of the mechanics of traditional fiction and a fellow experimenter with her characters' moment-by-moment consciousness. But she could hardly bear to read it. "An illiterate, underbred book it seems to me," she wrote in her diary on this day after working through the first two hundred pages, "the book of a self-taught working man, & we all know how distressing they are, how egotistic, insistent, raw, striking, & ultimately nauseating. When one can have cooked flesh, why have the raw?" Violently snobbish toward Joyce's "indecency" and no doubt competitive toward his innovations—"what I'm doing is probably being better done by Mr. Joyce," she once noted—she finished the book with impatient boredom, eager to get back to reading Proust and to writing *Mrs. Dalloway*, her own stream-of-consciousness novel set on a single June day.

August 17

BORN: 1932 V. S. Naipaul (*A House for Mr. Biswas*, *A Bend in the River*), Chaguanas, Trinidad

1959 Jonathan Franzen (*The Corrections*, *Freedom*), Western Spring, Ill.

DIED: 1935 Charlotte Perkins Gilman (*The Yellow Wallpaper*), 75, Pasadena, Calif.

1973 Conrad Aiken (*The Charnel Rose*, *Ushant*), 84, Savannah, Ga.

1854 Bigamy! Insanity! False identities! Arson! The thrillingly convoluted plot of *Lady Audley's Secret*, Mary Elizabeth Braddon's triple-decker novel of Victorian sensation and anxiety, made it one of the most popular novels of the age. Writing soon after the Constance Kent murder case captured English headlines with a similar story of family hatreds and high-profile detective work, Braddon constructed one of the first detective thrillers around the discovery that Lady Audley, the beautiful young wife of wealthy old Sir Michael Audley, wasn't who she said she was: she had abandoned her old identity (and her previous marriage) and on this day created a new one from scratch, a history, it soon turns out, she is prepared to murder to conceal.

1902 After praising her historical novel, *The Valley of Decision*, Henry James urged Edith Wharton to write about an American subject, contemporary New York: "the immediate, the real, the ours, the yours, the novelist's that it waits for . . . Profit, be warned, by my awful example of exile and ignorance."

1918 Louis Untermeyer, in the *New Republic*, on Ezra Pound's *Pavannes and Divisions*: "It is the record of a creative talent grown sterile, of a disorderly retreat into the mazes of technique and pedantry."

1924 A sixteenth-century alchemist who declares, "I am wiser by seventy than all such cod-merchants"; a Kansas City lawyer who thinks, "According to the mileage on the speedometer it was time once again to have the Reo lubricated"; his wife, "who was sure that in some way—because she willed it to be so—her wants and her expectations would be the same"; a San Francisco clerk besieged by the '60s, who fumes, "It could be that Hate is the only reality." These varied voices, and many others, came from the pen of Evan S. Connell, born on this day, who restlessly transformed himself in book after book, working odd jobs to support his writing for decades until his brilliantly expansive biography of Custer, *Son of the Morning Star*, became a late-career bestseller.

1936 The Macmillan Company announced that two printing plants were turning out copies of *Gone with the Wind* for three eight-hour shifts a day, and that if all the copies published so far were stacked, they would reach fifty times the height of the Empire State Building.

1958 Elizabeth Janeway, in the *New York Times*, on Vladimir Nabokov's *Lolita*: "The first time I read *Lolita* I thought it was one of the funniest books I'd ever come on . . . The second time I read it . . . I thought it was one of the saddest."

August 18

BORN: 1922 Alain Robbe-Grillet (*The Voyeur, The Erasers*), Brest, France
1974 Nicole Krauss (*The History of Love, Great House*), New York City
DIED: 1850 Honoré de Balzac (*Père Goriot, Eugénie Grandet*), 51, Paris
1981 Anita Loos (*Gentlemen Prefer Blondes*), 92, New York City

1563 Though as a teenager he wrote a political essay against tyranny, "On Voluntary Slavery," that is still read to this day, Étienne de La Boétie is largely remembered for one reason: as the bosom friend of Michel de Montaigne, who, having spent the previous ten days at La Boétie's side despite the threat of contagion, recorded his death from plague at 3 a.m. on this day. They had known each other only six years, but it's often been thought that Montaigne's retreat to a life of writing, almost a decade after La Boétie's death, was a way of keeping himself company in the absence of his friend, about whom he wrote, in the essay titled, naturally, "Of Friendship," "We were halves throughout, to a degree, I think, that by outliving him, I defraud him of his part."

1912 Among the dozens of poets she wrote to before the launch of her new magazine, *Poetry*, Harriet Monroe sent a short note to Ezra Pound (via his father, Homer L. Pound, assistant assayer at the U.S. Mint), and on this day Pound replied quickly from London. "I *am* interested," he began, sending two poems and offering to keep her "in touch with whatever is most dynamic in artistic thought . . . I *do* see nearly everyone that matters." Over the next few years he brought T. S. Eliot, Robert Frost, and H.D., among others, to *Poetry* before breaking with the magazine in a series of letters whose tone he hinted at in this first note when he added, "However I need not bore you with jeremiads."

1943 Orville Prescott, in the *New York Times*, on Betty Smith's *A Tree Grows in Brooklyn*: "If you miss 'A Tree Grows in Brooklyn' you will deny yourself a rich experience, many hours of delightful entertainment (for it is long), and the pleasant tingle that comes from a sense of discovery."

1974 It was getting late in the summer, and Rodney Parker, as always, was working the phones: a college basketball coach happy with the two players he sent his way; a fellow fixer who might know a junior college for some of his other kids; a high school coach despondent because Albert King, the impossibly talented 6′5″ fourteen-year-old, was slipping out of their influence. For a summer, when Brooklyn was a battle zone and the basketball talent pipeline was still a cottage industry, Rick Telander—a white jock nearly as young as the black kids he coached, played against, and wrote about—tried to keep up with Parker's hustling while gathering the stories for *Heaven Is a Playground*, a book that over time has gathered for itself some of the aura of the playground legends he chronicled.

August 19

BORN: 1902 Ogden Nash (*I'm a Stranger Here Myself*), Rye, N.Y.

1903 James Gould Cozzens (*Guard of Honor, By Love Possessed*), Chicago

DIED: 1662 Blaise Pascal (*Pensées, Provincial Letters*), 39, Paris

1936 Federico García Lorca (*Poet in New York, Blood Wedding*), 38, Alfacar, Spain

1890 "I was never fond of towns, houses, society or (it seems) civilization," Robert Louis Stevenson wrote to Henry James, predicting he'd only return to Britain once, to die (he never made it back at all). "I simply prefer Samoa."

1903 Did the bloody Battle of Rivington Street between Monk Eastman's gang and the hooligans loyal to his rival Paul Kelly take place in New York on this day or a month later? The historical evidence points to the latter, but that was of little concern to Jorge Luis Borges when he adjusted and compressed the facts and legends of Eastman's brutal life into "Monk Eastman, Purveyor of Iniquities," one of the bloody tales in *A Universal History of Infamy*, his first collection of fiction. In Borges's imagination Monk Eastman seems less a real-life Tammany enforcer than a character from Borges's library; more specifically from Herbert Asbury's *Gangs of New York*, from which Borges drew whatever facts about Eastman he didn't invent out of thin air.

1938 Antoine de Saint-Exupéry's card tricks convinced André Gide he must be clairvoyant.

1946 It tells you a lot about Rosa Burger's upbringing to know that her parents shoehorned their wedding on this day into the time between their arrest during the black miners' strike on the Witwatersrand and their court appearance ten days later. Two years afterward, in the same month that the charges were dropped and the Afrikaner nationalist government took office, Rosa, their only daughter, was born, beginning a life in which she has to learn to define for herself an identity as the child of Lionel and Carol Berger, famous enemies of the state, and as a white in the apartheid system, a story that Nadine Gordimer, in *Burger's Daughter*, based on the white South African activist families she knew around her.

2009 "Tommy," the letter Paul Haggis wrote to Scientology spokesman Tommy Davis on this day began. "For ten months now I have been writing to ask you to make a public statement denouncing the actions of the Church of Scientology of San Diego." And with the same opening began "The Apostate," Lawrence Wright's 2011 *New Yorker* profile of Haggis, the Oscar-winning screenwriter and director of *Crash*, which ended by quoting Haggis again: "I was in a cult for thirty-four years. Everyone else could see it. I don't know why I couldn't." Two years later, Wright published *Going Clear*, in which he embedded Haggis's story in a history of Scientology and its relationship to Hollywood, reported with the same intrepid and patient thoroughness Wright used for his Pulitzer-winning book on al-Qaeda, *The Looming Tower*.

August 20

BORN: **1890** H. P. Lovecraft (*At the Mountains of Madness*), Providence, R.I.
1951 Greg Bear (*The Forge of God, Darwin's Radio*), San Diego, Calif.
DIED: **1887** Jules Laforgue (*The Imitation of Our Lady the Moon*), 27, Paris
2001 Fred Hoyle (*The Black Cloud*), 86, Bournemouth, England

1950 Immanuel Velikovsky asks the reader at the opening of *Worlds in Collision* "to consider for himself whether he is reading a book of fiction or non-fiction"; the *New York Times*, at least for the purposes of its bestseller list, where *Worlds in Collision* spent the last of its eleven weeks at #1 on this day, chose nonfiction. A scientific scandal even before it was published, Velikovsky's book modestly proposed that as recently as 1500 B.C. Venus spun off as a comet from Jupiter and twice swept past Earth on its way to settling into planetary orbit, thereby explaining a host of ancient mythologies and refuting the theories of both Newton and Darwin. Velikovsky's conjectures, shaky at the time, have been further undermined by later discoveries, but one element of his thought has gained some acceptance: the importance of catastrophic events in shaping evolutionary and geological history.

1979 "So Farrah is a story," explained George W. S. Trow, "and Farrah having a problem is a story, and Farrah talking about her problem is a story." Many have called TV culture shallow, but none with the chilling insight—and cryptically imperious style—of Trow's 1980 *New Yorker* essay "Within the Context of No Context," which became a little book the following year. Among his evidence that America had given up cultural judgment and authority in favor of popularity: the cover of *People* on this day. Putting Farrah Fawcett and her problem—that she had split from Lee Majors—on the cover was not a statement of approval or disapproval of Farrah or her talent, as might have once been the case. Instead it was in the spirit of what Trow with grim relish called "the important moment in the history of television," when Richard Dawson asked *Family Feud* contestants to guess, not the correct answer to a question, but what a hundred other Americans had already guessed.

2004 Ben Ball, in the *TLS*, on Elliot Perlman's *Seven Types of Ambiguity*: "It paints a convincing portrait of Australia's cheerfully brazen appeal to greed and comfort; the universities honeycombed with deconstruction; the low hum of racism and sexism; the anxiety that, underneath, there is nothing there."

August 21

BORN: **1930** Joseph McElroy (*Women and Men*), New York City
1937 Robert Stone (*Dog Soldiers, Children of Light*), Brooklyn
DIED: **1940** Leon Trotsky (*The History of the Russian Revolution*), 60, Mexico City
2007 Siobhan Dowd (*Bog Child, The London Eye Mystery*), 47, Oxford, England

1888 William Seward Burroughs, founder of what became the Burroughs Corporation and grandfather of William S. Burroughs, received four patents for his adding machines.

1909 "Do you know what a pearl is and what an opal is?" James Joyce wrote to Nora Barnacle. "My soul when you came sauntering to me first through those sweet summer evenings was beautiful but with the pale passionless beauty of a pearl. Your love has passed through me and now I feel my mind something like an opal, that is, full of strange uncertain hues and colours, of warm lights and quick shadows and of broken music."

1921 On his first birthday, Christopher Milne, known later to everyone but family and friends as Christopher Robin, received a teddy bear that he called "Edward Bear" before settling on "Winnie-the-Pooh." Four years later, the first Pooh story appeared in print, a Christmastime tale based on the ones Christopher's father, A. A. Milne, told about him and his stuffed animals Pooh, Eeyore, and Piglet, and in 1926 the book *Winnie-the-Pooh* was published with illustrations by E. H. Shepard. Shepard based his drawings of Christopher Robin on the real Christopher Milne (who like his father would later weary of the way these stories defined him to the world), but as his model for the immortal Bear of Very Little Brain Shepard used not the real "Pooh" but a teddy bear, known as "Growler," owned by his own son Graham.

NO YEAR "My mother would not have wanted me to spend my life with this man." Ellen's mother, at this point in Amy Bloom's "Love Is Not a Pie," is a little box of ashes, but her memory and the presence at her funeral of those who loved her are enough to convince her daughter that "August 21 did not seem like a good date, John Wescott did not seem like a good person to marry, and I couldn't see myself in the long white silk gown Mrs. Wescott had offered me." Later that day she'll hear the words her mother once used to describe the rare and true path her own heart took, "Love is not a pie, dear," a motto that, like Bloom's story, happily confounds the limited expectations we—and no doubt John Westcott—often bring to plots involving marriage and adultery.

BORN: **1920** Ray Bradbury (*The Martian Chronicles, Fahrenheit 451*), Waukegan, Ill.
1935 Annie Proulx (*Brokeback Mountain, The Shipping News*), Norwich, Conn.
DIED: **1979** James T. Farrell (*Young Lonigan, Judgment Day*), 75, New York City
2007 Grace Paley (*Enormous Changes at the Last Minute*), 84, Thetford, Vt.

1603 "In brief, this is my case: I have completely lost the ability to think or speak coherently about anything at all," confessed young Philipp, Lord Chandos, in a letter on this day to the writer and philosopher Francis Bacon. Having once written with confidence from within a universe that seemed "one great unity," he was now overcome by skepticism. The world, especially its humblest elements—a watering can, earthworms under a rotting board, rats suffering death throes from poison—still spoke to him with thrilling intensity, but in a way he could no longer find the words for, so he had to give up writing. It's a fascinating and challenging declaration—that our words aren't equal to the world—but one made more ambiguous by the sheer eloquence with which its author proclaims the insufficiency of language. That its author was not the fictitious Lord Chandos, writing in 1603, but Hugo von Hofmannsthal, writing in 1902—and that Hofmannsthal did not give up writing after publishing it—only adds to the letter's ambiguity, and its fascination.

1762 Edward Gibbon dined with a Captain Perkins, who afterward led him "into an intemperance we have not known for some time past."

1903 One reason William James has remained an interesting thinker is that he paired a desire to establish a Big Idea with a skepticism that such a thing was possible or even worthwhile. "I am convinced that the desire to formulate truths is a virulent disease," he wrote a friend on this day while struggling to compose a major work of philosophy. "I actually dread to die until I have settled the Universe's hash in one more book . . . Childish idiot—as if formulas about the Universe could ruffle its majesty, and as if the common-sense world and its duties were not eternally the really real!" And so it's appropriate that the next book he published, *Pragmatism*, has ever since been taken by some as a slight work of little philosophical importance, and by others as every bit the "epochmaking" work James had childishly hoped for.

1930 After his horse bolted in Wyoming, Ernest Hemingway required stitches on his chin.

1934 Malcolm Cowley, in the *New Republic*, on the stories of Somerset Maugham: "Reading these thirty stories one after another is like sitting for a long time in a room where people are playing bridge and gossiping in even voices. The room may be east or west, in London or Singapore, but the people in it are always the same: they are the Britons of good family who administer the Empire under the direction of its actual rulers. They know what is done and what is not done."

August 23

BORN: 1926 Clifford Geertz (*The Interpretation of Cultures*), San Francisco
1975 Curtis Sittenfeld (*Prep*, *American Wife*), Cincinnati
DIED: 1723 Increase Mather (*A Further Account of the Tryals of the New-England Witches*), 84, Boston
2012 James Fogle (*Drugstore Cowboy*), 75, Monroe, Wash.

1872 The *Pickwick Portfolio*, the household newspaper written by the March girls in *Little Women*, is, Louisa May Alcott assures her readers, "a *bona fide* copy of one written by *bona fide* girls once upon a time"—one in fact, that Alcott and her sisters produced during her own childhood. Her story later came full circle when five sisters in Pennsylvania, the Lukens, were inspired by the March girls to start their own homemade journal, *Little Things*. Handwritten at first but typeset by its third issue, in two years the Lukens' journal had a thousand subscribers, including Miss Alcott herself, who wrote them on this day, "I admire your pluck and perseverance and heartily believe in women's right to any branch of labor for which they prove their fitness."

1948 Before he ever set out with Neal Cassady, Jack Kerouac jotted down in his journal an idea for a future book, "about two guys hitch-hiking to California in search of something they don't really find, and losing themselves on the road, and coming all the way back hopeful of something else."

1956 Attacked by the Nazis in Germany and hounded out of Norway in the '30s, Wilhelm Reich, the radical psychoanalyst who claimed to have discovered a life force known as "orgone energy," had a quieter time of it during his first eight years in the United States, where his work attracted the attention of, among others, Norman Mailer and William Steig. But after a series of articles in the *New Republic* in 1947 warned of a "growing Reich cult," the Federal Drug Administration challenged the medical claims for the therapeutic boxes he called "orgone accumulators," and in 1956 began the destruction of his work, arresting Reich, chopping up the orgone boxes at his headquarters in Orgonon, Maine, and, on this day, forcing his associates to feed six tons of his journals and books into the New York City Sanitation Department's Gansevoort Street incinerator in the West Village.

NO YEAR It was two years after Christopher's mother went to the hospital and died—or so he'd been told—that he found, in a box in his father's closet, a stack of letters he'd never been shown, all addressed to him and dated—May 3, September 18, August 23—after she died. Telling of her new life in London and explaining why she had to leave their family, the letters add another mystery to the ones Christopher, the autistic narrator of Mark Haddon's *The Curious Incident of the Dog in the Night-Time*, is already investigating: the death of the dog next door and the constant riddle of the human emotions he finds so incomprehensible.

August 24

BORN: **1899** Jorge Luis Borges (*A Universal History of Infamy*), Buenos Aires
1977 John Green (*Paper Towns, The Fault in Our Stars*), Indianapolis
DIED: **1943** Simone Weil (*Waiting for God, The Need for Roots*), 34, Ashford, England
2004 Elisabeth Kübler-Ross (*On Death and Dying*), 78, Scottsdale, Ariz.

1770 Thomas Chatterton gained little of the fame he desired during his life, but his apparent suicide by arsenic on this day at the age of seventeen has reverberated through the following centuries. The Romantics took up his memory—Keats wrote him a sonnet, and Wordsworth called him the "marvellous boy"—and in 1856 the painter Henry Wallis posed the poet George Meredith, sprawled red-haired in a garret, for his popular portrait *Death of Chatterton*. And in the following century Peter Ackroyd put the poet's death at the heart of *Chatterton*, a multilayered novel that takes advantage of the irresistible biographical detail that less than a year after Wallis painted Meredith, Meredith's wife, Mary, left her husband for the man who had posed him as the doomed poet.

1814 At the ugly house they had just been forced by poverty to rent in Switzerland, Mary and Percy Bysshe Shelley walked to the nearby lakeshore and read Tacitus's description of the Siege of Jerusalem. Then "we come home, look out the window, and go to bed."

1935 "The thing I think about most," Evelyn Waugh wrote to Laura Herbert from Ethiopia, "is your eyelashes making a noise like a bat on the pillow."

1962 Having traveled by bus up to northern California's Portola Valley from Mexico City, where he had secluded himself from the buzz created when his first novel, *V.*, was published that spring, Thomas Pynchon stood as best man in the wedding of his close college friend—and soon-to-be fellow novelist—Richard Fariña to Mimi Baez, the eighteen-year-old sister of Joan Baez (whose boyfriend Bob Dylan did not attend). In photographs taken by the mother of the groom but never publicly released, the reclusive best man, dressed in a dark suit, is said to sport a giant mustache that may or may not have been fake.

1975 "To learn to write at all," Joanna Russ wrote James Tiptree Jr. (who later revealed herself to be a woman named Alice Sheldon), "I had to begin by thinking of myself as a sort of fake man, something that ended only with feminism."

August 25

BORN: 1921 Brian Moore (*Black Robe, Lies of Silence*), Belfast, Northern Ireland
1949 Martin Amis (*Money, Time's Arrow*), Swansea, Wales
DIED: 1900 Friedrich Nietzsche (*Beyond Good and Evil*), 55, Weimar, Germany
1984 Truman Capote (*Breakfast at Tiffany's, In Cold Blood*), 59, Los Angeles

1793 When contemporary readers of Charles Brockden Brown's novel *Arthur Mervyn* saw its opening line, "I was resident in this city during the year 1793," they knew exactly what his narrator was speaking of. The city was Brown's own, Philadelphia, the largest in the new country. And the year 1793 meant fever: the yellow fever epidemic that killed over 4,000 of the city's 50,000 residents. Nearly half of those residents fled the city, especially after the local doctors on this day published a list of measures to corral the spread of the disease. Brockden Brown—not the first American novelist but the first good one—vividly describes that flight in *Arthur Mervyn*, a wonderfully intense Gothic drama in which urban disease and commerce are equal causes of anxiety and intrigue.

1900 In the last of a three-day match between Marylebone Cricket Club and London County, Arthur Conan Doyle, taking a turn at bowling, dismissed the batter considered the greatest cricketer of all time, W. G. Grace, for his only first-class wicket.

1909 Fat and thin, Catholic and skeptic, individualist and socialist, carnivore and vegetarian, tippler and teetotaler, mustachioed and bearded: G. K. Chesterton and G. B. Shaw were seen as almost comical opposites when they regularly and affectionately locked antlers at the turn of the twentieth century, a combat that culminated in Chesterton's biography of Shaw in 1909, which Shaw himself reviewed in the *Nation* on this day. Shaw called its "account of my doctrine" "either frankly deficient and uproariously careless or else recalcitrantly and . . . madly wrong," but nevertheless called himself "proud to have been the painter's model." Another reviewer, meanwhile, suggested that Shaw had wearied of his beliefs but couldn't give up the fame they had brought him, and so invented his amicable opponent, "Chesterton."

1938 Running as a Democrat for California assemblyman in the 59th District, Robert A. Heinlein lost to the incumbent by 450 votes.

1950 With an operating budget of $1,434,789 and the ambivalent support of its studio, MGM, John Huston's prestige production of *The Red Badge of Courage* began shooting its first battle scenes on a day in Chico, California, that reached 108 degrees. On the set was Lillian Ross, the *New Yorker* reporter whose genial unobtrusiveness and flawless recall of dialogue captured, among other details, the comments a few weeks later of an MGM publicity man: "Two things sell tickets. One, stars. Two, stories. No stars, no stories here." When preview audiences for the movie agreed and tore the picture to shreds, Ross had a story of her own to tell, and *Picture*, her groundbreaking inside account of the shooting of the movie (and its panicked re-editing), found a success its subject didn't.

August 26

BORN: 1880 Guillaume Apollinaire
(*Calligrammes*, *Alcools*), Rome
1941 Barbara Ehrenreich (*Nickel and
Dimed*, *Fear of Falling*), Butte, Mont.
DIED: 1945 Franz Werfel (*The Forty Days of
Musa Degh*), 54, Los Angeles
1989 Irving Stone (*Lust for Life*, *The Agony
and the Ecstasy*), 86, Los Angeles

1881 "I wonder again," Henry Holmes Goodpasture writes in his journal at the opening of Oakley Hall's *Warlock*, "how we manage to obtain deputies at all." Yet another has just been run off from the town of Warlock, a good one at that, but too prudent not to leave when Abe McQuown started firing into the air in the middle of town. Nevertheless, on this day the good Mr. Goodpasture can report that the ad hoc Citizens' Committee has brought in a man of significant reputation as marshal, one Clay Blaisedell, who carries a renown embodied in the gold-handled Colts he is known to brandish. A free-handed rewrite of the already-familiar events of the Gunfight at the OK Corral, *Warlock* is a refreshingly impure, almost effortlessly hilarious, and claustrophobically bleak epic of the West.

1945 On the last Saturday of August, with the war just over, they arrive to pay their respects at the large house on Long Island: the undertaker Bonasera, the baker Nazorine, the heartthrob crooner Johnny Fontane, the killer Luca Brasi, and the many other friends of Don Vito Corleone. It's the wedding of Connie, the Don's only daughter, and Mario Puzo uses the great event to introduce the three sons in a family that will become among the best-known in American fiction: Sonny the hothead, Freddo the dutiful coward, and Michael the skeptical independent, who sits at a far table with his future wife, Kay, and decides how much of his family's business to reveal to her while, back in his office, the Don blandly promises Johnny Fontane that he'll take care of the studio boss who's been giving him trouble: "I'll make him an offer he can't refuse."

1969 Jim Bouton had two questions when a call from manager Joe Schultz woke him up in his hotel room this morning to tell him he had been traded to the Houston Astros. First, what city was he in? (Baltimore, where his Seattle Pilots were playing the Orioles.) Second, who was he traded for? ("*Dooley Womack?* Holy mackerel.") For a washed-up former star making a comeback throwing knuckleballs for an expansion team, getting dealt into a pennant race, even for Dooley Womack, was not so bad, and by the end of the day, Bouton, whose notoriety for his taboo-breaking baseball memoir *Ball Four* can make you forget what a good book it is, found himself in St. Louis, pitching an inning for his new team and then learning the foulmouthed words to "Proud to Be an Astro" on the team bus back to the hotel.

August 27

BORN: 1871 Theodore Dreiser (*Sister Carrie,
An American Tragedy*), Terre Haute, Ind.
1959 Jeanette Winterson (*The Passion,
Sexing the Cherry*), Manchester, England

DIED: 1969 Ivy Compton-Burnett (*Pastors
and Masters, A House and Its Head*), 85,
London
1971 Bennett Cerf (*At Random, Shake Well
Before Using*), 73, Mount Kisco, N.Y.

1784 At Comely Gardens in Edinburgh, James Tytler, having just completed seven ill-paid years as the editor of the second edition of the *Encyclopædia Britannica*, floated his hot-air balloon 350 feet into the air before dropping suddenly into a pile of garbage outside of the city, thereby becoming the first Briton to fly. Despite these landmark achievements, Tytler was a figure of fun in Edinburgh, memorialized by his fellow Scotsman Robert Burns as "a mortal who, though he trudges about Edinburgh as a common printer, with leaky shoes, a skylighted hat and knee buckles as unlike as 'George-by-the-Grace-of-God and Solomon-the-Son-of-David,' yet that same unknown drunken mortal is author and compiler of three-fourths of Elliott's pompous 'Encyclopedia Britannica,' which he composed at half a guinea a week."

1920 Saying, "I have really no idea how a moving pictures story is composed," Joseph Conrad went with his agent to a movie adaptation of *Les Misérables*: they were being paid $1,500 by an American studio for a script of his story "Gaspar Ruiz." "I am ashamed to tell you this," he wrote a friend, "but one must live."

1959 Frank O'Hara was half-joking when, at lunch on this day with LeRoi Jones, he proposed a new literary movement, "Personism," and followed through a week later with "Personism: A Manifesto" for Jones's magazine, *Yugen*. In a tone as off-handedly and evocatively conversational as his poems, he promised nothing—"What can we expect of Personism? . . . Everything, but we won't get it"—but still managed to stand for his style as solidly as any red-blooded revolutionary. "To give you a vague idea," he shrugged, "one of its minimal aspects is to address itself to one person (other than the poet himself), thus evoking overtones of love without destroying love's life-giving vulgarity." He put his theory immediately into practice, writing after lunch that day his "Personal Poem," in which he's curious whether "one person out of the 8,000,000 is thinking of me."

1967 "Her Book to Be Published Soon, Tulsa Teen Keeps Cool," read the headline in the *Tulsa World* in April about local girl S. E. Hinton, whose new novel, *The Outsiders,* was written when she, like its subjects, was in high school. Early reviewers often didn't know that "S. E." was a "she," but as interest in her novel grew, the author, now identified as Susan Hinton, age nineteen, explained to the readers of the *New York Times Book Review* on this day that most books for teens were told "from a stand-off, I'm-a-little-scared-to-get-close-they're-hairy view" of grownups. The result: proms or gangs and no stories in between. "Sometimes," she added, "I wonder which extreme does the most harm."

BORN: **1749** Johann Wolfgang von Goethe (*The Sorrows of Young Werther*), Frankfurt
1828 Leo Tolstoy (*War and Peace*, *Anna Karenina*), Yasnaya Polyana, Russia
DIED: **1989** Joseph Alsop (*I've Seen the Best of It*), 78, Washington, D.C.
1993 E. P. Thompson (*The Making of the English Working Class*), 69, Worcester, England

1833 When William Wordsworth stood in his garden and, like a schoolboy, recited three of his sonnets to his visitor, Ralph Waldo Emerson, Emerson nearly laughed at first but soon thought better of it: after all, "I had come thus far to see a poet, and he was chaunting poems to me, I saw, that he was right, and I was wrong, and gladly gave myself up to hear."

1956 The scandal of *Peyton Place* was set in motion even before the book was published. Expecting a modest sale for the first novel of New Hampshire housewife Grace Metalious, her publisher indulged in a hired publicist who visited Metalious's small town of Gilmanton, got an earful of the local gossip, and realized what an asset he had in Metalious herself, who, a few months later, obliged by giving an Associated Press reporter a quote that would follow the book, and haunt Metalious, for years after it appeared on this day: "To a tourist these towns look as peaceful as a postcard picture. But if you go beneath that picture, it's like turning over a rock with your foot—all kinds of strange things crawl out." When *Peyton Place* was finally published the following month, it was already #4 on the *New York Times* bestseller list and its author—a "Pandora in blue jeans"—an instant celebrity.

NO YEAR It's a simple proposition at the end of a night of poker: cut the cards, and if Nashe and Pozzi get the high card, they get the $5,000 back they owe, but if Flower and Stone win, then Nashe and Pozzi are down $10,000 they don't have. The result—seven of hearts for Flower, four of diamonds for Nashe—leads to another proposition: the losers can pay off their debt by building a massive wall from the stones of a fifteenth-century castle on Flower and Stone's remote estate, where this disastrous card game has taken place. It's late August now. Working ten hours a day, they'll be square by mid-October, a date that looms ahead of them like a dream—at least until they reach it—in Paul Auster's elegant fable of fate and freedom, *The Music of Chance*.

August 29

BORN: 1929 Thom Gunn (*The Man with Night Sweats*), Gravesend, England

1947 Temple Grandin (*Thinking in Pictures*, *Animals in Translation*), Boston

DIED: 1769 Edmond Hoyle (*A Short Treatise on the Game of Whist*), c. 97, London

1981 Lowell Thomas (*With Lawrence in Arabia*), 89, Pawling, N.Y.

1948 Robert Caro, Lyndon Baines Johnson's eternal biographer, writes of the "bright and dark" threads—Johnson's bright achievements of equality and his dark hunger for power—that ran through his subject's career. In the period covered by Caro's second volume, *The Means of Ascent*, though, all the threads were dark. Stalled in his political ambition, LBJ used the 1940s—and his government influence—to make himself rich, but the darkest moment of that time for Caro, and the center of his book, was his race for Senate against "Mr. Texas," Coke Stevenson. Johnson stole the race, Caro establishes, when on this day, one day after the primary runoff and two days after his fortieth birthday, his men began to work the phones and stuff enough ballot boxes to ensure their candidate won by eighty-seven votes in a manner, Caro writes, that "violated even the notably loose boundaries of Texas politics."

1959 Robert Phelps, in the *National Review*, on Robert Lowell's *Life Studies*: "To hold out the palms of one's own hands, the veins in one's own wrists, the self-judgment in one's own heart, and at the same time to make surable, breathing structures out of words, is simply to make the rarest, the most permanent literature we are going to have."

1974 "It was August 29, 1974. The air smelled like somebody's arm up close." Nixon had just quit, and Dylan Ebdus, heading into fifth grade, and Mingus Rude, heading into sixth and new to the Brooklyn neighborhood—call it Boerum Hill or Gowanus, depending on whether you were trying to gentrify or not—had just met. Dylan, white, was local but uncomfortable there; Mingus, new, made himself at home, the son of a white, absent mom and a black dad whom, Dylan's mom had told him even before Mingus showed him the gold records, she had once seen open for the Stones. She also predicted to Dylan that he and Mingus were going to be best friends, and she was right, their alliance providing the central spine in Jonathan Lethem's sprawling novel *The Fortress of Solitude*.

2001 Near Lake Baikal, on his way across Siberia with two Russian guides, Ian Frazier's van caught fire.

August 30

BORN: 1797 Mary Shelley (*Frankenstein*),
London
1943 Robert Crumb (*Fritz the Cat, Zap Comix*), Philadelphia
DIED: 1989 Seymour Krim (*Shake It for the World, Smartass*), 67, New York City
2006 Naguib Mahfouz (*Palace Walk, Midaq Alley*), 94, Cairo

1869 By this last day of the Powell expedition, after three months and almost a thousand miles on rough and often uncharted canyon waters, their four small boats had been reduced to three, the ten explorers had attritted to six, and ten months of provisions had shrunk to ten pounds of flour, fifteen of dried apples, and seventy or so of coffee. Led by John Wesley Powell, the one-armed geology professor who recalled the journey years later in his laconic classic, *The Exploration of the Colorado River and Its Canyons*, the expedition made the first known passage through the Grand Canyon, where, just two days before the journey's end, three of its members balked at the river's last, unknown dangers and set out on their own, never to be seen again.

1923 Midway through writing *Mrs. Dalloway*, Virginia Woolf recorded a "discovery" about her way of writing: "How I dig out beautiful caves behind my characters: I think that gives exactly what I want; humanity, humour, depth. The idea is that the caves shall connect and each comes to daylight at the present moment."

1960 The juvenile authorities in Montana worked more slowly back then. Four days after his parents crossed over into North Dakota and robbed the Agricultural National Bank in Creekmore of $2,500, and two days after they were taken away in handcuffs for the crime, fifteen-year-old Del Parsons, alone at home after his twin sister decided to run away, is picked up by a family friend and driven north to Canada. His life has ruptured unimaginably twice in three days, and as he crosses the border, he accepts the changes—not the last he'll face before Richard Ford's *Canada* is over—with the question that strikes him as the only one he can ask, "What do I have to lose?" The answer is no less inevitable: "very little."

1968 Ten days or so after the Russian tanks rolled into Czechoslovakia, four days after Czech leader Alexander Dubček made his stuttering, humiliated return from Moscow, and seven years after Tereza, a young woman from the country, arrived in Prague and upset the comfortable bachelor life that Tomas had arranged for himself by making him fall in love with her, Tomas is given a choice: take a job in exile in Switzerland or remain in Prague. He chooses Switzerland because he thinks Tereza wants it too, but when she realizes she can't live in exile and returns, irrevocably, behind the Iron Curtain, Tomas has another choice: stay abroad and resume his old, light bachelor's way of life, or follow her back home and accept the weight of love in Milan Kundera's *The Unbearable Lightness of Being*.

August 31

BORN: 1885 DuBose Heyward (*Porgy,*
  Mamba's Daughters), Charleston, S.C.
  1908 William Saroyan (*The Human*
  Comedy), Fresno, Calif.
DIED: 1688 John Bunyan (*The Pilgrim's*
  Progress), 59, London
  1951 Abraham Cahan (*The Rise of David*
  Levinsky), 91, New York City

1872 Born of myth or a mother, Martin
Dressler entered the world on this day,
destined to reshape the cityscape of turn-
of-the-century Manhattan, or at least the
Manhattan imagined by Steven Millhauser
in *Martin Dressler*, one of the more gratifyingly odd tales to win the Pulitzer Prize
for Fiction. Buoyed by the pluck of a Horatio Alger hero, Dressler rises quickly in his
chosen art: the construction of a series of
ever more fantastic hotels. He opens the
Hotel Dressler on his twenty-seventh birthday and the New Dressler on his thirtieth,
but when his most fabulous creation, the
Grand Cosmo, with its indoor wooded
countrysides, lagoons, and even opium dens,
is delayed from opening on his thirty-third
birthday "by a flaw in the refrigerated-air
system," it's a sign that Martin may finally
have dreamed too large.

1925 Margaret Mead arrived for the first
time in Samoa.

1931 Isak Dinesen arrived home from
Africa, never to return.

1949 "Congratulations to Miss Alice Laidlaw," began a notice on this day in the *Wingham Advance-Times* itemizing the $1,350 in
scholarships earned by a local girl who was
"ranked first in English of all students apply-
ing for the University of Western Ontario."
Even then, though, Miss Laidlaw knew that
with no family money to support her, two
years at university would be all she could
afford, and at the end of that time, she and
her new husband headed west to Vancouver, where, writing under her married name
of Alice Munro, she began to draw on the
experience of being a scholarship student,
one of that "dribble of the children of the
poor who are brash & brainy & scornful &
lucky too sometimes under their meekness
in ways their betters can't suspect."

2005 Abdulrahman Zeitoun woke in the
tent on the roof of his garage and looked
out over the flood around him. The waters
from Hurricane Katrina had reached just
a foot deep in his neighborhood during
the storm and then receded, but on the
30th they had rushed back: the levees, he
knew, must have broken. Now, after his
first night on the roof, Zeitoun wondered
what he would do until he saw his canoe
floating nearby, nine feet above his yard. For
the rest of the day, he paddled through his
neighborhood, feeling a strange peace, and
helped five trapped neighbors to safety, and
when evening came he grilled chicken and
vegetables on his roof, prayed, and went to
sleep, exhausted, in his tent. The next six
days, as Dave Eggers recounts in *Zeitoun*, he
spent in much the same way, until, mistaken
for a looter, he began another, more terrible,
odyssey through the flooded city.

September, tucked modestly away three-quarters into the calendar, is the start of many things: school years, fall, football season, the return to work after the end of summer. It's also the beginning of months whose awkwardly Latinate names rhyme with little except themselves. Some poets, understandably, neglect them: in all his works, for instance, Shakespeare makes no mention of September, October, or November. But in a title "September" can stand squarely; it's weightier and more declarative than the short and flighty names of the summer and spring months. There's "September, 1819," for instance, in which Wordsworth found spring and summer "unfaded, yet prepared to fade." Transposing just two digits in her title a century later in "September, 1918," Amy Lowell caught the familiar beauties of early fall—including an afternoon that's "the colour of water falling through sunlight"—but she stored them away without tasting them, like a harvest of berries. With the war not yet over, she was too busy balancing herself "upon a broken world" to enjoy them yet.

The best-known September poem also was born in a broken world, at the beginning of the next world war. In the days after Germany invaded Poland, W. H. Auden wrote "September 1, 1939," in which the stench of war and dictatorship reached even those who might have considered themselves safe in his newly adopted home of New York City. Auden spent the rest of his life disowning the poem and its popularity, or at least "loathing" the "trash" of its hopeful line "We must love one another or die," which he quickly came to see as self-congratulatory (in one later version he substituted "We must love one another and die"). But that line, among others, is what has brought people back to the poem in later Septembers. Lyndon Johnson came close to quoting it, ending his apocalyptic "Daisy" ad (which aired just once, on September 7, 1964) with the words "We must either love each other, or we must die." And the entire poem began circulating again in mass media and in forwarded e-mails in September 2001, when its visions of Manhattan skyscrapers and death in September—along with those declarations of hope that had rung false so soon to Auden's ears—felt suddenly, movingly contemporary.

The House of Mirth by Edith Wharton (1905) ❧ September is early in the New York social season, but for Lily Bart it's getting a little late. She still has her beauty, but she's twenty-nine and has no money of her own, and the decisions she makes—and doesn't make—in the first month of Wharton's great novel will set her course for its remainder.

Harriet the Spy by Louise Fitzhugh (1964) ❧ "JANIE GETS STRANGER EVERY YEAR. MISS WHITEHEAD'S FEET LOOK LARGER THIS YEAR." Return to school with Harriet M. Welsch, self-appointed sixth-grade spy and future writer, who reckoned with the slippery ethics of observing and reporting long before Janet Malcolm wrote *The Journalist and the Murderer*.

Stoner by John Williams (1965) ❧ The "campus novel" is almost always a comedy, but *Stoner*, long overlooked but now becoming a classic, is a campus tragedy, and not less of one because of the petty academic quarrels, which in other hands might be turned into farce, that drive its hero's inexorable disappointment.

Deliverance by James Dickey (1970) ❧ It's a little weekend trip for four men from the suburbs into the nearby wilderness—canoeing down a Georgia river about to be dammed. If everything goes right, they'll get back in time for the second half of the Sunday football game on TV, and in the meantime, they might get in touch with something real.

Hotel du Lac by Anita Brookner (1984) ❧ All is gray: the garden, the lake beyond, "spreading like an anaesthetic towards the invisible farther shore." It's late September, well into the off-season, with reduced rates for the few visitors to the Hotel du Lac, where Edith, a romance novelist with a romance problem of her own, escapes for a "mild form of sanctuary." We're in Switzerland, but we're also in Brookner country, home of isolation, disappointment, and quiet determination.

White Noise by Don DeLillo (1985) ❧ Every September the station wagons—they'd now be minivans—arrive on campus, disgorging tanned kids and dorm supplies in a ritual that begins the school year at DeLillo's generic midwestern college, where education has become untethered from any meaning beyond a nervous self-consciousness.

Ms. Hempel Chronicles by Sarah Shun-lien Bynum (2008) ❧ Every September Ms. Hempel turns to write on the blackboard, "First Assignment," and soon, as in every other fall semester, the American colonists will rebel and the revolution will be won. Not much older than the middle-school kids she's teaching, and not much more sure of what she's becoming, Bynum's raw young teacher is open to experience and, most thrillingly, unprotected from it.

September 1

BORN: 1889 Herbert Asbury (*The Gangs of New York*), Farmington, Mo.
   1942 C. J. Cherryh (*Downbelow Station, Cyteen*), St. Louis
DIED: 1729 Richard Steele (*The Tatler, The Spectator*), 57, Carmarthen, Wales
   1967 Siegfried Sassoon (*Counter-Attack*), 80, Heytesbury, England

1605 Though he had been in good graces with James I, England's new Scottish king, Ben Jonson found himself writing pleading letters to a half-dozen courtiers from the "vile prison" where he had been committed without a hearing. The cause? "A Play, my Lord," he wrote the Earl of Salisbury, embarrassed to be imprisoned for so petty a cause (he was aware of better ones, having nearly been executed for manslaughter a few years before). The play was *Eastward Ho!*, whose apparent crime, in the tense political atmosphere two months before the foiled Gunpowder Plot, was making fun of Scots, embracing the idea, for instance, of sending "a hundred thousand of them" to the New World, "for we are all one Countrymen now, ye know; and we should find ten times more comfort of them there, then we do here." Though threatened with having his ears and nose cut, Jonson was freed by October.

1838 The astonishingly compressed inspiration under which Stendhal, locking himself away for fifty-three days in November and December, wrote his final masterpiece, *The Charterhouse of Parma*, is legendary, but he first composed the novel's opening under more leisurely circumstances. The scandalously witty author had taken to sitting with the daughters of the Countess de Montijo, Paca and Eugénie (who would grow up to marry Napoleon III and become the last empress of France), and telling them stories of his adventures with Napoleon's army. On this evening he began a tale of a young soldier wandering bewildered through the Battle of Waterloo, which soon became *Charterhouse*'s opening scene, at the end of which, in his own copy of the novel, he noted, "For you, Paca and Eugénie."

1938 "Was ever a book written under greater difficulty?" The book was *The Grapes of Wrath,* and John Steinbeck's difficulties were mostly those of success: selling his house and buying a ranch, hosting visitors (including Charlie Chaplin), and responding to requests for public statements. (There was also the pounding of that endless construction work on the house next door.) His main difficulty, though, was keeping up with the furious pace he'd set himself: "I am simply incapable of working any way but hard and fast." Twice before, with "The Oklahomans" and "L'Affaire Lettuceberg," he had tried and failed to write a novel about migrant farm workers, but after he sketched out this version in May, he averaged 2,000 words a day and was done with the book, his longest yet, by the end of October. The following year would bring a whole new set of difficulties: the "nightmare," Steinbeck called it, of *The Grapes of Wrath*'s phenomenal popularity.

BORN: **1894** Joseph Roth (*The Radetsky March*), Brody, Austro-Hungarian Empire
1918 Allen Drury (*Advise and Consent, Preserve and Protect*), Houston, Tex.
DIED: **1973** J. R. R. Tolkien (*The Lord of the Rings*), 81, Bournemouth, England
1997 Viktor Frankl (*Man's Search for Meaning*), 92, Vienna

1911 "Hey kids I'll be wit you Sunday," promised Flip, the green-faced, cigar-chomping, dream-disturbing rascal from Winsor McCay's *Little Nemo in Slumberland*, and the next day he, Nemo, and the Princess debuted in the color pages of the *New York American*. William Randolph Hearst paid top dollar for cartoonists, and he had induced McCay to bring his eye-poppingly intricate dreamscapes from the *New York Herald* to the *American* under the new title *In the Land of Wonderful Dreams*. Nemo and Flip only lasted a few years there, though: annoyed by McCay's lucrative sidelines in vaudeville and animated films, Hearst shut down his comics and forced him to focus on political cartooning.

1932 As Ray Bradbury often told it, on the day before his uncle's Labor Day funeral, young Ray, age twelve, walked down to a lakefront carnival in his hometown of Waukegan, Illinois, where, in a sideshow tent, he encountered a performer named Mr. Electrico who changed his life. Coursing with electricity that stood his hair on end, Mr. Electrico chose Ray from out of a crowd of children, tapped him with his electrified sword, and commanded him, "Live forever!" Certain he had been chosen for a reason, Bradbury took the words as a command to create: "Just weeks after Mr. Electrico said this to me, I started writing every day. I never stopped." Even his biographer's later discovery that his uncle actually died almost two months later never altered Bradbury's memory of that fateful moment when he chose life in the face of death.

1933 Virginia Woolf wrote in her diary about *Testament of Youth*: "I am reading with extreme greed a book by Vera Brittain. Not that I much like her. A stringy metallic mind, with I suppose, the sort of taste I should dislike in real life. But her story, told in detail, without reserve, of the war, and how she lost lover and brother, and dabbled her hands in entrails, and was forever seeing the dead, and eating scraps, and sitting five on one WC, runs rapidly, vividly across my eyes."

1940 Conrad Aiken, in the *New Republic*, on Federico García Lorca's *A Poet in New York*: "There has been no more terribly acute critic of America than this steel-conscious and death-conscious Spaniard . . . He hated us, and rightly, for the right reasons."

September 3

BORN: 1940 Eduardo Galeano (*Open Veins of Latin America*), Montevideo, Uruguay
1963 Malcolm Gladwell (*The Tipping Point, Outliers*), Fareham, England
DIED: 1883 Ivan Turgenev (*Fathers and Sons, Torrents of Spring*), 64, Bougival, France
2001 Pauline Kael (*I Lost It at the Movies*), 82, Great Barrington, Mass.

1838 One of the most momentous events in the *Narrative of the Life of Frederick Douglass* is also, by necessity, one of the most discreetly told. "On the third day of September, 1838," he wrote, "I left my chains, and succeeded in reaching New York without the slightest interruption of any kind. How I did so,—what means I adopted,—what direction I traveled, and by what mode of conveyance,—I must leave unexplained." Only in his third autobiography, the *Life and Times of Frederick Douglass*, published more than fifteen years after slavery's abolition, did he feel he could safely reveal the details

of his escape, which involved borrowing the documents of a friend (who did not much resemble him), dressing like a sailor (and speaking like an "old salt"), jumping on a train north from Baltimore, and facing the moment of truth when the conductor asked, "I suppose you have your free papers?"

NO YEAR They part at midnight. Rodolphe has the passports? And they will meet at the Hôtel de Provence at noon the next day? Of course, of course. Emma Bovary imagines that the moment they are borne off together in the mail coach will be like going off in a balloon, rising into the clouds. When Rodolphe returns home, though, he doesn't go to bed to dream but to his writing desk, to write the kind of letter he has written before. Forget me, Emma! Oh, we were lunatics! "Fate is to blame—only fate!" (Ah, "that is a word that always has a nice effect.") His duty done, he smokes three pipes and goes to bed, and the following morning places the letter at the bottom of a basket of apricots for delivery. Emma reads the letter in shock and despair. Her husband, Charles, enjoys the apricots.

1933 Storm Jameson, in the *Sunday Times*, on Vera Brittain's *Testament of Youth*: "Its mere pressure on mind and senses makes it unforgettable. The cumulative effect of these pages, on a contemporary, is indescribably troubling and exalting."

1947 Published: *Goodnight Moon* by Margaret Wise Brown (Harper & Bros., New York)

BORN: **1905** Mary Renault (*The King Must Die*), Forest Gate, England
1908 Richard Wright (*Black Boy*, *Uncle Tom's Children*), Roxie, Miss.

DIED: **1977** E. F. Schumacher (*Small Is Beautiful*), 66, Romont, Switzerland
1989 Georges Simenon (*Dirty Snow*, *My Friend Maigret*), 86, Lausanne, Switzerland

1907 Oh, how they pounced when Ambrose Bierce, the most poisonous pen in the West, wrote, for once, honeyed words of praise! When late in his career Bierce took a young writer named George Sterling under his wing and compared his poem "A Wine of Wizardry" to Keats, Coleridge, and Spenser with a purple fulsomeness matched only by the poem itself, the response was immediate and gleefully savage. The *San Francisco Examiner* claimed on this day that five lines from the poem "would drive a man to beat a cripple, and ten lines would send him to the bottom of the river." Under attack, Bierce was now in his element and returned fire with satisfaction: "Shall these Toms, Dicks and Harrys of the slums and cornfields set up their meager acquirements as metes and bounds beyond which a writer shall not go?"

1920 In the inscription in the copy of his first book of stories, *Flappers and Philosophers*, that F. Scott Fitzgerald sent his hero H. L. Mencken, he divided its contents into "Worth Reading" ("The Ice Palace," "The Cut-Glass Bowl," "Benediction," "Dalyrimple Goes Wrong"), "Amusing" ("The Offshore Pirate"), and "Trash" ("Head and Shoulders," "The Four Fists," "Bernice Bobs Her Hair").

1957 His publisher had heard there'd be a review of *On the Road* in the next day's *Times*, so just before midnight Jack Kerouac and Joyce Johnson climbed out of bed and bought the first copy off the truck at the newsstand at Sixty-sixth and Broadway. "It's good, isn't it?" Jack said. "Yes," said Joyce, and they took it to a bar and read it three more times "like students poring over a difficult text for which they sense they're going to be held responsible," as Johnson remembered in her memoir *Minor Characters*. Then they went back up to their apartment, where Jack, not sure why he wasn't happier at the news, "lay down obscure for the last time in his life."

1962 He was just fifteen, but on his second day of work as an assistant engineer at EMI's Abbey Road studios Geoff Emerick found himself in the control room when a young band from Liverpool—whose members were only a few years older than him—made their first recording, of "Love Me Do" and "How Do You Do It." For the rest of the decade, Emerick became increasingly important in forming the Beatles' sound—he took over as engineer in 1966 on *Revolver*, just as the band's urge to experiment began to explode—and his 2006 memoir, *Here, There, and Everywhere*, is a charming and insightful glimpse into what it was like to grow up inside the bubble of Beatlemania.

September 5

1893 The letter Beatrix Potter wrote on September 4 to Noel Moore, the eldest son of one of her closest friends, is understandably famous: in it, she told—and illustrated—the story that became her first book, *The Tale of Peter Rabbit*. But the following day, not wanting Noel's younger brother, Eric, to feel left out, she wrote one to him about "a frog called Mr. Jeremy Fisher" who tries and fails to catch a lunch of minnows for his friends and dines instead on "a roasted grasshopper with lady-bird sauce." ("I think it must have been nasty," she added.) Many years later, after her story became *The Tale of Mr. Jeremy Fisher*, she explained to another correspondent her standards for animal realism, in response to Kenneth Grahame's Toad, who combed his hair: "A frog may wear galoshes, but I don't hold with toads having beards or wigs."

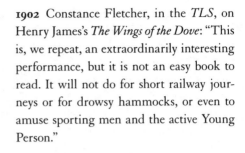

1902 Constance Fletcher, in the *TLS*, on Henry James's *The Wings of the Dove*: "This is, we repeat, an extraordinarily interesting performance, but it is not an easy book to read. It will not do for short railway journeys or for drowsy hammocks, or even to amuse sporting men and the active Young Person."

1914 "Out of sheer rage," D. H. Lawrence wrote his agent on this day, "I've begun my book about Thomas Hardy. It will be about anything but Thomas Hardy, I am afraid." Enraged less by Hardy than by the "colossal idiocy" of the war that had just begun, Lawrence was right about his *Study of Thomas Hardy* being about everything but its declared subject. Over eighty years later Geoff Dyer used Lawrence's letter for the epigraph and the title of *Out of Sheer Rage*, a book less about Lawrence than about Dyer's infinite postponement of his desire to "write a Lawrence book," which, as the quotation above implies, makes it very much about Lawrence after all, and also one of the most eccentrically enlightening books about books in recent memory.

2004 Gregory Maguire, in the *New York Times*, on Susanna Clarke's *Jonathan Strange and Mr. Norrell*: "Clarke's imagination is prodigious, her pacing is masterly and she knows how to employ dry humor in the service of majesty."

September 6

BORN: 1928 Robert M. Pirsig (*Zen and the Art of Motorcycle Maintenance*), Minneapolis
1972 China Miéville (*Perdido Street Station*), Norwich, England
DIED: 1939 Arthur Rackham (illustrator of *Grimm's Fairy Tales*), 71, Limpsfield, England
1994 James Clavell (*Shōgun, Noble House*), 69, Vevey, Switzerland

1888 "I shall have a fine book of travels," Robert Louis Stevenson wrote to a friend while steaming for the Pacific. "I feel sure; and will tell you more of the South Seas after very few months than any other writer has done—except Herman Melville perhaps, who is a howling cheese" (a compliment, by the way).

1914 Before Djuna Barnes moved to Paris and wrote her modernist masterpiece, *Nightwood*, she scribbled for nearly every newspaper in New York, interviewing celebrities from Florenz Ziegfeld and Billy Sunday to Jack Dempsey and Dinah the gorilla. And she wrote "stunt stories," most dramatically "How It Feels to Be Forcibly Fed," which appeared on this day in the *New York World*, and in which she submitted to the torturous punishment then being inflicted on hunger-striking British suffragists: first her nostrils were sprayed by the doctor "with a mixture of cocaine and disinfectant," then came the milk, through a red rubber tube: "Every drop seemed a quart, and every quart slid over and down into space. I had lapsed into a physical mechanism without power to oppose or resent the outrage to my will."

1958 As on every other morning at nine-thirty sharp, the desk clerk of the Prince Heinrich Hotel hands the key to the billiard room to Robert Faehmel, and the bell-boy brings up a double cognac and shuts the door behind them; they are not to be disturbed until eleven. On this morning, though, an old acquaintance from before the war—an enemy, in fact, though he'd like that forgotten—insists that he be shown in to see Faehmel, and throughout the day history's disturbances continue in Heinrich Böll's *Billiards at Half-Past Nine*: it's the day Robert's father, a fellow architect, celebrates his eightieth birthday, and it's the day Robert's mother comes out of the asylum where she's been held since she was judged insane for refusing to go along with the Nazi madness.

1976 Harry Mathews, the first American member of Oulipo, the French group of experimental writers known for constraining their language in various mechanical ways, made an experiment of another kind when he agreed to translate *The Laurels of Lake Constance*, the first novel by Marie Chaix. Smitten by her author photo, he drafted a handwritten note "in which I deployed every seductive wile my experience as a writer could supply." But when second thoughts made that approach seem "shabby," he sent instead a short, typed letter in his most formal French that, nonetheless, had the seductive effect he'd originally intended, thus confirming, to his delight, the power of "classical restraint." She left her marriage for him on this day, and they have remained together ever since.

September 7

BORN: 1900 Taylor Caldwell (*Captains and the Kings*), Manchester, England
1962 Jennifer Egan (*A Visit from the Goon Squad, Look at Me*), Chicago
DIED: 1962 Isak Dinesen (*Winter's Tales*), 77, Rungsted, Denmark
1990 A. J. P. Taylor (*The Struggle for Mastery in Europe*), 84, London

1923 Langston Hughes may have said, about Jean Toomer's first and only novel, "*Cane* contains the finest prose written by a Negro in America," but Toomer himself would have resisted such a description, and in a letter on this day to his publisher, Horace Liveright, he did. When Liveright said that in the biographical note to *Cane*, "there should be a definite note sounded about your colored blood," Toomer, who had grown up among blacks and whites and identified at times with each—and with neither—replied, "My racial composition and my position in the world are realities which I alone may determine." Liveright could "feature Negro" in ads for the book, he added, but shouldn't expect him to do the same: "For myself, I have sufficiently featured Negro in *Cane*."

1923 Published: *Harmonium* by Wallace Stevens (Knopf, New York)

1977 After more than four years in prison, the longest time served by any Watergate conspirator, G. Gordon Liddy was released on parole after President Carter commuted his sentence. Among the advocates for his release was an unlikely one: George V. Higgins, who had kept his legal practice even after he became the author of a series of crime-fiction bestsellers beginning with the masterful *Friends of Eddie Coyle* and whose previous high-profile client was the Black Panther Eldridge Cleaver. In April, having argued successfully for clemency from the president, Higgins expressed his confidence that his client would be the rare Watergate figure not to sign a lucrative book deal: "I'd bet on it. He's a standup guy. That's how he got into this mess in the first place." Three years later, Liddy's memoir, *Will*, spent fourteen weeks on the *New York Times* bestseller list.

2012 In an attempt to create a paper trail for his own imagination, Philip Roth on this day published an "Open Letter to Wikipedia" on *The New Yorker*'s website to establish, for the record, that he had *not* based the character Coleman Silk in his novel *The Human Stain* on the writer Anatole Broyard, who, like Silk, hid his black ancestry to identify as white. Having been told by a Wikipedia administrator that "we require secondary sources" when he tried to edit speculation about Broyard from the *Human Stain* entry, Roth wrote the source material himself, testifying that his story was inspired instead by his friend Melvin Tumin, a professor hounded, like Silk, for an innocuous use of the word "spooks," and listing in great detail many of the elements of his story that came from no specific source outside his own capacity for invention.

BORN: **1924** Grace Metalious (*Peyton Place, The Tight White Collar*), Manchester, N.H.
1947 Ann Beattie (*Chilly Scenes of Winter, Distortions*), Washington, D.C.
1954 Jon Scieszka (*The Stinky Cheese Man, Math Curse*), Flint, Mich.
DIED: **1995** Eileen Chang (*Lust, Caution; Love in a Fallen City*), 74, Los Angeles

1666 Samuel Pepys bought two eels near the Thames, spent much of the day talking with people whose homes had been spared or destroyed by the great London fire of the previous week, and then traveled out of the city to retrieve his diary, which he had taken out of harm's way during the conflagration (other valuables—his wine and Parmesan cheese—he had buried in a hole in his yard). The account he then recorded of the calamity—the Lord Mayor wailing at his inability to halt the fire's advance, pigeons hovering by their burning homes for so long their wings were singed—remains the most valuable record of the fire, and though Pepys's normal life resumed (he was soon visiting his mistresses again) for months he dreamed uneasily of flames.

1883 "You are quite right, little princess," Sigmund Freud wrote to his fiancée, Martha Bernays, about the book they were both reading, *Don Quixote*, "it is no reading matter for girls, I had quite forgotten the many coarse and in themselves nauseating passages when I sent it to you." But the book made him split his sides with laughter anyway, and he kept writing to her about it, insisting on this day, "Do finish *Don Quixote*; the second part contains many fewer of the shocking qualities than the first and is far more fantastic."

1968 "It must have cost at least two hundred thousand dollars to produce this scene": Arthur Ashe serving to Clark Graebner in the semifinals of the U.S. Open at Forest Hills. A few years after launching his career by profiling Bill Bradley at Princeton, John McPhee returned to sports with *Levels of the Game*, a double portrait of two American tennis stars—Ashe becoming a legend, Graebner at the peak of his short career—and the training and talent that brought them to center court. Born the same year and opponents and friends for much of their lives, they were opposites on the court and off, which they acknowledged as readily as anyone: black and white, liberal and conservative, artistic and businesslike, free-swinging and stiff, cool and anxious. McPhee's portrait was based on those opposites but subtly complicated by the precision of each profile and by the players' own thoughtful senses of who and where they were.

2002 Judith Shulevitz, in the *New York Times*, on Christopher Hitchens's *Why Orwell Matters*: "As Hitchens and just about every other political columnist knows, quoting Orwell is like quoting Scripture. You can find support for almost any argument if you leaf through his collected writings long enough, because he wrote about nearly everything that mattered and was never afraid to change his mind when circumstances proved some earlier assumption incorrect."

September 9

BORN: 1868 Mary Austin (*The Land of Little Rain*, *The Ford*), Carlinville, Ill.
1964 Aleksandar Hemon (*Nowhere Man*, *The Lazarus Project*), Sarajevo
DIED: 1898 Stéphane Mallarmé (*The Afternoon of a Faun*), 56, Valvins, France
1980 John Howard Griffin (*Black Like Me*, *Scattered Shadows*), 60, Fort Worth, Tex.

1876 The *Spectator* on George Eliot's *Daniel Deronda*: "No book of hers before this ever contained so little humour . . . On the other hand, . . . no book of hers was ever conceived on ideal lines so noble."

1907 "I may say," Alice B. Toklas was made to say by Gertrude Stein in *The Autobiography of Alice B. Toklas*, "that only three times in my life have I met a genius and each time a bell within me rang and I was not mistaken." Pablo Picasso and Alfred North Whitehead were two of the geniuses; the third she met when she arrived in Paris from San Francisco, not long after the earthquake everyone in Paris was eager to hear about, and called on her friends Michael and Sarah Stein. There with them was Michael's younger sister Gertrude, "a golden brown presence" in a "warm brown corduroy suit," as Alice recalled in her actual autobiography, with a voice "deep, full, velvety like a great contralto's, like two voices." Much later, with her two voices, she'd speak for Alice in the book that, finally, made them both famous.

1944 Sergeant J. D. Salinger's eleven months of combat in Europe, which began when he waded through the surf at Utah Beach on D-Day, were almost unrelentingly grim: in June alone two-thirds of his infantry regiment were killed or wounded. But on this day he wrote a letter home that was filled with joy. Not only was his regiment among the first to enter liberated Paris, he told Whit Burnett, his editor at *Story*, but he had met Hemingway. After word got out that the great writer was at the Ritz, Salinger drove there in his jeep and showed Hemingway one of his own war stories in a recent *Saturday Evening Post*. Hemingway praised the story, said he had already seen Salinger's picture in *Esquire*, and was "not big-shotty" at all to the writer twenty years his junior. The two remained in touch through the war, though the often-told story that Hemingway later visited Salinger's unit and shot the head off a chicken may not be true.

1958 Ralph Ellison reported back to Albert Murray on the Columbia Records concert later released as Miles Davis and Duke Ellington's *Jazz at the Plaza* records, "Duke signified on Davis all through his numbers and his trumpeters and saxophonists went after him like a bunch of hustlers in a Georgia skin game fighting with razors."

1975 After their second declaration of bankruptcy, Raymond and Maryann Carver were released from $24,390 in debts.

BORN: **1935** Mary Oliver (*American Primitive, Thirst*), Maple Heights, Ohio
1937 Jared Diamond (*Guns, Germs, and Steel; Collapse*), Boston
DIED: **1976** Dalton Trumbo (*Johnny Got His Gun, Eclipse*), 70, Los Angeles
1994 Amy Clampitt (*The Kingfisher, What the Light Was Like*), 74, Lenox, Mass.

1797 In late March, Mary Wollstonecraft and William Godwin, two political radicals in the age of revolution, having first met at the home of Tom Paine, were joined in marriage, a custom they had each become notorious for condemning. Five months later, Wollstonecraft gave birth to a daughter, whom they hoped to raise with the same independence they had brought to their marriage, but the mother quickly took ill after an infection, and on this day, after eleven days tenderly described by Godwin in the *Memoirs* of his wife (a book whose frankness would soon make him a pariah), she died. The baby girl, who survived, was named Mary like her mother, and two decades later, under her married name of Mary Shelley, she wrote *Frankenstein*.

1967 Djuna Barnes, author of the avant-garde landmarks *Nightwood* and *Ryder*, spent the last forty-two years of her life as "the most famous unknown in the world!" as she wrote to a friend on this day. From her tiny apartment in Greenwich Village, she guarded her legacy and her privacy with a ferocity that led one acquaintance to refer to her as "Madame Vitriol," refusing visits from some admirers, like Carson McCullers and Anaïs Nin, but not others: after Susan Sontag sent her a copy of *Against Interpretation*, Barnes wrote her, "I have been informed that seeing me on the village streets, you have refrained from addressing me, because someone has told you that I am a Demon, of some violence and invective. Please do me the pleasure of speaking with me the next time?"

NO YEAR Something was going on in the neglected building known as Old Meats, the chairman of the horticulture department noticed. The building, right in the middle of campus, had been locked up for years, but he saw a nondescript young man let himself in and out. What was going on in Old Meats, it turned out, was Earl Butz, a pearly white, eighteen-month-old, third-of-a-ton Landrace hog, and a secret experiment in porcine nutrition: what would happen if a pig, bred for the task, was encouraged to eat as much as he could for as long as he could? After transplanting Shakespearean tragedy to a midwestern hog farm in her Pulitzer-winning *A Thousand Acres*, Jane Smiley stayed in her adopted Iowa but turned to comedy in *Moo*, a land-grant-college novel with a cast of hundreds, at whose center sits Earl Butz, a massive metaphor as well as a living, feeling beast who knows to make a break for it when he can.

September 11

BORN: 1885 D. H. Lawrence (*Sons and Lovers, The Rainbow*), Eastwood, England
1959 Andre Dubus III (*The House of Sand and Fog, Townie*), Oceanside, Calif.
DIED: 1958 Robert W. Service ("The Cremation of Sam McGee"), 84, Lancieux, France
2009 Jim Carroll (*The Basketball Diaries, Forced Entries*), 60, New York City

1599 Swiss tourist Thomas Platter's mention of attending Shakespeare's *Julius Caesar* makes it the first recorded performance at the new Globe Theatre.

1888 "Medicine is my lawful wife and literature is my mistress," Anton Chekhov wrote to A. S. Souvorin. "When I get tired of one I spend the night with the other. Though it's disorderly, it's not so dull, and besides, neither of them loses anything from my infidelity."

1979 At the center of Janet Malcolm's *The Journalist and the Murderer* is a note of seduction so brazen it was nearly its author's undoing: a letter from reporter Joe McGinniss to Jeffrey MacDonald, who had just been convicted of the murder of his family, assuring him that "total strangers can recognize within five minutes that you did not receive a fair trial . . . It's a hell of a thing—spend the summer making a new friend and then the bastards come along and lock him up. But not for long, Jeffrey—not for long." But as McGinniss later made clear in his book on MacDonald, *Fatal Vision*, he was convinced even then of his subject's guilt. MacDonald sued McGinniss (they settled out of court), and Malcolm, herself recently sued by one of her own subjects, used their case to argue that no journalist can avoid the role of a seducer who carries an "unholy power" over those she writes about.

1992 Lorna Sage, in the *TLS*, on Michael Ondaatje's *The English Patient*: "With Ondaatje, togetherness is a momentary, present-tense phenomenon: as soon as people start developing pasts and futures, everything becomes fissile and flies apart."

2001 On the final afternoon of his (and his guide Sergei's) thirty-seven-day, 9,000-mile trip across Siberia by van and train, the longest of the five he took for his *Travels in Siberia,* Ian Frazier arrived at a Pacific beach of boulders, broken cement, and rusted iron, with a small black cow standing nearby, two wrecked ships in the bay, and a large rock spray-painted with the logos of the New York Yankees and Los Angeles Dodgers. Not until the next morning did he talk to his wife at home in New Jersey and learn of the events in Manhattan that day.

2001 That same evening, at the other end of Manhattan from the attacks, Alice Stewart Trillin, the addressee of the title imperative in her husband Calvin's *Alice, Let's Eat* and a level-headed presence in many of his other books—and, as he described her later in *About Alice*, an "incorrigible and ridiculous optimist"—died at New York Presbyterian Hospital of heart failure, caused by her radiation treatment for lung cancer twenty-five years before.

BORN: 1880 H. L. Mencken (*The American Language*, *Prejudices*), Baltimore
1943 Michael Ondaatje (*Coming Through Slaughter*), Colombo, Ceylon
DIED: 1869 Peter Mark Roget (*Thesaurus of English Words and Phrases*), 90, West Malvern, England
2008 David Foster Wallace (*Consider the Lobster*), 46, Claremont, Calif.

1560 It's an irresistible story: on this day Arnaud du Tilh was sentenced to death for impersonating Martin Guerre, a well-to-do peasant who had abandoned his wife and son only to return a dozen years later to find that du Tilh, claiming to be Guerre, had taken his place and fathered two sons with Guerre's wife. Ever since, this tale of bold imposture has drawn storytellers, from Michel de Montaigne, who may have been at du Tilh's sentencing, to local villagers who passed down the story for centuries, and finally to two slim, evocative retellings in the twentieth century: Janet Lewis's 1941 novel, *The Wife of Martin Guerre*, and Natalie Zemon Davis's historical investigation, *The Return of Martin Guerre*, written after she consulted on the Gérard Depardieu movie of the same name.

1867 The charges for the inquest into the death of eighteen-year-old Malcolm Melville, son of Herman, whose death by pistol was ruled a suicide "while laboring under temporary insanity of mind," totaled $11.31¼.

1895 George Bernard Shaw crashed his bicycle into Bertrand Russell, whose "knickerbockers were demolished."

1925 By eleven in the evening only a few of the guests remain at the Stoners' first party in their new, too-expensive house: the assistant dean and his wife, some friends from the English department, and, unexpectedly, Hollis Lomax, who has, in his year in the department, remained an opaque, ironic presence, declining all social invitations until this one. Well into the early hours of the next day, Lomax speaks openly as never before, confessing his personal struggles, and by the night's late end, just before Lomax gives Stoner's wife a chaste yet oddly intimate goodbye kiss, Stoner feels a kinship with this man who had been a stranger. The feeling lasts until the following Monday, when Lenox greets Stoner with an inexplicable iciness closer to anger than irony, the first sign of an enduring and crucial hostility in John Williams's modestly profound tragedy, *Stoner*.

1954 Following an invitation from a young employee at the Guinness Park Royal Brewery, who had known them as fellow runners at Oxford, Norris and Ross McWhirter, the proprietors of McWhirter Twins Ltd., a London fact-gathering agency, met Sir Hugh Beaver, the Guinness managing director, for lunch at the brewery. Sir Hugh had an idea, inspired by a debate with fellow sportsmen whether the golden plover was the fastest game bird in Europe: create a book of superlatives to answer the idle questions that pop up in pubs every day. Hired immediately for their "quirkish minds," the McWhirters spent a frantic year of research and by the next fall produced the first *Guinness Book of Records*, 198 pages in a special "beer-proof" binding.

September 13

BORN: 1916 Roald Dahl (*James and the Giant Peach*), Llandaff, Wales
    1920 Else Holmelund Minarik (*Father Bear Comes Home*), Denmark
DIED: 1592 Michel de Montaigne (*Essays*), 59, Château de Montaigne, France
    1928 Italo Svevo (*Zeno's Conscience*), 66, Motta di Livenza, Italy

NO YEAR The "sands," in Erskine Childers's *The Riddle of the Sands*, are not in the desert but in the shallows around the northern coastal islands of Germany. And the "riddle" is why a solo yachtsman named Davies, cruising his way innocently along the coast in search of ducks, was directed on this day by a fellow sailor into those treacherous shallows, where only luck saved his boat from being blown to pieces in a gale. The riddle's solution, Davies and his friend Carruthers discover on a return to the same coast, has to do with what is hiding among those coastal islands, an answer that would prove surprisingly influential as *The Riddle of the Sands*, after its release in 1903, became not only a template for the modern spy thriller but, read by Churchill and others, a major influence on the British military buildup for the First World War.

1939 His stove has reverted to an old gas-burner model that smells like burned grease. His refrigerator has become an obsolete, belt-driven monster. His TV set is now an AM radio in a wood cabinet, and his polyphonic audio set a Victrola playing a 78 of Ray Noble's "Turkish Delight." And his homeopape machine? That's just gone. *Ubik,* Philip K. Dick's reality-bending masterpiece, is set in the near-future of 1992, but suddenly all the modern conveniences in Joe Chip's conapt have deteriorated decades into the past, and time itself seems to have shifted back to this date. The only thing left for Joe to do is meet with the other employees of Runciter Associates and figure out how they've ended up in this half-life where time is slipping away from them. Was their founder, Glen Runciter, really killed in that moon explosion, or were they? And how can they get their hands on an aerosol can of that time-fixing Ubik spray they keep hearing about?

1940 The Nazi occupation of France didn't extend to the Mediterranean port city of Marseille, so in the days after the invasion its foreign consulates were besieged with those looking to flee into exile, including the novelists Heinrich Mann and Franz Werfel, German émigrés whose opposition to the Nazis had put them atop a Gestapo execution list. Finally, on a Friday the 13th that Werfel worried was bad luck, Mann (nearly seventy), Werfel, and their wives, Nelly Mann and Alma Mahler Werfel (widow of the composer Gustav Mahler), made a dramatic mountain climb on goat paths through the Pyrenees with the help of the clandestine American Rescue Committee and escaped to a friendly welcome in Spain. Within a month they had arrived by ship at Hoboken, New Jersey.

BORN: **1930** Allan Bloom (*The Closing of the American Mind*), Indianapolis

1934 Kate Millet (*Sexual Politics*, *The Loony-Bin Trip*), St. Paul, Minn.

DIED: **1321** Dante Alighieri (*The Divine Comedy*, *La vita nuovo*), c. 56, Ravenna, Italy

1982 John Gardner (*Grendel*, *The Art of Fiction*), 49, Susquehanna, Pa.

1953 The multiple rejections he had already received might explain the rather resigned cover letter a schoolteacher named William Golding sent to Faber and Faber on this day with the manuscript of his novel *Strangers from Within*, which, he said, "might be defined as an allegorical interpretation of a stock situation." Faber's reader was unimpressed, rejecting it too as an "absurd & uninteresting fantasy . . . A group of children who land in jungle-country near New Guinea. Rubbish & dull. Pointless." But later that month a young editor, Charles Monteith, picked the manuscript off the reject pile and was intrigued, and after significant revisions and an advance of £60 that "delighted" the debut author, Faber published the novel in 1954 under its new title, *Lord of the Flies*.

1968 For Nick Hornby, as for much of the rest of the world, 1968 was a year of upheaval, although the tremors in Hornby's life weren't assassinations, protests, and war, but divorce, a new home, and a new school. All of which left him vulnerable at age eleven, when his father took him to his first professional soccer game, to the strange mass lure of unrelenting sporting mediocrity—in other words, Arsenal in the late '60s. Young Nick had been a Manchester United fan for about three weeks, but that first visit to Highbury converted him immediately. "The fact that I was intruding on a marriage that had gone disastrously sour lent my afternoon a particularly thrilling prurience," he recalls in *Fever Pitch*, his memoir of the glorious and inexplicable tyranny that Arsenal football has held over his life ever since.

NO YEAR The first day of the canoe trip down the river in James Dickey's *Deliverance* is a quiet one, spent mainly in preparation. The four suburban men, Lewis, Ed, Bobby, and Drew, drive into the woods of north Georgia, make vaguely tense arrangements with the locals, and put their canoes in, steering and pulling down the river with amateur awkwardness until dusk forces them to make camp. And in his tent at night, stone dead from the paddling, Ed sleeps and then wakes in the absolute darkness when something hits the tent. He turns on his flashlight. Above his head the canvas is punctured, "and through it came one knuckle of a deformed fist, a long curving of claws that turned on themselves." Well, he almost laughs, "there was nothing, after all, so dangerous about an owl."

1972 A bookkeeper for the Committee to Re-Elect the President, an unnamed source in *All the President's Men*, tells Carl Bernstein, "If you could get John Mitchell, it would be beautiful."

September 15

BORN: 1789 James Fenimore Cooper (*The Last of the Mohicans*), Burlington, N.J.
1890 Agatha Christie (*The Murder of Roger Ackroyd*), Torquay, England
DIED: 1938 Thomas Wolfe (*Look Homeward, Angel; Of Time and the River*), 37, Baltimore
1989 Robert Penn Warren (*All the King's Men, Night Rider*), 84, Stratton, Vt.

1866 Anthony Trollope let nothing get in the way of his literary industry. He had trained himself to write in busy train cars, so working in the drawing room of the Athenaeum Club caused him no trouble until the time he overheard two clergymen there complaining of how often he reused the same characters, in particular the disagreeable Mrs. Proudie. To their surprise and embarrassment, he identified himself and declared, "As to Mrs. Proudie, I will go home and kill her before the week is over." Whatever the truth of the tale (he told it many different ways), kill Mrs. Proudie he did in *The Last Chronicle of Barset*, which he completed on this day under the working title "The Story of a Cheque for Twenty Pounds and of the Mischief which it did," and which he, and many others, considered the finest of his vast output of novels.

1883 Seventy-two years before Rosa Parks refused to give up her seat on an Alabama bus, Ida B. Wells refused the demand of a conductor on the Chesapeake & Ohio Railway to leave the first-class ladies carriage for the crowded colored car, and indeed scratched and bit the conductor as she was pulled forcibly out of her seat. Wells won a $500 court judgment against the railway—later overturned—but the incident also helped launch her new career in journalism: she recounted the case in her first column for the *Living Way*. Later she turned to a pugnacious crusade against lynching, first as the editor of the *Memphis Free Speech & Headlight* until its offices were destroyed by an angry white mob in 1892, and then as a writer and activist in Chicago.

1895 Thomas Hardy surprised the visiting novelist George Gissing by leaping up at the breakfast table and killing a wasp "with the flat of a table-knife!"

1945 When Isaiah Berlin, whose family had fled the Soviet Union when he was a child, returned as a British diplomat to one of the cities of his youth, now known as Leningrad, he asked after a poet from the past, Anna Akhmatova. To his shock, she was still alive, and he could meet her that day. In her tiny apartment they talked through the night, discussing literature and art, exchanging news of exiled Russians and those who had—often tragically—stayed, and unburdening themselves of their lives' intimate details. They met only once again, but the visit proved epochal for Akhmatova especially: Berlin immediately became a figure in her poetry as the "Guest from the Future," and nearly as quickly her persecution began, as the Soviet regime called Berlin a British spy and denounced Akhmatova as "half nun, half harlot."

BORN: 1898 H. A. Rey (*Curious George, The Stars*), Hamburg, Germany
1950 Henry Louis Gates Jr. (*Colored People, The Signifying Monkey*), Keyser, W.Va.
DIED: 1672 Anne Bradstreet (*The Tenth Muse Lately Sprung Up in America*), c. 60, North Andover, Mass.
2007 Robert Jordan (Wheel of Time series), 58, Charleston, S.C.

1704 Diderot and d'Alembert may have been given the lion's share of the credit for the great *Encyclopédie*, but the workhorse of the immense project was the Chevalier de Jaucourt, whom his colleagues mocked for his "merciless compiling" even as they were grateful for his industry. A wealthy nobleman whose mother excused his embarrassing scholarly efforts by saying, "A professor of medicine may be ridiculous, but it is not really a vice," de Jaucourt, who was born on this day, joined the *Encyclopédie* after his own work, a medical dictionary, was lost in a shipwreck after twenty years' labor. At his busiest, with the help of a handful of secretaries he once sold a house to keep paying, he composed over 15,000 encyclopedia articles in six years, covering subjects from Pharmacy to Hydraulics to Chess.

1896 Three years after writing *Maggie, a Girl of the Streets*, Stephen Crane found himself—whether by chance or design is still debated—taking the side of an alleged woman of the streets. In this day's early hours, Crane, a star reporter for the *New York Journal,* saw a woman named Dora Clark falsely arrested for soliciting and, despite the advice of the sergeant on duty that "if you monkey with this case, you are pretty sure to come out with mud all over you," testified successfully in her favor and wrote up his experience as a "reluctant witness" in the newspaper sketch "Adventures of a Novelist." A month later, though, Crane testified in her favor again, and this time the police were ready with the mud they'd promised, turning the trial into an inquisition into the reporter's own morals.

1936 Malcolm Cowley, in the *New Republic*, on Margaret Mitchell's *Gone with the Wind*: "I would never, never say that she has written a great novel, but in the midst of triteness and sentimentality her book has a simple-minded courage that suggests the great novelists of the past. No wonder it is going like the wind."

1944 It may have been that the only way Mary McCarthy could extract herself from her disastrous marriage with Edmund Wilson was to write her way out. Wilson, the most powerful critic of his day (with the possible exception of McCarthy), had already read "The Weeds," her blistering portrait of a woman who gets up the nerve to leave her domineering, Wilsonian husband only to return to him miserably at the end, but when *The New Yorker* published it on this day it ended their marriage for good. When McCarthy asked her husband why the story made him so mad now, since she had shown it to him before, he replied, "But you've improved it!"

September 17

1835 Charles Darwin, experimenting with the birds on Chatham Island in the Galápagos, which had never known human predators, pushed a large hawk off a branch with the end of his gun.

1963 It's like old times when childhood friends Guitar and Milkman get together and spend the day talking about how they might get the sack full of gold they are sure Pilate has hanging from the roof of her shack, and how they'll spend it once they have it. Guitar thinks he could bankroll a mission to avenge the bombing that killed four little girls in Birmingham the Sunday before; Milkman isn't sure what he'd do: he just wants to get away from town, from his past, or maybe he wants the excitement of doing a job with Guitar. Everything carries weight in Toni Morrison's *Song of Solomon*, symbolic and otherwise, but this sack, once they get it, turns out to be lighter than expected, filled with rocks and old bones rather than gold, thereby saving the thieves from seeing their desires fulfilled.

1992 Blue van Meer's memories of her mother are fleeting and sketchy, as they are of the day, when Blue was five, that her mother's white Plymouth Horizon went through a Mississippi State Highway guardrail into a line of trees. On any other day Blue would have been in that car too (and perhaps would have kept her mother from falling asleep at the wheel), but it's a hint of the story to come in Marisha Pessl's *Specialty Topics in Calamity Physics* that she had instead been whisked off from kindergarten that day by her mercurial, intellectual father to spend the afternoon learning about rural deer-management programs, the beginning, it turns out, of a vagabond fatherly tutorial that leaves Blue a precocious (and pedantic) student susceptible to the most dangerously baroque of intellectual plots.

2000 Sven Birkerts, in the *New York Times*, on Joseph Brodsky's *Collected Poems*: "Brodsky charged at the world with full intensity and wrestled his perceptions into lines that fairly vibrate with what they are asked to hold. There is no voice, no vision, remotely like it."

BORN: **1709** Samuel Johnson (*A Dictionary of the English Language*), Lichfield, England
1954 Steven Pinker (*The Language Instinct, The Blank Slate*), Montreal

DIED: **1830** William Hazlitt (*Table-Talk, The Spirit of the Age*), 52, London
1951 Gelett Burgess (*Goops, and How to Be Them*), 85, Carmel, Calif.

1768 "I have now begun the sixtieth year of my life," Samuel Johnson reflected on his birthday. "How the last year has passed I am unwilling to terrify myself with thinking . . . I have found myself somewhat relieved by reading, which I therefore intend to practise when I am able. This day it came into my mind to write the history of my melancholy. On this I purpose to deliberate. I know not whether it may not too much disturb me."

1840 Did Rafinesque—a friend of Audubon and correspondent of Jefferson who died on this day—really exist? His name sounds like an obsolete art movement or a vaguely disreputable adjective. And his life? It's the stuff of a fabulist, a Barth or Pynchon, even in John Jeremiah Sullivan's apparently factual biographical essay, first published as the Kentucky representative in the anthology *State by State*, and subsequently included in his collection *Pulphead*. Constantine Rafinesque, whose peers considered him ill-mannered and grotesquely corpulent, was, by his own measure, "Botanist, Naturalist, Geologist, Geographer, Historian, Poet, Philosopher, Philologist, Economist, Philanthropist." By Sullivan's measure he was a man both ahead of and behind his time, a polymath in the style of the previous century who held advanced but often incoherent ideas on evolution, nature, and race that in their ragged, hungry mystery make, to Sullivan's mind, as good a foundation as any for an American religion.

1917 The young writer Aldous Huxley took up residence at Eton, where he taught (poorly, by his own account) for a year. Among his pupils was Eric Blair, who would grow up to become his rival in dystopian fiction, George Orwell.

1959 Burns Singer, in the *TLS*, on Jack Kerouac's *The Dharma Bums*: "The way in which comfort is piled on comfort (there is a never-ending stream of drink) adds to the sense of the fairytale where everything can be had for the wishing."

1970 Peter Morris Green, in the *TLS*, on Gore Vidal's *Two Sisters*: "Even a mature and world-weary cat can be playfully wicked, and while always ending up by pouncing playfully into our laps, will pretend from time to time to aim for our throats."

September 19

BORN: 1920 Roger Angell (*The Summer Game, Let Me Finish*), New York City
1921 Paulo Freire (*The Pedagogy of the Oppressed*), Recife, Brazil
DIED: 1942 Condé Nast (publisher of *Vogue, Vanity Fair*), 69, New York City
1985 Italo Calvino (*If on a winter's night a traveler*), 61, Siena, Italy

1876 General Lew Wallace had already led an adventurous life—fighting at Fort Donelson and Shiloh as the youngest major general in the Union Army, meeting secretly with Billy the Kid as governor of New Mexico—when he turned to writing. Fascinated by the biblical story of the three wise men, he was drawn to turn that story into a book by an encounter on a train on this day with a fellow Shiloh veteran, Robert Ingersoll, known as the "Great Agnostic" and considered the finest orator of his day, whose love of arguing the finer points of belief drove Wallace, until then indifferent to religion, to study the life of Jesus and build a novel around it: *Ben-Hur: A Story of the Christ*, which became the biggest American blockbuster of the nineteenth century.

1935 Fiction may not get any harder-boiled than Horace McCoy's *They Shoot Horses, Don't They?* It's a crime novel as suicide note, and it's no spoiler to reveal that the title of the book is its last line too, spoken by the narrator, Robert Syverten, as he's arrested for murder. Throughout the book, as Robert and Gloria Beatty, his partner in dancing and death, shuffle toward their fate through a brutal and endless dance marathon on the outskirts of Hollywood at the bottom of the Depression, the voice of Robert's judge intones his final judgment, to be fulfilled "upon the 19th day of the month of September in the year of our Lord, 1935, in the manner provided by the laws of the State of California." Robert may not have known where their story was headed, but Gloria did, and she died with a smile on her face.

1963 Twelve years after their marriage and nine before their divorce, Alice and James Munro moved to Victoria, British Columbia, and opened Munro's Books.

1967 On this evening, CBS devoted an hour of its prime-time television schedule to Eric Sevareid's interview with a retired longshoreman, and was rewarded for it. Eric Hoffer had by then published four books of self-taught philosophy and social commentary, beginning with *The True Believer*, all written in a chiseled, aphoristic style during his off-hours as a San Francisco stevedore. As singular as Hoffer and his story might already have seemed on the page, his presence on the screen—smoking, shouting, mopping his brow, and nearly leaping out of his chair with intellectual passion—was charismatic and compelling and made Hoffer a national celebrity, drawing so much interest that the special was repeated two months later.

1979 Hermione Granger (from the Harry Potter series) is born.

BORN: 1948 George R. R. Martin (*A Game of Thrones*), Bayonne, N.J.
1951 Javier Marías (*Your Face Tomorrow*), Madrid
DIED: 1863 Jacob Grimm (*Grimm's Fairy Tales*, *Deutsches Wörterbuch*), 78, Berlin
1933 Annie Besant (*The Ancient Wisdom*, *Occult Chemistry*), 85, Adyar, India

1879 Though a "seven-percent solution" of cocaine in water was Sherlock Holmes's preferred vice, there is no evidence that Arthur Conan Doyle experimented with the drug himself, as so many did in the late nineteenth century before its harmful effects were understood. But he was not averse to testing other remedies on himself, as he reported as a twenty-year-old medical student in his first professional publication, "Gelseminum as a Poison," in the *British Medical Journal*. Curious about how much tincture of gelseminum, or jasmine root, a popular pain reliever at the time, he could take without poisoning himself, he investigated. Doubling the standard dose led to short-term giddiness; quadrupling it caused severe headache, depression, "extreme lassitude," and "diarrhoea . . . so persistent and prostrating" that he ceased the experiment.

1929 "Hell, in case you're interested," Jim Thompson once wrote, "is actually the College of Agriculture of the University of Nebraska," the institution at which Thompson matriculated on this day, just a month before the stock market crash brought the start of even harder times to the Great Plains. A twenty-two-year-old high school dropout and the family breadwinner as a hotel bellboy and oil-field roughneck, he had been told the ag school was the sensible route to steady work, but when his punishing schedule of part-time jobs dried up he had to drop out. He spent the next two years hoboing around the plains looking for work until, with the fact-gathering help of his mother, sister, and newlywed wife, he started churning out true-crime tales for magazines in a fifteen-year apprenticeship before his great crime novels of the 1950s.

1998 James McManus, in the *New York Times*, on Lorrie Moore's *Birds of America*: "Fluid, cracked, mordant, colloquial, Moore's sentences hold, even startle, us as they glide beneath the radar of ideological theories of behavior to evoke the messy, god-awful behavior itself."

2001 Teju Cole's *Open City* is the story of Julius, a Nigerian American psychiatry resident who wanders through New York, listening and observing. Julius's finely defined intelligence makes the listening and observing full of vitality, but never more so than when he leaves for a few weeks in Belgium and gets to know Farouq, the manager of an Internet shop who takes over the middle of the novel with his own intelligence. A self-taught intellectual from Morocco who reminds Julius both of Marx, anonymous in London, and De Niro as the young Vito Corleone, Farouq talks to Julius of Paul de Man, Edward Said, Hezbollah, and Mohammed and traces his angry disillusionment with the promise of Europe to this day, when his grad-school committee rejected his master's thesis without explanation, nine days after the Twin Towers fell.

September 21

BORN: 1866 H. G. Wells (*The War of the Worlds, Tono-Bungay*), Bromley, England
1947 Stephen King (*Carrie, The Stand, The Dark Tower*), Portland, Maine

DIED: 19 B.C. Virgil (*The Aeneid, The Eclogues*), 50, Brundisium, Roman Empire
1918 Jacqueline Susann (*Valley of the Dolls, The Love Machine*), 56, New York City

1853 Charles Dickens protested publicly that any similarity between his improvident friend Leigh Hunt and Harold Skimpole, the villainous sponger in *Bleak House*—a similarity that haunted Hunt for the last years of his life—was "the wildest delusions of the wildest lunatics." But in a letter to a friend on this day Dickens, a frequent target of Hunt's own sponging, confessed otherwise. "I suppose he is the most exact portrait that ever was painted in words!" he boasted. "There is not an atom of exaggeration or suppression. It is an absolute reproduction of a real man."

1891 For decades, biographies of Stephen Crane included a poignant romantic episode from his youth when, for a few intense weeks, he courted a "tall darkly pretty girl named Helen Trent." In conversation and letters he asked if she liked flowers and dogs, praised the virtues of naked ocean swimming, and told her, "You have the most beautiful arms I ever saw." She questioned his interest in the "vile" slums of the Bowery and then on this day informed him she was marrying someone else. But did "Helen Trent" even exist? Later scholars, especially Stanley Wertheim and Paul Sorrentino, have argued convincingly that Crane's friend and early biographer, Thomas Beer (best known as the author of an eccentrically memorable history of the 1890s, *The Mauve Decade*), concocted the letters Crane allegedly wrote her, and most likely invented the "well-bred" Miss Trent as well.

1939 Living in exile from the Nazis in London, with his suffering from terminal mouth cancer nearly unbearable, Sigmund Freud selected his reading from his library with care. On September 20, he read his final book, *La peau de chagrin*, Balzac's tale of a man who finds a magic hide that grants him wishes but shrinks, along with his remaining life, with each wish. "This was the proper book for me to read," he remarked to his doctor, Max Schur; "it deals with shrinking and starvation." The following day, he reminded Schur of his promise "not to forsake me when the time comes." Schur hadn't forgotten, and over the next two days administered doses of morphine strong enough that Freud never woke from their effects.

1973 John Spurling, in the *New Statesman*, on J. G. Farrell's *The Siege of Krishnapur*: "For a novel to be witty is one thing, to tell a good story is another, to be serious is yet another, but to be all three is surely enough to make it a masterpiece."

2005 The appearance of a copy of Flann O'Brien's *The Third Policeman*, carried by Desmond in the opening episode of the second season of *Lost*, caused sales of the 1967 novel to balloon.

BORN: 1924 Rosamunde Pilcher (*The Shell Seekers*), Lelant, England

1931 Fay Weldon (*The Lives and Loves of a She-Devil*), Birmingham, England

DIED: 1914 Henri Alain-Fournier (*The Lost Estate*), 27, Vaux-lès-Palameix, France

1968 Charles Jackson (*The Lost Weekend*), 65, New York City

YEAR 1401 (by Shire-reckoning) Even the unpleasant Sackville-Bagginses were invited to Bag End for the birthday celebrations for Bilbo Baggins, turning the venerable age of eleventy-one nearly sixty years after he returned from the travels celebrated in *The Hobbit*, and his adopted heir, Frodo, who was reaching his hobbit's "coming of age" at thirty-three. What a party it was, with fireworks, a great feast, presents for everyone, a rare appearance by Gandalf the Wizard, and, to the surprise of all, Bilbo's sudden disappearance in a flash of light. And late in the evening Frodo received the gift, left by Bilbo, that was the true reason for the entire affair, a golden ring that would be the cause of Frodo's own great adventure.

1598 Two days after his comedy *Every Man in His Humour* was first performed (with William Shakespeare in the cast), Ben Jonson set out with a fellow actor, Gabriel Spencer, to settle a quarrel with swords in Hoxton Fields. The two had been imprisoned together for their parts in a "lewd" and "seditious" production the year before, but now Jonson, after taking a cut on the arm, killed Spencer with a thrust into his side.

Sentenced to hang for murder, Johnson was able to avoid the noose by pleading "benefit of clergy," a privilege by then extended to anyone who could read from the Bible before the court. Jonson was set free, but his worldly goods were confiscated and a *T* was branded on his thumb to mark him, since no one could plead benefit of clergy twice.

1888 *National Geographic Magazine* made its debut.

1912 In the space of four days in September, Franz Kafka completed two short but momentous works: the first letter in what would become his passionately ambivalent correspondence with Felice Bauer and, two days later, his story "The Judgment." The letter, less than four hundred words long, took him ten careful days of composing before he could put it in the mail, while the more than four thousand words of the story poured out of him in a single night, from ten in the evening on this day to six in the morning the next, when he proudly burst into his sister Ottla's room to read the results. It "quite literally came out of me like a regular birth," he wrote, "covered with filth and slime," and, understanding perhaps who had loosed such powers within him, he dedicated it to "Miss Felice B."

1948 Leaving Hollywood for good to write serious books, James M. Cain rented a small house for $165 a month in Hyattsville, Maryland, "the churlish little state from which I fled."

September 23

BORN: 1865 Baroness Emmuska Orczy (*The Scarlet Pimpernel*), Tarnaörs, Hungary
1907 Pauline Réage (*The Story of O*), Rochefort, France

DIED: 1889 Wilkie Collins (*The Woman in White, The Moonstone*), 65, London
1939 Sigmund Freud (*Civilization and Its Discontents*), 83, London

1930 Aleister Crowley, the occultist, poet, mountaineer, libertine, and would-be prophet who by then had settled comfortably into his role as "the wickedest man in the world," arrived in Lisbon to begin what a friend called "some stunt," a round-the-world travelogue with his girlfriend. But when she left him, Crowley improvised another stunt entirely. With the assistance of Fernando Pessoa, a local writer who took an interest in mystical arcana (and who later would be recognized as the great Portuguese writer of his time), he composed a cryptic and woeful suicide note, laid it by a seaside chasm known as the Mouth of Hell at the moment of the autumnal equinox, and while Pessoa reported to the press that his friend had disappeared, he followed his girlfriend to Germany and watched with pleasure as the newspapers of Europe reported his death.

1957 The unlikely friendship between Henry Green, the enigmatic English manufacturer-novelist, and Terry Southern, the American satirist nineteen years his junior, began with a fan letter from the younger writer to his elder and may have reached its peak with their collaboration on Green's *Paris Review* interview in 1957. One of the finest in that venerable series, the interview is both deliciously sly (at one point Green purposefully mishears "suttee" for "subtle") and theoretically serious, and was clearly stage-managed by its participants. Though the introduction falsely claimed the discussion took place on a winter's night "in the author's firelit study" (it was composed via letter in the late summer), their put-on did not include Green's suggestion, in a letter on this day, that "The last sentence might be 'and at this Mr. Green drifted off into the rain as sad as a grey dead starved pigeon wet in the ash can.'"

1986 Nicholson Baker dreamed that John Updike, drunk in New Orleans, had to work his way back home as a train conductor.

2000 Like architects, comics artists build boxes to hold human lives, and no one has taken the architectural possibilities of the form farther than Chris Ware. To the intricately nested and diagrammed boxes in earlier books like *Jimmy Corrigan*, he added another in *Building Stories*: the briefcase-sized cardboard container that holds fourteen loose books and pamphlets inside. One of those books, "September 23, 2000," tells the story of a single day in an ordinary Chicago three-flat building: a sniping couple, a lonely young woman, the equally lonely landlady, a cat named Mr. Kitty, rain on the roof, plumbing problems, and a quiet Saturday that seems so morosely typical that it spins its inhabitants into despair until, for one of them at least, it becomes an anniversary to remember.

BORN: **1896** F. Scott Fitzgerald (*This Side of Paradise, The Great Gatsby*), St. Paul, Minn.
1944 Eavan Boland (*Against Love Poetry, In a Time of Violence*), Dublin
DIED: **1991** Dr. Seuss (*Green Eggs and Ham, The Lorax*), 87, La Jolla, Calif.
2004 Françoise Sagan (*Bonjour Tristesse, A Certain Smile*), 69, Honfleur, France

1853 George Brimley, in the *Spectator*, on Dickens's *Bleak House*: "*Bleak House* is, even more than any of its predecessors, chargeable with not simply faults, but absolute want of construction."

1854 Henry David Thoreau took a bath, likely his last of the year.

1920 J. M. Murry, in the *Athenaeum*, on Frank Harris's *Oscar Wilde: His Life and Confessions*: "The personal magnetism of a man dies with him; his solid achievement as an artist alone has substance in the eyes of posterity; and we, who are posterity for Wilde, must confess that he is rather a pale ghost as an artist."

1930 "Is success in any other profession," Moss Hart asks near the end of his memoir, *Act One*, "as dazzling, as deeply satisfying, as it is in the theatre?" By that point, you are more than willing to agree with him: certainly there are few successes more deeply satisfying to *read* about than the story Hart tells in *Act One*. Following a dramatic and unfailingly charming series of setbacks and breakthroughs, his transformation from stage-struck nobody to hit playwright climaxes in its final pages with the opening-night smash on this day of his Broadway debut, *Once in a Lifetime*. His later successes, from *You Can't Take It with You* to *A Star Is Born,* were left for another volume, which a fatal heart attack at age fifty-seven kept him from ever writing.

1952 Clarice Lispector arrived with her husband for a diplomatic posting in Washington, D.C., a "vague and inorganic city" that Lispector acknowledged was "beautiful, according to various laws of beauty that are not my own."

1956 Published: *Peyton Place* by Grace Metalious (Messner, New York)

1964 Eve Auchincloss, in the *New York Review of Books*, on Brigid Brophy's *The Snow Ball* and *The Finishing Touch*: "Brigid Brophy flings herself upon the novel as if it were an exercise machine and she a programmatic gymnast."

2001 Three weeks after his novel *The Corrections* was released to largely ecstatic reviews, Jonathan Franzen spent a day driving around St. Louis, the city of his youth and the lightly disguised terrain of much of the novel, to shoot B-roll footage for the *Oprah Winfrey Show*, awkwardly attempting to look contemplative at local and personal landmarks although he declined the one thing the producer most wanted, a visit to his old house. That same morning, Winfrey announced on her show that she had chosen *The Corrections* for her book club, but the footage never aired: she soon withdrew the invitation after Franzen, with similar awkwardness, expressed public ambivalence about his selection.

September 25

BORN: 1897 William Faulkner (*The Sound and the Fury, As I Lay Dying*), New Albany, Miss.

1930 Shel Silverstein (*Where the Sidewalk Ends, A Light in the Attic*), Chicago

DIED: 1968 Cornell Woolrich (*The Bride Wore Black*), 64, New York City

1970 Erich Maria Remarque (*All Quiet on the Western Front*), 72, Locarno, Switzerland

1930 As chairman of the selection committee of the Book Society, Britain's answer to the Book-of-the-Month Club, Hugh Walpole got an early look at Somerset Maugham's latest novel, *Cakes and Ale*. But after opening it up before bed on this night, he "read on with increasing horror. Unmistakable portrait of myself," he wrote in his diary. "Never slept!" Walpole saw himself—"the very accents of my voice"—in Alroy Kear, the favor-currying, self-promoting novelist of Maugham's sharp satire, and many other readers did too. Maugham, of course, demurred, telling Walpole that "nothing had been further from my thoughts than to describe you," but after Walpole's death he freely confessed to friends and in the introduction to a reissue of the book that he indeed had Walpole, that "ridiculous creature," in mind when he wrote what he would later say was his favorite of his own books.

1940 It was perhaps not naiveté but his too-knowing skepticism that delayed the flight of Walter Benjamin from occupied France until the last minute. An exile since the Nazis took power in Germany in 1932, Benjamin, a German Jewish essayist of unique brilliance, joined the flood of refugees heading to the south of France ahead of the Nazi invasion in 1940 and in September, though his papers were not quite in order, made an attempt to cross the Spanish border en route to America. The story of his death is incomplete, but it is thought that, fearing he would be sent back to France, he took enough morphine to kill himself. "In a situation with no way out, I have no choice but to end it. My life will finish in a little village in the Pyrenees where no one knows me," he is said to have written on a postcard to a friend on this night. "There is not enough time to write all the letters I had wanted to write."

1953 On the same day Saul Bellow called Anthony West, who had just panned *The Adventures of Augie March* in *The New Yorker*, a *mamzer* in a letter to his publisher, he protested to *The New Yorker*'s Katharine White that West had, "out of his own turbulence, thoughtlessness and pedantry," attacked a "mad symbolical novel" that Bellow had never written. A month later he happily thanked her for the magazine's "precedent-breaking offer" to let him respond in its pages, though he declined. The review's confusion was too "vast, involved and peculiar" to even argue with.

1959 After a quiet marriage ceremony in Beverly Hills, Helen Gurley, future author of *Sex and the Single Girl* and editor of *Cosmopolitan*, and her new husband, David Brown, went out for dinner and then to see Candy Barr on the Sunset Strip: "Candy is a damned fine stripper," said the new Mrs. Brown, "and I thought it a perfectly fine place to spend our wedding night."

September 26

BORN: 1888 T. S. Eliot (*The Waste Land, Four Quartets*), St. Louis

1949 Jane Smiley (*A Thousand Acres, The Age of Grief*), Los Angeles

DIED: 1936 Harriet Monroe (editor, *Poetry*), 75, Arequipa, Peru

1990 Alberto Moravia (*The Conformist, Contempt, Boredom*), 82, Rome

1929 "We very much like your title The Secret of the Old Clock," wrote L. F. Reed of Grosset & Dunlap to Edward Stratemeyer about his latest idea for a girl detective series. However, Reed didn't like most of the names Stratemeyer suggested for his teen heroine: "Stella Strong," "Nell Cody," and "Diana Dare." He preferred "Nancy Drew." Stratemeyer already had a thirty-year track record of creating series like the Rover Boys, Tom Swift, and, most recently, the Hardy Boys, so he confidently put the new sleuth in the hands of a young journalist named Mildred Wirt, and beginning with *The Secret of the Old Clock*, Wirt wrote nearly all of the first twenty-five Nancy Drew books published under the pen name of Carolyn Keene.

1950 Raymond Chandler accepted *Strangers on a Train*, his last job as a Hollywood screenwriter, out of curiosity: he wanted to work with Alfred Hitchcock, and Hitchcock wanted to work with him, even if it meant driving a hundred miles to Chandler's home in La Jolla for story meetings. But it didn't go well. On this day, after eight weeks and $40,000 (which nearly equaled the writer's lifetime book royalties to that point), Hitch fired Chandler. Later, when meeting with Chandler's replacement, Hitchcock is said to have held his nose and dropped Chandler's screenplay in the trash. Chandler, meanwhile, after he saw the final shooting script a couple of months later, wrote Hitch, "If you wanted something written in skim milk, why on earth did you bother to come to me in the first place?"

1964 John Updike, in the *New Republic*, on Vladimir Nabokov's *The Defense*: "His sentences are beautiful out of context and doubly beautiful in it. He writes prose the only way it should be written—that is, ecstatically."

1997 M. John Harrison, in the *TLS*, on Kurt Vonnegut's *Timequake*: "Kurt Vonnegut is old, and bored with the novel—do we have to be too?"

September 27

BORN: 1955 Charles Burns (*Black Hole*, *Big Baby*), Washington, D.C.
1958 Irvine Welsh (*Trainspotting*, *The Acid House*), Edinburgh
DIED: 1961 H.D. (*Helen in Egypt*, *Trilogy*), 75, Zurich
2009 William Safire (*On Language*, *Safire's Political Dictionary*), 79, Rockville, Md.

1912 When Rebecca West, not yet twenty, called H. G. Wells, one of the world's best-known writers and an apostle of free love in his married middle age, "the old maid among novelists" in a review of his latest book, *Marriage*, he was intrigued and invited her to lunch with his wife. In person, he was even more interested—"I had never met anything like her before"—and so was she: "I found him one of the most interesting men I have ever met. He talked straight on from 1:15 till 6:30 with immense vitality and a kind of hunger for ideas." (His wife, meanwhile, she thought was "charming, but a little effaced.") A year later, they began an affair that lasted a decade and produced a son, the writer Anthony West, who grew up with West but preferred Wells.

1960 Out of the invitation of the Soviet newspaper *Izvestia* to describe a single day in her life Christa Wolf made a life's obsession, returning every September 27 to record her day and thereby creating *One Day a Year*, a memoir accumulated from everyday moments lived amid the upheavals of history and the self-conscious drama of a life dedicated to writing. And what upheavals: from this day in 1960, when she prepared her daughter's birthday cake in Halle, East Germany, and discussed Lenin with her husband and a factory work brigade, to 2000, by which time Wolf had become the most prominent writer—a "loyal dissenter" controversial to all—in a country that no longer existed, subsumed in the unified Germany in which she now made her uneasy home.

1964 Not since *Ulysses* was a book analyzed more closely than the 888-page volume published on this day, officially titled the *Report of the President's Commission on the Assassination of President John F. Kennedy* but known almost immediately as the *Warren Report*. Selling 12,000 copies at government offices on its first day, the report, including its twenty-six volumes of supplementary documents published two months later, has been pored over ever since by historians, conspiracy theorists, and those who revere it as a magnificent repository of American life. It's "the *Oxford English Dictionary* of the assassination and also the Joycean novel," Don DeLillo said after mining it for *Libra*, "the one document that captures the full richness and madness and meaning of the event . . . When I came across the dental records of Jack Ruby's mother I felt a surge of admiration. Did they really put this in?"

1998 Courtney Weaver, in the *New York Times*, on Irvine Welsh's *Filth*: "Welsh writes with such vile, relentless intensity that he makes Louis-Ferdinand Céline, the French master of defilement, look like Little Miss Muffet."

BORN: 1943 George W. S. Trow (*Within the Context of No Context*), Greenwich, Conn. 1944 Simon Winchester (*The Professor and the Madman*), London

DIED: 1891 Herman Melville (*The Confidence-Man, Billy Budd*), 72, New York City 1970 John Dos Passos (*The 42nd Parallel, 1919, The Big Money*), 74, Baltimore

1909 The crowds are fearfully large but somehow reassuring: "Where there is no room, one needn't look for it." And above them all there is the open sky, "which is, after all, the thing that matters here." Franz Kafka and Max and Otto Brod have come to Italy, through the chaos of crowds, automobiles, and locomotives, to see an airplane show. It's less than two months since Blériot became the first to fly across the Channel, and he's here. Curtiss the American, with his massive biplane, is here. And in the crowd, celebrities: d'Annunzio, Puccini, and, according to Guy Davenport's retelling of the same episode, Wittgenstein. Kafka's report in *Bohemia* on this day, "The Aeroplanes at Brescia," one of his first published pieces, made him a pioneer of sorts too: the first in German literature to write about airplanes.

1959 It's the year of Debbie, Eddie, and Liz, and the influence of that archetypal Hollywood love triangle has seeped even into Miss Mandible's sixth-grade class at Horace Greeley Elementary: spurned Debbie Reynolds is Sue Ann Brownly, Liz Taylor the seductress is Miss Mandible herself, and disloyal Eddie Fisher is the unnamed diarist of Donald Barthelme's "Me and Miss Mandible," the breakout story in his playfully provocative career. The narrator has somehow been transported, at the age of thirty-five, from a failed career in insurance adjusting into a normal-sized kid's desk in Miss Mandible's classroom, where he hulks like Gulliver and causes passions to stir. Sue Ann, on this day, kicks him viciously in the shins, while Miss Mandible, even though she knows it will lead to her destruction, lets "her hands rest on my shoulders too warmly, and too long."

1984 Anthony Burgess, in the *TLS*, on Gore Vidal's *Lincoln*: "There is something in the puritanical American mind which is scared of the imaginative writer but not of the pedantic one who seems to humanize facts without committing himself to the inventions which are really lies."

2001 Robert Macfarlane, in the *TLS*, on Ian McEwan's *Atonement*: "The dust jacket proclaims *Atonement* his 'finest achievement,' and although publishers are prone to this Whiggishly perfectible view of their authors' talents, in this case they are triumphantly right."

September 29

BORN: 1547 Miguel de Cervantes (*Don Quixote*), Alcalá de Henares, Spain
1810 Elizabeth Gaskell (*Cranford, North and South*), London
DIED: 1902 Émile Zola (*Germinal, L'Assommoir, Nana*), 62, Paris
1967 Carson McCullers (*The Heart Is a Lonely Hunter*), 50, Nyack, N.Y.

1767 "On September 29, 1967," Alex Haley wrote in the final chapter of *Roots*, "I felt I should be nowhere else in the world except standing on a pier at Annapolis." And that's where he was, on the two-hundredth anniversary of the arrival there of a British slave ship, the *Lord Ligonier*, which had sailed from the mouth of the Gambia River with a cargo of 3,265 elephant tusks, 3,700 pounds of beeswax, 800 pounds of raw cotton, 32 ounces of gold, and 98 "choice healthy slaves," a journey whose documents allowed Haley to connect chains of oral history in his own family and in West Africa and imagine the story of his enslaved ancestor Kunta Kinte and the line of descendants to himself that became the bestselling book and epochal TV miniseries.

1929 Percy Hutchinson, in the *New York Times*, on Hemingway's *A Farewell to Arms*: "Mr. Hemingway's manner does not seem to be quite an enduring thing, any more than was Victorian heaviness enduring. But . . . seldom has a literary style so precisely jumped with the time."

1935 The history of *The Escapist* began with a failed escape. Josef Kavalier was just fourteen when he formally invited Prague's club of magicians "to witness another astounding feat of autoliberation by that prodigy of escapistry, Cavalieri, at Charles Bridge, Sunday, 29 September 1935." But his one rehearsal of his Houdini-like stunt failed—his younger brother nearly died in the cold River Moldau—and Josef's true escape had to wait until four years later, when, hidden in a coffin, he evaded the Nazi grip on Prague and made his way to New York, where, in Michael Chabon's *The Amazing Adventures of Kavalier & Clay,* he and his cousin Sammy Clay invent their Nazi-fighting comic-book superhero, the Escapist.

1939 One of the most unlikely—and successful—acts of Allied espionage in World War II was birthed in the mind of one spy-turned-novelist and promoted by another. In the early days of the war a top-secret intelligence memo written by future James Bond creator Ian Fleming suggested various far-fetched deceptions, including one scenario borrowed from *The Milliner's Hat Mystery*, a 1937 novel by former spycatcher Basil Thomson: the planting of false documents on the body of an apparent accident victim. Carried out with meticulous brilliance in 1943, the planting of such a body on the Spanish coast, as retold by Ben Macintyre in his thoroughly entertaining *Operation Mincemeat*, fooled the Nazis enough to open the door for the Allied invasion of Sicily.

1961 Burns Singer, in the *TLS*, on V. S. Naipaul's *A House for Mr. Biswas*: "Mr. Biswas is simply not worth all the detail that Mr. Naipaul spins so laboriously about him."

September 30

BORN: 1207 Rumi (*The Masnavi, The Shams*), Wakhsh, Persia
1924 Truman Capote (*Other Voices, Other Rooms*), New Orleans
DIED: 1990 Michel Leiris (*Manhood, The Rules of the Game*), 89, Saint-Hilaire, France
2006 André Schwartz-Bart (*The Last of the Just*), 78, Pointe-à-Pitre, Guadeloupe

1905 At the age of fifty-five, already granted a kind of immortality as one of the figures in Renoir's *Luncheon of the Boating Party* (he's the dandy in the top hat), Charles Ephrussi, art connoisseur and champion of the Impressionists, died in Paris after a short illness. In just a few years his friend Marcel Proust gave him further life as a model for Charles Swann, the Jewish aesthete in the first book of *In Search of Lost Time*. And a century later he returned, under his own name, as a central figure in *The Hare with Amber Eyes*, a dramatic family history by Edmund de Waal, a descendant of the Ephrussis who traces his family's rise and fall through the collection of tiny ceramic *netsuke* Charles imported from Japan, one of the few legacies that survived the family's destruction by the Nazis.

1934 In the apparently exhaustive list of the works of Pierre Menard enumerated by the narrator of Jorge Luis Borges's tale "Pierre Menard, Author of the *Quixote*" there is at least one document missing: the letter that Menard wrote the narrator on this day explaining his masterpiece, his unfinished attempt to write Cervantes's *Don Quixote*— not merely to copy it but to *write* it himself, word for word but as if from scratch, a task made admirable by its difficulty, for, as he points out, "composing the *Quixote* in the early seventeenth century was a reasonable, necessary, perhaps even inevitable undertaking; in the early twentieth, it is virtually impossible." It is a measure of Borges's audacious ingenuity that in this most delicious of his intellectual tales, he somehow convinces you that such a creation *would* be a masterpiece.

1944 It's his birthday (and it was his author's birthday too), but that's not why this September 30 sticks out for the narrator of Truman Capote's *Breakfast at Tiffany's* as "a day unlike any other I've lived." There's the runaway horse that carries him through Central Park until his friend Holly Golightly and a cop head it off. And then there are the headlines in the evening papers, alongside Holly's photograph: "PLAYGIRL ARRESTED IN NARCOTICS SCANDAL," "ARREST DOPE-SMUGGLING ACTRESS." "Don't forget," Holly says as the cops take her down the stairs, "please feed the cat." The cat sticks around, but Holly is soon gone—to Brazil, to Buenos Aires, to Africa, to another life, though she's impossible to forget. She may be a phony, it's true, but she's "a *real* phony, you know?"

October

If you like fall, you like October. It's the height of the season, the fieriest in its orange, the briskest in its breezes. "I'm so glad I live in a world where there are Octobers," exclaims the irrepressible Anne Shirley in *Anne of Green Gables*. "It would be terrible if we just skipped from September to November, wouldn't it?" October at Green Gables is "when the birches in the hollow turned as golden as sunshine and the maples behind the orchard were royal crimson" and "the fields sunned themselves in aftermaths": it's a "beautiful month."

Katherine Mansfield would have disagreed. October, she wrote in her journal, "is my unfortunate month. I dislike exceedingly to have to pass through it—each day fills me with terror." (It was the month of her birthday.) And Gabriel García Márquez's biographer notes that October, the month of the greatest disaster in his family history, when his grandfather killed a man in 1908, "would always be the gloomiest month, the time of evil augury" in his novels.

Some people, of course, seek out evil augury in October. It's the month in which we domesticate horror, as best we can, into costumes, candy, and slasher films. Frankenstein's monster may not have been animated until the full gloom of November, but it's in early October that Count Dracula visits Mina Harker in the night and forces her to drink his blood, making her flesh of his flesh. And it's in October that the Overlook Hotel shuts down for the season, leaving Jack Torrance alone for the winter with his family and his typewriter in *The Shining*, and it's in October that his son, Danny, starts saying "Redrum."

Can you domesticate horror by telling scary tales? Just as the camp counselor frightening the campers around the fire is likely the first one to get picked off when the murders begin, the four elderly members (who used to be five) of the Chowder Society in Peter Straub's *Ghost Story*, who have dealt with the disturbing death of one of their own the previous October by telling each other ghost stories, prove anything but immune to sudden terror themselves until they can trace their curse to a horrible secret they shared during an October fifty years before—just after, as it happens, another kind of modern horror, the stock market crash of 1929. In the odd patterns that human irrationality often follows, those financial terrors, the Black Thursdays and Black Mondays, tend to arrive in October too.

The Gambler by Fyodor Dostoyevsky (1867) ✎ Those planning to celebrate National Novel Writing Month in November can take heart—or heed—from Dostoyevsky's bold wager in October 1866, made to pay off his gambling debts, that if he couldn't write a novel in a month he would lose the rights to his next nine years of work. The subject he chose won't surprise you.

Ghost Stories of an Antiquary by M. R. James (1904) ✎ James had modest aims for the wittily unsettling tales, often set among the libraries and ancient archives that were his professional haunts, that he wrote to entertain his students at Eton and Cambridge. But their skillful manipulation of disgust has made them perennial favorites for connoisseurs of the macabre.

Ten Days That Shook the World by John Reed (1919) ✎ Oddly, one effect of the Russian Revolution was to modernize the calendar so the October Revolution, in retrospect, took place in November. But wherever you place those ten days, Reed, the partisan young American reporter, was there, moving through Petrograd— soon to be Leningrad—as the very ground shifted underneath him.

Peyton Place by Grace Metalious (1956) ✎ The leaves are turning red, brown, and yellow in the small New England town, while the sky is blue and the days are unseasonably warm: it must be Indian summer. But let's hear Grace Metalious tell it: "Indian summer is like a woman. Ripe, hotly passionate, but fickle."

A Wrinkle in Time by Madeleine L'Engle (1962) ✎ It's a dark and stormy October night when Meg comes downstairs to find Charles Wallace waiting precociously for her with milk warming on the stove. Soon after, blown in by the storm, arrives their strange new neighbor Mrs. Whatsit, "her mouth puckered like an autumn apple."

The Dog of the South by Charles Portis (1979) ✎ There's no particular reason to read *The Dog of the South* in October except that it begins in that month, when the leaves in Texas have gone straight from green to dead, and Ray Midge's wife, Norma, has run off with his credit cards, his Ford Torino, and his ex-friend Guy Dupree. Any month is a good month to read Charles Portis.

Black Robe by Brian Moore (1985) ✎ It's Indian summer in *Black Robe* too, but the warm days are ending and winter's coming on when Father Laforgue begins his journey to a remote Huron settlement. Based on the letters sent by seventeenth-century Jesuit missionaries in North America, *Black Robe* dramatizes the familiar clash of cultures in deeply unfamiliar but sympathetic ways.

The Road by Cormac McCarthy (2006) ✎ The landscape McCarthy's father and son travel has been razed of all civilization, and calendars have gone with it, but as their story begins the man thinks it might be October. All he knows is that they won't last another winter without finding their way south.

October 1

BORN: 1914 Daniel J. Boorstin (*The Image*, *The Discoverers*), Atlanta
1946 Tim O'Brien (*The Things They Carried*), Austin, Minn.
DIED: 2004 Richard Avedon (*Portraits*), 81, San Antonio
2012 Eric Hobsbawm (*The Age of Revolution*), 95, London

1835 "Doves & Finches swarmed round its margin," Charles Darwin wrote on this day about a tiny pool of water on Albemarle Island in the Galápagos, the only mention he made in the diaries of his five-year journey on the HMS *Beagle* of the birds that would play a central role in his theory of natural selection and that would later bear his name. Nevertheless, he brought samples of them home, as he did of countless of the islands' species, and by the time he published his account of the trip in *The Voyage of the Beagle* in 1839, he was able to theorize that the remarkable variation in the small group of bird species later known as "Darwin's finches" was due to their isolation from each other on the various islands of the archipelago.

1888 L. Frank Baum opened Baum's Bazaar on Main Street in Aberdeen, South Dakota, offering housewares, toys, and the "latest novelties in Japanese Goods, Plush, Oxidized Brass and Leather Novelties." It failed a year later.

NO YEAR *Danny the Champion of the World*, set in a countryside much like that in which Roald Dahl's tiny writing shed stood, was one of Dahl's own favorites. It's the least fantastic of his tales for children, except that few things are more fantastic for a boy than to have "the most marvelous and exciting father any boy ever had," especially one who conspires with his son to capture over a hundred tranquilized pheasants and construct a Special Extra-large Poacher's Model baby carriage to transport them, thereby ruining the grand shooting party hosted every year on the opening day of pheasant season by Mr. Victor Hazell, the piggy-eyed snob with the "glistening, gleaming Rolls-Royce" that won't be so glistening or gleaming once the pheasants have done with it.

2008 Having been named the "chief artist" of the newspaper *Izvestia* a year before on his 108th birthday, political cartoonist Boris Yefimov died on this day in Moscow at the age of 109. Born in Kiev at the end of the nineteenth century, he lived his childhood under the tsar and then for ninety years chronicled the tumultuous history of the Soviet Union and its dissolution, caricaturing its enemies as they changed and always keeping close enough to the party line to survive its many purges (his first book had a foreword by his friend Trotsky, whom he soon had to draw as an enemy of the state). After Stalin executed his brother, a famous journalist who was the model for Karkov in Hemingway's *For Whom the Bell Tolls*, Yefimov thought he'd be next, but he even survived the experience of having Stalin personally suggest and edit his cartoons.

October 2

BORN: 1879 Wallace Stevens (*Harmonium, Ideas of Order*), Reading, Pa.

1904 Graham Greene (*The Heart of the Matter*), Berkhamsted, England

DIED: 2002 Norman O. Brown (*Life Against Death*), 89, Santa Cruz, Calif.

2005 August Wilson (*The Piano Lesson, Fences*), 60, Seattle

1822 Mary Shelley began her journal again for the first time since Percy Bysshe Shelley drowned in July: "Now I am alone—oh, how alone! The stars may behold my tears, and the winds drink my sighs; but my thoughts are a sealed treasure, which I can confide to none."

1830 In the two days since she met the Reverend Edward Casaubon, who seemed at once the "most interesting man she had ever seen" and the "most distinguished-looking," young Dorothea Brooke's affection for this sallow, middle-aged bookworm has blossomed. After all, she notes decisively to her flightier sister, "Everything I see in him corresponds to his pamphlet on Biblical Cosmology." And when Mr. Casaubon, on making his goodbyes on this brisk day, alludes drily to his need for young companionship, Dorothea, glowing with the prospect of matrimony, prepares for an ill-fated decision that George Eliot is too good a novelist, and *Middlemarch* too great a novel, to make the end of her story.

1950 "Well! Here comes ol' Charlie Brown!" says Shermy to Patty in the first line in Charles M. Schulz's new comic strip. "How I hate him!"

1957 Julia Child wrote to Avis DeVoto that she had caught up with the bestselling *Peyton Place*: "Those women, stroked in the right places until they quiver like old Stradivarii! Quite enjoyed it, though feeling an underlying abyss of trash."

1968 Djuna Barnes remarked to a friend on Anaïs Nin: "Something of a pathological 'little girl' lost—sometimes a bit 'sticky,' she sees too much, she knows too much, it is intolerable."

1975 Ann Rule's career as the "Queen of True Crime" began with a haunting coincidence. A mother of four, she was writing for *True Detective* magazine under the pen name Andy Stark and taking forensic science classes when an old friend she had worked nights with on a crisis hotline called to ask if she knew why police were looking into his records. A few days later, on this day, that friend, Ted Bundy, was arrested in Utah for kidnapping, and the next morning wired a message to Rule in Seattle: "Ted Bundy wants you to know that he is all right, that things will work out." Rule's first book, *The Stranger Beside Me*, describes how things did work out, and how Rule came to learn the true story of the serial killer she had once thought of as "almost the perfect man."

October 3

BORN: 1924 Harvey Kurtzman (editor of *Mad* and *Help!*, *Little Annie Fanny*), Brooklyn
1925 Gore Vidal (*Burr*, *Julian*, *Myra Breckinridge*), West Point, N.Y.
DIED: 1896 William Morris (*News from Nowhere*, Kelmscott Press), 62, London
1967 Woody Guthrie (*Bound for Glory*), 55, New York City

1802 On the night before her brother, William, married her friend Mary Hutchinson, Dorothy Wordsworth wore Mary's wedding ring on her own finger while she slept.

1860 Sailing north from the equator toward San Francisco, his last novel published three years before, Herman Melville marked this passage in his copy of Chapman's Homer with an underline and an exclamation: "The work that I was born to do is done!"

1918 It wasn't until he was thirty-seven, with four novels published and one, *Maurice*, written but kept secret because of the gay relationship at its heart, that E. M. Forster first had sex. Stationed in Egypt with the Red Cross during the war, he confessed in coded language to a friend, "Yesterday, for the first time in my life I parted with respectability. I have felt the step would be taken for many months. I have tried to take it before. It has left me curiously sad." But he wasn't sad at all when, a few years later, he fell in love with an Egyptian man. "I am so happy," he wrote on this day. "I wish I was writing the latter half of *Maurice* now. I know so much more. It is awful to think of the thousands who go through youth without ever knowing."

1933 Lacking the $1.83 in postage to submit the manuscript of her first book, *Jonah's Gourd Vine*, to a publisher, Zora Neale Hurston prevailed upon the local chapter of the Daughter Elks to borrow the funds from their treasury.

1951 It's the set piece to end all set pieces: Sinatra, Gleason, and Hoover in the stands, Durocher, Maglie, Robinson, and Mays on the field, Ross Hodges on the mic, and the Giants and the Dodgers playing for the pennant. Branca throws to Thomson, Gleason throws up on Sinatra's shoes, Pafko goes back to the wall, the Giants win the pennant, and a kid named Cotter Martin runs off with the ball. Published as a special insert in *Harper's* in 1992 and as a book of its own in 2001, "Pafko at the Wall" also stands as the masterful prologue to Don DeLillo's 1997 epic, *Underworld*.

1999 Verlyn Klinkenborg, in the *New York Times*, on Kent Haruf's *Plainsong*: "Haruf has made a novel so foursquare, so delicate and lovely, that it has the power to exalt the reader."

2008 Will Heinrich, in the *New York Observer*, on Stieg Larsson's *The Girl with the Dragon Tattoo*: "To call the dialogue wooden would be an insult to longbows and violins. And yet, I had no trouble finishing the book—on the contrary, I raced through it, even while I disliked it, and myself for reading it."

October 4

BORN: 1937 Jackie Collins (*Hollywood Wives*, *The Stud*), London
1941 Anne Rice (*Interview with the Vampire*), New Orleans
DIED: 1974 Anne Sexton (*The Awful Rowing Toward God*), 45, Weston, Mass.
1988 Geoffrey Household (*Rogue Male*), 87, Banbury, England

1866 Made desperate by his debts, Fyodor Dostoyevsky reluctantly signed in July 1865 an agreement whose predatory conditions might well have come from a fairy tale: if he failed to complete a 160-page novel by November 1, 1866, his publisher would have the right to all his works for the next nine years without compensation. He paid off some creditors with the rubles and gambled away the rest, but, busy with another book, *Crime and Punishment*, he put off the contracted novel until this day, less than a month before his deadline, when he finally engaged a young stenographer, Anna Grigorievna, to help him. He dictated the story of *The Gambler* to her every afternoon, turned in the manuscript two hours before the deadline, and then, when they met a week later to resume his work on *Crime and Punishment*, asked for Anna's hand in marriage, which she granted.

1981 Bernd Heinrich was a quickly rising star professor in the field of entomology (he had published extensively on bumblebees), and was beginning a career in nature writing that would later include *The Mind of the Raven* and *Winter World*, but to the other runners at the start of the North American 100 km ultramarathon championship he was an unknown (though he had won the Masters Division of the Boston Marathon the year before). He'd never competed at any length beyond the marathon before, but, using his expertise in animal physiology, he'd trained all summer in the Maine woods while doing his biological fieldwork and by the end of the race he had set, at age forty-one, a new American 100 km record of 6:38:20 (that's sixty-two 6:40 miles), a mark that stood for over a decade and an experience that's the climax of his book on the human and animal capacities for endurance, *Why We Run*.

1986 The New York District Attorney's office may have eventually been satisfied that the wondrously bizarre attack on Dan Rather this evening—in which the CBS newsman was beaten by two well-dressed men shouting, "Kenneth, what is the frequency?"—was perpetrated by a paranoid delusional named William Tager, but Paul Limbert Allman has suggested another suspect: the late, bearded fabulist Donald Barthelme. Writing in *Harper's* in 2001 (and later adapting his article for the stage), Allman assembled his clues—the striking appearance of the phrase "What is the frequency?" and a character named Kenneth in Barthelme's *Sixty Stories*, along with the fact that Rather and Barthelme, Texans born just six months apart, likely knew each other as reporters in Houston in the 1960s—into a deadpan tale that, if it never quite reaches plausibility, at least has the makings of a good Barthelme story.

October 5

BORN: 1949 Bill James (*Bill James Baseball Abstract*), Holton, Kans.
1952 Clive Barker (*Books of Blood, Weaveworld, Abarat*), Liverpool
DIED: 1962 Sylvia Beach (Shakespeare & Company), 75, Paris
2003 Neil Postman (*Amusing Ourselves to Death*), 72, New York City

1814 Percy Bysshe Shelley read Coleridge's "Rime of the Ancient Mariner" aloud to Mary Godwin.

1927 She had been mulling the idea for months—a fictional biography of her friend Vita Sackville-West, with whom she'd had a short affair and a long fascination—and on this day, her other work done, Virginia Woolf allowed herself to begin it: "a biography beginning in the year 1500 & continuing to the present day, called Orlando: Vita; only with a change about from one sex to another." She quickly gave herself up "to the pure delight of this farce," and then asked her subject's permission to write about "the lusts of your flesh and the lure of your mind." Vita was equally delighted: "What fun for you; what fun for me," she replied. "Yes, go ahead, toss up your pancake, brown it nicely on both sides, pour brandy over it, and serve hot."

1937 Richard Wright, in the *New Masses*, on Zora Neale Hurston's *Their Eyes Were Watching God*:

"Her novel is not addressed to the Negro, but to a white audience whose chauvinistic tastes she knows how to satisfy."

1949 "Gentlemen: Your ad in the Saturday Review of Literature says that you specialize in out-of-print books." So began, with uncharacteristic formality, the first letter Helene Hanff, a television scriptwriter and book-loving Anglophile in New York, sent to Marks & Co., a London bookshop located at 84, Charing Cross Road, in search of essays by Hazlitt, Stevenson, and Hunt. She soon sloughed off her initial propriety ("I hope 'madam' doesn't mean over there what it does over here," she remarked in her second letter), but it took over two years for her London bookselling correspondent, Frank Doel, to drop the "Miss Hanff" for "Helene" and more than two decades for Hanff to cross the Atlantic for her long-promised visit to the shop. By that time Doel had died, but their letters had already been immortalized in the collection *84, Charing Cross Road*.

ORLANDO

144

Orlando on her return to England

BORN: 1895 Caroline Gordon (*None Shall Look Back*), Todd County, Ky.

1914 Thor Heyerdahl (*Kon-Tiki, Aku-Aku*), Larvik, Norway

DIED: 1892 Alfred Tennyson (*In Memoriam A.H.H., Idylls of the King*), 83, Lurgashall, England

1979 Elizabeth Bishop (*North & South, A Cold Spring*), 68, Boston

1536 The unapproved possession of a Bible translated into English was a crime in England punishable by excommunication or death when William Tyndale, a graduate of Oxford with half a dozen languages at his command, moved to Germany in 1524 and began his own translation of the New Testament. By 1526 copies of his translation were being smuggled back into England, and a decade later, while living in Antwerp, Tyndale was arrested and convicted of heresy by the Holy Roman Emperor. Tradition has it that this is the day he was strangled and burned to death, with the final words "Lord, open the King of England's eyes." Not long after, Henry VIII did indeed approve an English translation of the Bible, and when King James commissioned his own version in the next century, a majority of its words were taken from Tyndale's once-heretical translation.

1834 From 1832, when a woman in Odessa sent him an anonymous fan letter signed "The Stranger," to 1850, just months before his death, when he married his admirer, who turned out to be a Polish noblewoman named Eveline Hańska, Honoré de Balzac carried on the most passionate correspondence of his life. He had to wait for her hand until the death of her husband and then had to compete with, among others, Franz Liszt for her affections. In return, he always declared she only had one competitor for his heart: his work on the vast series of novels called the *Comédie humaine* he outlined to her on this day. "I have now shown you my real mistress," he confessed. "I have removed her veils . . . [T]here is she who takes my nights, my days, who puts a price on this very letter, taken from hours of study—but with delight."

1919 When she moved into shared lodgings with Ivy Compton-Burnett on this day, Margaret Jourdain was already a grand figure: a poet, an admired authority on English furniture and interior design, and the sharp-tongued center of an active social circle. Ivy was the opposite: withdrawn and drab, fading into the wallpaper (the provenance of which Margaret was no doubt an expert). So when Ivy began in the next decade to gain a small but shocking celebrity from her novels, their circle was horrified, not only at the vaguely disreputable activity of novel-writing, but that it was Ivy, the nonentity, who was becoming known by scribbling away behind her silent facade. Even Margaret claimed she had been unaware that her companion had published a novel at all until she produced *Pastors and Masters* "from under the bedclothes."

October 7

BORN: 1964 Dan Savage (*Savage Love, The Kid*), Chicago
1966 Sherman Alexie (*The Absolutely True Diary of a Part-Time Indian*), Wellpinit, Wash.
DIED: 1849 Edgar Allan Poe ("The Tell-Tale Heart," "The Purloined Letter"), 40, Baltimore
1943 Radclyffe Hall (*The Well of Loneliness, Adam's Breed*), 63, London

1804 It's not until halfway through his *Confessions of an English Opium-Eater* that Thomas de Quincey eats his first opium. After twenty days of unbearable pain from toothache and rheumatism he went out on a "wet and cheerless" London Sunday that one biographer places in early October, met a college friend who suggested opium, and obtained a tincture at a druggist. It did not merely ease his pain. "Here was a panacea," he remembered almost twenty years later when he was in the depths of addiction, "for all human woes . . . Happiness might now be bought for a penny, and carried in the waistcoat-pocket." His daily doses didn't begin for another decade, but the forty years after that were consumed in desperate cycles of consumption and withdrawal.

1924 Having finally read the manuscript of T. E. Lawrence's *Seven Pillars of Wisdom* after spending two years attempting to arrange its publication, George Bernard Shaw reprimanded the young soldier about his punctuation: "You practically do not use semicolons at all. This is a symptom of mental defectiveness, probably induced by camp life."

1955 Jack Kerouac, passing jugs of red wine around the audience, couldn't be convinced to come up and read his work, but the crowd of a hundred or so at a San Francisco auto-repair-shop-turned-performance-space called Six Gallery recognized that the five poets who did read—Philip Lamantia, Michael McClure, Philip Whalen, Allen Ginsberg, and Gary Snyder—had done something rare: they had changed poetry. Or rather Ginsberg had, in just his second public performance and his first reading of *Howl*, the first part of which he had composed a month and a half before in one blow, "sounding like you," he wrote Kerouac, "an imitation practically." At the reading, as Ginsberg built to his anguished and ecstatic climax, Kerouac drummed on a wine jug and yelled "Go!" from the audience for rhythm.

1971 Michael Ratcliffe, in the *Times*, on E. M. Forster's posthumous *Maurice*: "It doesn't work . . . Two of Forster's strongest cards—the spirit of place and the fringe of emasculating women—are scarcely played at all, though he holds them in his hand and needs them to win this particular game like no other."

BORN: **1917** Walter Lord (*A Night to Remember, Day of Infamy*), Baltimore

1920 Frank Herbert (*Dune, God Emperor of Dune*), Tacoma, Wash.

DIED: **1754** Henry Fielding (*Tom Jones, Joseph Andrews*), 47, Lisbon

1945 Felix Salten (*Bambi, Josephine Mutzenbacher*), 76, Zurich

1762 After receiving a turtle on his nomination to local office, Edward Gibbon hosted a dinner for forty-eight supporters consisting of "six dishes of turtle, eight of Game with jellies, Syllabubs, tarts, puddings, pine apples, in all three and twenty things besides a large piece of roast beef on the side."

1818 The vicious, class-baiting contempt with which John Keats's *Endymion* was greeted is well known: "Back to the shop Mr John, back to plasters, pills, and ointment boxes," scoffed *Blackwood's* about his "imperturbable drivelling idiocy." Some, including Lord Byron, have claimed the bad reviews drove the young poet to his death, but Keats himself, though wounded, showed a resilient indifference in a letter to his publisher on this day. He was his own fiercest critic, after all: "My own domestic criticism has given me pain without comparison beyond what Blackwood or the Quarterly could possibly inflict." With his "slipshod Endymion," he added, he had "leaped headlong into the Sea, and thereby have become better acquainted with the Soundings, the quicksands, and the rocks, than if I had stayed upon the green shore, and piped a silly pipe, and took tea and comfortable advice. I was never afraid of failure;

for I would sooner fail than not be among the greatest."

1846 To Louise Colet, jealous of a letter he had written an old flame, Gustave Flaubert protested that he didn't seriously love the other woman, or rather, that he did, "but *only when I was writing.*"

1945 One story begins, "He came into the world in the middle of a thicket, in one of those little, hidden forest glades." The other opens, "The saying is that young whores eventually become old religious crones, but that was not my case." During his prolific Viennese career, Felix Salten, who died on this day, was best known as the author of the first novel, *Bambi*, which became an American bestseller (translated by Alger Hiss's future antagonist, Whittaker Chambers) well before it found its way to Walt Disney. Disney adapted two more of Salten's stories, but he never would have touched the second book above: *Josephine Mutzenbacher*, a legendary, often banned, and anonymously published pornographic novel that has sold millions. Salten never acknowledged he wrote it, but scholars have come to believe the speculation that he did, and after his death his family even sued (unsuccessfully) to claim its significant royalties.

1964 His Canadian publisher, Jack McClelland, informed Mordecai Richler that "you are absolutely out of your mind. Why in hell anybody would turn down an offer of $7,000 to go to Africa to write a film script, I'm damned if I know. You must have more money than brains."

October 9

BORN: 1899 Bruce Catton (*A Stillness at Appomattox*), Petoskey, Mich.
  1934 Jill Ker Conway (*The Road from Coorain*), Hillston, Australia
DIED: 2003 Carolyn Heilbrun (*Writing a Woman's Life*, Amanda Cross novels), 77, New York City
  2004 Jacques Derrida (*Of Grammatology*), 74, Paris

1849 Rarely has the choice of a literary executor been so poorly made as when Edgar Allan Poe, ailing at age forty, asked a fellow editor—and sometimes rival—named Rufus W. Griswold to oversee the publication of his works after his death. When Poe died in a delirium a few months later, Griswold fulfilled his obligation by publishing a vicious obituary in the *New York Tribune* on this day that portrayed Poe as a talented but friendless madman whose death no one mourned. The following year, he continued his attack with an edition of Poe's works in which he made up scurrilous quotes from Poe's unpublished letters and falsely claimed the late author had plagiarized, been expelled from college, deserted the army, and seduced his stepmother, a portrait that became the dominant image of Poe for decades to come.

1890 The trouble with fictional chronologies is that sometimes the math just doesn't add up. It sharpens our sense of Sherlock Holmes as a living presence to read such concrete details as the posted notice in one of his best-loved cases that "THE RED-HEADED LEAGUE IS DISSOLVED, October 9, 1890." The problem, though, as generations of Holmesians have debated, is that Mr. Jabez Wilson, the red-headed dupe of the tale, says he only worked at the league for two months before it mysteriously dissolved, but also that he began there in April (six months before October). How to account for the discrepancy? Rather than blaming sloppy storytelling by Watson or his creator Arthur Conan Doyle, some imaginative readers like Brad Keefauver have credited it to a clumsy attempt by Wilson to hide the amount he earned at the league, in hopes of lowering the fee he'd owe Holmes.

1899 "With this pencil I wrote the MS. of 'The Emerald City.' Finished Oct. 9th, 1899." "The Emerald City" wasn't the only title L. Frank Baum considered for his manuscript—he tried "The Land of Oz," "From Kansas to Fairyland," and "The City of the Great Oz" before settling on *The Wonderful Wizard of Oz*—but he felt strongly enough he had created something memorable that he framed the message above, along with the pencil. The month before *Oz* was published, Baum told his brother it was "the best thing I ever have written" and that his publisher expected to sell a quarter of a million copies. Although *Oz* didn't match the sales of Baum's earlier *Father Goose* before his publisher went bankrupt in 1902, by the time its copyright expired in 1956 there were four million copies of *The Wonderful Wizard of Oz* in print.

BORN: **1950** Nora Roberts (*Angels Fall, Naked in Death*), Silver Spring, Md.

1959 Jaime Hernandez (*Love and Rockets, Locas*), Oxnard, Calif.

DIED: **1837** Charles Fourier (*The Theory of the Four Movements*), 65, Paris

1973 Ludwig von Mises (*The Theory of Money and Credit*), 92, New York City

1914 "Married life really is the greatest institution that ever was," P. G. Wodehouse declared ten days after his wedding. "When I look back and think of the rotten time I have been having all my life, compared with this, it makes me sick."

1939 George Orwell harvested five eggs from his hens and made two pounds of blackberry jelly.

1947 Fired as a publisher's assistant, William Styron reported to his father he was glad, since publishing is "only a counterfeit, a reflection, of really creative work."

1947 Edith Sitwell, in the *Spectator*, on Northrop Frye's *Fearful Symmetry: A Study of William Blake*: "To say it is a magnificent, extraordinary book is to praise it as it should be praised, but in doing so one gives little idea of the huge scope of the book and of its fiery understanding."

1986 J. D. Salinger had refused requests for an interview for over twenty years, since ending his publishing career and removing himself from the public eye in 1965, but on this day he submitted to one, under duress, at the Manhattan offices of his attorney at the Satterlee Stephens law firm. His interviewer was a lawyer representing Random House and its author Ian Hamilton, whose forthcoming biography of Salinger used quotations from his personal letters that Salinger objected to strongly enough that he was willing to sit through a deposition. The process was, by all accounts, excruciating, as the lawyer extracted from the reclusive author a description of what he had been writing since 1965—"Just a work of fiction. That's all."—and for hours walked him through the nearly one hundred letters Hamilton had quoted, which Salinger said were written by a "gauche" and "callow" young man he could hardly recognize.

2006 At the center of Anthony Swofford's third book, *Hotels, Hospitals, and Jails*, is a remarkable document, an eight-page handwritten letter from his father carrying six dates of composition between July and October and a final message added on this day: "I have sat on this for much too long . . . It is well past time to shred or mail. So mail here it comes. With Love, Your Father." And so it came: a bill of grievances both petty and substantial, each with an accounting at the end: "You get a pass on that" or "No pass here." And while Swofford's book, *Hotels, Hospitals, and Jails*, is in part a raw confession of his self-destructive misbehavior after his first book, *Jarhead*, made him rich and famous, it is also a bill of grievances of his own, a book-length reply to his father's letter that he feels he has to write before becoming a father himself.

October 11

BORN: 1925 Elmore Leonard (*Hombre, Rum Punch, Out of Sight*), New Orleans
   1962 Anne Enright (*The Gathering, What Are You Like?*), Dublin
DIED: 1809 Meriwether Lewis (*The Journals of Lewis and Clark*), 35, Hohenwald, Tenn.
   1963 Jean Cocteau (*The Holy Terrors*), 74, Milly-la-Forêt, France

1843 "Began the Chinese tale," Hans Christian Andersen noted tersely in his diary on this day. By the next evening he had finished "The Nightingale," the story of a songbird whose voice is so beautiful it draws death away from the dying emperor, a tale whose inspiration he'd recorded just a month before in the same diary, and with equal concision. "Jenny Lind's first performance as Alice," he wrote of the young singer already stirring a frenzy as the "Swedish Nightingale." "In love." He spent nearly all of the next ten days with her, giving her poems, a portrait of himself, a briefcase, and, just as she was leaving town, most likely a marriage proposal. She didn't accept the latter, remaining friends with Andersen for the rest of their lives but always being careful to refer to them as "brother" and "sister."

1928 Arthur Sydney McDowell, in the *TLS*, on Virginia Woolf's *Orlando*: "It is a fantasy, impossible but delicious; existing in its own right by the colour of imagination and an exuberance of life and wit."

1947 Published: *Se questo è un uomo* (*If This Is a Man/Survival in Auschwitz*) by Primo Levi (De Silva, Turin)

1949 Richard Wright had fielded offers before to turn *Native Son* into a movie (MGM, astoundingly, had once been interested in filming it with an all-white cast), but when French director Pierre Chenal suggested making the movie in Argentina, he accepted. But who would play the lead role of Bigger Thomas? Wright suggested Canada Lee, a sensation in Orson Welles's stage version, but Chenal had an improbable idea: why not Wright himself? Even more improbably, Wright took the role, and on this day, having trimmed twenty-five pounds on the voyage, he arrived in Buenos Aires to begin shooting what they hoped would be the biggest movie ever made in South America. Acclaimed in Argentina, the film was panned after being chopped by a third for U.S. and European distribution.

2007 Greeted by reporters on her London doorstep with the news that she had won the Nobel Prize for Literature at age eighty-seven, Doris Lessing put her grocery bags down and sighed, "Oh, Christ."

BORN: 1939 James Crumley (*The Last Good Kiss*), Three Rivers, Tex.
1949 Richard Price (*Clockers*, *Lush Life*), Bronx, N.Y.
DIED: 1926 Edwin A. Abbott (*Flatland*), 87, London
2010 Belva Plain (*Evergreen*, *Promises*), 95, Short Hills, N.J.

1713 Surely it's no coincidence that Neal Stephenson's Baroque Cycle, his three-volume, nearly 3,000-page epic of the Age of Enlightenment, begins on this day with the execution of a witch: the triumph of rationality is never a sure, or linear, outcome. On the same day, Enoch Root arrives at the bustling frontier outpost of Boston to deliver a letter to one of its many immigrants, Daniel Waterhouse. Waterhouse, once a friend of both Newton and Leibniz and now the founder of a misbegotten academy, the Massachusetts Bay Colony Institute of Technologickal Arts, has been summoned back to Europe to mediate the supremely irrational dispute between the two inventors of the calculus and thereby rescue the path toward progress that Root promises, with Stephenson's usual brand of anachronistic cheek, will ultimately make Waterhouse's own institute a glorious campus dedicated to the "art of automatic computing."

1927 Edith Wharton married Teddy Wharton and had her most passionate affair with Morton Fullerton, but it was about Walter Van Rensselaer Berry that she wrote in her diary after his death, "The Love of all my life died today, & I with him." Berry had not taken either of his two clear opportunities to propose to her, once when they first met in Maine in their youth and once after she finally divorced the miserable Teddy twenty years later, but they were close allies in public and private for the second half of her life. The social columnists considered him the model for Selden in *The House of Mirth*, and her friends assumed they were lovers, but her biographers have been less sure, in part because she got into his apartment soon after his death and burned nearly all the letters she'd written him.

1961 The loudest explosion in the salvo of contempt that greeted the publication of *Webster's Third New International Dictionary* was launched from the heights of the *New York Times* editorial page. Mocking the *Webster's* lexicographers with some of their own approved language as "double-domes" who "have been confabbing and yakking for twenty-seven years," the *Times* called for a return to the old *Webster's Second*. Outrage against the *Third*'s "permissiveness" became infectious: critics misled by the dictionary's own press release knocked it for okaying slang with headlines like "Saying Ain't Ain't Wrong," Dwight Macdonald published a twenty-page takedown of the dictionary in *The New Yorker*, and in *Gambit* Rex Stout had his fastidious sleuth Nero Wolfe feed pages from the *Third* into the fire.

1979 Published: *The Hitchhiker's Guide to the Galaxy* by Douglas Adams (Arthur Barker, London)

October 13

BORN: 1890 Conrad Richter (*The Light in the Forest*), Pine Grove, Pa.
  1902 Arna Bontemps (*Black Thunder*), Alexandria, La.
DIED: 1995 Henry Roth (*Call It Sleep*), 89, Albuquerque, N.M.
  2002 Stephen E. Ambrose (*Undaunted Courage*), 66, Bay St. Louis, Miss.

1819 John Keats, twenty-three, was already ill with the tuberculosis that would kill him less than two years later when his love for the young Fanny Brawne reached its feverish height. On this day, in a dash-filled letter, he struggled to find a language for his passion: "I have been astonished that Men could die Martyrs for religion—I have shudder'd at it—I shudder no more—I could be martyr'd for my Religion—Love is my religion—I could die for that—I could die for you." A few days later, it is thought, he gave her a ring to seal their secret engagement. It's also speculated that this was the same week he found a more disciplined language for his love in the sonnet that begins "Bright star! would I were steadfast as thou art," which for two centuries since has set its readers to swooning.

1926 "We have so many bedbugs," Isaac Babel wrote his mother from Moscow, "that it has become a legend among the other dwellers in our apartment."

1958 At a Buddhist temple on the Upper West Side on this day, as described in *How I Became Hettie Jones*, her memoir of bohemian life among the Beats, Hettie Cohen became Hettie Jones, marrying LeRoi Jones, a poet she'd met when they both worked for a small Greenwich Village magazine for record collectors. Her husband would later change his own name, to Amiri Baraka, when he moved to Harlem in 1965 and helped launch the Black Arts movement, while Hettie Jones (whom Baraka, to add to the confusion of names, called "Nellie Kohn" in his own memoir, *The Autobiography of LeRoi Jones*) stayed in lower Manhattan with their two daughters and remained Hettie Jones.

1958 Published: *A Bear Called Paddington* by Michael Bond (Collins, London)

1997 David Foster Wallace, in the *New York Observer*, on John Updike's *Toward the End of Time*: "A novel so mind-bendingly clunky and self-indulgent that it's hard to believe the author let it be published in this kind of shape."

2001 Chided again by critic James Wood for the "hysterical realism" he said her fiction shared with DeLillo, Rushdie, Wallace, and others, Zadie Smith wryly admitted in the *Guardian* that although in her first novel she may have aspired to the spareness of Kafka, she "wrote like a script editor for *The Simpsons* who'd briefly joined a religious cult and then discovered Foucault. Such is life." Now, though, in the weeks after September 11, she added, she was "sitting here in my pants, looking at a blank screen, finding nothing funny, scared out of my mind like everybody else."

BORN: **1894** E. E. Cummings (*The Enormous Room*), Cambridge, Mass.
1942 Péter Nádas (*A Book of Memories*), Budapest
DIED: **1959** Errol Flynn (*My Wicked, Wicked Ways*), 50, Vancouver, B.C.
1997 Harold Robbins (*The Carpetbaggers*), 81, Palm Springs, Calif.

1667 Having been expelled from his Jewish community in Amsterdam in 1656 for his heretical teachings, the philosopher Baruch Spinoza taught himself to grind lenses, a craft of newfound interest in that age of explorations with the telescope and the microscope, and one in keeping with his radical belief in a God of nature, not of man. Over time, his skills increased to where his fame as a lens grinder approached his infamy as the "atheist Jew"; in a letter on this day, Christiaan Huygens, the discoverer of Saturn's moon Titan, praised the lenses of "the Jew of Voorburg" for their "admirable polish." Over time, however, the grinding may have also hastened Spinoza's death from a lung disease often blamed on the glass dust he inhaled every day.

1939 Ambitious and prolific, Thomas Merton spent his twenty-fifth summer with two friends in a cottage in upstate New York, each writing a novel he thought would make his name. Back in New York City in the fall, Merton got a publisher's rejection slip for his novel on this day; when he called to ask why, they said it was dull and badly written, and Merton realized he agreed. But by that time his mind had moved on to other things: in a jazz club that same month, disgusted with his life, he realized he wanted to become a priest. A decade later he told the story of his awakening in *The Seven Storey Mountain*, a memoir written from his new life in a Trappist monastery that, neither dull nor badly written, became an immediate bestseller and a Catholic touchstone.

1972 The *New Republic* on Hunter S. Thompson's *Fear and Loathing in Las Vegas*: "This is more hype than book. It needs some humanity and a better idea of what time it is."

1994 As he did every Friday afternoon for years, Naguib Mahfouz, frail and nearly blind and deaf at age eighty-two, crossed from his apartment to the waiting car of a friend who would drive him to a café for his weekly meeting with other Cairo writers and intellectuals. From the sidewalk a young man greeted him, as many did, but when Mahfouz reached out through the open car window to shake his hand, the man stabbed him in the neck. The attack, which Mahfouz outlived by a dozen years, came on the sixth anniversary of his Nobel Prize for Literature—the first for an Arabic writer—but what was the cause? Mahfouz's condemnation of the fatwa against Salman Rushdie for *The Satanic Verses*, or his own controversial religious allegory, *Children of Gebelaawi*, which had been judged heretical and banned in Egypt thirty-five years before?

October 15

BORN: 1844 Friedrich Nietzsche (*Thus Spoke Zarathustra*), Röcken, Prussia
1881 P. G. Wodehouse (*Carry On, Jeeves*), Guildford, England
1923 Italo Calvino (*Invisible Cities*), Santiago de las Vegas, Cuba
DIED: 1968 Virginia Lee Burton (*Mike Mulligan and His Steam Shovel*), 59, Boston

1764 By his own account, Edward Gibbon, on his first visit to the Eternal City, was inspired to write *The History of the Decline and Fall of the Roman Empire* by the presence of its glorious but deteriorating past: "It was at Rome on the fifteenth of October 1764, as I sat musing amidst the ruins of the Capitol while the barefooted fryars were singing Vespers in the temple of Jupiter, that the idea of writing the decline and fall of the City first started to my mind." Some later historians have been skeptical of the exactness of this memory, which he didn't describe until thirty years later, but few were skeptical of the *Decline and Fall* itself, whose innovative use of primary sources created the standard for modern history.

1920 Katherine Mansfield, in the *Athenaeum*, on Gertrude Stein's *Three Lives*: "Miss Gertrude Stein has discovered a new way of writing stories. It is just to keep right on writing them. Don't mind how often you go back to the beginning, don't hesitate to say the same thing over and over again—people are always repeating themselves—don't be put off if the words sound funny at times: just keep right on, and by the time you've done writing you'll have produced your effect."

1967 The standing ovation Richard Burton received when he read from David Jones's *In Parenthesis* on the same stage as W. H. Auden left Auden with, at least according to Burton's diary, a "ghostly smile" and a look of "surprise, malice, and envy."

1976 Among the things Eleanor Coppola took note of on this day while her husband, Francis, was shooting thirty-eight takes of a scene at Colonel Kurtz's compound for *Apocalypse Now*: the severed heads played by local people, who were buried in the ground all day, drinking Cokes; a man giving a boa constrictor a sip of water; fake blood being used up fast at $35 a gallon; kids "putting chunks of dry ice in film cans and making the lids pop off." Coppola was on set in the Philippines to shoot a documentary about the making of the picture; the documentary, the wonderful *Hearts of Darkness*, wasn't released until 1991, but her diary of the production, *Notes*, was published in 1979, the same year the movie came out, and it's a calm and observant record of a tumultuous experience.

2012 James Wood, in *The New Yorker*, on Tom Wolfe's *Back to Blood*: "In the regime of the enforced exclamation mark, everyone is equal."

BORN: **1854** Oscar Wilde (*The Picture of Dorian Gray*), Dublin

1888 Eugene O'Neill (*A Long Day's Journey into Night*), New York City

DIED: **1997** James A. Michener (*Hawaii, Chesapeake, Space*), 90, Austin, Tex.

1999 Jean Shepherd (*In God We Trust, All Others Pay Cash*), 78, Sanibel Island, Fla.

1892 The *New York Times* on Arthur Conan Doyle's *Adventures of Sherlock Holmes*: "You may care for one detective story, but when there is a round dozen you may get a fit of indigestion . . . Sherlock Holmes, with all his *mise en scène*, has too much of premeditation about him. You weary of his perspicacity."

1933 Evicted from her Florida apartment for unpaid back rent of $18, Zora Neale Hurston received a wire from Lippincott offering her a $200 advance for her first novel, *Jonah's Gourd Vine*: "I never expect to have a greater thrill than that wire gave me. You know the feeling when you found your first pubic hair. Greater than that."

1935 Dismissed on this day by the Nazi regime from his position at the University of Marburg because he was a Jew, Erich Auerbach arranged to resume his career in exile at Istanbul University, where he continued his labors on one of the monumental works of literary analysis, *Mimesis*, an imaginative and approachable multilingual survey of the literary representation of reality from Dante to Virginia Woolf. His achievement was only made more impressive by his distance from the usual reference materials he would have had in Europe, a condition he modestly deflected in his epilogue to the book: "If it had been possible for me to acquaint myself with all the work that has been done on so many subjects, I might have never reached the point of writing."

1952 To his son in Rome, spending a year in residence at the American Academy, William Styron Sr. wrote, "Son, don't eat so much Italian food that you will grow gross and heavy like Thomas Wolfe. Extra weight certainly shortens our lives."

1961 Published: *Mastering the Art of French Cooking*, vol. 1, by Simone Beck, Louisette Bertholle, and Julia Child (Knopf, New York)

1995 However many men there actually were at the Million Man March at the National Mall in 1995, we only see a handful of them in Z. Z. Packer's story "An Ant of the Self" in *Drinking Coffee Elsewhere*, and we only learn the names of two: Ray Bivens Jr. and his son, Spurgeon, who are there on an ill-fated mission to sell some black men some birds. Spurgeon—"nerdy ol' Spurgeon"—can't explain what makes him skip his debate tournament to drive his dad to D.C. in his mom's car after bailing him out of a DUI, nor can he explain what drives him into a bloody battle with Ray Jr. on a suburban sidewalk in the middle of the night after the march, but there's something in him, alongside his ambition, that wants to know the feeling of scraping bottom.

October 17

BORN: 1903 Nathanael West (*Miss Lonelyhearts*, *The Day of the Locust*), New York City
1915 Arthur Miller (*Death of a Salesman*, *The Crucible*), New York City
DIED: 1973 Ingeborg Bachmann (*Malina*, *The Book of Franza*), 47, Rome
1979 S. J. Perelman (*Crazy Like a Fox*, *Westward Ha!*), 75, New York City

1861 E. S. Dennis, in the *Times*, on Charles Dickens's *Great Expectations*: "Faults there are in abundance, but who is going to find fault when the very essence of the fun is to commit faults?"

1945 On this day Ava Gardner became the fifth wife of the clarinet-playing lothario Artie Shaw, who put the starlet on a reading program so she might be worthy of the frequently bestowed title of "Mrs. Artie Shaw": *The Brothers Karamazov*, *Babbitt*, *Tropic of Cancer*, *The Origin of Species*. But he'd deny the story Gardner later loved to tell, that he mocked her when he caught her reading Kathleen Winsor's bodice-ripping bestseller *Forever Amber*. No doubt Gardner liked to tell it because just a few days after Shaw divorced her, he rushed down to Mexico, where Kathleen Winsor herself, sultry enough that some thought she should star in the movie of her own book, became Mrs. Artie Shaw number six.

1964 It was with great relief that Richard Hughes confirmed to his publisher on this day, after a visit to the Pinewood Studios, that "John *does* break his neck . . . , Emily *does* murder the prisoner and *does* bring the pirates to the gallows." Hughes's *A High Wind in Jamaica*, one of the strange and great novels of the century, had long drawn interest from movie producers, but only in 1964 did a big-budget production commence, starring Anthony Quinn and James Coburn as pirates and, as the doomed John, one of the children who prove more terrible than their pirate captors, a child actor in his only film role, the future novelist Martin Amis, who later recalled that the visiting author was "pleased, impressed, tickled" by the production, as well as "otiously tall."

1969 "The plain fact is, Mr. Hayes, I have earned this job—through great love of the short story and great labor to know it." Gordon Lish was thirty-five, a frustrated and restless textbook editor, when he heard that one of the biggest jobs in his little business, fiction editor at *Esquire*, was open. "I want this job," he declared in a long letter to editor in chief Harold Hayes, "and I want it with more eagerness than is becoming to a man of my age because this is the work I was meant to do, and because I have not been doing it." *Esquire* took a chance on him and for the next seven years, calling himself "Captain Fiction," Lish championed new writers like Barry Hannah, Richard Ford, and his old friend Raymond Carver.

1978 "The evidence of copying," expert witness Michael Wood testified in the trial of whether Alex Haley had plagiarized portions of *Roots* from Harold Courlander's *The African*, "is clear and irrefutable."

October 18

BORN: 1777 Heinrich von Kleist (*The Marquise of O—*), Frankfurt, Germany
1948 Ntozake Shange (*For Colored Girls Who Have Considered Suicide When the Rainbow Is Enuf*), Trenton, N.J.
DIED: 1973 Walt Kelly (*Pogo*), 60, Woodland Hills, Calif.
1973 Leo Strauss (*Natural Right and History*), 74, Annapolis, Md.

1831 Alexis de Tocqueville, living on "Street No. 3" while visiting Philadelphia, found the regularity of the city's design "tiresome but convenient." "Don't you find that only a people whose imagination is frozen could invent such a system?" he asked. "These people here know only arithmetic."

1859 Nine years after she stayed with the Swiss painter François d'Albert Durade while depressed after her father's death, George Eliot wrote to him of her success as a novelist, so he could know "that one whom you knew when she was not very happy and when her life seemed to serve no purpose of much worth, has been at last blessed with the sense that she has done something worth living and suffering for."

1917 Virginia Woolf, in the *TLS*, on Henry James's last memoir, *The Middle Years*: "He comes to his task with an indescribable air of one so charged and laden with precious stuff that he hardly knows how to divest himself of it all."

1921 Through six years in an orphanage, six more as a hobo, ten years as a travel-ing tree surgeon, and dozens of bouts as a professional featherweight, Jim Tully most wanted to be a writer, and finally, at the age of thirty-five, he received a telegram from Harcourt, Brace accepting his first novel, *Emmett Lawler*, launching one of the most unlikely literary careers of the century. His next book, *Beggars of Life*, became a bestsell-ing hobo classic, while Tully, charming and pugnacious at five foot three, became the toast of Hollywood. Admired by Mencken, employed by Chaplin, and befriended by Jack Dempsey and W. C. Fields, he knocked out matinee idol John Gilbert with one punch and then costarred with him in *Way for a Sailor* before his career flamed out in the thirties and left him forgotten by the fifties.

1980 At first he was described only as "a free-lance writer named Bill," one of the Kansas City locals who joined Roger Angell after the fourth game of the Royals-Phillies World Series for a dinner of ribs and base-ball talk that Angell distilled, in his lyrical way, into a "murmurous Missouri of base-ball memories" in *The New Yorker*. But by the time the essay reappeared in Angell's *Late Innings* two years later, "Bill" was further identified as "Bill James, a lanky, bearded, thirty-two-year-old baseball scholar who writes the invaluable *Baseball Abstract*." By then Daniel Okrent's profile of James in *Sports Illustrated* had made him nearly famous; by the end of the century, his iconoclastic statistical theories made him one of the most influential figures in the sport.

October 19

BORN: 1931 John le Carré (*Tinker, Tailor, Soldier, Spy*), Poole, England

1938 Renata Adler (*Speedboat, Reckless Disregard*), Milan, Italy

DIED: 1682 Thomas Browne (*Religio Medici, Urn Burial*), 77, Norwich, England

1745 Jonathan Swift (*Gulliver's Travels, A Modest Proposal*), 77, Dublin

1908 Before there was a Macondo, the legendary setting of *One Hundred Years of Solitude*, there was Aracataca, the remote Colombian town where Gabriel García Márquez was born, and where his maternal grandfather, Colonel Nicolás Márquez, loomed as its leading citizen. And before Aracataca there was the dark moment in the family history, when Colonel Márquez killed another man in a "matter of honor" in a manner that may or may not have been honorable. The details were hazy—was his victim armed or not?—but the outcome was clear: the colonel was forced to leave town and make his fortune on the other side of the mountains. For the young novelist, given puzzling pieces of the story as a child, it was "the first incident from real life that stirred my writer's instincts," and one he was never "able to exorcise," even after he transformed it, in *One Hundred Years of Solitude*, into the moment when José Arcadio Buendía hurls a spear "with the strength of a bull" into the neck of his rival.

1970 When Donald Goines was released from Jackson State Penitentiary in December 1970 after a stint for attempted larceny—following ones for armed robbery, abetting prostitution, and the unlicensed distilling of whiskey—he left with the manuscript of a novel and a contract for its publication, signed on this day. Inspired by the underworld stories of Iceberg Slim, Goines had signed with Slim's Los Angeles publisher, Holloway House, who released *Dopefiend* and *Whoreson*, the first two novels in Goines's short but prolific career as one of the pioneers of street fiction. Murdered in Detroit in 1974, Goines was rediscovered thirty years later by a new generation of hip-hop artists, with movies based on his works starring DMX, Ice-T, and Snoop Dogg.

1988 Three years after a forced marriage between two corporate titans, R. J. Reynolds and Nabisco, created RJR Nabisco, it was clear the awkward alliance between cigarettes and Oreos wasn't taking, and Russ Johnson, the company's flamboyant, mop-headed CEO, had an idea: a leveraged buyout that would split the two companies and, by the way, allow management to reap an obscene windfall. He sold his board on the plan at a meeting on this day, kicking off the greatest corporate frenzy of the go-go '80s, a bidding war that nearly tripled the company's stock price in six weeks and provided the dramatic material for one of the iconic narratives of the decade, Bryan Burrough and John Helyar's *Barbarians at the Gate*.

BORN: 1854 Arthur Rimbaud (*A Season in Hell*), Charleville, France
1946 Elfriede Jelinek (*The Piano Teacher*), Mürzzuschlag, Austria

DIED: 1890 Richard Francis Burton (*The Book of the Thousand Nights and a Night*), 69, Trieste
1994 Francis Steegmuller (*Flaubert and Madame Bovary*), 88, Naples, Italy

NO YEAR "Enough," the groom declares. "There will be no wedding to-day." The wedding is off, in this quiet country church, because a stranger has stepped forward to testify that on October 20, fifteen years before, the groom, Edward Fairfax Rochester of Thornfield Hall, married Bertha Antoinetta Mason in Spanish Town, Jamaica, and that Mrs. Bertha Rochester is still alive. In fact, she resides in, of all places, Thornfield Hall, and Rochester's thwarted second bride, Jane Eyre, is about to be introduced to her. Charlotte Brontë said little more about this earlier marriage in *Jane Eyre*, but in *Wide Sargasso Sea* Jean Rhys imagined the story of the first Mrs. Rochester and their doomed wedding, which in her telling Rochester greets with the words "So it was all over."

1854 Not long after their honeymoon, Brontë's new husband, the Reverend Arthur Bell Nicholls, took hold of the reins of her correspondence, telling his wife that letters like hers, which comment so freely about their acquaintances, "are dangerous as lucifer matches." She must refrain from writing her opinions to her good friend Ellen Nussey, he declared, or Ellen must burn her letters after reading. For the good fortune of later readers, neither woman obeyed, allowing us to read, among other things, Charlotte's comments about Arthur himself: "Men don't seem to understand making letters a vehicle of communication—they always seem to think us incautious . . . I can't help laughing—this seems to me so funny. Arthur however says he is quite 'serious' and looks it, I assure you—he is bending over the desk with his eyes full of concern."

1962 During a cultural thaw that had just a few months remaining, Soviet premier Nikita Khrushchev broke a decades-long taboo by approving the publication of *One Day in the Life of Ivan Denisovich*, an unsparing novel by former prisoner Aleksandr Solzhenitsyn about the brutal life in one of Stalin's labor camps. To those in the Politburo who feared its revelations about the camp, the premier retorted, as he proudly recounted on this day to Solzhenitsyn's editor, "What do you think it was, a holiday resort?" The novel was an immediate success in the USSR and in the West, but within two years Khrushchev was forced out of office by Brezhnev, within five *Ivan Denisovich* was quietly removed from Soviet libraries, and within twelve Solzhenitsyn himself was forcibly exiled to the West.

1973 John Updike, in *The New Yorker*, on Günter Grass's *From the Diary of a Snail*: "Imaginations seem to be as choosy as mollusks about the soil they inhabit; amid a great deal of mental travelogue, this one episode dankly, grotesquely lives."

October 21

BORN: 1772 Samuel Taylor Coleridge ("The Rime of the Ancient Mariner"), Ottery St. Mary, England
1929 Ursula K. Le Guin (*A Wizard of Earthsea*), Berkeley, Calif.
DIED: 1969 Jack Kerouac (*The Dharma Bums*), 47, St. Petersburg, Fla.
1974 Donald Goines (*Dopefiend, Whoreson*), 37, Detroit

1920 J. R. Ackerley's *My Father and Myself* is a disarmingly frank memoir of a life— or rather two lives—of secrecy. Ackerley's secrecy was forced on him—being a homosexual was a crime then in England—but in his writing he told all, both about his own life and what he learned of his father's, a prosperous and respectable Edwardian who once hinted to his son that "in the matter of sex there was nothing he had not done, no experience he hadn't tasted." Only after his death was that revealed to include bigamy: he left his son two letters, the first dated on this day, that confessed he had a second family, including three children who knew him only as Uncle Bodger. "I'm not going to make any excuses, old man," he added. Neither did his son.

1967 "How do you make a good movie in this country without being jumped on?" The critical tide had already turned in favor of *Bonnie and Clyde* when on this day *The New Yorker* published Pauline Kael's 7,000-word defense of the movie, which began with the plea above. Lively and combative, Kael's review ended up being an audition for the regular reviewing gig she kept at the magazine for the next twenty-three years. Meanwhile, in the *New York Times*, the movie and its stylish but unsettling violence forced the end of another career: Bosley Crowther's tone-deaf campaign against the picture, which he called a "cheap piece of bald-faced slapstick comedy," was the final straw that drove him out of the powerful reviewing chair he had held there for twenty-seven years.

1967 There is something of *The Red Badge of Courage* in *The Armies of the Night*, Norman Mailer's autobiographical history-as-novel: the confused and comic figure muddling through the periphery of a mass event with little control over its outcome. In this case, though, it's not a war the figure was muddling through but a protest against a war—the March on the Pentagon on this day—and the comic figure is Mailer, with a highly tuned sense of the absurd but also a drive to push to the center of things and make a spectacle of himself. The result is one of his best books: both grandiose and self-deflating, and attuned to the danger of something happening, or of nothing happening at all.

1990 Jay Parini, in the *New York Times*, on A. S. Byatt's *Possession*: "A. S. Byatt is a writer in mid-career whose time has certainly come, because 'Possession' is a tour de force that opens every narrative device of English fiction to inspection without, for a moment, ceasing to delight."

October 22

BORN: 1919 Doris Lessing (*The Golden Notebook*, *The Four-Gated City*), Kermanshah, Iran
1965 A. L. Kennedy (*Paradise*, *On Bullfighting*), Dundee, Scotland
DIED: 1982 Richard Hugo (*The Real West Marginal Way*), 58, Seattle
1998 Eric Ambler (*Journey into Fear*, *The Light of Day*), 89, London

1942 Raymond Chandler was always touchy about how his books were talked about, especially when it came to James M. Cain, with whom Chandler and Dashiell Hammett were often lumped as "hard-boiled" writers. Hammett, he wrote his publisher Blanche Knopf on this day, was "all right," but Cain? "He is every kind of writer I detest, a faux naif, a Proust in greasy overalls, a dirty little boy with a piece of chalk and a board fence and nobody look-ing . . . Do I, for God's sake, sound like that?" Despite this disdain, within a year Chandler was under contract to sound like Cain, as the co-writer of Billy Wilder's adap-tation of Cain's *Double Indemnity*, for which Chandler would share his first Academy Award nomination for best screenplay.

1961 Richard Stern, in the *New York Times*, on *Catch-22*: "Its author, Joseph Heller, is like a brilliant painter who decides to throw all the ideas in his sketchbooks onto one canvas, relying on their charm and shock to compensate for the lack of design."

1962 Well into his last years of drunken-ness, delusion, and lingering charisma, Del-more Schwartz read his poems at the first National Poetry Festival in Washington, D.C., in a tremulously declamatory voice. That evening he "hurt his hotel room" (in the words of Richard Wilbur) and was brought, raging, to a police station, where his release was arranged by Wilbur and John Berryman, whose waiting taxi Schwartz then rode off in alone. Later, his great friend Berryman recalled that night in grief—as well as Schwartz's earlier years of "unstained promise"—in "Dream Song #149."

1973 On a Himalayan slope in the morning sun, Peter Matthiessen glimpsed something "much too big for a red panda, too covert for a musk deer, too dark for wolf or leopard, and much quicker than a bear." Was it, he wondered in *The Snow Leopard*, a yeti?

1996 Forty-two years to the day after seeing his first opera—*Rigoletto*—on his eleventh birthday in Tokyo, Japanese industrialist Katsumi Hosokawa attends another musi-cal birthday celebration, a concert by his favorite soprano, Roxane Coss, that was organized to draw him, and his business, to an unnamed South American country. But just as a song ends, the lights are shut off, and the men with guns enter the room. In adapting the events of the Lima hostage crisis, in which Peruvian insurgents laid siege to a party at the Japanese embassy and held its guests hostage for four months, for her novel *Bel Canto*, Ann Patchett changed details large and small, reimagining the crisis as an ensemble piece in which cap-tives and captors are brought together by the "beautiful singing" of the title before the siege's violent end.

October 23

BORN: 1942 Michael Crichton (*The Andromeda Strain, Jurassic Park*), Chicago
1961 Laurie Halse Anderson (*Speak, Chains, Wintergirls*), Potsdam, N.Y.
DIED: 1939 Zane Grey (*Riders of the Purple Sage*), 67, Altadena, Calif.
1996 Diana Trilling (*We Must March My Darlings*), 91, New York City

1847 "I wish you had not sent me *Jane Eyre*," William Makepeace Thackeray wrote to the book's publishers a week after it was published under the pseudonym Currer Bell. "It interested me so much," he added, "that I have lost (or won, if you like) a whole day in reading it at the busiest period, with the printers I know waiting for copy." (They were waiting for the next installment of *Vanity Fair*, just then making Thackeray a literary celebrity as it was serialized in *Punch*.) "It is a woman's writing, but whose?" he speculated. In turn, when the second edition of *Jane Eyre* appeared, Charlotte Brontë (still writing as Currer Bell) dedicated it to Thackeray, "who, to my thinking, comes before the great ones of society, much as the son of Imlah came before the throned Kings of Judah and Israel."

1869 "I shall leave no memoirs," promised Isidore Ducasse, and he kept his word. Few writers left less for biographers than Ducasse, who wrote for a short, furious time as the Comte de Lautréamont, died of unknown causes in Paris at twenty-four, and left behind a poetic novel, *The Songs of Maldoror*, later embraced by the Surrealists. *Maldoror* breathes fire, declaring that unless the reader is "as fierce as what he is reading," "the deadly emanations of this book will dissolve his soul as water does sugar," but Ducasse took a milder tone in a rare surviving letter to his publisher, in which he argued his works were moral and shouldn't be censored: he "sings of despair only to cast down the reader and make him desire the good as the remedy."

1975 Inside, issue 198 of *Rolling Stone* may have been full of news of George Harrison's new record, Foghat's fall tour, and an unknown band called Talking Heads whose lead singer "looks like the bastard offspring of an unthinkable union between Lou Reed and Ralph Nader," but the front page had the scoop of the year. In "Tania's World," Howard Kohn and David Weir landed the story everyone wanted, an inside report on Patty Hearst, the heiress-turned-terrorist who had taken up arms with her kidnappers, the ragtag revolutionaries called the Symbionese Liberation Army. Hearst was arrested just before the article appeared, but "Tania's World" gave the first glimpse into the deliciously mundane details—the anxious road trips, takeout hamburgers, pay-phone rendezvous, safe-house skinny-dipping, and copy-shop communiqués—of her fugitive days.

1992 John Sutherland, in the *TLS*, on Donna Tartt's *The Secret History*: "It aims to be hypnotic and finally achieves something more like narcosis. Tartt might have been wise to show her manuscript to a ruthless editor as well as to her indulgent college friends."

BORN: **1933** Norman Rush (*Mating, Mortals, Whites*), San Francisco

1969 Emma Donoghue (*Room, Slammerkin*), Dublin

DIED: **1970** Richard Hofstadter (*The Paranoid Style in American Politics*), 54, New York City

1992 Laurie Colwin (*Home Cooking, A Big Storm Knocked It Over*), 48, New York City

1911 Whether "unsuitable reading material" was really one of the causes of the wave of teen suicides that swept across Germany before the First World War, as some claimed at the time, Rudolf Ditzen, who had taken to calling himself Harry after *The Picture of Dorian Gray*, was drawn to a literary death, along with his friend Hanss Dietrich von Necker. At first the Leipzig teens planned that the one whose writing was judged inferior (by a third party) would be shot, but then they decided instead to stage a suicide pact as if it were a duel over a girl. Ditzen survived the shots, Necker didn't, and on this day Ditzen was arrested for murder. The charges were dropped, but the scandal was still fresh enough that when he published his first novel after the war, he took a pen name, Hans Fallada, that he kept through his tormented but often successful career.

1962 On a fall night in Harlem, at the height of the Cuban Missile Crisis, James Brown recorded a show that turned him from a chitlin'-circuit headliner into a nationwide star. *Live at the Apollo* is the name of both the resulting record and a little book by Douglas Wolk about the record, one of the standout entries in the marvelous 33 1/3 series of books on individual albums. Cramming as much drama and abrupt intensity into his tiny book as Brown did into his thirty-one-minute LP, Wolk lovingly diagrams the intricate web of performers' lives, R&B riffs, and hit recordings that put that single night's performance into context and make even the most fleeting of pop pleasures seem full of meaning.

1992 At 11:00 p.m., James Frey, a recent graduate of local Denison University, was cited by Granville, Ohio, police for driving under the influence and driving without a license after he drove his tire up onto a curb. Five hours later, Frey was released and never jailed again, which means that, among other events described in his memoirs *A Million Little Pieces* and *My Friend Leonard,* he wasn't beaten by Granville cops with billy clubs or charged with Attempted Incitement of a Riot and Felony Mayhem, he did not get hit in the back of the head with a metal tray on the first of his eighty-seven days in a county facility for violent and felonious offenders by a three-hundred-pound illiterate black man named Porterhouse, nor did he read *Don Quixote, Leaves of Grass,* and *East of Eden* to Porterhouse, nor did Porterhouse cry when Anatole betrayed Natasha in *War and Peace,* nor did Porterhouse sleep with *War and Peace* and cradle it as if it were his child.

October 25

BORN: 1941 Anne Tyler (*The Accidental Tourist, Breathing Lessons*), Minneapolis
1975 Zadie Smith (*White Teeth, On Beauty, NW*), London
DIED: 1400 Geoffrey Chaucer (*The Canterbury Tales*), c. 57, London
1989 Mary McCarthy (*Memories of a Catholic Girlhood*), 77, New York City

1851 The *Athenaeum* on Herman Melville's *Moby-Dick*: An "ill-compounded mixture of romance and matter-of-fact . . . Mr. Melville has to thank himself only if his horrors and his heroics are flung aside by the general reader, as so much trash belonging to the worst school of Bedlam literature,—since he seems not so much unable to learn as disdainful of learning the craft of an artist."

1859 George Eliot read Balzac's *Père Goriot*, "a hateful book."

1946 Did Ludwig Wittgenstein threaten Karl Popper with a poker the only time they met, at a session of the Cambridge Moral Science Club on this afternoon—or did the two philosophers even attack each other, as some rumors soon had it? A more interesting question, as David Edmonds and John Eidinow explain in their enlightening history of the incident, *Wittgenstein's Poker*, was why the meeting exploded in undeniable hostility. The two men, both products of the cultural hothouse of Vienna, were spoiling for a fight: Wittgenstein impatient and exacting, engaged with puzzles of language and sure there were no other questions, and Popper certain that philosophy had an obligation to confront the political problems of the world, as he just had in *The Open Society and Its Enemies*, a defense of liberalism against the Fascism that had nearly consumed Europe.

1972 It was the lowest point in their Watergate investigation. Bob Woodward and Carl Bernstein woke to find their latest *Washington Post* story, which tied Nixon aide H. R. Haldeman to the slush fund that paid the Watergate burglars, denied by their main source and the *Post* pilloried as reckless and partisan like never before. By the end of the day, which also included a meeting pitching their book proposal for *All the President's Men* to their future publisher, the reporters were able to confirm that Haldeman did run the fund, but Deep Throat, Woodward's best inside source, was still worried. The next time they met, Deep Throat growled they had set back their story by months: "You've got people feeling sorry for Haldeman. I didn't think that was possible."

2012 Faulkner Literary Rights, LLC, filed suit in Mississippi against Sony Pictures Classics claiming that Owen Wilson's paraphrase in Woody Allen's *Midnight in Paris* of two sentences from *Requiem for a Nun*— "The past is not dead! Actually, it's not even past," in Wilson's version—violated the Faulkner estate's copyright on the sentences.

October 26

BORN: 1902 Beryl Markham (*West with the Night*), Ashwell, England
1945 Pat Conroy (*The Great Santini, The Prince of Tides*), Atlanta
DIED: 1957 Nikos Kazantzakis (*Zorba the Greek*), 74, Freiburg, Germany
2008 Tony Hillerman (*The Wailing Wind*), 83, Albuquerque, N.M.

1726 Published: *Travels into Several Remote Nations of the World* by Lemuel Gulliver, later revealed as Jonathan Swift (Benjamin Motte, London)

1849 When the time came for Flaubert to set off with his friend Maxime Du Camp for his long-imagined trip to Greece and Egypt, he nearly balked at the idea of leaving his mother for the two-year journey. The day they parted was "atrocious," "the worst I have ever spent"; finally he just kissed her and dashed away, listening to her screams from behind the door he shut behind him. After midnight he composed himself enough to write and send her a "thousand kisses," and after he woke, on this day, he wrote again, saying, "I keep thinking of your sad face." That evening, Du Camp returned to his Paris apartment to find his friend prostrate and sighing on the floor of his study. "Never again will I see my mother or my country! This journey is too long, too distant, it is tempting Providence! What madness!"

1913 When the body of Frederick Rolfe was discovered in his apartment in Venice after his death at age fifty-three the night before, he left behind, in the words of one biographer, "letters, drawings and notebooks sufficient to cause a hundred scandals," as well as a small army of literary pseudonyms and identities including Frederick Austin, Frank English, George Arthur Rose, Nicholas Crabbe, and, best known of all, Baron Corvo, under which he published *Hadrian the Seventh*, a novel of an Englishman living alone with his cat who, after being rejected from the priesthood, is suddenly elevated to the papacy. Two decades after his death, Rolfe was blessed with the most appropriately idiosyncratic of biographers, A. J. A. Symons, whose *Quest for Corvo* has gained a cult following equal to that of *Hadrian*'s. Fellow connoisseurs and eccentrics—and connoisseurs of eccentricity—Symons and Rolfe always seemed to reserve their greatest curiosity for themselves.

1977 "First wedding night. But first mourning night?" The day after Henriette Barthes died at eighty-four, her son Roland, who had lived with her most of his life, penciled those lines on a scrap of paper. There are common words for the moment of marriage, he seems to say, but not for the moment of loss, especially for an unmarried, gay man like Barthes, for whom an "innocently conjugal" affection for his mother (in Brian Dillon's words) is a kind of unspeakable scandal. Over the next year, curious but fearful about the idea of making literature of thoughts that often seemed banal, he tracked his grief in hundreds of similarly fragmentary notes, which twenty-five years later, long after his own death, were published as his *Mourning Diary*.

October 27

BORN: 1914 Dylan Thomas (*A Child's Christmas in Wales*), Swansea, Wales
1932 Sylvia Plath (*The Colossus, The Bell Jar*), Boston
DIED: 1975 Rex Stout (*Fer-de-Lance, Some Buried Caesar*), 88, Danbury, Conn.
1977 James M. Cain (*Double Indemnity, Mildred Pierce*), 85, University Park, Md.

1883 The *Spectator* on Anthony Trollope's *Autobiography*: "Mr. Trollope seems to be one of the few men who have fully reached their ideal, and enjoyed reaching it to the full."

1909 A short visit back to Dublin from Trieste made James Joyce eager to return to exile: "I felt proud to think that my son . . . will always be a foreigner in Ireland, a man speaking another language and bred in a different tradition. I loathe Ireland and the Irish. They themselves stare at me in the street though I was born among them. Perhaps they read my hatred of them in my eyes."

1917 The marriage of William Butler Yeats at fifty-two to twenty-five-year-old Georgie Hyde-Lees—just weeks after a different young woman had declined his proposal—plunged him into a torment of second thoughts until, in their hotel room a week later, Georgie declared an urge to write. The "automatic writing" she produced broke through his gloom with its message—"all is well at heart"—and its invitation into a realm of spiritual communication the poet had long yearned for. Their frequent writing sessions, in which Yeats asked for guidance from the "Instructors" she channeled, transformed their marriage and his own writing, culminating in *A Vision*, an occult autobiography of sorts that he considered the great work of his life and that was met with incomprehension and scorn when it was published in 1925.

1937 Stephen Spender, in the *New Republic*, on Franz Kafka's *The Trial* and *The Metamorphosis*: "However roundabout it may seem, his approach to reality is direct: he is not building up an allegory in order to illustrate a metaphysic, he is penetrating reality in order to discover a system of truth."

1948 Dropout anthropologist, failed reporter, and now a miserable junior PR man for General Electric, Kurt Vonnegut couldn't sell the stories he wrote on mornings and weekends until the day that, he would later say, "looms like Stonehenge beside my own little footpath from birth to death." Arriving home after work, he found a check for $675 in the mail from *Collier's* magazine for "Report on the Barnhouse Effect," his first published story. The next day, he wrote his father that when he sold a few more, "I will then quit this goddamn nightmare job, and never take another one so long as I live, so help me God," a letter his father put up on his mantel with a quote from *The Merchant of Venice* written on the back, "An oath, I have an oath in Heaven: Shall I lay perjury on my soul?"

BORN: **1818** Ivan Turgenev (*A Sportsman's Notebook, First Love*), Oryol, Russia

1903 Evelyn Waugh (*Decline and Fall, Vile Bodies*), London

DIED: **1704** John Locke (*Two Treatises of Government*), 72, Essex, England

1998 Ted Hughes (*The Hawk in the Rain, Birthday Letters*), 68, London

1882 The engagement of Edith Jones to young millionaire heir Henry Stevens was broken, according to *Town Topics*, because of "an alleged preponderance of intellectuality on the part of the intended bride. Miss Jones is an ambitious authoress, and it is said that, in the eyes of Mr. Stevens, ambition is a grievous fault." (Miss Jones instead married Teddy Wharton in 1885.)

1910 At eighty-two, oppressed by the rivalry between his wife and his disciples and unhappy with the luxury in which they all lived, Leo Tolstoy stole away from his rural estate in the darkness of the early morning, leaving a note to his wife, Sophia, asking "to live the last days of my life in peace and solitude." After a day of railway travel while Sophia tried to kill herself by wading into a pond, Tolstoy wrote to his daughter asking for the books he was reading, including Montaigne's *Essays*, The

Brothers Karamazov, and Maupassant's *A Woman's Life*. He soon grew ill, though, and took refuge in the house of the stationmaster in Astopovo, where his presence drew not the peace he had sought but a horde of journalists, photographers, dignitaries, and other onlookers for the final days before his death on November 7.

1937 In what may be the most notorious of all movie reviews, Graham Greene took on a sacred object: Shirley Temple. Having the year before compared her "oddly precocious body" to Marlene Dietrich's, Greene wrote that in *Wee Willie Winkie* Miss Temple, age nine, was now "a complete totsy," measuring "a man with agile studio eyes, with dimpled depravity." Temple's studio sued for libel in London and won, and Greene had to pay the tot and Twentieth Century Fox £500, which equaled the advance for his next book. For years after, until his house was destroyed in the war, he proudly displayed on his bathroom wall the studio's legal complaint that he had falsely accused them of "procuring" the child star "for immoral purposes."

1952 Flannery O'Connor told Robie Macauley she had purchased a hen and rooster peafowl and four peachicks from Florida.

October 29

BORN: 1740 James Boswell (*Life of Johnson*), Edinburgh

1905 Henry Green (*Living, Loving, Party Going*), Tewkesbury, England

DIED: 1911 Joseph Pulitzer (publisher, *New York World*), 64, Charleston, S.C.

1924 Frances Hodgson Burnett (*The Secret Garden*), 74, Plandome, N.Y.

1692 A tireless and ambitious businessman, Daniel Defoe invested in a variety of enterprises: wholesale hosiery, cargo shipping, trade in spirits and tobacco, a diving bell to recover sunken treasure, and most memorably, seventy civet cats from which he planned to manufacture perfume from the musk recovered, by spatula, from their anal glands. His losses accumulated, however, and with the cats already seized for nonpayment, his creditors had him committed to the Fleet Prison with £17,000 in debts. He negotiated with his creditors to secure his release, but for the rest of his life they hounded him for the debts, even after he left business behind for the new and more successful profession of authorship.

1888 Hoping to capitalize on *Alice's Adventures in Wonderland*, Lewis Carroll designed the "Wonderland Postage-Stamp Case," including illustrations of Alice holding a pig and the Cheshire Cat, slots for various stamp denominations, and a short essay, "Eight or Nine Wise Words About Letter-Writing."

1962 After nearly a dozen years living in Brazil with her partner, Lota de Macedo Soares, Elizabeth Bishop found a new acquaintance of interest with a "wonderful name": Clarice Lispector, a neighbor down the street. "Her 2 or 3 novels I don't think are so good but her short stories are almost like the stories I've always thought should be written about Brazil—Tchekovian, slightly sinister and fantastic." Lispector was already gaining recognition as Brazil's best writer since Machado de Assis, but she was unknown in the United States, and Bishop's interest led to a first novel translated into English, *The Apple in the Dark*, and to the glamorous but reserved Lispector's appearance on this day at a conference in Texas, where her translator marveled at this "rare person who looked like Marlene Dietrich and wrote like Virginia Woolf."

2004 Five days after his church in Haiti was burned down by an armed gang, Rev. Joseph Dantica boarded a flight to Miami. He had traveled to the United States over thirty times in the decades since his brother immigrated there; this time, although he possessed a valid tourist visa, he requested asylum out of fear of the gang at home, and the border machinery caught him in its gears. Two days later, vomiting but deprived of immediate medical treatment—"I think he's faking," a Customs medic said—and with his niece, the novelist Edwidge Danticat, still unable to see him, Dantica died, a nightmare that Danticat recounts with calm anger in *Brother, I'm Dying*, a memoir of the parallel lives of her father in Brooklyn and her uncle in Haiti, the "second father" who raised her after her parents moved to America.

BORN: **1821** Fyodor Dostoyevsky (*Crime and Punishment, The Brothers Karamazov*), Moscow

1877 Irma Rombauer (*The Joy of Cooking*), St. Louis

DIED: **1987** Joseph Campbell (*The Hero with a Thousand Faces*), 83, Honolulu

2009 Claude Lévi-Strauss (*Tristes Tropiques, The Raw and the Cooked*), 100, Paris

1772 On October 29, Karl Wilhelm Jerusalem, a young German law student who favored a blue coat and yellow breeches and had developed an affection for the wife of a friend, shot himself; he died the next day. A few days later the news reached an acquaintance of his, Johann Wolfgang von Goethe, who had been struggling to put his own flirtation with suicide into words after a similar unrequited love. "At that moment," Goethe later wrote, "the plan of 'Werther' was formed . . . just as water in a vessel, which stands upon the point of freezing, is converted into hard ice by the most gentle shake." *The Sorrows of Young Werther* became the sensation of the Romantic age, sparking copycat suicides, a fashion for blue coats and yellow breeches, and, once word got out about its author's inspiration, pilgrimages to the grave of Karl Wilhelm Jerusalem.

1915 Francis Hackett, in the *New Republic*, on Robert Grant's *The High Priestess*: "To describe a rigid, humorless, mean, pretentious woman is certainly worth while, but to imply that her essentially low qualities are merely the hind side of feminism is to flatter the conservative view of feminism with a vengeance."

1933 "I work, I spend money as if my future were secure. Yet every hour I receive a warning from my heart, and I believe that my health is close to collapse and that either the tyranny will last for a long time yet or be superseded by chaos." Nine months after Hitler became chancellor, Victor Klemperer still had his job as a professor of French in Dresden, but he had few illusions about the catastrophe building around him, and over the next dozen years, spared the Nazis' worst cruelties as a war veteran and the husband of a non-Jew, he turned his scholarly energy to his diary, where he documented the everyday humiliations, the relentlessly incremental restrictions, and the perversions of language of the Reich. Improbably, he survived the war and so did his diaries, which, published as *I Will Bear Witness*, remain one of the most thorough and moving personal records of the Nazi years.

October 31

BORN: 1795 John Keats ("Ode to a
Nightingale," "Ode to Melancholy"),
London
1959 Neal Stephenson (*Cryptonomicon*,
The Baroque Cycle), Fort Meade, Md.
DIED: 1960 H. L. Davis (*Honey in the Horn*,
Beulah Land), 66, San Antonio, Tex.
2008 Studs Terkel (*Working*, *The Great
War*), 96, Chicago

1615 Miguel de Cervantes hinted at the end
of the first book of *Don Quixote* that further adventures might be forthcoming, but
before he could complete his own sequel, a
rival appeared that credited another author,
Alonso Fernández de Avellaneda, on the
title page and insulted Cervantes as old,
friendless, and boring. Cervantes, meanwhile, took advantage of being second
by adding a scene in which Don Quixote
and Sancho Panza themselves mock the
false sequel. In the second book's dedication, written on this day, he mentioned "the
loathing and disgust caused by another
Don Quixote," and in the book's preface he
completed his revenge: humbly declining to
abuse his usurper, he instead told a tale of
a madman who, after inflating a dog from
behind through a hollow reed, asks, "Do
your worships think, now, that it is an easy
thing to blow up a dog?" "Does your worship think now," added Cervantes, "that it
is an easy thing to write a book?"

1967 Published: *Trout Fishing in America*
by Richard Brautigan (Four Seasons, San
Francisco)

1980 "Does it matter that he is 20 years
old? That he grew up in rural West Virginia and later on the streets of San Francisco?" Catherine Texier asked about the
author in her *New York Times* review of JT
Leroy's debut novel, *Sarah*. "It does. And
yet it shouldn't." Those sorts of questions
were asked throughout the heady, mysterious rise of Leroy, who claimed to have
been born on this day into a childhood of
abuse and street hustling, until it became
clear that behind his veiled persona wasn't
the twiggy, bewigged figure who made shy
public appearances as JT but a forty-year-
old woman named Laura Albert, who said
she invented Leroy's identity as an "avatar"
for her fiction, not a hoax. Did it matter that
he *wasn't* twenty years old? It did. And yet,
perhaps, it shouldn't.

1981 As you might expect among wizards,
October 31 is a celebrated day in the calendar. There is the traditional Halloween
feast at Hogwarts, with candy-filled pump-
kins, decorations, masses of live bats, and,
at Harry Potter's fourth Hogwarts Halloween, the Goblet of Fire, which declares
him the surprise fourth Triwizard champion. It's also the anniversary of the incomplete decapitation in 1492 of Sir Nicholas
de Mimsy-Porpington, whose ghost was
known forever after as Nearly Headless
Nick. And of course it's on this day that
Lord Voldemort himself stepped into the
Potter cottage and with the Killing Curse—
"Avada Kedavra!"—murdered James and
Lily Potter but failed to kill the baby Harry,
nearly destroying himself in the process and
leaving behind, in the lightning-shaped scar
on Harry's forehead, a part of his soul.

November is the anti-April: gray and dreary, the beginning of the end of things rather than their rebirth. It's the month you hunker down—that is, if you don't give up entirely. When Ishmael leaves Manhattan for New Bedford and the sea in *Moby-Dick*, it may be December on the calendar, but he's driven there, to the openness of oceans, by "a damp, drizzly November in my soul." And where else could Dickens's *Bleak House* begin but, bleakly, in "implacable November," with dogs and horses mired in mud, pedestrians "jostling one another's umbrellas in a general infection of ill temper" (not unlike Ishmael "deliberately stepping into the street, and methodically knocking people's hats off"), and, of course, the English fog:

"Fog everywhere. Fog up the river, where it flows among green aits and meadows; fog down the river, where it rolls defiled among the tiers of shipping and the waterside pollutions of a great (and dirty) city. Fog on the Essex marshes, fog on the Kentish heights. Fog creeping into the cabooses of collier-brigs; fog lying out on the yards and hovering in the rigging of great ships; fog drooping on the gunwales of barges and small boats."

Shall I go on? *Jane Eyre* begins on a "drear November day," with a "pale blank of mist and cloud" and "ceaseless rain sweeping away wildly before a long and lamentable blast." And it's on a "dreary night in November," as "rain pattered dismally against the panes," that Victor Frankenstein, blindly engrossed in his profane labors as the seasons have passed by outside, first sees the spark of life in the watery eyes of his creation. Is it any wonder that Meg in *Little Women* thinks that "November is the most disagreeable month in the whole year"?

Not everyone agrees that it's disagreeable. In his *Sand County Almanac*, Aldo Leopold, who finds value in each of the seasons, calls November "the month for the axe" because, in Wisconsin at least, it's "warm enough to grind an axe without freezing, but cold enough to fell a tree in comfort." With the hardwoods having lost their leaves, he can see the year's growth for the first time: "Without this clear view of treetops, one cannot be sure which tree, if any, needs felling for the good of the land." The season's first starkness, in other words, brings clarity to the work of the conservationist, whose labors in managing his forest are done with axe not pen, "humbly aware that with each stroke he is writing his signature on the face of his land."

Frankenstein by Mary Shelley (1818) ☙ The horrified, fascinated romance between creator and created begins with an electric spark in the gloom of November and ends on the September ice of the Arctic, with the monster, having outlived the man who called him into being, heading out to perish in the darkness.

Bleak House by Charles Dickens (1853) ☙ Not quite as muddy and befogged as the November afternoon on which it begins—nor as interminable as the legal case, *Jarndyce v. Jarndyce*, in which its story is enmeshed—*Bleak House* is actually one of Dickens's sharpest and best-constructed tales.

New Grub Street by George Gissing (1891) ☙ Set in a London institution nearly as foggy as Dickens's Chancery—the world of small-time literary foragers that Gissing knew from intimate experience—*New Grub Street* is a bracingly and winningly unsentimental look at two delicate and unpromising financial propositions: literature and marriage.

The Friends of Eddie Coyle by George V. Higgins (1970) ☙ Eddie Coyle was caught driving a truck through New Hampshire with about two hundred cases of Canadian Club that didn't belong to him, and now he has a court date in January. So he spends the fall trying to make a deal—trying to make a number of deals, in fact, in Higgins's debut, glorious with conversation and double-crossing, which Elmore Leonard has, correctly, called "the best crime novel ever written."

The Death of Jim Loney by James Welch (1979) ☙ The fall is indeed bleak in the Montana of Welch's second novel, in which Loney, a young man with a white father and an Indian mother—both lost to him—stumbles toward his fate like Ivan Ilyich, unsure of what it means to live.

The Ice Storm by Rick Moody (1994) ☙ Thanksgiving and family dysfunction go together like turkey and gravy, but Moody deftly sidesteps the usual holiday plot in his Watergate-era tale of suburbanites unmoored by affluence and moral rot by setting his domestic implosion on the day and night after Thanksgiving, as an early-winter storm seals Connecticut in ice.

A Century of November by W. D. Wetherell (2004) ☙ November 1918 may have meant the end of the Great War, but for Charles Marden, who lost his wife to the flu and his son to the trenches, it means a pilgrimage, driven by unspoken despair, from his orchard on Vancouver Island to the muddy field in Belgium where his son died, an expanse still blanketed with barbed wire and mustard-gas mist that seem to carry another hundred years' worth of war in them.

November 1

BORN: 1959 Susanna Clarke (*Jonathan Strange and Mr. Norrell*), Nottingham, England
1965 James Wood (*How Fiction Works*, *The Broken Estate*), Durham, England
DIED: 1907 Alfred Jarry (*Ubu Roi*, *The Supermale*), 34, Paris
1972 Ezra Pound (*The Cantos*, *Hugh Selwyn Mauberley*), 89, Venice, Italy

1604 The King's Men gave *The Tragedy of Othello, the Moor of Venice* its first recorded performance at Whitehall Palace in London.

1755 Would it be too much to say that the terrible earthquake and tsunami in Lisbon, which leveled one of the great cities of Europe and killed a fifth of its inhabitants, laid equal waste to European philosophy? Hundreds of writers attempted to make sense of the quake, including the young Immanuel Kant, who, unlike most, blamed the upheaval on geological forces rather than God, and the popular, optimistic theory of God's benevolence, summed up by Leibniz's claim that we live in "the best of all possible worlds," could hardly hold against the arbitrary suffering of thousands—on All Saints' Day, no less. Nor could it withstand the withering assaults of Voltaire, who wrote his skeptical "Poem on the Lisbon Disaster" within a month of the calamity and made the earthquake central to his sarcastic masterpiece, *Candide*.

1930 Ernest Hemingway swerved into a ditch in Billings, Montana, and broke his arm. His passenger, John Dos Passos, was unhurt.

1976 Justice, for once, moved swiftly in the case of Gary Gilmore, but not as fast as he wanted. In July he shot two men in Utah, and by early October he was convicted and sentenced to death. His case would have made headlines anyway, since no one had been executed in the United States in nearly ten years, but when on this day he waived his right to appeal and demanded to die, it became a circus. Reviled and celebrated for his outlaw nihilism, Gilmore was executed in January, but his notoriety didn't end there. He had sold the rights to his story to reporter Lawrence Schiller, whose researches became the foundation of Norman Mailer's epic "true life novel," *The Executioner's Song*. And years later, Gilmore's younger brother, Mikal, a *Rolling Stone* writer, reckoned with his family's history of violence and his own attempt to escape it in the harrowing memoir *Shot in the Heart*.

1993 It is November 1, 1993, and somewhere in Britain Hazel Burns and Spencer Kelly are born. But it's also November 1, 1993, when Hazel and Spencer, as young adults, wake up together in his bed after their first, life-changing night together. Using two narrative conceits for his story—all its events, past, present, and future, take place on November 1, 1993 (the day the European Union was founded), and all its nouns (with only twelve exceptions, he assures us) are borrowed from those used in the *Times* on that day—Richard Beard constructed *Damascus*, a serious and playful novel of time, fate, love, and chance; of crowds, countries, and a few individual lives.

November 2

BORN: **1927** Steve Ditko (*The Amazing Spider-Man, Tales to Astonish*), Johnstown, Pa.
1949 Lois McMaster Bujold (*Paladin of Souls*), Columbus, Ohio
DIED: **1950** George Bernard Shaw (*Pygmalion*), 94, Ayot St. Lawrence, England
1961 James Thurber (*My Life and Hard Times, The 13 Clocks*), 66, New York City

1918 F.H., in the *New Republic*, on Booth Tarkington's *The Magnificent Ambersons*: "Almost nothing that is necessary to creating a study of this American reality is lacking in Mr. Tarkington except the temper of a master novelist."

1938 Malcolm and Jan Lowry arrived in Mexico for the first time on October 30, 1936, though Malcolm, superstitious, liked to say it was three days later, on the Day of the Dead. The next day Malcolm, whose alcoholism had already led him to check into Bellevue Hospital in New York in May, had his first taste of mescal; by the middle of the month they had settled in the resort town of Cuernavaca, in the shadow of its two nearby volcanoes; and by the end of the next year Jan had left him when he refused to stop drinking. By then, he had already completed a rough draft of *Under the Volcano*, which, after many revisions, would begin on the Day of the Dead 1939, as two men in white tennis flannels recall the destruction and death of the mescal-soaked consul, Geoffrey Fermin, on the same day the year before.

1962 Stanley Kubrick was well into preproduction for his seventh feature, *Red Alert*, an atom-bomb thriller based on the novel by the same name by Peter George, when he realized he had to radically shift its tone: the only way to express the absurd reality of nuclear holocaust was with what he would call "nightmare comedy." He knew where to go for help, to a writer whose satirical novel *The Magic Christian* Peter Sellers had given him while they were making *Lolita*, and so on this day he sent Terry Southern a telegram reading, "I have a proposition which would profitably occupy you in London for next eight weeks." *Red Alert* soon became *Dr. Strangelove*, and Southern, for better or worse for his writing career and his health, soon became one of the hottest screenwriters in the business.

November 3

BORN: 1903 Walker Evans (*Let Us Now Praise Famous Men*), St. Louis
1942 Martin Cruz Smith (*Gorky Park, Stalin's Ghost*), Reading, Pa.
DIED: 1957 Wilhelm Reich (*The Mass Psychology of Fascism*), 60, Lewisburg, Pa.
2001 E. H. Gombrich (*The Story of Art, Art and Illusion*), 92, London

1793 The quotation for which Olympe de Gouges is best remembered—"Women have the right to mount the scaffold; they must also have the right to mount the speaker's platform"—proved dismayingly prophetic. De Gouges transformed herself from a small-town butcher's daughter into a wealthy and sophisticated Parisian socialite, playwright, and political activist, culminating in her "Declaration of the Rights of Women," which, with pointed irony, exposed the absence of women in the French Revolution's doctrine of universal equality, the "Declaration of the Rights of Man." But on this day, for her stubborn public protests against the radicals who had taken over the revolution, she was guillotined by the Jacobins, who ridiculed her as an example of what could happen if women neglected the domestic duties given them by nature.

1844 After the success of *A Christmas Carol*, Charles Dickens struggled to repeat his holiday hit the next year until he came upon the idea for *The Chimes,* a similar tale in which a father watches as a ghost as his loved ones are crushed by poverty, only to wake, as if from a dream, to a happy ending. Dickens wrote the story in less than a month and reported that he finished it on this day at 2:30 p.m. with "what women call 'a real good cry.'" When he read it aloud to friends in December—his first taste of the public performances that came to consume the last decades of his life—he thrilled when they shared his tears: "If you had seen Macready last night—undisguisedly sobbing and crying on the sofa, as I read—you would have felt (as I did) what a thing it is to have Power."

2002 A. O. Scott, in the *New York Times,* on Donna Tartt's *The Little Friend*: "'The Little Friend' seems destined to become a special kind of classic—a book that precocious young readers pluck from their parents' shelves and devour with surreptitious eagerness, thrilled to discover a writer who seems at once to read their minds and to offer up the sweet-and-sour fruits of exotic, forbidden knowledge."

BORN: 1879 Will Rogers (*Letters of a Self-Made Diplomat to His President*), Oologah, Okla.

1950 Charles Frazier (*Cold Mountain, Nightwoods*), Asheville, N.C.

DIED: 1918 Wilfred Owen ("Anthem for Doomed Youth"), 25, Sambre-Oise Canal, France

1933 John Jay Chapman (*Emerson and Other Essays*), 71, Poughkeepsie, N.Y.

1899 Published: *Die Traumdeutung* (*The Interpretation of Dreams*) by Sigmund Freud (Franz Deuticke, Leipzig). Only six hundred copies were sold in the next eight years.

1911 The *Athenaeum* on Max Beerbohm's *Zuleika Dobson*: "This is the wittiest and most amusing of extravaganzas."

1968 Eight months after signing a blood oath to defend the Fatherland with eleven young followers, and a few weeks after the Nobel Prize for Literature, which many had expected would go to him, was given to his mentor Yasunari Kawabata, Yukio Mishima held a press conference in uniform to announce the formation of the Tatenokai (the "Shield Society"), a small private army organized to protect the emperor. The press mocked "Captain Mishima's Toy Army," but Mishima was deadly serious, and two years later, after a halfhearted coup attempt, he committed the ritual suicide of seppuku with the help of his closest followers, having been given the courage to "die a hero's death" by the ferocity of the young warriors he had assembled around him.

NO YEAR "Was—was it always like this?" It's Thursday, just after midnight in the firehouse, and the playing cards are ticking on the tabletop and the Mechanical Hound is quiet in its kennel, sleeping but not sleeping. And Montag the fireman is starting to ask questions. "Didn't firemen *prevent* fires rather than stoke them up and get them going?" But there's hardly enough time for the other firemen to pull out their rulebooks and reply before the next alarm sounds, calling them out in their "mighty metal thunder" to douse a house full of forbidden books with kerosene in *Fahrenheit 451*, a novel Ray Bradbury wrote surrounded by books, feeding dimes to keep the typewriter humming in the basement of the UCLA library and walking through the stacks touching the books when the dimes ran out.

NO YEAR "Is it cold yet?" his fiancée asks from the absolute cold of orbit. "Is Manhattan beautiful?" They have, in his words, "the greatest long-distance relationship in the history of the cosmos. Or at least the long-distantest": Chase Insteadman, once a child TV star and now a dinner-party ornament, and Janice Trumbull, the lost astronaut, trapped on the international space station. Her letters to him make human-interest headlines, and they make Chase—well, the more public their sad romance becomes, the farther away it feels. Meanwhile Chase finds distractions closer to home as he and his new friend Perkus Tooth make their way through the bohemian edges and power-hungry center (which, oddly, often abut each other) of Manhattan in Jonathan Lethem's *Chronic City*.

November 5

BORN: 1926 John Berger (*Ways of Seeing, G.*), London
1943 Sam Shepard (*Buried Child, True West*), Fort Sheridan, Ill.
DIED: 1977 René Goscinny (*Asterix, Lucky Luke*), 51, Paris
2005 John Fowles (*The French Lieutenant's Woman*), 79, Lyme Regis, England

1718 Tristram Shandy, Gentleman, according to his *Life and Opinions*, was "brought forth into this scurvy and disastrous world of ours."

NO YEAR The fires of Bonfire Night, lit across the Wessex heath, give a pagan glow to the opening and closing of Thomas Hardy's *The Return of the Native*. In the opening chapters, Eustacia Vye, the restless and bewitching "Queen of Night," presides over the final bonfire of the evening, with which she hopes to draw a former lover, Damon Wildeve, away from his marriage to another. A year later to the day, with her own marriage to the earnest Clym Yeobright in trouble, another fire draws Eustacia and Damon together again and sets off the chain of events through which, in their restlessness, they will be destroyed.

1949 Jean Rhys had fallen out of the literary life since her last novel was published a decade earlier, but not far enough that she didn't see a notice placed in the *New Statesman and Nation* on this day: "Jean Rhys (Mrs Tilden Smith) author of *Voyage in the Dark, After Leaving Mr Mackenzie, Good Morning, Midnight*, etc. Will anyone knowing her whereabouts kindly communicate with Dr

H. W. Egli." Replying to the ad led Rhys to Selma Vaz Dias, Dr. Egli's wife, who had adapted *Good Morning, Midnight* for the stage, and who would become a domineering champion of her work through Rhys's many more years of poverty, drunkenness, illness, and obscurity until late in life—too late, Rhys always said—her novel *Wide Sargasso Sea* made her a literary celebrity in 1966.

1986 The giddiest moment in Alan Hollinghurst's Man Booker Prize–winning novel, *The Line of Beauty*, comes at a silver anniversary party for a politically ambitious couple when a lower-class friend of the family, Nick Guest, the aptly named hero of the story whose confidence has just been boosted by a bump of cocaine, asks the party's guest of honor, whose arrival has sent the entire house into near hysterics of excitement, to dance. The guest of honor is Prime Minister Margaret Thatcher, the song is "Get Off of My Cloud," and the moment is giddy not just because of Nick's daringly successful impudence, but also because of Hollinghurst's own audacity in pulling recent history into his own story with such style.

1987 Thomas R. Edwards, in the *New York Review of Books*, on Toni Morrison's *Beloved*: "One can only try to suggest something of what it is like to find one's way through an extraordinary act of imagination while knowing that one has missed much, that later reading will find more, and that no reader will ever see all the way in."

BORN: 1921 James Jones (*From Here to Eternity, The Thin Red Line*), Robinson, Ill.
1952 Michael Cunningham (*The Hours*), Cincinnati

DIED: 1901 Kate Greenaway (*Under the Window, Marigold Garden*), 55, London
1999 George V. Higgins (*The Friends of Eddie Coyle*), 59, Milton, Mass.

1699 The only survivor of a shipwreck somewhere northwest of Tasmania, Lemuel Gulliver awakens bound to the ground, unable to move any part of his body and with forty or so tiny men, armed with bows and arrows, advancing across his prone torso. The men scatter at his roar but, bravely, they soon return, and what follows is a small miracle of cross-cultural communication, in which Gulliver and his captors, though they share no language, agree that he will not murder scores of them with the sweep of his giant hand and they, in return, will not torment him with the piercings of a thousand tiny arrows. The Lilliputians feed the giant as best they can and comprehend his needs well enough to loosen his bonds so that he can, to the peril of those nearby, "ease myself with making water; which I very plentifully did, to the great astonishment of the people."

1839 At noon on this fall Wednesday, twenty-five New England women assembled in the Boston apartment of Mary Peabody for the first "Conversation" in a new series hosted by Margaret Fuller, already gaining at age twenty-nine a reputation as a remarkable intellect. Scheduled on Wednesdays so the attendees could stay in town for her friend Emerson's "Present Age" lecture series in the evening, the Conversations began as more of a monologue by the charismatic Fuller on her subject of the Greek myths, but in the five years she led the discussions she became the "nucleus of conversation," "call[ing] out the thought of others" toward her aim that women should not just be superficially educated but, like men, should "reproduce" what they learn, in conversation with each other if not out in the public world where they were less free to operate.

1932 Over 3,000 people died in the Cuba hurricane of 1932, one of the century's deadliest, but none of them were aboard the SS *Phemius*, a 7,400-ton merchant steamer whose massive central funnel was blown overboard by winds topping 200 mph. The ship and crew were dragged across the sea by the storm for five brutal days, and the captain's report on their improbable survival so moved the chairman of his shipping line that he passed it along to novelist Richard Hughes, whose strange sea story, *A High Wind in Jamaica*, had just been a great success, in hopes he could record an event "that must never be forgotten." Six years later, Hughes produced *In Hazard*, a short, taut novel that holds tight to the dramatic details of the *Phemius*'s ordeal.

1944 J. R. R. Tolkien buried a hen and grease-banded his apple trees.

November 7

BORN: 1913 Albert Camus (*The Stranger, The Plague, The Fall*), Dréan, French Algeria
1954 Guy Gavriel Kay (*Tigana, The Summer Tree*), Weyburn, Sask.
DIED: 1910 Leo Tolstoy (*The Death of Ivan Ilyich*), 82, Astapovo, Russia
1992 Richard Yates (*Revolutionary Road*), 66, Birmingham, Ala.

1874 In the *Times* of London, Arthur Rimbaud placed an advertisement: "A PARISIAN (20), of high literary and linguistic attainments, excellent conversation, will be glad to ACCOMPANY a GENTLEMAN (artists preferred) or a family wishing to travel in southern or eastern countries. Good references. A.R. No. 165, King's-road, Reading."

1896 Eleven-year-old Ezra Pound published his first poem in the *Jenkintown Times-Chronicle*, a limerick on the defeat of Williams Jennings Bryan by William McKinley that begins "There was a young man from the West."

1900 Perhaps it was his immersion in the culture of the twelfth century for the study that would become *Mont Saint Michel and Chartres* that made Henry Adams so receptive to the shock of the new twentieth century at the Paris Exhibition of 1900. In a November letter to his old friend John Hay, Adams marveled at the mysterious power of the electric dynamos on display there, and over the next seven years this shock became the engine behind his singular autobiography, *The Education of Henry Adams*, driven by the contrast between the forces of medieval and modern life ("the Virgin and the Dynamo," in his words) and by Adams's own history as a child of the colonial era making his way in the modern one, "his historical neck broken by the sudden irruption of forces totally new."

1955 While traveling the country for what would become one of the most influential photography books of the century, *The Americans*, Robert Frank was arrested in McGehee, Arkansas, and interrogated for twelve hours in the city jail—"Who are you? Where are you going? Why do you have foreign whiskey in your glove compartment? Are you Jewish? Why did they let you shoot photos at the Ford plant? Why did you take pictures in Scottsboro? Do you know what a commie is?"—before being released.

1972 Flying home from Rome to Colorado on this day to vote for McGovern, James Salter assured Robert Phelps, "Your life is the correct life . . . Your desk is the desk of a man who cannot be bought." In their mutually affectionate and admiring correspondence, which began with a fan letter from Phelps about Salter's novel *A Sport and a Pastime*, Salter was the novelist more admired than popular and Phelps the impossibly well-read journalist who lived in fear of never rising above what he considered hackwork to write something great: "You are wrong about my 'life,'" he replied to Salter. "For 20 years, I have only scrounged at making a living . . . Somewhere I took a wrong turning. I should not have tried to earn my living with my typewriter. I should have become a surveyor, or an airline ticket salesman, or a cat burglar."

BORN: **1900** Margaret Mitchell (*Gone with the Wind*), Atlanta

1954 Kazuo Ishiguro (*Never Let Me Go*), Nagasaki, Japan

DIED: **1674** John Milton (*Paradise Regained, Samson Agonistes*), 65, London

1998 Rumer Godden (*Black Narcissus*), 90, Courance, Scotland

1602 The Oxford University library, having been emptied in an anti-Catholic purge, was reborn with money from Sir Thomas Bodley, who had married a widow made wealthy by the sardine trade, and reopened on this day as the Bodleian Library.

1623 The booksellers Edward Blount and Isaac Jaggard registered on this day at the Stationers' Company a new publication: "Master William Shakspears *Comedyes, Histories, and Tragedies*." "As where (before) you were abus'd with diverse stolne, and surreptitious copies, maimed, and deformed by the frauds and stealthes of injurious impostors," the editors promised, the plays "are now offer'd to your view cur'd, and perfect of their limbes." Copies of what became known as the First Folio sold for roughly fifteen shillings (binding was extra), but the late author's reputation was slow in climbing to the level of his peers like Ben Jonson. The first recorded auction sale of a secondhand First Folio, which would later command upwards of $6 million, was for eight and a half shillings, barely half its original price.

1763 It says something about the market for intellectuals in the eighteenth century that Adam Smith, having made his philosophical reputation by publishing his *Theory of Moral Sentiments*, found it an easy decision to resign his post as Professor of Moral Philosophy at the University of Glasgow to become instead the tutor to a teenager, the young, wealthy, and well-connected Duke of Buccleuch. The benefits of his new position included a doubled salary, a lifetime pension, a new appreciation for expensive clothes and the opera, and entree to the intellectual salons of Europe, where he met Voltaire and others and further developed the ideas he would spend the ten years after his return to Great Britain in 1766 fashioning into his masterwork, *The Wealth of Nations*.

1975 The Washerwomen had run before. Calling themselves "priests without a parish," the Washerwomen—three middle-aged sisters, Gina, Karen, and Rose—rewrote the Bible (replacing "Israelites" with "Negroes," among other things) and preached, with a vitality that attracted a loyal few, that "every church was broken" except their own. They first fled from Jacksonville, Florida—where they had, in their righteousness, murdered the rest of their family—to found their church in Queens, and now they were packed and ready, along with their tiny flock, to run again. But with the police at the door, their flight became another massacre, a "Night of Thunder" from which few escaped, among them Ricky Rice, a child who, in Victor LaValle's intricate novel of doubt and belief, *Big Machine*, grows up to find himself in battle against another suicidal cult.

November 9

BORN: 1924 Robert Frank (*The Americans, The Lines of My Hand*), Zurich
1934 Carl Sagan (*Cosmos, Contact, The Dragons of Eden*), Brooklyn
DIED: 2001 Dorothy Dunnett (*The Game of Kings*), 78, Edinburgh
2004 Stieg Larsson (*The Girl with the Dragon Tattoo*), 50, Stockholm

NO YEAR You might wonder at first what the *Quicksand* in the title of Nella Larsen's first novel, which made her a bright light of the Harlem Renaissance before she suddenly abandoned writing a few years later, refers to, since Helga Crane, her heroine, is always on the move, from the South to Chicago to Harlem to Denmark and back to Harlem again, restlessly unsure of where she belongs. But on a rainy day in New York, humiliated by her desires the night before, she stumbles into a storefront church and, against her judgment, is consumed by the orgy of faith around her and—either lost or saved, she doesn't know—makes a choice that mires her into a life from which there's no escape. But which was the quicksand—the restless whirlpool of her earlier life, or the thoughtless sinking toward its end?

1965 "You're wasting your time. What you got there," Frank Sinatra said on this day as he watched himself sing on a TV studio monitor, "is a man with a cold." It's part of the legend of Gay Talese's great profile, "Frank Sinatra Has a Cold," that he never spoke directly with Sinatra while reporting it, but he didn't need to hear it straight from Frank to know his health. "A Sinatra with a cold can," Talese wrote, "in a small way, send vibrations through the entertainment industry and beyond." With its portrait of a celebrity through those whose lives orbit around him—the bodyguard scanning a room for approaching trouble, the staffers repainting his jeep in the middle of the night in response to an offhand remark—"Frank Sinatra Has a Cold" made its own waves when it appeared in *Esquire* in 1966.

1967 *Rolling Stone*, called "sort of a magazine and sort of a newspaper" by editor Jann Wenner, debuted.

2011 Christopher Hitchens's hospital room in the M. D. Anderson Cancer Center in Houston was, as Ian McEwan put it, raised temporarily "to the condition of a good university library." It was Hitch's last home, and when McEwan made his final visit there Hitchens borrowed the Peter Ackroyd book his friend had been reading on the plane and finished it that night. Hitchens would be dead in a little more than a month—and had few illusions it would be otherwise—but still he worked away, weakened by pain and morphine, at a 3,000-word review of a Chesterton biography, while talking of Dreiser, Browning, and *The Magic Mountain* with his friends. McEwan, by Hitchens's request, read Larkin's "Whitsun Weddings" aloud, and their debate about its ending's ambiguous arrows continued, unresolved, into the last e-mails that followed their in-person goodbyes.

BORN: **1893** John P. Marquand (*The Late George Apley*), Wilmington, Del.
1960 Neil Gaiman (*The Sandman, American Gods*), Portchester, England
DIED: **1995** Ken Saro-Wiwa (*Sozaboy, A Month and a Day*), 54, Port Harcourt, Nigeria
2007 Norman Mailer (*The Armies of the Night*), 84, New York City

NO YEAR Long before historians confirmed that Thomas Jefferson was the father of his slave Sally Hemings's children, the rumors of his paternity were common enough that William Wells Brown could make the fate of two such children the basis of his 1853 novel, *Clotel; or, The President's Daughter.* Brown's novel, the first by an African American, opens with the sale at a slave auction on this day of Currer, once Jefferson's laundress, and her teenage daughters, Clotel and Althesa, and nears its end, after each has succumbed to the savage caprices of slavery, with the matter-of-fact declaration, "Thus died Clotel, the daughter of Thomas Jefferson, a president of the United States; a man distinguished as the author of the Declaration of American Independence, and one of the first statesmen of that country."

1855 The second edition of Walt Whitman's *Leaves of Grass* is best known for carrying the most famous blurb in American publishing history: "I greet you at the Beginning of a Great Career—R. W. Emerson," which, to Emerson's dismay, Whitman put right on the cover. But inside the book, alongside Emerson's admiring letter and other raves for the first edition of *Leaves,*

he quoted the pans, including Rufus Griswold's judgment on this day that the *Leaves* were "a mass of stupid filth": "It is impossible to imagine how any man's fancy could have conceived it, unless he were possessed of the soul of a sentimental donkey that had died of disappointed love."

1880 Is Arthur Rimbaud better remembered for the precocious age at which his poetic career began or the age, nearly as young, at which he ended it? Cut short not by death like Keats or Chatterton but by his own restlessness, Rimbaud's voice flourished in his late teens and then fell silent. Rimbaud later surfaced as a coffee trader in Aden and then, on this day, signed a contract to become his firm's representative in Harar, Ethiopia, where until his death of cancer in 1891 he sent a variety of goods—ivory, frankincense, panther skins, rifles—in camel caravans across the desert while in Paris the reputation of his abandoned poetry grew.

1905 Alexander Innes Shand, in the *TLS,* on President Theodore Roosevelt's *Outdoor Pastimes of an American Hunter*: "It may be said that he risks a valuable life too freely in treading dizzy ledges after the bighorn, in rushing in through the worrying pack of savage hounds to drive his hunting knife between the shoulders of the cougar, or in galloping a half-broken pony over slopes of shale or ground that is honeycombed with the burrows of the prairie dog. But that is the way it pleases him to take his well-earned holidays."

November 11

BORN: 1922 Kurt Vonnegut (*Slaughterhouse-Five, Cat's Cradle*), Indianapolis
1954 Mary Gaitskill (*Bad Behavior, Veronica*), Lexington, Ky.
DIED: 1999 Jacobo Timerman (*Prisoner Without a Name, Cell Without a Number*), 76, Buenos Aires
2005 Peter Drucker (*Concept of the Corporation*), 95, Claremont, Calif.

NO YEAR Rarely in literature does a life of reading come to such a bad end as in the case of Leonard Bast, the doomed young insurance clerk in whom the Schlegel sisters "take an interest" in E. M. Forster's *Howards End*. Twenty years old when they meet him—today is his birthday—and living "at the extreme verge of gentility" (with the anonymous abyss of poverty gaping on the other side), Leonard tries to improve himself by reading Ruskin and Ibsen, but for the Schlegels he always seems less a man than a "cause," and when he dies in the entry hall of their house, smothered by their books, one isn't sure who is the clumsier: Leonard for pulling over the bookcase, or Forster for ending his life with such heavy symbolism.

NO YEAR In Argentina, according to Pippi Longstocking, Christmas vacation begins on this day, ten days after the end of summer vacation.

1948 "Hey, boy!" From his table at Les Deux Magots Richard Wright offered his familiar, smiling greeting when James Baldwin arrived in Paris for the first time.

Baldwin, in fear that his hometown of New York would destroy him if he stayed, went into exile with Wright as his model, but their "pleased and conspiratorial" embrace at the café would be one of their last. Just a few months later Baldwin published "Everybody's Protest Novel," an essay that appeared to everyone but Baldwin to be an attack on Wright's *Native Son*. Wright certainly thought so, and lit into Baldwin at another café on the day it came out. "Richard was right to be hurt," Baldwin later admitted, when he better understood his own Oedipal motivations: "His work was a road-block in my road, the sphinx, really, whose riddles I had to answer before I could become myself."

196- The eleventh of November of this vaguely enumerated year (which matches the 1962 of the history books) is a Sunday, which means that Fred Exley, the narrator of the "fictional memoir" by Frederick Exley called *A Fan's Notes*, is getting ready to watch a New York Giants football game at the bar of the New Parrot Restaurant in Watertown, N.Y. Exley, an English teacher and a drunk and, above all else perhaps, a Giants fan, doesn't make it to kickoff, though: he suffers what he takes to be a heart attack but what a nurse at the nearby hospital informs him are the pains of "drinking too much." Exley's novel begins at this point and circles back to return to it, much the way Exley's own sodden life is now inextricably linked to this great and graceful book.

BORN: 1915 Roland Barthes (*Mythologies, S/Z*), Cherbourg, France
1945 Tracy Kidder (*Mountains Beyond Mountains*), New York City
DIED: 1984 Chester Himes (*If He Hollers Let Him Go*), 75, Moraira, Spain
2007 Ira Levin (*Rosemary's Baby, The Stepford Wives*), 78, New York City

1828 A symphony wasn't all that Franz Schubert left unfinished when he died at the age of thirty-one. On this day, quickly deteriorating, he made a special request to his friend and librettist Franz von Schober in what turned out to be his final letter, "Please be so good as to come to my aid in this desperate condition with something to read. I have read Cooper's *Last of the Mohicans*, *The Spy*, *The Pilot*, and *The Pioneers*. If by any chance you have anything else of his, I beg you to leave it for me at the coffee-house with Frau von Bogner." It's not known if his request was granted—Europe was mad for James Fenimore Cooper in those days, and *The Prairie* and *The Red Rover* were translated into German as soon as they were published in English—but Schubert quickly fell further into spells of delirium and fever and died a week later.

1969 It wasn't quite a secret that American troops had massacred hundreds of unarmed civilians in a Vietnamese hamlet known as My Lai on March 16, 1968. Word soon got out within the army, and thanks to an ex-soldier whistle-blower, the following summer Lieutenant William Calley was quietly charged with murder. But no reporter had talked to Calley himself until Seymour Hersh followed a tip and traveled to Fort Benning, where, after midnight, he shared a few drinks with the young lieutenant, who had the look of "an earnest freshman one might find at an agricultural college, anxious about making a fraternity." Later on this day, Hersh wrote up his findings for the first of a series of newspaper articles that, as photographs of the incident and further eyewitness testimony appeared, broke open one of the biggest scandals of the war.

2008 Jonathan Lethem, in the *New York Times*, on Roberto Bolaño's *2666*: "By writing across the grain of his doubts about what literature can do, how much it can discover or dare pronounce the names of our world's disasters, Bolaño has proven it can do anything, and for an instant, at least, given a name to the unnamable."

November 13

BORN: 354 St. Augustine (*Confessions*, *City of God*), Thagaste, Roman Africa
1850 Robert Louis Stevenson (*Treasure Island*, *Kidnapped*), Edinburgh
DIED: 1955 Bernard DeVoto (*Across the Wide Missouri*), 58, New York City
2012 Jack Gilbert (*Views of Jeopardy*, *Refusing Heaven*), 87, Berkeley, Calif.

1797 They had thought to make some money by collaborating on a popular poem for the new *Monthly Magazine*, so on a winter's walk on this evening Samuel Taylor Coleridge and William Wordsworth began to plan a ballad about a sea journey. Wordsworth quickly realized how different their working styles were and dropped out of the project, but not before making a suggestion, involving the giant albatrosses he had read about in sailors' tales: "'Suppose,' said I, 'you represent him as having killed one of these birds on entering the South Sea, and that the tutelary Spirits of these regions take upon them to avenge the crime.'" After further walking and talking, and then five months of intense poetic labor, Coleridge completed "The Rime of the Ancient Mariner."

1849 Herman Melville paid half a crown to stand on an adjacent roof to watch the execution of Mr. and Mrs. Manning, convicted murderers, in London: "The man & wife were hung side by side—still unreconciled to each other—What a change from the time they stood up to be married, together!"

1874 Mark Twain was just a few books into his remarkable career, but his celebrity was advanced enough that when he announced by telegram that he and his good friend Rev. Joseph Twichell would be walking from his home in Hartford to Boston, over a hundred miles away, the Associated Press sent out bulletins on their progress. Whether they actually planned to complete the stunt or not, the pilgrims lasted a day and a half and thirty-five miles and finished the journey by train. William Dean Howells welcomed the weary travelers with a feast in Boston and reported, "I never saw a more used-up, hungrier man than Clemens. It was something fearful to see him eat escalloped oysters."

1952 Though she was just forty-two, Margaret Wise Brown had nearly a hundred children's books to her name when she took ill while traveling in Europe. Treated for an ovarian cyst, she grew fond of the nuns at the hospital and, to show one how well she was doing before being released, kicked a foot high in the air from her hospital bed, dislodging a blood clot in her leg that quickly traveled to her brain and killed her. With typically impulsive generosity—and little imagining it would take effect so soon or that its value would increase so significantly—she had recently revised her will to leave the copyright to most of her books, including *Goodnight Moon* and *The Runaway Bunny*, to a friend's eight-year-old son, who spent most of his adult life as a drifter, arrested for petty crimes and living off his ever-growing royalty checks.

November 14

BORN: **1907** Astrid Lindgren (*Pippi Longstocking*), Vimmerby, Sweden
1907 William Steig (*Shrek!*, *Sylvester and the Magic Pebble*), Brooklyn

DIED: **1831** G. W. F. Hegel (*Phenomenology of Spirit*), 61, Berlin
1965 Dawn Powell (*The Locusts Have No King*), 68, New York City

1851 "I should have a paper-mill established at one end of my house, and so have an endless riband of foolscap rolling in upon my desk; and upon that endless riband I should write a thousand—a million—billion thoughts, all under the form of a letter to you. The divine magnet is on you, and my magnet responds. Which is the biggest? A foolish question—they are *One.*" Is that Kerouac writing ecstatically to Ginsberg in the 1950s? No, it was Herman Melville gushing to Nathaniel Hawthorne a century before, replying to the letter—lost to history—Hawthorne sent him after he received his copy of *Moby-Dick*, the book Melville published on this day and dedicated to his new friend Hawthorne "in token of my admiration for his genius."

1916 During a break in the dark early-morning hours of the Battle of the Ancre, H. H. Munro, a lance sergeant known under the pen name Saki, spoke his last words to a fellow soldier before being shot by a German sniper: "Put that bloody cigarette out."

1928 The tales of F. Scott Fitzgerald's drinking are "exaggerated" and he's "a very nice chap indeed," P. G. Wodehouse reported to his stepdaughter. "The only thing is, he goes into New York with a scruffy chin, looking perfectly foul. I suppose he gets a shave when he arrives there, but it doesn't show him at his best in Great Neck."

1930 After three years in Paris, where he worked with James Joyce and published his first essays, Samuel Beckett returned to Dublin as a lecturer in French at his old university, Trinity College. Bored and restless, he diverted his energies into a spoof lecture he presented in French to the Modern Language Society there on Jean du Chas, a poet he had invented. He gave du Chas his own birthday, April 13, 1906, and concocted for him a literary movement, "Le Concentrisme," whose central concept was the hotel concierge as a figure of God. "That amused me for a couple of days," he wrote a friend on this day. "I wish to God I were in Paris again, even Germany, Nuremberg, annulled in beer."

November 15

BORN: 1930 J. G. Ballard (*Crash*, *Empire of the Sun*), Shanghai
1941 Daniel Pinkwater (*The Hoboken Chicken Emergency*), Memphis
DIED: 1932 Charles W. Chesnutt (*The Marrow of Tradition*), 74, Cleveland
1978 Margaret Mead (*Coming of Age in Samoa*), 76, New York City

1854 The elopement of Marian Evans (not yet known as George Eliot, the novelist she'd become) with George Henry Lewes, a married man, caused a fizz of scandal among their friends in England. Perhaps the most offended was George Combe, the leading English exponent of the new science of phrenology, the assessment of character through brain measurement. It was bad enough that she had run off with Lewes, a skeptic of phrenology. But worse: how could a woman with "*her* brain," which Combe had once judged among the most impressive of any woman's he'd measured, have so degraded herself? He searched for an explanation, and in a letter on this day he asked, is there "insanity in Miss Evans's family?"

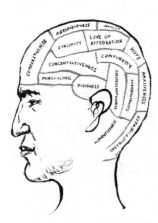

1905 "For the first time the veil has been lifted from New York society," promised the ad wrapped around Edith Wharton's *The House of Mirth*, and on the *New York Times* letters page controversy soon erupted between readers who named themselves after society enclaves Wharton knew well, "Newport" and "Lenox." After Newport argued on this day that the book, with its "detestable story" and "Henry Jamesey style," should be retitled "The House of Lies," Lenox came to the defense of Wharton's "true literature." Newport then admitted that what irked him wasn't so much the truth of Wharton's portrait as the airing of it: "In society, we regale ourselves with the latest scandal about Mrs. X., but we don't shout it out in a Subway car."

1945 Albert Camus's *The Stranger* was his "American" novel, breaking from French traditions with a hard-boiled style borrowed from Hemingway, Steinbeck, Erskine Caldwell, and James M. Cain. Camus acknowledged his debts in an interview on this day, three years after *The Stranger* was published, but he assured French readers his borrowing was a one-time thing. Writing only in the American style would create merely a "universe of robots and of instincts." He would trade a hundred Hemingways, he added, for a single one of his countrymen like Stendhal or Benjamin Constant.

1947 Maurice Lane Richardson, in the *TLS*, on Ayn Rand's *The Fountainhead*: "In spite of all its pretentiousness and affectation, its total humourlessness, the book does impart a feeling of sincerity, a genuine concern for architecture."

November 16

BORN: **1930** Chinua Achebe (*Things Fall Apart, No Longer at Ease*), Ogidi, Nigeria
1954 Andrea Barrett (*Ship Fever, The Voyage of the Narwhal*), Boston

DIED: **1973** Alan Watts (*The Way of Zen*), 58, Druid Heights, Calif.
2006 Milton Friedman (*Capitalism and Freedom*), 94, San Francisco

1865 "It has been a melancholy task to read this book; and it is a still more melancholy one to write about it." Just a year into his literary career, Henry James reviewed in the *Nation* a new book of verse: *Drum-Taps*, by Walt Whitman. James's melancholy mood was brought on not by the poems' solemn subject, the Civil War, but by their "monstrous" author: "It is not enough," he wrote, "to be aggressively careless, inelegant, and ignorant, and to be constantly preoccupied with yourself. It is not enough to be rude, lugubrious, and grim. You must also be serious. You must forget yourself in your ideas." Certainly the self-submerging James must have found Whitman's celebration of himself disconcerting, but he'd come to regret this review as a "little atrocity perpetrated in the gross impudence of youth."

1928 Three months after James Douglas, the editor of the *Sunday Express*, launched a campaign against "A Book That Must Be Suppressed," Chief Magistrate Sir Chartres Biron agreed, ruling Radclyffe Hall's novel *The Well of Loneliness* obscene for portraying the physical love between women "in the most alluring terms." The defense counsel at first had tried to argue the book wasn't about sex at all but later in the trial admitted, after Hall insisted he do so, that in fact it *was* about sex. Meanwhile, Sir Chartres rejected the dozens of expert witnesses prepared to defend the book, including Virginia Woolf and E. M. Forster, remarking, "I don't think people are entitled to express an opinion upon a matter which is the decision of the court." When Sir Chartres gave his verdict, Hall, unable to testify herself, expressed her own opinion from the gallery: "It is shameful."

1952 Humbert Humbert, in *Lolita*, dies from coronary thrombosis, a few days before his trial for murder was to begin.

1961 Robert A. Heinlein reported to his agent that his "bomb shelter is completed and stocked."

1970 With the money from the film of his bestselling novel, *The Liberation of Lord Byron Jones*, the story of a black undertaker shot by a white policeman who was sleeping with his wife, Jesse Hill Ford built an estate in Tennessee he called Canterfield, and there, on this day, his novel found an awful parallel in his own life when he shot and killed the black driver of a car parked in his driveway. Having written a novel about a white man acquitted of murder in the death of a black man, Ford was himself acquitted in a trial whose ironies drew the attention and scorn of the national press and, by his own account, sapped his capacity to imagine the complex and empathetic fiction that had once made his name.

November 17

BORN: 1916 Shelby Foote (*The Civil War*, *Shiloh*), Greenville, Miss.
 1983 Christopher Paolini (*Eragon*, *Eldest*), Los Angeles
DIED: 1968 Mervyn Peake (*Titus Groan*, *Gormenghast*), 57, Burcot, England
 1992 Audre Lorde (*Zami*, *Sister Outsider*), 58, St. Croix

1868 Anthony Trollope, running as a Liberal candidate for Parliament in what turned out to be "the most wretched fortnight of my manhood," finished fourth among four candidates.

2003 Of the thirty-seven courses in the eleven-hour lunch the novelist Jim Harrison shared with eleven fellow gourmands in France and later chronicled for *The New Yorker*, he declined only one: oysters and cream of Camembert on toast, a combination that turns his tummy. The other thirty-six, all based on archival recipes from the history of French cookery, he happily and/or dutifully consumed; he particularly enjoyed

the "tart of calf's brains with shelled peas" and the "filet of sole with champagne sauce accompanied by monkfish livers." And to those who might question the excess of a meal that "cost as much as a new Volvo station wagon," he can only reply, "Life is a near-death experience, and our devious minds will do anything to make it interesting."

2006 Emma Tinker, in the *TLS*, on Alison Bechdel's *Fun Home*: "*Fun Home* is a reminder of why the graphic form is so well suited to memoir: like a quarrelling couple, words and images do not always collaborate, but undermine each other and reveal each other's lies."

YEAR OF THE DEPENDS ADULT UNDERGARMENT David Foster Wallace deflected questions about how he knew so much about the drug and alcohol recovery culture in *Infinite Jest*, saying he'd visited AA meetings as a "voyeur." Only after his death did it become widely known that he had spent most of his adult life in recovery, including a stay at a Boston halfway house called Granada House, the model for Ennet House in the novel, where on this morning (in the book's corporate-sponsored yearly calendar) Hal Incandenza, the brainiac high school tennis star and pot addict who is the closest thing to a stand-in for the author, nervously knocks at the front door, radiating, to the jaded eye of Ennet's director, "high-maintenance upkeep and privilege and schools where nobody carried weapons, pretty much a whole planet of privilege away from" the lives of the house's usual clientele.

BORN: **1939** Margaret Atwood (*The Handmaid's Tale, Cat's Eye*), Ottawa, Ont.
1953 Alan Moore (*Watchmen, V for Vendetta*), Northampton, England

DIED: **1922** Marcel Proust (*In Search of Lost Time*), 51, Paris
1999 Paul Bowles (*The Sheltering Sky*), 88, Tangier, Morocco

1842 "Never was any thing more promising," Dr. Matthew Allen, the proprietor of an insane asylum, assured Alfred Tennyson and his family about his plan to produce machine-carved wooden furniture. "All things are a lie and all things are false if this fails." Fail it did, though, after Tennyson and his relations poured much of their inheritance into the project—on this day Tennyson attempted to intervene when he heard his brother Septimus was about to lend the doctor another £1,000, on top of the £8,000 they had already lost—although the Tennysons did regain much of their money a few years later, when a life insurance policy signed over to them was redeemed at the death of the broken Dr. Allen.

1911 G. K. Chesterton, in the *Nation*, on J. M. Barrie's *Peter Pan*: "There is something almost anonymous about its popularity; we feel as if we had all written it. It is made out of fragments of our own forgotten dreams, and stirs the heart with sleepy unquiet, like pictures from a previous existence."

1963 They have the money, the plan, and the expert marksmen. All they need is a patsy and a map of the motorcade. At the end of *American Tabloid*, the first installment of Underworld USA, James Ellroy's fictional trilogy of conspiracy and repression, hard guys Pete Bondurant, Kemper Boyd, and Ward Littell converge in a room at the Miami Fontainebleau. Too many people want the president dead for it not to happen—"there's supposed to be a half-dozen or six dozen or two dozen more" plots in the works—and it's set to go down in Miami, on November 18, until word arrives that there's been a change of plans.

1975 *The Savage Detectives*, the first of Roberto Bolaño's two vast masterpieces, begins with one character making his way through Mexico City. Juan García Madero is seventeen, curious and companionable, studying law but idly consumed by poetry, conversation, and sex. For two months in the fall he's drawn into a circle of poets, talkers, and lovers, and on this date he records in his diary a day (and a night) that in its passivity and pleasure—talking about poetry and shoplifting, pining for one of the lovely Font sisters and then being seduced by the other—could be exchanged for many of the others. It's an idyll that will be upset in the coming pages, as the novel leaves García Madero behind to follow a multitude of voices and characters from Chile to Liberia, but never quite forgotten.

2005 "I'm in awe of his productivity," David Foster Wallace e-mailed Jonathan Franzen about their fellow novelist William T. Vollmann. "How many hours a day does this guy work?"

November 19

BORN: 1929 Norman Cantor (*Inventing the Middle Ages*), Winnipeg, Man.
1942 Sharon Olds (*The Dead and the Living, The Father*), San Francisco
DIED: 1974 Louise Fitzhugh (*Harriet the Spy*), 46, New Milford, Conn.
1975 Elizabeth Taylor (*Mrs. Palfrey at the Claremont*), 63, Penn, England

1845 Published: *The Raven and Other Poems* by Edgar Allan Poe (Wiley & Putnam, New York)

1849 Søren Kierkegaard's ending of his engagement with Regine Olsen was one of the great literary breakups. Kierkegaard certainly thought so: having renounced their mutual passion on this day in favor of his vocations for writing and for God, he kept his thoughts of her aflame in his philosophical works for the rest of his life, while she, heartbroken, married another. After eight years of seeing her around Copenhagen without being able to speak to her, he could bear it no longer and wrote to her husband, giving him the choice of passing on to Regine a letter he had enclosed for her. Her husband returned the second letter unopened. Six years later, when Kierkegaard died and willed everything to Regine "as if I had been married to her," it was her turn to say no.

1956 Ernest Hemingway often promised he would write his memoirs of Paris, especially after Gertrude Stein slighted him in her *Autobiography of Alice B. Toklas*. "I have a rat trap memory," he told Maxwell Perkins then, "and the documents." But his recollections got a boost when on this day the baggage men at the Ritz Hotel in Paris told him that two trunks he had stored there since the '20s would be thrown into the garbage if he didn't reclaim them. They turned out to be a "treasure trove" of old manuscripts and notebooks (and sandals and sweatshirts) that gave Hemingway the raw material for the reminiscences of *A Moveable Feast*, which settled scores with Stein, Dos Passos, and Fitzgerald and helped define—and name—an era.

2000 Anthony Quinn, in the *New York Times*, on Michel Houellebecq's *The Elementary Particles*: "One can only assume that France's literary scene must have been suffering a profound torpor if it responded with such outrage to this bilious, hysterical and oddly juvenile book."

2008 On her fiftieth birthday, law and history professor Annette Gordon-Reed won the National Book Award for Nonfiction for *The Hemingses of Monticello*, which kicked off an avalanche of awards for her work, including the Pulitzer Prize, a MacArthur Foundation "genius" grant, and the National Humanities Medal, all of which honored her decades of research that established to a near certainty the once-dismissed assertion that Thomas Jefferson was the father of his slave Sally Hemings's children. In *The Hemingses of Monticello*, though, she went much further, painting a rich history of the family of free and enslaved blacks who shared—and helped build—the president's hilltop home.

BORN: 1923 Nadine Gordimer (*July's People*), Springs, South Africa

1936 Don DeLillo (*Libra*, *White Noise*, *Underworld*), Bronx, N.Y.

DIED: 1947 Wolfgang Borchert (*The Man Outside*), 26, Basel, Switzerland

1995 Robie Macauley (*The End of Pity*, *Technique in Fiction*), 76, Boston

1942 Were they a macho lark, or serious business? Ernest Hemingway's wartime sea patrols have drawn mockery from biographers and friends alike—including his wife at the time, Martha Gellhorn—and one Cuban captain in the same waters later called him "a playboy who hunted submarines off the Cuban coast as a whim." But however much Hemingway was prone to self-mythology, when he took his thirty-eight-foot sportfishing boat, the *Pilar* (named after a character in *For Whom the Bell Tolls*), out of Havana harbor in search of German U-boats for the first time on this day with a crew of five and an insufficient arsenal of guns and grenades, they were not just playing at war. German subs downed hundreds of ships in the Caribbean during the war and dozens in the Straits of Florida alone, and Hemingway's was just one of the many civilian vessels, dubbed the Hooligan Navy, officially deputized to patrol sectors of the coastal waters.

1951 "Dear Mr. Leonard," began the letter from Marguerite E. Harper, Literary Agent. Harper had come across Elmore Leonard's first published story, "Trail of the Apaches,"

in a copy of *Argosy* magazine and was impressed at how well he told a long story with hardly any dialogue. Was he interested in having an agent? At twenty-six, Leonard was, but to make sure he wouldn't let the excitement get to his head, Harper warned in a letter nine days later, "DON'T GIVE UP YOUR JOB TO WRITE. I say this very seriously." He didn't: for another twenty years he paid the bills with advertising work in Detroit until, with the market for Westerns drying up, he made his entrance into crime fiction—and became known as one of its great masters of dialogue—with *The Big Bounce* in 1969.

NO YEAR On November 19, Jerome Belsey e-mailed his father from London, "We're in love! The Kipps girl and me! I'm going to ask her to marry me, Dad!" On November 21, he e-mailed again, "Dad—mistake. Shouldn't have said anything. Completely over—if it ever began." In between, though, Howard Belsey, his father, an English academic in Massachusetts, has already set out across the Atlantic in an anxious fury to confront his errant son as well as Monte Kipps, the father of the "Kipps girl" and his eternal academic rival in Zadie Smith's *On Beauty*, her "homage" to E. M. Forster's *Howards End*, which also begins with two messages, "I do not know what you will say: Paul and I are in love" and "All over. Wish I had never written. Tell no one," that come before and after a journey that, once begun, can't be called back.

November 21

BORN: 1694 Voltaire (*Candide, Philosophical Dictionary*), Paris
  1932 Beryl Bainbridge (*An Awfully Big Adventure*), Liverpool, England
DIED: 1970 Anzia Yezierska (*Bread Givers, Hungry Hearts*), c. 85, Ontario, Calif.
  2011 Anne McCaffrey (*The Dragonriders of Pern*), 85, County Wicklow, Ireland

1811 Fulfilling a suicide pact both delirious and deliberate, Heinrich von Kleist, a young dramatist and novelist considered by his family a parasite and a wastrel, shot Henriette Vogel, a woman with terminal cancer who had captivated him with her passion for death, and then himself at a rural inn outside Berlin. The two spent their final moments drinking coffee and rum and chasing each other like children, after writing letters of reconciliation and explanation to family and friends, assuring them that their souls were about to ascend "like two joyous balloonists" and making arrangements for their death, including, in Vogel's case, ordering a commemorative cup for her husband's Christmas present and, in Kleist's, asking the Prussian secretary of war to pay a final barber's bill he had forgotten.

1829 To the question "Whether the poems of Shelley have an immoral tendency" at a meeting of the Cambridge Apostles, Arthur Hallam and Alfred Tennyson voted "no."

1853 Charles Dickens updated his wife on Wilkie Collins's growing mustache: 'You remember how the corners of his mouth go down, and how he looks through his spectacles and manages his legs. I don't know how it is, but the moustache is a horrible aggravation of all this. He smoothes it down over his mouth, in imitation of the present great Original, and in all kinds of carriages is continually doing it."

1959 Hugh Kenner, in the *National Review*, on Richard Ellmann's *James Joyce*: "Much energy has gone into chronicling the shillings various men lent him, how many, on what date, and whether they were repaid; but as for his books, it suffices to inventory their scenes and identify their characters . . . So much for the thirty-five years of a great writer's time."

NO YEAR "Mr. Ewell, would you tell us in your own words what happened on the evening of November twenty-first, please?" asks the prosecutor, Mr. Gilmer. What happened at the Ewell home on that evening is what the jury, with the guidance of Mr. Gilmer and the defense attorney, Mr. Atticus Finch, must judge in Harper Lee's *To Kill a Mockingbird*. Did Tom Robinson beat and rape Mayella Ewell, as Mayella and her father tell the court, or, as Tom testifies, did her father beat Mayella after she asked Tom in to do a chore and tried to kiss him? The jury—"twelve reasonable men in everyday life"—is out a long time considering its verdict, almost long enough to offer the hope that justice might, this time, prevail.

1982 On the same night the killer of J. R. Ewing was revealed on *Dallas*, rock critic Lester Bangs and the Delinquents opened for Talking Heads at the Armadillo World Headquarters in Austin.

BORN: **1819** George Eliot (*Adam Bede, The Mill on the Floss*), Nuneaton, England
1969 Marjane Satrapi (*Persepolis, Chicken with Plums*), Rasht, Iran
DIED: **1916** Jack London (*The Call of the Wild*), 40, Glen Ellen, Calif.
1993 Anthony Burgess (*A Clockwork Orange*), 76, London

1890 "My wretched birthday," George Gissing wrote in his diary, in the midst of writing his greatest book, *New Grub Street.* "Am 33 yrs old."

1907 One of the most fascinating invented characters in recent American writing was born on this day. Duke Wolff is the main character in one novelist's book, Geoffrey Wolff's *The Duke of Deception*, and a supporting character in another, Tobias Wolff's *This Boy's Life*, but in both cases—the books are memoirs—the inventing was done not by the authors, Duke's two sons, but by the Duke himself, who claimed to have graduated from Yale and the Sorbonne, piloted test planes, and parachuted into Normandy. Records show that he did none of the above, and instead skipped out on bills, jumped bail, and committed check fraud in a lifelong con that makes him, in his sons' superb memoirs, both a monster and a wonder.

1963 Aldous Huxley, dying of laryngeal cancer and speaking only with difficulty, wrote a request to his wife, Laura, for a final injection: "Try LSD 100 mm intramuscular." She went to retrieve the drug from the next room, where Huxley's doctor and nurse, as well as the rest of the household, were watching a television that was rarely used. "This is madness," Laura thought, "these people looking at television when Aldous is dying," but as she opened the box of LSD vials, she heard that President Kennedy had been shot. Despite the doctor's uneasiness and her own trembling hands, Laura injected the psychedelic herself and said to her husband, much as Susila says to the dying Lakshmi in Huxley's last novel, *Island*, "Light and free you let go, darling; forward and up." Huxley spoke or wrote no more before dying peacefully six hours later.

1963 On the same day Huxley died in Los Angeles and the president died in Dallas, C. S. Lewis collapsed and died in London, two days after telling his brother, "I have done all that I was sent into the world to do, and I am ready to go."

1998 Michael Wood, in the *New York Times*, on Michael Cunningham's *The Hours*: "The connections between the two books, after the initial, perhaps overelaborate laying out of repetitions and divergences, are so rich and subtle and offbeat that not to read 'Mrs. Dalloway' after we've read 'The Hours' seems like a horrible denial of a readily available pleasure—as if we were to leave a concert just when the variations were getting interesting."

November 23

BORN: 1920 Paul Celan ("Death Fugue"),
Cernauti, Romania
1949 Gayl Jones (*Corregidora*, *The Healing*),
Lexington, Ky.
DIED: 1976 André Malraux (*Man's Fate*), 75,
Créteil, France
1990 Roald Dahl (*Fantastic Mr. Fox*, *The Twits*), 74, Oxford, England

1833 Honoré de Balzac's chair broke from overwork, the second to collapse under him in recent days.

1859 On the day before its publication, George Eliot began reading Darwin's *On the Origin of Species*. "Not impressive," she recorded at first, although two days later she realized the book "makes an epoch."

1905 Sometimes your brother is not your best reader. William and Henry James were well into their celebrated, but dissimilar, writing careers when William confessed his puzzlement at the "interminable elaboration of suggestive reference" in his younger brother's novel *The Golden Bowl*. "But why won't you, just to please Brother, sit down and write a new book, with no twilight or mustiness in the plot, with great vigor and decisiveness in the action ... Publish it in my name, I will acknowledge it, and give you half the proceeds." Henry, replying on this day, was a little miffed: "I shall greatly be humiliated if you *do* like it, & thereby lump it, in your affection, with things, of the current age, that I have heard you express admiration for & that I would sooner descend to a dishonoured grave than have written."

1973 "The bowl," on this cold Friday night, the day after Thanksgiving in New Canaan, Connecticut, "went around like the wine at Eucharist." The soundtrack from *Hair* is on the hi-fi, talk of Milton Friedman and *Jonathan Livingston Seagull* is in the air, and a key party is, it seems, what you're supposed to be open-minded enough to try as the straggly ends of the '60s reach the suburbs in Rick Moody's *The Ice Storm*, where the parents have no more idea what do with their desires and their dismay than their children do. In the Halfords' living room, hands reach eagerly or anxiously or indifferently into the white salad bowl for the house keys of someone else's spouse, as the roads and power lines outside become treacherous with ice.

1987 Lawrence Weschler's impishly serious curiosity has rarely had such room to operate as it did in *Boggs*, his profile of the artist J. S. G. Boggs, whose trial for illegally reproducing Her Majesty's paper currency began at the Old Bailey in London on this day. Boggs made a provocative conceptual career out of attempting to pay for goods and services with his own drawings of money, which meticulously matched the details of an official bill on one side but usually left the other side blank. (It was a good bargain for those who accepted: his bills were worth more as pieces of art than their face value.) The Bank of England was not amused, but Boggs's jury acquitted and then congratulated him.

BORN: 1888 Dale Carnegie (*How to Win Friends and Influence People*), Maryville, Mo.

1961 Arundhati Roy (*The God of Small Things*), Shillong, India

DIED: 2002 Harriet Doerr (*Stones for Ibarra*), 92, Pasadena, Calif.

2003 Hugh Kenner (*The Pound Era*), 80, Athens, Ga.

1859 Published: *On the Origin of Species by Means of Natural Selection, or the Preservation of Favoured Races in the Struggle for Life* by Charles Darwin (Murray, London)

1903 Just before midday, a well-dressed man who gave his name as George F. Robinson presented himself at the offices of the Bank of England and asked for the governor of the bank. Brought instead to the bank secretary, Kenneth Grahame (known then, until *The Wind in the Willows* came out five years later, as the author of *The Golden Age*, whose admirers included Theodore Roosevelt), he presented him with a manuscript tied with black and white ribbon. When Grahame refused to read the manuscript as asked, Robinson raised a revolver, shooting and missing three times as Grahame fled. Subdued and arrested, the gunman expressed "Socialist views" and declared that by grasping the end of the manuscript with the black ribbon rather than the white one Grahame had proved "that Fate demanded his immediate demise."

1922 It was an unlikely path that led Erskine Childers to stand blindfolded on this day in front of a firing squad in Dublin. Born in England but raised partly in Ireland, he gained early fame when his novel, *The Riddle of the Sands*, became a sensation with its spy-thriller plot and its warning of a German buildup to war. He left fiction behind, though, to focus on military affairs and then, with a convert's zeal, became consumed with home rule for Ireland, running guns on his yacht and becoming a leader of Irish independence. But when he resisted the compromise that created the Irish Free State, Childers, suspected a spy by some Irish and a traitor by the British, was arrested and executed by the Irish government. His last words, spoken with typical empathy and aplomb to the young men on the firing squad, were "Take a step or two forwards, lads. It will be easier that way."

1977 When a few fans followed the trail of the pen name James Tiptree Jr., which some had speculated hid a CIA professional or even Henry Kissinger but few had imagined was a woman, to a sixty-two-year-old psychologist in northern Virginia named Alice Sheldon, she felt she had to out herself, and so began writing to the colleagues she'd been corresponding with for years as Tiptree. On this day she confessed to Ursula Le Guin her fear that she'd lose her friends, especially among women, after her "put-on" was revealed. But Le Guin wrote back with excitement and affection: "Oh strange, most strange, most wonderful, beautiful, improbable . . . It would take an extraordinarily small soul to resent so immense, so funny, so effective and fantastic and ETHICAL a put-on."

November 25

BORN: 1909 P. D. Eastman (*Go, Dog. Go!*; *Are You My Mother?*), Amherst, Mass.
1951 Charlaine Harris (*Dead Until Dark*), Tunica, Miss.
DIED: 1968 Upton Sinclair (*The Jungle, Oil!, King Coal*), 90, Bound Brook, N.J.
1970 Yukio Mishima (*Spring Snow, The Sound of Waves*), 45, Tokyo

1862 "I had a real funny interview" with President Lincoln, Harriet Beecher Stowe reported to her husband, "the particulars of which I will tell you." The particulars, though, have been lost to history, including whether he greeted her with the words that have since become attached to her name, "So this is the little woman who made the great war?"

1889 After two editors rejected his new novel called *Too Late, Beloved!* as morally unsuitable, Thomas Hardy tried a third, Mowbray Morris at *Macmillan's Magazine*, who turned it down too. "You use the word *succulent* more than once," Morris replied. "Perhaps I might say that the general impression left on me by reading your story—so far as it has gone—is one of rather too much succulence." When the novel, which does have its moments of succulence, was eventually published as *Tess of the d'Urbervilles*, Morris weighed in again, in a review that said it told "a coarse and disagreeable story in a coarse and disagreeable manner." Hardy, always rubbed raw by bad notices, was nearly fed up: "Well, if this sort of thing continues no more novel-writing for me." Two novels later, the further hostility that met *Jude the Obscure* drove him to stick to poetry.

1921 Having entered Tufts University on the strength of a forged transcript for a high school he never graduated from, Nathan Weinstein did hardly a lick of work and by Thanksgiving was encouraged by the university to withdraw with failing grades in all his classes, among them a "double F" in French and a "Not Attending" record in phys ed (his lethargy would earn him the ironic nickname "Pep"). No matter. Helping himself to the credits of a more diligent Tufts student who shared his name, Weinstein fraudulently transferred to Brown University as a sophomore, and this time managed to graduate. Two years later, before leaving for Paris to become a writer, he chose a new identity of his own by changing his name, legally this time, to Nathanael West.

2004 For the soldiers of Bravo Squad touring the country after an Iraqi firefight made them celebrity heroes in Ben Fountain's satire of the home front, *Billy Lynn's Long Halftime Walk*, Texas Stadium on Thanksgiving Day is their Inferno, a bewildering extravaganza of Jack and Cokes, cell-phone Hollywood rumors, and backslaps and quavering thank-yous from Cowboys fans for their service. At halftime they descend to its deepest pit of hell, in which Destiny's Child, the Prairie View A&M marching band, and infinite armies of drill girls, flag twirlers, and ROTC extras strut and gyrate around them as they stand at attention at midfield, one day before being shipped back to their desert war zone.

BORN: 1922 Charles M. Schulz (*Peanuts*), Minneapolis

1943 Marilynne Robinson (*Housekeeping, Gilead, Home*), Sandpoint, Idaho

DIED: 1974 Cyril Connolly (*Enemies of Promise*), 71, Eastbourne, England

2005 Stan Berenstain (The Berenstain Bears), 82, Solebury, Pa.

1791 "There will be very few Dates in this History," the young author promised in her *History of England*, and indeed there were almost none until the final page, where she wrote, "Finis, Saturday Nov. 26 1791." The author was Jane Austen, age fifteen, and her *History*, written for the pleasure of her family, summed up two and a half centuries of British rulers with a breezy impertinence promised by her opening line, "Henry the 4th ascended the throne of England much to his own satisfaction in the year 1399, after having prevailed on his cousin and predecessor Richard the 2d, to resign it to him, and to retire for the rest of his Life to Pomfret Castle, where he happened to be murdered." Illustrated by her sister Cassandra, Austen's schoolgirl romp was likely inspired by the marginal notes—"Detestable Monster!" "Sweet Man!"—she left in the family copy of Goldsmith's *History of England*, and by her Stuart contempt for Queen Elizabeth, "that pest of society."

NO YEAR "The prospect of the Netherfield ball was extremely agreeable to every female" of the Bennet family, but none is so disappointed in its outcome as the second-eldest daughter, Elizabeth. She had looked forward to dancing with the charming Mr. Wickham, who had just informed her of the perfidy of his former friend Mr. Darcy, but instead, with Wickham nowhere to be found, she finds herself paired first with the dreary clergyman Mr. Collins and then with the hated Darcy himself, whose ironic sally, "What think you of books?" gets him nowhere. The following day brings no improvement, only an unwanted but insistent proposal from Mr. Collins. Darcy's proposal, and Elizabeth's awakened love for him, will have to await a later season in Austen's *Pride and Prejudice*.

1922 Howard Carter had excavated in Egypt's Valley of the Kings for five seasons with little to show for it when a workman discovered a step cut into the rock. Carter's team soon unearthed twelve steps leading down to a door, but rather than continue, they covered up what they had found and waited for their patron Lord Carnarvon to arrive. Three weeks later, they removed the door and cleared the passage behind it, and on this day, "one whose like I can never hope to see again," as Carter wrote in *The Tomb of Tutankhamen*, he made a small breach in another sealed door, held a candle in the opening, and looked through. "Can you see anything?" asked Carnarvon from behind. "Yes, wonderful things."

1993 Natasha Walter, in the *TLS*, on Annie Proulx's *The Shipping News*: "Now that Proulx has made her mark, she should aim higher and get herself some characters she can respect."

November 27

BORN: 1909 James Agee (*Let Us Now Praise Famous Men*), Knoxville, Tenn.
1964 David Rakoff (*Half Empty*, *Don't Get Too Comfortable*), Montreal
DIED: 8 B.C. Horace (*Satires*, *Odes*, *Epistles*), 56, Rome
2006 Bebe Moore Campbell (*Your Blues Ain't Like Mine*), 56, Los Angeles

1886 It's not out of rage or vengeance that Baron Innstetten challenges Major Crampas to a duel in Theodor Fontane's *Effi Briest*, but a stubborn, sullen submission to the demands of Prussian society. Once the baron discovers Crampas's love letters to the baron's young wife, Effi, the rules of honor leave him, and his rival, no choice. And so they proceed to the dunes and mark ten paces, and so the shots ring out, and so Effi proceeds to her own inexorable, socially decreed doom. But things turned out differently for the real-life Effi. Fontane based the novel, which made him a belated success at age seventy-five, on a well-known case that ended in a similar duel on this day, but the object of that duel, Elisabeth von Ardenne, chose another fate entirely: cast out from society like Effi and deprived of her children, she gave her life to nursing and lived another sixty-five years.

19– Tom Ripley slept well on the train to Naples—confident and content as never before—and after disposing of Dickie's toothbrush, hairbrush, raincoat, and blood-stained trousers in an alley, he takes the bus to the town they'd left a few days before.

Tom hadn't planned to kill Dickie, or rather he had planned it just a few hours before he took the oar in his hand and did it, and from now on he'll have to keep improvising, keep looking just a little ahead of himself. It begins right away, when Dickie's girlfriend, Marge, asks, "Where's Dickie?" Tom, calm and prepared, has the answer ready: "He's in Rome." Soon, in Patricia Highsmith's *The Talented Mr. Ripley*, Tom himself will be in Rome, living Dickie's wonderful life.

1947 Over the Thanksgiving holiday, after Saul Bellow's second novel, *The Victim*, was published, his father offered to make him a mine supervisor at $10,000 a year.

2006 Only nine months before, Boss Wang and Boss Gao had opened their new bra-ring factory in Lishui, taking advantage of a new expressway from the coast to the southern Chinese town, but by November 28, the auspicious eighth day of the Chinese lunar month, they were ready to move to a different city. They didn't tell the workers until the 26th, which left this day for Master Luo to negotiate with the Tao family about whether their efficient teenage daughters— "Yufeng can do ten thousand pairs of wires in a day. Where are you going to find a new worker who's that fast?"—would move with the factory, just one of the everyday moments through which Peter Hessler, in his brilliantly observed *Country Driving*, tells the story of China's massive and sudden transformations as well as any epic history could.

BORN: 1757 William Blake (*Songs of Innocence and Experience*), London
1881 Stefan Zweig (*Beware of Pity*, *The World of Yesterday*), Vienna
DIED: 1859 Washington Irving (*The Legend of Sleepy Hollow*), 76, Tarrytown, N.Y.
1968 Enid Blyton (*Five on a Treasure Island*), 71, Hampstead, England

1582 William Shakespeare paid £40 for a license for his marriage to Anne Hathaway.

1928 At twenty-one, with her mother dead and her father dying, Virginia Woolf had written in her diary, "If your father & mother die you have lost something that the longest life can never bring again." A quarter century later, though, she was ruthlessly grateful that at least her father, Leslie Stephen, was gone. On his birthday this day, she noted he could still have been alive—he would have been ninety-six—"but mercifully was not." Though he had encouraged her, "his life would have entirely ended mine. What would have happened? No writing, no books;—inconceivable." Now, having buried her "unhealthy" obsession with her parents in *To the Lighthouse*, she can think of him safely again: "He comes back now more as a contemporary. I must read him some day."

1947 When a letter from his uncle Alex landed on the desk of Kurt Vonnegut, a junior PR man at General Electric, requesting a photo of his nephew (and Kurt's brother) Bernard, a famous scientist there, Kurt decided to have some fun. "We have a lot more to do than piddle with penny-ante requests like yours," he wrote back as "Guy Fawkes." "This office made your nephew, and we can break him in a minute—like an egg shell." His uncle, Vonnegut later recalled, neither got nor appreciated the joke.

1966 "Mr. Truman Capote requests the pleasure of your company at a Black and White Dance on Monday, the twenty-eighth of November at ten o'clock, Grand Ballroom, The Plaza." Norman Mailer, Marianne Moore, and Ralph Ellison were there, along with Frank Sinatra and Mia Farrow, the Maharajah of Jaipur, and eleven friends Capote made in Kansas while researching *In Cold Blood*. Greta Garbo, Jackie Kennedy, and Robert McNamara declined, and Carson McCullers, to her fury, was not invited. For months leading up to the night, Capote carried around a composition book filled not with notes for his next book but with the names on his ever-changing guest list. The Black and White Ball, crowning the year of his incredible success with *In Cold Blood*, was, as many have said, Capote's last great work.

November 29

BORN: 1898 C. S. Lewis (The Chronicles of
Narnia, *The Screwtape Letters*), Belfast,
Ireland
1918 Madeleine L'Engle (*A Wrinkle in
Time*), New York City
DIED: 1980 Dorothy Day (*The Long
Loneliness*), 83, New York City
1991 Frank Yerby (*The Foxes of Harrow*),
75, Madrid

1921 "I like being a detective, like the work," Dashiell Hammett's Continental Op once said. "I can't imagine a pleasanter future than twenty-some years more of it." Hammett himself only lasted about six years as a detective for the legendary Pinkerton agency—strike-breaking, snooping at roadhouses, nabbing pickpockets—until, too sick with TB to continue, he turned to writing stories. Hammett liked to say his career ended on this day with the cracking of the *Sonoma* gold-specie case, in which a quarter of a million dollars in gold coins disappeared from the strongroom of a Pacific freighter. Set for a cushy undercover job investigating the theft on the ship's return trip to Hawaii and Australia, he cost himself a free trip across the Pacific when he discovered the coins hidden onboard just before they sailed.

1934 On the same day she went to see the first sound movie of her novel *Anne of Green Gables*, starring Dawn O'Day (who from that point on took the name of her character, Anne Shirley, as her stage name), L. M. Montgomery pasted into her journal the photo she had used years before as a model for Anne, "a photograph of a real girl somewhere in the U.S., but I have no idea who she was or where she lived." As scholars have since pointed out, the "real girl" was Evelyn Nesbit, the most famous model of her day and the subject of its most notorious scandal when her husband, Harry Thaw, murdered the architect Stanford White for "ruining" Nesbit when he seduced her at age sixteen, the same age she was when she posed for the photograph that inspired Anne.

1948 Fired as general secretary of the Poetry Society and editor of the *Poetry Review*, Muriel Spark spent her final days there copying the group's mailing list to use for a new journal she planned to edit.

1967 When Ralph and Fanny Ellison bought their first house, a 246-year-old summer home on ninety-seven acres in Plainfield, Massachusetts, in the spring of 1967, he had already been working on his second novel, after *Invisible Man*, for fourteen years, distracted at times by his public role in the debates of the '50s and '60s and burdened by characters that struggled to cohere into a story. Ellison piled up hundreds of pages and sent out word he was nearly done with the novel, but on this day they returned to their house on a sunny afternoon to find it engulfed in smoke and flames, his manuscript inside. What did he lose? At first he told friends he only lost the work he'd done that summer, but over time, as the novel remained unfinished, the loss, in his telling, would grow.

BORN: **1667** Jonathan Swift (*A Tale of the Tub*), Dublin
1835 Mark Twain (*Tom Sawyer, Huckleberry Finn*), Florida, Mo.
DIED: **1900** Oscar Wilde (*The Importance of Being Earnest*), 46, Paris
1997 Kathy Acker (*Blood and Guts in High School*), c. 50, Tijuana, Mexico

1951 Struggling with alcoholic binges in New York, Elizabeth Bishop took advantage of a fellowship to embark by freighter for a trip around South America. Arriving in Rio on this day, she planned a two-week visit but ended up staying far longer. While visiting with acquaintances from New York, including an aristocratic Brazilian named Lota de Macedo Soares, something, possibly a cashew, caused Bishop's face to swell so much she couldn't see—"I didn't know one *could* swell so much"—and as Lota nursed her back to health, they fell in love. Soon Bishop acquired a toucan, moved into a writing studio Lota built near her country home, and stayed for sixteen often blissful and sometimes alcoholic years until Lota's overdose of tranquilizers in 1967.

1954 "I like it less than anything else of yours I have read," Edmund Wilson wrote to his good friend Vladimir Nabokov after "hastily" reading the manuscript of *Lolita*. "Nasty subjects may make fine books; but I don't feel you have got away with this."

1979 Rosemary Dinnage, in the *TLS*, on Joan Didion's *The White Album*: "Didion has been around—Hollywood, Waikiki, Bogotá; she has a superb sense of place—

and has come back with a message: *It doesn't matter*."

1982 At 4 a.m. on the day of her deadline, Sandra Cisneros finished the last of the stories for her first book of fiction, *The House on Mango Street*. She had started them in 1977 at the Iowa Writers' Workshop, "to write about something my classmates couldn't," and she continued composing her spare and evocative vignettes in Chicago and Massachusetts, finishing the last of them— "Mango Says Goodbye Sometimes," "The Monkey Garden," and the most difficult, "Red Clowns"—on an island in Greece. Soon after she wrote a friend, "I will have to live with its permanent imperfections," but she spent the next two years revising and perfecting the book that, since its first, tiny publication with Arte Publico Press, has sold over two million copies.

NO YEAR The Advent calendar Enid Lambert brings out every year on the last day of November is not the usual cardboard-windowed model. It's hand-sewn of green felt and canvas, with two rows of twelve pockets. Each pocket holds an ornament for the tree, and the last is always reserved for the Christ child, a tiny plastic baby in a gold-painted walnut shell. As the ornaments go on the tree and Enid's grown-up children straggle across the country toward their hometown of St. Jude, Jonathan Franzen's *The Corrections* turns out, despite its every satirical impulse, to be a Christmas story, one that bends ever so slightly toward Enid's outdated but fierce will.

December

Did Dickens invent Christmas? It's often said he did, rescuing the holiday from the neglect that Puritanism, Utilitarianism, and the Scrooge-like forces of the Industrial Revolution had imposed on it. But Dickens himself would hardly have said he invented the traditions he celebrated: the mission of his Ghost of Christmas Present, after all, is to show that the spirit and the customs of the holiday are alive among the people, and no humbug at all. But the appearance of *A Christmas Carol* in 1843 did coincide with the arrival in Victorian England of some of the modern traditions of the holiday. That same year the first commercial Christmas cards were printed in England, two years after Prince Albert brought the German custom of the Christmas tree with him to England following his marriage to Queen Victoria.

Christmas was undoubtedly Dickens's favorite holiday, and he made it a tradition of his own. *A Christmas Carol* was the first of his five almost-annual Christmas books (when he skipped a year in 1847 while working on *Dombey and Son*, he was "very loath to lose the money. And still more so to leave any gap at Christmas firesides which I ought to fill"), and for eighteen more years he published Christmas editions of his magazines *Household Words* and *All the Year Round*. And the popular and exhausting activity that nearly took over the last decades of his career, his public reading of his own works, began with his Christmas stories. For years they remained his favorite texts to perform, whether it was December or not.

One of the Christmas traditions Dickens most wanted to celebrate was storytelling itself. The early Christmas numbers of *Household Words* were imagined as stories told around the fireplace, often ghost stories like *A Christmas Carol*. The best-known American ghost tale is told around the Christmas hearth too: "The story had held us, round the fire, sufficiently breathless," it begins, "gruesome, as, on Christmas Eve in an old house, a strange tale should essentially be." We learn little more about that first gruesome story, except that the one that follows is even stranger and more unsettling, a ratcheting of dread that gave Henry James its title, *The Turn of the Screw*.

Telling ghost stories around the hearth might have declined since Dickens's and James's times, but it's striking how important the voice of the storyteller remains in more recent Christmas traditions: Dylan Thomas, nostalgic for the winters of his childhood in "A Child's Christmas in Wales"; Jean Shepherd, nostalgic for the Red Ryder air rifles of his own childhood in *In God We Trust, All Others Pay Cash*, later adapted, with Shepherd's own narration, into the holiday TV staple *A Christmas Story*; and David Sedaris, nostalgic for absolutely nothing from his years as an underpaid elf in the "SantaLand Diaries," the NPR monologue that launched his storytelling career.

The Chemical History of a Candle by Michael Faraday (1861) ✒ Dickens was not the only Victorian with a taste for public speaking: Faraday created the series of Christmastime scientific lectures for young people at the Royal Institution, the best known of which remains his own, a classic of scientific explanation for readers of any age.

Little Women by Louisa May Alcott (1868) ✒ If you were one of the March girls, you'd read the copies of *The Pilgrim's Progress* you found under your pillow on Christmas morning, but we'll excuse you if you prefer to read about the Marches themselves instead.

The Catcher in the Rye by J. D. Salinger (1951) ✒ Holden's not supposed to be back from Pencey Prep for Christmas vacation until Wednesday, but since he's been kicked out anyway, he heads to the city early, figuring on taking it easy in some inexpensive hotel and going home all rested up and feeling swell.

Chilly Scenes of Winter by Ann Beattie (1976) ✒ Want to extend *The Catcher in the Rye*'s feeling of holiday ennui well into your twenties? Spend the days before New Year's with Charles, love-struck over a married woman whom he keeps giving Salinger books until she can't bear it anymore.

The Ghost Writer by Philip Roth (1979) ✒ The brash and eventful fictional life of Nathan Zuckerman, which Roth followed through another eight books, starts quietly, with his abashed arrival on a December afternoon at the country retreat of his idol, the reclusive novelist E. I. Lonoff, where, by the end of this short novel (one of Roth's best), he will think he's falling in love with a young woman he's sure is, yes, Anne Frank.

The Orchid Thief by Susan Orlean (1998) ✒ Head south with the snowbirds to the swamps of Florida as Orlean investigates the December theft of over two hundred orchids from state swampland and, in particular, its strangely charismatic primary perpetrator, John Laroche.

Stalingrad by Antony Beevor (1998) ✒ Or perhaps your December isn't cold enough. Beevor's authoritative account of the siege of Stalingrad, the wintry graveyard of Hitler's plans to conquer Russia, captures the nearly incomprehensible human drama that changed the course of the war at a cost of a million lives.

December by Alexander Kluge and Gerhard Richter (2012) ✒ Two German artists reinvent the calendar book, with Richter's photographs of snowy, implacable winter and Kluge's enigmatic anecdotes from Decembers past, drawing from 21,999 B.C. to 2009 A.D. but circling back obsessively to the two empires, Nazi and Soviet, that met at Stalingrad.

December 1

BORN: 1935 Woody Allen (*Getting Even, Without Feathers*), Bronx, N.Y.
1958 Candace Bushnell (*Sex and the City*), Glastonbury, Conn.
DIED: 1947 Aleister Crowley (*The Book of the Law, The Book of Lies*), 72, Hastings, England
2011 Christa Wolf (*Cassandra, The Quest for Christa T.*), 82, Berlin

1816 Leigh Hunt, in the *Examiner*, on John Keats: "He has not yet published any thing except in a newspaper; but a set of his manuscripts was handed us the other day, and fairly surprised us with the truth of their ambition, and ardent grappling with Nature."

1825 Setting out for St. Petersburg after the death of the tsar, Alexander Pushkin was saved from joining the doomed Decembrist uprising when he took a pack of hares running across the path of his carriage as an omen of bad luck and turned back.

1911 Edgar Rice Burroughs had either a diligent habit of personal recordkeeping or a premonition of his later fame when, not long after the failure of his latest business venture (selling wholesale pencil sharpeners), he noted that at 8 p.m. on December 1, 1911, he wrote the opening words of his second serial for *The All-Story* magazine: "I had this story from one who had no business to tell it to me, or to any other." Six months later, he recorded that at 10:25 p.m. on May 14, 1912, he wrote the final words of the tale: "'My mother was an ape, and of course she couldn't tell me anything about it—and I never knew who my father was.'" The first installment of "Tarzan of the Apes" appeared in *All-Story* in October; Tarzan made his movie debut in 1918.

1948 The death of an unidentified man found on Somerton Beach in Adelaide, South Australia, on this day might not have remained one of Australia's most intriguing unsolved mysteries were it not for the two words on a piece of paper found in the fob pocket of his trousers: *tamam shud*, Persian for "the end" and the final line torn from a copy of one of the most popular books of the age, *The Rubaiyat of Omar Khayyam*.

1960 David Halberstam opened *The Best and the Brightest*, his history of the American ensnarement in Vietnam, with the entrance of a figure who would play almost no direct role in the rest of the book. On a "cold day in December," Robert A. Lovett, one of the "wise men" of establishment Washington, arrived at the Georgetown home of a man two decades his junior, John F. Kennedy, who was building his cabinet after his election the previous month. Kennedy, or so he told reporters, was willing to offer Lovett his choice of Defense (a job he'd held under Truman), State, or Treasury; Lovett declined them all but suggested the men, including Dean Rusk for State and Robert McNamara for Defense, who would become the central figures in the administration's stumble toward a disastrous war.

BORN: 1958 George Saunders (*CivilWarLand in Bad Decline*), Amarillo, Tex.
1963 Ann Patchett (*Bel Canto, State of Wonder*), Los Angeles

DIED: 1814 Marquis de Sade (*Justine, The 120 Days of Sodom*), 74, Charenton, France
1995 Robertson Davies (*Fifth Business*), 82, Orangeville, Ont.

1793 Samuel Taylor Coleridge enlisted with the 15th Light Dragoons as "Silas Tomkyn Comberbach." In April, with his brother's help, he was discharged as "insane."

1805 At the end of the Battle of Austerlitz, and the close of book three of *War and Peace*, Prince Andrei lies unconscious, left to die from his wounds. Napoleon himself makes a cameo appearance, remarking, "That's a fine death!" Hearing him, Andrei finds the little emperor, until now his hero, suddenly insignificant compared to the beauty of the "lofty and everlasting sky" he has just glimpsed at the point of death. Like Napoleon, Tolstoy at first thought Andrei wouldn't survive, as he explained to a friend as he worked on the novel: "I needed a brilliant young man to be killed at the battle of Austerlitz . . . Then he began to interest me; I imagined a part for him to play in the further course of the novel and I took pity on him, merely wounding him seriously instead of killing him."

1919 Having lost the manuscript for *Seven Pillars of Wisdom*, his memoir of his role in the Arab revolt against the Turks, when he left it in a briefcase at Reading station, T. E. Lawrence began on this day to write the book again. Working day and night from memory and battle reports while wearing a flying suit to keep warm in an unheated office and living off sandwiches purchased at nearby railway stations, he rewrote nearly all of a draft of 400,000 words in thirty days. He spent the next few years obsessively revising the book before publishing it—perversely, given the worldwide interest in his story, or shrewdly, given the way it added to his mystique—only in a limited edition whose lavish production put him into debt for years.

1945 At a party at the Hollywood estate of Preston Sturges while en route to Mexico from his beach shack in British Columbia, Malcolm Lowry defeated a national Ping-Pong champion, twice.

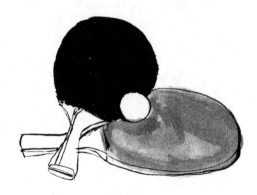

2001 Patrick McGrath, in the *New York Times*, on Peter Ackroyd's *London: A Biography*: "Just what is it about this damp, gray town, the suicide capital of Europe in the 19th century, that can make a grown man cry, or at least inspire him to write such a robust, passionate and exhaustively researched book as this?"

December 3

BORN: 1857 Joseph Conrad (*Heart of Darkness, Lord Jim*), Berdychiv, Russian Empire
1953 Patrick Chamoiseau (*Texaco, School Days*), Fort-de-France, Martinique

DIED: 1910 Mary Baker Eddy (*Science and Health with Key to the Scriptures*), 89, Newton, Mass.
2000 Gwendolyn Brooks (*Annie Allen, Maud Martha*), 83, Chicago

1897 Edith Wharton published her first book, *The Decoration of Houses,* an illustrated guide for wealthy homeowners, co-written with Ogden Codman, that argued against the excesses of the Gilded Age and proved a surprising success.

1926 Late on this evening, the young novelist Agatha Christie left her country home without explanation. The discovery of her abandoned car five miles away the next morning made her disappearance the talk of England, drawing thousands, including Arthur Conan Doyle and Dorothy Sayers, to search for her body before she was finally discovered residing under a pseudonym at a luxury spa, where she claimed temporary amnesia. The mystery has never been definitively solved, though scholar Jared Cade has argued convincingly that she staged her disappearance—never suspecting it would cause such an uproar—to embarrass her husband, whose affair was ending their marriage, a scenario made only more plausible by the name under which she registered at the spa: Mrs. Teresa Neele, which borrowed a last name from Nancy Neele, the rival her husband soon married after their divorce.

1929 C. S. Lewis had known the new Professor of Anglo-Saxon at Oxford for more than three years before a late night of talk about northern myths sealed their friendship. "I was up till 2.30 on Monday, talking to the Anglo Saxon professor Tolkien," he recounted in a letter to a friend on this day, "discoursing of the gods and giants of Asgard for three hours, then departing in the wind and rain." Lewis and J. R. R. Tolkien shared many more late-night discussions in their three decades as Oxford colleagues, including another in 1931 whose importance Lewis described in a letter to that same friend: "I have just passed from believing in God to definitely believing in Christ . . . My long night talk with Dyson and Tolkien had a good deal to do with it."

2006 Erica Wagner, in the *New York Times*, on Roald Dahl's *Collected Stories*: "These stories are never less than enjoyable; most are also utterly heartless. That doesn't matter."

BORN: **1795** Thomas Carlyle (*Sartor Resartus*), Ecclefechan, Scotland
1875 Rainer Maria Rilke (*Duino Elegies*), Prague
DIED: **1975** Hannah Arendt (*The Origins of Totalitarianism*), 69, New York City
1987 Arnold Lobel (*Frog and Toad Are Friends*), 54, New York City

17– The game theorists of nuclear war who conceived of Mutually Assured Destruction two centuries later would have understood the Vicomte de Valmont in Choderlos de Laclos's *Dangerous Liaisons* when he writes to the Marquise de Merteuil "that each of us possesses what we need to ruin the other, and that we must mutually consider each other's interests." Throughout the novel Valmont and Merteuil have played their amoral, amorous games of manipulation on others, but now they are left to face each other. The Marquise, valuing her self-made independence from such entanglements, tries to put off Valmont, but he won't have it any longer. It's either yes or no, love or hate, peace or war, he demands. "Very well, then," she replies. "War!"

1875 Entering New York harbor after thirty-eight years in Europe, Charles Schermerhorn Schuyler can't help but think in terms of the stories he might be paid to write about his return: "The United States in the Year of the Centennial," "Old New York: A Knickerbocker's Memories." In *1876*, the third novel in his fictional romp through American history (published, impishly, during the self-congratulation of the Bicentennial year), Gore Vidal skewered both his country's habitual corruption and his own scribbling profession as Schuyler, a refined gentleman forced by a financial collapse to "ply his wares on foot, as it were, in streets where once triumphantly he rode," takes to his lowlier calling, as did the aristocratic Vidal himself, with shrugging aplomb: "Well, no self-pity. The world is not easy."

NO YEAR The season has turned sharply for the worse, and so it seems has nature itself. The birds, more restless than usual all fall, are now massing in the sudden cold of winter, species joining with species and *attacking*. Hitchcock transplanted the unsettling idea of mass avian malevolence in Daphne du Maurier's story "The Birds" from the blustery coast of England to the Technicolor brightness of California, but du Maurier's original, told with the terse modesty of postwar austerity, still carries a greater horror, as Nat, a rural handyman, survives an early attack and quickly adapts to the tidal rhythms of the giant waiting flocks, making a fortress of his family's small cottage while his neighbors outside fall prey. But the birds are adapting too . . .

2009 *Moshi Kōkō Yakyū no Joshi Manager ga Drucker no "Management" o Yondara* (*What If the Female Manager of a High School Baseball Team Read Drucker's Management*), a fictional guide to economics by Natsumi Iwasaki with a plot summarized exactly by its title, was published on this day and became the bestselling book in Japan in 2010, with a spin-off film and animated series.

December 5

BORN: 1934 Joan Didion (*Slouching Toward Bethlehem*), Sacramento, Calif.
1935 Calvin Trillin (*Killings*; *Alice, Let's Eat*), Kansas City, Mo.
DIED: 1784 Phillis Wheatley (*Poems on Various Subjects, Religious and Moral*), 31, Boston
1870 Alexandre Dumas *père* (*The Count of Monte Cristo*), 68, Puys, France

1890 His last novel, his eighth already at age thirty-three, had sold no better than the others, forcing George Gissing to sell the books off of his shelves to support his meager existence. The subject of his next novel, *New Grub Street*, was one he knew well, the degrading poverty of the scribblers on the edges of commercial literary life, and on the same day he wrote the final page of the book he also noted in his diary an invitation to a respectable dinner party: "Of course I must refuse. I have sold my dress-suit, so that I couldn't go, even if I had no other reason. But I suppose I shall never again sit at a civilized table." *New Grub Street* made him little more money than his previous books, but it made his reputation, and he was able to return to civilized tables and look forward to a place in the posterity he always said he was writing for.

1945 Fresh off his successful screenplay adaptations of *Pride and Prejudice* and *Jane Eyre* and looking forward to a Hollywood version of his novel *Brave New World*, Aldous Huxley contracted with Disney to turn *Alice in Wonderland* into a film script. It was not a good match. His script changed Alice's rabbit hole into a Narnian cabinet door and brought Lewis Carroll into the story to tell Alice, in words that sound like Huxley's later psychedelic experiments, "You've got to find the little door inside your own head first." After an awkward meeting, Walt Disney rejected Huxley's scenario as "so literary I could understand only every third word," and when Disney's animated version appeared in 1951, Huxley was not credited.

NO YEAR Charles Highway, in Martin Amis's *The Rachel Papers*, has "five hours of teenage to go" before he turns twenty, five hours left "to re-experience the tail-end of my youth." Amis wasn't much past his own teenage himself when he wrote this tale of an Oxford-cramming adolescent who, like his creator, wears his withering precocity on his snotty sleeves. Charles spends much of the novel, when he's not plotting the seduction of the Rachel of the title, ginning up a bitter "Letter to My Father," but the whole book can be seen as a (less bitter) letter to Amis's own father, a declaration that like his dad, Kingsley (who made a precociously disillusioned debut with *Lucky Jim* nineteen years before), he can write.

2012 Dwight Garner, in the *New York Times*, on Richard Bradford's *Martin Amis*: "Reading 'Martin Amis: The Biography' is like watching a moose try to describe a leopard, using only its front hooves."

BORN: 1919 Eric Newby (*A Short Walk in the Hindu Kush*), London
1942 Peter Handke (*The Goalie's Anxiety at the Penalty Kick*), Griffen, Austria
DIED: 1951 Harold Ross (editor, *The New Yorker*), 59, Boston
1961 Frantz Fanon (*The Wretched of the Earth*), 35, Bethesda, Md.

1885 Witty, independent, and opinionated, Clover Adams was once called by Henry James "a perfect Voltaire in petticoats" and has often been thought a model for his lively American heroines Daisy Miller and Isabel Archer, as well as, more directly, for the title character of the anonymously published novel *Esther*, by her husband, Henry Adams. (Her sharp wit also caused her to be suspected as the author of Adams's scandalous Washington satire, *Democracy*.) But she has become best known as a literary absence: after she killed herself following months of harrowing depression after the death of her father, her mourning husband burned all her letters to him and is said to have never spoken her name again. And nowhere in the many pages of that most ironically detached of American autobiographies, *The Education of Henry Adams*, is there a mention of her name.

1902 James Joyce, age twenty, reported to his family that Yeats, the famous poet, had spent the day making introductions for him in London and, best of all, had paid for their breakfast, lunch, and dinner together and all their cab and bus fares.

1925 At twenty-three, Langston Hughes had had his first book of poems, *The Weary Blues*, accepted by Knopf and been the subject of a feature in *Vanity Fair*, but he still had to earn a living. Dissatisfied with his position as assistant to historian Carter G. Woodson, he took a job as a hotel busboy in Washington, D.C., for lower pay but better hours for writing. There, spotting the famous poet Vachel Lindsay in the dining room, he slipped him a few of his poems and woke up the next day to find himself "discovered" again, after Lindsay praised the "bellboy poet" at a public reading the night before. Newspaper photographers wanted Hughes's picture, while Lindsay left behind an inscribed book for him with the message "Do not let any lionizers stampede you. Hide and write and study and think."

1947 G. W. Stonier, in the *New Statesman and Nation*, on Frederic Wertham's *Dark Legend: A Study of Murder*: "A murder story, psychological detection, myth, taboo, insanity, literary creation: such are the stages of Dr. Wertham's exploring. *Dark Legend* may well, I feel, become a classic of its kind."

1990 John Banville, in the *New York Review of Books*, on John McGahern's *Amongst Women*: "*Amongst Women*, despite the quietness of its tone and the limits deliberately imposed upon it by the author, is an example of the novelist's art at its finest, a work the heart of which beats to the rhythm of the world and of life itself. It will endure."

December 7

BORN: **1873** Willa Cather (*My Ántonia, Death Comes for the Archbishop*), Gore, Va.
1928 Noam Chomsky (*Syntactic Structures, Manufacturing Consent*), Philadelphia

DIED: **1975** Thornton Wilder (*Our Town, The Bridge of San Luis Rey*), 78, Hamden, Conn.
1985 Robert Graves (*I, Claudius; Good-bye to All That*), 90, Deià, Spain

1853 Harper & Bros. paid Herman Melville a $300 advance for a book, which he never completed, "on 'Tortoises' and 'Tortoise Hunting.'"

1976 It's among the most familiar tales of discovery in American literature, and among the most inspiring to the unpublished (though few would want to emulate its sad path to success): Mrs. Thelma Toole, who had been unable by phone to convince Walker Percy to read the novel left behind by her son after his suicide, arrived in a limousine at Percy's Loyola University office with a box full of smudged typescript. Percy finally read the novel, first with reluctance and then excitement, and wrote her back on this day, saying that Ignatius Reilly, the book's hero, "is an original—a cross between Don Quixote and W. C. Fields." He later added "a mad Oliver Hardy" and "a perverse Thomas Aquinas" to those forebears when he wrote the foreword to the published edition of John Kennedy Toole's *A Confederacy of Dunces*, which went on to win the Pulitzer Prize for Fiction, something Percy himself never achieved.

1976 "In 1976," Tom Clark wrote in *No Big Deal*, "Mark Fidrych hit baseball in the face with a pie containing money." Fidrych, you may remember, was the Bird, a gangly and guileless rookie pitcher who came out of nowhere to thrill and charm baseball for one improbable summer. Before he blew out his arm the next spring, he holed up with Clark in the L.A. Hilton for five days in December to produce *No Big Deal*, a quickie jock autobiography far better than most. A phenom once himself—he became the poetry editor of the *Paris Review* in his early twenties—Clark had written poems on pitchers Vic Raschi and Dock Ellis and an entire book on the Charlie Finley A's and knew enough in *No Big Deal* to step out of the way and let the Bird's fresh torrent of language flow.

1986 William Hamilton, in the *New York Times*, on Art Spiegelman's *Maus*: "To express yourself as an artist, you must find a form that leaves you in control but doesn't leave you by yourself. That's how 'Maus' looks to me—a way Mr. Spiegelman found of making art."

BORN: 1945 John Banville (*The Book of Evidence, The Sea*), Wexford, Ireland

1951 Bill Bryson (*A Walk in the Woods*), Des Moines, Iowa

DIED: 1859 Thomas de Quincey (*Confessions of an English Opium-Eater*), 74, Edinburgh

1992 William Shawn (editor, *The New Yorker*), 85, New York City

1888 "During the last six weeks, I have had to wrap a kerchief round my left hand while I wrote because I couldn't even bear the sensation of my own breath on it." Starving and driven nearly mad, the unnamed narrator of Knut Hamsun's *Hunger* struggles in a desperate cycle of poverty and exhaustion, not eating enough to write and not writing enough to eat. The struggles were Hamsun's own, but unlike the novel's narrator, Hamsun found his life immediately transformed when the first fragment of *Hunger* appeared in a Danish journal. While fielding offers from publishers and seeing himself compared to Dostoyevsky, Hamsun on this day warmly thanked one publisher for an advance of 200 kroner, recalling the madness of his poverty in the words above, which he would later reuse, almost verbatim, in the novel.

1927 The party of the first part, Charlotte L. Mason, contracted on this day to pay the party of the second part, Zora Hurston, $200 a month and provide "one moving picture camera and one Ford automobile." In return, Hurston would "lay before" Mrs. Mason all the material relating to the "music, folklore, poetry, voodoo, conjure, manifestations of art, and kindred matters existing among American Negroes" she could collect, and was forbidden to share it with anyone else without permission. Mason, a wealthy white patron of the Harlem Renaissance who liked to be called "Godmother" by those she helped, drove Langston Hughes, another of her so-called children, away with her overbearing insistence on "primitive" expression, but Hurston lasted five ambivalent years in her employ before setting out on her own.

1939 Margaret Mead, by then the world's best-known anthropologist and an expert in rituals, did not leave the arrangements to chance when, at age thirty-seven, she gave birth to her only child. Having completed an article for the *Encyclopædia Britannica* the day before (as, she noted, her mother had before her own birth), Mead was joined in her delivery room by a team of nurses who had already been shown her short film "First Days in the Life of a New Guinea Baby," a movie photographer, an obstetrician, a child psychologist, and the baby's pediatrician, Dr. Benjamin Spock, whose later bestselling manual, *Baby and Child Care*, would incorporate some of Mead's ideas about child rearing. The procedure must be deemed a success: her daughter, Mary Catherine Bateson, went on to become a prominent anthropologist herself.

1955 Commissioned by the Ford Motor Company to suggest names for their new car, which they eventually called the Edsel, Marianne Moore, having already sent "Thunderblender," "Mongoose Civique," and dozens more, submitted her last, "Utopian Turtletop."

December 9

BORN: 1608 John Milton (*Lycidas*, *Paradise Lost*), London
1899 Jean de Brunhoff (*The Story of Babar*), Paris
DIED: 1977 Clarice Lispector (*The Passion According to G.H.*), 56, Rio de Janeiro
1995 Toni Cade Bambara (*The Salt Eaters*; *Gorilla, My Love*), 56, Philadelphia

1825 In *Vivian Grey*, the bookish father Horace Grey warns his son, "Vivian, beware of endeavoring to become a great man in a hurry." But Vivian is very much in a hurry, as was his creator, Benjamin Disraeli, also the son of a literary man. Before he was twenty—not even old enough to take out a loan by himself—young Disraeli got caught up in the English mania for South American mining investments that finally collapsed at the end of 1825, with four London banks failing on this day. Saddled with a debt it took him decades to repay, Disraeli turned to fiction, publishing *Vivian Grey* the following year, an anonymous but autobiographical novel that didn't stay anonymous for long, and the first of the more than a dozen novels he wrote before twice becoming prime minister.

1874 "I DON'T KNOW WHETHER I AM OGING TO MAKE THIS TYPE-WRITING MACHINE GO OR NTO," Mark Twain wrote William Dean Howells on his new capital-letters-only typewriter. "THAT LAST WORD WAS INTENDRED FOR N-NOT: BUT I GUESS I SHALL MAKE SOME SORT OF A SUCC SS OF IT BEFORE I RUN IT VERY LO G. I AM SO THICK-FINGERED THAT I MISS THE KEYS."

1934 In a full-page ad in his own magazine, *New Yorker* columnist Alexander Woollcott endorsed the 1934 Airflow Chrysler, calling it "the world's first sensible motor car." In the following week's issue, E. B. White mocked him as "that fabulous old motorist . . . admittedly the country's leading exponent of the flagging torso."

1935 You might not associate Minnesota with mob murders, but in the '30s and '40s, three reporters were gunned down in Minneapolis while investigating ties between organized crime and government, most famously Walter W. Liggett, who in the space of a few months in 1935 was beaten by gangsters, framed on a morals charge, and finally shot five times in an alley after returning home with his family from the offices of the crusading newspaper he'd founded, the *Midwest American*. Though his wife and another eyewitness identified Kid Cann, whose violently maintained interests in gambling and liquor made him the Al Capone of the Twin Cities, as the shooter, Cann was acquitted and continued to flourish in the rackets there for another twenty-five years.

1961 Whitney Balliett, in *The New Yorker*, on Patrick White's *Riders in the Chariot*: "Writers who attract cults are, like lap dogs, a pitiable lot. Their worshippers coddle them, overcelebrate their virtues, shush their faults, and frighten away prospective and perhaps skeptical readers with an apologist's fervor."

BORN: **1830** Emily Dickinson (*Poems*), Amherst, Mass.

1949 August Kleinzahler (*Sleeping It Off in Rapid City*), Jersey City, N.J.

DIED: **1936** Luigi Pirandello (*Six Characters in Search of an Author*), 69, Rome

1946 Damon Runyon (*Guys and Dolls*), 66, New York City

1513 Overthrown as a Florentine statesman and then imprisoned, tortured, and exiled, Niccolò Machiavelli had to settle for a more contemplative political life at his estate in Tuscany. Writing to a friend in Rome, he described his daily life in retreat: overseeing his woodcutters, reading Petrarch by a spring, gambling with townspeople, and then in the evening entering his study: "On the threshold I take off my workday clothes, covered with mud and dirt, and put on the garments of court and palace. Fitted out appropriately, I step inside the venerable courts of the ancients . . . and for four hours at a time I feel no boredom, I forget all my troubles, I do not dread poverty, and I am not terrified by death." He had, he added, "composed a short study, *De principatibus*," a treatise known to us as *The Prince*.

1896 The tumult that erupted when Fermin Gémier, costumed in an enormous papier-mâché belly, stepped onstage at the Theatre l'Oeuvre and pronounced the first word of Alfred Jarry's play *Ubu Roi*—"Merdre!"—was not entirely spontaneous. In addition to much of literary Paris—Colette, Yeats, and Gide were all there—Jarry packed his opening night with a friendly rabble he instructed to howl if the rest of the crowd was applauding or cheer if the others were booing: "The performance must not be allowed to reach its conclusion, the theater must explode." The play did finish, amid shouts, whistles, and fistfights, and Jarry himself was thoroughly satisfied at the spectacle, though *Ubu* would never be performed again in his short lifetime.

1924 Edwin Muir, in the *New Republic*, on James Joyce's *Ulysses*: "The danger is not that it will become unrecognized, but that in time it will overshadow every other potentiality of our age."

1924 Witter Bynner, in the *New Republic*, on Edna St. Vincent Millay's "Renascence": "Where there had been nothing, no whisper of her, stood a whole poet. Few were aware, but how aware were those few."

NO YEAR Cruelty and kindness fill the stories of George Saunders, each amplified by the presence, or at least the possibility, of the other: that we can be cruel to each other makes the kindness more heroic; that we could be kind makes our cruelty more terrible. So when, in "Tenth of December," the title story in Saunders's fourth collection, an overweight, dreamy boy wanders out into the snowy woods and chances his way across the wet ice of a pond, crossing paths with a chemo-wracked old man planning to hasten his own demise, you are not sure whether the world's well-practiced viciousness toward them will only be increased by their encounter, or whether their suffering, shared, will be lessened.

December 11

BORN: 1922 Grace Paley (*The Little
Disturbances of Man*), Bronx, N.Y.
1937 Jim Harrison (*Dalva*, *Legends of the
Fall*), Grayling, Mich.
1939 Thomas McGuane (*Ninety-Two in the
Shade*), Wyandotte, Mich.
DIED: 1757 Colley Cibber (*An Apology for the
Life of Mr. Colley Cibber*), 86, London
1920 Olive Schreiner (*The Story of an
African Farm*), 65, Wynberg, South Africa

1920 Colette's path to literary respectability, via the scandalous schoolgirl novels she ghostwrote for her husband and an even more disreputable career as a dance hall performer, wasn't the usual one, but when she finished *Chéri*, she was sure that for the first time she had "written a novel for which I need neither blush nor doubt." Some thought the story of an aging courtesan and her young lover was vulgar, but others were won over, often to their surprise, including the novelist André Gide. "I am myself completely astonished to be writing to you, completely astonished by the great pleasure I've had in reading you," he confessed to her on this day. "I already want to reread it, and I'm afraid to. Suppose I liked it less? Quick, let me post this letter before I throw it into a drawer."

1934 In a movement built on personal testimony, the first confession was Bill W.'s, the stock investor in New York who on this day, with his drinking destroying his career and his life, bought four beers at a grocery to keep himself from going into withdrawal on the way to a Manhattan drying-out clinic. He'd checked into the clinic three times before, but this time those beers he bought became his last, on a day whose anniversary he would celebrate thirty-six times. Five years later, "Bill's Story" became the opening chapter of *Alcoholics Anonymous*, the book, often known as *The Big Book*, that became the bible of the organization Bill W. founded.

1974 "Harvey St. Jean had it made." That was Edna Buchanan's lead in the *Miami Herald* after St. Jean, the city's top defense lawyer, was found shot to death in his Cadillac, and it was the title Calvin Trillin chose for his chapter on the murder in *Killings*, a collection of his *New Yorker* crime reporting. Most of the murders he wrote about were the kind found in small, wire-service newspaper reports, but Harvey St. Jean lived on the front page, and that's where he landed in death too; as Buchanan wrote, in a title she used for her own crime collection, "the corpse had a familiar face."

December 12

BORN: 1821 Gustave Flaubert
(*Madame Bovary, Salammbô*),
Rouen, France
1905 Vasily Grossman (*Life
and Fate*), Berdychiv, Russian
Empire
DIED: 1889 Robert Browning
(*The Ring and the Book*), 77,
Venice
1995 Andrew Lytle (*The Velvet
Horn*), 92, Monteagle, Tenn.

1775 Gilbert White, the great English naturalist of his day, whose *Natural History and Antiquities of Selborne*, a collection of letters to two fellow zoologists, has never been out of print—through hundreds of editions—since 1789, was a humble and patient observer of local fauna from tortoises to swallows, but he had an eye for human behavior as well, as on this day, when he described an "idiot-boy" in the village who thought and cared only about bees, or, rather, their honey. He'd spend the winter torpid like his quarry, but in the summer he would take the bees bare-handed, "disarm them of their weapons, and suck their bodies for the sake of their honey-bags," filling his shirt with their bodies and making "a humming noise with his lips, resembling the buzzing of bees."

1970 The Brynmor Jones Library at the University of Hull, whose construction Philip Larkin, as head librarian, had carefully oversaw for fifteen years, and which he described to Barbara Pym the year before as "an odd building with a curious glaring drabness and far too little space," was officially opened.

1997 It was a rainy, gray day on the Gulf Coast when Frederick and Steven Barthelme, on the advice of their attorney, drove down from Hattiesburg, Mississippi, where they taught fiction at the university, to surrender at the Harrison County Jail in Gulfport on a felony charge of conspiring to defraud the nearby Grand Casino. The fraud was alleged, bewilderingly, to have been committed with a blackjack dealer they hardly knew, on a night they lost nearly ten grand between them, during a period in which they gambled away hundreds of thousands of dollars of their inheritances. The only good fortune is that such a tale fell into the hands of two skilled storytellers, who used the same laconic, heart-weary humor of their fiction to write *Double Down*, the story of their gambling mania and the even more irrational workings of the justice system that eventually cleared them.

1999 James R. Kincaid, in the *New York Times*, on Charles Palliser's *The Unburied*: "You won't want a plot summary, but I went to such trouble getting it straight that I'm not going to throw it all away."

December 13

BORN: 1871 Emily Carr (*Klee Wyck, The House of All Sorts*), Victoria, B.C.
1915 Ross Macdonald (*The Drowning Pool*), Los Gatos, Calif.
DIED: 1784 Samuel Johnson (*The Idler, Lives of the Poets*), 75, London
1972 L. P. Hartley (*The Go-Between, Eustace and Hilda*), 76, London

1908 When Willa Cather first met Sarah Orne Jewett in February 1908, Cather was a spirited young journalist at *McClure's Magazine*, and Jewett, though nearly sixty, still looked to Cather "very much like the youthful picture of herself in the game of 'Authors' I had played as a child." By December Jewett took the liberty of writing a long and remarkable letter full of kind advice to her new friend. "I do think it is impossible for you to work so hard and yet have your gifts mature as they should," she wrote. "Your vivid, exciting companionship in the office must not be your audience, you must find your own quiet centre of life." She struck a nerve: Cather replied quickly, confessing her fear that she remained a beginner at writing fiction, unable to learn and too busy with journalism to try.

1936 Knowing only the abstract characters and landscapes of Samuel Beckett's plays, it's surprising to learn that earlier in his career, long before *Waiting for Godot* was first produced, he filled notebooks with his plans for a play about the relationship between Samuel Johnson and Hester Thrale. "Can't think why there hasn't been a film of Johnson, with [Charles] Laughton," he wrote to a friend on this day. "There are 50 plays in

his life." In a later letter to the same friend, though, he sounds more like the Beckett we know: "It isn't Boswell's wit and wisdom machine that means anything to me, but the miseries that he never talked of . . . The horror of annihilation, the horror of madness, the horrified love of Mrs. Thrale, the whole mental monster ridden swamp that after hours of silence could only give some ghastly bubble like 'Lord have mercy upon us.'"

2001 Andrew O'Hagan, in the *London Review of Books*, on Jonathan Franzen's *The Corrections*: "Today's big novel is the type of book which aims at bigness with the notion that all other big books are folded inside. The example is not *War and Peace* but the World Wide Web."

NO YEAR "Greetings from sunny Seattle," Bernadette's letter begins. "Have I mentioned how much I hate it here?" To this point, Maria Semple's *Where'd You Go, Bernadette?* has been an on-the-nose, up-to-the-minute satirical flurry of e-mails, text messages, invoices, and emergency-room bills, and for much of Bernadette's letter to Paul Jellinek, an old architecture colleague in L.A., the mood is the same: bristling, scattershot one-liners about the rain, the ugliness, and the slow-moving, self-satisfied, Subaru-driving boredom of her adopted home. Then, in the middle of the letter—in the middle of the book—Bernadette sighs, "Oh, Paul," and begins to reveal depths beneath her frantic facade, and the satire becomes a story.

BORN: 1916 Shirley Jackson ("The Lottery," *The Haunting of Hill House*), San Francisco

1951 Amy Hempel (*Reasons to Live, The Dog of the Marriage*), Chicago

DIED: 1953 Marjorie Kinnan Rawlings (*The Yearling*), 57, St. Augustine, Fla.

2001 W. G. Sebald (*Vertigo, Austerlitz*), 57, Norfolk, England

1882 As Henry James Sr., the mercurial patriarch who cultivated a family of geniuses, approached his death, his daughter, Alice, took to her bed, his son Henry embarked for home by ship from London, and his son William, also in London, wrote a farewell letter on this day that, like Henry Jr., arrived in Boston too late to greet his "blessed old father" before he passed. William's letter is as accepting of death ("If you go, it will not be an inharmonious thing") as his father, who welcomed it, and touchingly Jamesian in its combination of affection and analysis: "It comes strangely over me in bidding you good bye, how a life is but a day and expresses mainly but a single note—it is so much like the act of bidding an ordinary good night. Good night my sacred old Father."

1951 The "quiet American" in Graham Greene's novel by that name is Alden Pyle, the disastrously idealistic Harvard grad full of theories about Indochina, but the ugliest American in the book is the bullying, cynical reporter named Granger. Greene denied the other characters in *The Quiet American* had real-life models, but Granger, he admitted, was based directly on an American reporter named Larry Allen, whose "harsh rudeness" at a press conference in Hanoi Greene recorded in his journal on this day. Allen had won a Pulitzer for his fearless reporting in World War II, but to Greene's eye he had become lazy and "oafish," the sort who could proudly growl, as Granger does, "Stephen Crane could describe a war without seeing one. Why shouldn't I?"

1972 After two months marooned with a band of survivors on the side of a mountain following the plane crash in the Andes described in *Alive*, Piers Paul Read's survival classic, Nando Parrado climbed to the top of a ridge only to find on the other side, not the green valleys of Chile he had hoped for, but more icy peaks as far as he could see. After a day and night of debate, Parrado, the calm and determined leader of the survivors, and Roberto Canessa, his tempestuous and stubborn fellow scout, finally sent a third colleague back to camp to conserve their only sustenance (the meat from the bodies of those who hadn't survived the crash) and set out through the mountains with Roberto's words, as Parrado recalled in his 2006 memoir, *Miracle in the Andes*, "You and I are friends, Nando. Now let's go die together."

1999 Suffering from cancer and a series of strokes, Charles M. Schulz announced his retirement and the end of *Peanuts*, whose last Sunday strip appeared in newspapers the following February 13, alongside news of Schulz's death the night before.

December 15

BORN: **1930** Edna O'Brien (*The Country Girls*),
Tuamgraney, Ireland

1943 Peter Guralnick (*Sweet Soul Music,
Last Train to Memphis*), Boston

DIED: **1683** Izaak Walton (*The Compleat
Angler*), 90, Winchester, England

2011 Christopher Hitchens (*God Is Not
Great, Hitch-22*), 62, Houston, Tex.

1850 From France, Gustave Flaubert's mother asked the eternal maternal question: When would he be married? Never, he declared from Constantinople. Travel might change a man, he said, but not him. He would bring home "a few less hairs on my head and considerably more landscapes within it" (and a venereal disease too, though he didn't mention that), but the idea of marriage remained "an apostasy which it appalls me to think of." As an artist, he had no choice: "You can depict wine, love, and women on the condition that you are not a drunkard, a lover, or a husband. If you are involved in life, you see it badly." No, he assured her, she would never have a rival. "Some will perhaps mount to the threshold of the temple, but none will enter."

1960 On the third day of the unsuccessful coup against Ethiopian emperor Haile Selassie, with the emperor still absent from the capital city and his inner circle held hostage in the palace, General Mengistu Newal, a leader of the coup, held up a piece of dry bread to the students at Haile Selassie University and said, "This is what we fed to the dignitaries today, so they will know what our people live on. You must help us." It's a rare moment of direct confrontation in *The Emperor*, Ryszard Kapuściński's account of the decline of Selassie's long reign, which is otherwise full of the whispers of palace protocol and intrigue, a subtly damning portrait that is among the finest in Kapuściński's career of either transcending the limits of journalism or abusing its standards of truth, depending on whom you ask.

1963 Inspired by a roll of adding-machine tape in a store—"narrow, long, / unbroken"—A. R. Ammons conceived a "fool use for it": a poem, *Tape for the Turn of the Year*, he would type on the fly for as long as the tape lasted, fitting his days and thoughts into its slim margins. On his tenth day of typing, Ammons had to go out of town, so he took the poem with him, reversing the unspooled yards back across the platen and stowing it in a paper bag in his glove compartment and then rewinding it back into the machine at the end of the day to make his record. It was a shorter entry than most because, reluctantly, he'd given "the day to myself & not / to the poem."

BORN: **1775** Jane Austen (*Sense and Sensibility, Pride and Prejudice*), Steventon, England
1899 Noel Coward (*Blithe Spirit, Private Lives*), Teddington, England
1928 Philip K. Dick (*The Man in the High Castle, Martian Time Slip*), Chicago
DIED: **1897** Alphonse Daudet (*Letters from My Windmill*), 57, Paris
1965 Somerset Maugham (*The Moon and Sixpence*), 91, Nice, France

1850 In the vasty deeps of *Moby-Dick*, the author himself surfaces just once, when noting in the chapter "The Fountain" that the contents of a whale's spout have remained a mystery through thousands of years of whale-observing "down to this blessed minute (fifteen and a quarter minutes past one o'clock p.m. of this sixteenth day of December, A.D. 1850)." Is it a coincidence that Melville presents himself with such sudden specificity in a chapter concerning the unknowability—and the danger—of the whale and its spout? "I have heard it said," he relates, "and I do not doubt it, that if the jet is fairly spouted into your eyes, it will blind you. The wisest thing the investigator can do then, it seems to me, is to let this deadly spout alone." And so is it best, too, to let the author alone to his unfathomable submarine life and content ourselves with what he shows us on the surface?

1865 The *Athenaeum* on *Alice's Adventures in Wonderland* by Lewis Carroll: "We fancy that any child might be more puzzled than enchanted by this stiff, overwrought story."

1901 Published: *The Tale of Peter Rabbit* by Beatrix Potter, in a privately printed edition of 250.

1955 In a warehouse the size of a football field, from a calmly authoritative man with white hair, white mustache, and an impeccable black suit, Loren Haris learns that he is, or was, or may be Enzo Samax. Born on this day, he was orphaned once, when his mother gave him up for adoption as a baby and died soon after, and orphaned again when his adoptive parents were killed in an accident, but now, on his tenth birthday, he's been reclaimed—well, "kidnapped" is the legal term for it—by his extended birth family, pulled away from a trip to a Manhattan planetarium into a waiting sedan and spirited off with his mysteriously prosperous new uncle to Las Vegas, the first of many transformations and adventures in Nicholas Christopher's lavishly learned, near-magical novel *A Trip to the Stars*.

1971 Christopher Ricks, in the *New York Review of Books*, on John Updike's *Rabbit Redux*: "It never decides just what the artistic reasons (sales and nostalgia are another matter) were for bringing back Rabbit instead of starting anew; its existence is likely to do retroactive damage to that better book *Rabbit, Run*."

2001 Andrew Sullivan, in the *New York Times*, on Nadine Gordimer's *The Pickup*: "It's extremely hard to write beautifully about the power of sex, of its capacity to elevate humans out of worlds that would divide them, of its occasionally transcendent quality. But Gordimer writes about it so easily we barely notice the accomplishment."

December 17

BORN: 1873 Ford Madox Ford (*The Good
Soldier, Parade's End*), Merton, England
1916 Penelope Fitzgerald (*The Blue Flower,
The Bookshop*), Lincoln, England
DIED: 1957 Dorothy L. Sayers (*Gaudy Night,
Whose Body?*), 64, Witham, England
1999 C. Vann Woodward (*The Strange
Career of Jim Crow*), 91, Hamden, Conn.

1920 Anzia Yezierska may have been a greenhorn when publishing her first book, *Hungry Hearts*, but she was wise enough to amend her contract to retain the motion picture rights to her stories of immigrants in New York City, and it was no doubt with some pride that she wrote to her editor at Houghton Mifflin on this day to let him know that she had been offered $10,000 for the film rights to the book, dwarfing the $200 she had received as an advance. A month later she was on the train to Hollywood, where, despite being celebrated as the "sweatshop Cinderella," she soon lost her taste for the huckster Babylon she found there and returned east to focus on her fiction, writing five more books, including *Bread Givers,* before falling back into the silence of obscurity.

1929 *Toad of Toad Hall*, A. A. Milne's stage adaptation of *The Wind in the Willows*, premiered in London.

1944 "'Tell me, Mr. Pyle, how does it feel to be an assault correspondent?' Being a man of few words, I said, 'It feels awful.'" Professionally, of course, Ernie Pyle couldn't be a man of few words: he had to file his column for the Scripps-Howard papers six times a week. But his laconic modesty endeared him to readers and the soldiers he wrote about, as did his willingness to endure the danger and deprivation of the front lines along with them. His columns made him a symbol of the infantrymen he celebrated, and his second collection, *Brave Men*, which followed the Allied invasions of Sicily and Normandy through to the liberation of Paris, reached #1 on the *New York Times* bestseller list on this day. It was still at the top of the list four months later when Pyle, who had left his beloved infantry to chronicle the naval war in the Pacific, was killed by a Japanese sniper on a small island west of Okinawa.

1956 William Esty, in the *New Republic*, on James Baldwin's *Giovanni's Room*: "This sounds like a painful novel, which it certainly is. It also sounds like a meretriciously fashionable-sensational one, which it is not."

BORN: 1939 Michael Moorcock (*Mother London*), London
1961 A. M. Homes (*Music for Torching*), Washington, D.C.
DIED: 2002 Lucy Grealy (*Autobiography of a Face*), 39, New York City
2011 Václav Havel (*The Power of the Powerless*), 75, Hrádeček, Czech Republic

1679 The business of poetic satire became a dangerous one when John Dryden, the poet laureate of England, was beaten by three men in London's Rose Alley while walking home from a coffeehouse. The extent of his injuries has remained unknown, as have the identity and motives of his attackers, even though Dryden offered a £50 reward for their names. While some have suspected they were sent by the Duchess of Portsmouth, one of the mistresses of Charles II, most have pointed the finger at the Earl of Rochester, a courtier, poet, and shameless libertine, who, though he was dying at the time of syphilis, gonorrhea, and/or alcoholism, may have sought revenge for Dryden's satirical jabs, which themselves were payment for Rochester once calling the plump poet laureate the "Poet Squab," an insult that lasted longer than his bruises.

1818 A month or so after writing to his brother and sister-in-law, newly emigrated to America, that the "generality of women . . . appear to me as children to whom I would rather give a Sugar Plum than my time," John Keats met Fanny Brawne.

"Shall I give you Miss Brawne?" he wrote on this day in his next long letter to America. His assessment: "Her mouth is bad and good . . . Her shape is very graceful and so are her movements. Her Arms are good, her hands baddish, her feet tolerable. She is not seventeen [she was eighteen, in fact], but she is ignorant, monstrous in her behaviour, flying out in all directions, calling people such names that I was forced lately to make use of the term *Minx*." As both the familiarity of "lately" and the fascinated flirtiness of "*Minx*" imply, Miss Brawne was, for Keats, not among the mere generality of women.

1967 In "Vanadium," the second-to-last of the autobiographical tales that make up Primo Levi's *Periodic Table*, the two main threads of his story—his career as a chemist and his ordeal under the Nazis in Auschwitz—come together in the person of "Dr. Müller," a fellow chemist with a German company who writes Levi on business and who Levi imagines—correctly it turns out—is the same Dr. Müller who treated him with less inhumanity than his other supervisors in the small lab where Levi worked at Auschwitz. They exchange letters—Müller's with a clumsy mix of repentance and self-justification, Levi's formal and ambivalent—but before they can meet, Levi receives word of Müller's death, just as, on this day in real life, Levi heard of the death of Ferdinand Meyer, the model for Müller.

December 19

BORN: 1910 Jean Genet (*The Thief's Journal*, *The Maids*), Paris
1924 Michel Tournier (*The Ogre*, *Friday*, *Gemini*), Paris
DIED: 1848 Emily Brontë (*Wuthering Heights*), 30, Haworth, England
1982 Dwight Macdonald (*Discriminations*), 76, New York City

1931 In the time Eric Blair—not yet writing as George Orwell—had spent living with and writing about the poor, one experience he hadn't shared with his tramping acquaintances was jail, and his plan was to spend Christmas there and write about it. But how to get inside? He considered arson and theft before deciding to get as drunk in public as he could. He managed to get himself arrested, rather gently, on this day, but after caroling with fellow prisoners in the Black Maria on the way to court, he found himself put back out on the street just a couple of days later. Neither drunkenness nor begging could get him jailed again in time for the holiday, nor did he find a taker for "Clink," the article he wrote about his efforts.

1936 Zora Neale Hurston traveled to Haiti on a Guggenheim Fellowship to collect the folklore she'd describe in *Tell My Horse*, but for a short time there she was consumed instead with her second novel, *Their Eyes Were Watching God*, which she finished on this day. "It was dammed up in me," she recalled, "and I wrote it under internal pressure in seven weeks." What was pushing to be expressed? Memories of her Florida hometown of Eatonville, perhaps, and the distinctive voice of her heroine, Janie Crawford, but also the love of a younger man she'd set aside for her career, a Columbia grad student named Percy Punter who shared his youth with Janie's love, Tea Cake.

1967 Before Jerry Kramer, all-pro right guard of the Green Bay Packers, kept a diary of his 1967 season, there had been few glimpses into the mind of an offensive lineman (in fact, few suspected linemen *had* minds). But in *Instant Replay*, Kramer quoted Shakespeare without shame, analyzed the motivational genius of his coach, Vince Lombardi, observed the NFL growing from a part-time job into a big business, and revealed his weekly obsession with the defensive linemen he lined up against each Sunday. This week, it was Merlin Olsen of the Los Angeles Rams: "All I keep thinking is: Olsen, Olsen, Olsen," he wrote, plotting how he'd react to each of Olsen's moves while acknowledging his job was often just a matter of pushing the other guy back as hard as he could. "It's a simple game, really."

1986 Asked for a blurb for *The Broom of the System*, the debut novel by his MFA student David Foster Wallace, Richard Elman replied that he didn't consider Wallace's work original, but "if you want to publish really good writing you should publish mine."

BORN: **1954** Sandra Cisneros (*The House on Mango Street, Caramelo*), Chicago
1960 Nalo Hopkinson (*The Salt Roads*), Kingston, Jamaica

DIED: **1961** Moss Hart (*Act One, The Man Who Came to Dinner*), 57, Palm Springs, Calif.
1997 Denise Levertov (*Breathing the Water*), 74, Seattle

1915 *The Evil Eye: A Musical Comedy in Two Acts* was presented by the Princeton University Triangle Club, with book by Edmund Wilson Jr., class of 1916, and lyrics by F. Scott Fitzgerald, class of 1917.

1998 Mary Gordon, in the *New York Times*, on John Bayley's *Elegy for Iris*: "Its dominant notes are humility, modesty, patience and humor. The heroism is all the more admirable for its reluctance to acknowledge that heroism might be defined in such terms."

2002 When their client asks, "So what can you tell me about Mikael Blomkvist?" Lisbeth Salander, Milton Security's best researcher, reports that Blomkvist is a careful reporter, was likely set up for the libel conviction that got him sentenced to three months in prison that very morning, and hates the nickname the newspapers have given him, "Kalle" Blomkvist, after Astrid Lindgren's boy detective. "Somebody'd get a fat lip if they ever called me Pippi Longstocking," Salander adds. They could hardly be blamed for doing so, though, since Stieg Larsson said he created her character—tattooed, abrupt to the point of surliness, and with red hair dyed black and cut "short as a fuse"—in *The Girl with the Dragon Tattoo* by imagining what Lindgren's headstrong, red-haired Pippi would have become when she grew up.

NO YEAR "Last day or not, he has to stick to the checklist." Manny DeLeon is a sort of saint of the corporate economy, the manager of a Connecticut Red Lobster who follows the dictates from headquarters but keeps a kind eye on his employees and his customers too. That didn't stop corporate from letting him know that on December 20 his location, despite a decent year of receipts, is shutting down. He'll get a transfer to an Olive Garden in Bristol, and he can take five of his people with him, but he's going to need a lot more than five to work the last day, even with a blizzard on its way. Set from the opening of Manny's shift to the end, Stewart O'Nan's *Last Day at the Red Lobster* is, like Manny, a modest and steady marvel.

December 21

BORN: 1917 Heinrich Böll (*Billiards at Half-Past Nine*), Cologne, Germany
1932 Edward Hoagland (*Cat Man, Sex and the River Styx*), New York City
DIED: 1375 Giovanni Boccaccio (*The Decameron*), 62, Certaldo, Italy
1940 F. Scott Fitzgerald (*Tender Is the Night*), 44, Los Angeles

1872 The readers of *Le Temps* were not discouraged from believing that the daring journey of the English gentleman-adventurer Phileas Fogg and his servant Jean Passepartout, as described in the newspaper's daily installments of Jules Verne's *Around the World in Eighty Days*, was actually taking place. After all, the dispatches ended just when the journey does, on December 22, 1872, with the travelers' arrival in London just after the deadline for Fogg's £20,000 wager. Or are they late after all? As Passepartout realizes in the nick of time, because they traveled east across the International Date Line, the day they believed was the 22nd was actually the 21st, and Fogg has just enough time to make it through the doors of the Reform Club and declare to those who had bet against him, "Here I am, gentlemen!"

1958 An unsentimental account of an emotional roller coaster, Diana Athill's *Instead of a Letter* recounts a blissful childhood and adolescence that turned suddenly into "twenty years of unhappiness" when her fiancé wrote to say he was marrying someone else, just before he died in the war. But those "years leprous with boredom, drained by the war of meaning," ended on this day, Athill's forty-first birthday, when the small happiness she had found in writing was "fanned into a glorious glow" by the news she had won the *Observer*'s short-story prize: "Bury me, dear friends, with a copy of the *Observer* folded under my head, for it was the *Observer*'s prize that woke me up to the fact that I had become happy."

1994 It was a small notice in a newspaper—that four men, one white and three Seminole, had been arrested on this day while leaving the Fakahatchee swamp with four pillowcases full of orchids and other endangered flowers—that drew reporter Susan Orlean from New York to Florida, and it was John Laroche who kept her there for two years to follow his story. Skinny, bedraggled, oddly handsome, and eccentrically passionate, Laroche was the sort of person who would tell the judge in his trial, "I'm probably the smartest person I know," and his quixotic pursuit of a rare plant, the ghost orchid, became the center of Orlean's *The Orchid Thief* (and, a decade later, embedded in layers of self-reflexive fiction, Spike Jonze and Charlie Kaufman's movie adaptation, *Adaptation*).

1999 A week after Charles M. Schulz announced he was retiring from *Peanuts*, Bill Watterson, who ended *Calvin and Hobbes* four years before, lauded him in the *Los Angeles Times*. "How a cartoonist maintains this level of quality decade after decade," wrote the cartoonist whose own strip lasted just a single decade, "I have no insight."

BORN: **1935** Donald Harington (*The Architecture of the Arkansas Ozarks*), Little Rock, Ark.

1951 Charles de Lint (*Moonheart, Jack of Kinrowan*), Bussum, the Netherlands

DIED: **1880** George Eliot (*Middlemarch, Daniel Deronda*), 61, London

1989 Samuel Beckett (*Endgame, Krapp's Last Tape*), 83, Paris

1849 For a harrowing few minutes he later retold in *The Idiot*, Fyodor Dostoyevsky and twenty-two of his fellow prisoners thought their lives were about to end in front of a firing squad. Only after the first three men were tied to stakes and the rifles aimed—with Dostoyevsky next in line for execution—did an aide to Nicholas I arrive with a reprieve, completing the bit of theater the tsar had planned a month before for these members of a secret society who had been arrested for reading and discussing forbidden literature. Dostoyevsky, twenty-eight and with just a handful of published stories to his name, was immediately shackled for his sentence of four years of hard labor in Siberia; in a letter he was permitted to write to his brother, he said, "There are few things left now that can frighten me."

1940 Nathanael West was a notoriously bad driver, and he likely wasn't paying attention when, speeding back to Los Angeles from a hunting trip in Mexico—perhaps to attend the funeral of his friend and fellow Hollywood novelist F. Scott Fitzgerald, who had died the day before—he ran a stop sign outside El Centro, California, and collided with another car. The reports of his death called him a "Hollywood scenarist" and took little note of his poor-selling novels, including *Miss Lonelyhearts* and *The Day of the Locust*; they focused instead on his wife, Eileen, who died in the crash too, just four days before *My Sister Eileen*, the Broadway play based on her sister Ruth McKenney's bestselling memoir (and later the source for the musical *Wonderful Town*), had its hit opening night.

1993 While they were in Italy on her husband Douglas's sabbatical, Carol Ann Brush Hofstadter died without warning of a brain tumor at the age of forty-two. In his shock and grief, her husband turned again to the questions of human consciousness and pattern-making that had consumed him since his first book, *Gödel, Escher, Bach*. What, exactly, was he grieving? What of this lost person remained? He braided memories of her, and the thoughts they had shared, into his book on translation, *Le Ton Beau de Marot*, and when he considered what makes a "self"—an "I"—in his next major book, *I Am a Strange Loop*, she was central again. The self, for Hofstadter, is a permeable thing, constructed by the web of thoughts we share with others, and in *I Am a Strange Loop* he argues poignantly and convincingly that in his own mind and those of others who knew her, Carol's consciousness remains alive in a real, if limited, way.

December 23

1951 Working as a poet and a critic had only earned her £31 the previous year, but Muriel Spark had given little thought to writing fiction before she entered a Christmas story competition in the *Observer*, sending in a quickly written entry on a lark, drawn by the £250 prize. Two months later, after she had forgotten about the contest, the editor of the *Observer* arrived at her flat early this morning with the paper containing her story, "The Seraph and the Zambesi," and the news that she had bested 7,000 competitors to win the prize. Set in a fiercely hot Christmas season in southern Africa, where Spark had once lived, the story convinced the paper's editors they had found a new talent, and their confidence convinced Spark as well, though her first novel, *The Comforters*, wouldn't appear until 1957.

NO YEAR Angus Wilson was an admirer, and later a biographer, of Charles Dickens, and at the opening of his novel *Anglo-Saxon Attitudes*, he makes his main character, Gerald Middleton, a bit of a Scrooge. Gerald is "a man of mildly but persistently depressive temperament," and "such men are not at their best at breakfast, nor is the week before Christmas their happiest time." He's only a bit of a Scrooge, though. He may be, by his own sour measure, a "sixty-year-old failure," but he's "that most boring kind, a failure with a conscience." Whether that conscience means he'll reckon, Scrooge-style, with the ghosts of his own past or just continue on his comfortably dyspeptic way becomes the small question at the heart of Wilson's brilliantly expansive and humanely satirical portrait of postwar Britain.

1974 Douglas Adams, a young screenwriter who had not yet concocted *The Hitchhiker's Guide to the Galaxy*, sat in the audience for the first taping of *Fawlty Towers* and was disappointed it wasn't more like *Monty Python*.

2005 Daniel Swift, in the *TLS*, on Joan Didion's *The Year of Magical Thinking*: "That suffering has given a great writer a great subject seems a cold, formal observation, but *The Year of Magical Thinking* is a profoundly formal book."

December 24

BORN: 1944 Karl Marlantes (*Matterhorn*), Astoria, Ore.

1973 Stephenie Meyer (*Twilight, New Moon, Eclipse*), Hartford, Conn.

DIED: 1994 John Osborne (*Look Back in Anger*), 65, Clunton, England

2008 Harold Pinter (*The Homecoming, The Birthday Party*), 78, London

NO YEAR *Great Expectations* was not one of Charles Dickens's Christmas tales, but it opens on a "raw" Christmas Eve when young Pip walks out to the graveyard in the marshes where his parents are buried and a man with a convict's iron on his legs and the mud of the marshes all over him accosts Pip among the graves and demands food and a file to break his chains. Out of fear and kindness, Pip sneaks the man a hearty Christmas breakfast the next morning, an act of mercy that the convict, arrested again that day and transported to Australia, remembers well when he makes his fortune abroad, only revealing his true name to Pip when he returns to England a wealthy though haunted man.

1936 George Orwell spent his Christmas traveling to Barcelona to join in the fight against Fascism in Spain, but on the way he stopped in Paris and met Henry Miller for the first time. Orwell had called Miller's *Tropic of Cancer* a "remarkable book" the previous year, but the two, one ascetic and the other hedonistic, had little else in common, especially concerning Orwell's destination. Going to Spain, Miller told the Englishman, was the "act of an idiot," and the idea of combating Fascism was "baloney." Orwell defended self-sacrifice and argued that the liberty Miller celebrated sometimes required defending. They agreed to disagree and parted amicably, with Miller giving Orwell a corduroy coat that surely would be better for fighting in than the blue suit he had on.

1948 Robert Lowell celebrated Christmas Eve at Yaddo by reading *Pride and Prejudice* to Flannery O'Connor and Clifford Wright.

1953 "Men's courses will foreshadow certain ends, to which, if persevered in, they must lead. But if the courses be departed from, the ends will change. Say it is thus with what you show me." So says Ebenezer Scrooge to the Ghost of Christmas Yet to Come, and so says Mr. Fish to Owen Meany as they play those roles in the Gravesend Players production of *A Christmas Carol* in John Irving's *Prayer for Owen Meany*. But while playing the ghost Owen has a vision of his own future, seeing his own name and the date of his death on the tombstone prop meant for Scrooge and fainting onstage. "IT SAID THE WHOLE THING," he cries afterward in his odd, high-pitched voice, and once again Owen's story bends itself toward an end that may be his to choose, or that may have been chosen for him.

1970 After putting the Vargas Llosa children to bed in their apartment in Barcelona, Julio Cortázar and Mario Vargas Llosa raced the electric cars the children had been given for Christmas.

December 25

BORN: 1924 Rod Serling (*Stories from the Twilight Zone*), Syracuse, N.Y.
1925 Carlos Castaneda (*The Teachings of Don Juan*), Cajamarca, Peru
DIED: 1938 Karel Čapek (*R.U.R. [Rossum's Universal Robots]*), 48, Prague
1956 Robert Walser (*Jakob von Gunten*), 78, Herisau, Switzerland

NO YEAR The morning is bright and mild when the children leave for their grandmother's house in the village on the other side of the mountain pass, but as they set out to return after Christmas Eve dinner with their packs full of food and gifts snowflakes begin to fall, first lightly and then with a blinding whiteness. *Rock Crystal*, Adalbert Stifter's 1845 novella, is a Christmas tale of sparkling simplicity, in which a small brother and sister find their familiar path home made strange and spend a wakeful night in an ice cave on a glacier as the Northern Lights—which the girl takes as a visit from the Holy Child—flood the dark skies above them.

1905 Jessie Chambers gave Blake's *Songs of Innocence and Experience* to D. H. Lawrence for Christmas.

1915 Theodore Dreiser, in the *New Republic*, on Somerset Maugham's *On Human Bondage*: "It is as though a symphony of great beauty by a master, Strauss or Beethoven, had just been completed and the bud notes and flower tones were filling the air with their elusive message, fluttering and dying."

1932 Christmas morning comes early at the Normandie Hotel. "Are you asleep?" Nora Charles asks Nick at what he soon discovers is almost five o'clock in the morning. She's been up all night reading the memoirs of a Russian opera star, and he's still drunk from Christmas Eve. When the phone rings announcing that Dorothy Wynant, a beautiful young blonde from a mixed-up and possibly murderous family, is on her way up, it's time to order sandwiches and coffee to go with the Scotch and soda Nick already has in his hand. Breakfast can wait until the afternoon in *The Thin Man*, Dashiell Hammett's final novel, published when he was just thirty-nine before Hollywood, left-wing politics, and booze kept him busy for the last decades of his life.

1956 Kept from going home to Alabama for Christmas by her job as an airline ticket agent, Harper Lee spent the holiday in New York with Broadway songwriter Michael Brown and his wife, Joy, close friends she had met through Truman Capote. Because Lee didn't have much money they had agreed to exchange inexpensive gifts, but when they woke on Christmas morning the Browns presented her with an envelope containing this note: "You have one year off from your job to write whatever you please. Merry Christmas." Given the humbling gift of "paper, pen, and privacy," Lee quit her job and set to work, and by the end of February she had written a couple of hundred pages of a manuscript that was first called *Go Set a Watchman*, then *Atticus*, and finally *To Kill a Mockingbird*.

December 26

BORN: 1891 Henry Miller (*Tropic of Cancer*, *Black Spring*), New York City

1956 David Sedaris (*Me Talk Pretty One Day*), Johnson City, N.Y.

DIED: 1931 Melvil Dewey (founder, *Library Journal* and Dewey Decimal System), 80, Lake Placid, Fla.

1933 H. W. Fowler (*A Dictionary of Modern English Usage*), 75, Hinton St. George, England

1915 Planning to spend Boxing Day with her fiancé, Roland Leighton, who had been given a short Christmas leave from the trenches of northern France, Vera Brittain was called to the telephone, where she learned instead that he had died three days before, shot while inspecting the barbed wire in a stretch of No Man's Land that had otherwise seen little action for months. By the time the armistice arrived, Brittain would also get news of the deaths in the war of her brother, Edward, and his and Roland's two closest friends, the loss of a generation that became the centerpiece of her memoir *Testament of Youth*, a bestseller at the time and a wartime classic ever since.

1930 "Julian, lost in the coonskins, felt the tremendous excitement, the great thrilling lump in the chest and abdomen that comes before the administering of an unknown, well-deserved punishment. He knew he was in for it." It's the end of a long night—Christmas night, in fact—that Julian spent at a roadhouse and then in his car in the parking lot with a gangster's girl, and he knows, as he's driven home, that he's been a bad boy. Julian English's three-day spiral to a lonely end in John O'Hara's *Appointment in Samarra* is inexplicable, inevitable, and compelling, the inexplicability of his self-destruction only adding to his isolation. He spends one more day burning every bridge he can in Gibbsville, Pennsylvania, and then calls out to his empty home before heading out to the garage to administer his final self-punishment, "Anybody in this house? Any, body, in, this, *house?*"

1952 Four days after her mother signed a consent form for her lobotomy and just days before it was scheduled to be performed, newspapers across New Zealand carried the news that Janet Frame had won the country's most prestigious literary prize, the Hubert Church Memorial Award, for her first book, *Lagoon and Other Stories*. The prize, which she had never heard of, earned her £25, and a reprieve. The superintendent of her mental hospital happened to see one of the articles and called off the surgery, telling her, "I've decided that you should stay as you are. I don't want you changed." Two and a half years later, she was released to a literary life that made her the most celebrated New Zealand writer since Katherine Mansfield, writing books that often drew from her time in the institutions where she had spent most of the first decade of her adult life.

December 27

BORN: 1910 Charles Olson (*The Maximus Poems*), Worcester, Mass.
1969 Sarah Vowell (*Assassination Vacation*), Muskogee, Okla.
DIED: 1992 Kay Boyle (*My Next Bride, 50 Stories*), 90, Mill Valley, Calif.
1997 Brendan Gill (*Here at The New Yorker*), 83, New York City

1817 There have been many terms for the idea—"disinterestedness," "receptivity"—but the name that has stuck was used just once by its creator, John Keats, in a letter to his brothers most likely on this day: "I mean *Negative Capability*, that is when man is capable of being in uncertainties, Mysteries, doubts, without any irritable reaching after fact and reason." Shakespeare had it, Keats added, but Coleridge, "incapable of remaining content with half knowledge," didn't, and neither did Keats's obstinate friend Charles Wentworth Dilke. A walk with Dilke, in fact, had inspired Keats's insight: "pleasant" though Dilke might be, he was someone, as Keats summed him up elsewhere, "who cannot feel he has a personal identity unless he has made his mind up about everything."

1908 Dunny Ramsay, like any boy where it's cold enough to snow, has a sense of when a snowball is coming, and so, naturally, he ducks, and the snowball, carrying inside it an egg-shaped stone hidden there by his antagonist, Percy Staunton, instead hits Mrs. Mary Dempster, the pregnant young wife of the Baptist minister, knocking her to the ground, bringing on a lifelong madness, and hastening the birth of her son Paul, who grows up to be the famous magician Magnus Eisengrim, and who, in the circular way of Robertson Davies's *Fifth Business*, may well be the one who, almost sixty years later, places that same egg-shaped stone in Percy's mouth when he is found drowned in his convertible in Toronto harbor.

1950 Neal Cassady's survival in literary history has mainly been secondhand, as a character in *The Electric Kool-Aid Acid Test* and inspiration for *On the Road*'s Dean Moriarty and *One Flew over the Cuckoo's Nest*'s Randle McMurphy, but at least for a moment his friend Jack Kerouac thought he'd make it there as a writer. On this day Kerouac, having found a massive letter from Cassady on his doorstep, wrote back in awe of "your poolhall musings, your excruciating details about streets, appointment times, hotel rooms, bar locations, window measurements, smells, heights of trees." Allen Ginsberg loved the letter too, but Cassady modestly, and accurately, replied, "All the crazy falldarall you two boys make over my Big Letter just thrills the gurgles out of me, but we still know I'm a whiff and a dream." The letter also became a whiff and a dream: it's been lost to history except for fragments.

1950 A conversation with Ralph Ellison, who was working with diligent focus on *Invisible Man,* made Langston Hughes feel that, many decades into his writing career, he was still spreading his talents too thin. "I am a literary sharecropper," he wrote Arna Bontemps.

BORN: 1922 Stan Lee (*Spider-Man*, *Fantastic Four*, *X-Men*), New York City
1967 Chris Ware (*Jimmy Corrigan*, *Building Stories*), Omaha, Neb.

DIED: 1903 George Gissing (*New Grub Street*, *The Odd Women*), 46, Ispoure, France
1963 A. J. Liebling (*The Sweet Science*, *Between Meals*), 59, New York City

1896 On his first wedding anniversary, Robert Frost pled guilty to assaulting his friend and tenant for calling him a coward. The judge called Frost "riffraff" and fined him $10.

NO YEAR Everything is orderly and comfortable in the Dutch home of Kees Popinga, the head manager for a prosperous ship's outfitters, until by chance on this winter evening he discovers that the firm is bankrupt and its owner is fleeing its ruin. With chaos seeping into his tidy life, Kees suddenly decides to break it open entirely, setting out on a greedily debauched course across Europe that begins with an accidental murder. *The Man Who Watched Trains Go By* was just one of a dozen or so novels the impossibly prolific Georges Simenon published in 1938 and one of hundreds he wrote in his lifetime, divided mostly between his Maigret mysteries and his *romans durs* ("hard novels"), of which *The Man Who Watched Trains Go By* is a memorably flinty example.

1949 "E, F, and I interrogated God this evening at six." How young was Susan Sontag when she sat in her car with friends, "immobilized with awe" outside Thomas Mann's house in Los Angeles, practicing her questions before being welcomed into his study to discuss Nietzsche, Joyce, and her favorite book, *The Magic Mountain*? Her diary places the meeting on this day, when she was sixteen and already at the University of Chicago, but in a later memoir she said she was only fourteen when Mann, with his German formality, asked about her studies and she thought, stricken with embarrassment, "Could he imagine what a world away from the Gymnasium in his native Lübeck . . . was North Hollywood High School, alma mater of Alan Ladd and Farley Granger?"

1969 "DICK GIBSON MAGNIFICENT STOP CONGRATULATIONS AND ADMIRATION," cabled Random House editor Joe Fox to Stanley Elkin on receipt of the manuscript for his third novel, *The Dick Gibson Show*, a story made of the voices of Dick Gibson and his obsessive guests, floating out over the midwestern night on high-wattage radio waves. Elkin's own voice was irrepressible, but even his admiring editor tried to rein him in at times. "Less is more," Fox wrote in the margins when striking out a paragraph, but Elkin, who believed that "*more* is more . . . less is less, fat fat, thin thin, and enough is enough," stetted him right back: "You *can't* cut this. It's really as good as I get." And it stayed, although *Dick Gibson*, in the end, continued Elkin's lifelong struggle with magnificence unmatched by readership.

December 29

BORN: 1893 Vera Brittain (*Testament of Youth*),
Newcastle-under-Lyme, England
1922 William Gaddis (*The Recognitions, J R*), New York City
DIED: 1894 Christina Rossetti (*Goblin Market*),
64, London
1926 Rainer Maria Rilke (*Sonnets to Orpheus*), 51, Montreux, Switzerland

1881 Baum's Opera House, built for L. Frank Baum by his oil-rich father, opened in Richburg, New York, two months before burning down.

1913 Its stiff-upper-lip bravado has made it the subject of T-shirts as well as the first entry in Julian Watkins's *100 Greatest Advertisements*, but it may be too good to be true that polar explorer Ernest Shackleton ever ran a classified ad reading, "MEN WANTED for hazardous journey. Small wages, bitter cold, long months of complete darkness, constant danger, safe return doubtful. Honor and recognition in case of success." It is true, though, that a letter from Shackleton, announcing the expedition to make the first crossing of Antarctica that he later recounted in the adventure classic *South*, appeared in the *Times* on this day. What may also be apocryphal, however, is the claim of one early Shackleton biographer that the explorer classified the responses to this letter into "three large drawers labeled respectively, 'Mad,' 'Hopeless,' and 'Possible.'"

1962 Whitney Balliett, in *The New Yorker*, on Henry Miller's *Tropic of Capricorn*: "Publicly celebrating one's libido is closely related to that other parlor pastime—recounting one's most recent operation."

1989 A year of European miracles ended with the unlikely ascent of a dissident playwright to the presidency of Czechoslovakia. One year before, Václav Havel was in police custody, unable to attend his play, *Tomorrow*, which imagined how Alois Rašín, one of the country's founders, experienced the first hours of Czech independence in 1918. Now, as the Soviet empire collapsed, Havel found himself preparing to take power himself, but he said it felt more like watching *Ubu Roi* than his own play to see the Communist members of the federal assembly, who had approved his imprisonment just weeks before, unanimously endorse his election. In his first days in Prague Castle, he laughed with his friends in the new government at this absurd turn of history and thought that even as president he could carry on some semblance of his former life as a citizen. He learned otherwise, though: "The Castle swallowed me up whole."

BORN: 1869 Stephen Leacock (*Sunshine Sketches of a Little Town*), Swanmore, England

1961 Douglas Coupland (*Generation X*, *Microserfs*), Baden-Söllingen, West Germany

DIED: 1948 Denton Welch (*In Youth Is Pleasure*), 33, Sevenoaks, England

2005 Rona Jaffe (*The Best of Everything*), 74, London

1935 The legend of Antoine de Saint-Exupéry the aviator was built on his failures. The last of these was his final disappearance over the Mediterranean in 1944, but it was an earlier crash in the sands of the Sahara while attempting, with laughably casual preparation, to claim a prize for the fastest flight from Paris to Saigon, that he was able to transform into a legend himself. A month afterward he began a series of newspaper articles on the crash and his trek through the desert for survival that became *Wind, Sand, and Stars*, an acclaimed bestseller in France and the United States. And in 1942, living unhappily by then in New York, he was once again inspired by the idea of an aviator stranded in the dunes, making it the beginning of his fanciful tale for children, *The Little Prince*.

1983 "In the end," Mme. Landau tells the narrator of W. G. Sebald's *The Emigrants*, "it is hard to know what it is that someone dies of." Paul Bereyter died on this day at the age of seventy-four by lying down on the railway tracks outside his German hometown. Like the other three men profiled in Sebald's novel—if "novel" is what you want to call it—Bereyter emigrated from Germany, but he was the only one of the four to return, becoming a soldier and then a teacher again in the town where his family had once been condemned for their Jewish ancestry. But what did he die of? What caused him to lie down on the tracks? Sebald's narrator, once a student of Bereyter's and an emigrant himself, claims no answer, merely writing down what he knows of his former teacher: his interest in railways, his lonely melancholy, his passionately inventive teaching, and the coarse attacks on his family during the Nazi years.

2003 "You sit down to dinner and life as you know it ends. The question of self-pity." A few days after her husband, John Gregory Dunne, died suddenly of a heart attack as she tossed the salad for dinner, Joan Didion—known for, among many things, her essay "On Keeping a Notebook"—opened a Word file called "Notes on change.doc" and recorded the thoughts above, but they were the last words she wrote for months. Finally, in the fall, she began to gather notes again on her husband's sudden death, their daughter's equally sudden illness at the same time, and what she called *The Year of Magical Thinking*, which lasted from this day until December 31, 2004, the first day, she realized to her sorrow, that John hadn't seen the year before.

December 31

BORN: 1945 Connie Willis (*Doomsday Book*),
   Denver, Colo.
   1968 Junot Díaz (*Drown, The Brief
   Wondrous Life of Oscar Wao*), Santo
   Domingo, D.R.
DIED: 1980 Marshall McLuhan
   (*Understanding Media*), 69, Toronto
   2008 Donald E. Westlake (*The Hot Rock,
   The Hunter*), 75, San Tancho, Mexico

1867 Mark Twain, out for the first time with his future wife (and her family), was disappointed by Charles Dickens's public reading in New York from *David Copperfield*, which, Twain thought, was "glittering frost-work, with no heart."

1908 Invited to a New Year's party at Max Brod's, Franz Kafka told him he'd rather stay home and read Flaubert's *Temptation of St. Anthony*.

1979 It should have been his big break; maybe it was. Harvey Pekar, always scrounging for recognition for his slice-of-life *American Splendor* comic books, got a lengthy and perceptive rave from Carola Dibbell in the *Village Voice*. What did it lead to? Not much, he sourly reported in a later comic, just wasted time and money, as short-lived enthusiasts (and movie producers) promised work but never followed up. It was just the first in a series of "big breaks" for Pekar—including his grouchy Letterman appearances in the late '80s and the Oscar-nominated *American Splendor* movie in the early 2000s—that never quite made Pekar the star he would have been uncomfortable being.

1997 New Year's Eve in Sing Sing prison was quiet but wakeful as the night began. "Another year," one inmate said. "Yeah," replied a neighbor, "another year closer to goin' home, you heard?" Ted Conover, meanwhile, *was* going home. He'd already handed in his resignation as a corrections officer, but he signed up for one last shift to see what New Year's was like on the cell block. "The first fires," he wrote in *Newjack*, his memoir of a year working as a prison guard, "started maybe ten minutes before midnight," and soon blazes in the galleries, made of trash and papers lit by matches flicked from the cells, were five feet high and filling the prison with smoke: not quite dangerous, but not comfortable either for those on guard.

NO YEAR The narrative clock in Michael Chabon's *The Yiddish Policemen's Union* ticks not only toward the resolution of its mystery—in this case detective Meyer Landsman's investigation of the murder of Mendel Shpilman, who may or may not have been the Messiah—but toward an outcome more uncertain and ominous, known as the Reversion. In Chabon's invented history (based on an actual proposal to make a temporary homeland for European Jews in Alaska), the federal Jewish settlement in Sitka, Alaska, which has grown to over three million after taking in refugees from the Nazis and the destruction of Israel, is set, after a sixty-year "interim," to revert to state control at the end of the year. The weary despair of its Jewish residents, preparing to join the diaspora again, is matched only by Chabon's clear delight in the alternative world he has created.

Acknowledgments

THANKS first to my collaborators. To Matt Weiland, editor, friend, and co-conspirator: thank you for believing there are books in my book-drunk head. To Joanna Neborsky: the moment I saw "A Partial Inventory of Gustave Flaubert's Personal Effects" was the first time I could imagine what this book could look like, and the moment I saw Theodore Dreiser with his hot dogs I knew I was right. To Morgan Davies, wading through the stacks in Morningside Heights while I was doing the same in Seattle, whose marginal comments on the gems she found were as delightful as Miss Austen's in her family copy of Goldsmith's *History of England*. To India Cooper, ToC '92, for close reading and Harper Lee fact-checking. To Jim Rutman, for when things get more complicated after this. To Sam MacLaughlin, for good humor and that little bit of Anne Carson when I needed it, and to everyone else at Norton.

THANKS to the institutions that, without knowing they were doing so, made this book possible. Most of all, to the Suzzallo and Allen Libraries at the University of Washington, where I burrowed in an earlier life and never expected I would again, for full, open stacks, generous alumni borrowing privileges, and the loveliest working space I could hope for. To the Seattle Public Library, for a superb, accessible collection and an equally lovely downtown reading room. (And to Peet's in Fremont and Zoka in Tangletown, my other favorite offices.) To the hundreds and thousands of biographers and editors this book depended on, and whose meticulous labor I appreciate like never before. To Wikipedia, mocked and mistrusted and, by now, absolutely indispensable: almost never the end of my search, but more often than not the beginning. To search engines that make the world's knowledge porous and available, and to the old-fashioned physical books that continue to make it readable.

AND thanks to all of my reading friends, many of whom I thought of when writing about the books I know you love. To Connie and Peter Nissley for making my first book-filled house, and to Elinor Nissley, once and future collaborator and calendar- and book-making inspiration. And to Laura, Henry, and Peter Silverstein, who stepped around my stacks of books (while making a few of their own), who thought that when I left my job that might mean they would see more of me, and whose excitement for this book, and for everything else we share, always increases my own.

Index